CATHOLICS/U.S.A.:

Perspectives on Social Change

WILLIAM T. LIU

is Professor of Sociology and Director, Social Science Training and Research Laboratory, University of Notre Dame. His previous books include *Chinese Society under Communism* (Wiley, 1966) and *Family and Fertility*. He has contributed to *Social Forces, American Journal of Sociology, Journal of Marriage and the Family, Sociological Analysis, Social Order, Social Compass, Asian Survey, American Catholic Sociological Review*, and other scholarly reviews.

NATHANIEL J. PALLONE

is Professor and Chairman, Department of Counselor Education, New York University. His previous books include *Guidance and Counseling in Schools, Guidance and Other Personnel Services, Readings in Guidance and Counseling*, and *Readings for Catholic Counselors*. He has contributed to the *Journal of Social Psychology, Journal of Counseling Psychology, Acta Psychologica, Insight, The Critic, Personnel and Guidance Journal, Catholic Educational Review*, and other professional journals. For four years, he edited the *Journal* of the National Catholic Guidance Conference.

CATHOLICS/ U.S.A.

Perspectives on Social Change

WILLIAM T. LIU

University of Notre Dame

NATHANIEL J. PALLONE

New York University

JOHN WILEY & SONS, INC.
New York · London · Sydney · Toronto

10 9 8 7 6 5 4 3 2 1

Library of Congress Catalogue Card Number: 72-93299

SBN 471 54149 4

Printed in the United States of America

For May and for Nicolina

Preface

This book developed from the collaboration of a sociologist and a psychologist, each of whom is concerned about the ways in which organized, pervasive social institutions affect the life experience and behavior pattern of the individual person. Both personally and professionally, we have been interested in the Catholic community in America, as a social institution, as a social phenomenon, and as a setting for the study of social change and its portents.

What we have endeavored to do in this volume is to provide a representative sample of research investigations by behavioral scientists that suggests a framework for the interpretation of the massive social changes that have occurred in a particular, pervasive social institution. We have been less concerned with the nature of those changes than with providing a series of perspectives for the general reader and for the student of the sociology and social psychology of religion through which social change becomes understandable. Our position is that social change is triggered not by a single event—for example, Vatican II—nor by a single personality, not even one as magnetic and engaging as John XXIII. Rather, we regard social change as the product of complex social and psychological forces governed by general behavioral laws that are discernible by the research methods of the sciences of behavior. It is a moot question indeed whether such forces congeal around events and personalities, or whether these forces create climates that lead inevitably to certain events and to the ascendance of certain personalities.

The collection of studies represented in this volume is not intended to exhaust the universe of research on the American Catholic community but, instead, to provide in a single repository investigations that contribute to developing perspectives on social change as a behavioral process. Nor have we, in the main, attempted to duplicate discussions of social change in certain aspects of the Catholic community already available in book-length studies by such scholars as Joseph Fichter, S.J., on the Catholic religious; John D. Donovan, on the professor in Catholic universities; Andrew M. Greeley, Peter H. Rossi, and James W. Trent, on the effects of Catholic education; Augusta Neal, on the formation of the nun; and James M. Lee and Leo Putz, C.S.C., on the Catholic seminary. Instead, we have contented ourselves that, within certain limitations of space, the collection in this volume is representative and sufficient to its purpose.

We are deeply indebted to those behavioral scientists who have contributed original studies to this volume and to those authors and editors who have graciously granted permission for republication of studies that originally appeared in other sources. For their helpful and critical comments, we are indebted to Professors Thomas McAvoy, C.S.C., William V. D'Antonio, Richard LaManna, and Donald Kommers, of the University of Notre Dame; and to Professors Martin Hamburger and Bernard Katz, of New York University. We are especially grateful to Professors Morris Janowitz, University of Chicago, John Kosa, Harvard Medical School, and George N. Shuster, Notre Dame, for their support and suggestions.

The preparation of this manuscript depended totally on the efficiency and dispatch of Mrs. Irene Leifer at New York University and Mrs. Marion Metzger and Mrs. Carol Evans at Notre Dame, whose secretarial excellence is matched only by their unflagging good humor. Finally, we must express our continuing gratitude to our wives, to whom this volume is dedicated, for maintaining their own perspectives throughout the rigors of a collaboration that extended halfway across the country.

William T. Liu

Nathaniel J. Pallone

Contents

Part V

MARGINALITY, TRANSITION, AND RENEWAL   421

CATHOLICS/U.S.A.:

Perspectives on Social Change

Overture: Perspectives on Social Change

That a providential God exists; that he created the universe; that Jesus Christ, his only begotten son, redeemed mankind after Adam's fall; that Christ founded an earthly Church under the vicarage of the Bishop of Rome—these comprise fundamental beliefs within the social institution that calls itself the Roman Catholic Church.

Insofar as behavior follows from belief, if at all, it is to be anticipated that some or all communicants of the Catholic faith habitually or occasionally behave in consequence of these beliefs. But it is not clear that a one-to-one causal relationship obtains between belief and behavior. And even superficial observation suggests that there are other engines for the behavior of Catholics—especially of Catholic Americans, who until recently found themselves cast politically and socially in a minority role, even suspected of owing spiritual allegiance to a foreign crown.

It is to these "other engines" that this volume endeavors to address itself, through the examination of the forces that generate the social and psychological behavior of Catholic Americans specifically as Catholic *Americans*. With the fundamental beliefs that comprise the core of their faith, and with the religious behaviors that may or may not flow therefrom, this volume remains largely unconcerned.

INDICATORS OF SOCIAL CHANGE

On Sunday, September 22, 1968, Patrick, Cardinal O'Boyle, Prince of the Holy Roman Church, Archbishop of Washington,

1

D.C., mounted to his episcopal pulpit and began to intone the harsh sounds of a repressive pastoral letter condemning clergymen and laymen alike who had voiced opposition to the then-recently published papal encyclical *Humanae Vitae*. In a prearranged demonstration, some 200 members of an "underground church" movement called the Washington Laymen's Association rose quietly and left the Cathedral. After the Cardinal-Archbishop had finished his pastoral letter and his sermon, they returned to the Celebration of the Eucharist. They had exercised their right to dissent—a right guaranteed them in their nation's Constitution, but a right quite alien to the traditional structure of discipline and decorum in their Church. Within a few hours, the spectacle was telecast throughout the nation, arrayed in the glorious spectrum of the rainbow.

That such behavior would have been well-nigh inconceivable 10 years earlier probably requires little documentation. Dissent in American Catholicism on anything resembling a public scale is a rare phenomenon. Private dissent, leading to the conditions known to theologians as "apostasy," is more common: while no fewer than 46 million Americans identified themselves as Catholic during the 1960 U.S. census, the rolls of American Catholic parishes accounted for only slightly more than half that number as members of the institutional church. There was a time when the dissenter sought refuge from an unacceptable belief system or a repressive Church structure; today, he escapes instead into the underground church, where he finds other laymen and even clergymen who believe as he does, or into the columns of the *National Catholic Reporter*. Why was yesterday's dissenter moved toward apostasy, while today's is moved to remain within the institutional church, if at its margin? It is our contention that today's dissenter, layman or cleric, remains within the church in consequence of a viable prospect for further massive or even radical social change—a prospect absent from American Catholic life during much of its history.

More and less dramatic examples of social change within the institutional church and in the American Catholic community can be offered almost without limit. Evidence that massive change has occurred both in the American Catholic community and in the larger American "host" society abounds. But it is not the purpose of this volume to catalogue, to describe, or to evaluate social change in American Catholicism. Instead, this volume seeks to provide the reader with a series of insights and perspectives from the behavioral sciences from which the reader can extrapolate a conceptually sound frame of reference through which to interpret and assess present and future social change in American Catholicism. Or, put more simply, it is the intent of this volume to provide the reader with those perspectives through which he is able to observe that 200 Catholic Americans in the nation's capital are led to dissent publicly and en bloc from the beliefs of their spiritual shepherd, no less than a Cardinal-Archbishop, not simply in response to the fresh breath of John XXIII and Vatican II, but because they respond to John XXIII and to Vatican II as Catholic *Americans*.

FROM CULTURAL DIFFERENCE TO AMERICAN HOMOGENEITY

The black American is a member of the most obvious, visible minority in American life. He may be rich or poor, suburbanite or ghetto-captive, content or angry with his experience of life. But his experience of life, his social class membership, his level of education, his occupational skill are determined if not solely then at least in large measure by the color of his skin.

The Catholic American belongs to a far, far less visible minority. Unlike the black American, he is bound to his fellow Catholic American not by skin coloration nor, indeed, by ethnicity or political persuasion or social class membership, but only by a commonality of belief and/or behavior related to certain religious convictions. The Catholic American is rich or poor, suburbanite or ghetto-captive, content or angry, not so much in consequence of his religious belief and/or behavior as in consequence of his ethnicity, his social class membership, his level of education, his occupational skill—factors relatively independent of his membership in a Catholic minority.

Is the notion of a "Catholic minority" in American life a viable one? Are Catholic Americans more conscious of their Catholicism than of their ethnicity, political persuasion, social class? Were the early waves of Catholic immigrants to the United State conscious of their Catholicity, or only of their German-ness, or Irish-ness, or Italian-ness—of the fact that they were culturally and linguistically "different" from the Yankee members of their host country? Was it necessary for the disparate groups of Catholic immigrants first to achieve a degree of American-ness, of cultural and linguistic homogeneity with the Yankee and with each other, before they felt a sense of communion with members of other ethnic groups who shared their religious beliefs and/or behavior?

A panoply of forces shaped the life situations confronted by European and Mediterranean Catholics who emigrated to the United

States in the great waves of the nineteenth century. Catholic immigrants dispersed primarily into the massive cities of the East, where they faced the problems of a burgeoning industrialized society, often quite alien to the folkways of the "old" country—the problems not only of assimilation but of cultural reorientation. There were notable exceptions—for example, the planned resettlement of Bavarian farmers in the midwest, with language and culture intact well into the twentieth century.

But, in the main, the Catholic immigrant found himself alien in an alien culture, unequipped for any but the more menial tasks in the labor force, usually illiterate and unschooled, at once suspicious and envious of the Yankee's position and influence. Soon enough, he set aside the traditional folkways of responding to the conditions of life learned in the old country, for they were no longer viable in responding to the new conditions that confronted him, and he learned to emulate the ways of his Yankee betters, if only to vie with them for the seats of power and influence.

THE CATHOLIC COMMUNITY IN A CHANGING AMERICAN SOCIETY

The same forces that shaped the life experience of the early immigrants had already begun to assault the dominant Yankee culture. Soon these forces would merge with new forces unleashed by the assimilation of Catholic and other immigrants to produce patterns of massive social change in American society, apart from which social change in American Catholicism can be viewed only in fragmentary fashion. Four principal trends can be discerned in the patterns of social change ascendant in American society from the middle of the nineteenth century to the final third of the twentieth century.

From Proprietary to Corporational Economy

The entrepreneurial system reached its zenith in the late 1800's, when the United States was a nation of independent farmers and small businessmen. By 1940, the United States had become a nation of employees; a corporational base had replaced a manufacturing base for the nation's economy. For all practical purposes, the American worker had become what William Foote Whyte has called the organizational man. With what social consequences? Most importantly, the emphasis on the development of an independent spirit, essential to an entrepreneurial economy, was eroded and replaced by an emphasis on cooperation with one's peers to achieve a common end. Attitudes, values, beliefs, and behavior patterns began to emerge which emphasized conformity to the norms of the group at the expense of economic and social self-sufficiency.

From Urbanization to Suburbanization

Most American cities outside the deep South represent microcosmically the total American society. Social change in the American urban community mirrors social change in the larger society. What major changes are observable in the social system of the American city?

First, the urban population exceeded the rural population for the first time in the 1920 census, following the influx of immigrants in new waves from central and eastern Europe during the preceding generation. Most of the new immigrants settled in the cities dotting America's ocean shores. Second, the increased urban population produced patterns of functional and structural differentiation in the urban community. Functionally, increasing complexity and division in work produced increased stratification in the American labor force. Structurally, the urban populated tended to locate according to the homogeneity of ethnic and cultural background, creating what are now called the "urban ghettos." Third, urbanization provided opportunities for married women to work outside the home; such opportunities, in turn, have produced a decline in fertility rates.

During the first four decades of this century, American society was characterized by rapid urbanization. Since 1940, however, and especially since World War II and its baby boom, the suburban population has grown far more rapidly than the urban population, and usually at the expense of the urban population, so that the suburban population had all but equalled the urban population in the 1960 census and surpassed it in the following decade.

Suburbanization has evoked a number of important social and economic consequences. There has emerged a mass middle-class suburban culture, centered around phenomena akin to what Philip Wylie calls "Momism." Factors obtain in the suburban microculture favoring greater other-reliance among adults (the residence-to-commuter-train car pool) and among children, especially on "Mom," who must chauffeur the child, for example, to the meeting of his Boy Scout Troop, where at age 11 he will be taught the values of self-reliance! In view of the massive changes in patterns of child rearing occasioned by the abandonment of the urban center to marginal families and by increasing Momism in the suburbs, it is likely that traditional theories of the psychological development of children and adolescents are no longer viable in either psychosocial environment.

Not only has a distinctly suburban family, characterized by a largely absentee father and centered around mother, appeared in American society but the American suburban community has emerged as a cultural subsystem. Distinct characteristics are observable in political behavior (in the main, washing one's hands of the problems of the urban center and its ghettos), in consumer behavior (for example, the rise of shopping centers or, even more recently, of totally enclosed and weather-conditioned enclaves of retail outlets called "shopping malls," whose stores welcome informally clad shoppers seeking to purchase milk by the gallon rather than the quart, cigarettes by the carton, whiskey by the case), and even in religious behavior. In what Andrew M. Greeley calls the suburban church, priests find that the roles they are expected to play center more often around family companionship and support and community leadership than they do around spiritual leadership or the conduct of religious rituals.

From Asceticism to Mass Affluence and Leisure

One of the most dramatic changes in American society has been the unprecedented increase in the availability of leisure on a scale never before experienced in any society. The Puritan fathers worked an average of 12 hours per day, six days per week. The modern American works an average of seven hours per day, five days per week—even if the suburbanite spends two hours a day travelling from home to work and back.

Mass leisure differs fundamentally from the leisure of the elite described by Thorstein Veblen: mass leisure is to be enjoyed in and of itself—its prime value conflicts directly with Puritan asceticism. Work no longer preempts the sacredness and meaning of life.

Mass leisure evokes mass involvement and multiple involvements as well, which imply the fragmentation of one's commitments. Thus, in earlier days the parish served spiritual, social, and communal functions. But mass leisure allows direct personal activity in a variety of distinct social and cultural institutions, not mediated through a central nexus for commitment. Paradoxically, multiple involvements result in the fragmentation of personal effect and thus, perhaps, breed alienation, while at the same time providing an illusory feeling that the individual person controls his environment. For its part, mass affluence has evoked frantic systems of marginal differentiation, evident in what Vance Packard has called the creation or discovery of new cultural symbols signifying consumptive power—often for its own sake.

The End of Ideology

The spread of mass education, the rapid upsurge in adult education, and new technologies for rapid news dissemination have eventuated in what is popularly called the massive "knowledge explosion" of the mid-twentieth century. American society has become more technologically knowledgeable in the past generation than even the wildest or most fantastic ruminations of the science fictionalists of the 1930's would have led anyone to reasonably expect. A "knowledgeable society" can ill tolerate ideological conflict. Segmented groups can no longer rely on ideology or passion in making decisions or solving problems, but rather must attend to technical competence in producing and utilizing factual information. The labor-management wars of the early 1900's were ideological conflicts, but today's disputes center primarily on the impact of technology and automation.

Ideological conflict is still occasionally injected into American political life—whether by a Goldwater in 1964 or a Wallace in 1968. However, political conflict over liberal versus reactionary belief systems appears to reflect a generation gap in American life more than genuine tension between conflicting ideologies. In such circumstances, as the results of the national elections of 1964 and 1968 attest, the day is customarily carried by the ideological moderate who projects himself as the master technician. Those clusters of ultraconservatism or superpatriotism, no less than the clusters of radical anarchism, in American life that still display the characteristics of what Robert Redfield called the "sacred" or "folk" society seem to reflect what is really a minor lag in social change, as the trend toward the end of ideology courses through the social system.

THE CHANGING CATHOLIC COMMUNITY
IN AMERICAN SOCIETY

Social change characteristic of American society in general has been reflected in the American Catholic community as a part of the total social system, even when certain trends appear to have differentially affected American Catholics. But certain patterns of social change, if not specific to the American Catholic community, have produced particularly noteworthy trends.

Class Membership

Prior to and during the mid-1940's, Protestants ranked above Catholics in income, occupation, and education; by the mid-1960's, these relative positions had been reversed. Within two decades, there appears to have occurred a wholesale change in class membership among Catholic Americans. In view of a pace for upward social mobility more accelerated among Catholics than among Protestants, a differential impact is likely to be felt in the next generation of Catholic Americans. Similarly, Catholics no longer find themselves in a socially inferior status which, for many of them, was intertwined with religious separatism. Many Catholics have now achieved affluence and influence without abandoning their religious identification to gain upward social mobility, an approach to socioeconomic advancement relatively common a generation ago. While the institutional church was earlier identified with the working class in American society, it has more recently been accused, with justification, of an insensitivity to members of the lower socioeconomic strata.

Decline in Fertility

Several demographic studies of the 1950's and 1960's reported rather consistent differentiation in fertility patterns between Catholics and Protestants, but the decline in the number of births given and expected by Catholic women has now substantially closed the "fertility gap." Apparently, the ideal of the large family, once widely preached from American pulpits and more recently advanced by some prominent Vatican figures, is no longer accepted as a viable model among American Catholics. There is, as well, some evidence that the role of the woman is interpreted quite differently by middle-class suburban Catholics, especially in view of the opportunity for meaningful employment outside the home. Perhaps the most important implication in the decline in fertility, however, is that the emphasis in family life among American Catholics seems to be shifting from parenthood coupled with total sacrifice of self-interest for the welfare of the children—under the benign smile of the Holy Mother, the Church, ever ready to proscribe the limitation of family size—to conjugal love and/or companionship between a man and a woman—a family system characteristic of industrially advanced societies.

The Catholic Family

Several trends are observable in the American family in general and in the Catholic family in particular, triggered by such forces as the change in the American economy, medical advances in conception control, especially through oral contraceptives, and the change from an "extended" to a "nuclear" family system. Although differences still obtain between Protestant and Catholic families in divorces and fertility rates, these "gaps" have substantially narrowed. While there is little hard evidence to determine whether the structure of the Catholic family approximates that of the Protestant family, some indicators suggest the prevalence of an "American" family pattern across religious, if not yet across class, lines. Thus, under the impetus of such groups as the Christian Family Movement, the "children's mass"—a phenomenon advocated by and oriented toward the institutional church—has given way to mass attendance by the "nuclear" family and, in many advanced parishes, religious instruction preparatory to the child's first reception of the Eucharist is given in the home, not in the church or the school.

IDENTITY TRANSFORMATION: ETHNIC TO AMERICAN TO CATHOLIC-AMERICAN

In his *Protestant, Catholic, Jew,* Will Herberg suggests that the renascence of interest and activity in "old country" religious denominations in the 1950's resulted from the third-generation American's security in his identity as an American. The first, immigrant generation was obviously culturally and linguistically different from the host society; their adherence to "old country" religion represented for them an island of cultural familiarity and security. In contrast, the second generation strived painfully for identity as Americans: not only were names changed or shortened and ethnic foods abandoned, but the old country religion and its language were forsaken. However, the successful pursuit of American-ness by the second generation made it possible for the members of the third generation to pursue an interest in the quaint folkways of their grandparents. The third generation was born not only assimilated but even homogeneous; their interest in old country ways may be interpreted as a search for differentiation. Membership in old country religious groups began to increase at about the same time that ethnic foodstuffs appeared on the shelves of suburban supermarkets, rendering it unnecessary to return to the small shops of the urban ghetto in search of ricotta or Lasagna noodles. Hence, Herberg seems to believe, the availability of bottled Borscht and frozen pizza and the membership growth of, for example, the Augustana Lutherans represent related aspects of a single social phenomenon.

It is difficult to assess the precise social dynamics at play in American Catholicism. But the confluence of trends in social change in American society and in the American Catholic community suggest the following type of paradigm.

The immigrant generation held tenaciously to the old country culture which had crossed the sea with them; religion represented an important, integral part of their culture. In the ethnic ghettos of the great cities, the Catholic parish was customarily organized on an ethnic, not a geographic basis, reserved for Irish-Catholics or for German-Catholics. The ethnic language was used in the pulpit, the confessional, the parish house, and perhaps in the parochial school. The "Irish" church might be located across the street from the "Italian" church—a condition that persists in some inner city areas—but never the twain met. The sense of identity was essentially, if not totally, ethnic, not religious—even though the ethnic identity might include identification with a particular version of old-country Catholicism.

At about the same time that the American population began to shift toward the suburbs, the Catholic population began its rapid ascent up the ladder of social mobility. The third-generation Italian-American-Catholic, for example, carried his own sense of American identity as a birthright. It was no longer necessary psychologically that he belong to an ethnic parish; linguistically, it was impossible, for he knew little if anything of the language of his grandfather. Furthermore, because of suburban dispersion, it was no longer feasible economically to maintain ethnically disparate parishes. Many of the old country religious communities initially established in the United States to serve the needs of a particular ethnic group of Catholics—for example, to conduct schools in Polish for Polish Catholic children—were forced to modify their institutional goals to include service to the entire American Catholic community. The substitution of the living vernacular for a dead language in church ritual seemed to underscore the homogeneity, not the ethnic disparity, of American Catholics. Today, it appears that the Catholic American of Irish, Italian, German, Polish, or Spanish ancestry is more conscious of his religious than of his ethnic identity—but only because he or his parents first achieved an *American* identity.

PART I

SOCIAL MOBILITY AMONG CATHOLIC AMERICANS

A surge toward upward social mobility has characterized much of the American Catholic experience, as it has the experience of other ethnic and religious groups. But Catholic tradition specifically minimizes the goods and glories of this life, counseling that goods are to be stored for the treasure-house of the next. Upward social mobility is an American, not a Catholic, phenomenon, predicated upon a Puritan ethos quite antagonistic to authentic Catholic beliefs.

During the last half of the nineteenth century and the first quarter of the twentieth, successive waves of immigration brought more and more Catholics to the United States. Even as the earlier Irish and European Catholic immigrant moved up and out of the lower ec-

13

onomic strata of American society, new Mediterranean and Latin arrivals entered these strata in greater numbers. The trend toward massive upward social movement became evident only after economic forces began to transform American society from an agrarian and small-business base to an industrialized technocratic base, where social and economic position is widely accessible.

But the trend toward upward social mobility seems to have differentially affected certain segments of the American Catholic community. In his investigation KOSA explores the social mobility rates apparent in the occupational aspirations of Catholic youth in relation to the social class membership of their parents. He concludes that social mobility relates inversely both to social class and to time-of-arrival in the United States, suggesting a leveling-off process in social mobility.

In a now-classic study, STRODTBECK investigates the relationship between values, achievement, and family interaction among Jewish and Italian-Catholic adolescents in a New England city. Strodtbeck concludes that certain values are basic to achievement in the American culture, irrespective of family interaction or social status; some of these values are compatible with, but others are antagonistic to, traditional Catholic beliefs.

By the mid-1960's, report GLENN and HYLAND Catholics tended to rank above Protestants on most indices to socioeconomic status. However, Glenn and Hyland contend that the dramatic strides made by Catholics in the last quarter of a century are attributable to the economic and social opportunities embedded in the structure of those communities where Catholic population is dense, rather than to elements of religious behavior or belief. Thus, social mobility indeed emerges as an American phenomenon—but one which has disproportionately benefited Catholic Americans.

1

The Emergence of a Catholic Middle Class

JOHN KOSA

Harvard University

SOURCE. "Patterns of Social Mobility among American Catholics," *Social Compass* (Netherlands), 1962, 9, 361-371. Reprinted by permission.

In the 1820's the immigration of Catholics to the United States turned into a mass movement. The newcomers from Ireland, now arriving in sizable numbers, took up their abodes in the cities of New England and the adjacent states, in an old settlement area of the country, marked by a distinct social order. It was the social order of a well-established Protestant middle class, of small independent entrepreneurs, proud of their achievements in pioneering and political organization, and determined in their Puritanical principles.

15

Placed against this background, the Irish immigrant appeared to be conspicuously different. He appeared to be the man of the laboring or lower class and earned names, such as "shanty Irish" and "Paddy," which clearly referred to his different way of life.[1]

The immigrant is likely to be different from the established resident, and one may rightly ask some questions about the true nature of this difference. Was the Irish Catholic any lowlier in wealth, power and prestige, was he any slower in the pursuit of worldly success than the Scottish Protestant who arrived in America about the same time in equally large numbers? Or was it a matter of religion, mores, and perhaps clannishness that set apart the Irish Catholic and associated his name with that of the lower class?

The questions are rather academic since the early immigrants from Ireland were followed by a succession of other Catholics coming from the various countries of Europe. The century from 1820 to 1920 witnessed a great influx of Catholic immigrants, growing in volume as time passed. Thus, while Protestant Americans made impressive social and financial advances, the Catholic population of the country was constantly replenished by masses of newcomers who, by virtue of their recent arrival, had to take the lowest place of the social pyramid. Moreover, many Catholic newcomers hailed from the countries of Southern and Eastern Europe and brought along a language, culture, and standard of living which not only separated them from the old Americans, but also seriously hindered their success.[2] Hence, the Protestant-Catholic differences of the early period became accentuated and stabilized. Although many families managed to advance themselves, the Catholic population of America had a noticeably lower socio-economic status than the Protestant population of the country.

The situation, as it existed in our times, was well appraised by three nationwide surveys, taken between 1939 and 1952. The results indicated that American Catholics, when compared to Protestants, were greatly underrepresented in the upper class, somewhat under-represented in the middle class, but overrepresented in the lower

---

[1] Carl Russel Fish, *The Rise of the Common Man*, New York, Macmillan, 1927, pp. 20-27, 112-13; Oscar Handlin, *Boston's Immigrants*, Cambridge, Harvard University Press, 1959; Carl F. Wittke, *The Irish in America*, Baton Rouge, State University, Press, 1956.

[2] François Houtart, *Aspects sociologiques du catholicisme américain*, Paris, Editions *Ouvrières*, 1957, pp. 22-59; John L. Thomas, *The American Catholic Family*, Englewood Cliffs, Prentice Hall, 1956, pp. 99-147; Milton M. Gordon, "Kitty Foyle and the Concept of Class as Culture," *American Journal of Sociology*, 53, November 1947, pp. 210-17.

class.[3] Similarly, a study of college attendance found that proportionally less Catholics than Protestants attended college.[4] Some sociologists, investigating locally restricted samples, concluded that the Catholics were less successful than the Protestants in the pursuit of worldly success, and the same scholars explained the finding with the aid of Max Weber's theory on the basic affinity of Protestantism and the spirit of capitalism.[5]

Whatever the empirical findings might be, it should not be overlooked that during the last few decades essential changes took place in American society, and the changes fundamentally altered the very same social forces which in the past had relegated the Catholics to a relatively low socio-economic status. As a foremost change, the occupational structure of the country was transformed, and the nation of small independent entrepreneurs was replaced by that of employees. The Catholics who always had been concentrated among the wage earners were now joined by many Protestants in the same type of employment. Members of the two religious groups worked in the same blue-collar and white-collar occupations, receiving similar wages and sharing a similar way of life.

The changes in the immigration policy contributed to the same effect. About 1920 the United States halted the free entrance of immigrants and drastically reduced the number of immigrants admitted to the country. The few newcomers who arrived after this date did not noticeably depress the socio-economic standards of the Catholic population.[6] The old force that had pulled down the social standing of Catholics was eliminated, and, at the same time, new

---

[3] Hadley Cantril, "Educational and Economic Composition of Religious Groups," *American Journal of Sociology,* 47, March 1943, pp. 574-79; Liston Pope, "Religion and the Class Structure," *Annals of the American Academy of Political and Social Science,* 256, March 1948, pp. 84-91; "Who Belongs to What Church?", *Catholic Digest,* 17, January 1953, pp. 2-8.

[4] Elmo Roper, *Factors Affecting the Admission of High School Seniors to College,* Washington, American Council on Education, 1949, p. XV.

[5] Gerhard Lenski, *The Religious Factor,* New York, Doubleday, 1961, pp. 86 sequ.; Albert J. Mayer and Harry Sharp, "Religious Preference and Worldly Success," *American Sociological Review,* 27, April 1962, pp. 218-227. For a different view see Joseph Veroff, Shella Feld and Gerald Gurin, "Achievement Motivation and Religious Background," *American Sociological Review,* 27, April 1962, pp. 205-217; and John Kosa and Leo D. Rachiele, *Spirit of Capitalism, Traditionalism and the Catholics,* paper presented at the 57th annual meeting of the American Sociological Association, Washington, D. C., 1962.

[6] In the present context we tend to overlook the Puerto-Ricans and other Spanish-Americans who seem to represent a special problem with racial (rather than religious) overtones. See William Petersen, "Is America Still the Land of Opportunity?," *Commentary,* 16, November 1953, pp. 477-86.

forces started to operate which helped to improve the Catholics' status. Such innovations of American life as the social policy initiated during the great depression, the growing influence of organized labor, and the emergence of an affluent mass society worked as great social levellers, eliminating many of those sharp inequalities that once had separated the top and bottom layers of society.

The total effect of these changes has been a betterment in the status of Catholics, and some common-sense observations, general and impressionistic as they are, give telling evidences. One may note, for example, the growing interest that the national press takes in the affairs of the church, giving increasing prominence and coverage to Catholic news items. One may note the election of the first Catholic to the Presidency as another sign of old barriers falling down. As far as the way of life of Catholics is concerned, one may note such changes as a rapid move into the suburbs, a switch in the political loyalty from the Democratic to the Republican party, and an increasing role in business leadership.[7] A trivial, yet characteristic, sign should also be noted: the sudden appearance of Catholics among the "titled Americans," due mainly to those refugee aristocrats who fled from the Communist-dominated countries to the safety offered by America.

Sociological studies present more systematic evidence of the fact that in the life time of the present generation a social mobility of considerable extent is taking place within the Catholic population, raising the status of large masses.[8] It is apparent, however, that certain sectors of American Catholicism are more successful, others less successful, in benefiting from this mass-like mobility. Accordingly, the present research attempted to explore the patterns of social ascendence and specify the more mobile, and the less mobile, sectors within the Catholic population.

The data were collected in two Catholic colleges, located in New York City and Upstate New York, where 328 male undergraduate students completed a questionnaire and furnished information about themselves, their fathers and parental grandfathers. One question asked: "What kind of work or occupation do you intend to take up after your education?" and subsequent questions inquired about the occupation of the father and grandfather. The first question re-

---

[7] For some critical remarks regarding this trend see Daniel Bell, (ed.), *The New American Right,* New York, Criterion, 1955.

[8] John Kosa and John Nash, "Social Ascent of Catholics," *Social Order,* 8, March 1958, pp. 98-103; John Kosa, Leo D. Rachiele and Cyril O. Schommer, "The Self-Image and Performance of Socially Mobile College Students," *Journal of Social Psychology,* 56, April 1962, pp. 301-16.

ferred to the intended occupation of the respondent at the beginning of his career, while the subsequent questions referred to actual achievements during the entire work career. Nevertheless, the question yielded answers which are comparable within the sample and indicate a trend in intergenerational social mobility. For the purpose of analysis, the occupations named in the questionnaires were evaluated on the North-Hatt scale of occupational prestige.[9] This procedure enabled us to compute a mean occupational prestige score for the three generations in any sub-group of the sample.

TABLE 1   MEAN OCCUPATIONAL PRESTIGE SCORES BY GENERATIONS AND SOCIAL CLASS OF THE RESPONDENTS

		Social Class of the Respondents		
	Total Sample (N = 338)	Upper and Upper-middle (N = 71)	Middle (N = 198)	Working and Lower (N = 69)
Respondent	79.1	82.7	79.1	75.5
Father	68.5	81.9	69.3	66.8
Grandfather	66.0	73.6	64.4	62.0

Table 1 presents the mean prestige scores of the three generations for the total sample and for the social classes represented by the respondents. The sample as a whole gives a picture of considerable social mobility. The grandfathers, with a mean score of 66.0, were on the level of a cabinet maker, the fathers advanced a few points to the level of a bookkeeper, while the respondents intend to advance more and begin their work career on the level of a contractor or economist.

Within this general trend, however, the specific performance of the social classes should also be considered. Table 1 shows a clear patterning for generations as well as for social classes. The occupational prestige score increases within each class with each subsequent generation and it also increases within each generation with each higher class. In fact, the classes are characterized by their specific patterns of mobility. The upper and upper-middle class (denoted as U. C. in the following text) shows a relatively high occupational

---

[9] Cecil C. North and Paul Hatt, "Jobs and Occupations: A Popular Evaluation," *Opinion News,* 9, September 1947, pp. 3-13. In addition, we used an extended North-Hatt scale prepared by Prof. Russel R. Dynes as well as further interpolations prepared by a panel of sociologists.

status as far back as the generation of the grandfathers; the grandfathers in this class reached about the same occupational level as
the present students from the working and lower class (L. C. in the
following) hope to reach at the end of their higher education. Hence,
the U. C. families show a relatively small social mobility over three
generations (9.1 points on the North-Hatt scale), while the same
mobility is relatively great in the middle class (M. C. in the following) and L. C. families (14.7 and 13.9 points, resp.). The aspirations
of the respondents reflect well this situation. The U. C. students
plan to start their career on about the same level as their fathers
occupy, but the M. C. and L. C. students expect to begin their work
career at a notably higher level than their fathers' present status.

It appears that social mobility, as evidenced by this sample, is
a process extending over generations, and the career expectations of
the students are determined by the achievements of their fathers
as well as of their grandfathers. Hence, each social class shows a
specific mobility pattern, and the respondent, who selected the name
of a social class to describe his background, made a choice that
aptly referred to the mobility pattern of his family.

If the social mobility of college students is determined by the
achievements of their ancestors, then it must also be effected by the
length of the American residency of their families. In this respect it
has been repeatedly observed that the upper classes in any segment
of American society are likely to contain a high proportion of "old
families," while the lower classes, an equally high proportion of
families which are, relatively speaking, newcomers on the American
scene.[10] In view of this problem we asked the respondents when
their paternal ancestor came to the United States. Based on this
information, Table 2 shows the mean occupational prestige scores by
period of immigration. It indicates that the prestige scores of the
respondents are independent of the length of the family's American
residence; they show chance variations, and the small group of students coming from recently arrived families reach the highest score.
For the fathers and grandfathers, however, the prestige scores are
correlated with the period of immigration, and those who come from
old families, score consistently higher than those from new families.
In other words, the time of immigration clearly differentiates the

10 W. Lloyd Warner and Leo Srole, *The Social Systems of American Ethnic
    Groups,* New York, Yale University Press, 1945; John Kosa, *Land of Choice:
    The Hungarians in Canada,* Toronto, University of Toronto Press, 1957;
    Bernard Barber, *Social Stratification,* New York, Harcourt, Brace, 1957, pp.
    428-29, 454-60.

career achievements of the older generations, but does not differentiate the aspirations of the present college students.

TABLE 2   MEAN OCCUPATIONAL PRESTIGE SCORES BY GENERATIONS AND PERIOD OF IMMIGRATION

	Period of Immigration			
	-1860 ($N = 113$)	1861-1890 ($N = 90$)	1891-1920 ($N = 99$)	1921- ($N = 17$)
Respondent	79.4	80.1	76.8	82.0
Father	71.3	69.2	65.6	65.3
Grandfather	69.0	66.5	63.0	62.8

We may investigate the intergenerational social mobility for each immigrant group separately. The oldest families (which arrived before 1860) show a rise of 10.4 points in occupational prestige from grandfathers to respondents, the next group of families (which arrived between 1861 and 1890) show a rise of 13.6, and the most recent group (which arrived after 1921), a rise of 19.2. Thus, the rise is negatively correlated with the length of American residency. The recently arrived families appear to move upward at the fastest rate, the oldest families at the slowest rate.

To present this trend in a simple form, we computed the occupational mobility rates for the subgroups of the sample.[11] If this rate is greater than 1.0, the subgroup moves upward faster than the total sample; if it is less than 1.0, the subgroup moves slower. The data presented in Table 2, yield the following occupational mobility rates:

Period of Immigration	Mobility Rate
-1860	0.87
1861-1890	1.04
1891-1920	1.05
1921-	1.51

The mobility rate increases for each more recent group of immigrants. The newcomers move fast, the oldtimers slowly; and the two groups are seemingly destined to meet on a common level where

[11] It was computed with the aid of the following formula:

$$\text{Occupational mobility} = \frac{M_{rg} - M_{gg}}{M_{rs} - M_{gs}}$$

where Mrg denotes the mean score of the respondents in any subgroup of the sample, Mgg the mean of the grandfathers in the subgroup, Mrs the mean score of the respondents in the total sample, and Mgs the mean of the grandfathers in the total sample.

the social differences that separated the fathers' and grandfathers' generations will be practically eliminated. In other words, the initial advantage enjoyed by earlier immigrants seems to be leveling off.

The problem of immigration cannot be entirely separated from that of ethnic origin, and particularly not in the present sample. The Catholic population is composed of many ethnic groups each of them displaying its characteristic social and psychological features.[12] For example, the Irish and Italian gorups are known to differ in temperament, scholastic achievements, and religiousness. Hence, it is reasonable to inquire whether they differ in their patterns of social mobility.

TABLE 3   OCCUPATIONAL MOBILITY RATES BY ETHNIC GROUPS

	Occupational Mobility Rate		Occupational Mobility Rate
Old stock, total (199) [a]	.90	New stock, total (135)	1.04
Irish (124)	.96	Italian (68)	1.11
English (33)	.87	French (21)	1.06
German (26)	.76	Polish (27)	.97
Dutch (16)	.83	Ukrainian (17)	.93

[a] Figures in parenthesis indicate the N for each group.

As the data presented in Table 3 indicate, the new immigrant stock has a higher occupational mobility rate than the old immigrant stock, and the ethnic groups of the new stock have higher rates than ethnic groups of the old stock. Within the two stocks further differences appear: the Irish seem to move faster than the Germans, and the Italians faster than the Ukrainians. One may assume that the social success of an ethnic group is interrelated with the particular ethnic culture of the group.[13] In the present context it is sufficient to note that the differences in the mobility of ethnic groups point,

12 August B. Hollingshead, "Trends in Social Stratification," *American Sociological Review,* 17 December 1952, pp. 679-86; Francis J. Brown and Joseph S. Roucek, *One America,* 3rd Ed., New York, Prentice Hall, 1952; John Kosa, Leo D. Rachiele and Cyril O. Schommer, "Psychological Characteristics of Ethnic Groups in a College Population," *Journal of Psychology,* 46, October 1958, pp. 265-75.

13 Bernard C. Rosen, "Race, Ethnicity, and Achievement," *American Sociological Review,* 24, February, 1959, pp. 47-60; Nathan Hurvitz, "Sources of Motivation and Achievement of American Jews," *Jewish Social Studies,* 23, October 1961, pp. 217-234; V. J. Kaye, "Participation of Ukrainians in the Political Life of Canada," *Revue de l'Université d'Ottawa,* 27, October 1956, pp. 3-24.

TABLE 4   EDUCATIONAL MOBILITY RATES BY SOCIAL CLASS, PERIOD OF
IMMIGRATION AND ETHNIC GROUP

	Educational Mobility Rate		Educational Mobility Rate
Social Class		Ethnic Groups	
of the Respondent		*Old stock, total*	0.87
Upper and		Irish	0.95
Upper middle	0.59	English	0.75
Middle	1.00	German	0.83
Working and lower	1.48	Dutch	1.08
Period of Immigration		*New stock, total*	1.19
-1860	0.89	Italian	1.20
1861-1891	0.98	French	0.99
1891-1920	1.23	Polish	1.24
1920-	0.86	Ukrainian	1.33

again, to a leveling-off process which seems to bring the children
of the new immigrant stock to the same socio-economic level as the
one occupied by the children of the old immigrant stock.

Since education is a relevant part of social status, our problem
can be approached through another avenue by investigating the educational achievements. We may compare the mean years of schooling
within the sample, measuring the actual time spent in education and
disregarding aspirations. Thus, every respondent who was a freshman was counted as having 13 years of schooling, without considering
his further educational plans.[14] From the means we computed the
educational mobility rates for the sub-groups of the sample.[15] The
results, presented in Table 4, outline the same trend as the one
observed in occupational mobility: the lower classes have a higher
mobility rate than the upper classes, the recently arrived immigrants
a somewhat higher rate than the old immigrants, and the new immigrant stock a higher rate than the old stock. Both in occupation
and education, the formerly disadvantaged groups (lower classes,
recent immigrants) are rapidly improving their status.

At this point some comments might be helpful to interpret the
results. The patterns of social mobility, evidenced by this sample,
suggest a trend toward leveling off the formerly conspicuous social
differences, caused by the time of immigration and ethnic origin.

[14] No correction was taken for the slight variations in the mean length of
schooling of the respondents in the various subgroups of the sample, due to
the varying proportion of freshmen and seniors in the subgroups.
[15] The formula given in Note 11 was used.

This trend, however, is not a specific Catholic phenomenon. Rather, it is a general feature of present-day American society, supported by such forces as popular affluency, replacement of human labor with the work of machines, and growing need for highly trained manpower in many new occupations. While the trend is general, its impact is particularly felt among the formerly underprivileged groups; thus, it is felt more among Catholics than among Protestants.

It is in this context that we think that the Catholic population of America (with the restriction used in this study) cannot be any longer equated with socio-economic inferiority. The Catholics are in the process of establishing a social stratification which is basically similar to that of the Protestant majority; they might even be near to the point of achieving equality in status.

The unanticipated consequences of this change can and will be felt in the whole structure of American Catholicism. In the past, the life of the American Catholics was to a great extent determined by a self-imposed segregation, well shown by the many "Tipperary Hills," "Germantowns," "Little Italies," and other ethnic settlements in the cities of the country. With social equality achieved, this type of segregation cannot be maintained and, in fact, is disappearing. Its end will necsesitate some fundamental changes in the fabric of Catholic life of America; it will raise problems with which the Catholics have to cope in the near future.[16]

Instead of making predictions, let us sum up our findings: (1) In the present sample of college students it was found that those coming from lower classes show a faster social mobility than those coming from the upper classes. (2) Children of recently arrived families have a higher mobility rate than those from old-immigrant families. (3) Children coming from the new immigrant stock move upward faster than those from the old immigrant stock. (4) It is suggested that this leveling-off process is a part of a general trend in America which is likely to place the Catholic population on a socio-economic level comparable to that of the Protestant population.

[16] See Thomas F. O'Dea, *American Catholic Dilemma*, New York, Sheed and Ward, 1958.

2

Catholic Values and the
Achievement Motive

FRED L. STRODTBECK

University of Chicago

SOURCE. Excerpted from "Family Interaction, Values, and Achievement," in David C. McClelland, Alfred L. Baldwin, Urie Bronfenbrenner, and Fred L. Strodtbeck, *Talent and Society* (Princeton: D. Van Norstrand, 1958), pp. 135-194. Reprinted by permission.

By the early 1950's, progress on the problem of the identification, understanding, and development of talented persons was believed to have reached a plateau. The resources of the Social Science Research Council's Committee on Identification of Talent were thus to be used in search for new perspectives. At Yale, the writer had been engaged in studies of family relationships and cultural values.

The implications of such research for the identification of talented persons or groups was believed to be a frontier area worthy of exploration.

It was not appropriate to think in terms of long-term designs. Terman had earlier, and inspiringly, demonstrated that to follow a set of young persons through a life career takes a life career. Like Terman, we faced the problem of relating whatever *analytic* variables we chose to work with to *outcome* variables, but the requirement of a "within-three-years" reporting date foreclosed to us the use of a longitudinal design. In retrospect, our ultimate decision on an outcome, or criterion, variable appears to have dictated the details of much of the remainder of the design.

The criterion problem consisted of a search for a way of evaluating performance in the larger community. We sought a community criterion which is as broadly understood and accepted as grades are in the academic community. The stubborn difficulty and appropriateness of the question, "What is talent?", was recognized and only uneasily resolved. The Committee came to use the term "talent" to refer to the *exercise* of an ability in a social setting, i.e., a talented performance. Mere possession of ability was not enough; activity of social consequence was required.

In small-group literature it has become commonplace to speak of social *rank* (in the group) as being a product of activities which have been carried out in conformity with group norms (4, p. 140). With regard to the larger society, although it is somewhat more difficult to demonstrate in particular cases, it is believed that rewards, prestige, and control of important resources also tend to be allocated in terms of the importance of the job and the length of training required to perform it. Through time, it appears that more responsible positions in society come to be coveted, in part, because of the consensus which exists concerning their worth to the group.

Unusual attainment in community service, the professions, or business generally results in high social status. More modest advances of the order of the shift from immigrant laborer to small business operator have similar, though not identical, status consequences. There is, of course, always some difficulty in distinguishing between status which is gained by personal effort and status which accrues from family membership. When the mobility of groups is under consideration, this difficulty is somewhat less serious. For example, if one of two groups who arrived in this country at about the same time has been markedly more upwardly mobile than the other, our inability to attribute the mobility exactly to the responsible generation does not foreclose a between-group comparison. The essential strategy in a "group" approach is that it enables us to utilize an indicant of performance which arises within society itself: status. The assumption is that the abilities of the more mobile groups have been used in activities of greater social consequence. Many difficulties, such as would arise when one attempts to compare the work of a chemist and a devoted nurse, are not squarely met. So long as the values of different men, or the same men at different times, are to be reconciled, it is doubtful that any fully satisfactory criterion can be found. "Relative rise in the status structure" appears to have the advantage of being a ubiquitous measure which both has application to many activities and implies the operation of a community-wide evaluation system. By this reasoning we have concluded that *status mobility* deserves serious consideration as a criterion of talented performance by groups.

This decision, made early in the research, at first seemed to create more problems than it solved. If social mobility were to be the criterion of differential talent development, how were we to get data helpful in understanding and identifying talented adolescents? Were we to be dependent in our research on the recall by adults of the attitudinal dispositions—and interpersonal relations—they believed themselves to have had as early adolescents? Since our time limitations no more permitted us to follow groups of adolescents in their status climb than in other forms of talent expression, was there an alternative to longitudinal research available? Could we not seek groups with differential mobility rates just as Durkheim had sought groups with differential suicide rates? Social group rates have the disadvantage that, since they are based upon the average of acts by many persons, they ordinarily have low predictive value for particular individuals. It is nonetheless possible that theoretical understanding of factors involved in talent development may be advanced by the study of factors associated with difference in group rates. For even if group predictions fall far short of the desired predictive efficiency, the mechanisms believed to differentiate among groups may later be found to differentiate among families within particular groups and thus provide a more crucial test of our understanding.

To illustrate, there is a popular impression that Presbyterians, Quakers, and Mormons are outstandingly industrious and successful, and they are believed to have produced a disproportionately high number of public leaders and men of science. Presbyterians historically represented the prototype of ascetic Protestantism which

Weber suggests is particularly consistent with the requirements for modern capitalism. Quakers and Mormons represent, in differing degrees, slight departures from ideal-type ascetic Protestantism, but there are still common emphases in the teaching of all three. From the standpoint of a research design, it would be desirable to have a classificatory typology of cultural groupings such that extreme cases could be selected with markedly different achievement rates. Hopefully, differences might be found between such groups which would clarify understanding of the requirements for achievement in particular situations. While such a design leaves much uncontrolled, it is to be considered first as a source of new hypotheses. Whatever findings result may be verified by other means.

In New Haven, where our research was to be conducted, there were only two large ethnic groups with similar periods of residence in this country: Southern Italians and Jews. Irish were also numerous, but they had been in New Haven a longer period. When it became apparent that for Italians and Jews it would be possible to locate second-generation families with early-adolescent (third-generation) sons in the public and parochial schools, an effort was made to review in detail the general demographic data relating to the time of arrival, respective economic situation upon arrival, and their subsequent socio-economic attainment. From the results of this inquiry we concluded that while Jews upon arrival had a slight advantage in terms of occupational status and urban skills, this original advantage has been appreciably widened during the period 1910-1940. Jews consistently have higher occupational status than the population at large, while, in contrast, Italians are consistently lower.

The next problem was to make decisions as to how to go about discovering what differences there might be between Italians and Jews in values, beliefs about nature, child-training practices, and family structure. To decide on research instruments, sample characteristics, and the like, it was necessary to be guided by working hypotheses suggested by the literature. Three sources were of particular importance: (a) studies of religion and social activity; (b) studies of child rearing and adult character; and (c) studies of small face-to-face group behavior. . . .

ITALIAN-JEWISH CULTURAL VALUES

It is to be assumed that the subsequent generations of Italians and Jews in this country have progressively become more acculturated and more like one another. For guidance in the formulation of hypotheses about the way in which value differences between these cultures may have influenced their differential achievement, one may turn first to the description of the original cultures from which they had emigrated. For the Southern Italian background there were some nine substantive sources (2, 3, 7–13). To the extent that they have been used in our quick overview, these sources were quite consistent. For the Jews, the relevant literature is much larger. In the present account, Zborowski and Herzog's *Life is With People* is the primary reference (16). Their treatment of *shtetl* culture is sympathetic—perhaps idealized—but sharply focused on attitude dimensions of great relevance to Italian-Jewish contrasts.

To begin with one of the most striking differences, Jews have traditionally placed a very high value upon *education and intellectual attainment*. The Jewish parent was expected to provide education, but not in a ritualistic manner. As much education was to be provided as the sons showed themselves capable of absorbing. Learning in the *shtetl* society gave the individual prestige, respect, authority—and the chance for a better marriage. The Jewish folk saying that "parents will bend the sky to educate their sons," and the heroic stories every first-generation Jewish parent can tell of the sacrifices made by fellow-parents to educate their children, illustrate the cultural legitimation of sacrifice for education.

The legitimation of education is further bound up with prestige associated with intellectual "brainwork," and the corresponding *lack* of prestige associated with physical accomplishments. This pattern of evaluation starts early in the child's career. Traditionally, a three- or four-year-old starting *kheyder* (elementary religious school) was regarded as a serious student. Brilliant students were treated with a deference ordinarily reserved for important adults. The weight of the opinion of the young scholar is reflected by the fact that a bearded man will not be ashamed to bring a difficult Talmudic question to a boy of thirteen.

Religious learning and the satisfactions of family life were not separated as they were in monastic Catholicism. It was the custom to arrange the young scholar's marriage while he was in his middle teens. In order that such scholars might give more attention to their studies, many of the economic responsibilities of the family were assumed by the wife.

In Southern Italian culture, the traditional attitude toward education was (and is) very different. School and book-learning environments were alien and remote from everyday experiences. Priests were taken from their families and villages to be educated.

To the typical Southern Italian peasant, school was an upper-class institution and potentially a threat to his desire to retain his family about him. While education might well serve for some as a means of social advancement, the peasant was disposed to believe that this avenue was not open to his children—in their case education was not functional. For each age there is a proper behavior. Family life, local political power, and other objectives were stressed as alternative goals to learning.

Even in this country, the first-generation Southern Italian parents' attitude was, in part, negative to education. As an Italian educator reports: "Mother believed you would go mad if you read too many books and father was of the opinion that too much school makes children lazy and opens the mind for unhealthy dreams." Intellectualism, in itself, was not valued in Southern Italian communities. Learned men were of another class, or alternatively, they were men of the church. Status in the community changed slowly; property was in all cases more important. Property could be gotten faster by a trickster-trader than a scholar (1). Scholars were like monks: good men but not of the real world.

La famiglia in the Southern Italian culture was an inclusive social world. The basic mores of this society were primarily family mores —everyone outside the family was viewed with suspicion. The basic code was family solidarity, and there was strong feeling that the family should stay together—physically close together. The essence of the ethos has been most forcefully captured by Edward C. Benfield. He states the one premise from which the "family vs. all others" political orientation would seem to flow: "Choose so as to maximize the short-run advantage of the family and assume others will do likewise."

The Jewish family was traditionally a close-knit one, but it was the entire Jewish *shtetl* community rather than the family which was considered the inclusive social unit and world. Although relatives were more important than friends, all Jews were considered to be bound to each other. The primary unit was the family of procreation. Physical proximity was not so heavily stressed. Mandelbaum (6, pp. 28, 31) and Joffe (5) have pointed out that the dynamics of benefice for the Jews was not of the reciprocal exchange nature. Parents' gift to their children are to be parallel for the next generation. In the home, as in the community, giving must move in a descending spiral. Giving serves not only to enrich the donor and succor the recipient, but it also maintains the constituency of fundamentally equal persons—and in this way enriches the community. In American Jewish communities today, the sizeable and highly publicized charitable contributions owe much to this tradition.

For the Jewish parents there was in the *Alles für die Kinder* theme an emphasis upon a bettered condition in the *future* which made them more willing to let children leave the community for opportunities elsewhere. Much less emphasis on the future existed in the Italian families' evaluation of alternatives.

The external world for the Jews was hostile to be sure, but it was by nature solvable. For all goods there is a proper price, for all labor there is a best way of doing it. For the Italian the equivalent phrasing is perhaps: "There is work which must be done." One might go further to say there are ways of doing the work which are more expeditious—but no matter how the work is done, there is always the chance that fate may intervene. The unpredictable intervention of fate may be for good or evil, but *Destino* is omnipresent. If a man works all his life for something which *Destino* may deny him, well then, why should men look so far ahead? There is always the present, and one might have a lucky break.

Zborowski, in his study in this country of the reactions of hospitalized Jewish and Italian veterans to pain, employs Florence Kluckhohn's well-known *time* orientation to differentiate the cultural responses (15). First, he finds that both Jews and Italians complain more about pain than "Old Americans." But, more importantly, sedation alone is enough to allay Italians. For the Jew sedation is not enough. He continues to be pessimistic and concerned about the implication of the sedation for his eventual recovery. For the Italian there is a *present-oriented* apprehension of the sensation of pain; for the Jew there is a *future-oriented* anxiety concerning the symptomatic meaning of the pain. Neither group wishes to suffer alone, neither group believes it is necessarily masculine to deny the existence of pain, and neither group believes that suffering is an end in itself.

In the use of folk medicines, belief in the "evil eye," and the like, Jewish and Italian culture shared many common irrational elements. Religious ritual was strong in both cultures. However, the complex of behavior involved in the individual's participation in his own salvation deserves separate attention.

In Italian folk theology, Catholic doctrine was popularly understood as requiring sheer obedience to arbitrary prescriptions for the sake of an arbitrary reward. Where the formula did not apply, the matter was of no real significance. Faith in the mystery of the Trinity and the timely interventions of the priest were all that was required. For the Jews, religious improvement was always possible and perfection always denied. The scholar proceeded at his own rate after becoming a rabbi. There was no one to grant the learned and respected man a more advanced degree; his job was ever undone. During the middle years he might have had to give more attention to business, but as he grew older he could spend his full time in discussion, study, and prayers.

In the East European *shtetl*, no man could occupy a position so humble that it could not in part be redeemed by his religious scholarship. Without the religious scholarship a man of means could be *prost*—simple, common, vulgar. A diploma of any type which signified learning in non-religious fields came to be accorded respect like that accorded religious scholarship. It is important to stress that if Talmudic scholarship taught precision, juridic care, and dedication, it taught attitudes toward learning which might, with a growth of heterodoxy, be transferred to other learning. So long as the ghetto confined the area of attainment, goals of religious scholarship were highly coveted. Upon release from the ghetto, the status and financial rewards available in the disciplines of law and medicine were also attainable by work of an intellectual character similar to Talmudic scholarship. Jewish mobility has in all probability been facilitated by the transformation of a complex of behavior which had not existed for the Italians.

A peasant's mistrust of books in contrast with the veneration of learning does not exist in isolation from other attitudes. Zborowski and Herzog tell us that in the *shtetl* the hair line of babies would in some instances be shaved back so that the child would have a high forehead—hence, appear intelligent. Short, thick hands were thought to be inappropriate and ugly—*prost*. The Jewish attitude toward the body was not ascetic, the body was neither ugly nor inherently evil. It was rather that the body was a vessel for containing the spirit. Rest, food, and procreation on the Sabbath were legitimated to keep the body at full efficiency, but a specialized interest in physical development *per se* was improper. For the Jews the mind was a great tool, but ever under discipline and purposeful direction. In the early morning prayers the mind is turned to sacred matters, on the Sabbath to non-business matters—it is never a question of whether the mind can win over impulse.

It is perhaps equally true that the Italian emphasis on good food and proper relaxation is superficially similar to Jewish practice, and, for that matter, to practices in many cultures. The essential difference as we perceive it is that the Italian manual worker was never ashamed of his strength; to keep his body fit was a desirable end in itself, for it was never perceived to be in competition with other necessarily more important activities.

To supplement the old-culture Italian-Jewish child training contrast there is just one comparative American study which has come to our attention. Field interviewers from the Harvard University Laboratory of Human Development contacted an area sample of families in greater Boston concerning methods of child rearing. With regard to second-generation Italians and Jews, the division of the families by social class was as follows:

	Italian	*Jewish*
Middle	7	64
Lower	36	15

This is consistent with the predicted differential status mobility: Jews are concentrated in the middle classes, Italians in the lower. Unfortunately, this distribution does not provide many middle-class Italian, and only relatively few lower-class Jewish families, though the frequencies for lower-class Italians and middle-class Jews are sizeable. Since this class distribution appears to be roughly "modal" for second-generation members of these ethnic groups, comparisons between these groups are of particular interest. The main points made are as follows:

(a) The amount of time spent in caretaking and in affectionate interaction with the child, the warmth of the mother-child relationship, and the amount of enjoyment in child-care is not different for the two groups. Both are relatively high in infant nurturance save only for the greater severity of the Italian mothers in toilet training. For sexual play with other children, masturbation, or nudity in the home, Italians are markedly less permissive than Jews.

(b) Italians are less permissive of aggression to parents and impose more requirements on the child's table manners, conversations with adults, acting as "boy" or "girl," caution around furniture, and freedom of movement from the home than do Jews. Italians were more prone to report they followed through and demanded obedience, although in terms of authority patterns such as mother-dominant, shared, father-dominant, or divided—no differences between Italian and Jewish families were reported. Family structure from the perspective of the child is reflected indirectly in the fact that Jewish children admit deviant behavior more frequently than Italian children, and, in addition, tend to require more attention from adults.

(c) In terms of current dependency, and this is focused at about the five-year level, both groups of children are about equally dependent, but the Jewish mother is significantly more accepting of dependent behavior. In general, the emotional atmosphere of parent-child relations is somewhat warmer in Jewish than in Italian families, while at the same time Jewish families place a higher evaluation on the benefits to be gained by spanking.

(d) In terms of expected school attendance, Jews expect much longer school attendance, but there is a corresponding lesser insistence on the child's "doing well in school." Perhaps this implies a disposition to permit the child to set his own level for quality of performance.

It should be noted that there were some marked differences between the 64 middle-class Jewish and the 15 lower-class Jewish families. While this latter number is small, the lower-class families were significantly more severe in weaning and toilet-training, took less pleasure in caring for babies, interacted less, and were less warm and nurturant when the child was an infant. At the current behavior level, they were also less demonstrative, much less permissive of sexual behavior, and in general more severe in their socialization practices. Italian-Jewish differences are greatly attenuated when class level is constant; hence, since class level is not controlled in the comparisons above, the exact contribution of "class" in contrast with "culture" cannot be ascertained.

Out of all this material, all too briefly summarized, we must now pick those values which appear most likely to have accounted for the differential occupational achievement of the two "old cultures" when they came to the United States. This task necessarily involves a comparison of Italian-Jewish value differences with the values we arrived at for a description of the Protestant-U.S. achievement ethic. It finally resolved itself into a comparison at five points, as follows:

1. *Man's sense of personal responsibility in relation to the external world.* The Protestant's world was the work of God, its mysteries were profound and not to be understood by the slacker. To work to understand and transform this world was the true Christian's personal responsibility. Misfortunes have a definite place in the scheme; they are the tests which God sets before men. By such logic, hard work was understood to be behind all worldly accomplishment, but there was still no guarantee that even a lifetime of hard work would necessarily be rewarded.

For the "U. S. achiever"—the successful scientist, executive, or professional person—rational mastery of the situation has been equated with the "hard work" of the Protestants, and threat of almost continuous review of his record has been equated with anxiety over eventual salvation. There is no necessary personal deprivation which must be endured; one's accomplishment can be facilitated by "breaks," but importantly breaks are of the individual's own making. It is a matter of being available with what is needed at the right place and at the right time. Just as breaks are not given by a beneficent power, neither are failures. Whatever failure an individual has suffered could always have been foreseen and hedged against if the individual were sufficiently alert. One might commiserate with an unforseen person, but for the "U. S. achiever" there is no legitimate excuse. His sense of personal responsibility for controlling his destiny is very great.

"Old-culture" Jewish beliefs appear to be congruent in many if not all respects with the "U. S. achiever" belief in rational mastery of the world presented above and at marked variance with that of the Southern Italian. For the "old-culture" Jew, there was the expectation that everything could be understood if perhaps not always controlled. Emphasis on learning as a means of control was strong. Religious or secular learning, once attained, unlike the Protestant's salvation and the "U. S. achiever's" status, was not in continual jeopardy. For men who were learned in trades but not specialized religious scholars, the expectations of charity to others of the community who were less fortunate was a continuing goad to keep working, but if misfortune befell a former benefactor, the community would understand. The "old culture" sense of personal responsibility coexisted with a responsibility of the community for the individual which eases somewhat the precariousness associated with "all or none" expectations on the individual.

For the Italian, the best laid plans of man might twist awry. Misfortune originated "out there," not inside the individual. The term *Destino* suggests that it has been written that a particular event will or will not come to pass. A sort of passive alertness is inculcated; no one knows when he is going to get a lucky break, but at the same time there is no motivation for a heroic rational undertaking, for such an undertaking may be *destined* to fail.

2. *Familism versus loyalty to a larger collectivity.* The essence of familism is an emphasis on filial obedience and parental authority. Calvinism was anti-familistic in its emphasis upon a first obedience to one's own soul and to God. Familistic social organization tends to involve a particular locus of activity and hierarchy of responsibility based upon age and kinship relations rather than upon impersonal technical requirements. For this reason the "U. S. achiever" tends

to be anti-familistic like the Calvinist. That is, the desire to keep two or more generations together would compete with the job and educational opportunities which require residential moves. The "U. S. achiever" moves with his wife and children on the basis of his technical qualifications to wherever he believes he can maximize his opportunities. At the early stages of his career he may even avoid the line of work where his father might help him, so as to win for himself the privilege of being judged for his own competence.

The "old-culture" Jewish pattern involved separations for business and educational reasons and a heightened consciousness that a man's first responsibility was for his children. That is, obligations were primarily from those that have more to those that have less, which, practically speaking, meant that children need not always stay to nurture parents who might be better off than they were. The Jewish pattern of weaker ties to parents is not seen to be as extreme as the pattern for the "U. S. achiever," but in some ways it contrasts sharply with the Southern Italian pattern.

Under great economic duress the Southern Italian familial organization may shrink to the nuclear unit—but this is atypical. The successful Italian wishes to draw his extended family about him, and in the process some are lifted in status just as others are secured in the status of the large-family complex.

3. *Perfectability of man.* An aspect of Calvinism, perhaps best captured for popular consumption in *Poor Richard's Almanac* by Benjamin Franklin, is the emphasis that at every moment of every day a person should work to improve himself. "Old-culture" Jewish emphases on religious scholarship and study represented a similar belief in the responsibility for self-improvement. For the "U. S. achiever" this perfectability requirement has, in one sense, been relaxed, but insofar as it remains, it has become even more stringent. Now, the improvement should take place in a relaxed manner with no apparent effort. The self-improvement should be "enjoyed," not "endured" as it might have been earlier. In all of these cases interest in education should be (and has been) high because it is one of the ways in which man obviously perfects himself.

For the Southern Italian there was considerable doubt as to whether man could perfect himself or, indeed, that he need try to. According to his interpretation of Catholicism, he must conscientiously fulfill his duties, but his "good works" did not form a rationalized system of life. Good works could be used to atone for particular sins, or, as Weber points out, stored up as a sort of insurance toward the end of his life, but there was no need to live in every detail the ideal life, for there was ever the sacrament of absolution. Furthermore, the Southern Italian really felt that man lived at an uneasy peace with his passions and that from time to time one had to expect them to break through. Man is really not perfectable—he is all too human, and he had better not drive himself or his mind too hard in trying to reach perfection.

4. *Consciousness of the larger community.* The Protestants' "each man his brother's keeper" has given way in the "U. S. achiever" to a less moralistic rationale for social consciousness based upon a recognition of the interdependencies in modern society. Just as the "old-culture" Jewish community could vicariously participate in the charities of its wealthiest members, there is a sense in which the strengthening of various aspects of American society are recognized to contribute to the common good.

The "old-culture" Jew, enabled by his success to assume a responsibility for the community, had little choice in the matter. The social pressures were great, and they were ordinarily responded to with pride and rewarded by prominence in the community forum. The identification went beyond the extended family. The giver was not to be rewarded in kind; his reward came from community recognition. Such community identification—as contrasted with family identification—was not highly developed among Southern Italians. Reduced sensitivity to community goals is believed to inhibit the near-altruistic orientations which in adolescence and early maturity lead individuals to make prolonged personal sacrifices to enter such professions as medicine or the law.

5. *Power relations.* Analysis of the requirements for success in America suggests that insofar as differences in status may be perceived to be legitimate because the high-status person is technically more competent, then the person in the subordinate position can still gives his full commitment to organizational goals without feeling or acting as if he were being dominated by his superior. Early Protestantism laid the groundwork for such limited and specific relationships by insisting that each man had a post assigned him by God so that no one should feel inferior or superior. The modern bureaucracies create for "U. S. achievers" a greatly increased number of positions in our society where a person has a specific role in a larger impersonal system to perform.

On the other hand, the "old-culture" Jew did not see power in the context of some external system of pre-established impersonal relationships. He tended, like the Protestant, to reduce power questions to other terms, to the equity of a particular bargain, for example; but unlike the Protestant, these relationships were always specific both as to persons and content involved, and *not* part of a larger system. His primary concern was to make his relationships good with others with whom he was in close contact over a particular issue. The specificity of his relations with others, including his separation of business and family matters, is also like the functional specificity of modern bureaucratic society, but again unlike it in overlooking the *system* of such functional relationships.

The "old-culture" Italian tends to see power entirely in immediate interpersonal terms and as a direct expression of who can *control* the behavior of another rather than who knows more for a job in an impersonal system. He is constantly interested in "who's boss?" and with turning every relationship into a "for me-against me" or "over me-under me" polarity.

THE NEW HAVEN SAMPLE

In the process of developing the sampling frame in New Haven, certain further data were obtained which bear upon Italian-Jewish cultural differences. A questionnaire was administered to over 1,000 boys between 14 and 17 in the New Haven public and parochial schools (and a somewhat larger number of girls). Data obtained on this questionnaire were utilized primarily to identify a set of third-generation Italian and Jewish boys who were in turn stratified by their school performance and socio-economic status. The questionnaire touched generally upon values and more particularly upon materials relating to occupational choice, parental expectations, parental control, educational aspirations, and balance of power in family interaction.

Boys from Catholic families who reported one or more paternal and one or more maternal grandparent born in Italy were considered Italian. Boys who reported the religion of both their parents as Jewish were considered Jewish. Determination of socio-economic status was made from information provided by the son relating to the parents' education and the father's occupation. Classification was made in terms of seven groupings. . . . In terms of these two criteria the following frequencies were obtained:

Socio-economic Status	Italian	Jewish	Other
High (classes 1 and 2)	8	24	52
Medium (classes 3 and 4)	80	66	213
Low (classes 5, 6, and 7)	182	17	455
Unclassified	15	2	59
	285	109	779

It may be noted that there were very few *High* (major and minor professional, owners of very large business) Italians, and relatively few *Low* (laborers through skilled workers) Jews. For both groups there were a substantial number of families who owned or managed small businesses, or were engaged in white-collar or supervisory positions—here classified *Medium.*

To demonstrate more clearly the way in which this distribution confirms the differential status distribution of the two groups, one may construct an index number using the distribution of "others" as a base. For example, 52 of 720 (excluding unclassified "Others") are of high socio-economic status. On a pro-rata basis 19.5 Italians of high status would be expected. Actually significantly fewer than this, only 8, or 41 per cent of the expected, are observed. For the Jews of high status 310 percent of the expected are observed. The full set of indices are as follows:

Socio-economic Status	Italian	Jewish
High	41%	310%
Middle	100	209
Low	107	25

It was desirable to use the boy's achievement in school as a criterion of his own performance just as the status of the family might be used as a criterion of the father's performance. Toward this end, each boy's performance on prior intelligence and school achievement tests was inspected and his grade performance in terms of the norms of the particular school predicted. When the boy's school grades exceeded the expected performance, he was considered an over-achiever and when his grades fell short of the predicted performance, he was classified as an under-achiever. . . . A total of 48 Italian and Jewish boys, matched according to SES and divided equally as between over-achievers and under-achievers were selected for intensive analysis. In addition to the questionnaire administered in the schools, questionnaires were given to the father, mother, and son in each of these 48 households. An experimental procedure designed to measure family interaction was also utilized in each household. . . .

THE V-SCALE

Fifteen items were included in the original screening questionnaire. These items, adapted from the Harvard Social Mobility seminar, dealt very generally with the types of value differences which have been previously described as characterizing "old-culture" Italian-Jewish differences. Not all points in the value analysis were covered in the questionnaire because the analysis was completed only after the intensive study had been made and the questionnaire was used in selecting the subjects for intensive study. In the first stage of the analysis, search was made for items which would discriminate at the .05 level between over-achieving and under-achieving students (both Italians and Jews being excluded from this comparison). The original set of fifteen items was reduced to eight. In this process a set of items of uneven coverage resulted.

Since neither the Italians nor the Jews had been involved in the original computations, an inspection of Italian-Jewish differences on V-items provides an independent check on the distribution of one type of "achievement potential" in the two populations. As an operation to corroborate the inferences which had been made on the basis of status mobility, it was predicted that Jews would have higher achievement-related responses than Italians. It may be seen in Table 1 that this prediction was significantly confirmed for six of the eight items, and that no differences were observed in the other two cases.

A factor analysis reveals that items relating to the rejection of subjugation to fate—the first three—have a high loading on Factor I (Mastery), and the fourth through sixth items (relating to Independence of Family) have a high loading on Factors II. The item treating of organizational vs. individual credit discriminates between Italians and Jews and is not highly related to the other alternatives. The eighth item, dealing with postponed gratification, which like the other seven had discriminated between over- and under-achieving students, did not discriminate between Italians and Jews nor did it correlate significantly with other items in the set. The third of the Mastery items also did not discriminate between Italians and Jews. The items dealing with control of one's destiny, separation from the family, and working for a group, differentiate between Italians and Jews as predicted in the introductory ethnographic contrasts. . . .

SUMMARY

Complicated though the task may be, we must now somehow integrate our empirical findings into the larger theoretical questions which lay behind our original research design. In its simplest terms, our plans started with the hypothesis that the American social sys-

TABLE 1 V-SCALE ITEMS, FACTOR LOADINGS AND ITALIAN-JEWISH RE-
SPONSE LEVELS

Factor Loading			Per Cent Dis-agree by Ethnicity	
Factor I "Mas-tery"	Factor II "Inde-pendence of Family"	Items	Jews	Italians
.64	.00	Planning only makes a person unhappy since your plans hardly ever work out anyhow.	90	62
.49	.28	When a man is born, the success he's going to have is already in the cards, so he might as well accept it and not fight against it.	98	85
.58	.15	Nowadays, with world conditions the way they are, the wise person lives for today and lets tomorrow take care of itself.	(80)[a]	(79)
.04	.60	Even when teen-agers get married, their main loyalty still belongs to their fathers and mothers.	64	46
.21	.60	When the time comes for a boy to take a job, he should stay near his parents, even if it means giving up a good job opportunity.	91	82
.29	.68	Nothing in life is worth the sacrifice of moving away from your parents.	82	59
—.02	.28	The best kind of job to have is one where you are part of an organization all working together even if you don't get individual credit.	54	28
—.05	.00	It's silly for a teen-ager to put money into a car when the money could be used to get started in business or for an education.[b]	(65)	(63)

[a] The difference is not significant at the .05 level for pairs of values in parentheses; for the remaining values the differences are significant at the .05 level or greater.

[b] Per Cent "Agree" reported for this item.

tem contained certain inherent requirements for the achievement of individuals in it, requirements inherited to a considerable extent from the Protestant Ethic as described by Weber, Parsons, and others, but also evolved into new forms. Then, since it was impractical to do longitudinal research, we decided to pick subcultures which had been conspicuously more and less successful in adapting *as groups* to the U. S. requirements for achievement of high status and to search their value systems and family life for clues as to why they differed in the production of achievant individuals in the United States.

Before summarizing the clues we discovered, it is necessary to stress that no one should impute an evaluative tone to our comparison of Italians and Jews—the two differentially achieving groups chosen for study. In the first place, the emphasis on status mobility as the criterion of "success" in this study should not be perceived as the only criterion by which one might recognize activities of social value. There are many alternative philosophies of life which would suggest quite different criteria of success to be investigated by the behavioral scientist. Our reason for choosing status mobility as the criterion rests primarily on the fact that it is a societal means of evaluating people which applies to a very broad range of social activities in the United States today.

Furthermore, we were not primarily motivated by a desire to study these subcultures *per se* with the notion of predicting which groups would show the most status mobility from now on. Rather our interest was in the extent to which each of these "old cultures" was *initially* adaptive to the U.S. social setting as we analyzed it. In fact, there is considerable evidence in our data to support the notion that whatever differences in values and family interaction initially existed, they are disappearing as both groups get more assimilated into American life. For example, we found no qualitative differences in family interaction between Italians and Jews using the Bales categories, and no V-score differences in our stratified sample (with effects of socio-economic status removed). Also, while Jews were more mobility-oriented in their favorable attitudes toward higher education and prestige occupations, there was no evidence that Italians differed from the rest of the population in this respect. Finally, we know that socio-economic status affects socialization practices and power balance in the family, both of which are factors which are related to subsequent achievement. But both ethnic groups are changing in socio-economic status. To take just one possible effect of this as an illustration: more Jews are moving into high status where the fathers are more powerful and may therefore, according to our data, tend to produce sons who have values *less* conducive to upward mobility. On the other hand, more Italians may be moving into medium status where family power may be more conducive to mobility than in the lower status where many of them are now. Thus one might on this basis predict a reversal in the mobility rates of the past, with a trend toward greater mobility for the Italians in the future. So, lest the analysis be misunderstood, the interest in "old culture" differences is not at all to predict group mobility rates, but to identify clues which might have explained differences in their initial adjustment to American life.

The clues we found consist in part of the value differences based on ethnographic evidence summarized earlier, and whatever further support for them we uncovered in the empirical study. Each of these value differences were selected because we thought it should promote status mobility in the United States, and not because it was necessarily the best way of comparing Italian and Jewish subcultures. In each case, our expectations were largely confirmed by the data. Three of the five expected value differences turned up in the V-scale which differentiated Italians from Jews and which also reflected differences in past status mobility (i.e., as represented by higher scores for fathers with higher social status) and probably *future* status mobility (i.e., as represented by higher scores for over-achieving sons). There is, then, evidence from three sources that the following three values contained in the V-scale are important for achievement in the United States:

1. A belief that the world is orderly and amenable to rational mastery, and that, therefore, a person can and should make plans which will control his destiny (three items in the V-scale). By way of contrast, the notion that man is subjugated to a destiny beyond his control probably impeded Southern Italians in their early adjustment to the United States, just as it impeded boys in school or less successful fathers in their occupations in this study. Unfortunately we cannot say with any assurance whether the poor performance of the Italians and the less successful fathers or sons was the result of the belief in fate or whether the belief in fate was the result of the poor performance. However, since we know—in the case of the Italians —that the belief was part of the "old culture" and therefore antedated their performance, we may feel justified in predicting that while beliefs and performance undoubtedly modify each other, it is the belief which came first so far as the adjustment of Southern Italians to the United States is concerned.

2. A willingness to leave home to make one's way in life. Again, by contrast, the South Italian stress on "familism" which we found evidence for in the V-scale should have interfered with upward mobility and contributed to the lower occupational achievement of Italians as compared with Jews. Family balance of power also affects the willingness to leave home, a fact which demonstrates that one's position in life can produce a value disposition as well as the reverse. But whether the willingness to break up the family comes from an "old culture," from power balance in the family, from the father's or son's relative lack of success in job or school, it is certainly a value of importance in the "achievement complex."

3. A preference for individualistic rather than collective credit for work done. On the one item in the V-scale which dealt with this value, the Jews showed greater preference for individualistic, the Italians for collective rewards, as one would perhaps expect from the greater "familism" of the Italians. Some loyalty to an abstract system of relations—to a collectivity—is essential in modern bureau-cratic organizations. Hence, the greater collective emphasis of the Italians here would appear to have *favored* their quick adaptation to American life (although perhaps more now when bureaucracies are better developed than earlier). On the other hand these same bureaucracies stress individualistic rewards and impersonal relations between superiors and subordinates, both of which do not fit very well with the Italian emphases on *non-individualized* collateral loyal-ties and on very personal dominance-striving in face-to-face relation-ships. Although the questionnaire does not provide much information on this point, it is also clear that while the Jewish emphasis on individualized rewards *is* adaptive to the bureaucratic system, it also contains an element which does not fit the system so well—i.e., the stress on *personal* rather than impersonal individualistic relation-ships. But again, our main concern is not with Italian-Jewish differ-ences, but with the elements in those differences which may explain their differential achievement. Here it seems to be the stress on individualistic reward among the Jews, although the case is not so clear-cut as with the other values in the V-scale, because there is only one item and because there are at this point elements in both "old cultures" working both for and against quick adaptation to the U.S. social system.

Aside from the V-scale results, which are most impressive because they reflect differential achievement of cultures (Jews over Italians), of fathers (high over low SES) and of sons (over- vs. under-achieve-ment in school), there are two facts from the larger questionnaire study which relate to a fourth expected value difference between Italians and Jews—namely, the value placed on the *perfectability of man*. The Jews definitely had higher educational and occupational expectations for their sons. Practically speaking, this would appear to mean they believed that man could improve himself more by education and that one should not readily submit to fate and accept a lower station in life, the way the Italians were more prepared to do.

The fifth and final expected Italian-Jewish value difference had to do with power relationships. We had been led to believe by ethnographic reports and other studies that Italians would be more concerned than Jews with establishing dominance in face-to-face relationships, and such turned out to be the case. Both in the boys' reports of who was dominant at home and in the actual decision-winning in the 48 homes we studied intensively, the Italians showed greater variations from equality of power than the Jews. While this finding is probably of lesser importance than those presented above, it nonetheless sharpens our curiosity about what effects the power balance through time in particular families will have on the son's achievement. Is it possible that when relatively equalitarian relations persist in the home, the son can move to new loyalties in larger systems of relationships such as those provided by college or a job without an outright "rupture" of family controls? Or conversely, is such an adjustment to new institutions outside the home harder the more the home has tended to be dominated by one parent or the other? Furthermore, what would be the cost of such a rupture to the son in terms of performance and motivation to continue on his own? Would the conflict not be less, the frustration less, when the break came, and consequently the emotional and intellectual adjustment more efficient if he had come from a home where controls were already diffuse and equalitarian as they are in many situations in life? The present design involved only a single visit with the families; in subsequent research it is to be hoped more can be arranged as the child is growing up, so that one can follow the effects of power balance on the child's adjustment inside the family and subsequently to life outside it. . . .

Our purpose has been to break some new ground in the study of talent potential. We have tried to do so both theoretically and empirically by focusing on three fairly novel aspects of the problem: *the requirements of the U.S. social system for success, the role of values in achievement, and family power* as a determinant of some of the child's most fundamental adjustments to life. If our preceding pages have succeeded either through theoretical argument or empirical fact in convincing people that these are problems *relevant to talent identification and worthy of being pursued by further research along the same lines,* our major objective will have been reached.

REFERENCES

1. Brown, N. O. *Hermes the thief.* Madison: Univer. Wisc. Press, 1947.
2. D'Alesandre, J. J. Occupational trends of Italians in New York City. *Italy American Monthly,* 1935, **2**, 11-12.
3. Guilds' Committee for Federal Writers Publications. *The Italians of New York.* New York: Random House, 1938.
4. Homans, G. C. *The human group.* New York: Harcourt, Brace, 1950.
5. Joffe, N. F. The dynamics of benefice among East European Jews. *Social Forces,* 1948-49, **27**, 239-247.
6. Mandelbaum, D. G. *Change and continuity in Jewish life.* Glencoe, Ill.: Oscar Hillel Plotkin Library, 1955.
7. Mangione, J. *Mount Allegro.* New York: Houghton Mifflin, 1942.
8. Mangione, J. *Reunion in Sicily.* New York: Houghton Mifflin, 1950.
9. Mariano, J. H. *The second generation of Italians in New York City.* New York: Christopher, 1921.
10. Pellegrini, A. *Immigrant's Return.* New York: Macmillan, 1951.
11. Radin, P. *The Italians of San Francisco: their adjustment and acculturation, Monographs* 1 and 2, S.E.R.A. Project, Cultural Anthropology, San Francisco, 1935.
12. Sangree, W. and Hybleum, M. A study of the people of Middletown of Sicilian extraction with special emphasis on the changes in their values resulting from assimilation into the Middletown community. Unpublished Master's thesis, Wesleyan Univer., 1952.
13. Sartorio, E. C. *Social and religious life of Italians in America.* New York: Christopher, 1918.
14. Snyder, C. R. Culture and sobriety. *Quart. J. Studies on Alcohol,* 1955, **16**, 101-177, 263-289, 504-532; 1956, **17**, 124-143.
15. Zborowski, M. Cultural components in responses to pain. *J. Social Issues,* 1952, **8**, 16-30.
16. Zborowski, M. and Herzog, E. *Life is with people.* New York: International Univer. Press, 1952.

3

Religious Identity and the Conventional Wisdom

NORVAL D. GLENN
University of Texas

RUTH HYLAND
University of Texas

SOURCE. "Religious Preferences and Worldly Success: Some Evidence from National Surveys," *American Sociological Review,* 1967, **32**, 73-85. Reprinted by permission.

The relationship of religion to economic.and occupational success is the most viable topic of debate in the sociology of religion in the United States.[1] The issues raised by Weber in his famous essay on the Protestant Ethic continue to evoke vociferous exchanges. During recent years the controversy has become centered on the influence

[1] Much of the debate deals not directly with economic and occupational success but with achievement motivation, deferred gratification, and similar variables that are assumed to underlie success.

of religion in contemporary American society.[2] Some scholars who accept Weber's basic thesis object to its application, in modified form, to contemporary societies.

The focus of the present controversy is on the relative rates of upward mobility of Protestants and Catholics, since there is clearcut evidence that Jews, for reasons that may or may not be essentially religious, experienced more rapid upward movement for several decades than either Protestants or Catholics.[3] Although there are some "hard data" that throw light on the relative advancement of Protestants and Catholics, these data are somewhat contradictory, or at least are subject to contradictory interpretations. One national study found no difference between the upward mobility of Protestant and of Catholic men;[4] this finding has been interpreted to mean both that religious differences do not lead to differences in mobility and that the Catholics equalled the Protestants in spite of palpable handicaps.[5] A study in the Detroit metropolitan area found greater upward mobility of Protestants than of Catholics;[6] this finding has been interpreted both as an indication of the importance of the

[2] For instance, see Raymond W. Mack, Raymond J. Murphy, and Seymour Yellin, "The Protestant Ethic, Level of Aspiration, and Social Mobility: An Empirical Test," *American Sociological Review,* 21 (June, 1956), pp. 295-300; Bernard C. Rosen, "Race, Ethnicity, and the Achievement Syndrome," *American Sociological Review,* 26 (February, 1959), pp. 47-60; Gerhard Lenski, *The Religious Factor,* rev. ed., Garden City, New York: Doubleday, 1963; Joseph Veroff, Sheila Feld, and Gerald Gurin, "Achievement Motivation and Religious Background," *American Sociological Review,* 27 (April, 1962), pp. 205-217; Albert J. Mayer and Harry Sharp, "Religious Preference and Worldly Success," *American Sociological Review,* 27 (April, 1962), pp. 218-227; Andrew M. Greeley, "Influence of the 'Religious Factor' on the Career Plans and Occupational Values of College Students," *American Journal of Sociology,* 68 (May, 1963), pp. 658-671; Marvin Bressler and Charles F. Westoff, "Catholic Education, Economic Values, and Achievement," *American Journal of Sociology,* 69 (November, 1963), pp. 225-233; Andrew M. Greeley, "The Protestant Ethic: Time for a Moratorium," *Sociological Analysis,* 25 (Spring, 1964), pp. 20-33; Ralph Lane, Jr., "Research on Catholics as a Status Group," *Sociological Analysis,* 26 (Summer, 1965); and Seymour Warkov and Andrew M. Greeley, "Parochial School Origins and Educational Achievement," *American Sociological Review,* 31 (June, 1966), pp. 406-414.

[3] See Nathan Glazer, "The American Jew and the Attainment of Middle-Class Rank: Some Trends and Explanations," in Marshall Sklare, ed., *The Jews,* New York: The Free Press of Glencoe, 1958, pp. 138-146.

[4] Seymour Martin Lipset and Reinhard Bendix, *Social Mobility in Industrial Society,* Berkeley and Los Angeles: University of California Press, 1959, pp. 48-56.

[5] Lenski, *op. cit.,* p. 84.

[6] *Ibid.*

religious factor and as a mere reflection of sampling variability or differences in ethnic background.[7] One author, in reporting selectively the findings of a national survey, noted that an equal percentage of Protestant and Catholic men under age 40 in metropolitan areas had incomes of $8,000 or more; he used these data to support a claim that Catholicism is not detrimental to worldly success.[8] However, he could have selected data from the same survey to support the opposite conclusion.[9]

It is not our ambition to end the controversy once and for all in this article; a secondary analysis of national survey data not gathered for the purpose of assessing mobility cannot provide conclusive evidence. However, we are convinced that the potential of such an analysis to help resolve the controversy has not been realized. All too frequently partisans in the debate have judiciously selected national survey data to support preconceived conclusions. Never, to our knowledge, has anyone done a comprehensive, thorough and objective analysis of the relevant national data.[10] Although the analysis reported here is not completely comprehensive, we strive for an objective treatment of the most relevant information.

Using data from 18 national surveys conducted from 1943 to 1965, we first assess trends in the relative economic, occupational, and educational status of Protestants and Catholics. Then, we take a close look at the contemporary distributions, first for the nation as a whole and then with regional, age, and community-size controls. Finally we scrutinize the evidence concerning the relative persistence of Protestant and Catholic students in school and college. We also include data for Jews and, on occasion, for those with no religious

---

[7] Greeley, "The Protestant Ethic . . . ," *op. cit.*

[8] *Ibid.*

[9] Our similar national data show important differences in the distributions of Protestants and Catholics above this level (see Table 9). Also, one could point out that Protestants equalled Catholics in spite of the heavy concentration of the former in the South and in the smaller metropolitan areas, where incomes in general were relatively low.

[10] The best treatments of national data on status differences by religious preference are primarily descriptive rather than attempts to assess the relative impact of Protestantism and Catholicism on worldly success. See Hadley Cantril, "Education and Economic Composition of Religious Groups: An Analysis of Poll Data," *American Journal of Sociology*, 47 (March, 1943), pp. 574-579; Donald J. Bogue, "Religious Affiliation," *The Population of the United States*, New York: The Free Press of Glencoe, 1959, pp. 688-709; and Bernard Lazerwitz, "A Comparison of Major United States Religious Groups," *Journal of the American Statistical Association*, 56 (September, 1961), 568-579. Lazerwitz's data are the most recent and come from two 1957 samples and one 1958 sample.

preference, but the sample sizes usually allow reasonably confident conclusions only for Protestants and Catholics. In order to control influences related to race, we analyze data only for white respondents.

Seventeen of the surveys were conducted by the Gallup Organization (also known as the American Institute of Public Opinion) and one was conducted by the National Opinion Research Center. The two earliest polls (1943 and 1945) used quota samples; all of the others used some kind of probability sample.[11] Four of the surveys were selected expressly for this study; they were the four most recent Gallup polls using national probability samples which were available from the Roper Public Opinion Research Center when we started our research. The data from the other surveys were on hand for other purposes. In no case did we have any knowledge of the relevant frequency distributions before we selected a survey, and in no case did we exclude a survey after we examined the data.

POSTWAR TRENDS

Since the mid-1940's, the relative standings of white Protestants and Catholics in the country as a whole have changed dramatically (see Tables 1, 2, and 3). For instance, in 1943 Protestants were well above Catholics in economic status, whereas by 1964 Catholics were clearly above Protestants (Table 1). The differences between the proportions of Protestants and Catholics at both the highest and lowest economic levels around 1964 are statistically significant. Since the 1943 data come from a quota sample, they do not meet the strict requirements for tests of significance, but the difference in the proportions of Protestants and Catholics at the lowest level is so large that we are rather confident that it did not result solely from sampling error.

The change in relative economic status may not have been quite as great as these data suggest. We delineated the 1964 levels on the basis of the income data in Table 6, whereas the levels for the

11 None of the samples are simple random samples, however; they are therefore not amenable to analysis with the usual textbook statistical formulae. The standard errors for the more recent Gallup polls are estimated to be usually about 1.4 to 1.6 times the standard errors for simple random samples. In addition, the recent Gallup samples are inflated about 100 percent by a weighting procedure used instead of callbacks; therefore the N's reported for the combined 1963, 1964, and 1965 data in the tables of this article are usually about twice the number of respondents represented. For statistical procedures for analysis of these samples, see Leslie Kish, *Survey Sampling,* New York: John Wiley and Co., 1965. We are indebted to Mr. Andrew Kohut of the Gallup Organization for additional guidance in analyzing the Gallup data.

TABLE 1   DISTRIBUTION (%) BY ECONOMIC LEVEL OF WHITE RESPONDENTS
TO A 1943 NORC SURVEY AND TO FOUR RECENT GALLUP POLLS, BY RELI-
GIOUS PREFERENCE [a]

1943 NORC Survey				
Economic Level	Protestants	Catholics	Jews	Total
Upper	26.3	21.6	50.0	25.9
Middle	51.4	48.1	41.2	50.2
Lower	22.3	30.2	8.8	23.9
	100.0	100.0	100.0	100.0
N	1,638	485	67	2,190

Four Recent Gallup Polls
(December, 1963 to March, 1965)

Economic Level	Protestants	Catholics	Jews	Total
Upper	35.9	41.0	58.0	37.8
Middle	41.5	43.3	26.7	41.5
Lower	22.7	15.6	15.3	20.7
	100.0	100.0	100.0	100.0
N	8,660	2,884	435	12,209

[a] The respondents to the 1943 NORC survey were divided into four economic levels largely on the basis of rent or, if they were home owners, estimated rental value of home. Here the two upper levels are combined into one. The Gallup respondents were divided into economic levels on the basis of the income data in Table 6. The upper level starts at $7,000 and the lower level is below $3,000.

The original 1943 NORC data give religious identification for church members only. The nonmembers had lower average status than the members; they were allocated between the Protestants and Catholics on the basis of information on church membership from a 1945 Gallup poll. Jewish members and nonmembers do not differ appreciably in economic status; therefore in 1943 Jewish data presented here are for members only.

1943 respondents were determined at least partly on the basis of the interviewers' impressions of the life styles of the respondents and their families. Consequently the standards of placement of the 1943 respondents may have varied somewhat by community and region according to the average level of affluence. If so, the effect undoubtedly was to raise the Protestants relative to the Catholics, because Protestants were (and still are) disproportionately more

TABLE 2   RATIO OF ACTUAL TO EXPECTED PROPORTION OF WHITE PROTESTANT, CATHOLIC, AND JEWISH HEADS OF HOUSEHOLDS AT BROAD URBAN OCCUPATIONAL LEVELS, 1945, 1953, AND 1964 [a]

	Protestants			Catholics			Jews		
	1945	1953	1964	1945	1953	1964	1945	1963	1964
Upper nonmanual [b]	.99	.99	.94	.81	.82	.98	1.86	2.11	2.11
Lower nonmanual [c]	.95	.92	.92	1.06	1.08	1.17	1.60	1.64	1.60
Upper manual [d]	.89	.99	1.03	1.37	1.10	1.04	.86	.56	.22
Lower manual [e]	.95	.95	.97	1.23	1.03	1.14	.57	.51	.49
N	1,748	4,178	7,150	587	1,616	2,462	121	286	341

[a] The 1945 data are from one Gallup poll, the "1953" data are from five Gallup polls ranging in date from October, 1953 to March, 1954, and the "1964" data are from four Gallup polls ranging in date from December, 1963, to March, 1965.

The "expected" proportion at each occupational level is the proportion of white heads of households of all religious preferences at that level.

[b] Professional and semi-professional workers, businessmen, and executives.
[c] Clerical and sales workers.
[d] Skilled workers.
[e] Service workers, operatives, and laborers.

South and in small communities, where average incomes are relatively low.[12]

Nevertheless a marked change in relative economic status undoubtedly resulted from the pronounced changes in relative occupational and educational standings. The occupational changes are shown in Table 2. The "expected" proportion of each religious category at each occupational level is simply the proportion of respondents of all religions at that level; accordingly ratios below and above unity indicate disproportionately low and high representation. Whereas Protestant representation decreased at both levels of nonmanual occupations and increased at both manual levels, Catholic representation increased sharply in nonmanual occupations and declined in manual work.[13] In 1945 and 1954 Protestants were more

[12] See Tables 4 and 5. One should not place much confidence in the apparent increase, in Table 1, in the proportion of Jewish families at the lowest economic level. The Jewish samples for both dates are small and subject to considerable sampling variability, and the occupational and educational data in Tables 2 and 3 show an increase in the relative standing of Jews.

[13] The underrepresentation of Protestants in 1945 and 1954 at all levels in Table 2 results from their overrepresentation in the farm category, which is not shown in the table.

TABLE 3 RATIO OF ACTUAL TO EXPECTED PROPORTION OF WHITE PRO-
TESTANTS, CATHOLICS, AND JEWS AT EACH BROAD EDUCATIONAL LEVEL,
AGES 30 AND OVER, 1945 AND 1964 [a]

	Protestants		Catholics		Jews	
Educational Level	1945	1964	1945	1964	1945	1964
No more than 8 years of school	.96	1.04	1.09	.95	.70	.55
At least some high school but no college	1.00	.97	1.08	1.11	1.11	.94
At least some college	1.05	.98	.75	.82	1.26	2.09
N	1,473	7,294	426	2,274	93	376

[a] The 1945 data are from one Gallup poll and the "1964" data are from four Gallup polls ranging in date from December, 1963, to March, 1965.

The "expected" proportion at each educational level is the proportion of white respondents of all religious preferences at that level.

highly represented than Catholics at the upper nonmanual level, but in 1964 representation of Catholics at this level slightly exceeded that of Protestants. Although the small N's do not allow us to place much confidence in the Jewish data, it appears that Jews gained on Christians during the two decades. According to the data, Jewish representation increased at the highest level, remained the same at the lower nonmanual level, and declined at both manual levels.[14]

The changes in representation at three broad educational levels were similar to the occupational changes (Table 3). Protestant representation increased at the lowest level and declined at the two higher levels, while Catholic representation declined at the lowest level and increased at the high school and college levels. Protestants ranked clearly ahead of Catholics in educational status in 1945, but by 1964 the relative standings of the two religious categories had become ambiguous. Catholics had moved ahead in median years of school completed (see Table 8) but were still underrepresented at the college level. During the 20-year period Jewish representation apparently increased at the college level and declined at all lower levels.

It is clear that Catholics as a whole have experienced more net upward mobility during the postwar period than Protestants. In

[14] The fact that Jewish representation declined from 1954 to 1964 in three of the urban levels and stayed the same in the other reflects decreased total representation of Jews in urban occupations as Christians became more urbanized.

part, this is simply a matter of Catholics overcoming an initial disadvantage growing out of their more recent immigration. The Catholic immigrants, as all others, usually became employed at first at the lower occupational levels, and as long as they were incompletely acculturated in nonreligious American culture, many of their cultural characteristics may have impeded their upward movement. Culture not detrimental to worldly success in the home country became detrimental in the context of American culture; probably some of the culture of the Southern and Eastern Europeans in its original context was adverse to economic advancement. Consequently the acculturation of European immigrant groups during the past few decades has, in the absence of many new immigrants, tended in itself to close the socioeconomic gap between Protestants and Catholics.

However, Catholics are now pulling ahead of Protestants; their greater advancement is therefore more than just a catching-up process. If, as is widely believed, the values, beliefs and practices of Protestantism are more conducive to worldly success than those of Catholicism, then clearly the Catholics have some advantage that more than offsets their religiously-based disadvantage.

Catholics in the United States do have one obvious and important advantage. They are highly concentrated in the larger metropolitan areas in the non-Southern regions (Tables 4 and 5)—precisely the communities with the highest average incomes, most favorable occupational distributions, and highest average educational attain-

TABLE 4   DISTRIBUTION (%) BY SIZE OF COMMUNITY OF RESIDENCE OF WHITE RESPONDENTS TO FOUR RECENT GALLUP POLLS, BY RELIGIOUS PREFERENCE [a]

Community Size	Protestants	Catholics	Jews	No Religion	Total
Rural	39.5	15.1	2.9	18.8	32.1
2,500-9,999	9.4	5.8	. . .	9.0	8.3
10,000-49,000	9.3	7.6	1.4	12.6	8.7
50,000-249,999	15.0	19.8	11.9	16.3	16.1
250,000-999,999	16.2	22.1	15.6	15.8	17.6
1,000,000 and over	10.5	29.5	68.1	27.4	17.2
Total	100.0	100.0	100.0	100.0	100.0
N	9,097	2,940	436	277	12,750

[a] Dates of the polls range from December, 1963, to March, 1965. Therefore, the data are essentially for 1964.

TABLE 5   DISTRIBUTION (%) BY REGION OF RESIDENCE OF WHITE RE-
SPONDENTS TO FOUR RECENT GALLUP POLLS, BY RELIGIOUS PREFERENCE [a]

Region	Prot-estants	Catholics	Jews	No Religion	Total
New England	2.5	12.3	7.8	5.8	5.0
Middle Atlantic	16.7	39.0	70.1	11.9	23.6
East Central	18.4	18.6	5.7	18.4	18.0
West Central	12.7	8.4	1.1	8.3	11.2
South	34.4	7.8	7.1	14.8	26.9
Rocky Mountain	4.3	3.2	0.9	12.3	4.1
Pacific	10.9	10.6	7.1	28.5	11.1
Total	100.0	100.0	100.0	100.0	100.0
N	9,099	2,940	435	277	12,751

[a] Dates of the polls range from December, 1963, to March, 1965. Therefore, the data are essentially for 1964.

ments.[15]   Thus, if Catholics in each community only equal or approach their Protestant neighbors in these status variables, Cath-

[15] For 1960 census data showing variation in income, occupation, and education by community size, see Leo F. Schnore, "Some Correlates of Urban Size: A Replication," *American Journal of Sociology*, 69 (September, 1963), pp. 185-193. The relationship between community size and median family income was monotonic, the median varying from $5,222 in urban places with 2,500 to 10,000 residents to $6,863 in urbanized areas with 3,000,000 or more residents. The relationship between community size and percentage of workers in nonmanual occupations was not as simple, but the percentages were generally higher in the larger classes of communities. Percentage of high school graduates did not vary consistently with community size, but the smallest percentage was in the communities with only 2,500 to 10,000 residents.

The median income of white persons with income in 1959 was $3,332 in the Northeast, $3,099 in the North Central Region, $3,322 in the West, but only $2,529 in the South. The percentage of employed white males in nonmanual occupations in 1960 was 39.4 in the Northeast, 33.7 in the North Central Region, 39.4 in the West, and 36.9 in the South. Median years of school completed by white persons 25 years old and older in 1960 were 10.8 in the Northeast and North Central Regions, 12.1 in the West, and 10.4 in the South. The more pronounced disadvantage of Southerners in income than in occupation and education reflects lower earnings within occupations in the South.

Bogue presents data from a 1955 NORC survey showing lower incomes for Protestants than for Catholics within broad occupational categories and educational levels (*op. cit.,* pp. 705-707). The variation in income within occupations by community size and region can account for this difference; therefore it is not, as Greeley argues ("The Protestant Ethic . . . , *op. cit.,* p. 32), evidence against an adverse economic effect of Catholicism.

olics in the country as a whole will exceed Protestants by a fairly wide margin. Furthermore, the probability of upward mobility of sons of manual workers apparently varies directly with size of community of orientation.[16] Consequently, with other relevant factors held constant, one would expect upward mobility to be substantially greater for Catholics than for Protestants. If this were not the case, then indeed it would seem that religiously-related values, ethnicity, high fertility, or some other factor or factors were holding Catholics back. However, Catholics apparently *are* advancing more rapidly than Protestants, and one cannot tell from the greater Catholic mobility alone whether or not it is occurring *in spite of* religiously-based handicaps. For clues we turn to a detailed comparison of the contemporary status of Protestants and Catholics.

CONTEMPORARY STATUS DIFFERENCES BY RELIGIOUS PREFERENCE

Income, occupational, and educational distributions of whites by religious preference around 1964 are shown in Tables 6, 7, and 8.

Median family income was nearly $900 higher for Catholics than for Protestants, and the proportion of families with incomes below $3,000 was 7.1 percentage points greater for Protestants—a statistically significant difference. However, a slightly larger percentage of Protestant families were at the very highest income level. Jewish families ranked well above all other religious categories, and the respondents with no religious preference came from families that ranked only above Protestants in median income but only below Jews in the percentage with very high incomes.

The low economic standing of Protestants resulted partly from the lower earnings in each occupation and at each educational level in the South and in small communities,[17] but also from the fact that Protestants ranked lowest in summary measures of occupational and educational status.

The only marked occupational difference between Protestants and Catholics was in the proportion of heads of households who were farmers. The two religious categories were about equally represented in upper-manual occupations, and Catholics were more highly represented in both nonmanual and lower-manual occupations. As one would expect, Jews were highly represented in all nonmanual occupa-

[16] Lipset and Bendix, *op. cit.,* chapter 8.
[17] See footnote 15.

TABLE 6 DISTRIBUTION (%) BY REPORTED OR ESTIMATED ANNUAL IN-
COME OF FAMILIES OF WHITE RESPONDENTS TO FOUR RECENT GALLUP
POLLS, BY RELIGIOUS PREFERENCE [a]

Income	Prot-estants	Catholics	Jews	No Religion	Total
Under $1,000	4.7	2.3	1.6	4.2	4.0
1,000-1,999	9.0	6.4	6.2	5.4	8.2
2,000-2,999	9.0	6.9	7.5	7.2	8.5
3,000-3,999	10.1	6.7	6.2	7.3	9.1
4,000-4,999	11.7	9.6	5.3	13.1	11.0
5,000-6,999	19.7	27.0	15.2	22.7	21.4
7,000-9,999	19.3	25.3	24.4	18.5	20.7
10,000-14,999	11.6	12.3	24.4	12.7	12.3
15,000 and Over	5.0	3.4	9.2	8.8	4.8
Total	100.0	100.0	100.0	100.0	100.0
Under $3,000	22.7	15.6	15.3	16.8	20.7
$7,000 and Over	35.9	41.0	58.0	40.0	37.8
$10,000 and Over	16.6	15.7	33.6	21.5	17.1
Median ($)	5,460	6,338	7,990	6,118	5,856
N	8,660	2,884	435	260	12,209

[a] Income was estimated by interviewer if respondent refused to report income.
Income is reported or estimated for 1963 or 1964 depending on the date of the
poll.

tions except clerical workers, were less than proportionately represented in all urban manual occupations, and were virtually absent
from the farm category.[18]

[18] The respondents with no religious preference, or the heads of their households, had a bimodal distribution along the scale of occupational prestige.
They had more than 2½ times their proportional share of the professional
and semi-professional jobs and were slightly overrepresented as laborers and
operatives and unskilled workers. In contrast, their representation was very
low as farmers, businessmen and executives, and clerical workers. Although
the sample size allows only a tentative conclusion, it seems that religious
apostasy is most common at the upper end of the occupational hierarchy but
more common at the bottom than in the middle.

Bogue's data agree with ours in showing a bimodal distribution but show a
much larger percentage of the respondents with no religion as farmers and
businessmen and executives (*op. cit.,* p. 703). Lazerwitz also shows a bimodal
distribution and high representation of the no-religion respondents in the farm
category (*op. cit.,* p. 574). These data are consistent with Lenski's finding of a
curvilinear relationship between income and religious interest, with the smallest religious interest at the upper income level and the greatest at the middle
levels. See Gerhard Lenski, "Social Correlates of Religious Interest," *American
Sociological Review,* 18 (October, 1953), pp. 533-544.

TABLE 7   DISTRIBUTION (%) BY OCCUPATION OF HEAD OF HOUSEHOLD
BY WHITE RESPONDENTS TO FOUR RECENT GALLUP POLLS, BY RELIGIOUS
PREFERENCE [a]

Occupation	Prot- estants	Catholics	Jews	No Religion	Total
Professional and semi-professional workers	12.8	13.1	27.6	38.7	14.0
Farmers and farm managers	10.8	2.2	0.3	1.8	8.2
Businessmen and executives	13.5	14.3	31.4	6.3	14.1
Clerical workers	6.6	8.9	9.4	2.7	7.2
Sales workers	6.4	7.6	13.2	5.0	6.9
Skilled workers	22.1	22.3	4.7	15.8	21.5
Operatives and un- skilled workers	17.3	18.1	11.7	18.9	17.3
Service workers	4.9	7.3	0.6	4.5	5.3
Laborers	5.5	6.2	1.2	6.3	5.5
Total	100.0	100.0	100.0	100.0	100.0
Nonmanual workers	39.3	43.9	81.6	52.7	42.2
Lower manual workers	27.7	31.6	13.5	29.7	28.1
Duncan's socioeco- nomic index	36.1	37.8	53.1	46.0	37.4
N	7,150	2,462	341	222	10,175

[a] Only those respondents reporting an occupation are included here. The dates
of the polls range from December, 1963, to March, 1965. Therefore, the data
are essentially for 1964.

The educational data in Table 8, which are limited to respondents
age 30 and older to exclude most persons who had not completed
their formal education, show that Catholics slightly exceeded Protestants in median years of school completed and that a larger
percentage of Protestants were at the lowest educational levels.
However, Protestants were ahead of Catholics in one important
respect—the percentage who had at least some college. Although the
difference only borders on statistical significance, we show below
that it almost certainly did not result from sampling error.[19]

[19] Both Jews and respondents with no religion ranked well above Christians in
educational status, and both had more than double the proportional representation as college graduates. Furthermore, the percentage who had finished
of those who had started college was much higher for Jews and no-religion

TABLE 8   DISTRIBUTION (%) BY EDUCATIONAL ATTAINMENT OF WHITE
RESPONDENTS TO FOUR RECENT GALLUP POLLS, AGES 30 AND OVER, BY
RELIGIOUS PREFERENCE [a]

Years of School Completed	Prot- estants	Catholics	Jews	No Religion	Total
0-7	15.5	14.1	9.5	9.0	14.8
8	22.4	20.4	10.6	23.2	21.5
1-3 high school	16.9	19.6	8.2	13.6	17.2
4 high school	28.4	31.9	35.7	21.5	29.3
1-3 college	8.2	6.2	15.4	9.6	8.0
College graduate	8.7	7.9	20.5	23.2	9.2
Total	100.0	100.0	100.0	100.0	100.0
No more than 8 years of school	37.9	34.5	20.1	31.2	36.3
At least some college	16.9	14.1	35.9	32.8	17.2
Median years of school completed	11.1	11.4	12.6	12.2	11.4
N	7,294	2,274	376	177	10,121

[a] Dates of the polls range from December, 1963, to March, 1965. Therefore, the
data are essentially for 1964.

These national data are useful for some purposes, but if we are
to make even tentative intelligent inferences about the influence of
religious factors, we must control for region and community size.
Also desirable is control for age, since Catholics are somewhat younger
than Protestants on the average.[20]   Therefore, we present the data
in Tables 9, 10, and 11 for young adults in non-Southern metropolitan
areas with 250,000 or more residents. In order to avoid including a
large number of people who had not completed their formal education, we use a different age range for education than for income and
occupation.[21]

respondents than for Christians. The persons who said they had no religion
had a bimodal distribution similar to their distribution along the scale of occupational prestige; they were highly overrepresented at the college level,
slightly overrepresented at the eight-year level, and underrepresented at all
other levels. Bogue and Lazerwitz report similar distributions.

[20] See Leonard Broom and Norval D. Glenn, "Religious Differences in Reported
Attitudes and Behavior," (forthcoming). Six of seven national surveys showed
a larger percentage of Catholics below age 40.

[21] In the case of income and occupation, our controls for age are imprecise,
since the age data are for the respondents themselves, the income data are

TABLE 9   DISTRIBUTION (%) BY REPORTED OR ESTIMATED ANNUAL IN-
COME OF FAMILIES OF WHITE RESPONDENTS TO FOUR RECENT GALLUP
POLLS, AGES 20-39, IN NON-SOUTHERN METROPOLITAN AREAS OF 250,000
OR MORE PEOPLE, BY RELIGIOUS PREFERENCE [a]

Income	Prot-estants	Catholics	Jews	No Religion	Total
Under $1,000	0.7	0.2	1.9	8.5	0.9
1,000-1,999	2.0	2.8	4.7	...	2.5
2,000-2,999	2.3	1.3	...	1.7	1.6
3,000-3,999	8.0	3.9	3.8	3.4	5.7
4,000-4,999	8.4	9.5	...	6.8	8.2
5,000-6,999	25.6	30.0	18.9	42.4	27.8
7,000-9,999	29.2	34.8	38.7	13.6	31.7
10,000-14,999	19.1	13.6	23.6	11.9	16.7
15,000 and over	4.6	3.9	8.5	11.9	4.9
Total	100.0	100.0	100.0	100.0	100.0
Under $3,000	5.0	4.3	6.6	10.2	5.0
$7,000 and over	52.9	52.3	70.8	37.4	53.3
$10,000 and over	23.7	17.5	32.1	23.8	21.6
Median ($)	7,292	7,198	8,610	6,440	7,319
N	586	610	106	59	1,361

[a] Income was estimated by interviewer if respondent refused to report income.
Income is reported or estimated for 1963 or 1964 depending on the date of the
poll.

With these controls, Protestants ranked slightly above Catholics
in summary measures of each variable. Jews ranked highest, well
above each category of Christians in each variable; respondents with
no religion ranked second in occupation and education and last in
income.

One could easily use the Protestant and Catholic income data
selectively, as Greeley did with similar data, to argue that the two
religious categories had the same earning power. The percentages
with incomes of $7,000 or more were virtually the same. However,
a more detailed examination of the data reveals that below the $7,000
level Catholics were somewhat better off than Protestants, while at

for their families, and the occupational data are for heads of households.
However, most of the respondents were either heads of households or spouses
of heads; the inclusion of a few young adults living with their parents probably affects the different religious categories in a similar manner. If there is
any differential effect, it is probably to lower slightly the apparent relative
standing of Catholics, since there is a wider Protestant-Catholic gap at the
older ages.

TABLE 10   DISTRIBUTION (%) BY OCCUPATION OF HEAD OF HOUSEHOLD
REPORTED BY WHITE RESPONDENTS TO FOUR RECENT GALLUP POLLS,
AGES 20-39, IN NON-SOUTHERN METROPOLITAN AREAS OF 250,000 OR MORE
PEOPLE, BY RELIGIOUS PREFERENCE [a]

Occupation	Prot-estants	Catholics	Jews	No Religion	Total
Professional and semi-professional workers	21.9	16.0	46.5	52.8	22.4
Farmers and farm managers	0.9	....	....	....	0.4
Businessmen and executives	16.2	14.8	32.7	....	16.2
Clerical workers	6.3	10.2	8.9	9.4	8.4
Sales workers	7.8	11.9	6.9	....	9.3
Skilled workers	22.8	22.7	5.0	15.1	21.1
Operatives and un-skilled workers	14.5	10.6	....	5.7	11.3
Service workers	7.1	11.8	....	13.2	8.9
Laborers	2.6	1.9	....	3.8	2.1
Total	100.0	100.0	100.0	100.0	100.0
Nonmanual workers	52.2	52.9	95.0	62.2	56.3
Lower manual workers	24.2	24.3	....	22.7	22.3
Duncan's socioeco-nomic index	43.5	41.9	62.5	52.0	44.7
N	588	586	101	53	1,328

[a] Only those respondents reporting an occupation are included here. The dates
of the polls range from December, 1963, to March, 1965. Therefore, the data
are essentially for 1964.

the level of $7,000 or more Protestants were decidedly more pros-
perous than Catholics. For instance, the proportion of Protestants
with incomes of $10,000 or more was six percentage points greater—
a statistically significant difference. The higher representation of
Protestants at the lowest income level can be explained by their
higher representation at the very lowest occupational and educational
levels (Tables 10 and 11), which in turn probably resulted from a
larger percentage of the Protestants being migrants from the South
and from small towns and rural areas. The lower representation of
Catholics at the highest income levels can be explained by their

TABLE 11   DISTRIBUTION (%) BY EDUCATIONAL ATTAINMENT OF WHITE RESPONDENTS TO FOUR RECENT GALLUP POLLS, AGES 25-44, IN NON-SOUTHERN METROPOLITAN AREAS OF 250,000 OR MORE PEOPLE, BY RELIGIOUS PREFERENCE [a]

Years of school completed	Protestants	Catholics	Jews	No Religion	Total
0-7	2.3	1.9	3.5	....	2.1
8	4.3	5.2	....	....	4.3
1-3 high school	14.1	17.9	....	3.6	14.4
4 high school	44.8	50.7	30.7	28.6	45.7
1-3 college	16.5	10.7	26.3	14.3	14.6
College graduate	18.0	13.6	39.4	53.6	18.9
Total	100.0	100.0	100.0	100.0	100.0
No more than 8 years of school	6.6	7.1	3.5	....	6.4
At least some college	34.5	24.3	65.7	67.9	33.5
Median years of school completed	12.7	12.5	14.8	14.5	12.6
N	693	689	114	56	1,552

[a] Dates of the polls range from December, 1963, to March, 1965. Therefore, the data are essentially for 1964.

lower representation at the highest educational levels and in turn in professional, semi-professional, business, and executive occupations. We attempt to account for these differences below.

One could also use the occupational data selectively to show practically no Protestant-Catholic difference. The percentages of Protestants and Catholics in non-manual, upper-manual, and lower-manual occupations were almost identical. However, Protestants had a marked advantage within the nonmanual level; 38.1 percent of them, compared with 30.8 percent of the Catholics, were in professional, semi-professional, business, and executive occupations—a statistically significant difference.

As we have indicated above, this occupational difference can be attributed to the educational difference (Table 11). Similar percentages of Protestants and Catholics had completed the eighth grade, but the high school dropout rate was substantially higher for Catholics. Of those who had completed high school, a substantially higher percentage of Protestants had started and completed college. Most of these differences approach but fall below statistical significance, but the difference in the percentages who had started to college is significant well beyond the 0.05 level.

Clearly, the differences in status between young metropolitan Protestants and Catholics grew primarily out of differential persistence in the educational process. This difference is so crucial that we scrutinize it carefully below. Before we do, however, it is important to point out that we cannot, from the data at hand, attribute the educational difference to religious or religiously-related influences, although Lenski's data from his Detroit study point toward a religious interpretation.[22] We cannot say that by controlling region, community-size, and age we are comparing people who have had equal opportunities for upward mobility. We know that more of the Catholics were offspring of immigrants, but, on the other hand, more of the Protestants were undoubtedly migrants from the South and from small towns and rural areas. Unfortunately, there is no way to assess accurately the relative importance of these two handicaps. Parental economic, occupational, and educational status is a crucial unknown, and thus uncontrolled, aspect of the opportunity structure, but the earlier data on Protestant-Catholic status differences suggest that this factor favored the Protestants.

PERSISTENCE IN SCHOOL AND COLLEGE

Some of the most important and interesting data presented by Lenski in *The Religious Factor* concern the relative dropout rates of white Protestants, white Catholics, Jews, and Negro Protestants. In his Detroit sample he found that Jews were least likely to have dropped out of a unit of school before completing it and that white Protestants, white Catholics, and Negro Protestants followed in that order.[23] The Protestant-Catholic difference was large enough that it probably did not result from sampling error, and it could not be explained by differences in parental status, because a larger percentage of the Catholics had middle-class parents. Weller, also using a Detroit sample, obtained similar results.[24] These data suggest

[22] *The Religious Factor*, chapter 6.

[23] *Ibid.*, pp. 263-266. The percentages who did not drop out were 79, 61, 48, and 33 respectively.

[24] Neil J. Weller, *Religion and Social Mobility in Industrial Society,* unpublished doctoral dissertation, University of Michigan, 1960, chapter 4, as cited by Lenski, *The Religious Factor,* p. 263. Weller found that 51 percent of the white Protestants but only 38 percent of the Catholics in his sample of 1100 men had completed their last unit of education.

that some difference in socialization may have given the Protestants a greater degree of "educational tenacity," which in turn might be a manifestation of the ability and willnigness to defer gratification. As an alternative explanation, Lenski suggests that the larger average size of Catholic families may produce a Protestant-Catholic difference in average IQ and thus place Catholic students at a competitive disadvantage.[25]

Neither our recent national data nor our non-Southern metropolitan data agree with Lenski's findings on relative dropout rates. Nationally, about the same percentage of Protestant and Catholic respondents had completed the last unit of school they entered (59.5 and 60.2 percent), although the percentages for Jews and respondents with no religion were somewhat higher (66.8 and 67.9 percent). In the large non-Southern metropolitan areas, where we expected the greatest similarity to Lenski's findings, the percentage of Catholics who had not dropped out of a unit of school (69.5) was higher than the Protestant percentage (67.1) and virtually the same as the Jewish percentage (70.1). Only the percentage for those with no religion (82.2) differed much from the others. The differences between our findings and Lenski's are so great that it is unlikely that they resulted from sampling variability; they indicate that Detroit is not representative of the nation nor even of large non-Southern metropolitan areas.

Still our data do show important educational differences among Protestants, Catholics, and Jews. Though the respondents of each religion were about equally likely to have finished the last unit of school entered, on the average they had terminated their education at different levels. In the large non-Southern metropolitan areas, the young Jews ranked far above the young Protestants in educational attainments, and the Protestants in turn ranked well above the Catholics. If one looks only at the percentages who had entered and completed college, the same ranking obtained in the nation as a whole.

So important are these differences that we have analyzed data from eleven Gallup polls conducted in 1960 or later to gain confidence in our findings. Four of these are the polls on which our "1964" data are based, and the remaining seven were on hand for other purposes. Using data from each of these polls we compare Protestants and Catholics in: (1) percentage who had completed high school; (2)

[25] A negative association of number of siblings with measured intelligence is well established and apparently is not simply the result of higher fertility at the lower socioeconomic levels. See Lipset and Bendix, *op. cit.*, p. 243.

percentage who had started to college; and (3) percentage of those who had started to college who had finished. Then, using the eleven comparisons for each variable, we use a Wilcoxon matched-pairs signed-rank test to test the null hypothesis that no difference existed in the universe.

Apparently, about the same percentage of Protestants and Catholics had completed high school; the average on the eleven polls was 47.1 percent for Protestants and 46.9 percent for Catholics—of course the Wilcoxon test does not reveal a significant difference. However, nine of the eleven polls show that a larger percentage of Protestants had started to college, and the difference is statistically significant. The average percentage shown by the polls is 17.6 for Protestants and 14.6 for Catholics. Of those who had started, the polls show that on the average 52.9 percent of the Protestants and 50.9 percent of the Catholics had graduated, but the difference is not significant.[26]

This analysis gives us a high degree of confidence that, among persons who were 30 years of age and older during the early 1960's, a larger percentage of Protestants than of Catholics had some college training. When it is remembered that there was a wide gap between Protestants and Catholics in all major status variables when these people were growing up, it becomes evident that differences in parental status may account for the greater college attendance of Protestants. Certainly there is ample evidence that nonmanual parents are more likely to instill in their children aspirations to go to college,[27] and of course these parents are usually more able to help pay the costs. If status differences of families of orientation do largely account for the differing rates of college attendance, then one would expect convergence of Protestant and Catholic college attendance rates with the convergence in income and occupation.

[26] When Jews are compared with Protestants, all of the polls show that a considerably larger percentage of the former had completed high school, and there is virtually no chance that this consistent large difference resulted from sampling error. The average percentage is 75.7 for Jews compared with 47.1 for Protestants. All but one of the polls show that a larger percentage of Jews had started to college, and the difference is significant (p.=0.002). The average percentages are 34.7 and 17.6 for Jews and Protestants respectively. Seven of the polls show a smaller college dropout rate for Jews; although this difference is not significant (p=0.108), the Catholic-Jewish difference is (p=0.013). On the average, the polls show that 59.7 percent of the Jews who had started to college had finished.

[27] For instance, see Herbert H. Hyman, "The Value Systems of Different Classes: A Social Psychological Contribution to the Analysis of Stratification," in Reinhard Bendix and Seymour Martin Lipset, eds., *Class, Status and Power*, New York: The Free Press of Glencoe, 1953, pp. 426-442.

In order to estimate whether or not such convergence has occurred, we tabulated educational data for the youngest respondents
(ages 20 through 25) to the six most recent Gallup polls included in
the analysis. The N's of the Protestant and Catholic subsamples are
fairly small (1182 and 492), but the data from these respondents
suggest that the traditional difference in college attendance has
been reversed. Whereas 33 percent of the Catholics had started to
college, only 29 percent of the Protestants had done so. Although
this difference is not statistically significant, it is unlikely that there
was a substantial difference in the opposite direction in the universe,
as there almost certainly was among persons aged 30 and older. Of
those who had started to college, 40 percent of the Protestants and
36 percent of the Catholics had graduated, but, since many of the
respondents were still enrolled in college, these percentages do not
indicate relative dropout rates. Twenty-seven percent of the Protestants and twenty percent of the Catholics had not completed high
school—a statistically significant difference.

The Catholic educational advantage at the young adult level can
be attributed partially to the concentration of Catholics in large non-
Southern metropolitan areas, where a larger percentage of the young
respondents of all religions had finished high school (83 percent
compared with 72 percent of the other young respondents) and had
started to college (36 percent compared with 28 percent). However
young Catholics in the large non-Southern metropolitan areas had
almost attained parity with Protestants. The percentages who had
completed high school were 84 for Protestants and 82 for Catholics,
and the percentages who had started to college were 37 and 35.[28]
These small differences are in sharp contrast to the wide Protestant-
Catholic disparities among the older respondents (see Table 11).
Among the young respondents in the South and in smaller communities, the Catholics were well ahead of the Protestants. Seventy-
nine percent of the former and seventy percent of the latter had
finished high school—a statistically significant difference; 31 percent
of the Catholics and 27 percent of the Protestants had started to
college. The Catholic advantage in this broad category of communities may have resulted from the more favorable distribution by
community size of Catholics within it.[29] Given the magnitude of

[28] The Protestant *N* is 241; the Catholic *N* is 223.

[29] Of the respondents to the four most recent Gallup polls included in this
study, 54 percent of the Protestants who lived in communities with fewer
than 250,000 residents were rural. The comparable percentage of Catholics
was only 31.3. Forty-one percent of the Catholics but only 20.5 percent of the
Protestants lived in communities with 50,000 to 249,000 residents.

the overall Catholic lead, it is improbable that Protestants had a marked advantage in communities of any size.

If, as the above findings suggest, the last remnants of a Protestant educational advantage are disappearing, then serious doubts are cast on the belief that religiously-based and religiously-related influences have an important differential effect on the worldly success of Protestants and Catholics in contemporary American society. Parental status differences, which undoubtedly existed, are the most reasonable explanation for the educational differences among the older (over age 25) adults, and the educational differences can in turn account for the remaining Protestant advantage in income and occupation in the large non-Southern metropolitan areas. Therefore, one simply does not need to invoke a differential effect of religious factors to explain any of the data presented in this paper.

SUMMARY AND CONCLUSIONS

At the end of World War II, Protestants in the United States ranked well above Catholics in income, occupation and education; since then Catholics have gained dramatically and have surpassed Protestants in most aspects of status. A lingering crucial difference is in the percentages who have been to college. However, this may be only a residue of lower parental status, and even this difference seems to have disappeared among the youngest adults.

An important reason for the more rapid advancement of Catholics is their heavy concentration in the larger non-Southern metropolitan areas, where earnings, occupational distributions, educational opportunities, and rates of upward mobility are more favorable than in the typical home communities of Protestants. Protestants still rank above Catholics in the large non-Southern metropolitan areas, but among young adults the gap in most aspects of status is not great. If the recent trend continues, Catholics in the nation as a whole will surge well ahead of Protestants in all major status variables in the next few years. However, Catholics may continue to lag slightly behind Protestants in their home communities.

Our primary concern here is with a Protestant-Catholic comparison, and therefore we refer only incidentally to the Jewish data. It is important to note, however, that Jews are maintaining a wide lead over other religious categories and apparently have improved their relative standing since World War II.

Our findings are consonant with the belief, expressed by Greeley and others, that religious influences do not handicap Catholics in their competition with Protestants. However, we must stress that these findings by themselves do not rule out a possible differential average impact of religious factors on the worldly success of Protestants and Catholics. The more favorable distribution of Catholics by region and community size could mask a religiously-based Catholic handicap, and there are reasons to believe that it does. In spite of the evidence presented here that Detroit is not typical of the country or of large metropolitan areas, one must not ignore Lenski's data showing greater upward mobility of Protestants. Even if one dismisses Lenski's findings as the result of sampling error or of peculiar Protestant-Catholic ethnic differences in Detroit, there remains the national study by Lipset and Bendix showing equal rates of upward mobility among Protestants and Catholics in spite of the greater mobility predicted for Catholics by their higher concentration in large communities. The Catholic handicap indicated by these data might be ethnic rather than religious; if so, it may have disappeared in recent years. However, religion itself should be important in at least one respect. The probability of upward mobility apparently varies inversely with number of siblings;[30] therefore the higher fertility of Catholics should give Protestants at least a slight advantage.

Analysis of national survey data for young adults during the next few years can provide more nearly conclusive evidence either for or against a differential impact of Protestantism and Catholicism on achievement. If it is found, as our data suggest, that the traditional differences in educational attainment are disappearing in each region and size of community, then sociologists should turn to more fruitful hypotheses concerning the relationship of religion to worldly status. Even if there should be some small remaining difference in Protestant and Catholic achievements, much of the recent attention devoted to Protestant-Catholic differences in mobility and aspirations could more fruitfully be directed to other topics.[31] This study shows that the effects of any Protestant-Catholic differences in influence on worldly status are small in relation to the effects of other influences that on balance favor Catholics.[32] Any

---

[30] Lipset and Bendix, *op. cit.*, pp. 238-243.

[31] Among the lines of inquiry that seem more fruitful is the study of the possible differential impact of different kinds of Protestantism on worldly status. For instance, a worthwhile project would be a rigorous test of Johnson's intriguing hypotheses concerning the effects of the Holiness sects. See Benton Johnson, "Do Holiness Sects Socialize in Dominant Values?" *Social Forces*, 39 (May, 1961), pp. 309-316.

[32] It is possible that even the religious influences favor the Catholics, but we doubt that this is the case.

differential impact of Protestantism and Catholicism on income, occupation, and education explains at best only a small fraction of the variance. Our analysis provides no conclusive answer to the question that has commanded so much sociological attention in recent years, but it suggests that arriving at a more nearly conclusive answer is not very important.

PART II

SOCIAL INSTITUTIONS AND DIFFERENTIATED ROLES

Social institutions customarily develop when the members of a group become convinced that functions which are important to maintaining the group or to satisfying the purpose for which the group exists, but which are initially performed by the individual, can be accomplished more efficiently or more conveniently through concerted, cooperative group effort. When social institutions are established, roles within the "parent" society become more clearly differentiated as some members assume specific responsibility for the efficient operation of the social institutions in question and as other members, freed from responsibility for these functions now within the domain of the institutions in question, assume responsi-

bility for the discharge of other specific social functions. In a participatory democracy, social institutions arise from consensus among peers; in hierarchical societies, they seem to arise in consequence of the decisions of the "power elite" among the leader corps. But even in an hierarchical society, social institutions cannot operate effectively without, at the least, the active cooperation of some members of the follower corps and the tacit approval of a majority of other members of that corps.

The school provides an illustration of the origin of social institutions and of the concomitant differentiation of social roles. For civilized society to maintain itself, it is necessary that its members master certain cognitive skills and that they be introduced to the culture (the habitual patterns of response) characteristic of the society. Initially, the development of cognitive skills and the transmission of the culture was accomplished through the efforts of the individual family. At a point not far distant in anthropological time, it became inefficient, for a variety of reasons, to continue to duplicate similar activities carried out in individual families. Thus, the school arose as a social institution to replace the efforts of the individual family in the development of certain skills and to complement the family in the transmission of the culture. Its establishment as a social institution freed certain family members for other, differentiated social functions, while at the same time creating or formalizing a number of differentiated social roles—teacher, school administrator, and the like.

This section considers both certain characteristics of social institutions and certain differentiated social roles in American Catholicism. The most clearly differentiated social roles in the Catholic community are those of members of the clergy and the religious life, even those whose roles have been subject to considerable modification following Vatican II and its aftermath. DEWEY *examines the role perceptions of priests in relation to a variety of social variables. Relatively sharp differences emerge in the way "progressives," "moderates," and "traditionalists" perceive the role of priest in a Church undergoing wide-scale renewal under the stimulation of Vatican II. In a complementary article,* PALLONE, DRISCOLL, *and* DROBA *explore the relationship between perceptions of self and perceptions of the religious role held by brothers and by nuns to determine the correlates of role satisfaction in the religious life.*

Reports by NEUWEIN *and by* HASSENGER *examine the current status of, and differentiated social roles within, American Catholic schools from the elementary level to the university. Although, as*

Hassenger observes, Catholic colleges often sprouted haphazardly, elementary and secondary schools were established systematically following the decisions of the hierarchy at the Second Plenary Council of Baltimore (1864). Their origins date from a time when the American public school, accurately representing the culture that supported it, was in essence a Protestant school. From a religious perspective, the public school was perceived as a threat to the faith of the Catholic American; from a behavioral science perspective, the public school and its Protestant culture served to underscore the immigrant Catholic's isolation from the mainstream of American life, while a Catholic school represented an avenue toward positive identification with religious tradition. Neuwein reports that the 1960's have seen a steady decline in Catholic school enrollment. Apparently, as Catholic Americans have become more Americanized, their need for an educationally separate, culturally distinct school system has gradually diminished.

Control of mass communication media within a society has far-reaching effects on the beliefs and behavior of its members—for the very constructs through which members assess and appraise events is thereby limited by those in control. In his study of the patterning of the Catholic press in America, GREENE *observes that the Catholic press "was born in a spirit of apology," serving psychological needs similar to those served by the separate religious school.*

4

Role-Conflict: The Priest in a Postconciliar Church

GERALD J. DEWEY

Loyola College (Montreal)

SOURCE. Prepared especially for this volume.

The problem to be investigated here is whether individuals who hold similar positions in an organization also share similar conceptions of its attendant role. As Dennis Wrong has recently argued, there has been a tendency among sociologists to assume that human behavior is exclusively social and only incidentally individual. This "over-socialized" view of man, he suggests, is the consequence of literal (if implicit) adherence to Durkheim's dictum that society is constitutive rather than regulative of human behavior.[1] To this view, social structural arrangements are highly stable and individuals either well or poorly socialized. The application of this perspective to role phenomena, according to Levinson, has led to the postulate of congruency in which such discrete elements as role-conception, structural demands and role performance are assumed to be congruent. He puts it this way:

The organizationally given requirements will be internalized by the members and will thus be mirrored in their role-conceptions. People will know, and will want to do, what is expected of them. The agencies of role socialization will succeed except with a deviant minority—who constitute a separate problem for study. Individual action will in turn reflect the structural norms, since the appropriate role-conceptions will have been internalized and since the sanctions system rewards normative behavior and punishes deviant behavior. Thus, it is assumed that structural norms, individual role-conceptions and individual role-performance are three isomorphic reflections of a single entity: "The" role appropriate to a given organizational position.[2]

That socialization is not necessarily quite this automatic, however, has been shown by much recent study of formal organizations and occupations. Not only do individuals enter an organization with already formed ideas and dispositions, but they also come under the influence of complex norms once inside the organization. In sum, this suggests that personal role-conceptions are rather unlikely to be "given." Perhaps the most exhaustive investigation of the research on this subject is that of Gross and his associates in *Explorations in Role Analysis.* In an altogether lucid exposition of the "postulate of role consensus," the authors consider various anthropological and social psychological as well as sociological assessments. Their conclusion is instructive:

In attempting to place the problem of role consensus in its social science setting we observed that the postulate of consensus is still enmeshed in the analyses of many students of social behavior. Since their analyses assume consensus on role definitions among members of a group or "society," they have ignored its possible significance as a variable for social science inquiry. We also observed, however, that during the past decade there has been an increasing tendency to consider role consensus an important variable for the study of individual social behavior, the functioning of social systems, and cultural organization.

[1] Dennis Wrong, 'The Oversocialized Conception of Man in Modern Sociology," *American Sociological Review,* XXVI, pp. 184-193.

[2] Daniel J. Levinson, "Role, Personality and Social Structure," in Lewis Coser and Bernard Rosenberg (eds.), *Sociological Theory,* MacMillan Company, 1964, p. 285.

That the members of a social system, whether a dyad or a total society, must agree among themselves to *some extent* on values or expectations is a matter of definition. The point we have been trying to underscore is that the degree of consensus on expectations associated with positions is an empirical variable, whose theoretical possibilities until recently have remained relatively untapped.[3]

In order to bring this problem into empirical focus, our investigation is directed to the pastoral role of the Catholic priest. This decision has been based on several considerations. First, pastoral activities are highly codified and directly accessible to all priests by virtue of their ordination. Presumably, then, the pastoral role is more amenable to social analysis than those of more protean character. Second, it is mainly his pastoral role that puts the priest in contact with all levels of Catholic life. The manifold pressures toward change now at work in the postconciliar Church, therefore, probably make the pastoral role more sensitive to redefinition than most others. It was thought this would amplify the problems of personal role conception. And, third, the pastoral role is perhaps more embedded in the authoritarian structures of Catholicism than other priestly roles. Since these established arrangements have become targets of criticism, both from outside the Church and within, it again seemed that role conceptions would prove especially problematic. Surely, the presence of varying role-conceptions among priests in this context would raise serious questions to *a priori* assertions that role-conceptions and structural demands are congruent.

Our perspective on the pastoral role, then, is intended to deal with role conception as a variable rather than constant element in priestly behavior. As stated elsewhere, we assume that the structural demands of the role and its personal conception are analytically separate. Moreover, we further assume that structural demands comprise (a) particular behavioral expectations and (b) institutional involvement. These assumptions are derived from recent appraisals of role behavior in complex organizations which have focused on the disparity between official expectations and the individual's response to them. Perhaps the seminal insight into this issue was Stouffer's remark upon concluding his study of conflicting social norms and role behavior:

From the theoretical standpoint, the most important implication of this paper may stem from its stress on variability. In essay writing in this field it is common and convenient to think of a social norm as a point

[3] Neal Gross, Ward Mason, and Alexander McEachern, *Explorations in Role Analysis*, John Wiley & Sons, Inc., 1958, pp. 42-43.

or at least as a very narrow band on either side of a point. This probably is quite unrealistic as to most of our social behavior. And it may be precisely the ranges of permissible behavior which most need examination, if we are to make progress in this realm which is so central in social science. For it may be the very existence of some flexibility or social slippage—but not too much—which makes behavior in groups possible.[4]

Stouffer, of course, is speaking mainly about the varying expectations made of individuals by others in a situation. What he does not explicate, however, is the complexity of these norms or expectations. This has been done by Levinson, fortunately, who suggests that structural demands confront individual role-players on at least two levels. First, there is the level of specific behavioral expectations: those activities expected of an individual by virtue of his position vis-à-vis others in the system. Second, there is the level of social arrangements which refer to the structured relationships between the individual and others—superiors, for instance, or clients and peers.[5] And, as Merton has shown, these two levels sometimes are incongruous or maladapted. Consequently, individual behavior may be subject to considerable strain because the structural relationships in which it is implicated are such that particular activities may be difficult to perform.[6] Gouldner, moreover, suggests that it may be this which leads individuals to evolve for themselves a role-conception the function of which may be to provide themselves a legitimation for resultant role performance. This is particularly likely to occur, according to Gouldner, during periods or organizational change and stress.[7] Finally, a recent essay by Brim on role socialization cogently argues that individuals may acquire a predisposition to such variant role-conceptions because their experiences with authority, peer groups and significant reference groups present contrary norms during the critical process of early preparation for the role.[8]

In sum, then, these studies provided the rationale for our in-

---

[4] Samuel C. Stouffer, "An Analysis of Conflicting Social Norms," *American Sociological Review*, XIV, p. 717.

[5] See, for example, Daniel J. Levinson, "Role, Personality, and Social Structure in the Organizational Setting," *Journal of Abnormal and Social Psychology*, Vol. 58, pp. 172-177.

[6] Merton's emphasis on "anomie" as an important condition of deviant behavior is generally quite relevant, although here his specific consideration of "innovators" is more to the point. See Robert K. Merton, *Social Theory and Social Structure*, The Free Press, 1964, pp. 131-160.

[7] Alvin Gouldner, "Reciprocity and Autonomy in Functional Theory," in L. Gross (ed.), *Symposium on Sociological Theory*, Row, Peterson and Company, 1959, pp. 92-118.

[8] Orville Brim and Stanton Wheeler, *Socialization After Childhood*, John Wiley & Sons, Inc., 1967, pp. 18-46.

vestigation of personal role conceptions among priests. What we wish to do is develop a typology which comprises both the individual's definition of specific role expectations (namely, what he feels a priest ought to do) and his institutional involvement (namely, what arrangements he wishes to preserve or reject). Afterward two questions will be addressed: (1) Are varying role-conceptions random or structural phenomena? (2) Are there any discernable consequences of varying role-conceptions?

RESEARCH SETTING AND METHODOLOGY

Research was conducted among priests in the Oklahoma City-Tulsa diocese, the boundaries of which include the entire state of Oklahoma. The diocese was formally established by the Vatican in 1905 and has grown since then from a clergy population of 81 to its present size of approximately 250 full-time priests.[9] Of these, about 210 are diocesan clergy with 186 presently engaged in some pastoral activities. These 186 diocesan priests, then, constitute the target population of the study. Permission was received from the bishop of the diocese to focus the investigation on the pastoral functions of clergymen in the post-Vatican Council II period, and his interest in the project helped to assure its success.

Field-work took place in two phases: trial interviews and mailed precoded questionnaires. Personal interviews were held with a small number of priests selected for their strong views concerning the pastoral role in the postconciliar age.[10] They were conducted at the respondents' residences, were tape recorded, and lasted on the

[9] There were in 1966 a total of approximately 256 clergymen in the diocese, 46 of whom were members of religious orders. The latter were excluded from the study because their rules of life, vows, and preparation introduce factors outside the purview of the analysis. Of the 210 *diocesan* clergy, 24 were unavailable because of assignments outside the diocese (graduate school, South American missions, etc.) Thus a total of 186 diocesan priests represent the population to which the research was directed. All are presently active in the pastoral ministry of the Church in Oklahoma.

[10] The selection of these respondents was made with the assistance of a knowledgeable "judge" whose work puts him into frequent contact with these priests. Selections were based on the known attitudes of respondents toward change in the post-Vatican II period. The nine selected were classified as "conservatives," "moderates," and "liberals." Of those eventually interviewed, 6 were full-time parish priests (4 pastors, 2 curates) and 3 were engaged in administrative or chaplain's work (the two chaplains were actually "pastors" of Newman Club Centers at state universities). Care was taken to make sure that respondents were from different age groups (6 under 45, 3 over 45) and from different areas (5 urban and 4 from small towns).

average about 2 hours. Rapport was excellent as judged by respondents' interest in the project and their unqualified cooperation in discussing many topics of a quite sensitive nature. Questions used in the interviews were designed carefully in advance to probe the issue of personal role-conception and were derived from an extensive review of relevant literature.[11]

Certain items emerged which seemed to distinguish between liberal and conservative role-definitions: liberals, for example, believed that celebrating daily Mass was rather unimportant while conservatives thought it was absolutely central to the pastoral role. During the interviews it also became evident, moreover, that priests do not uniformly feel obliged to observe certain well-established Church norms. Liberals, for instance, seemed more critical of ecclesiastical authority; conservatives, on the other hand, seemed more careful than liberals to conform their behavior to clearly established command-obedience arrangements. These two dimensions— *subjective definitions of role-activities* and *involvement in institutional arrangements*—were then selected as critical factors in the formation of personal role-conceptions.

The second phase of the research, then, consisted of a mailed questionnaire comprising instruments devised to measure personal role-conceptions together with other questions designed to elicit information about personal background and related matters. Questionnaires were sent to all 186 diocesan priests; included were personal letters describing the purpose of the research and prepaid envelopes to encourage prompt replies. Later, two subsequent attempts were made to increase responses.[12] In all, 119 (64%) of those contacted submitted returns, nearly all being diligently completed. Comparisons of respondents with the total population as to age, present assignment, and residence revealed no substantial bias. Further comparison of personal role-conceptions, employing the ratings of knowl-

---

[11] Papal documents on various aspects of the priesthood from Pope Pius X to Pope Pius XII have been edited by Archbishop Pierre Veuillot, *The Catholic Priesthood,* The Newman Press, 1965. Also useful are: Raymond A. Tartre, *The Postconciliar Priest,* P. J. Kenedy and Sons, 1966; Gregory Baum, (ed.), *The Constitution on The Church of Vatican Council II,* Paulist Press, 1965; *Decree on The Ministry and Life of Priests of Vatican Council II,* National Catholic Welfare Council, 1965; Hans Kung, *The Council, Reform and Reunion,* Sheed and Ward, 1961; Abbe Michonneau, *Revolution in a City Parish,* Newman Press, 1949.

[12] Prior to these efforts, however, the author was given the opportunity to explain the project to the entire diocesan clergy at a meeting of the Diocesan Little Council. Although this was done with permission of the bishop, extreme care was taken to emphasize the independent nature of the project.

edgeable judges, indicated that "traditionalists" were underrepresented among respondents.[13] This, of course, limits any generalization of the findings.

Role Definition Instrument

In general, the pastoral role includes

... functions related to preaching, teaching, administering the sacraments, carrying out the ritual that embodies the doctrine, regulating, directing and leading in all activities perceived as the work of the Church.[14]

Each of these functions has been institutionalized so that clearly established rubrics specify how each is to be performed. Formal role socialization is designed to teach prospective priests the meaning of such activities and the traditional means of implementing them.[15] Besides these traditional behaviors, however, others of a more progressive nature seem to evolve in response to changing social situations.[16] While not formally incorporated in the system, these progressive norms tend to become important to its adaptation even though their appropriateness may not be *officially* acknowledged. Not infrequently, though, traditional and progressive pastoral norms are discordant and thus generate some measure of ambivalence among actors. The irony of this process has been stated by Merton:

Only through such structures of norms and counter-norms, we suggest, can the various functions of a role be effectively discharged. This is not merely a matter of social psychology but of role-structure. Potentially conflicting norms are built into the social definition of roles that provide for normatively acceptable alternations of behavior as the state of a social

[13] Two knowledgeable informants were asked to rate each priest in the diocese according to an index derived from our formulation of varying role-conception. Agreement between judges was remarkably high (92%), and a cross-check of their ratings and our own classification revealed that in 21 cases where respondents identified themselves on the questionnaire there were 20 instances of the same rating. In sum, it may be said that only traditional priests were proportionately under-represented among respondents. Presumably, such clergymen tend to disparage empirical inquiries of this kind. Some supporting evidence is provided in a study of priests in the Boston archdiocese. See Sister Marie Augusta Neal, *Values and Interests in Social Change,* Prentice-Hall, 1966.

[14] *Ibid.,* p. 17.

[15] See, for example, Joseph H. Fichter, *Religion as a Profession,* University of Notre Dame Press, 1957.

[16] For an excellent report of such developments within the postconciliar Church see Xavier Rynne, *Letters From Vatican City,* 4 volumes, Farrar, Strauss and Geroux, 1962-1966.

relation changes. This is a major basis for that oscillation between differing role-requirements that makes for sociological ambivalence.[17]

It should be noted that counter-norms, or what we have called progressive norms, are not generally very radical. On the basis of preliminary interviews and a review of pertinent literature, progressive counter-norms seem to evolve from the contemporary secular ethos. Since this constitutes the social-cultural milieu of the American Church, it seems to have become imperative that the Church adapt itself to it. These counter-norms, however, do not necessarily *replace* those already well-established in the system. It is, of course, doubtful that the Church could maintain itself as an institution if orthodox behavior patterns were to be preempted by emergent norms. As Merton puts it, "only through such structures of norms and counter-norms . . . can the various functions of a role be effectively discharged." Thus, what is really pertinent is that progressive norms evolve as functional extensions of traditional norms, and that the performance of both is necessary.

Hence, during preliminary interviews respondents whose attitudes toward the postconciliar were known in advance were asked: "In your opinion, what are the most important functions or duties as a priest?" Their responses were codified as follows.

(a) Progressive normative obligations. These include the specific behavioral items accepted as "very important" by all three known progressive respondents and rejected in the sense of being "not very important" by all three known traditional respondents.

(b) Traditional normative obligations. These include the specific behavioral items accepted as "very important" by all three known traditional respondents and rejected in the sense of being "not very important" by all three known progressive respondents.

(c) Moderate normative obligations. These include the specific behavioral items accepted as "moderately important" or "very important" by all three known moderate respondents and also accepted by known traditional or progressive respondents.

From an original list containing some 50 items, a total of 14 eventually were retained as satisfying the criteria specified.[18] It was felt that these consistently differentiated known progressives from known traditionalists. Furthermore, it was felt that the items

---

[17] Robert K. Merton and Elinore Barber, "Sociological Ambivalence," in Edward A. Eiryakian (ed.), *Sociological Theory, Values, and Socio-Cultural Change,* The Free Press, 1963, p. 108.

[18] These items were selected from the publications cited in footnote 11 above and other pertinent sources.

would yield a satisfactory definition of moderates in the sense that each one could be accepted by respondents known to be moderates in their attitudes toward pastoral activities. Although frankly heuristic, it was decided that this method would be a useful operational device for classifying subjects according to their subjective role definitions.[19]

After pretesting the items on a sample of priests in another diocese, who were again selected for their known traditional-moderate-progressive attitudes, it was determined that all 14 items sufficiently discriminated between high and low scores to be retained in the final instrument.[20] The items (each providing four response categories: very important, moderately important, slightly important, and of no importance) were as follows:[21]

Progressive Items

(a) How important do you think it is for a priest to read and study modern theology?

(b) How important do you think it is for a priest to speak out against social injustice?

(c) How important do you think it is for a priest to participate in ecumenical activities in the community?

(d) How important do you think it is for a priest to support the anti-poverty program?

(e) How important do you think it is for a priest to encourage lay people to seek a greater voice in parish and diocesan affairs?

(f) How important do you think it is for a priest to work for liturgical reform?

(g) How important do you think it is for a priest to participate in the implementation of the teachings of Vatican Council II?

[19] The rationale for this approach was deduced from Rose Laub Coser's discussion of Erving Goffman's concept of role distance, which suggests that actors may withhold commitment from certain aspects of their role without rejecting the role as such. Rose Laub Coser, "Role Distance, Ambivalence, and Transition-Status," *American Journal of Sociology*, Vol. 42, pp. 173-188.

[20] For a discussion of the "discriminatory power" of scale items see William Goode and Paul Hatt, *Methods in Social Research*, McGraw-Hill Book Company, Inc., 1952, pp. 275-76.

[21] After combining scale items, the traditional responses scaled in a Guttman-type model with reproducibility of .90, and the progressive items with a reproducibility of .88. For a good presentation of this method see Goode and Hatt, *op. cit.*

Traditional Items

(a) How important do you think it is for a priest to encourage private prayers and devotions among lay people?

(b) How important do you think it is for a priest to direct parish societies?

(c) How important do you think it is for a priest to disperse the sacraments?

(d) How important do you think it is for a priest to administer parish finances?

(e) How important do you think it is for a priest to seek converts to Catholicism?

(f) How important do you think it is for a priest to (spend time in) private prayer and meditation?

(g) How important do you think it is for a priest to say Mass daily?

As mentioned before, it was assumed that the combination of items accepted and rejected would permit a classification of subjects as traditional or moderate or progressive in role definition. The technique used for scoring and coding each subject was based on a continuum for each set of items, with the possible range of scores being 7-28. To accept as "very important" every traditional item, for example, would equal a score of 28 while to reject every item as "of no importance" would equal a score of 7. The same formula would apply to the progressive items. It was arbitrarily decided that a total score of 21 on either set of items would represent the cut-off point in classifying each case. This meant that the following categories would obtain:[22]

(a) Progressive role definition. A total score of *21 or higher* on progressive items and a total score of *less than 21* on the traditional items.

(b) Traditional role definition. A total score of *21 or higher* on traditional items and a total score of *less than 21* on the progressive items.

(c) Moderate role definition. A total score of *21 or higher* on *both* the traditional items *and* the progressive items.

While it is *logically* possible for an individual to have a score of *less than* 21 on both sets of items, this combination did not occur among respondents. It may be possible to assume that the empirical basis upon which items were finally selected was such that only

[22] A similar approach may be found in Maurice Zeitlin, "Alienation and Revolution," *Social Forces*, Vol. 45, pp. 224-236.

salient behavioral dimensions were in fact being tapped. Whether or not there are other equally relevant items that were missed in the course of the preliminary investigations remains, of course, an open question. To give some idea of the actual range of scores of respondents to the sets of items, Table 1 provides a classification of personal role definition types.

TABLE 1 DISTRIBUTION OF SCORES ON TRADITIONAL, MODERATE, AND PROGRESSIVE ROLE DEFINITIONS FOR RESPONDENTS TO THE QUESTIONNAIRE SENT TO ALL PRIESTS IN THE OKLAHOMA CITY-TULSA DIOCESE

Role Definition	Number of Respondents	Percent
Progressive	50	42
Moderate	50	42
Traditional	19	16
Total	119	100

Institutional Involvement Instrument

It has been suggested that the question of individual role definition is perhaps only partly the basis of personal role-conception. That is to say, there is some reason to believe that a verbal statement about which obligations are or are not important may involve a certain stereotypic response. As such, it may not represent what the person is actually prepared to do in his role-performance. The latter may result in part from the authority of others to secure compliance with their expectations quite apart from whatever may be regarded as personally important.

All things being equal, the individual tends to accept the legitimacy of the expectations held by those to whom he is accountable. This is probably the result of socialization and thus constitutes a structural mechanism for assuring conformity to established normative prescriptions. Therefore, in order to avoid the bias possibly inherent in the respondent's manifest choice of one set of norms over another (a choice which may involve a tendency to express a favorable self-image), it was decided to seek a more balanced view of personal role-conception by taking into account also the factor of involvement in the organization. The operational idea here is that the individual ordinarily will believe himself accountable to the *established* normative arrangements. In specific situations, therefore, he would tend to behave in the traditionally orthodox manner;

and, perhaps, seek for some justification when such behavior conflicts with his subjective role-definition.

Consequently, it was necessary to probe the question of involvement before accepting the role-definition scores as an appropriate descriptive index of personal role-conception. John Donovan's study of academic roles provided a clue as to how this might be done.

. . . the role preferences of the Catholic academic men are suggestive but incomplete. They point the directions of professional values, but their reliability as indices may be suspect because they express self-images and because they may be projections of stereotypes rather than functional bases of behavior. The research problem, therefore, was to neutralize this possibility by identifying the professor's value orientation in concrete professional situations which would elicit clear-cut value responses.[23]

As in Donovan's investigation, the problem here is to "neutralize" projections and get at the objective functional basis of role performance. What he calls value-orientation, however, is perhaps more elusive than the question of involvement. Operationally, we shall regard high involvement as the individual's tendency to choose an *established* alternative when faced with a hypothetical conflict-situation comprising traditional and progressive options. Unlike the role definition scale items, these hypothetical situations consist of choices which more or less directly raise the issue of legitimate authority and one's accountability to it. Such authority, of course, may refer either to the established (traditional) structures of pastoral activities *or* to the specific obedience owed to institutional authorities. In either instance, the dominant motif is whether or not the individual is disposed to behave in accord with institutional orthodoxy. Put differently, this has something to do with the dialectic interplay between charismatic and institutional legitimacy and its affect on pastoral role-conceptions. Does the individual priest see himself as accountable to the established (traditional) social structure, or does he instead find himself caught up in some paradox of institutionalization? If the latter, how far is he prepared to go in acting outside the boundaries of traditional arrangements? Each test situation, then, was designed to probe this issue.[24] It is assumed that the individual's pattern of responses will represent his *relative* in-

---

[23] John Donovan, *The Academic Man in The Catholic College*, Sheed and Ward, 1964, p. 124.

[24] The relevance of these value-conflicts was adduced by preliminary field interviews.

volvement in the established routine of pastoral life.[25] A presentation of these situations may be sufficient to indicate the general approach.

Situation A—Social Protest vs. Accommodation To The Status Quo

Father Smith is the pastor of a well-established city parish in an all white predominately middle-class neighborhood. Members of the parish were vehemently opposed to having Negroes move into their area. Father Smith was asked by the local human relations council to support an attempt to help integrate the area.

What should Father Smith have done?

1. (A)   He definitely should not have helped to integrate the area.

2. (A)   He probably should not have helped to integrate the area.

3. (SP)   He probably should have helped to integrate the area.

4. (SP)   He definitely should have helped to integrate the area.

Situation B—Independence vs. Submissiveness

Msgr. Black was an experienced member of the diocesan clergy. Two former assistants of his were being considered by the Bishop for appointment to an important city pastorate. Only one would receive the appointment. Msgr. Black's opinion was solicited by the Bishop.

Father A. was reasonably intelligent and had always gotten along well with Msgr. Black. He worked hard at whatever tasks he was given and caused neither the Msgr. nor his parishioners any trouble. His most important qualities were reliability and respect for authority. Father A. was also quite successful at gaining converts.

Father B. was a brilliant young man who had acted rather independently as Msgr. Black's assistant. His sermons often dealt with controversial social issues but were always penetrating and well prepared. He had also taken an active interest in working among the poor and underprivileged members of the city, frequently to the point of causing parishioners to wonder if he wasn't spending too much time away from the parish.

Which of the priests should Msgr. Black have recommended?

1. (S)   He definitely should have recommended Father A.

[25] For a similar approach to social changes in ecclesiastical settings, see Sister Marie Augusta Neal, *op. cit.*

2. (S)   He probably should have recommended Father A.

3. (I)   He probably should have recommended Father B.

4. (I)   He definitely should have recommended Father B.

Situation C—Authority vs. Personal Conscience

Father Francis was just appointed assistant to a very conservative pastor in a well supported city parish where parishioners were known to hold very traditional religious and political attitudes. Father Francis was ordered by the pastor to do nothing that might cause disharmony or confusion among parishioners. He was specifically told not to give sermons on controversial social issues and to avoid making any changes in the liturgy unless explicitly approved by the pastor.

What should Father Francis have done?

1. (A)   He should have done exactly as he was told and said nothing to the pastor about his own feelings in this matter.

2. (A)   He should have done exactly as he was told after first informing the pastor of his own feelings in this matter.

3. (PC)   He should have told the pastor that he could not in good conscience do as he was ordered and attempted to persuade the pastor to change his instructions.

4. (PC)   He should have followed his own conscience in this matter even though it meant disobeying the explicit orders of the pastor.

Situation D—Innovation vs. Conformity

Father Green was called in by his Bishop to discuss his new appointment. Two positions were open and the Bishop wished to know which one Father Green preferred.

Position X was a pastorate in a city parish with about 150 families, most of them rather middle-class and somewhat progressive. The parish had a good school, an active CFM group, a successful liturgical program, and a very small debt.

Position Y was an appointment to an experimental city pastorate. Father Green's duties would involve working with a relatively small group of very active and progressive lay people dedicated to social justice and liturgical renewal. He would be given a free hand in developing this "parish" as he wished.

What should Father Green have done?

1. (C) He definitely should have chosen Position X.
2. (C) He probably should have chosen Position X.
3. (I)   He probably should have chosen Position Y.
4. (I)   He definitely should have chosen Position Y.

An index of "institutional involvement" was constructed from the responses to these situations by coding all orthodox responses as 1 and others as 0 (zero). Scores from 2-4, then, arbitrarily were assigned "high" involvement and scores of less than 2 "low" involvement.[26] To give some idea of the distribution of scores Table 2 shows the frequency of types of involvement among respondents.

TABLE 2 DISTRIBUTION OF SCORES ON "HIGH" AND "LOW" INVOLVEMENT FOR RESPONDENTS TO THE QUESTIONNAIRE SENT TO ALL PRIESTS IN THE OKLAHOMA CITY-TULSA DIOCESE

Involvement	Number of Respondents	Percent
High	74	62
Low	45	38
Totals	119	100

FINDINGS: VARYING ROLE CONCEPTIONS

Here, then, the question of personal role-conceptions among priests is examined to see what it yields. The general assumption is that sociological ambivalence caused by the confluence of (orthodox) norms and (evolving) counter-norms exposes priests to divergent structural demands; consequently, there is likely to be incongruity in personal role-conceptions. Correlatively these will most probably reflect not only social psychological differences (particularly with respect to reference groups) but also lead to varying consequences for the social structure.

As previously noted, calculations of responses to the *subjective role-definition* scale yielded the following results: progressives—42%, moderates—42%, and traditionalists—16%. These types were constructed on the basis of the importance ascribed to each item in the progressive—traditional sets.[27]

---

[26] See Zeitlin, *op. cit.*

[27] The importance of assessing obverse sides of sociological phenomena is brilliantly presented in Reinhard Bendix and Bennet Berger, "Images of Society and Problems of Concept Formation in Sociology," in L. Gross (ed.), *op. cit.*, pp. 92-118.

(a) *Progressive role definition.* General acceptance of progressive items as important and rejection of traditional items as unimportant.

(b) *Moderate role definition.* General acceptance of both sets of items as important.

(c) *Traditional role definition.* General acceptance of traditional items as important and rejection of progressive items as unimportant.

In sum, it seems that progressive priests see pastoral role-demands mainly in terms of social action and as essentially "this worldly." Quite obviously the familiar image of the pastoral function holds little attraction for them. Well-established sacerdotal activities and parish routine are thought to have little importance, apparently, when seen against the persistent demands of human needs in the "secular city." Traditional priests, on the other hand, take the reverse position. They appear to regard their primary obligations in terms of conventional parochial functions and as essentially "other-worldly." Seemingly, the traditional priests regard themselves as separate from secular society and chiefly responsible for maintaining the *status quo* in the Church. Moderates, in turn, seem to view pastoral role-demands as obligatory in both directions. How effectively they manage to reconcile these somewhat divergent orientations is problematic, of course; but, in any event, their image of the pastoral role is indeed complex. Perhaps this question might be clarified somewhat when considered in the light of *institutional involvement,* the other element of personal role-conception.

As stated elsewhere, responses to hypothetical value-conflict situations were used to discern institutional involvement. There were four different precoded answers that respondents could choose in each instance. While these choices reflected varying degrees of commitment to established institutional arrangements, responses were dichotomously coded as either "high" or "low" involvement. High involvement denotes an unwillingness to question or challenge traditional Catholic mores and ecclesiastical arrangements. Low involvement, then, denotes the reverse tendency. Our general hypothesis was that role definition (as measured above) and institutional involvement would be associated: (a) progressive role-definition and low involvement; (b) moderate role-definition and intermediate involvement; (c) traditional role-definition and high involvement. These assumptions are investigated below.

Table 3 shows the distribution of progressive, moderate, and traditional responses to the hypothetical situations. According to the hypothesis, the institutional involvement of progressiveness should

TABLE 3   SUBJECTIVE ROLE-DEFINITION AND INSTITUTIONAL INVOLVEMENT
AMONG OKLAHOMA CLERGY

Role-Definition	High Involvement		Low Involvement		Total	
	N	%	N	%	N	%
Progressive	13	26	37	74	50	100
Moderate	42	84	8	16	50	100
Traditional	17	90	2	10	19	100
Total	72		47		119	

$X^2 = 43.85$ 2 df p .001

be lower than the traditionalists' while moderates should be intermediate. The data indicate that this is indeed the case. Perhaps a
description of the four "involvement" situations will place this
relationship in sharper focus.

Table 4 indicates that progressive priests nearly unanimously
reject the traditional practice of accommodation to segregated hous-
ing. Not surprisingly, moderates also tend to question the legitimacy
of such acquiescence. However, traditionalists are rather divided
on the issue. It may be that the strong position officially taken by
the Church on the immorality of racial discrimination has effectively
challenged the legitimacy of unofficial (i.e., "de facto") accommodation to established social arrangements.[28] That a significant number
of traditional priests still adhere in some degree to segregated neigh-

TABLE 4   SUBJECTIVE ROLE-DEFINITION AND ACCOMMODATION TO STATUS
QUO OF SEGREGATED NEIGHBORHOODS AMONG OKLAHOMA CLERGY

Role-Definition	High Involvement Choice		Low Involvement Choice		Total	
	N	%	N	%	N	%
Progressive	2	4	48	96	50	100
Moderate	10	20	40	80	50	100
Traditional	10	53	9	47	19	100
Total	22		97		119	

$X^2 = 18.17$ 2 df p .001

[28] See, for example, Thomas Merton, *Seeds of Destruction,* Farrar, Strauss and
Geroux, 1961. Also, William Ferree, *The Act of Social Justice,* Marianist
Publications, 1951.

TABLE 5   SUBJECTIVE ROLE-DEFINITION AND ACCEPTANCE OF SUBMISSIVE-
NESS AMONG OKLAHOMA CLERGY

Role-Definition	High Involve-ment Choice		Low Involve-ment Choice		Total	
	N	%	N	%	N	%
Progressive	7	14	43	86	50	100
Moderate	32	64	18	36	50	100
Traditional	16	84	3	16	19	100
Total	55		64		119	

$X^2 = 37.47$ 2 df p .001

borhoods, however, suggests that accommodation remains latent in the system.

The next conflict-situation concerns the issue of independence v. submissiveness in Catholic life. Several critics have demonstrated the historical importance attached to submissiveness with the Church, particularly in relationships between superiors and subordinates.[29] Table 5 shows the distribution of responses for this situation. Especially significant is the degree to which progressive priests opt for the norm of independence. Moderates, and particularly traditionalists, however, still appear to accept the legitimacy of being submissive —at least as measured by the situation. Comments from many respondents indicated that the behavior of the hypothetical Father B. seemed to them irresponsible and arbitrary, asserting, in effect, that a priest's first duty is acquiescence to tradition. Still, independence does involve the risk of some arbitrariness and often creates some disorder. Perhaps the greater one's involvement in the system the less willing he is to accept these hazards. Conversely, to be less involved in established institutional arrangements may pre-dispose one to emphasize the priority of personal decision-making over institutional order whenever the conflict arises.[30]

Next, the conflict between hierarchic authority and individual conscience is sharply posed. Significantly, progressives and traditionalists are deeply divided on which is the more legitimate norm. Table 6 shows that 89% of the traditionalists align themselves with established authority, while 90% of the progressives repudiate it. Moderates, too, seem to question the legitimacy of unalloyed obedience. It seems important to observe here that the bishop of the

[29] See the discussion of this point in Sister Marie Augusta Neal, *op. cit.*
[30] *Ibid.*

TABLE 6 SUBJECTIVE ROLE-DEFINITION AND ACQUIESCENCE TO HIER-
ARCHIC AUTHORITY AMONG OKLAHOMA CLERGY

Role-Definition	High Involvement Choice		Low Involvement Choice		Total	
	N	%	N	%	N	%
Progressive	5	10	45	90	50	100
Moderate	19	38	31	62	50	100
Traditional	17	89	2	11	19	100
Total	41		78		119	

$X^2 = 35.50$ 2 df   p .001

diocese has a reputation for permissiveness, which perhaps helps to
explain the moderate's pattern of relatively low involvement on this
issue.[31]

The territorial parish has, of course, been the rule in Catholic
social structure.[32] Consequently, even to consider innovations would
seem to imply some disenchantment with the system. Similarly, the
experimental attitude seems on the ascendency among contemporary
progressives in the Church.[33] Table 7 again discloses sharp differences between respondents, with progressives displaying significantly
less involvement in the established system than moderates and
(especially) traditionalists.

TABLE 7 SUBJECTIVE ROLE-DEFINITION AND CONFORMITY TO ESTABLISHED
PARISH STRUCTURE AMONG OKLAHOMA CLERGY

Role-Definition	High Involvement Choice		Low Involvement Choice		Total	
	N	%	N	%	N	%
Progressive	9	18	41	82	50	100
Moderate	29	58	21	42	50	100
Traditional	18	95	1	5	19	100
Total	56		63		119	

$X^2 = 37.12$ 2 df   p .001

[31] For an excellent assessment of latent authoritarianism in the Church see
Thomas O'Dea, *The American Catholic Dilemma,* Sheed and Ward, 1958.
[32] Joseph H. Fichter, *Social Relations in The Urban Parish,* University of
Chicago Press, 1954.
[33] This seems to be implicit in the Vatican Council II document on *The Pastoral
Constitution of The Church in The Modern World.*

TABLE 8   COMPARISON OF CLASSIFICATIONS BY ROLE DEFINITION AND INSTITUTIONAL INVOLVEMENT

Role Definition	Institutional Involvement	N	%
1. Progressive	Low	37	31
2. Progressive	High	13	11
3. Moderate	Low	8	7
4. Moderate	High	42	36
5. Traditional	Low	2	1
6. Traditional	High	17	14

As an index of personal role-conception, then, subjective definitions and institutional involvement were combined to form composite types.[34]

Table 8 gives the breakdown of respondents classified according to scores on both instruments. Since our operational theme is derived from the perspective of normative ambivalence, it was decided that personal role-conception types adequately should reflect the individual's disposition to norms and counter-norms in the pastoral role. That is, the typology would have to discriminate between priests as to whether they were responsive to established norms, to evolving counter-norms, or both. Thus, cases falling into cells 2, 3, 4, and 5 above were classified together as a single type. Whatever loss this may entail in logical elegance seems more than compensated by its empirical usefulness. In sum, this construction yields the following composite types: Progressives—31%; moderates—55%; and traditionalists—14%.[35] Each may be described as follows:

(a) *Progressives* accept progressive role-behaviors as more important than traditional ones. Also are relatively uninvolved in the established institutional norms of Catholic social structure. Tend to prefer social change over accommodation to the *status quo*, independence over submissiveness, personal decision-making over obedience, and experimentation over preservation of established structures.

(b) *Traditionalists* accept traditional role-behaviors as more important than progressive ones. Also are highly involved in the established institutional norms of Catholic social structure. Tend

---

[34] The degree to which this typology may be said to reflect real empirical differences is considered below.

[35] According to the rating of independent judges (see footnote 13 above), the distribution for the entire diocese is: Progressives—30%, Moderates—42%, Traditionalists—28%.

to prefer accommodation to the *status quo* over social change, submissiveness over independence, obedience over personal decision-making, and preservation of established structures over experimentation.

(c) *Moderates* accept both traditional and progressive role demands. Also are rather highly involved in the established institutional norms of Catholic social structure, though not so highly involved as traditionalists. Tend to prefer social change over accommodation to the *status quo* and personal decision-making over obedience, but also prefer submissiveness over independence and preservation of established structures over experimentation. [Classified also as moderates are 15 ambivalent cases in which subjective role definition and institutional involvement are sharply dissonant (e.g., progressive with high involvement).]

SOCIAL CORRELATES OF VARYING ROLE-CONCEPTIONS

Prior research has indicated that age is significantly related to openness toward change, particularly within formal organizations like the Catholic Church.[36] Among progressives, 86% are under 45 years of age—indicating a generally favorable and open attitude toward change among younger clergy. Moderates also seem well disposed toward change and here again age is significant—61% being less than 45 years old. Only traditionalists are on the whole older —65% age 45 or over.

As Table 9 shows, age and role-conception are strikingly related for these respondents. This seems especially important in view of the average age of priests in the diocese, which is about 42 years. It suggests that critical jobs (e.g., pastor) will have to be assigned to men still quite young; and since these priests are very likely change-oriented, the entire system will perhaps tend to be generally open.[37]

However, this supposition requires more rigorous investigation. Table 10 indicates the relationship between varying role-conceptions and present assignments. Immediately evident is the trend among pastors to be either moderates or traditionalists. Progressives, on

---

[36] Sister Marie Augusta Neal, *op. cit.*

[37] Since the Oklahoma City-Tulsa diocese is relatively small, it takes from 2-3 years before recently ordained priests are assigned to pastorates. This may be contrasted with larger dioceses where it may be 15-20 years before curates become pastors.

TABLE 9   PERSONAL ROLE-CONCEPTIONS AND AGE AMONG OKLAHOMA CLERGY

Personal Role-Conceptions	Under 45		Age 45 and Over		Total	
	N	%	N	%	N	%
Progressives	32	86	5	14	37	100
Moderates	40	62	25	38	65	100
Traditionals	6	35	11	65	17	100
Total	78		41		119	

$X^2 = 14.63$ 2 df p .001

the other hand, are more often found as curates or in administrative positions. Thus, while there is little to warrant the conclusion that progressive role-conceptions prove untenable after one becomes a pastor, it does seem that an interest in innovations might prove difficult to retain in a pastorate.[38]

Similarly, the evidence indicates that role-conception is related to the length of time one has been a priest. As Table 11 shows, traditionalists and moderates are generally the more experienced priests; progressives, on the whole, have been priests for less than ten years. Taken together, then, it seems that role-conception is a function of age and time spent in the social structure.[39] As younger clergy spend more time in the Church, particularly as they move from the peripheral position of curate to the central position of

TABLE 10   PERSONAL ROLE-CONCEPTIONS AND PRESENT ASSIGNMENTS AMONG OKLAHOMA CLERGY

Personal Role-Conceptions	Pastor		Curate		Administrative		Total	
	N	%	N	%	N	%	N	%
Progressives	11	30	16	43	10	27	37	100
Moderates	39	60	11	17	15	23	65	100
Traditionals	12	70	2	12	3	18	17	100
Total	62		29		28		119	

$X^2 = 13.60$ 4 df p .01

[38] See the discussion of innovation among higher level members of formal organizations in Amatai Etzioni, *A Comparative Analysis of Complex Organizations,* The Free Press, 1961.
[39] *Ibid.*

TABLE 11 PERSONAL ROLE-CONCEPTIONS AND YEARS IN PRIESTHOOD AMONG OKLAHOMA CLERGY

Personal Role-Conceptions	Less than 10		10 or More		Total	
	N	%	N	%	N	%
Progressives	23	62	14	38	37	100
Moderates	21	32	44	68	65	100
Traditionals	2	12	15	88	17	100
Total	46		73		119	

$X^2 = 16.42$ 2 df   p .001

pastor, it appears likely that their progressive role-conceptions may change to a more moderate (or perhaps traditional) type.

On the other hand, however, other data suggest a qualification. Table 12 shows that social class background, as measured by father's occupation, is significantly related to role-conceptions. Progressives, and to some extent moderates, are more likely to come from the middle-classes than traditionalists. This relationship holds with age held constant and is generally consistent with studies of lower-class authoritarianism.[40]

Furthermore, there is also a slight but significant relationship between role-conception and region. Table 13, for example, shows that progressives generally are native born Oklahomans while moderates and traditionalists more frequently come from other regions

TABLE 12 PERSONAL ROLE-CONCEPTIONS AND FATHER'S OCCUPATION AMONG OKLAHOMA CLERGY

Personal Role-Conceptions	White Collar		Blue Collar		Total	
	N	%	N	%	N	%
Progressives	33	90	4	10	37	100
Moderates	41	65	22	35	63 [a]	100
Traditionals	9	52	8	48	17	100
Total	83		34		117 [a]	

$X^2 = 10.11$ 2 df   p .01

[a] No answers in two cases.

[40] Seymour Martin Lipset, "Religion and Politics in American History," in Earl Kobb (ed.), *Religious Conflict in America,* Doubleday and Company, 1964.

TABLE 13   PERSONAL ROLE-CONCEPTIONS AND PRE-SEMINARY RESIDENCE
AMONG OKLAHOMA CLERGY

Personal Role-Conceptions	Oklahoma		Outside Oklahoma		Total	
	N	%	N	%	N	%
Progressives	27	73	10	27	37	100
Moderates	31	48	34	52	65	100
Traditionals	9	52	8	48	17	100
Total	67		52		119	

$X^2 = 6.45$ 2 df p .05

(very often from Eastern states). There are perhaps many reasons
for this but several factors seem especially relevant: (a) American
Catholicism seems to have been more progressive in the Middle-West
than in the East.[41] Native-born clergy, therefore, might have been
reared in a more permissive religious atmosphere and thus acquired
progressive dispositions toward the pastoral role. (b) The history
of the Church in Oklahoma seems to reflect a rather untypical
American experience. For example, the earliest clergy in the diocese
were Belgian rather than Irish. From this it could be argued that
the ethnic character of the Church in Oklahoma was not strictly
part of the Eastern establishment, which was largely Irish-American,
and this may have had an effect on its development.[42] (c) Catholics in Oklahoma always have been a small minority. Perhaps this
produced a more flexible and open attitude among Catholics, one
permitting them to adapt to their rural-Protestant milieu. Since
their numbers were never large enough to constitute a serious threat
to the Protestant majority, Oklahoma Catholics perhaps were not
exposed to the ghetto-like influences which often result in militant
in-group feelings and personal insecurity.[43]

Less speculative is the evidence concerning the relationship between reading habits and role-conceptions (see Table 14). Progressives prefer and read publications highly critical of the *status
quo* in the Church. Traditionalists, however, eschew such journals
and select instead those supportive of established Catholic norms

[41] See Robert D. Cross, *The Emergence of Liberal Catholicism in America,*
Harvard University Press, 1958.
[42] This is discussed in historical perspective by John Tracy Ellis, *American
Catholicism,* University of Chicago Press, 1956.
[43] See, for example, the suggestive treatment in Lewis A. Coser, *The Functions
of Social Conflict,* The Free Press, 1961.

TABLE 14 PERSONAL ROLE-CONCEPTIONS AND READING HABITS AMONG
OKLAHOMA CLERGY

Personal Role-Conceptions	Open-Critical Journals		Traditional Journals		Total	
	N	%	N	%	N	%
Progressives	31	84	6	16	37	100
Moderates	39	60	26	40	65	100
Traditionals	3	18	14	82	17	100
Total	73		46		119	

$X^2 = 19.31$ 2 df   p .001

and structures. Moderates, in turn, follow an intermediate pattern. Although this relationship obtains even with age held constant, it does not of course tell us whether reading certain journals leads one to develop a certain role-conception, or whether an existing conception leads one to select congenial journals.[44] What it does suggest, however, is that reading a particular kind of publication may be one way in which (a) progressives can retain their role-conception over time, or (b) other clergy may become exposed to ideas dissonant with those already held.

This finding is especially illuminating when viewed in the context of reference groups. It is well-known, of course, that reading can represent an important socialization influence—particularly in a highly literate, technological society. It would seem appropriate, therefore, to suggest that reading habits constitute one's (symbolic) form of interaction with "significant others." [45] An indirect check on this relationship would require evidence showing that varying role-conceptions are also related to similarly varying reference groups.

Table 15 is suggestive along these lines. Progressives consistently select outstanding Church liberals as persons they most admire; moderates are almost evenly split in whom they admire; and traditionalists nearly unanimously select outstanding Church conservatives. Perhaps the primary (though not exclusive) source of information concerning these personages is the publication media. It is entirely possible, then, that what one reads is a structural link to

[44] Similar findings are reported by Sister Marie Augusta Neal, *op. cit.*

[45] This point is cogently argued in Timotsu Shibutani, "Reference Groups as Perspectives," *American Journal of Sociology*, Vol. 61, pp. 567-569.

TABLE 15   PERSONAL ROLE-CONCEPTIONS AND "PROFESSIONAL" REFERENCE
GROUPS AMONG OKLAHOMA CLERGY

| Personal Role-Conceptions | Which Members of Church Hierarchy Most Admired by Respondents | | | | | |
| | Liberals | | Conservatives | | Total | |
	N	%	N	%	N	%
Progressives	34	92	3	8	37	100
Moderates	33	60	26	40	59	100
Traditionals	1	8	12	92	13 [a]	100
Total	68		41		109 [a]	

$X^2 = 29.05$ 2 df p .001

[a] Four traditionals did not answer.

the sort of reference groups he acquires in the course of his experience.[46]

Of further interest here are the findings presented in Table 16.
The operational motif of these data has to do with whether or not
various groups *in the diocese* constitute "significant" references for
each role-conception type. First, the progressives and moderates are

TABLE 16   PERSONAL ROLE-CONCEPTIONS AND "MEMBERSHIP" REFERENCE
GROUPS AMONG OKLAHOMA CLERGY

| Reference Groups [a] | Role-Conceptions | | | | | | | |
| | Progressives | | Moderates | | Traditionalists | | | |
	N	%	N	%	N	%	X^2 [b]	P
The Bishop	33	89	59	91	11	65	10.45	.01
Conservative clergy	3	8	18	28	7	41	9.01	.05
Liberal clergy	15	42	21	32	—	—	9.21	.01
Traditional laity	8	22	23	35	4	24	N.S.	—
Liberal laity	23	62	30	46	1	6	15.47	.001

[a] Respondents were asked: "How important do you think it is to do what——
expects?" Table includes percentages of "very important" responses for each
role-conception type.
[b] Chi square tests involve 2 df in each instance.

[46] The seminal discussion of this is, of course, Davis Reisman, *The Lonely
Crowd,* Doubleday and Company, 1959.

more likely than traditionalists to consider their bishop's expectations important. Since the present bishop has the reputation of being permissive and rather progressive, it is not altogether surprising that progressives and moderates should hold themselves responsible to his expectations. That traditionalists should be less attentive to them, however, is important: since the bishop is the established and *legitimate* authority in the diocese, to whom priests take a vow of obedience, it would seem that traditionalists would feel especially compelled (by their very conception of the pastoral role) to advert to his claims.[47] To do otherwise would attest the importance of other reference groups as a support for personal role-conception. Also interesting—and less perplexing—are the findings that: (a) moderates and traditionalists are significantly more likely than progressives to accept "conservative clergy" as reference groups; (b) progressives and moderates are similarly well disposed to the expectations of "liberal clergy;" (c) progressives—and to some extent moderates—generally accept "liberal lay-people" as reference groups. Surprisingly, there is no significant difference between varying role-conceptions and "traditional lay people" as a reference group—nobody being especially likely to regard them as such. Sociologically, then, it seems accurate to say that membership groups (i.e., within the diocesan structure) are likely to serve also as reference groups mainly when they support a personal role-conception.[48] However, the precise nature of this relationship is another matter: Whether one is cause or effect of the other can not be demonstrated by the data here available.

Other factors: (1) parents' religion and early family atmosphere, (2) educational background, (3) rural-urban differences, (4) voluntary group participation, (5) degree of inter-personal association, and the like—were not significantly related to varying role-conceptions, or were only apparently related, the relationship not holding when age or years in the priesthood were controlled.

Generally, then, it seems that important social structural differences underlay varying role-conceptions. Whether the latter lead

[47] What may throw some light on this problem is an observation made often by conservative respondents during personal interviews, the substance of which being that "I'm just not sure what the bishop expects me to do." In other words, it may be that traditionalists can justify their apparent indifference to "legitimate authority" by invoking its purported ambiguity. But this, of course, requires further investigation.

[48] For a lucid discussion of reference groups and role-taking, see Ralph Turner, "Role-Taking, Role Standpoint, and Reference Group Behavior," *American Journal of Sociology,* Vol. 61, pp. 316-328.

to any consequences for the diocesan system is another question, of course, and will now be considered in some detail.

ANALYSIS AND DISCUSSION

The principal theme of our delineation of varying role-conceptions concerns the issue of change vs. stability in pastoral activities. Progressives are well-disposed toward change, rather uninvolved in established institutional arrangements, and moved primarily by a concern for the social dimensions of the pastoral role. Traditionalists, obversely, are opposed to change, rather deeply involved in the preservation of established arrangements within the Church, and moved primarily by a concern for the sacerdotal and parochial dimensions of the pastoral role. Moderates, however, display a more temperate attitude toward change and continuity. In some (so far) indeterminate way, they seem to constitute a rather pragmatic approach to pastoral life—perhaps linking together their seemingly more ideological peers. In brief, this provides the context for investigating the following hypotheses.

H:1. Progressives will consistently hold attitudes that support changing specific structural arrangements in the Church, while traditionalists will consistently hold opposite attitudes. Moderates, however, will hold ambivalent attitudes: generally supporting only those structural changes for which there are official guidelines.

H:2. Progressives will perceive functional alternatives to a career in the priesthood, while moderates and traditionalists will perceive the priesthood as the only vocation meaningful to them. Corollary to this: Progressives will be critical of their formal seminary preparation, while moderates and traditionalists will regard it as adequate.

H:3. Progressives will experience greater "strain" in the performance of their pastoral role than either moderates or traditionalists. Corollary to this: progressives will be *least* likely to advise other young men, who feel they have a vocation, to enter the priesthood.

Varying Role Conceptions and Attitudes toward Structural Change

The first hypothesis contends that innovations are not likely to occur "accidentally" but probably because there are individuals whose role-conception supports change as an important and necessary objective. Table 17 shows the percentage of favorable responses to the question "Do you think (viz., territorial parishes) ought to be changed in some way?"

TABLE 17   PERSONAL ROLE-CONCEPTIONS AND AFFIRMATIVE RESPONSES
TO QUESTIONS CONCERNING STRUCTURAL CHANGES IN THE CHURCH AMONG
OKLAHOMA CLERGY

"Structures" Requiring change	Personal Role-Conceptions			X^2	P
	Progressives ($N = 37$)	Moderates ($N = 65$)	Traditionalists ($N = 17$)		
Territorial parish	84%	52%	24%	20.76	.001
Present form of confession	89	48	12	29.85	.001
Exclusion of women from clergy	38	15	—	10.24	.01
Parish schools	92	57	24	25.01	.001
Status of curates	84	55	24	12.61	.01
Church ownership of property	68	28	24	17.52	.001
Obligatory Sunday mass	81	32	18	28.25	.001
Command-Obedience relations	92	49	12	29.87	.001
Status of lay people	100	72	35	28.48	.001
Compulsory celibacy	81	52	29	15.99	.001
Use of religious titles	70	22	12	29.59	.001

2 df in each case.

The data indicate that the predicted patterns do, in fact, obtain: progressives *consistently* support structural changes, traditionalists *consistently* oppose them, and moderates tend to support changes when officially approved (i.e., territorial parishes, parish schools, status of curates, and status of lay people in the Church) and tend to reject others (i.e., present form of Confession, exclusion of women from the sacrament of Holy Orders, ownership of property by the Church, obligatory attendance at Sunday Mass, value of emphasis on obedience in the Church, and the use of religious titles).[49]

[49] By "officially approved" is meant that the formal authority of the diocese supports such changes in some measure. The notable exception here is the issue of celibacy. So far as it could be determined during the field-work, this issue has not been placed on the agenda for discussion and study—at least not in the public activities of the diocesan Little Council. Nor was this issue open for discussion at the recent Vatican Council II. That moderates should favor some change, then, would seem to suggest the saliency of the issue.

These moderates, it would seem, constitute a critical element in the diocese since their numbers and position (as pastors and diocesan administrators) put them at the center of the social structure. Also they would appear to be a less ideological, more issue-oriented element in the diocese. Unlike progressives and traditionalists, who seem to take a position on the ecclesiastical "left" or "right," moderates appear on the whole rather pragmatic.[50] For example: on the issue of territorial parishes moderates resemble progressives. This would seem practical in view of changes which have occurred in the larger society, where urbanization has created a fluid yet concentrated population. Under these circumstances territorial parishes are often impractical for at least two reasons: (a) Shifts in population and changing ethnic-religious ecological patterns tend to make the heavy investment involved in building new parishes or maintaining existing ones extremely burdensome, if not impossible. Non-territorial parishes therefore would offer a feasible alternative in many instances. (b) The concentration of population frequently results in the growth of large and impersonal parishes from which any sense of community is practically excluded. In consequence, the parish may become little more than a bureaucratic service agency. Again non-territorial parishes, based perhaps on common interests and directed by an itinerant clergy, may offer a practical solution.[51]

With respect to Church ownership of property, however, moderates are more like traditionalists. And, again, the pragmatic issue-conscious approach would appear operative. For the Church to begin liquidating its considerable holdings would appear rather unlikely, to say the least. The progressive's seeming impatience would, if acted upon, present immense difficulties and possibly result in some loss of service to the community (parochial schools, hospitals, etc.).[52] The traditionalist's intransigence to change and the progressive's commitment to innovation and experimentation, then, may

[50] This suggests an interesting parallel between political attitudes toward federal programs and clerical attitudes toward official change in the Church. Perhaps it presages an "end to ideology" movement in ecclesiastical affairs. This oversimplifies the problem, to be sure; still, it would appear to merit further study. For a suggestive analogy see William V. D'Antonio, "Community Leadership in an Economic Crisis," *American Journal of Sociology*, LXXI, pp. 688-700.

[51] A nonterritorial parish has since been established in the diocese with the bishop's approval and encouragement. See Jack M. Bickham, "The Community of John XXIII," *The Oklahoma Courier*, Vol. 47, Numbers 4 and 5, 1967.

[52] For an informative, though not always impartial, consideration see Edward Wakin and Joseph Scheuer, *The De-Romanization of The American Catholic Church*, MacMillan and Company, 1966.

be contrasted with the moderate's prudent gradualism as an important consequence of varying role-conceptions in the context of social structural change.

The use of this political idiom, incidentally, should not imply that one role-conception is necessarily "better" or any more "right" than the others. It is, rather, that each type describes a different normative involvement in the institutional Church: progressives are primarily concerned with norms not entirely legitimatized in the structures of Catholic life, while traditionalists accept the legitimacy of the established norms. Moderates, as the empirical definition indicates, tend to look for some institutional basis before they accept emergent norms and generally attribute legitimacy to the established ones.

Varying Role Conceptions And Functional Alternatives

The next hypothesis asserts first that progressives will perceive functional alternatives to the pastoral role, and second that their previous training will seem to them rather inappropriate to the tasks at hand. Ironically, this means that progressives will perceive existing structures as obstacles instead of means to the realization of pastoral functions. Presumably they will regard as inadequate their preparation for the role because such preparation has been designed to conform them to the system. Since the system has dubious value to progressives, it would follow that their preparation to function in it will now seem to them inadequate and inappropriate to what is believed really obligatory.[53]

Respondents were asked: "Do you think there are other careers you might have chosen that would give you more opportunity to do the things you would like to accomplish?"

Table 18 shows the frequency of "yes" responses for each type of role conception. Clearly, progressives tend to perceive alternatives to their formal position as priests in the Church's formal organization. But it cannot be concluded from this that these priests are "misfits" or rebels with no real interest in the pastoral role.

The data presented in Table 19 indicate that it is chiefly progressives who are most deeply committed to the spirit of renewal epitomized by Vatican Council II. Briefly, to conjecture, it would appear that a progressive is concerned that the persistence of established conditions may vitiate his commitment to pastoral obligations.[54]

[53] See Joseph H. Fichter, *Religion as a Profession, op. cit.*
[54] The implications of such normative ambivalence for role theory is superbly developed in Merton and Barber, *op. cit.*

TABLE 18   PERSONAL ROLE-CONCEPTIONS AND ALTERNATIVES TO PRIESTLY CAREER AMONG OKLAHOMA CLERGY

| Personal Role-Conceptions | "Would other careers give you a greater opportunity to do the things you consider important?" | | | | | |
| | Yes | | No | | Total | |
	N	%	N	%	N	%
Progressives	21	57	16	43	37	100
Moderates	7	11	58	89	65	100
Traditionals	2	12	15	88	17	100
Total	30		89		119	

$X^2 = 29.16$ 2 df p .001

The corollary to this hypothesis is that progressives will be more critical of their seminary training than either moderates or traditionalists. Table 20 indicates that such is the case. Progressives are obviously more critical of their training, especially in those areas most relevant to the pastoral function (i.e., pastoral training, academic preparation in psychology and social science, isolation of seminary life). Conversely, moderates and traditionalists regard their preparation as generally adequate and appropriate to their present obligations. Because progressives are younger than others, it is perhaps fair to wonder whether later, when older, their training might upon reflection seem better. Nevertheless, unless time and experience modify the progressive's role-conception, there are grounds to suspect his estrangement from the system if he cannot change

TABLE 19   PERSONAL ROLE-CONCEPTIONS AND COMMITMENT TO CHURCH RENEWAL AS TAUGHT BY VATICAN COUNCIL II AMONG OKLAHOMA CLERGY

| Personal Role-Conceptions | Yes, Renewal Is Important | | Renewal Is Not Important | | Total | |
	N	%	N	%	N	%
Progressives	34	92	3	8	37	100
Moderates	55	85	10	15	65	100
Traditionals	7	59	10	41	17	100
Total	96		23		119	

$X^2 = 15.98$ 2 df p .001

it from within.[55] In either case, there is sharp discontinuity in the system in the sense that a significant minority of deeply committed priests are critical of both the structural context of their pastoral role and their systematic preparation for it.

Varying Role Conceptions and Strain

The latest hypothesis asserts that progressives will experience greater "strain" in the performance of the pastoral role than either traditionalists or moderates. Our indicator of role strain here is adapted from the *Job Related Tension Index* developed by the Survey Research Center, which includes a number of questions designed to measure the tension and dissatisfaction experienced in one's occupational role.[56]

This notion comes into sharper focus if considered from the perspective of Robert Merton's theory of normative ambivalence.[57] Merton observes that ordinarily individuals are expected to perform their roles in accordance with traditionally established norms; not

TABLE 20   PERSONAL ROLE-CONCEPTION AND BELIEF THAT SEMINARY TRAINING WAS INADEQUATE OR INAPPROPRIATE AMONG OKLAHOMA CLERGY

Aspects of Seminary Training	Personal Role-Conceptions			X^2	P
	Progressives ($N = 37$)	Moderates ($N = 65$)	Traditionals ($N = 17$)		
Philosophy and theology	54	35	12	12.90	.01
Pastoral training	76	40	29	15.14	.001
Strict discipline	57	28	12	12.50	.01
Isolation from laity	68	31	24	16.48	.001
Isolation from parish	70	28	29	22.79	.001
Lack of experience	46	20	35	8.46	.02
Psychology and social science	73	46	41	7.25	.05
Spiritual training	57	35	18	8.48	.02

2 df

[55] Some aspects of this are touched upon in Robert Brooks, "The Former-Major Seminarian," unpublished doctoral dissertation, University of Notre Dame, 1958.

[56] This instrument is discussed in J. Diedrick Snock, "Role Strain in Diversified Role-Sets," *American Journal of Sociology,* LXXI, pp. 363-372.

[57] Merton and Barber, *op. cit.*

infrequently, however, such norms are poorly adapted to the situations in which individuals find themselves. Put somewhat differently, the established role-expectations may contribute much to the preservation of institutional stability but little to the satisfaction of individual needs and interests. Consequently, novel arrangements are evolved which often conflict with those already legitimatized. The by-product of this may be role strain among individuals whose role-conception makes them more sensitive to the progressive than to the traditional norms.

The data in Table 21 show that progressives are indeed more likely than others to experience role strain. In view of his indifference to established pastoral rubrics, it is not surprising that the progressive should experience difficulty in his work. What is surprising, however, is that differences in strain among types are not greater. Perhaps the permissive uses to which authority is put in this diocese mitigates the otherwise adverse consequences of normative ambivalence. Quite possibly in a more authoritarian diocese both moderates *and* progressives would experience considerably greater tension than they do in Oklahoma. To conjecture further, it also seems likely that traditionalists would experience less strain in a more authoritarian diocese.[58]

More pertinently, the corollary to the hypothesis is that *one* of the consequences of role strain may be some measure of disenchant-

TABLE 21   PERSONAL ROLE-CONCEPTION AND ROLE STRAIN AMONG OKLA-
HOMA CLERGY

Personal Role-Conceptions	"High" Strain [a]		"Low" Strain		Total	
	N	%	N	%	N	%
Progressives	23	62	14	38	37	100
Moderates	20	32	42	68	62	100
Traditionals	5	33	10	67	15	100
Total	48		66		114 [b]	

$X^2 = 8.04$ 2 df p 0.1

[a] Respondent's scores on the instrument can range from 1-5. "High" strain refers to scores of 2.5 and over, "low" strain refers to scores of less than 2.5.

[b] Three moderates and two traditionals did not complete this part of the questionnaire.

[58] Some supporting evidence of this may be found in Sister Marie Augusta Neal, *op. cit.*

TABLE 22   PERSONAL ROLE-CONCEPTION AND RESPONSES TO QUESTIONS CONCERNING ADVICE GIVEN TO YOUTH WHO THINK THEY HAVE A VOCATION AMONG OKLAHOMA CLERGY

Personal Role-Conceptions	Would Probably Encourage Vocation		Would Probably Not Encourage Vocation		Total	
	N	%	N	%	N	%
Progressives	8	22	29	78	37	100
Moderates	28	43	37	57	65	100
Traditionals	12	71	5	29	17	100
Total	48		71		119	

$X^2 = 11.80$ 2 df p .01

ment with the priesthood as evidenced in the advice given by priests to prospective seminarians. Respondents were asked the question: "In the light of your own experience as a priest, how would you advise a high-school student who feels he has a vocation to enter the priesthood?"

As Table 22 indicates, progressives are significantly more likely to dissuade the prospective priest—or, at least, less likely to encourage the vocation. It is important to recall at this point that there is little evidence to say that these priests are "spoiled" or "misfits." By their own admission they are deeply committed to the program of Church renewal and seem to possess a real sense of Christian witness. Their apparent "alienation" (i.e., relatively low involvement in the system) is perhaps the unanticipated consequence of the purposive reform undertaken by the postconciliar Church. And one result of this seems to be an unwillingness to recruit others for an on-going system regarded as antiquated.

SUMMARY

The results of this study must of course be considered tentative until comparable investigations provide further support. What seems evident at this juncture, however, is that: (a) varying personal conceptions of the pastoral role are presently discernable among priests; (b) such differences refer to whether individual priests are primarily concerned with established normative arrangements, evolving role-demands, or both.

There is, moreover, some evidence to indicate that varying role-conceptions reflect social structural differences. Progressives, for instance, tend to be younger and more peripherally located in the system than either moderates or traditionalists. But besides these differences progressives also seem more likely to be native Oklahomans from rather middle-class families. They are more likely to read journals critical of the *status quo* and, perhaps because of this, appear to relate themselves to reference groups which symbolize change and permissive authority. This difference seems to endure through time, for it obtains among older as well as younger priests and among pastors as well as others.

Finally, progressives are consistently in favor of structural changes and more likely than moderates or traditionalists to perceive alternatives to priestly life. Correlatively, they are rather critical of their formal preparation for pastoral life, experience greater strain than others in the performance of pastoral activities, and are least likely to encourage vocations among youth.

By way of conjecture, a case might be made that the dissensus in role-conceptions reflects a dialectic tension between charismatic and institutional legitimacy.[59] Progressives, and to some degree moderates, seem primarily responsive to charismatic norms and question the traditional bases of legitimacy in Catholic life. To the degree that traditional authority becomes untenable and is replaced by charisma, often identified outside the diocesan structure—to this extent the social system would rest upon an unstable, quite precarious base.

[59] Thomas O'Dea, "Five Paradoxes: The Dilemmas of Institutionalization," in Tiryakin (ed.), *op. cit.*

5

Self, Role, and Satisfaction in the Religious Life

NATHANIEL J. PALLONE
New York University

JOHN DRISCOLL, C.S.C.
Holy Cross Junior College

MARIAN DROBA, S.S.J.
Office of the Delegate for Religious, Archdiocese of Detroit

SOURCE. Prepared especially for this volume.

Psychological study of priests, nuns, and brothers has drawn its impetus largely from the pioneering work of Dom Thomas Verner Moore (1936), who investigated the incidence of mental illness among the clergy. On the basis of his findings, Moore urged that applicants for the religious life be routinely screened on a battery of diagnostic psychological tests to detect incipient emotional disorder.

On the basis of clinical evidence from psychodiagnostic tests, a number of investigators have attempted to predict "persistence" in or "defection" from the religious life among candidates for the priesthood, sisterhood, or brotherhood (Aloyse, 1961; Arnold, 1962; Barry, 1960; Bier, 1965; Coville, 1964; McCarthy and Dondero, 1963; Sweeney, 1964; Tageson, 1964; Vaughan, 1963). Such investigations, however, have yielded disappointing results. Indeed, some voices have objected to the routine diagnostic screening of religious candidates both on theologic and on psychological grounds. Vaughan (1961), for example, has asserted that the majority of those who "defect" are healthier mentally than most who remain, since the "defector" possesses sufficient ego-strength to determine incompatibility between his own personality or needs and the demands associated with the religious role. Kobler (1964) regards the diagnostic screening approach as inappropriate in the selection of religious candidates, for he believes that selection of the religious life represents the culmination of a process of "occupational" choice and adjustment involving normal rather than pathological drives and motivations.

Other investigators, following the methods of differential psychology rather than those of clinical psychology as championed by Moore, have sought to determine differences in personality, values, or interests between nuns and members of the "general" adult female population (Becker, 1962; D'Arcy, 1962; McKenna, 1961; Rice, 1962), or between priests or brothers and members of the general adult male population (Dunn, 1965; Fichter, 1957; McCarthy, 1961, 1963; Weisberger, 1962). However, results of these investigations remain largely inconclusive. Hence, McCarthy (1960) has suggested that some personal characteristics vary quite as widely among persons in the religious life as among members of the general population, or among members of other "occupational" groups. McCarthy also believes that it is likely that those who elect the religious life share in common certain interests, values, or personality features. But as yet psychological research has failed to identify such common characteristics.

A PROBLEM IN VOCATIONAL PSYCHOLOGY

Thus a body of research by differential psychologists suggests that Catholic religious do not differ significantly from otherwise similar members of the general population, while research by clinical psychologists has failed to illuminate the dynamics of attraction to or withdrawal from the religious life, even though some commentators (cf. Finch, 1965) continue to regard attraction as a particular form of psychopathology. Yet it need not be documented that the problem of "defection" from the religious life persists, with consequent manpower shortages in many communities.

Even though neither differential nor clinical psychological research has proved fruitful, however, rarely have researchers addressed the choice of the religious life as a "normal" process of occupational (vocational) development and adjustment. Resistance to the application of the theoretical constructs and research methods of vocational development psychology to those engaged in the religious life may rest upon the traditional Catholic belief that, in its religious sense, "vocation" implies a divine calling, by definition not amenable to empirical investigation.

On the basis of current theory and research in vocational development psychology, one might expect that the decision of a religious or a religious candidate to remain within ("persist") or to leave ("defect from") the religious life hinges largely upon the degree of vocational or occupational satisfaction he experiences.

Super's (1957) well-known formulation holds that *"In choosing an occupation, one is, in effect, choosing a means of implementing a self-concept."* Super's (1957, 1963) theory of vocational development conceptualizes that process as the progressive implementation of the person's self-concept through an occupational role or series of roles which the person elects to play; the role or series of roles is elected in consonance with the person's perceptions of himself, of self-realities and self-possibilities. From Super's theoretical formulation, Pallone and Banks (1968) have drawn an operational corollary which holds that "vocational satisfaction consists in relatively high congruence between one's self-concept" on the one hand and "the demands, requirements, and self-actualizing possibilities inhering in the occupational role one has elected."

Operationalization of the construct of vocational satisfaction advanced in this corollary, however, presents certain methodological problems: how can one determine with accuracy the "demands, requirements, and self-actualizing possibilities" associated with an occupational role? Perhaps the perceptions of the role held by successful members of an occupation could be called into play. These perceptions might be regarded as "standards" against which the perceptions held by persons who aspire to the occupation might be gauged. But this procedure carries certain inherent disadvantages. For example, the procedure makes the assumption that the role perceptions of successful members of an occupation are adequate reflections of the "realities" of that occupation.

An avenue toward an operational *approximation* to the vocational satisfaction construct hinges upon relating a subject's perception of himself to his perception of the "ideal" occupant of an occupational role to which the subject aspires or in which he is engaged, successfully or no. Partial support for this approach can be found in a conclusion reached in a study of vocational development among nurses by Pallone and Hosinski (1967) that "vocational choice . . . may be regarded as a point in life at which the person states definitely both 'This is the kind of person I would like to be (or become)' and 'As I perceive my contemplated or implemented occupation role, it will allow me to be (or become) that kind of person.' "

PARALLEL STUDIES: MINISTERS, NUNS, BROTHERS

In an effort to apply the research methods of vocational development psychology to the religious life, three parallel investigations were conducted to study the correlates of vocational satisfaction among Protestant ministerial students and among Catholic brothers and nuns respectively. Specifically, these investigations explored, among members-in-training of the three religious occupations, certain correlates of congruence between the subject's self-concept and his perception of the "ideal" occupant of the religious role he or she was preparing to enter—as a reasonable approximation to the construct "vocational satisfaction." Operationally, these studies sought to differentiate between subjects who exhibited markedly high and markedly low levels of congruence between self-concept and occupational role percept (i.e., percept of the "ideal" member of the respective occupation) in terms of personality factors, vocational interests, authoritarianism or dogmatism, values, and selected elements of social and educational history. The present article reports results of the investigation of correlates of vocational satisfaction among nuns and brothers; the investigation of correlates of vocational satisfaction among graduates students in a Protestant theological seminary have been reported elsewhere (Pallone and Banks, 1968).

SELF AND ROLE PERCEPTIONS AMONG BROTHERS

Some 121 student brothers attending scholasticates of the three American provinces of the Brothers' Society, Congregation of the Holy Cross, were studied. Since they were engaged in a program of specific educational preparation for particular roles within the religious life (e.g., teaching or youth work), Ss may be regarded as having progressed to what Super (1964) has called the "implementation" stage in their vocational development.

Measures of self-concept and of perceptions of the "ideal" Holy Cross brother were obtained from Ss' responses, under differential sets of instructions, to a Q-sort instrument constructed by Suziedilis (1957) but adapted by Tageson (1960) for use with adolescent male religious. This instrument contains 50 socially neutral, self-relevant, behaviorally descriptive statements. To obtain a measure of self-concept, Ss were required to sort statements into a normalized, forced distribution with nine intervals, ranging from "most like me" to "most unlike me." To obtain a measure of perception of the "ideal" occupant of the religious role which Ss had elected and for which they were preparing, Ss were similarly required to sort statements into nine intervals, ranging from "most like the ideal Holy Cross brother" to "most unlike the ideal Holy Cross brother." Test-retest reliability was reported by Suziedilis at +.66.

Coefficients of correlation were computed between each S's self- and occupational role percept sorts according to formulae proposed by Stephenson (1953) for use with Q-technique. Resultant r's were converted to z' transformations, arrayed, and partitioned at quartiles. Mean r for the first quartile $= +.040$, while mean r for the fourth quartile $= +.839$, with t significant beyond .01. Accordingly, Ss in the fourth and first quartiles were regarded as significantly "more" and "less" congruent ("vocationally satisfied"), respectively.

Mean ratings for more and less congruent Ss on each Q-statement in self- and occupational role percept sorts were compared through t, as reported in Table 1. Significant differences emerged *neither* in self-perceptions *nor* in perceptions of the "ideal" Holy Cross brother between more and less satisfied Ss. Hence, brother-subjects perceived themselves and the "ideal" brother in surprisingly uniform fashion. Since no significant differences emerge, it is evident that Ss substantially agreed in their perceptions of those elements of the

TABLE 1   MEAN RATINGS FOR SELF AND OCCUPATIONAL ROLE PERCEPTS—BROTHERS

Q-Prelicates: *I am a person who . . .* OR *The ideal Holy Cross brother is a person who . . .*	Self Sort			Occupational Role Sort		
	Satisfaction Level			Satisfaction Level		
	More	Less	t	More	Less	t
1. believes in the destiny of fate.	2.6	3.4	0.50	2.7	3.4	0.43
2. never gets excited.	4.9	3.8	0.70	5.5	5.3	0.15
3. won't share some things with anybody.	3.2	4.3	0.74	2.9	3.4	0.35
4. tries to make life as easy as possible for himself.	3.4	6.2	1.97	2.6	2.5	0.75
5. is extraordinary.	4.9	4.0	0.57	6.6	5.2	0.95
6. lets his heart decide where his reason has difficulty.	4.6	5.6	0.68	4.2	4.0	0.13
7. believes that things will always turn out well.	7.0	5.2	1.69	6.8	6.6	0.18
8. keeps always on the go.	6.4	4.5	1.43	6.3	6.3	0.00
9. regards suffering as a necessary part of life.	7.5	6.5	0.63	7.8	7.5	0.18
10. goes along with the majority.	5.4	5.2	0.14	5.3	4.7	0.54
11. always laughs off an insult.	5.5	3.4	1.38	6.9	6.2	0.25
12. is dominant in a group.	4.3	4.6	0.17	4.8	4.3	0.42
13. follows traditions and customs most faithfully.	5.4	5.1	0.28	5.7	6.1	0.36
14. is very firm with children.	5.1	4.3	0.80	5.3	5.4	0.11
15. has few, but very close, friends.	4.6	5.4	0.55	4.2	4.5	0.24
16. worries a great deal about the future.	4.0	4.8	0.50	3.5	3.7	0.20
17. regards sex as a very tricky aspect of life.	4.0	5.3	0.89	3.9	4.5	0.48
18. always does things in a uniform manner.	4.9	4.7	0.20	5.3	5.7	0.53
19. never gets too emotionally involved with others.	4.0	4.5	0.35	3.6	5.1	1.05
20. frequently compares his abilities with those of others.	4.7	7.2	1.93	3.9	3.6	0.26
21. is sensitive.	5.7	6.7	0.62	4.9	5.2	0.20
22. never rests satisfied with himself.	6.8	5.0	1.12	7.2	6.8	0.33

23. tolerates no deviation from the law.	4.2	4.4	0.16	4.2	4.9	0.58
24. is carefree most of the time.	4.9	5.2	0.23	4.7	5.1	0.33
25. is generous at the expense of his own welfare.	7.1	4.4	1.76	7.6	7.2	0.28
26. is eager to surpass others.	4.1	5.1	1.81	3.9	3.3	0.42
27. never in the least modifies his principles.	4.2	3.8	0.30	4.1	5.1	0.62
28. is reserved.	5.8	5.3	0.31	5.9	5.8	0.10
29. imposes himself on others at times.	4.6	4.9	0.25	4.5	4.4	0.09
30. likes to do things on the spur of the moment.	4.7	5.4	0.63	4.6	4.1	0.60
31. rarely asks anybody for a favor.	5.0	5.3	0.27	4.9	4.6	0.29
32. seeks advice a great deal.	4.9	4.9	0.00	4.8	4.9	0.09
33. once decided on a plan of action, carries it out, no matter what.	4.3	4.0	0.25	4.2	4.7	0.35
34. is always informal.	5.1	5.1	0.00	5.2	4.9	0.29
35. hates nothing and nobody.	5.8	4.8	0.55	6.8	5.7	0.68
36. does things always on his own.	4.2	5.2	0.83	4.1	3.7	0.36
37. is satisfied and contented with what life provides.	6.8	5.1	1.41	6.9	6.8	0.08
38. never talks back to superiors.	5.7	5.6	0.71	5.6	5.3	0.23
39. lets everyone do as he wishes.	4.0	4.8	0.66	3.7	3.5	0.21
40. always likes things to be perfect.	5.7	5.5	0.13	5.3	5.7	0.43
41. trusts no one as much as himself.	3.1	5.4	1.91	2.8	3.1	0.23
42. always unquestioningly obeys orders.	5.5	4.8	0.58	5.9	6.4	0.41
43. does things very rapidly.	5.0	5.0	0.00	5.2	4.9	0.41
44. freely expresses emotions.	4.3	5.1	0.57	4.3	4.0	0.27
45. has a high opinion of himself.	3.9	5.5	1.06	3.7	3.7	0.00
46. regards sex as an important aspect of life.	6.2	5.7	0.41	6.2	5.6	0.50
47. drives himself hard.	6.2	3.9	1.76	6.6	6.2	0.44
48. is constantly concerned with preserving his health.	3.7	3.6	0.08	4.0	4.2	0.18
49. takes no chances.	4.3	4.3	0.00	4.3	4.2	0.10
50. lets his conscience be his guide.	6.2	5.6	0.46	6.2	6.7	0.35

religious life approximated in the Q-items: they not only agreed in their perceptions of the "ideal" brother, but they perceived themselves as very similar persons. Thus, vocational satisfaction for these Ss appears to inhere precisely in the *relationship* between self and role.

SELF AND ROLE PERCEPTION AMONG NUNS

Ninety-seven novices and postulants from three provinces of the Franciscan Sisters of St. Joseph were also studied. Measures of self-concept and of perceptions of the "ideal" Sister of St. Joseph were similarly obtained from Ss' responses, under differential sets of instructions, to a Q-instrument constructed for use in this investigation. The final version of the instrument contained 50 self-relevant, socially neutral statements. Some 100 statements—50 from Tageson's (1960) modification of the Suziedelis instrument and 50 extracted from essays about the "ideal" Sister of St. Joseph written by members of the community at the request of the investigators—were first sorted into a parametric, nine-interval distribution for social desirability by 21 young, professed sisters of the community. In accordance with procedures suggested by Kerlinger (1964), the 50 statements whose mean ratings did not differ significantly from the midpoint (5) of the social desirability scale, but which demonstrated sizable variances, were incorporated in the final instrument.

Ss sorted these 50 Q-statements into a parametric, nine-interval distribution ranging from "most like me" to "most unlike me" to obtain a measure of self-concept and from "most like the ideal Sister of St. Joseph" to "most unlike the ideal Sister of St. Joseph" to obtain a measure of occupational role percept. Coefficients of correlation were computed between each S's self- and occupational role percept sorts, according to Stephenson's (1953) formulae. Resultant r's were again converted to z', arrayed, and partitioned at quartiles. Mean r for the first quartile $= +.13$, while mean r for the fourth quartile $= +.64$, with $t = 16.7$, significant beyond .001. Accordingly, Ss in the fourth and first quartiles were again regarded as significantly "more" and "less" congruent (vocationally satisfied), respectively.

Mean ratings for more and less satisfied Ss on each Q-statement in self- and occupational role percept sorts were again compared through t, as reported in Table 2. While mean ratings for brother-subjects differed significantly on none of the 50 Q-statements used to measure their self- and occupational role percepts, moderate variation in both sets of perceptions is evident among sister-subjects.

Inspection of Table 2 reveals significant differences between more and less satisfied Ss on 13 statements in the self-sort and on three in the occupational role percept sort. More satisfied Ss perceived themselves, in contract to less satisfied Ss, as more able to love impartially (Q-statement 4); as more often on the go (6); as less willing to assent to majority opinion (9); as having many, rather than few, friends (15); as only moderately sensitive (16); as more generous at the expense of their own welfare (20); as more able to communicate with a variety of persons (23); as more likely to remain open-minded (25); as less spontaneous (26); as more willing to innovate or to experiment (39); as less free to express emotion (43); as more willing to sacrifice personal interests to the common good (43); and as less willing to face risks (49). More satisfied Ss perceived the ideal nun as less involved with persons outside her own community (Q-statement 7); as less attentive to her own ideals and goals (8); and less approachable (34) than she was perceived by less satisfied Ss.

While it bears repetition that brother-subjects and sister-subjects responded to two distinct Q-instruments, each appropriate to the population under investigation, differences in self- and role-perception are nonetheless striking. Apparently both self and role are perceived less uniformly by nuns than by brothers, perhaps due only to a sex difference—women are customarily less predictable or more variant than are men! No significant differences emerged either in the self- or in the role perceptions of brothers, while significant differences were observed among nuns on fully 13 statements in the self-percept sort. However, in the role percept sort, only three significant differences were noted among the 50 Q-statements, suggesting relatively uniform perception of the ideal role occupant.

CORRELATES OF "VOCATIONAL SATISFACTION"

Correlates of the level of congruence between self- and occupational role-percepts among both brother-subjects and nun-subjects were sought in personality factors, degree of open- or closed-mindedness (authoritarianism or dogmatism, respectively), dominant values, vocational interests, and selected elements of social and educational history. Table 3 reports mean raw scores for "more" and "less" congruent nun-subjects and brother-subjects, along with associated t values, for each psychometric variable investigated.

TABLE 2 MEAN RATINGS FOR SELF AND OCCUPATIONAL ROLE PERCEPTS—NUNS

Q-Predicates:
I am a person who . . .
OR The ideal Sister of St. Joseph is a person who . . .

| | Self Sort | | | Occupational Role Sort | | |
| | Satisfaction Level | | | | | |
	More	Less	t	More	Less	t
1. acts with characteristic delicacy of manners.	5.04	4.76	0.46	5.24	4.96	0.67
2. is extraordinary.	3.88	3.28	1.10	3.24	4.28	1.79
3. lets her heart decide where her reason has difficulty.	4.56	5.48	1.44	3.68	3.68	0.00
4. possesses the freedom of impartial love.	5.40	4.20	2.45*	6.16	5.80	0.68
5. believes that things will always turn out well.	5.16	5.12	0.07	5.12	5.04	0.22
6. always keeps on the go.	6.20	4.84	2.81**	5.20	4.40	2.00
7. becomes involved with mankind outside the community.	4.56	4.52	0.81	5.20	6.32	2.42*
8. has her own ideals and goals.	5.76	6.24	1.05	5.44	6.56	2.19*
9. goes along with the majority.	3.80	5.04	2.45*	2.88	3.08	0.51
10. is a practical woman.	6.20	5.32	1.79	6.00	6.16	0.33
11. always laughs off an insult.	4.64	4.20	0.76	5.00	5.68	0.72
12. is dominant in a group.	3.92	2.96	1.77	3.60	3.76	0.39
13. follows customs and traditions most faithfully.	4.40	5.00	1.22	5.16	5.12	0.07
14. is very firm with children.	3.64	3.68	0.09	3.96	3.96	0.00
15. has few, but very close, friends.	3.80	5.92	4.07***	3.12	3.40	0.65
16. is sensitive.	5.24	7.08	3.01**	4.00	3.60	0.79
17. distinguishes uniformity from conformity.	5.12	4.84	0.62	5.44	6.04	1.76
18. never rests satisfied with herself.	5.36	6.28	1.61	4.48	4.81	0.57
19. cultivates a taste for the finer aspects of music, art, and drama.	5.84	6.00	0.32	5.48	5.32	0.51
20. is generous at the expense of her own welfare.	6.52	5.36	2.68**	6.08	6.28	0.43
21. accepts and supports change in her traditional mode of living.	5.08	4.88	0.54	5.96	5.68	0.70
22. is a lively person, welcome in any group.	4.96	4.68	0.48	5.32	5.20	0.41

23. is able to communicate with difficult persons.	6.04	4.20	4.28***	5.96	6.04	0.41
24. is reserved.	4.56	5.52	1.54	4.76	4.56	0.41
25. probes into various sides of an issue and keeps an open mind.	5.56	4.72	2.15*	6.56	6.40	0.45
26. likes to do things on the spur of the moment.	3.04	4.60	3.34**	2.92	3.20	0.64
27. recognizes the role of the laity.	5.36	5.32	0.13	5.56	5.64	0.27
28. lets herself be known and gets to know others.	5.28	5.00	0.50	5.92	5.68	0.60
29. is identified with the poor.	4.68	4.96	0.58	5.44	5.72	0.60
30. hates nothing and nobody.	4.80	5.32	1.06	5.04	4.80	0.47
31. is satisfied and contented with what life provides.	4.92	4.96	0.07	4.92	4.16	1.28
32. responds to the contemporary demands of her.	5.84	5.40	1.08	6.40	6.32	0.18
33. never openly disagrees with superiors.	5.44	5.80	0.58	5.28	4.52	1.49
34. is approachable.	6.36	5.72	1.68	6.64	7.40	2.05*
35. is ready and willing to accept any task given her.	6.64	5.88	1.62	7.28	6.84	1.09
36. always likes things to be perfect.	5.29	5.48	0.31	4.00	3.60	1.03
37. overlooks the faults of others.	5.96	4.96	1.90	6.56	6.36	0.44
38. never lets "I don't want" or "I don't like" cross her lips.	4.40	3.84	1.25	5.36	4.84	1.24
39. is willing to try new things.	6.60	5.40	2.54*	5.88	5.76	0.34
40. does things very rapidly.	3.76	4.40	1.10	3.04	3.36	0.77
41. is immersed in the things of this world because nothing is profane.	3.88	4.24	0.68	3.92	3.84	0.12
42. freely expresses emotions.	3.16	4.92	2.77**	2.44	3.04	1.55
43. puts the common good before her individual needs.	6.24	5.28	2.75**	7.44	7.20	0.60
44. regards sex as an important aspect of life.	3.60	3.68	0.20	4.32	4.44	0.27
45. participates actively in professional organizations.	3.60	3.68	0.20	4.40	4.52	0.31
46. drives herself hard.	5.44	5.16	0.54	4.64	3.72	1.89
47. goes beyond immediate duties to meet others on a personal level.	6.24	5.40	1.74	6.68	7.04	0.74
48. works cooperatively with members of the opposite sex.	5.00	4.96	0.15	4.92	5.08	0.52
49. takes no chances.	3.24	4.44	2.69*	2.84	3.28	0.96
50. regards the lay person as an equal.	5.12	5.55	1.00	4.64	4.92	0.82

*t significant at .05; **t significant at .01; ***t significant at .001.

TABLE 3   MEANS FOR PERSONALITY, VALUES, AND INTERESTS VERSUS ROLE SATISFACTION LEVEL AMONG NUNS AND BROTHERS

| | Nuns | | Brothers | |
| | Satisfaction Level | | Satisfaction Level | |
Variable	"More" (N = 25)	"Less" (N = 25)	"More" (N = 30)	"Less" (N = 30)
Personality Factors				
Cyclothymia	5.00	5.12	7.00	6.66
Intellectual awareness	7.10	6.00	6.43	6.96
Ego strength	6.00	4.75*	4.90	4.63
Dominance	5.10	4.85	4.46	4.86
Enthusiasm	5.30	4.80	4.86	5.16
Superego strength	7.00	5.66	6.70	5.60*
Adventuresomeness	6.00	3.90***	5.06	4.23
Sensitivity	6.00	5.00	6.10	6.53
Suspiciousness	5.00	6.15	4.83	6.30*
Unconventionality	6.10	6.10	6.50	6.20
Shrewdness	6.20	4.85***	5.36	4.76
Guilt proneness	4.75	7.20***	5.70	7.06*
Radicalism	5.10	7.10**	4.50	4.80
Self-sufficiency	5.00	5.90	5.63	6.56
Self-sentiment level	7.00	4.90**	6.83	4.93***
Ergic tension level	4.90	6.10*	5.63	6.96**
Authoritarianism			80.66	79.03
Dogmatism	3.27	3.50		
Values				
Theoretical	34.24	32.37	38.66	36.66
Economic	29.00	30.87	33.06	34.23
Aesthetic	38.00	41.54	44.06	44.33
Social	49.95	46.91	35.56	37.76
Political	34.08	34.50	39.23	37.43
Religious	53.12	51.00	51.36	49.36
Vocational Interests				
Outdoor	44.54	42.20	38.66	39.50
Mechanical	23.20	24.91	31.33	29.93
Computational	21.66	17.45	24.13	26.40
Scientific	37.12	29.08*	37.13	35.73
Persuasive	27.58	30.75	34.06	31.43
Artistic	27.83	31.79	24.76	24.16
Literary	24.12	18.20	18.33	23.23

TABLE 3   MEANS FOR PERSONALITY, VALUES, AND INTERESTS VERSUS ROLE
SATISFACTION LEVEL AMONG NUNS AND BROTHERS—Continued

| | Nuns | | Brothers | |
| | Satisfaction Level | | Satisfaction Level | |
Variable	"More" (N = 25)	"Less" (N = 25)	"More" (N = 30)	"Less" (N = 30)
Musical	26.37	16.41	16.20	14.10
Social service	66.00	61.91	60.60	54.26
Clerical	40.41	42.33	44.16	44.10

*for *t* significant at .05
**for *t* significant at .01
***for *t* significant at .001

Personality Factors

Measures of personality source traits were obtained through the
Cattell (1962) 16 Personality Factor Questionnaire, an instrument
which measures traits of personality described as "functionally uni-
tary" and "psychologically significant." Inspection of Table 3 reveals
that seven of the 16 factors differentiate more from less congruent
nuns and that six factors differentiate more from less congruent
brothers.

More congruent nuns demonstrated higher ego-strength, greater
adventuresomeness, greater shrewdness, and a higher level of self-
sentiment than their less congruent counterparts. But less congruent
nuns demonstrate considerably greater levels of proneness toward
guilt and (curiously) of radicalism and a higher level of ergic tension
(generalized feeling of frustration).

More congruent brothers demonstrate higher superego-strength
and a higher level of self-sentiment than their less congruent confreres.
Less congruent brothers exhibit higher levels of suspiciousness, guilt
proneness, self-sufficiency, and ergic tension.

It is perhaps instructive to compare these results with those
reported by Pallone and Banks (1968) in their parallel study of
correlates of vocational satisfaction among Seventh-day Adventist
ministerial students. They found that more congruent subjects were
more adventuresome, but less shrewd and less generally frustrated.

Ergic tension (generalized frustration) emerges as a dimension
of some interest. A higher level of ergic tension significantly differentiates less from more congruent nuns, brothers, and Protestant
ministerial students. It is impossible to speculate whether tension

or satisfaction is antecedent, or to determine whether less satisfied subjects feel more generally frustrated in consequence of a lower degree of vocational satisfaction or experience less satisfaction in consequence of their relatively free-floating frustration. Whatever the relationship, however, the dynamics implied appear to differ little from what one might expect to observe among more and less satisfied workers in any occupational role.

Higher levels of self-sentiment differentiate more from less satisfied subjects among both nuns and brothers. This finding may suggest a dimension of particular interest among Catholic religious, whose theology views a vocation as oriented first to achieving one's personal salvation and only secondly to serving one's fellows. Similarly, higher levels of guilt proneness differentiate less from more congruent nuns and brothers. It may be speculated that a proneness toward guilt embedded within the structure of the personality propels one to embrace a religious vocation as a means of expiation. But the realities of the religious life, especially in the active communities engaged in welfare, service, or educational activities, may provide little opportunity for a focus of attention upon self salvation, and expiation of personal guilt; hence, vocational dissatisfaction. No such relationship was observed among Seventh-day Adventist ministerial students. In fact, the mean levels of guilt proneness for both more and less satisfied ministerial students (Pallone and Banks, 1968) were lower than for any of the four Catholic groups. Seventh-day Adventist theology, in contrast, regards a religious calling as oriented essentially to the service of one's fellow, not to personal salvation.

Open- vs. Closed-Mindedness

Among brothers, this dimension was measured through the California F-Scale (Adorno et al., 1950); among nuns, through Schulze's (1962) D-10 Scale, a modified version of Rokeach's Dogmatism Scale (1960). Although these instruments measure somewhat variant aspects of orientation toward authority, neither differentiates more from less congruent subjects among nuns or brothers respectively. The F-Scale also failed to differentiate more from less satisfied ministerial students (Pallone and Banks, 1968).

Dominant Values

Value orientation was measured among both Catholic and Protestant subjects through the Allport-Vernon-Lindzey Study of Values (1960). None of the instrument's six scale discriminate between more and less satisfied nuns and brothers. However, mean scores were significantly higher for more satisfied ministerial students on the social value scale (Pallone and Banks, 1968).

Vocational Interests

Expressed preferences for certain occupational activities were measured through the familiar Kuder Vocational Preference Record (1960), Form CH, which assesses vocational interests in 10 broad areas of occupational endeavor. Among brothers, more satisfied subjects demonstrated a significantly higher mean level of interest in scientific pursuits than did less satisfied subjects. None of the 10 scale discriminated among nuns. The social service scale significantly differented more from less satisfied ministerial students (Pallone and Banks, 1968).

Social-Educational History

Subjects completed a questionnaire designed for use in these investigations which elicited self-reports concerning number of years of elementary and secondary education completed under church auspices; average weekly attendance at religious services; extracurricular activities in school, parish, or community; past honors and awards; quartile high school rank; whether the (Catholic) subject had attended a school conducted by the community of which he was now a member; college grade point average; number of siblings; birth order; number of siblings themselves engaged in the religious life; number and relationship of other relatives themselves engaged in the religious life; age at which serious consideration was first given to a religious occupation; age at entry to the subject's present community; history of prior affiliation with another community; source of information about the subject's present community; preference for life-work within that community; parental church affiliation; parental ethnic identification; employment prior to entrance to the religious life; size of community of upbringing; and age at which serious consideration was first given to entrance to the present community. Data were analyzed through chi-square.

Among nuns, significant differences were found on but two of these elements of social-educational history: (1) More satisfied nuns reported that they engaged significantly more often in parish and community activities. (2) More satisfied nuns reported significantly more often a preference for teaching rather than health services as a life-work choice within their community.

Among brothers, a significant difference was found on only one of these elements: More satisfied brothers reported significantly more often that they had graduated from a school conducted by the community of which they were now members.

Protestant ministerial students were differented on two elements: (1) More satisfied subjects reported significantly more often a longer period of their pre-college education in church schools. (2) More satisfied subjects reported significantly more often a vocational preference for the ministry during high school (Pallone and Banks 1968).

SUMMARY AND DISCUSSION

This report has summarized parallel investigations of the correlates of vocational satisfaction among Roman Catholic nuns and brothers, comparing the results obtained in these studies with those obtained in an investigation of vocational satisfaction of Protestant ministerial students.

It has been reported that neither self- nor occupational role percepts differed significantly between more and less satisfied brothers. More satisfied brothers exhibited higher levels of superego strength, self-sentiment, and scientific interest, and reported more often that they had graduated from schools conducted by the community of which they are now members. Less satisfied brothers demonstrated higher levels of suspiciousness, guilt proneness, self-sufficiency, and ergic tension (generalized feeling of frustration).

Among nuns, more and less satisfied subjects perceived themselves differently on 13 of 50 Q-statements and perceived the ideal nun differently on 3 of 50 statements. More satisfied nuns demonstrated higher levels of ego strength, adventuresomeness, shrewdness, and self-sentiment, and reported that they had engaged significantly more often in parish and community activities. They also evinced significantly more often a preference for teaching over health service as a lifework within the religious lifeway. Less satisfied nuns demonstrated higher levels of guilt proneness, radicalism, and ergic tension.

Apparently, the "ideal" occupant of a religious role is well understood by those preparing for that role. Male religious (both brothers and ministerial students) differed on none of the statements employed to measure their perceptions of the ideal role occupant, while female religious differed on only 3 of 50 statements. Unanimity and near-unanimity testify to the "public" character of the occupation as it is perceived by those who are in the "implementation" stage in their own vocational development. Since, however, levels of congruence between self- and occupational role percept sorts differed between extreme quartiles at .01 or beyond in each of the three groups investigated, there is some justification for regarding the notion of vocational satisfaction as represented essentially by the *relationship* between the self-as-perceived and the occupational-role-as-perceived as a tenable one.

Though these investigations have considered a large number of variables in relation to vocational satisfaction, few have emerged as significant. This fact alone suggests that those variables which indeed discriminate more from less satisfied members of religious occupations may represent decisive dimensions of satisfaction in the religious life. For example, among Roman Catholic subjects, higher levels of self-sentiment distinguish more from less satisfied religious; self-sentiment may represent an engine or generator of satisfaction with the religious life among nuns and brothers. Guilt proneness, on the other hand, may represent a key generator of dissatisfaction with the religious life among nuns and brothers. And generalized frustration indeed cuts across denominational lines as it influences dissatisfaction with the religious life among nuns, brothers, and ministerial students. Speculation about the dynamics at play here has been offered earlier.

It should be noted that dogmatism apparently is not a relevant variable in satisfaction or dissatisfaction with the religious life. A popular clinical hypothesis suggests that persons enter the religious life in response to strong authoritarian needs both to control and to be controlled in dogmatic fashion. The results of the three investigations reviewed in this report offer no support to such an hypothesis. Indeed, there is little indication of psychopathology as a relevant dimension among more or among less satisfied nuns, brothers, or ministerial students. Rather, these investigations suggest that satisfaction in the religious life appears to be triggered by "normal" processes of occupational development and adjustment equally observable among members of many occupational groups. By the same token, while there is no evidence of pathological dynamics, neither is there evidence that satisfaction or dissatisfaction in the religious life is influenced by spiritual or religious factors apart from or in addition to psychological factors quite amenable to empirical investigation.

REFERENCES

Adorno, T., Frenkel-Brunswik, Else, Levinson, D., and Sanford, R. N. *The authoritarian personality*. New York: Harper, 1950.

Allport, G. W., Vernon, P. E., and Lindzey, G. *Manual: study of values*, 3rd ed. Boston: Houghton-Mifflin, 1960.

Aloyse, M. Evaluation of candidates for the religious life. *Bulletin Guild of Catholic Psychiatrists*, 1964, **11**, 221-223.

Arnold, Magda B. A screening test for candidates for religious life. In V. Herr, *Screening candidates for the priesthood and religious life*. Chicago: Loyola Univ. Press, 1962, pp. 1-63.

Barry, W. A. An MMPI scale for seminary candidates. Unpublished thesis, Fordham Univ., 1950.

Becker, A. J. A study of personality traits of successful religious women of teaching orders. Unpublished thesis, Loyola Univ. (Chicago), 1962.

Bier, W. C. Selection of seminarians. In J. M. Lee and L. J. Putz, *Seminary education in a time of change*. Notre Dame: Fides, 1965, pp. 170-204.

Cattell, R. B., and Eber, H. W. *Handbook for the sixteen personality factor questionnaire*. Champaign: Institute for Personality & Ability Testing, 1962.

Coville, W. J. Personality assessment of candidates to seminaries: a study of clinical and psychometric methods and their effectiveness. In S. W. Cook, *The research planning workshop*. New York: Religious Education Association, 1962, pp. 175-288.

D'Arcy, P. F. Review of research on the vocational interests of priests, brothers, and sisters. In V. Herr, *Screening candidates for the priesthood and religious life*. Chicago: Loyola Univ. Press, 1962, pp. 149-203.

Dunn, R. F. Personality patterns among religious personnel: a review. *Catholic Psychological Record*, 1965, **3**, 125-136.

Fichter, J. H. *Religion as an occupation*. Notre Dame: Univ. Notre Dame Press, 1961.

Finch, J. G. Motivations for the ministry—a pathological view. *Insight*, 1965, **4**, 26-31.

Kerlinger, F. B. *Foundations of behavioral research*. New York: Holt, Rinehart, Winston, 1964.

Kobler, F. J. Screening applicants for religious life. *Journal of Religion and Health*, 1964, **3**, 161-170.

Kuder, G. F. *Administrator's manual: Kuder preference record*. Chicago: Science Research Associates, 1960.

McCarthy, T. N. *Psychological assessment in the religious vocation*. Philadelphia: LaSalle College, 1960.

McCarthy, T. N. *Characteristics of the promising candidate*. Philadelphia: LaSalle College, 1961.

McCarthy, T. N. *Characteristics of the psychologically healthy brother*. Philadelphia: LaSalle College, 1963.

McCarthy, T. N., and Dondero, A. Predictor variables and criteria of success in religious life: needed research. *Catholic Psychological Record,* 1963, **1**, 71-80.

McKenna, Helen, Religious attitudes and personality traits. *Journal of Social Psychology,* 1961, **54**, 379-388.

Moore, T. V. Insanity in priests and religious: the rate of insanity in priests and religious. *American Ecclesiastical Review,* 1936, **95**, 485-498.

Pallone, N. J., and Hosinski, Marion. Reality-testing a vocational choice: congruence between self, ideal, and occupational percepts among student nurses. *Personnel and Guidance Journal,* 1967, **45**, 666-670.

Pallone, N. J., and Banks, R. R. Vocational satisfaction among ministerial students. *Personnel and Guidance Journal,* 1968, **46**, 870-875.

Rice, P. J. MMPI performances of well adjusted and poorly adjusted religious women. Unpublished thesis, Loyola Univ. (Chicago), 1962.

Rokeach, M. *The open and closed mind.* New York: Basic Books, 1960.

Schulze, R. A shortened version of the Rokeach dogmatism scale. *Journal of Psychological Studies,* 1962, **13**, 93-97.

Stephenson, W. *The study of behavior: Q-technique and its methodology.* Chicago: Univ. Chicago Press, 1953.

Super, D. E. *The psychology of careers.* New York: Harper, 1957.

Super, D. E. *Career development: self-concept theory.* New York: College Entrance Examination Board, 1963.

Sweeney, R. H. Testing seminarians with MMPI and Kuder: a report on ten years of testing. Unpublished thesis Loyola Univ. (Chicago). 1964.

Tageson, C. F. *The relationship of self-perceptions to realism of vocational choice.* Washington: Catholic Univ. Press, 1960.

Vaughan, R. P. Specificity in programs of psychological evaluation. *Bulletin Guild of Catholic Psychiatrists,* 1961, **8**, 149-155.

Vaughan, R. P. A psychological assessment program for candidates to the religious life: validation study. *Catholic Psychological Record,* 1963, **1**, 65-70.

Weisberger, C. A. Survey of psychological screening programs in a clerical order. In V. Herr, *Screening candidates for the priesthood and religious life.* Chicago: Loyola Univ. Press, 1962, pp. 107-146.

6

American Catholic Schools
after the First 100 Years

REGINALD A. NEUWEIN

University of Notre Dame

SOURCE. Prepared especially for this volume. Based on *Catholic Schools in Action* (Notre Dame: University of Notre Dame Press, 1966).

The question "why do Catholic schools exist" may now be asked at a deeper, more philosophical level. Are there valid reasons why the Church should not have been content to follow the Protestant example and establish Sunday Schools to provide the religious instruction that the public school could not usually offer? It may seem strange at first glance that the question is very difficult to answer. A simple, uncomplicated reply is readily found. But an elaboration must take into account differences of orientation that have three main identifiable sources.

The first is "diversity." A school "system" that is not systematic cannot easily achieve unity in terms of either philosophy or practice. Public education in the United States also does not conform with any one pattern. We can, however, identify special Catholic problems. Some of these are often referred to in the pertinent literature. Diocesan superintendents have limited authority. They have no status in the canon law, whereas the pastor of a parish does. In many instances the decision about what to do in a given local situation depends on generally silent but protracted discussions or even altercations between a bishop and his parish priests or between the bishop and religious communities. Frequently there is neither the time nor the training to deal effectively with educational problems. A considerable number of the clergy and religious of the United States read widely, take an interest in current discussion of ideas, and follow the debates that make some leading periodicals lively organs of opinion. If they do so they are likely to differ about virtually all matters that are not definitely doctrines of the Church. But in many rectories intellectual life may proceed pretty much in terms of seminary manuals and diocesan newspapers (some of which, incidentally, are better than their reputations). Therefore, although the exploration of educational objectives is being conducted vigorously at the level of university discussion, with the support of diocesan superintendents, the actual conduct of the schools may be quite routine in character.

The second of the three sources is the fact that at present the study of administrative, curricular, and guidance problems by persons serving the public school so far outstrips that under Catholic auspices that the influence of the first is dominant. There is a growing quantity of reputable Catholic research, but most of it is being conducted in collaboration with scholars who serve public and secular education. The inevitable result is that in several areas there is no recognizable difference between the two systems. For instance, new methods of teaching mathematics and physics have been adopted by Catholic and public schools alike, and there is even some reason to conclude from statistics compiled by the National Science Foundation that these methods are being used more widely in Catholic than in other schools. But they are the same methods, and on the whole approximation to common standards tends to blunt the edges of separatism. This is most noticeable in curriculum building. One has only to compare the course of study used in a typical Catholic elementary or secondary school of forty years ago with that in effect today to note the influence of public education on the Catholic school.

The third source is the unevenness of teacher preparation. As has been indicated, the great efforts made to improve the training given to religious have been notably successful. But the demands made on the communities have been so heavy that young men and women have been assigned to schools far earlier than is desirable, in the hope that summer session work would fill in the educational gaps. That being the situation, it is not remarkable that differences in outlook and orientation should exist. Meanwhile the religious community itself may be undergoing a transformation of its rule and structure. The major cause of unevenness is, however, the fact that the increasing number of lay teachers are being recruited haphazardly. Even the question of whether they are truly committed to Catholic education sometimes remains open.

Of course there are manifest similarities. Every Catholic school teaches religion, although it may by no means do so in the way others do. In all, symbols associated with the liturgy and prayer are intimately associated with the school day. The very presence of the religious is in itself a dominant, unforgettable symbol. Here are persons set apart from the world reminding that world not merely of sin, of justice, and of judgment, but also of the unavoidable choice between the holy and the unholy, between the things that are of time and the things that transcend time. One may rebel against all this, as many have, but even those who do not surrender to the school cannot erase its imprint from the texture of their minds. This one remembers about Catholic education when virtually all else may have been forgotten.

But whether this unity is properly one of intensified parish life rather than of the school is a question asked more and more often. It cannot be answered because research has provided no basis for a valid comparison between parish life in which the school occupies a central position and, hypothetically, parish life that exists so rich in terms of liturgy and action that a school might be of peripheral concern. Even so there is ample evidence that if what has just been said about the purpose of the Catholic school were all that could be said, the philosophical basis on which that school rests would be relatively insubstantial.

I. THE ENROLLMENT OF CATHOLIC SCHOOLS

Any look at schools in action must be concerned with that segment of youth being served. This Study examined the enrollment of the Catholic elementary and secondary schools in the United States for the 1962-63 school year. The enrollment statistics collected annually by the National Catholic Welfore Conference were analyzed for the 9-year period from the school year 1953-54 to the school year 1962-63. This period was used because the statistical method of collecting data was changed in 1953 and remained constant through 1962.

The enrollment data were first analyzed by individual dioceses and then by dioceses grouped into 9 standard statistical regions. The analyses showed a clear pattern of continued growth in both the elementary and secondary enrollment during this 9-year period. A few individual dioceses showed a drop in enrollment, but in each of these subdivision to form new dioceses accounted for the decrease in enrollment.

The second clear outcome of the analysis was that the rate of growth of secondary enrollment greatly exceeded that of elementary enrollment. During the 9-year period secondary enrollment increased 59.9% whereas elementary enrollment increased 38.7% (Tables 1 and 2).

In further analysis of the 9-year period broke down in 2 parts. The first 6 years, 1953-54 to 1959-60, showed a rather even rate of growth for both elementary and secondary enrollments. During this period the elementary enrollment increased by 27.2% and the secondary by 30.0%. However, the 3 years 1960-61 to 1962-63 show a complete change in the rate of enrollment growth. During this period secondary enrollment increased by 23.0% while elementary enrollment increased by only 9.0%. The average growth per year in elementary school enrollment over the full 9-year period was 138,671, and in secondary schools 43,294; for the first 6-year period the average growth per year was 146,329 in elementary schools, and 30,867 in secondary schools; during the subsequent 3-year period the elementary growth per year was 123,356, compared with 68,149 in secondary schools (Table 3); a further look at these enrollment growth rates is presented in Table 4.

From these statistics it seems clear that greater provision for secondary schools was made from about 1959, near the end of the first 6-year period. This change in emphasis could not have been the result of a change in total population, because the percentage of increase in upcoming secondary school population was far out-

TABLE 1 GROWTH IN ELEMENTARY ENROLLMENT BY REGIONS, 1953-62

Region	1953	1962	Change	Change %	1953	1959	Change	Change %	1959	1962	Change	Change %
1	303,693	354,779	51,086	16.8	303,693	350,020	46,327	15.2	350,020	354,779	4,759	1.3
2	1,016,167	1,365,530	349,363	34.3	1,016,167	1,236,269	220,102	21.6	1,236,269	1,365,530	129,261	11.2
3	902,696	1,264,469	361,773	40.0	902,696	1,182,486	279,790	30.9	1,182,486	1,264,469	81,983	6.9
4	293,900	425,958	132,058	44.9	293,900	378,365	84,465	28.7	378,365	425,958	47,593	12.5
5	162,999	259,556	96,557	59.2	162,999	215,289	52,290	32.0	215,289	259,556	44,267	20.5
6	78,720	116,784	38,064	48.3	78,720	110,814	32,094	40.7	110,814	116,784	5,970	5.3
7	187,280	242,278	54,998	29.3	187,280	236,873	49,593	26.4	236,873	242,278	5,405	2.3
8	66,774	98,008	31,234	46.7	66,774	95,389	28,615	42.8	95,389	98,008	2,619	2.7
9	212,099	345,013	132,914	62.6	212,099	296,800	84,701	39.9	296,800	345,013	48,213	16.2
Total	3,224,328	4,472,375	1,248,047	38.7	3,224,328	4,102,305	877,977	27.2	4,102,305	4,472,375	370,070	9.0

Legend: Region 1 = Maine, New Hampshire, Vermont, Massachusetts, Rhode Island, Connecticut; 2 = New York, New Jersey, Pennsylvania; 3 = Ohio, Indiana, Illinois, Michigan; 4 = Minnesota, Iowa, Missouri, North Dakota, South Dakota, Nebraska, Kansas; 5 = Delaware, Maryland, District of Columbia, Virginia, West Virginia, North Carolina, South Carolina, Georgia, Florida; 6 = Kentucky, Tennessee, Alabama, Mississippi; 7 = Arkansas, Louisiana, Oklahoma, Texas; 8 = Montana, Idaho, Wyoming, Colorado, New Mexico, Arizona, Utah, Nevada; 9 = Washington, Oregon, California, Alaska.

TABLE 2   GROWTH IN SECONDARY ENROLLMENT BY REGIONS, 1953-62

Region	1953	1962	Change	Change %	1953	1959	Change	Change %	1959	1962	Change	Change %
1	55,762	88,968	33,206	59.5	55,762	72,885	17,123	30.7	72,885	88,968	16,083	22.1
2	186,949	296,358	109,409	58.5	186,949	243,442	56,493	30.2	243,442	296,358	52,916	21.7
3	177,509	274,027	96,518	54.3	177,509	227,423	49,914	28.1	227,423	274,027	46,604	20.4
4	61,262	90,477	29,215	47.7	61,262	75,109	13,847	22.6	75,109	90,477	15,368	20.5
5	26,909	54,974	28,065	104.3	26,909	36,420	9,511	35.3	36,420	54,974	18,554	50.9
6	19,631	31,106	11,475	58.5	19,631	24,752	5,121	26.1	24,752	31,106	6,354	25.7
7	32,198	49,347	17,149	53.3	32,198	41,947	9,749	30.3	41,947	49,347	7,400	17.6
8	12,567	20,365	7,798	62.1	12,567	18,164	5,597	44.5	18,164	20,365	2,201	12.1
9	46,642	84,891	38,249	82.0	46,642	64,492	17,850	38.3	64,492	84,891	20,399	31.6
Total	619,429	990,513	371,084	59.9	169,429	804,634	185,205	30.0	804,634	990,513	185,879	23.0

stripped by the increase in the provision for secondary schools; and further, the decreased provision for elementary schools cannot be accounted for by a corresponding decrease in elementary-age population.

TABLE 3   AVERAGE GROWTH PER YEAR IN ELEMENTARY AND SECONDARY ENROLLMENT

	1953-54—1962-63	1953-54—1959-60	1960-61—1962-63
Elementary	138,671	146,329	123,356
Secondary	43,294	30,867	68,149

TABLE 4   PERCENTAGE OF ENROLLMENT GROWTH BY REGIONS

	1953-1962		1953-1959		1959-1962	
Region	Elementary	Secondary	Elementary	Secondary	Elementary	Secondary
1	16.8	59.5	15.2	30.7	1.3	22.1
2	34.4	58.5	21.6	30.2	10.4	21.7
3	40.0	54.3	30.9	28.1	6.9	20.4
4	44.9	47.7	28.7	22.6	12.6	20.5
5	59.2	104.3	32.0	35.3	20.5	50.9
6	48.3	58.5	40.7	26.1	5.3	25.7
7	29.3	53.3	26.4	30.3	2.3	17.6
8	46.7	62.1	42.8	44.5	2.7	12.1
9	62.6	82.0	39.9	38.3	16.5	31.6
National	38.7	62.8	27.2	29.9	9.0	20.2

Projected vs. Actual Enrollment, 1968-69

In looking toward the possible future Catholic school enrollment, the percentages of those eligible and of those who were enrolled in the school year 1962-63, as shown in Table 5, were used in making projections for the school year 1968-69. This future year was used because it was the latest for which previous infant baptism figures were available to project first-grade eligibles. The control factors in the 1962-63 enrollment were held constant. The projection assumes: that no change in the percentage of eligibles enrolled will be made; that the ratio of staff to pupils will be unchanged; and that the use of school space will continue at the 1962-63 level. The procedure was to move the "Eligible infant baptisms" for 1962-63 ahead

6 years, applying the survivorship ratios; by this method the 1962-63 eligibles for grade one became the eligibles for grade seven, the sixth-grade became the twelfth-grade eligibles and so with each grade level advanced 6 years. To complete the total eligible group, 6 yearly groups were moved into the grade 1-6 positions; the results are shown in Table 5.

TABLE 5   PROJECTED SCHOOL ENROLLMENT FOR 1968-69

Elementary Schools, Grades 1-8	
	Enrollment at 1962-63
Eligible Infant Baptisms	Percentage (52.21)
9,770,108	5,100,973 [a]
Secondary Schools, Grades 9-12	
	Enrollment at 1962-63
Eligible Infant Baptisms	Percentage (32.22)
4,154,080	1,338,444 [a]

[a] Percentage applied against total grades, not grade by grade.

However, the Office of the Executive Secretary, National Catholic Educational Association, reported the following figures as the actual enrollments of Catholic elementary and secondary schools for 1968 to 1969.

> *Actual Elementary School Enrollment (1 to 8) in 1968 to 1969:* 3,899,000
> *Actual Secondary School Enrollment (9 to 12) in 1968 to 1969:* 1,085,000

In other words, the actual enrollment of Catholic elementary schools represented only 76 percent of the number we had projected (Table 5) on the basis of our 1962 data and proportions, although the actual enrollment of Catholic secondary schools represented in 1968 to 1969 approximately 138 percent of the number we had estimated on the basis of the 1962 data and percentages. Thus, it seems clear that in a scant six years Catholic elementary schools have sharply receded in the proportion of the Catholic children they serve.

It is most instructive to contrast the actual enrollment figures for 1968 to 1969 with those reported in Tables 1 and 2 for 1962 and for 1953. In 1962, about 4,472,000 pupils were enrolled in Catholic elementary schools (Table 1), but in 1968 to 1969 the enrollment had shrunk to only 3,900,000. These figures show a *decline in the enrollment in Catholic elementary schools of nearly one half million pupils in the seven-year period between 1962 and 1969.* In fact, *half the increase in enrollment in Catholic elementary schools between 1953 and 1962 (Table 1) had been lost by 1969.*

The picture reverses sharply in the secondary school. In 1962, approximately 990,000 students were enrolled in Catholic secondary schools (Table 2), but in 1968 to 1969 the enrollment had increased to 1,080,000. These figures show an *increase in the enrollment in Catholic secondary schools of nearly 160,000 pupils in the period between 1962 and 1969. Between 1953 (Table 2) and 1969, the enrollment of Catholic secondary schools very nearly doubled.* This growth is all the more impressive when we observe that the enrollment of Catholic elementary schools has shown an absolute net increase of only 18 percent during the same years.

Admission Policies

At this point a review of the schools' admission policies as of 1962 is in order. The review of these policies is based on responses from 9451 elementary school principals and 2075 secondary principals which were recorded.

The general admission policies can be summarized as follows, with the percentage of schools using each policy:

1. Attendance limited to parish membership
   Elementary schools   70%
   Secondary schools   14
2. Limitation of space
   Elementary schools   42
   Secondary schools   52
3. Limited to Catholics
   Elementary schools   20
   Secondary schools   17
4. Academic standards
   Elementary schools   13
   Secondary schools   53
5. Lack of maturity of students
   Elementary schools   25
   Secondary schools   26
6. Admission tests
   Elementary schools   16
   Secondary schools   68
7. Direct tuition charges
   Elementary schools   50
   Secondary schools   77

TABLE 6   OWNERSHIP OF CATHOLIC ELEMENTARY SCHOOLS IN 1962-63

Elementary	Totals	%
Total reporting	9451	100.0
No response	288	3.0
Parish	8211	86.9
Private	394	4.2
Diocesan	359	3.8
Interparish	80	0.8
Institutional	119	1.3

The use of parish membership as a requisite for school enrollment is more common among elementary schools because the parish-administered school is the usual type of elementary school; 86% of the reporting elementary schools were parish schools, whereas only 37% of the reporting secondary schools were parish administered.

When space is a factor in limiting enrollment, the policies are usually established by the individual schools. However, a growing number of dioceses have diocesan policies governing class size in the elementary schools, and in most of these the policy is followed strictly. This definite trend seems to go through 2 stages: the control is first a strong suggestion and then a strict policy. This trend is not so evident at the secondary level, because in most dioceses such administrative control of secondary schools is slight.

Only a small percentage of the reporting schools indicated a policy of limiting attendance to Catholic children. This Study did not collect information on the number of non-Catholic students in the schools, but it was not rare to find schools which had non-Catholic boys and girls in enrollment. In some systems that had separate schools for Negroes, which were in the process of integration, there were secondary schools that had non-Catholic enrollments as high as 50%. The policy of not enrolling a non-Catholic child was most often effected when there was a lack of space for Catholic applicants.

Admission tests in the elementary schools are used primarily to assist in better placement of the child, although in some of the private elementary schools the admission test is used as a screening for enrollment. Only 4% of the 9541 elementary schools reporting were classed as private schools, and only some of these screened applicants by testing. Tests administered prior to admission to the secondary schools are also used for student placement, but in 53% they are used chiefly for acceptance or rejection of the applicants (Tables 7 and 8).

TABLE 7 GRADE ORGANIZATION OF SECONDARY SCHOOLS [a]

Grade organization	Total Schools	%	Not Identified	%	Parish	%	Private	%	Inter-parish	%	Diocesan	%
No response	47	2.3	6	9.4	23	3.0	10	1.3	2	1.9	2	0.6
7- 8	0	0.0	0	0.0	0	0.0	0	0.0	0	0.0	0	0.0
7- 9	26	1.3	0	0.0	25	3.2	0	0.0	1	1.0	0	0.0
7-12	84	4.0	0	0.0	21	2.7	45	5.9	4	3.8	3	0.9
8-12	192	9.3	4	6.3	67	8.7	79	10.4	6	5.7	34	9.9
9-12	1666	80.3	52	81.3	607	78.8	610	79.9	91	86.7	297	86.3
10-12	14	0.7	1	1.6	5	0.6	5	0.7	1	1.0	2	0.6
Others	46	2.2	1	1.6	22	2.9	14	1.8	0	0.0	6	1.7
Total	2075	100.0	64	3.1	770	37.1	763	36.8	105	5.1	344	16.6

[a] Not Included—29 institutional schools, 1.4% of total.

TABLE 8   SECONDARY SCHOOL DIRECTION OF CATHOLIC ELEMENTARY
SCHOOL GRADUATES, JUNE 1962

	Graduates	%	To Catholic High Schools	%
Total	388,683	100.0	239,351	61.5
Boys	189,843	48.8	114,005	60.0
Girls	198,840	51.2	125,346	63.0

Additional admission policies are developed in parish schools
when in spite of the policies outlined there are too many eligible
applicants for the available space. In many of these schools the
parish membership requirement is extended to include some or all of
the following qualifications:

1. Parents of applicants must be regular envelope contributors
to the support of the parish.

2. Longer parish membership receives priority for enrollment.

3. Parish activity and service of parents also establish priority.

4. In some parishes having a child already in the school establishes priority for the younger children; in others only one child in
a family is admitted.

In some parish elementary schools 4 times as many children are
enrolled in the Confraternity of Christian Doctrine classes as are
enrolled in the full-time elementary school because of lack of space.
In a lighter vein, some pastors have observed that the school enrollment period would be the ideal time for pastors to take their annual
vacations.

Tuition Costs

The additional factor in the enrollment of children in Catholic
schools is the direct payment of tuition and fees by the parents to
assist in financing the school operation. Fifty percent of the elementary schools reported direct tuition charges, with the median payment at $25 or less. Among private elementary schools, accounting
for only 4% of the total, the median tuition payment was between
$76 and $100. Also in the elementary schools, fees in addition to
tuition were reported by 69% of the schools, the median fee being
$25 or less. Direct tuition payment is more common at the secondary
school level, where this is levied in 77% of the reporting schools,
with the median tuition between $76 and $100. In the private

secondary schools the median tuition charge is between $150 and $200. The median additional fee charge in 79% of all secondary schools is $25 or less.

In many elementary schools and in some secondary schools tuition charges are scaled down when more than one child in a family attends the school. Principals of 61% of the elementary schools estimated that income from tuition covered less than 25% of the cost of school operation. Principals of 38% of the secondary schools estimated that tuition income covered between 76% and 100% of the cost of school operation.

School Organization Patterns

The Study considered the organization of Catholic schools under 3 classifications. The first identification was by ownership, the second by administrative grade organization, and the third by student organization. Elementary and secondary schools were considered separately, and the information reported here has been processed from the responses of 9451 elementary and 2075 secondary schools to Schedule II—Elementary Principal's Report, and to Schedule III—Secondary Principal's Report.

OWNERSHIP PATTERNS. Broken down by ownership there are 4 groups of schools: those owned by individual parishes; those owned by a group of parishes; those owned by individual religious communities; and those owned by the dioceses. One rather clear way of identifying ownership is to determine which agency would receive insurance benefits in case of fire or other damage.

The principals' reports on ownership of elementary schools in 1962-63 are given in Table 6.

It is obvious from the summary of ownership of elementary schools that the most common is the parish-owned school. This is understandable because these schools are located closest to the homes of the young elementary school children. The establishment of the parish elementary school also tends to provide some social and recreational facilities that could be used by both the school and the parish.

Most of the private elementary schools are downward extensions of existing private secondary schools; only a few operate as separate elementary schools.

GRADE ORGANIZATION PATTERNS. In the elementary schools the prevailing administrative organization is by grades 1 through 8. However, 22% of the reporting schools indicated that they had kindergartens in their programs. The organization by sexes is primarily coeducational, although approximately 6% of the schools limited enrollment to either boys or girls.

Grade organization at the secondary school level is slightly more complicated than at the elementary school level.

Table 7 shows that although there is a wide variety of grade organization in secondary schools, the predominant organization is by grades 9 through 12, which matches with the elementary structure of kindergarten or grade 1 through grade 8. We can assume that other grade spans are provided to meet local situations, such as 7-12 and 8-12 organizations, which probably serve parish and private schools that have corresponding elementary divisions.

It is interesting that the junior high school organization, which is part of that popularly known as the 6-3-3 breakdown, is not present in appreciable numbers; only 26 schools, or 1.3%, report this organization. In numbers enrolled, only 1.5% of the total secondary enrollment is designated as grades 7 and 8.

STUDENT ORGANIZATION PATTERNS. The more complicated structure within the secondary school pattern is the organization by sexes. This includes 4 types of school organization, which we will define, although they might appear obvious.

1. *All-boy schools* enroll boys only.
2. *All-girl schools* enroll girls only.
3. *Coeducational schools* enroll boys and girls and provide a common educational program for boys and girls in the same classrooms under the same instructors. The obvious exception to this type of instruction would be physical education, intramural and extramural.
4. *Coinstitutional schools* are almost unique to Catholic secondary school organization. In this type of organization, 2 schools share a single administrative structure. The total educational program is offered separately to boys and girls, with women instructors for girls and men instructors for boys. In the general academic program separate physical facilities are used for boys and girls, although they make use of the same specialized facilities, such as science laboratories, but under separate instruction. Somewhat less clear are the conditions under which boys and girls use such facilities as diningrooms, libraries, and auditoriums. The aim is to provide a separate education for boys and girls more economically in a single school plant than could be provided in 2 separate schools.

A slight variance of the coinstitutional school is the coinstructional school, in which the organization remains the same for the faculty, men or women serving boys or girls or both in separate classes. The purpose of this type of organization is to provide separate education and to take advantage of the special abilities of the teaching staff, most frequently in science, mathematics, foreign languages, art, and music. This plan is limited by the fact that the constitutions of many religious communities for men do not allow their members to teach girls, and some religious communities for women have a similar prohibition.

Size of Catholic Schools

The size of a school is not in itself the most important factor in controlling quality or effectiveness of the school. In fact, an ideal school was described in earlier times as "Mark Hopkins on one end of a log and a student on the other," a description that implies that the complete education exists in a one-to-one relationship of teacher to student. Because our society makes ever-broadening demands for more and better education for an ever-increasing number of students, the one-to-one relationship becomes more and more impossible. The picture of Mark Hopkins and his student emphasizes the continuing importance of the quality of the teacher. The importance of the teacher and his effectiveness are controlled by the circumstances under which he meets his students. The good teacher's effectiveness will be conditioned by good or bad physical surroundings. A good first-grade teacher can produce good results in good physical surroundings, with good instructional tools, working with a reasonable number of children; the same first-grade teacher working under less favorable circumstances will not achieve optimum results. The completely good or the very poor first-grade situation, each with the same good teacher, can occur in either a very small school or a very large school. The parallel exists at the secondary school level.

The median size for elementary schools reporting falls in the interval of 301-400 in enrollment. It is interesting that the combined enrollment of 802 schools reporting enrollments at 100 or less, 8.6% of all schools, is only 1.1% of the enrollment of all schools. Also notable is the fact that the 12 schools reporting enrollments of over 2000 enroll more than half as many as the 802 small schools.

Among the chief drawbacks of the small elementary schools, those with 400 or less enrollment, are the lack of a nonteaching principal and of adequate clerical assistance. An elementary school of this size usually has 8 classrooms and a total staff of 8, 1 of whom has the responsibility of the principalship as well as a full-time teaching load. The function of the elementary school principal will be treated more fully in the section devoted to school staff.

The Study has found little evidence of any movement toward interparish school planning or toward diocesan central schools for the elementary school population. The advantages of such planning might outweigh any disadvantages and might even make it possible to provide Catholic schools for a larger number of the youth.

In common with other types of American secondary schools, the Catholic secondary schools reviewed here have an appreciable number of small schools and a significant number of very small schools. The *very small* schools are those with an enrollment of 100 or less. There are 258 of these schools among those reporting, or 12.9% of the total 1997 schools being considered. The small schools are those with an enrollment between 101 and 200; these added to the very small schools make a total of 704 schools, or 35.3% of all secondary schools reporting. The group with an enrollment between 101 and 200 considered separately were 446, or 22.4% of the total schools reporting. However, the small and very small schools enroll only 10% of the total students. The median enrollment figure for all schools is in the interval of 201-300.

The problems in the operation of the small and very small secondary schools can be overcome, but too often they are not. Both groups are seriously handicapped in attempting to provide a broad curriculum. It is almost impossible to maintain a thoroughly competent staff within a reasonable ratio of total staff to students; to provide a full program of English in language structure, literature, and development of writing ability; the social sciences; mathematics; the sciences in biology, chemistry, and physics; more than one modern foreign language; art, and music.

A further necessity for a good secondary school is an adequate library with a competent person to operate it. The library needs of a small secondary school are not greatly different from those of a secondary school with 500 students. The major difference might be less need for multiple copies of volumes.

Other special competent staff are necessary in physical education, guidance, and school administration. Intramural sports, if considered important, also need staff and pupil personnel.

Specialized space, facilities, and equipment necessary to implement the total school program are also among the problems of the small schools.

Each of these problems and others not identified can be overcome. If adequate finances were available most of the problems could be eliminated, but in view of the short supply of well-trained teachers staffing problems would remain. In other situations, interschool cooperative programs for sharing staff and facilities have been developed. One of these is the Western States Small Schools Project, by which the departments of education of several Rocky Mountain states have attempted to improve the educational offering in the small high schools.

In a number of dioceses, long-term plans have been implemented to develop central schools and to replace small parish high schools with new interparish schools. One of these plans is described in a monograph prepared by Monsignor Justin A. Driscoll of the Archdiocesan Schools of Dubuque, Iowa.

Medium-sized secondary schools, with enrollments between 201 and 600, number 856, 42.8% of the responding schools with 38% of the total enrollment in all schools.

The greater part of the total enrollment is served by the large school group, those with enrollments of 601 or more, which enroll 52% of all secondary students. There are only 436 of these schools, which is 21.8% of the total. The enrollment of these large schools extends from just over 600 to over 4000 students.

Just as size is not an absolute factor limiting quality in the small schools, it does not guarantee quality in the largest school. The control of positive factors can be illustrated by a closer look at the largest schools in the secondary group, the 38 with enrollments in excess of 1600. Of the 38 schools, 16 are located in 1 archdiocese and the remaining 22 in 13 individual dioceses. Using the ratio of staff to students as an indicator of quality, there is a wide range in the 38 schools, from 1 staff to 20 students in the most favorable school, to 1 to 42 in the 2 least favorable schools. The ratio in the 16 schools in the single archdiocese ranges from 1 staff member to 38 students to 1 staff member to 42 students, and in the remaining 13 dioceses the range is from 1 to 20 up to 1 to 34. It would seem that in the single large archdiocese there is a policy of establishing very large schools with a limited faculty. This combination policy could be a deterrent to operating a quality school. One of the potential advantages of the large school is the possibility of having trained and specialized teachers in such fields as physical science, biological sciences, modern language, religion, and other subject areas. However, ,some of this advantage could be dissipated by seriously handicapping the teachers with heavy student loads. This overload would be likely in secondary schools with a staff to student ratio of 1 to 42, where academic class size would be regularly in excess of 60 students.

One other gauge of secondary school size is the twelfth-grade enrollment. Of the total number of schools reporting, 907 schools, or 47%, identified their twelfth-grade enrollment at less than 39 students. This group represented 17% of the total twelfth-grade enrollment.

Graduates of Catholic Schools

At the end of grade 8 Catholic school students and their parents must make a decision about the continuation of their education. That some students make this decision at the end of either grade 6 or 7 is evidenced by a consistent drop in enrollment from grade 6 to 7 and from grade 7 to 8. It is highly improbable that these students are giving up further education; they are entering either a Catholic secondary school with a different grade organization or a public school with a junior high school organization. Validating this assumption, 11.4% of parish secondary schools begin with grade 7 or 8 and 16.3% of the private secondary schools begin with grade 7 or 8.

Elementary schools responding to an inquiry about their graduates of June 1962 reported that 61.5% of those graduates went on to Catholic secondary schools, boys and girls in about equal percentages.

The graduates of parish, interparish, and diocesan elementary schools went to Catholic high schools in about equal percentages, but of the private school graduates 73.9% entered Catholic high schools, in comparison with the total percentage of 61.5. This difference might indicate the greater ability and willingness of the parents of private students to provide for tuition costs.

Secondary school principals were asked to identify the type of degree-granting institution their graduates planned to attend. The request, made in October 1962, did not require a follow-up to determine whether the graduates' intentions were fulfilled. An analysis of the principals' responses is given in Table 9.

The figures indicating the postsecondary directions of Catholic high school graduates of 1962 include an appreciable number of young people whose next step was to a junior college. This is increasingly true in areas where state-supported and community junior colleges make higher education financially possible for increasing numbers of our youth. Under these circumstances the junior college is becoming less a terminal institution and more an intermediate institution between secondary education and the possible achieving of a degree.

There is the possibility that the plans of the graduate will change, that he may never continue a program of further formal education, or that he will follow his plans on a deferred-time basis. There is also the possibility, although true of smaller numbers, that some

TABLE 9   POSTSECONDARY DIRECTION OF CATHOLIC HIGH SCHOOL GRADUATES JUNE 1962 (2075 SCHOOLS)

Total graduates	155,698	
To college:		
Catholic college	40,922	48.42%
Private college	7,773	9.20%
Public college	30,401	35.97%
Religious life	4,441	5.60%
Diocesan seminary	968	.20%
Total postsecondary	84,505	

54.29% of the total graduates planned to go on to postsecondary education.

Total girl graduates	87,177	
To college:		
Catholic college	19,529	48.14%
Private college	3,151	7.80%
Public college	14,681	36.21%
Religious life	3,205	8.00%
Total	40,566	

46.53% of the total of girl graduates planned to go on to postsecondary education.

Total boy graduates	68,521	
To college:		
Catholic college	21,393	48.76%
Private college	4,622	10.51%
Public college	15,720	35.77%
Religious life	1,236	2.30%
Diocesan seminary	968	2.01%
Total	43,939	

64.15% of the total of boy graduates planned to go on to postsecondary education.

graduates who do not have this as their plan in June of their graduating year, will go on to higher education.

On the premise that it is important to know what the graduates of secondary schools do after their graduation and, more important, how well they succeed, the Study developed a means by which success of the college-bound graduates could be judged. Although educators are interested in the in-school progress and success of their students, the purpose of this follow-up was to determine how well the graduates had been prepared for success in their later study. The Study did not assume that only the college-bound were important in a follow-up. The inquiry checked the graduates of June 1956 and June 1958 in their college graduating years, June of 1960 and 1962. The areas of inquiry considered most significant included: did the student graduate; did he transfer; was he dropped; grade point average at leaving or graduation; grade point average in his graduating class; persistency rate of entering class; did the student go on to graduate work; honors achieved. These items were selected not only because of their importance but also because of their general availability in college student records.

The 104 secondary schools involved in this follow-up procedure were willing to cooperate but the accumulated returns were so few that they could not produce significant results. The major problem was that the high-school pupil records generally did not show the college into which the graduate was accepted and subsequently entered but only showed the colleges to which transcripts had been sent. Because most students requested more than one transcript and some as many as 8, the following went no further.

As the Study staff visited high schools in the 13 selected dioceses, conferences with principals and guidance personnel showed that a strong effort was made to guide the college-bound student toward Catholic colleges. Some principals and guidance counselors indicated that very strong guidance was given the academically superior graduates toward Catholic colleges. It is difficult to evaluate the success of this guidance activity; if it were completely effective large numbers of the academically apt would continue their future education in Catholic colleges and the lesser academically apt graduates' success in non-Catholic colleges, on a comparative basis, would be somewhat obscured. Thus a new dimension would have to be added to any comparative studies of the college success of Catholic high-school graduates.

Sources of Financial Support

The original design of the Study considered the problem of financing Catholic schools of utmost importance. However, it became evident that this aspect could not be given adequate treatment within the time of the Study. The fiscal information presented here is limited to identification of major sources of income for current operation of the schools.

The principals of the elementary and secondary schools were asked to estimate the sources of finance for their operation. The request included a suggestion that they reinforce their estimates with the judgment of others who might be more knowledgeable. The request did not require any validation by the principal, and it represented his conditioned thinking. Whether these estimates would be proved by a complete financial analysis or not, the importance of the summary is that it shows what the principals think.

The principals were asked to estimate the percentage of financial support derived from the following sources: tuition and fees, parish subsidy, diocesan subsidy, and miscellaneous—endowments, gifts, et cetera. A fifth category presented to the secondary principals only was the percentage of their operating expenditure subsidized by their religious communities; this percentage was not to include any allowance for contributed services.

The analysis of the elementary principals' responses shows two general patterns: first, the parish, interparish, and diocesan schools get their major support from parish subsidy; second, the private schools get their major support from direct tuition. It can also be seen that very little financial support for the elementary schools comes from the diocesan level. Surprising was the small number of parish, interparish and diocesan schools that ascribed any considerable income to miscellaneous receipts including gifts and money-raising events. The surprise is occasioned by the stereotype of the Catholic school and its bingo games.

At the secondary level a similar pattern of income source prevails, although direct tuition becomes more important for the parish, interparish, and diocesan high schools. Parish subsidy remains the greatest source of income for the parish and interparish schools, and it is the second most important source for the diocesan high school. The private schools report direct tuition as the major source of income; the other important sources are the operating religious communities and miscellaneous receipts, although, in the elementary schools, these were reported as a relatively unimportant source of support.

This analysis of the sources of income reported by the principals should be considered very carefully. The principals were in fact estimating, by request, what might be considered a cash statement. In both elementary and secondary schools there probably are actual costs that were not included in these estimates. These costs would include interest and amortization on capital investments and costs of operation and maintenance which in many parish schools are included in the regular parish budget for heat, power, cleaning and care of grounds. Other costs not normally included would be the real costs to religious communities not covered by the nominal stipend paid for each sister, brother, or priest who works in the school. These hidden costs absorbed by the community include the cost of educating each teacher, health care costs, and retirement costs for community members.

Perhaps the basic information in this analysis will stimulate further interest in the total fiscal operation of the schools.

II. THE STAFF OF CATHOLIC SCHOOLS

This section of the study, concerned with the staffing of Catholic elementary and secondary schools, is based on 2 separate activities. The first was an attempt to gather statistical data about each of the staff members in the schools. Since this was a first attempt, only information that is most fundamental and informative and could be most reliably determined in a national survey was requested. The Study staff hopes that these basic findings might stimulate further inquiry.

The second activity was a more intimate view of teachers and administrators as the Study staff met them face to face in a representative group of Catholic schools in action. The firsthand experience also gave the staff an opportunity to observe the interesting relationship of students and schools.

This depth study of Catholic schools in action observed 218 elementary and 104 secondary representative schools in 13 dioceses. The results will not be presented statistically but will be offered as observations to support and broaden the statistical reports.

In each of the 2 activities the Study staff met with wholehearted cooperation from all the people concerned with the schools—the hierarchy, the diocesan superintendents, the religious communities, the principals and teachers, and the pastors of parish schools. Only 3 dioceses and 1 archdiocese—in New Jersey—decided not to cooperate with the Study. This decision affected returns from approximately 100 secondary and 475 elementary schools, served by about 8500 staff members.

In the nationwide collection of data 92% of the total elementary staff, 84% of the secondary staff, 88% of the elementary schools, and 85% of the secondary schools made returns that could be handled in the processing of national data. There were other returns in each category that could not be handled in the Study's data-processing procedure.

In processing the accumulated data, elementary and secondary staff are treated separately, and each staff group is presented under 5 categories: priest, brother, sister, layman, and laywoman.

Tables 10 and 11 present the basic findings: total number reporting, the category of each, and the position of each respondent.

Table 10 shows the responses of 103,779 elementary school staff members that could be processed. The largest number of staff members consist of sisters, who represent 66.2% of the total; the second largest group is laywomen, 27.9% of the total. The small number of priests is somewhat surprising; these reports came from 9451 schools, and one might assume the number of priests who render some teaching or supervisory service would be closer to 9500 than the 2036 shown here. It is clear that communities of teaching brothers are not extensively engaged in elementary education; they represent only 0.5% of the total elementary group.

A gross ratio of lay to religious teachers developed from Table 11 shows 1 lay teacher to 2.24 religious in the elementary schools. This ratio is based on the total number of persons reporting and does not take into account the fact that some of them participate only on a part-time basis.

Preparation of Teachers

The median training level of the total elementary staff is the B. S. degree, with 49.8% having less than a degree and 50.2% having a bachelor's degree or more. As noted in Table 12, the medians are developed without including the "no response" category. Laywomen teaching in the elementary school have less formal training than any of the other 4 categories, 23.2% having only 1 year of college or less and only 31.8% having a bachelor's degree or better; 56.7% of the sisters have a bachelor's degree or better.

Table 13 shows that the secondary staff has more training than does the elementary staff. The median training level for the total group is the B. S. degree plus and is the same for each of the 5 categories. The sisters have the highest percentage of 47.7% at the advanced training level of a master's degree or more. Also, each of the religious categories outranks the lay teachers in advanced training. Of the brothers and priests, 41.5% and 41.3%, respectively, have master's degrees or more, whereas only 19.5% of the laymen and 15.1% of the laywomen have this advanced training.

In a separate analysis not presented in tabular form, the Study identified those elementary and seconadry staff members who earned their undergraduate diplomas from Catholic institutions. Of the total elementary group, 85% were awarded their undergraduate degrees by a Catholic institution, whereas only 50.8% of the lay teachers were awarded undergraduate degrees in a Catholic institution. Similarly, in the total secondary group, 84% were graduates

TABLE 10   TOTAL ELEMENTARY STAFF RESPONDENTS BY CATEGORY AND POSITION, OCTOBER 1962

Position	Total	No Response		Priest		Brother		Sister		Layman		Laywoman	
		No.	%	No.	%	No.	%	No.	%	No.	%	No.	%
No response	5,152	123	14.4	953	46.8	23	4.8	2,470	3.6	163	5.8	1,420	4.9
Teacher	89,576	660	77.4	968	47.5	389	81.9	57,449	83.7	2,645	93.9	27,465	94.9
Administrator	2,055	22	2.6	40	2.0	38	8.0	1,947	2.8	2	0.1	6	0.0
Teacher and administrator	6,996	48	5.6	75	3.7	25	5.3	6,807	9.9	6	0.2	35	0.1
Total	103,779	853	0.8	2,036	2.0	475	0.5	68,673	66.2	2,816	2.7	28,926	27.9

TABLE 11   TOTAL SECONDARY STAFF RESPONDENTS BY CATEGORY AND POSITION, OCTOBER 1962

Position	Total	No response		Priest		Brother		Sister		Layman		Laywoman	
		No.	%	No.	%	No.	%	No.	%	No.	%	No.	%
No response	2,984	75	16.9	906	16.5	264	7.9	1,162	5.9	273	4.6	304	6.3
Teacher	34,310	350	78.8	4,001	72.8	2,839	84.5	16,931	85.9	5,654	95.0	4,535	93.5
Administrator	1,290	3	0.7	352	6.4	188	5.6	719	3.6	19	0.3	9	0.2
Teacher and administrator	1,225	16	3.6	238	4.3	68	2.0	896	4.5	5	0.1	2	0.0
Total	39,809	444	1.1	5,497	13.8	3,359	8.4	19,708	49.5	5,951	14.9	4,850	12.2

TABLE 12 PREPARATION OF ELEMENTARY SCHOOL STAFF, OCTOBER 1962

Education	Total	No response		Priest		Brother		Sister		Layman		Laywoman	
		No.	%	No.	%	No.	%	No.	%	No.	%	No.	%
No response	1,439	42	4.9	254	12.5	6	1.3	767	1.1	29	1.0	341	1.2
High school only	2,669	32	3.8	4	0.2	12	2.5	1,065	1.6	40	1.4	1,516	5.2
Less than 1 yr. college	3,977	39	4.6	1	0.0	6	1.3	1,383	2.0	51	1.8	2,497	8.6
1 yr. college	5,131	40	4.7	3	0.1	16	3.4	2,341	3.4	95	3.4	2,636	9.1
2 yr. college	39,209	318	37.3	219	10.8	142	29.9	24,603	35.8	1,108	39.3	12,819 [a]	44.3
B.S. degree	17,408 [a]	153	17.9	314	15.4	72 [a]	15.2	12,123 [a]	17.7	475 [a]	16.9	4,271	14.8
B.S.+	27,005	179	21.0	680 [a]	33.4	146	30.7	21,078	30.7	827	29.4	4,095	14.2
M.S.	4,994	33	3.9	292	14.3	48	10.1	3,936	5.7	123	4.4	562	1.9
M.S.+	1,947	17	2.0	269	13.2	27	5.7	1,377	2.0	68	2.4	189	0.7
Total	103,779	853	0.8	2,036	2.0	475	0.5	68,673	66.2	2,816	2.7	28,926	27.9

[a] Median, not including "No response."

TABLE 13 PREPARATION OF SECONDARY SCHOOL STAFF, OCTOBER 1962

Education	Total	No response		Priest		Brother		Sister		Layman		Laywoman	
		No.	%	No.	%	No.	%	No.	%	No.	%	No.	%
No response	305	23	5.2	101	1.8	9	0.3	76	0.4	28	0.5	68	1.4
High school only	153	5	1.1	5	0.1	13	0.4	18	0.1	38	0.6	74	1.5
Less than 1 yr. college	115	1	0.2	0	0.0	6	0.2	33	0.2	21	0.4	54	1.1
1 yr. college	132	3	0.7	1	0.0	6	0.2	35	0.2	17	0.3	70	1.4
2 yr. college	2,246	35	7.9	237	4.3	172	5.1	1,050	5.3	291	4.9	461	9.5
B.S. degree	5,851	57	12.8	660	12.0	424	12.6	1,591	8.1	1,599	26.9	1,520	31.3
B.S.+	15,901 [a]	153	34.5	2,227 [a]	40.5	1,333 [a]	39.7	7,523 [a]	38.2	2,794 [a]	47.0	1,871 [a]	38.6
M.S.	9,447	113	25.5	1,378	25.1	827	24.6	5,866	29.8	762	12.8	501	10.3
M.S.+	5,659	54	12.2	888	16.2	569	16.9	3,516	17.8	401	6.7	231	4.8
Total	39,809	444	1.1	5,497	13.8	3,359	8.4	19,708	49.5	5,951	14.9	4,850	12.2

[a] Median, not including "No response."

of Catholic institutions, whereas only 55% of the lay teachers got their undergraduate degrees from a Catholic college or university. A similar inquiry aimed at identifying the number of non-Catholic teachers in the schools showed that in the elementary schools 3.8% of laymen teachers and 4.4% of laywomen teachers were non-Catholic. In the secondary schools there was a much larger percentage of non-Catholic teachers, 6.8% of the laymen and 15.1% of the laywomen.

Preparation for sisters and laywomen in the elementary schools is about equal in the 20-24 age interval, but the in-service advancement of the sisters brings them to the bachelor's degree plus in the 35-44 age interval. The median preparation level for laywomen in the 20-24 year interval is 2 years of college, and it remains at that level throughout the scale. On the other hand, although the median preparation level of the sisters has the same beginning, it increases continuously throughout the age scale, up to the 69-or-over age group. The required educational programs of religious communities and the lack of comparable programs for lay teachers, either required or highly motivated, probably account for this difference in continuing in-service training. Also, the cost of this additional formal education might be a deterrent to lay teachers, in view of the level of their salaries.

It seems important to establish the important characteristics of the 2 parts of this dichotomous staff of the Catholic schools, the religious members and lay members. In this identification of characteristics of staff at both the elementary and secondary levels, the sisters will be used as representative of all religious and the laywomen as representative of all lay teachers. In most important characteristics, the sisters are truly representative of the religious and the laywomen of the lay faculty. The characteristics considered are age, preparation, and experience.

A small but significant number of sisters and laywomen in the elementary schools are less than 20 years of age; for the teachers in each of these categories the median preparation level is 1 year of college. The presence of these very young and lesser trained people seems to prove the difficulty of Catholic schools to secure an adequate supply of teachers.

As a group the sisters in the elementary schools are older than the laywomen; only 14.6% of the sisters are less than 25 years of age, whereas 27% of the lay teachers fall in that age group. The largest number of sisters, 28.6%, are in the 25-34 year category.

The median training level of the elementary sisters does not rise above 2 years of college until age 35-44 years. The training level of sisters moves from the 2-year college level in the 25-34 year interval to a bachelor's degree plus in the 35-44 interval. This slow but steady movement up by the sisters can be ascribed in great part to the positive influence of the Sister Formation Movement years, compared with 27.0% of the sisters. The median training level for both sisters and laywomen is the same through the interval of 35-44 years. Beyond this point the median training level of the sisters advances to the master's degree plus. In addition the sisters' training beyond the master's degree far exceeds that of the laywomen.

Experience of Teachers

Experience is an important characteristic of any school staff; This study investigated this characteristic among the staff in the Catholic elementary schools and secondary schools. The types of experience presented are years in Catholic schools, in public schools, in other independent schools, total experience, and years in present position. Some respondents (the number is not known) did not count the school year 1962-63, the year within which they were teaching, as a year of experience. This might affect the figures which relate to the first 3 experience ranges: years in Catholic schools, total experience and years in present position.

Most easily identified is the high median of sisters' total years of experience in both elementary and secondary schools. The sisters' median for total experience in elementary schools is 15-19 years. In secondary schools, sisters' medians for total experience and experience in Catholic schools is 20-29 years.

It is important that in the elementary schools only 19.6% of the laywomen and 21.7% of the sisters have been in their present positions for more than 4 years. In the secondary schools, only 36.2% of the sisters and 18.5% of the laywomen have been in their present positions for more than 4 years. Even considering the number of newly established schools, this is a relatively high rate of turnover that must cause serious problems at both levels. The median total experience of laywomen in secondary schools is the 3-4 year interval.

The short tenure of the sisters can be ascribed partly to the policy of religious communities to review annually the assignments of each of their members. Many changes in assignments are made to meet the overall needs and commitments of the individual communities. This change in assignment particularly affects school principals who often are also the spiritual superiors of local communities. The canonical rules that govern religious communities require that a spiritual superior may not continue in this capacity for a period longer than 6 years.. Some communities have adopted a policy under which a religious other than the superior is assigned the responsibility of principal. This usually happens at the secondary school level and in larger schools.

In the elementary schools 35% of the laywomen and 23.3% of the laymen have had some teaching experience in public schools, and 5.1% of the sisters also have had public school teaching experience. At the secondary school level, 37.3% of the laywomen, and 24.2% of the laymen, and 8.8% of the sisters have taught in public schools.

School Principals

We find that 1752 of the 9451 elementary schools are staffed by full-time nonteaching principals. Of the 2075 secondary schools reporting, 1077 are staffed by full-time nonteaching principals. The assignment of full-time principals in both elementary and secondary schools is conditioned by the size of the schools.

In the elementary schools some additional administrative assistance available to the school principal was reported under the heading "Assistant Principals"; 444 schools, or 4.7% of the total, showed from one-tenth to 1 full-time assistant. Similarly, 606, or 29.2% of the secondary schools showed from one-tenth to 4 full-time assistants. Although this item was not cross-tabulated with school size, we assume that these assistant principals are in the larger schools.

Part of the administrative duties within any school is purely clerical, so we attempted to determine the availability of clerical assistance in elementary and secondary schools. Of the 9451 elementary schools, 86.1% reported they had no full-time clerical help, and 80.9% reported they had no full- or part-time clerical help. Among 2075 secondary schools 53.7% had no full-time clerical help, and 69.1% had no full- or part-time clerical help. It was a firsthand observation of the Study staff that the small schools with full-time teaching principals had no clerical assistance, and the schools that were fairly staffed and had at least a part-time nonteaching principal also had clerical help.

The Study staff had planned to survey the persistency rate of students in Catholic elementary schools, but the plan was abandoned because of the method by which student records were filed. All former students, both graduates and transfers, were placed in a single alphabetical file. A complete reorganization of files by year in schools that were in many cases 25 years old or older was obviously impossible. As mentioned earlier, a planned follow-up of college-bound high school graduates was not completed because most school records showed the colleges to which students requested transcripts be sent, but not the schools they eventually entered. The Study staff ascribed these inadequacies not only to lack of adequate clerical help but also to lack of guidance personnel.

Ratio of Staff to Students

A review of the schoolday organization and the teaching load assignment in the secondary schools is presented in Table 14.

TABLE 14 SECONDARY TEACHERS' CLASS LOAD, SCHOOL DAY ORGANIZATION, OCTOBER 1962

Teaching Load (2075 Schools)								
Teaching Periods			Other assigned Periods			Total Periods		
	Total	%		Total	%		Total	%
No response	124	6.0	No response	465	22.4	No response	237	11.4
4	189	9.1	1	1226	59.1	4	32	1.5
5	1035	49.9	2	305	14.7	5	275	13.3
6	510	24.6	3	46	2.2	6	799	38.5
>6	217	10.5	>3	33	1.6	7	535	25.8
						8	165	8.0
						9	32	1.5

School Day					
Daily Hours			Daily Periods		
	Total	%		Total	%
No response	41	2.0	No response	32	1.5
4	2	0.1	4	0	0.0
5	162	7.8	5	35	1.7
6	1246	60.0	6	331	16.0
7	569	27.4	7	910	43.9
>7	55	2.7	8	676	32.6
			9	91	4.4

The teaching load medians appear normal—5 teaching periods and 1 additional assigned period in a 6- or 7-period day. However,

35% of the schools report 6 or more teaching periods, and an additional 35% report 7 or more total assignment periods. These loads would be excessive for teachers who must make varied preparation and evaluate written work of students.

In considering the numerical relationship of teachers to pupils, the Study first developed the ratio of total staff to total enrollment within each school. This was followed by a digest of the practices followed by each school to control the number of students assigned to a single class.

Table 15, which presents the ratio of total staff to pupils in elementary schools, shows the national median in the interval of 36-40 pupils.

TABLE 15   ELEMENTARY SCHOOL PRINCIPALS' REPORTS, STUDENT PER STAFF MEMBER, OCTOBER 1962 (9280 SCHOOLS)

Number of Students per Staff Member	Number of Schools	% of Schools
25 or less	853	9.2
26-30	832	8.9
31-35	1490	16.0
36-40	2068	22.2
41-45	1990	21.4
46-50	1207	13.0
51-55	415	4.4
56-60	187	2.0
61-65	86	.9
66-70	34	.3
71 or more	118	1.2

Table 16 gives a strong indication of class size in its report of the maximum size control in each school. Although the table does not tabulate enrollment room by room in each school, one can assume that individual room enrollments will not be greatly above or below the indicated maximum control figure. In this light the median class size for grades 1-3 falls in the interval of 46-50 pupils; 21.4% of the schools report maximum controls above 50 pupils.

Many dioceses have policies on class size in the elementary school which vary from strong directives to suggested practices. Frequently these are newly developed policies being implemented by control of the registration of the incoming first grades. From

TABLE 16   ELEMENTARY SCHOOL PRINCIPALS' REPORTS, CONTROL OF MAXIMUM CLASS SIZE, OCTOBER 1962

Maximum Size	Total Schools	%	Maximum Size	Total Schools	%
Grades 1-3	8179	100.0	Grades 4-8	8159	100.0
Less than 26	748	9.1	Less than 26	823	10.0
26-30	399	4.8	26-30	403	4.9
31-35	477	5.8	31-35	521	6.3
36-40	1135	13.8	36-40	1265	15.5
41-45	1039	12.7	41-45	1126	13.8
46-50	2604	31.8	46-50	2621	32.1
51-55	878	10.7	51-55	775	9.4
56-60	563	6.8	56-60	386	4.7
61-65	112	1.3	61-65	93	1.1
66-70	86	1.0	66-70	61	0.7
More than 70	138	1.6	More than 70	85	1.0

observation and discussions with many educators, the Study staff is certain of a growing concern in Catholic schools about the size of classes in the elementary schools. The major block to the control and reduction of class size is at the parish level, where more children are applying for admission than can be accommodated at existing class sizes. The problem of expanding facilities at the parish level is a serious one because of the financial difficulties and the difficulty of obtaining adequate staff. The supply of religious teachers is limited, and it is frequently difficult to find a religious community able to accept the staffing of a new school or the expansion of an existing one. If a religious community does accept the responsibility of a school, it is usually with the understanding that the staff will include a certain number of lay teachers. This increases the operating costs because the direct salary payment to a lay teacher greatly exceeds the stipend to a religious.

Large classes are not new to the religious communities that prepare teachers for the Catholic elementary schools. Although the sister who faces a first-grade class of 60 or more would probably rather have fewer, in her training she may be exposed to techniques for minimizing the problems in handling such large groups. Members of the Study staff visited first grades in 218 elementary schools at various times in the school year from October through May, and it was a rare classroom with fewer than 40 students. The majority had more than 50 youngsters and many had more than 60. The most evident characteristic was the prevailing order and the ready response of the children to a change in classroom activity.

In some first grades of 60 or more, the teacher had as many as 5 reading groups. While she worked with each of these groups separately, the rest of the class was busy with reading workbooks and other assigned work. As the teacher spent about 15 minutes with each group, by the time the fifth group came for its reading activity the youngsters had been at work independently for more than an hour. Although there was no evidence of unrest among the children, there surely can be some question of the effectiveness of this hour of independent work. However, the reading achievement of pupils in these schools, as measured by standard tests at the second-, fourth-, and sixth-grade levels, was significantly above their grade norms, though no controls were exercised over IQ inputs.

In the middle and upper grades of the elementary schools a great part of the educational program is carried on within a catechetical framework, a procedure adopted as an answer to the very large class. As in the primary grades, the results of standard achievement batteries show that the students are achieving at or above grade level. The observer cannot help wondering how much more these same teachers could do with smaller classes and the opportunity to give more attention to the individual, or whether these findings could stand the scrutiny of input controls over ability.

The Lay Teacher

The rapid growth of Catholic schools during the past 15 years has made necessary an expanded use of the lay teacher at both the elementary and the secondary school levels. During this period the number of religious who became available as teachers did not keep pace with the expanding needs of the schools. In 1950 there were a total of 27,770 teachers in the secondary schools, 23,147 religious and 4623 lay teachers. By 1961 the total number of teachers had risen to 46,623, an increase of 67.9%. In this period the number of religious increased from 23,147 to 34,153, a growth of 47.5%, while the number of lay teachers advanced from 4623 to 12,470, an increase of 169%.

A similar expansion took place in the elementary schools, with an increase of total staff from 66,525 in 1950 to 110,911 in 1961, a growth of 66.7%. The number of religious increased 26.5% from 61,778 to 78,188, but the great increase was in the number of lay teachers from 4747 to 32,723, a 589% increase. This meant that

TABLE 17 LAYMEN TEACHERS' SALARIES AND TOTAL TEACHING EXPERIENCE, ELEMENTARY SCHOOLS, OCTOBER 1962 (N = 2338)

Salary	<$2500 (%)	2500-2999 (%)	3000-3499 (%)	3500-3999 (%)	4000-4499 (%)	4500-4999 (%)	5000-5499 (%)	5500-5999 (%)	6000+ (%)
No response and 0	2.38	19.0	25.3	25.1	18.5	16.9	1.3	0.0	0.0
1- 2 years	30.3	33.6	29.4	33.8	36.5	36.6	29.9	14.3	6.7
3- 4 years	12.6	13.8	15.9	14.9	22.6	20.4	29.9	21.4	6.7
5- 9 years	14.4	14.2	13.6	11.2	12.4	18.3	29.9	50.0	40.0
10-14 years	6.5	8.3	5.8	6.6	5.4	5.6	2.6	0.0	36.7
15-19 years	3.2	3.6	3.5	3.6	1.2	0.0	0.0	7.1	3.3
20-29 years	4.0	2.8	3.7	2.7	2.4	1.4	6.5	7.1	0.0
30-39 years	1.8	2.0	1.4	1.1	0.5	0.0	0.0	0.0	6.7
>39 years	3.2	2.8	1.4	1.1	0.5	0.7	0.0	0.0	0.0

whereas there were 13 religious for every lay teacher in 1950, in 1961 there were 2.38 religious for each lay teacher.

Because of the increasing numbers of lay teachers in Catholic schools, an inquiry was made to determine the salary levels of lay teachers during the 1962-63 school year (see Table 17). It is easily determined that teachers in the secondary schools receive salaries higher than those paid to elementary teachers.

The median salaries fall in the following intervals: for elementary women, $3000-3499, by inspection $3145; elementary men, $3500-3999, by inspection $3555; secondary women, $4000-4499, by inspection $4010; secondary men, $4500-4999, by inspection $4803. Combining men and women, 2.4% of the teachers at the elementary level are paid more than $4500, whereas 46.4% of the teachers at the secondary level receive more. In addition, 0.2% of all elementary teachers and 9.4% of all secondary teachers receive salaries greater than $6000.

Half of the elementary principals and 65% of the secondary principals indicated that lay teachers were paid on a salary schedule determined by training and teaching experience. However, analysis of the relation between salary payments and teaching experience and further analysis related to teacher training showed little connection between the training and experience of the teachers and salaries paid. This lack of correlation may be due to the slight spread between the minimum and maximum salaries reported.

Because of the great increase in the numbers of lay teachers in both the elementary and secondary schools during the period between 1950 and 1961 when, as cited earlier, the lay teachers in secondary schools increased 169% and in the elementary schools the increase was 589%, an attempt was made to identify the role and status of lay teachers in these separate schools. In pursuit of these identifications small group structured conferences were held with 1,200 elementary lay teachers in 218 schools and with 650 lay teachers in 104 secondary schools and similar conferences were held with a corresponding number of religious in the same schools.

Based on these interviews, and on the observation of these lay teachers at work in the schools, and on the developed statistical data related to the lay teacher, the following factors are strong limiting controls in the most effective utilization of these teachers in Catholic schools, and these factors need careful consideration by Catholic school leaders:

1. As the number of lay teachers continues to grow, greater efforts must be made to provide more adequate salaries to attract

and retain better-trained teachers. This effort should be aimed at both elementary and secondary schools but more intensely at the elementary level.

2. There is a general lack of organized orientation and in-service programs for lay teachers to assist them in reaching a level equal to that of the religious. The training of religious teachers prepares them to work toward the special goals of Catholic schools that are the only reason for their existence. To work effectively toward these goals the lay teacher must first be made aware of them and then be assisted in developing the methods by which they can be achieved.

3. Almost always the number of lay teachers in a given school is the result of a problem of numbers. The first factor is the total number of teachers needed for the school staff; the second factor is the number of religious teachers available. The number of lay teachers that must be employed is determined by subtracting. To improve the position of lay teachers in Catholic schools and to capitalize best on their potential an evaluation should be made of those contributions that are peculiar to them and those they can accomplish more effectively than could the religious.

4. The negligible participation by lay teachers in the administration of Catholic schools strongly affects the status of the lay teacher. Careful consideration should be given to determining whether a lay principal is anomalous to the concept of a Catholic school staffed by lay and religious teachers.

5. In the elementary schools particularly, parents do not understand or accept fully the concept of the lay teacher. If the lay teacher is accepted by Catholic school leadership as something more than a necessity, a program informing parents of the true place of these teachers should be developed.

III. SUMMARY AND DISCUSSION

All of the foregoing data and observations were accumulated and developed against the scene of the Catholic school as it was played in 1963, and even though comparable data have not been accumulated objectively for the 1970 situation of these schools, it seems important to report on the current operation even from a subjective vantage point. The interest and involvement of those responsible for the 1962-63 Study of Catholic schools did not cease with the publication of the original findings in 1966. Following this publication the University of Notre Dame established an *Office for Educational Research,* and while the overall purpose of this research office is to pursue and serve the needs of the total educational efforts of all

American schools, it has the built-in purpose of a continuing analysis of the separate Catholic schools.

With this as a background a series of observations is offered as representative of the current Catholic school situation.

During the past four years the enrollment pattern in the Catholic schools has changed radically. During the three year period ending with 1962 the average yearly enrollment growth in elementary schools was 123,000, but during the three year period ending with 1966 the elementary school enrollment decreased. The major reasons which affect this decrease include: policies adopted by many dioceses which restrict class size; closing of selected grades or of entire schools; and fewer applicants for admission.

By early September 1969, the situation relative to the financing of Catholic education in one state with a heavily Catholic population had grown so drastic that eight ordinaries were moved to an extraordinary measure. Eight bishops in New York composed a joint pastoral to be read to the congregations in their respective dioceses urging the latter to petition members of Congress to support federal aid for church schools. This action has few parallels in recent decades; the pulpit has been decreasingly used in modern times for political suasion. Coupled with the growth in Catholic secondary schools between 1962 and 1969 on a national basis, (observed earlier in this chapter) and the extraordinary decline in the enrollment of Catholic elementary schools, this official ecclesiastical push for government support seems, indeed, to portend that the shape of Catholic elementary and secondary education in the United States will undergo wholesale change as it enters its second 100 years.

There is a wide spread position being taken by those presently responsible for the operation of Catholic schools, that the Church cannot support financially the present school operation and certainly is not in a position to support an expansion of the present program. The factors which are used to support this position include the diminishing supply of religious available for service to the schools with the consequent increasing need for more expensive lay teachers; and the increasing overall costs of quality education.

The position that the Church is financially unable to support a broad educational effort within the existing establishment is taken without the realization that the laity is the financial support of the Church.

Because of the present indecisive situation surrounding the total program of Catholic Education it is proposed that a careful and objective look be taken at the total situation to include:

1. A reassessment of the current reasons for the existence of the school establishment, the Confraternity of Christian Doctrine, adult education programs, and any other formal programs of Catholic education.

2. An evaluation of the way in which these formal programs are meeting the established goals.

3. A scientific assessment of the ability and willingness of the laity to support the existing programs or expanded programs of education.

4. A careful and imaginative search for the ways in which the established goals may be achieved more effectively for more people within the financial ability of the total Church.

7

Catholic Colleges and Universities after the Second 100 Years

ROBERT HASSENGER

University of Notre Dame

SOURCE. Prepared especially for this volume.

Catholic higher education had perhaps never received as much attention as it was getting when this chapter was written. At the same time as Catholic colleges and universities found themselves in the public eye because of renewed hostilities centering around the use of federal and state funds to aid private, religiously-affiliated schools, the changing patterns of control in several key institutions served to move the Catholic colleges upstage.[1] These events have also pro-

---

[1] To avoid the constant use of the phrase "colleges and universities," I shall use "colleges" to refer to higher educational institutions generally, unless otherwise noted.

vided the impetus for a spate of new books on Catholics and their schools.[2] And in reading these, one begins to realize how little is really know about the largest private "system" of higher education in the world.

The quotation marks are used advisedly. Catholic colleges and universities have never been an official project of the American Church, but were founded hither and yon by separate groups—usually orders of religious sisters, brothers, and priests—with little systematic attention to what the others were doing. For most such groups, having their own colleges simply seemed a good idea. Any expectation of sketching even the broad outlines of this far-flung enterprise in a single chapter would, of course, be presumptuous; a recent volume about the same size as the present book was concerned only with this type of profile—with the *shape* of Catholic higher education—and barely covered its most obvious features.[3] The title chosen for that volume by its editor—the present writer—is indicative of the approach which will be taken here. In this chapter, I shall attempt only to hit some high points, referring the reader to the more complete discussions in other published and unpublished sources, and to my fellow contributors' chapters in this book.

---

[2] Realizing that "school" is most accurately used to refer to a secondary educational institution, I use this as I do "college," to avoid repetition. As the volume is being prepared, several books were either just out or in preparation. The two Carnegie-backed studies of Catholic education (Andrew M. Greeley and Peter H. Rossi, *The Education of Catholic Americans,* Aldine, 1966; Reginald A. Neuwien, *Catholic Schools in Action,* Notre Dame, 1966) concentrated on primary and secondary education, although the former book casts some light on Catholic higher education. See also Manning M. Pattillo, Jr. and Donald M. Mackenzie, *Church-Sponsored Higher Education in the United States,* American Council on Education, 1966.

Just published are *The Changing Catholic College,* by Andrew Greeley, the report of a Carnegie-financed study of some 30 institutions; the report of the study of Catholic higher education by the National Catholic Education Association, directed by Charles Ford; a chapter on "Catholic and their Colleges," in *The Academic Revolution,* by Christopher Jencks and David Reisman (Doubleday); James Trent's *Catholics in College* [University of Chicago Press]; Hassengers' *The Shape of Catholic Higher Education* (also from Chicago); and a number of dissertations at Minnesota, Michigan, and Catholic University of America.

The climate and impact of the Catholic college are touched on in, respectively, *The American Student's Freedom of Expression,* by E. G. Williamson and J. L. Cowan, University of Minnesota Press, 1966; and Theodore M. Newcomb and Kenneth Feldman, *The Impact of College.*

[3] Robert Hassenger (ed). *The Shape of Catholic Higher Education.* University of Chicago Press, 1967.

Choice of the term "shape" reflects my concern with the present, with the way things look now. But for anything like a complete understanding of how the present patterns in Catholic higher education came about, one must consider the colleges in historical perspective. Happily, this has recently been done by Philip Gleason, and one can here only refer the reader to his excellent discussion of the effects in the schools of American Catholics' situation as newcomers to a foreign and somewhat hostile host culture, and the social, institutional, and ideological adjustments which have been called forth by accommodation to the norms and requirements of American society.[4] All of the evidence indicates that the colleges—often, in their early days, more appropriately described as secondary schools —were founded primarily to achieve the two-pronged purpose of preparing Catholics for entrance into the mainstream of American society, and providing them with spiritual water-wings, that they might not be lost to the Church there. David Riesman's description of these schools as "decompression chambers" is particularly appropriate. But as the children and grandchildren of the immigrants no longer find it necessary to hold on to the distinctive customs and values characterizing the hyphenated Americans, the colleges and universities under Catholic auspices are no longer able to count on a ready-made clientele. Somewhat as have the Negro colleges, the Catholic institutions are finding that many from among formely minority groups prefer to attend the best schools of the larger society, leaving those colleges established exclusively for their group to those who are less acculturated. These schools were in some sense *too* successful in adapting earlier generations to the host culture.[5]

THE INSTITUTIONS

First, then, a look at the physical shape of Catholic higher education. This must be seen as part of the broader picture.

Two decades ago, private colleges and universities comprised the majority of American educational institutions, but the trend toward public higher education has so accelerated that, by Autumn of 1965, only 1,032,312 of the 5,967,411 students in college were in church-

---

[4] Philip J. Gleason, "Catholic Higher Education: A Historical Perspective," in *ibid.*, pp. 15-53.

[5] See Jencks and Riesman, *Academic Revolution,* for an elaboration of this point.

related institutions.[6] Although these colleges had only 17.3 percent of the total enrollment, they awarded more than a quarter of the bachelor's and first professional degrees.[7]

Of the 817 schools having definite present connections with religious bodies, the largest segment is Roman Catholic (41.5 percent), according to the Danforth Report. This would mean 339 colleges and universities under Catholic auspices. But the Committee on Catholic Higher Education of the National Catholic Educational Association reports 457 Catholic institutions of higher learning.[8] Two hundred of these are conducted primarily for clergy and religious, 257 for lay men and women. The Ford study was the first to attempt compilation of complete statistics on some of the basic aspects of Catholic higher education. The research team found that more than a third of the Catholic institutions had fewer than 100 full-time students; the vast majority of these were for religious men or women, but some were for lay students. More than half had fewer than 300-full-time students. Only about six percent had more than 2,000 full-time students, and nearly a third have been founded since 1950. All but three of the institutions founded since 1950 had fewer than 300 full-time students. In a statistical sense, the "typical" Catholic college was for women, with between 301 and 750 full-time students.

ENROLLMENT PATTERNS

While it is difficult to find reliable statistics on the exact distribution of Catholic collegians on Catholic and secular[9] campuses, it is

---

6 And only 935,159 more were in other private colleges. (Pattillo and Mackenzie, *Church-Sponsored Higher Education,* p. 16.) Enrollment was higher in 1966-67, although freshman enrollment was down slightly (.9%) for the first time since 1951, Garland G. Parker, "Statistics of Attendance in American Universities and Colleges, 1966-67," *School and Society, 95,* 9-24, (January 7, 1967) with later supplements as additional data became available. The decline in male freshman enrollment (2.3% down, compared to an increase of .8% for women) was undoubtedly a reflection of the increased Selective Service calls. Junior and community colleges showed the greatest growth, enrolling 1,500,000 in 1966-67, compared to 1,200,000 in 1965-66.

7 Pattillo and Mackenzie, *Church-Sponsored Higher Education,* pp. 16 and 27. The attrition rate is lower in such schools. See note 10.

8 Charles E. Ford and Edgar L. Roy, Jr. "Working Paper for the Advisory Committee, NCEA Study of Catholic Higher Education," St. Louis, September 15, 1966 (mimeographed).

9 Needless to say, "secular" is not used pejoratively, here, but to describe non-church-related institutions. Since Harvey Cox (*The Secular City,* Macmillan, 1965), the term is often an honorific one, especially among Catholic liberals.

the consensus of many who have tried to decipher the various reported enrollments that somewhat less than a third of the Catholics in college, or about 400,000 in 1966-67, attended schools affiliated with their church. Jencks and Riesman estimate about 30 percent enter Catholic colleges, although the percentage of those receiving degrees from Catholic schools is slightly higher.[10] Somewhere between nine and twelve percent of the bachelor's degrees each year in the United States are awarded by Catholic institutions, and about 92-95 percent of these are to Catholics.[11] This proportion within Catholic schools will probably decrease to somewhere between 85 and 90 percent, as efforts are made to diversify Catholic college enrollment, with federal money becoming available for more students from less advantaged socioeconomic groups. And fewer and fewer of the total Catholic population in college will be in Church-sponsored institutions in the years ahead, probably only about twenty percent by 1985.[12]

Most likely to attend Catholic schools are girls. In 1965, the U.S. Office of Education listed 136 four-year Catholic women's colleges, in addition to more than forty junior colleges. There are, by comparison, only about 100 non-Catholic colleges enrolling women exclusively. Taken together, five out of six Catholic schools are sex-segregated, nearly half of the colleges admitting women only, an additional third serving men exclusively.[13] But the big coeduca-

---

[10] Jencks and Riesman have calculated that about 35% of the Catholics in college received their degrees from Catholic colleges in 1965. The discrepancy is accounted for by the greater likelihood of those in Catholic colleges actually getting degrees than Catholics in the large public institutions with higher attrition rates (which may be even higher for Catholics in these schools). Of those Catholics receiving degrees, then—which is of course a smaller number than those entering college—about 35% obtained these from Catholic schools in 1965.

[11] Andrew Greeley (*Religion and Career*, Sheed and Ward, 1963) estimated on the basis of his (National Opinion Research Center) sample that 13.3 percent of the 1961 B.A.'s were awarded by Catholic colleges, but there are indications his sample may be slightly skewed. See Jencks and Riesman, *Academic Revolution*, and Trent, *Catholics in College*.

[12] See R. J. Clifford, S. J. and W. R. Callahan, S. J., "Catholics in Higher Education," *America*, 111, 288-91 (1964); and J. W. Evans, "Catholic Higher Education on the Secular Campus," in Hassenger, *op. cit.*, 275-93. Some of the reasons for this decreasing proportion are discussed at the end of this chapter.

[13] As late as 1929, Piux XI wrote, in his encyclical on "The Christian Education of Youth," that "there is not in nature itself . . . anything to suggest that there can or ought to be promiscuity, and much less equality of the two sexes." He declared it "False . . . and harmful to Christian education," that "the so-called method of 'coeducation' " was suggested.

tional universities enroll such large numbers that considerably more than one in six Catholic *students* is in a coeducational setting. Only about one quarter of the Catholic college women attend Catholic women's colleges. More than half of those who attend college at all go to Catholic schools, a much higher proportion than for men. This rate has been steadily decreasing however, as more formerly male colleges admit women. Only a handful of the Jesuit schools still do not allow women on the undergraduate level (although all do, on the graduate level, where programs exist), and there are few remaining non-Jesuit institutions which are still for men only. Even at these, there are an increasing number of cooperative ventures, from joint cultural and area studies programs to sharing of faculty and cross-enrollment of students.[14]

DIFFERENCES IN QUALITY

Another connatation of shape is quality: in what "shape" are Catholic colleges and universities?

More than four out of five of those schools with fewer than 100 full-time students did *not* have regional accreditation, according to NCEA Report. Most of these were run primarily for religious or clergy. Nearly half of those institutions with between 101 and 300 full-time students, and one in ten of those in the 301-750 range, still sought the accreditation of their regional associations. All of the colleges and universities with more than 750 students were regionally accredited. When age of institution was considered, the Ford team found that three-fourths of the schools founded before 1950 were accredited, compared to one-quarter founded since that time. Again, most of the latter were run for religious or clergy. More than half of the schools not accredited were junior colleges. Some of the obvious implications of these data will be discussed at the end of this chapter.

One clear index of quality is the number of National Merit Scholars an institution enrolls. As of 1966, here is the way Catholic schools ranked, by the number of their National Merit Scholars, and the number which were enrolled in 1965-66 (Table 1).[15]

It would of course be expected that, in schools which have been

---

14 More will be said about this later in this chapter.

15 National Merit Scholarship Corporation, *The Merit Program: 1955-65,* NMSC, 1966.

"good" longer, there would be more Merit Scholars who have been graduated than are presently enrolled; if a school were to have more Scholars currently enrolled than have been graduated, this would be an indication the institution was on the upswing; and if earlier totals were not matched currently, one might reason that the over-all quality of the school had declined, or at least was so perceived by potential students. By these criteria, Notre Dame would seem to have been and to have remained most attractive to bright students (men, at least); Georgetown, St. Louis, Boston College, Rosary, Villanova, Catholic University and Fordham to be on the rise; Marquette, Holy Cross, and St. Mary's of Notre Dame

TABLE 1   CATHOLIC COLLEGES FROM WHICH MERIT SCHOLARS HAVE BEEN GRADUATED AND COLLEGE ENROLLMENT OF MERIT AND ACHIEVEMENT SCHOLARS, 1965-66 [a]

School	Graduated	Enrolled
Notre Dame	53	40
St. Louis	17	18
Georgetown	16	34
Marquette	15	12
Holy Cross	10	8
Detroit	8	—
Loyola of the South	7	—
Boston College	6	12
Catholic University	6	9
Fordham	6	8
St. Mary's of Notre Dame	5	6
Rosary	—	10
Villanova	—	8

[a] *Source.* National Merit Scholarship Corp., *The Merit Program: 1955-65* (Evanston: National Merit Scholarship Corp., 1966).

to be holding steady; and Detroit and Loyola of the South perhaps declining in quality. An even better measure would control for the size of the freshman class, indicating how an institution stands when its popularity with high-ability students relative to its size is determined. Robert Nichols has computed indices of popularity for various colleges, showing those schools which are over-chosen by high-ability students, taking into account the number of places available in the freshman class, for both men and women.[16] Notre Dame is most frequently over-chosen by high-ability men, ranking eighteenth among all American colleges enrolling men; Georgetown is next, among Catholic schools. Women over-chose Georgetown and Catholic University most frequently, but LeMoyne College, Boston College, Fordham, St. Louis, Canisius, San Francisco, Villanova, and Marquette are also picked often by high-ability women. One of the reasons there are so many institutions in the latter group is the comparatively small number of places for women in the freshman classes of many of the Jesuit schools (all but two of those in this group are run by Jesuits). And it should be noted that Catholic men were only about half as likely as non-Catholics to win NMSC awards between 1956 and 1959.[17]

Notre Dame also looks good in other measures. By 1962, it was tied with Harvard for the largest number of Danforth Fellowships received;[18] by 1966, its graduates had been awarded 122 Woodrow Wilson Fellowships, far more than any other Catholic college;[19] yet Notre Dame was not adjudged worthy of membership in Phi Beta Kappa until 1967, after four other Catholic schools.[20] Remnants of an aggressive, "fighting Irish" climate lingered long after it had outlived its usefulness to immigrant Catholics. As late as the mid-1950's, CEEB scores were unimpressive, although considerable progress has been made since (Table 2). While still "Number One" as this is written, Notre Dame may have to run very hard to stay ahead of such fast-moving schools as Fordham, which is recruiting new academic stars (such as Elizabeth Sewell, Robert Havighurst, and Marshall McLuhan); Boston College, radically upgrading faculty salaries and attracting some stars of their own; and Immaculate

---

16 Robert C. Nichols, "College Preferences of Eleventh Grade Students," *NMSC Research Reports*, **2** (9), 1966.

17 See Jencks and Riesman, *Academic Revolution;* and T.R. McConnell, E. D. Farwell, and J. R. Warren, "Student Personality Characteristics Associated with Groups of Colleges and Fields of Study," *College and University,* (1962).

18 Fifteen each, according to Pattillo and Meckenzie, *Church-Sponsored Higher Education,* p. 115.

19 As Edward Wakin put it (*The Catholic Campus,* Macmillan, 1963): "Notre Dame has been awarded more Woodrow Wilson scholarships, Danforth Fellowships, Marshall Fellowships and Rhodes Scholarships than all other Catholic universities *combined*" (p. 35, my italics). Between 1952 and 1966, Notre Dame was awarded 23 Danforths, 9 Root-Tilden Fellowships, and 6 Rhodes Scholarships.

20 Catholic University, Fordham, Georgetown, and the College of St. Catherine.

TABLE 2   CEEB SCORES FOR NOTRE DAME FRESHMEN IN 1955, 1960, AND 1965 [a]

Year	Verbal Mean	Quantitative Mean
1955-56	481.78	528.61
	(1,095)	(1,095)
1960-61	532.32	576.86
	(1,536)	(1,550)
1965-66	576.31	629.51
	(1,550)	(1,550)

[a] Numbers of students in parentheses.

Heart of Los Angeles, already characterized by a distinctive climate, and to become a member of the Associated Claremont Colleges in 1969 or 1970.[21]

Even among the Catholic women's colleges, distinct differences can be seen, as the College Entrance Examination Board Scores for twenty of these schools indicate (Table 3). The 1964 mean scores at Manhattanville were 632 (Verbal) and 599 (Quantitative) compared with, for example, 570 (V) and 529 (Q) at Rosary; 535 (V) and 505 (Q) at Mundelein, or 479 (V) and 450 (Q) at Marylhurst. Unfortunately, few Catholic parents are aware of such differences among schools.

The term "climate" which was introduced above is seen more and more often, when differences among colleges are discussed. A number of research studies in the 1950's[22] have led to the development of several ways of assessing the over-all "feel" or atmosphere

---

[21] Two other indications of Notre Dame's leadership can be found in the section on graduate education below. But Boston College had the largest number of Woodrow Wilsons awarded its seniors in 1967: 8, compared to 7 at Fordham, 5 each at Georgetown and Notre Dame, 4 at Emmanuel in Boston. For B.C.'s new leadership in the area of faculty salaries, see below.

[22] C. R. Pace and G. G. Stern, "An Approach to the Measurement of Psychological Characteristics of College Environments," *Journal of Educational Psychology,* **49** 269-77 (1958); D. L. Thistlewaithe, "College Press and Student Achievement," *Journal of Educational Psychology,* **50** 183-91 (1959), and "College Press and Changes in Study Plans of Talented Students," *ibid.,* **51** 222-34 (1960).

TABLE 3   DISTRIBUTION OF CEEB SCORES FOR ENTERING FRESHMEN AT
TWENTY CATHOLIC WOMEN'S COLLEGES, 1964 [a]

College (Number Entering in Parentheses)	Verbal [b]			Quantitative [b]		
	650+	600-649	—450	650+	550-649	—450
Barat (120)	9	12	4	8	20	15
Clarke (215)	3	11	39	4	13	39
Dunbarton (141)	7	11	5	6	18	20
Immaculate Heart (108)	13	16	18	6	25	31
Loretto Hts. (338)	5	5	9	2	15	14
Manhattanville (234)	38	27	0	18	58	0
Marygrove (301)	13	11	9	7	24	17
Marymount at Tarrytown (224)	11	15	3	6	37	9
Mount Mercy (227)	3	7	34	2	17	35
New Rochelle (250)	28	17	2	13	37	7
Newton College of Sacred Heart (222)	20	28	1	10	58	3
Rosary (215)	20	16	7	6	37	17
Rosary Hill (332)	5	8	27	5	19	36
St. Catherine (354)	9	12	15	6	24	33
St. Mary's of Notre Dame (303)	16	12	6	10	37	12
St. Xavier, Ill. (197)	11	15	7	9	27	16
Salve Regina (240)	3	10	14	1	21	19
Seton Hill (209)	12	13	10	7	27	14
Trinity (270)	29	25	0	16	40	1
Webster (230)	11	9	24	2	17	40

[a] In percentages. *Source. Manual of Freshmen Class Profiles, 1965-67*, College
Entrance Examination Board.

[b] Since women are typically higher in verbal scores and lower in quantitative
scores, it was thought to be more useful to concentrate on the distribution at
the upper end of the latter, and at the high and low ends of the former.

of an educational institution.[23] The best term to summarize such dimensions as degree of student autonomy; accessibility of facultv and administrators, freedom of choice in courses, paternalistic or maternalistic control, student self-government, and the like, seems to be "climate." Robert F. Weiss, S. J., had pulled together the results of all the available research on Catholic college climates to 1965.[24] The reader who would learn more of the differences in approach of the College Characteristics Index, the College and University Environment Scales, and the Environmental Assessment Technique is referred to the Weiss effort. Results for Catholic colleges and universities do not differ significantly from one approach to another, and we shall content ourselves with a summary of the major patterns here. While a fairly strong feeling of group solidarity and identity is found on most Catholic campuses—particularly in the women's colleges—there is at the same time a high degree of organization and structure, both with regard to curriculum and to extra-curricular matters of student life. Politeness, protocol, and proper forms of dress and address are considered important. There appear to be few institutional attempts to preserve student freedom and maximize student responsibility. Conduct is regulated by legislative codes and administrative fiats.

The academic climate is characterized more by a rather instrumental vocationalism than by intellectual or esthetic concerns. Little stress seems to be placed on academic achievement and scholarship, on interest in ideas as ideas. Liberal educational goals seem to be held by a minority.[25]

The women's colleges are, as noted, highest in sense of community; they also appear more intellectually alive: they are about average in the various "intellectualism" scales, while the men's

---

[23] See G. G. Stern, "Environments for Learning," in N. Sanford (ed.), *The American College* John Wiley, 1962 690-730, and *Scoring Instructions and College Norms: Activities Index-College Characteristics Index,* 1963; C. R. Pace, *CUES: College and University Environment Scales—Preliminary Technical Manual,* Educational Testing Service, 1963; A. W. Astin, "An Empirical Characterization of Higher Educational Institutions," *Journal of Educational Psychology,* **53**, 224-35 (1962); A. W. Astin and J. L. Holland, "The Environmental Assessment Technique: A Way to Measure College Environments," *Journal of Educational Psychology,* **52**, 308-16 (1961); A. W. Astin, *Who Goes Where to College?* Science Research Associates, 1965.

[24] Robert F. Weiss, S. J., "The Environment for Learning on the Catholic College Campus," in Hassenger, *Shape of Catholic Higher Education,* pp. 57-82.

[25] Perhaps because of this, cheating seems to be taken rather lightly on many Catholic campuses. See below.

and coed colleges and universities rank below two-thirds of the American colleges in the samples. Surprising to some will be the extremely low scores of many Jesuit schools, which seem characterized by a heavy entrepreneurial, "practical" emphasis.[26] Although considerably higher in the measures of intellectuality and sensitivity, the women's colleges are nevertheless very high in propriety and organization, with little apparent tolerance for deviant, off-beat, convention-flouting behavior.[27] Small schools often appear more interesting places than large universities—and B.A.-granting institutions than many granting doctorates—but this may be due in large part to the instrumental concerns of the more recently arrived ethnic groups, a large client-segment of the urban, commuter university. (The importance of social class should not be underestimated, in discussing Catholic higher education; more will be said about this below.)

It should be clear that real pluralism can usually be found *within* institutions; even small colleges typically are characterized by several distinct sub-cultures. This can be illustrated by the data in Table 4, showing how the perceived climate of the pseudonomous "Mary College" studied by Hassenger varied by college major.[28] Compar-

---

26 See the portraits of specific Jesuit institutions in J. Foster, R. Stanek, and W. Krassowski, "The Impact of a Value-Oriented University on Student Attitudes and Thinking," Cooperative Research Project No. 729, Office of Education, Department of Health, Education, and Welfare, 1961, and J. Foster, "Some Effects of Jesuit Education: A Case Study," in Hassenger, *Shape of Catholic Higher Education*, pp. 163-90; F. Kearns, "Social Consciousness and Academic Freedom in Catholic Higher Education," *ibid.*, pp. 223-49; G. J. DiRenzo, "Student Imagery at Fairfield University, 1963-64," Mimeographed at Fairfield University, 1965; R. F. Weiss, S. J., "Student and Faculty Perceptions of Institutional Press at St. Louis University," Unpublished doctoral dissertation, University of Minnesota, 1964, and summarized in Weiss, 'The Environment for Learning."

27 Andrew Greeley found that self-identification as "conventional" (choice of this term in a list of adjectives the respondent felt characterized himself) seemed to be somewhat associated with Catholic college attendance (Greeley, *Religion and Career*).

28 Robert Hassenger, "The Impact of a Value-Oriented College on the Religious Orientations of Students with Various Traits, Background, and College Exposures," Unpublished doctoral dissertation, University of Chicago, 1965, summarized in Hassenger, "Portrait of a Catholic Women's College," in Hassenger, *Shape of Catholic Higher Education*, pp. 83-106. The description of an instrument for the study of college sub-cultures can be found in C. R. Pace and L. Baird, "Attainment Patterns in the Environmental Press of College Sub-cultures," in T. M. Newcomb and E. K. Wilson, *The Study of College Peer Groups*, Aldine, 1966, pp. 215-42.

TABLE 4 RANKINGS IN COLLEGE CHARACTERISTICS INDEX FACTORS, BY COLLEGE TYPE AND "MARY COLLEGE" MAJOR [a]

	Intellectual Climate							
	Work	Non-vocational Climate	Aspiration Level	Intellectual Atmosphere	Student Dignity	Academic Climate	Academic Achievement	Self-Expression
Liberal arts colleges	4	1	1	1	1	1	1	2
"Mary College"								
Science	2	6	2	4	4	2	3	5
Humanities	1	3	6	3	2	6	4	4
Social science	3	5	7	5	3	7	5	3
Education	5	4	3	2	5	5	2	1
Denominational schools	6	7	5	7	7	4	7	6
Teachers' colleges	7	2	4	6	6	3	6	7

	Non-Intellectual Climate					
	Self-Expression	Group Life	Academic Organization	Social Form	Play	Vocational Climate
Liberal arts colleges	2	7	7	7	4	7
"Mary College"						
Science	5	4	3	2	6	2
Humanities	4	5	1	4	7	5
Social science	3	.2	4	5	5	3
Education	1	3	2	3	3	4
Denominational schools	6	1	5	1	2	1
Teachers' colleges	7	6	6	6	1	6

[a] "Rank" refers to "how much" of a factor a group reports.

isons of the perceived climates of "Mary College" science, social science, humanities and education majors to those reported for denominational schools, teachers' colleges, and for first-rate liberal arts colleges can be made.[29] In general, four "Mary College" groups can be seen to rank [30] between the liberal arts colleges, which are highest in intellectual climate and lowest in non-intellectual climate, and the denominational schools and teachers' colleges, which ranked lowest in intellectual climate, highest in non-intellectual climate. There were interesting departures from this pattern, however. Humanities and social science majors reported a very low "aspiration level" (college encouragement of self-prescribed high student standards) and "academic climate" (institutional stress on academic excellence), while science majors ranked immediately behind the liberal arts colleges here. Education students reported numerous opportunities available for the development of leadership potential and self-assurance ("self-expression"), and ranked second in both "academic achievement" and in perceived "intellectual atmosphere." In the non-intellectual climate, "Mary College" groups held the first four ranks on "academic organization" (a highly structured academic environment, with little freedom to substitute courses and make other changes), with humanities majors first. The school was also high in "vocational climate," an emphasis on practical, applied activities with comparative rejection of esthetic experience, and all but the education students were conspicuously low on "play," activities associated with dating, athletics, or other forms of collegiate amusement. The other data found in Hassenger [31] support the findings presented here.

Another angle of vision allows the investigator to discover the difference between the expected climate at an institution, and that found actually to obtain. Loveless has compared the freshmen ex-

---

[29] Stern (*College Norms*) groups schools into three categories in one analysis. Denominational schools comprise "major Protestant" colleges, i.e., those founded by major denominations, such as Congregationalists and Presbyterians (e.g., Denison, Emory); "minor Protestant" schools established by smaller denominational groups (e.g., Northwest Christian College); and Catholic colleges (there were eight in the original sample). First-rate liberal arts colleges are those like Antioch and Swarthmore. Teachers' colleges are those preparing primary and secondary school teachers exclusively. It is important to realize that it is perceived press or climate which is being investigated here, although Stern has presented evidence that his instrument is independent of students' needs: personal traits do not distort perceived press. For the problem of reference groups, however, see below.

[30] Rank refers to "how much" of a factor a group reports. Thus, liberal arts colleges rank first on six of the eight dimensions of the Intellectual Climate; "Mary College" humanities majors rank first on Work, third on Non-Vocational Climate, etc.

[31] Chapter 4, *The Shape of Catholic Higher Education.*

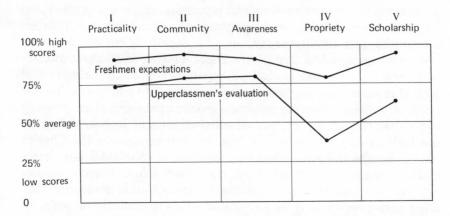

| | I
Practicality | II
Community | III
Awareness | IV
Propriety | V
Scholarship |

pectations of Notre Dame with the climate as described by upper-classmen [32]; differences for the five CUES factors are shown in Figure 1. It is interesting—but not surprising: similar studies elsewhere show this is typically the case—that freshmen entering Notre Dame in 1966 expected "more of" each factor than upperclassmen reported was to be found. As can be seen in the standard scores, Notre Dame is apparently characterized by a fairly high level of appreciation for and involvement in public issues and problems (Awareness), and a high sense of friendly cohesiveness (Community). The Scholarship score is above average, but rather lower than many faculty would undoubtedly prefer; with such a high Practicality score, however, this is not surprising: apparently Notre Dame has not entirely shaken off the instrumental vocationalism seen above to characterize so many of the Jesuit colleges.[33] The greatest discrep-

---

[32] Eugene Loveless, "Differences Between Expected and Perceived Climate, University of Notre Dame," unpublished paper.

[33] Although it should be pointed out that a carefully stratified sample of 152 Notre Dame students studied the following year by Hassenger reported considerably more Practicality and Propriety press than the Loveless respondents. (Scores on the Community scale were directly comparable, but the Hassenger sample reported slightly higher Scholarship press, and slightly lower Awareness press, than students in the Loveless sample.) Scores on all five scales were below what entering freshmen apparently expected, however. This raises the question as to whether there is not an exaggeration of all dimensions of a college, by the entering freshmen, who paint in the bold colors of the mass media, rather than the shades of gray of more realistic observers. In the present case, entering Notre Dame students perceived the school as high in *both* intellectualism and vocationalism (although these are mean scores, and it might turn out that different perceivers are involved, here).

ancy was between expected and reported Propriety scores—the extent to which conventionalism and organization are anticipated and found. So the entering student apparently found less emphasis on community and intellectuality than he expected, but at the same time, was surprised to find Notre Dame placing less importance on monitoring his life than he had anticipated. One of the uncontrolled factors in such research, however, is the extent to which self-descriptions are influenced by the reference groups of the reporters. Greeley notes that the self-reported intellectual climate of Boston College is not high, perhaps because they look too intently across the Charles River, despite the more objective indications that B.C. is a fairly exciting place, intellectually; on the other hand, Carroll College reporters describe their school as much higher in this dimension than other measures show it to be, probably because of the absence of anything like Harvard near Helena, Montana.[34] Development of better instruments and their use on the Catholic campus will allow us to learn much more about the differences in climates among and within Catholic institutions. But this is the way the Catholic schools look at present. What effects do they have?

IMPACT OF CATHOLIC COLLEGES AND UNIVERSITIES

One of the reasons for the separate existence of church-sponsored colleges and universities is the purported difference they make in the lives of their students. Whether or not it is reasonable to expect four years of college to affect appreciably the values and attitudes of one who is exposed to so much pre- and post-college experience is

---

[34] Greeley, *Changing Catholic College* (schools not identified by name there, however). A. W. Astin has been developing an instrument which attempts to deal with the problem of self-report devices, by an elaboration of the Environmental Assessment Technique, which would incorporate the best of both the objective and subjective approaches. In his Inventory of College Activities, observable events are still concentrated upon, although an effort is made to pick up some of the more subtle stimuli approached by the CCI and CUES (see Astin's paper read in the symposium, "Recent Research on the Characteristics of College Environments," at the 1965 Meetings of the American Psychological Association, Chicago).

often debated; I have discussed this elsewhere.[35] But a careful examination of the available data is showing that, the Jacob Report to the contrary notwithstanding,[36] certain students do undergo considerable change within certain colleges and their sub-cultures.[37] The longest chapter of *The Shape of Catholic Higher Education* was given over to discussion of the impact of the Catholic colleges and universities; only some broad summaries will be attempted here.

There is a general pattern of association between Catholic college attendance and what might be called "conservative" social and political attitudes. Or at least there *has* been: the recent data of Greeley and Rossi seem to indicate that Catholic college Catholics were significantly lower than those in secular colleges in anti-Semitism and in opposition to civil liberties.[38]

What can again be called "conservatism" or "orthodoxy" has also been consistently found in the religious values, attitudes and behavior of Catholic college students and graduates. The general decrease in religious concern found among American collegians has not been characteristic of Catholics. Whether the criterion was church attendance, or self-reported religiosity, or indices of religious knowledge and understanding, Catholic college products have been found most "religious." [39] One can suggest, from a number of past studies, that results which might be expected to be associated with real religious commitment have not been very visible, for Catholic college graduates; their involvement in what can be termed the "social apostolate" has not been impressive. The greatest impact of the schools and colleges has seemed to be less on social consciousness than on doctrinal and ethical matters and those which had, in

---

[35] Chapter 5 of *Shape* and "A Rationale for Changing Student Values," *Educational Record*, **48**, 61-67 (1967).

[36] Philip Jacob, *Changing Values in College*, Harper, 1957; for critiques of Jacob, see A. H. Barton, *Studying the Effects of College Education*, Hazen Foundation, 1959; and David Riesman, "A Review of the Jacob Report," *American Sociological Review*, **23**, 732-39 (1958).

[37] Newcomb and Feldman, *The Impact of College.*

[38] Greeley and Rossi, *Education of Catholic Americans.* The support of civil liberties was little higher for this group than for those educated in Catholic grade and high schools, suggesting that the college itself has little impact (comparing Tables 7.1 and 7.8).

[39] On their test of religious knowledge, e.g., Pattillo and Meckenzie found that seniors at Catholic and Conservative Protestant colleges scored much higher than either seniors at liberal Protestant and at public colleges, or freshmen at their own institutions (*Church-Sponsored Higher Education*, pp. 142 ff.).

Greeley and Rossi's words, "crucial symbolic importance for American Catholicism—church attendance, sexual morality, and organizational 'loyalty' (to the Papacy and to the teaching authority of the Church)." [40]

Closely linked to specifically religious values and attitudes are those better termed moral and ethical. The same general patterns as above can be found, although some of the most recent work suggests that young Catholics, at least, are beginning to separate religious from moral concerns. All of the past research has found Catholics to be more strict in their sexual morality than Protestants, Jews, and non-believers. As late as the early 1960's, one study even showed that Catholic students took sexual misconduct much more seriously than they did intellectual integrity. [41] Not only was sex looked at with considerable reverence, it was perceived to be essentially procreative. [42] This was reflected in the desired and actual family size of Catholics; in fact, an earlier study seemed to find that

---

[40] This quotation is from the preliminary report ("The Social Effects of Catholic Education," by Greeley, Rossi, and L. J. Pinto), p. 54, although it also appears in the 1966 volume.

[41] In his Cornell doctoral dissertation (1963), Robert McNamara, S. J., found that cheating on terms papers and examinations was judged more harshly by men at Cornell and Columbia than by those at Fordham and Notre Dame, who were more concerned with sexual morality. In addition, great differences in cheating behavior existed. At both Catholic colleges, more than 40 percent admitted to cheating more than once, while less than 20 percent on the secular campuses did so ("The Interplay of Intellectual and Religious Values"). The Cornell-Columbia percentages are directly comparable to those for eleven colleges in the Goldsen survey (Rose K. Goldsen, M. Rosenberg, R. Williams, and E. A. Suchman, *What College Students Think,* Van Nostrand, 1960). Even if it is argued that only the admission is greater, with the incidence of cheating not necessarily higher on the Catholic campuses, the rejoinder can be made that this higher frequency of admission indicates that fewer Catholic collegians think this behavior seriously wrong. But it is perhaps worthwhile to consider the suggestion of David Riesman to the writer: "Are the exams in the Catholic colleges more factual, less free-wheeling, and therefore easier to cheat on?"

[42] For years, the Roman Catholic Church taught that the primary end or object of marriage was "the procreation and education of children"; a secondary end was "the mutual love of husband and wife." This is no longer the case: the teaching now is that there are "two primary ends" of marriage. Some may quibble with such wording, wondering how there can be *two primary* ends or goals, but the point here is that a change in emphasis has occurred.

the number of children desired was directly related to the extent of an individual's education in the Catholic school system: even with ethnicity controlled, the more Catholic education, the greater was the desired family size.[43] A more carefully-designed follow-up study indicates, however, that the "college effects" reported in Westoff *et al.* are more accurately seen as due to the differential selectivity of women with larger-family orientations into Catholic colleges, with these schools apparently counteracting influences that might otherwise prevail. Women from Catholic high schools attending non-Catholic colleges were found to desire smaller families as seniors than they had as freshmen.[44]

Other recent data indicate that there has been a dramatic shift in Catholic attitudes toward family planning and artificial contraception. Westoff and Ryder found that a majority of married Catholic women aged 18-39 were not conforming to Catholic doctrine on birth control,[45] and an as yet unpublished survey of 283 Catholic couples in fifteen states discovered that very few were satisfied with the rhythm method: 86 percent would use other methods if they were approved by the Catholic church.[46] Among younger couples,

---

[43] C. Westoff, R. Potter, and P. Sagi, *The Third Child*, Princeton University Press, 1963. Degree of religiosity worked in opposite ways for Catholics and Protestants, with highly religious Catholics having more, and Protestants *fewer*, children.

[44] C. Westoff and R. H. Potvin, "Higher Education, Religion and Women's Family-Size Orientations," *American Sociological Review*, **31**, 489-96 (1966). The same kind of reinforcement effects the Catholics on secular campuses who are active members of Catholic campus organizations, such as Newman Centers or student parishes. Lawrence Menard ("Effect of the Newman Club on the Religious Commitment of its Members," Paper read at the 1966 Meetings of the American Catholic Sociological Society, Miami) found that such students in five New York City colleges underwent less decrease in traditional belief and practice than Catholic non-members. Some attrition from traditional Catholicism occurred, but it was less for Newman participants than non-participants (and of the members, less for women than for men).

[45] C. F. Westoff and N. B. Ryder, "Methods of Fertility Control in the United States: 1955-65," Paper read at the Conference on Population, University of Notre Dame, November, 1966.

[46] This survey is presently being conducted on a more comprehensive basis, and thus cannot be further identified at this time. The writer expresses his appreciation to Dennis J. Geaney, O.S.A., for making results available to him.

and those in college today, there are indications that many are already acting as their own theologians in this regard.[47]

There is a considerable fund of data on the effects of the colleges on the personality traits of Catholic students. The earlier research almost unanimously found that Catholics were higher in measured authoritarianism, dogmatism, and general conservatism, than those on secular campuses, with Catholics in Catholic schools higher than Catholics on non-Catholic campuses.[48] More recent investigations provide mixed results. Stern and Trent found a general constraint and restrictiveness in the Catholic schools in their samples;[49] in the Trent research, seniors in the five Pacific Coast Catholic colleges he studied looked little different from freshmen, despite the general movement toward a freer expression of impulses and concern with intellectual and esthetic matters found for non-Catholic colleges in the sample.[50] But other studies suggest that at least some Catholic collegians are no higher in dogmatism than their non-Catholic peers,[51] and that changes do take place on some Catholic campuses. Hassenger found that authoritarianism and dogmatism decreased significantly during the first two years students spent in a Catholic women's college, and corresponding increases occurred on scales assessing social maturity and concern with civil liberties.[52] Questioning of the Catholic teaching on birth control increased four-fold, from twenty to eighty percent who expressed ,serious reservations

---

[47] And in many other ways. See Daniel Callahan, *The New Church,* Scribner's, 1966; and the contribution (Chapter 7C) to *Shape of Catholic Higher Education,* by Rauch and Hassenger.

[48] Summarized in Chapter 5 of Hassenger, pp. 128-41.

[49] G. G. Stern, "Psychological Characteristics of Denominational Colleges," Paper read at the 1965 Meetings of the American Catholic Psychological Association, Chicago; J. W. Trent, "Dimensions of Intellectual Productivity Among Sectarian and Non-Sectarian College Students," Paper read at the 1964 Convention of the American Personnel and Guidance Association; and J. W. Trent, "Religious and Dispositional Characteristics of Catholic Intellectuals," Paper read at the 1965 Meetings of the American Catholic Sociological Society, Chicago.

[50] Using the Omnibus Personality Inventory developed at the Center for the Study of Higher Education, Trent has been studying samples of Catholics and non-Catholics in California State Colleges, at Berkeley, and in five West Coast Catholic colleges.

[51] See, for example, Barbara Long, "Catholic-Protestant Differences in Acceptance of Others," *Sociology and Social Research,* **49,** 166-71 (1965); and R. Hassenger, "Catholic College Impact on Religious Orientations," *Sociological Analysis,* **27,** 67-79 (1966).

[52] See Hassenger dissertation, "Impact of a Catholic College" and Chapter 5 of *The Shape of Catholic Higher Education.*

about the traditional position. But very little in the way of hard data is available, and it is only when many longitudinal studies have been done that we shall be able to speak with any authority here.

DIFFERENTIAL COLLEGE IMPACT

It was noted above that *some* students seem to change, in *some* Catholic colleges. As more research is done on higher education, it becomes clear that college impact is a function not only of student characteristics, but of institutional exposures. It would not be expected, for example, that a given Catholic college would have the same effect on Irish as on Polish students, taken collectively. Seventy years separate their times of peak arrival in this country.[53] Greeley found that 43 percent of the Irish and German students in his sample had taken college for granted when growing up, compared to less than a third of the Polish and Italian Catholics, with the former two groups also seeming to have a higher estimate of their own abilities.[54] When a control for social class is introduced, however, it appears that planning to attend college is primarily a function of middle class standing, although self-appraisal of competence seems more closely linked to ethnicity.[55] Hassenger found that the impact

---

[53] The peak years of immigration for the most visible Catholic ethnic groups: Irish, 1851; Germans, 1882; Italians, 1907; and Poles, 1921 (from John L. Thomas, S. J., "Nationalities and American Catholicism," in *Catholic Church, U.S.A.*, ed. Louis Putz, C.S.C., Fides Press, 1956, pp. 155-176).

[54] Thirty-three percent of the Irish and Germans, compared to 23 percent of the Italians and Poles (*Religion and Career*). Regarding plans for their later careers, however, the split was another way, with 28 percent of the Poles and 21 percent of the Germans (compared to 13 and 12 percent of the Irish and Italians, respectively) indicating an intention to pursue academic fields; Irish and Italians were more interested in law and engineering, respectively. It is interesting that, in the later Greeley work with Rossi (*op. cit.*), third-and-later-generation Irish, German, and Polish Catholics are equally likely to be found in Catholic schools, but Italians are less frequently found there (although percentages do increase with length of stay in the U.S.).

[55] Here is how it breaks down:

	Irish-German (College Taken for Granted)		Italian-Polish	
Middle upper class	52 [a]	(424) [b]	45	(80)
Working lower class	15	(132)	19	(67)
	High Estimate of Ability			
Middle upper class	35	(286)	27	(15)
Working lower class	32	(283)	18	(63)

[a] In percentages. From A. M. Greeley, "Anti-Intellectualism in Catholic Colleges."

[b] Numbers of students. *Amer. Cath. Sociol. Rev.*, **23**, 350-68 (1962).

of a Catholic women's college was much greater on Italian and Polish than on Irish and German girls, contrary to his expectations.[56] Public high school girls coming to "Mary College" were also found to be more open and receptive to change.[57]

A particular college may have considerable impact on students' values and attitudes in one dimension (e.g., political), without appreciably affecting those in another (e.g. religious); such differential Catholic college effects can be found in McNamara and Hassenger.[58] Or an institution may greatly change students characterized by one set of qualities (e.g. intellectualism), but have little effect on others.[59] Different factors operate in individual cases, which is not surprising, since students come to college with years of interpersonal influence and unique past experiences. To really understand the impact of Catholic colleges, information will have to be gathered to determine what happens to whom in which settings. As a number of investigations have shown, changes in students' values and attitudes are often associated with differential college exposures.[60] To further complicate matters, one must be able to determine whether differences

---

[56] The reader is referred to Chapter 5, *The Shape of Catholic Higher Education,* and to the Hassenger dissertation, "Impact."

[57] *Ibid.* See also J. T. Fox, "Authoritarianism and the St. Ambrose College Student," *Religious Education,* 60, 272-76 (1965), for a similar finding. David Riesman reminds us that "in considering the impact of colleges, it is, of course, all too common and easy to focus on the students they turn out rather than to compare in detail the finished product with the entering freshmen. It is in these latter terms of what economists would call 'value added' that colleges should really be appraised. And it is in such terms that Immaculate Heart and Webster are distinguished colleges, even though they do not produce many " 'distinguished' graduates" (from the Foreword to *Shape of Catholic Higher Education,* p.v.).

[58] See McNamara, "Interplay," and his "Intellectual Values and Instrumental Religion," *Sociological Analysis,* 25 (1964), 99-107; Robert Hassenger, "Religious Values and Personality Traits of Catholic College Women," *Insight,* 3(2), 37-48 (1964), and Hassenger, "Varieties of Religious Orientation," *Sociological Analysis,* 25, 189-199 (1965), as well as Hassenger, *op. cit.* (1966) (note 50).

[59] *Ibid.,* and Chapter 5 of *Shape;* Trent, *Catholics in College.*

[60] C. D. Bolton and K. Kammeyer, *The University Student: A Study of Student Behavior and Values,* College and University Press, 1967; Goldsen *et al., College Students;* D. Gottlieb and B. Hogdkins, "College Student Sub-

which appear are due to college impact, or to differential selectivity, which draws students of certain traits or dispositions to particular campuses, or to specific sub-cultures within a campus.[61] There are simply no investigations with which the writer is familiar that have explored the impact of a Catholic college with the kind of care which would control for such confounding variables; what indications we have of differential college impact must be inferred from less rigorous studies. These have been summarized in Hassenger.[62]

What impact have the Catholic colleges? We just do not know. There are a few indications that religiously affiliated colleges do

---

cultures, *School Review*, **71**, 291-99 (1963); Esther Lloyd-Jones, and H. Estrin, *The American Student and His College*, Houghton Mifflin Co., 1967; T. M. Newcomb, Kathryn E. Koenig, R. Flacks, and D. P. Warwick, *Persistence and Change: Bennington Students After 25 Years*, John Wiley, Inc., 1967; L. A. Pervin, L. E. Reik, and W. Dalrymple, *The College Dropout and the Utilization of Talent*, Princeton University Press, 1966; B. E. Segal, "Fraternities, Social Distance, and Anti-Semitism Among Jewish and Non-Jewish Undergraduates," *Sociology of Education*, **38**, 251-64 (1965); H. Selvin and W. Hagstrom, "Sources of Support for Civil Liberties," *British Journal of Sociology*, **11**, 51-73 (1960); C. H. Stember, *Education and Attitude Change*, Institute of Human Relations Press, 1961; Rebecca Vreeland and C. E. Bidwell, "Organizational Effects on Student Attitudes: A Study of the Harvard Houses," *Sociology of Education*, **38**, 233-50 (1965). These and other studies are summarized in Newcomb and Feldman, *Impact of College*.

61 A. W. Astin, for example, was able to show that the earlier Knapp studies on the "productivity" of small liberal arts colleges was largely a function of college input ("A Re-examination of College Productivity," *Journal of Educational Psychology*, **52**, 173-78, 1961). For some of the evidence that personality types cluster in different college sub-cultures, see M. Rosenberg, *Occupations and Values*, Free Press, 1957; W. A. Scott, *Values and Organizations*, Rand McNally, 1965; B. Sternberg, "Personality Traits of College Students Majoring in Different Fields," *Psychological Monographs*, **69**, 1-21 (1955); P. C. Teevan, "Personality Correlates of Undergraduate Field of Specialization," *Journal of Consulting Psychology*, **18**, 212-14 (1964); C. E. Bidwell, S. H. King, B. Finnie, and H. A. Scarr, "Undergraduate Careers: Alternatives and Determinants," *School Review*, **71**, 299-316 (1963); D. Brown, "Personality, College Enivronment and Academic Productivity," in *The American College*, ed. N. Sanford, John Wiley, 1962, pp. 536-62; C. MacArthur, "Sub-culture and Personality During the College Years," *Journal of Educational Sociology*, **33**, 260-68 (1960); and Chapter 4 of *The Shape of Catholic Higher Education*.

62 *Ibid.*, Chapter 5.

not change their students so much as they reinforce the formation which has occurred in the home, and to some extent in primary and secondary school.[63] To date, the colleges seem to have been most successful at—to quote the preliminary report of the NORC research— "inculcating precisely those norms already reasonably well accepted among American Catholics." [64] This behavior derives from the historical situation of the group: "Parochial school Catholics perform especially well in those aspects of Catholicism—attendance at Mass, sexual morality, acceptance of authority—that were immensely important to the American Church in the last century." [65] A summary of Catholic college impact a decade hence—one which takes into account the differential effects of various institutions and the subcultures within them—may provide us with dramatically different conclusions. But this will depend in large measure not only on the kinds of socializing experiences available on the Catholic campus— the distinctiveness of the program, the structuring of the curriculum and of student life, the charisma of priests and professors—but on the student input: what kinds of students will go there?

CATHOLIC COLLEGE CLIENTELE

Early in this chapter it was suggested that an increasingly smaller proportion of the Catholics in college will be enrolled in Catholic institutions, in the years to come. There are several reasons for this. For one, it is not at all clear that Catholics will continue to support their colleges as in the past. Founded, as we noted, to defend the faith of their student-clients, the colleges and universities no longer are called upon by an embattled, defensive minority to perform this function. As they have made it in the larger society, Catholics—like other Americans—appear to be more interested in providing their sons and daughters with the kinds of education which will equip them for competition in the status race. And with the wider world view of young Americans who have been exposed to the effects of

---

[63] Greeley and Rossi (*Education of Catholic Americans*) found that the Catholic schools were effective reinforcers of the religious training received in highly religious homes, but had little effect on those from less religious backgrounds. Catholic colleges seemed to make a difference only for those who had attended Catholic grade and high schools. Similar findings are those of Westoff and Potvin, "Family Size"; and Menard, "Effects of Newman."

[64] Greeley *et al.,* "Social Effects," p. 79. But see the similar results for the one Catholic school in the study of "the future of liberal arts colleges," financed by the Carnegie Corp., and directed by Morris Keeton of Antioch College.

[65] *Ibid.*

McLuhan's electronic revolution,[66] colleges resembling their Catholic high schools look less and less attractive.

Further, with the mushrooming of public education, it becomes not only cheaper to commute to the large public urban institutions like CUNY and Illinois at Chicago, but even less expensive to go away to a state institution, than to commute to a Catholic college. As Jencks and Riesman point out, growth in college enrollment during the past generation has been due in large part to the greater number from less educated and less affluent families. Irish and German Catholics who sent their sons to Notre Dame and Georgetown in the 1940's and 'fifties are more inclined now to look to Princeton, Stanford, and Northwestern; and Catholic colleges have lately been attracting more Italian and Polish students—the sons and grandsons of those in the "second wave" of immigration, in the early years of the present century. Commuter colleges, particularly, have drawn them. But these are the institutions which will have most difficulty competing with the new public colleges and junior colleges, particularly since the larger and larger proportions of lay faculty in these schools has meant increased tuition charges.[67] As the Catholic colleges become more and more like their secular counterparts, there are fewer and fewer reasons to pay twice as much for the same education.[68]

Given these developments, many expect the Catholic colleges to become institutions attracting predominantly upper-middle class students, particularly if public funds do not become available to provide scholarships to less advantaged youngsters. More and more of these may come from the more recently arrived ethnic groups, however, as third-and-fourth generation Italian- and Polish-Americans reach the affluence levels of the Irish and German Catholics who

---

[66] Marshall McLuhan, *Understanding Media,* McGraw-Hill, 1965.

[67] Jencks and Riesman provide a useful illustration of how the proportional increase in costs of attending a commuter college are greater than those for a residential institution, since it is tuition which is escalating, compared to relatively moderate increases in room and board. Thus, for the student paying only tuition, incidentals, and transportation, tuition increases mean a much faster rise, proportionately, of his total educational expenses, than comparable tuition increases in schools where students pay room and board and greater travel expenses, as well. For those attending commuter colleges because they are the only places they can afford, the already higher rates of Catholic institutions may become prohibitive with tuition increases.

[68] State aid to Catholic education—or scholarships to students for attending the institutions of their choice—might change this argument, but the recent decisions of the Supreme Court would seem to provide little reason for Catholic educators to count on receiving public funds.

preceded them.[69] Or perhaps not, if the disinterest in Catholic primary and secondary Catholic education that Greeley and Rossi found among Italians is manifested on the college level.[70] But whichever ethnic groups are represented, it is almost certain that the heavy Irish concentration of the past will greatly diminish. Using data provided by Andrew Greeley, Jencks and Riesman show that nearly half of the Irish Catholics in the early 1960's were in Catholic colleges, compared to less than a quarter of the non-Irish Catholics.[71] But as tuitions increase, both the Irish and the other Catholic groups will be less eager to pay Ivy League rates for educations in less posh settings, particularly if the Catholic colleges seem to be providing essentially the same curricular offerings, and if an education including Catholic theology and philosophy is no longer judged essential in the post-Vatican II world. Both the predominantly working-class, commuter schools, then, and the traditionally middle-class colleges, may be hard put to survive by the 1970's and 'eighties.[72]

Even if they can retain a clientele, however, there are many Catholic colleges and universities that will not have the resources to survive as four-year colleges. There is just too much competition. It is instructive to cite here the Jesuit administrator quoted by Neil McCluskey in a recent paper:

---

[69] As an aside, it is interesting to speculate to what extent the Catholic colleges which do continue to attract students—the Georgetowns, Fordhams, Notre Dames—will be changed with the increasing numbers from Italian and Polish families. Not only are students generally more rebellious today, even on the Catholic campuses (E. G. Williamson and J. L. Cowan [*The American Student's Freedom of Expression,* University of Minnesota Press, 1966] report that 70 percent of the Catholic college presidents in their study stated that their students were becoming increasingly more demonstrative), a case might also be made that the greater proportion of students from Italian families will lead to a less-inhibited and docile campus climate than prevailed in the largely Irish-dominated Catholic colleges in the past. Where the Irish mother tends to dominate—at least in the literature of the Irish-Americans—the Italian father is traditionally boss in his family. It is tempting to suggest that Italian males will be more likely to rebel against the institutional authorities, particularly if they are "fathers." Polish students remain an unknown quantity, although the high independence of one group of Polish girls was demonstrated in chapter 4, "Portrait of a Catholic Women's College," in Hassenger, *The Shape of Catholic Higher Education.*

[70] Greeley and Rossi (*Education of Catholic Americans*) found that, even with a control for generation, Italian Catholics were less likely than Irish, Germans, French, or Poles to attend Catholic grade and high schools although the proportions attending did increase, the longer the Italian had been in the United States.

[71] In Chapter 7 of *The Academic Revolution.*

Recently I sat as a member of the Board of Review for the North Central Association. Our task was to evaluate the resources of institutions seeking accreditation for new doctoral programs. Frankly, the experience was shattering! The new state universities (the teachers' colleges of ten years ago) have resources in many areas far beyond those we hope to have. A private institution (I have always considered it second-rate) could point to three gifts from trustees of the institutions. These three gifts were well over twice the total of our first five years priority campaign.[73]

The resources may well exist in a Catholic community largely indistinguishable from other Americans, in socio-economic terms. But whether these will be channeled into Catholic higher education—and if so, into the nearly three hundred colleges and universities—is another question.

One of the recommendations of the NCEA Committee on Catholic Higher Education is that many of the marginal four-year colleges become junior colleges, or pool resources with neighboring institutions. I have elsewhere discussed some of the cooperative ventures in Catholic higher education, and a rather complete description of the programs existing in 1965 can be found in Salerno.[74] Only a few will be mentioned here. Thomas More College within Fordham University (Bronx Campus) enrolls women, and has a lay woman dean, the first in Fordham's history, although the remainder of the undergraduate student body is entirely male. St. Thomas (men) and St. Catherine (women) in Minnesota have exchanged students since 1957, and male St. John's (Collegeville) and female St. Benedict's have more recently inaugurated such a venture. In the Spring of 1967, 115 Notre Dame students were enrolled in 144 courses at St. Mary's, with 171 belles making the trip the other way, to take 243 Notre Dame courses (obviously, the same students tend to

---

72 Some schools may follow the evolution of Chicago's Mundelein College, overwhelmingly Irish in the 1930's, with Italian and Polish girls attending in such numbers in the 1960's that, by 1963, the largest ethnic segment was Polish. But as the College re-structured its program and mission, and acquired additional dormitory space to accommodate more out-of-Chicago students, it underwent further evolution, changing back from a primarily commuter, working-class school, to a heavily resident, middle-class College (see "Portrait of a Catholic Women's College," in Hassenger, *Shape*).

73 Cited in Neil G. McCluskey, S. J., "Vatican II and Catholic Higher Education," talk given at the University of Dayton, February 28, 1967, and published in modified form as "The New Catholic College," *America*, **116**, 414-17 (1967).

74 "The Future Shape of Catholic Higher Education," in Hassenger, *Shape*, pp. 300-301; Sr. M. Dolores Salerno, D. M., "Patterns of Interinstitutional Cooperation in American Catholic Higher Education," *National Catholic Educational Association Bulletin*, **62**(4), 1-31 (May, 1966).

take more than one offering). Every indication is that such cooperative ventures will continue, and perhaps be expanded. But it often seems as though the men's colleges and universities are more eager for this than their counterparts, which would appear to have at least as much—if not more—to gain. Many of the women's colleges, especially those located near front-rank Catholic universities, apparently fear that cooperation will lead to absorbtion; they are also concerned, quite legitimately, about what will become of the bottom half of a faculty, people who are typically not qualified to teach in a university, and yet to whom the college has some moral obligations. Often such people would be qualified to teach lower division courses—more so than the increasing numbers of graduate students who are pushed into instruction as institutions on the make begin to garner more research funds—but this would mean giving up "their" courses, and teaching freshmen and sophomores (who may well, of course, be brighter and more sophisticated than the upperclassmen they have been teaching). If such problems can be solved, it is likely that we shall see even more articulation, and some amalgamation, in the years ahead.

This may not improve the colleges' atmospheric conditions, nor increase the impact on their students. Schools which do seem to have an unmistakable effect on their students are those which have allocated considerable resources to just this end.[75] If Catholic schools fail to exert the influence many feel they should have,[76] it may well be due to an inability to provide the necessary funds, which have gone to bolster graduate programs.

GRADUATE EDUCATION

Although post-baccalaureate programs seem to be attracting an increasingly larger proportion of the available funds, Catholic graduate education has not, even recently, been impressive. Although 26 Catholic institutions award either the Master's or Ph.D., only twenty graduate departments were ranked in the recent Cartter

---

[75] By most criteria, such schools as Amherst, Antioch, Bennington, Oberlin, Reed, Sarah Lawrence, Shimer, and Swarthmore. See G. G. Stern, "Characteristics of the Intellectual Climate in College Environments," *Harvard Educational Review,* **33**, 5-41 (1963).

[76] See R. Hassenger, "A Rationale for Changing Student Values," *Educational Record,* **48**, 61-67 (1967).

survey,[77] with but three of these considered outstanding.[78] Not a single social science department in a Catholic graduate school was ranked.[79] This is reflected in the paucity of research and scholarship money that has been available to Catholic graduate programs. Of 775 fellowships distributed by the National Science Foundation in 1956, only 17 went to Catholic colleges; in 1957, 19 out of 845 fellowships were awarded to students from Catholic schools. In 1962, no Catholic university ranked among the top 75 recipients of federal research money, and three of the four in the first 100 had medical schools, which obtained the largest share of this money.[80] Nor has the situation improved much since: the data available from the National Science Foundation as late as 1965 would indicate that Catholic schools are no better off than in 1962.[81] Only 147 of 5,996

---

[77] Allan M. Cartter, *An Assessment of Quality in Graduate Education,* American Council on Education, 1966. Notre Dame led the list of Catholic schools in total departments listed, with six (chemistry, English, history, mathematics, philosophy, and physics); St. Louis was next, with five (bacteriology-microbiology, biochemistry, English, philosophy, and physiology). Four departments were ranked at Fordham (Classics, English, French, and philosophy); there were three at Catholic University (Classics, French, and Spanish), and two at Georgetown (astronomy and pharmacology). No other Catholic graduate departments were considered strong enough to be awarding Ph.D. degrees.

[78] Spanish at Catholic University, biochemistry at St. Louis, and Chemistry at Notre Dame were rated "Good." The levels in this survey were "Distinguished," usually only a handful of programs; "Strong," the next 8 to 10; "Good," 10 or 12 departments in major fields; and "Adequate Plus," meaning they were considered worthy of granting Ph.D.'s.

[79] Suggesting that, if Catholics made their peace with Galileo and Darwin, it took somwhat longer for Durkheim, Weber, Freud, and Skinner.

[80] From Jencks and Riesman, *Academic Revolution,* who cite the House Committee on Education and Labor, *The Federal Government and Education,* Washington, 1963. The medical schools of Georgetown and St. Louis contain some of the ranked departments at these institutions, but are rumored to be considerable financial drains on these universities. One of the tragedies of heavy professional school commitment in many Catholic institutions is the wrong reasons for this involvement, historically; some struggling Catholic colleges at the turn of the century hankered after instant university standing, doing so by buying up nearly-bankrupt dentistry, pharmacy, medical, and law schools. Today, these provide nothing distinctively "Catholic," and take great expenditures to remain up-to-date. They do allow fund-raisers in urban Jesuit institutions to appeal to civic pride and pragmatism, however, telling the local or state citzenry that "half of the lawyers in——are the products of ——."

[81] National Science Foundation, *Federal Support for Academic Science and Other Educational Activities in Universities and Colleges, Fiscal Year 1965.* Even Notre Dame was not among the top 100 grant and contract recipients.

National Defense Education Act Fellowships were allocated to Catholic universities in 1966-67, less than three percent of the total.[82] But this is not surprising, considering the fact that Catholic schools award only about three percent of the nation's doctorates.[83]

The Greeley data indicate that Catholics now go to graduate school in proportion to their numbers in the U.S. population.[84] And all available evidence shows that they persist to the Ph.D.[85] Jencks and Riesman estimate that, even if all doctoral candidates in Catholic universities were themselves Catholics—and an actual count would most likely show that about 75-80 percent are [86]—only a third of the Catholic Ph.D. candidates would be accounted for, indicating that about two-thirds are seeking degrees in non-Catholic graduate departments.[87]

One of the reasons for this is undoubtedly that the professionally-oriented faculty in Catholic colleges often feel obliged to suggest that their best students go to the ranking graduate departments.[88] These have not been in Catholic universities. One seems to find today that the graduate departments in the best of the Catholic universities pull students from the less visible Catholic liberal arts colleges, such as St. Ambrose, Rockhurst, St. Thomas, or the Marymounts, and from second-level Catholic universities (e.g., Fairfield, Detroit). Perhaps Fordham, St. Louis, and Notre Dame are attractive to those who have spent four years in less exciting college climates; but the best of the Fordham, St. Louis, and Notre Dame undergraduates head off for Berkeley, Chicago, and Harvard. (And

---

82 Numbers, for the leaders: Notre Dame, 45; Catholic University, 40.

83 Compared to 11 percent of all B.A.'s, 8 percent of the M.A.'s, and 7 percent of the professional degrees. National Catholic Welfare Conference, *Summary of Catholic Education,* 1963; U.S. Office of Education, *Digest of Educational Statistics,* 1965. According to J. L. Chase and Marguerite G. Wensel ("Doctor's Degrees Awarded in All U.S. Institutions: By State and By Institutions," U.S. Department of Health, Education, and Welfare, 1964), only Catholic University, Notre Dame, Fordham, and St. Louis are among the top 50 producers of Ph.D.'s. Even the three percent figure represents a significant increase over a decade earlier, however,

84 *Religion and Career.*

85 S. Warkov and A. M. Greeley, "Parochial School Origins and Educational Achievement," *American Sociological Review,* **31,** 406-14 (1966).

86 The proportion at the Catholic universities with which the writer is familiar, including Notre Dame, where 98.5% of the *under*graduates are Catholic.

87 In Chapter 7 of *Academic Revolution.*

88 And it appears that faculty at Catholic institutions play a crucial role in orienting students toward graduate school. See A. M. Greeley, "Criticism of Undergraduate Faculty by Graduates of Catholic Colleges," *Review of Religious Research,* **6,** 97-106 (1965).

often come back with shiny Ph.D.'s to Fordham, St. Louis, and Notre Dame, and send their best students to Berkeley, Chicago, and Harvard.)

Some, of course, believe that the Catholic graduate school has a distinctive mission. One spokesman asserted that

a university is incomplete without a theology department, and . . . only in a true university which encompasses the complete spectrum of scholarly pursuits can an embryonic scholar absorb the proper view of his own subject and its place in the totality of man's knowledge. Perhaps only in Catholic graduate schools can the competent, committed Catholic scholar and future teacher be trained.[89]

Most young Catholics with professional orientations would disagree, holding that any "synthesizing" of Christian principles and "secular" knowledge can only be done after a complete grounding in an academic discipline, requiring the best possible preparation, which is rarely to be found in the Catholic university. The social sciences, especially, have so recently fought loose from the past encroachments of philosophy and theology that there would seem to be real disadvantages accruing to any attempts at a premature synthesis. What is perhaps more significant, many young scholars who are Catholics in belief and practice are concerned to separate their professional work as far as possible from their religious commitments. These are the people who often suggest throwing out all but a small number of doctoral programs in Catholic higher education, to concentrate on top-quality sequences in a handful of universities.[90] But—unfortunately, from the point of view of the present writer— this is unlikely to happen, for at least six hard-nosed reasons.

First, graduate school attendance has never been higher. The number of people taking the Graduate Record Examination for admission to graduate school—not counting exams for professional schools, nor the GRE's taken at many schools as part of their institutional testing programs—jumped from 57,922 in 1962-63 to 81,768 in 1963-64, and 106,100 to 1964-65[91] No doubt many take the examinations without actually enrolling. But some of those who take the exams as part of the institutional testing programs have

---

[89] J. F. Mulligan, S. J., "The Catholic Campus Today," *Commonweal,* **83,** 499 (1966).

[90] Not only "secularized" Catholics make such recommendations: The NCEA research team—including Paul Reinert, S. J., President of St. Louis University—come out for this in their *Report.* See also James M. Lee (ed.) *Catholic Education in the Western World,* Notre Dame Press, 1967.

[91] Educational Testing Service, *Annual Reports: 1964-65,* E.T.S., 1966, pp. 81-82.

their scores forwarded to graduate schools, and a few graduate programs do not require the GRE's, preferring such measures as the Miller Analogies Test. With this fantastic jump in the graduate school-going—and the usefulness of graduate school to extend the moratorium on commitment, or to avoid a trip to Southeast Asia—it would be unrealistic to expect Catholic colleges and second-rate universities with higher aspirations not to start still more graduate programs.

Second, even those universities with fairly good programs have their sights set on higher things. Whatever "excellence" is, it seems to be currently denoted by foundation grants and research projects, which go to institutions with the men who prefer to concentrate on training graduate students. There are a lot of indications that this situation is at least partly dysfunctional for the over-all educational picture, as the Berkeley rebels would be the first to insist.[92] Nevertheless, it *is* the name of the game, as presently played, and it would be naive in the extreme to expect those Catholic university presidents who have this kind of "excellence" within their grasp to pull out of the race now.

Third, some suggest with Wallis that those schools which confine their efforts to undergraduates will become, in effect, prep schools for the universities.[93]

Fourth, there is the eminently pragmatic consideration of the need to staff the myriad of second-rate Catholic colleges and universities. The vast majority of these will, alas, not amalgamate, coordinate, or disappear, whatever the recommendations of the planners,[94] and faculty will probably continue to come predominantly from Catholic universities.

Fifth, graduate students provide cheap help for teaching the huge freshman classes of schools on the make. A university like St. John's on Long Island *needs* graduate programs, not only for its

---

[92] One of the dangers in rating graduate schools, as in the Cartter Report and its predecessors, is that institutions and departments on the edge of that kind of excellence are constrained to follow the "tried-and-true" path to this exalted state, and become fearful of innovative programs.

[93] W. A. Wallis, "The Plight of the Small College," *Atlantic,* **216,** 126 (November, 1965). Jaques Barzun would agree with—and lament—this line of reasoning: "College to University—and After," *The American Scholar,* **33,** 212-219 [1964].

[94] NCEA *Report,* 1967.

pretensions to intellectual respectability, but to staff the many course sections required by their penchant for bigness.[95]

Sixth, despite the changing patterns of control in Catholic higher education (about which more below), religious orders will be heavily involved for the foreseeable future, and many members with more pastoral than intellectual concerns will prefer less rigorous programs or second-rate doctoral programs. In addition, it will probably be less expensive for orders to send the majority of their men to Catholic schools, where rebates on tuition usually exist.

This is not an inspiring list of reasons for continued graduate departments in Catholic higher education; but the writer believes they are more cogent ones, in 1967, than those Mulligan suggests.

One cannot resist entering the hope, however, that graduate programs would be cut back in most Catholic universities, and that the availability of government and foundation grants does not determine the shape graduate education takes. It would be ironic, indeed, if the Catholic colleges within a few major universities which are presently considerably superior to the graduate schools in the same institutions—at least in the students they attract, for the best of them go to leading graduate schools, while the Catholic graduate programs are attended in large part by the products of second-rate Catholic colleges—will not suffer while graduate sequences are begun higglety-pigglety. Some of the graduate schools seem to be building their social science departments, particularly, in a helter-skelter manner, depending on what kinds of research funds are available, following a main chance kind of curricular philosophy. It would be tragic if the best of the undergraduate programs began to suffer, in this mad scramble for top twenty membership.

Catholic universities should strengthen their doctoral sequences to be sure—particularly do the social sciences need drastic upgrading. But they must resign themselves to the impossibility of providing programs in every conceivable area, and map out some kind of strategy whereby the best men in an area concentrate in one institution, avoiding needless duplication and the spreading thin of resources. While such duplication is no monopoly of Catholic graduate education, institutions with limited resources must be especially prudent, and must give up trying to compete in every graduate discipline. They have something to learn from the seven English

---

[95] Full-time enrollment increased from about 6,000 in 1946 to about 12,000 in 1965 (from "Academic Freedom and Tenure: St. John's University," *Bulletin of the American Association of University Professors,* **52,** 12-19 [Spring, 1966]). Enrollment in 1966-67 was down in the wake of the St. John's controversy.

universities formed in the 1960's; each of the institutions is building in some areas only, having abandoned the notion that each school has to offer every academic discipline.[96] One of the developments which may contribute to more rational planning in the Consortium of Universities in the Washington Metropolitan Area, with five participating institutions: American University, Catholic University, Georgetown, George Washington, and Howard. Cooperation at the graduate level will work for the upgrading of programs without unnecessary new facilities, the elimination of duplication so that each school may specialize in greater depth, and the over-all improvement of graduate study and research.

More such ventures—and some radical surgery—will be necessary if Catholic graduate education is to decently survive.

FACULTY

Less need be said about the faculty in Catholic colleges, since John Donovan has treated this topic at greater length elsewhere in some depth.[97] But it is essential to point out a few things here, to put in perspective the discussions of lay-clerical relations, and the changing patterns of institutional control, which follow.

In his discussion of the "changing functions" of the college professor, Robert Knapp suggested that the academician has historically been called upon to perform three tasks: teaching, research, and character-building.[98] In Catholic higher education, character-build-

---

96 E. g., Sussex, York, Warwick. While they are at it, they might look at the new way Sussex is structured, and the radical innovations which link faculty and students in schools, not departments (see D. Daiches, *The Idea of a New University*, Andre Deutsch, London, 1964). They might also think about offering graduate programs building on what Daniel Bell terms the "third tier" (*The Reforming of General Education*, Columbia, 1966, pp. 208 ff.), and would get some help here by reading W. Arrowsmith "The Future of Teaching," *The Public Interest*, 6, 53-67 (Winter, 1967).

Many Catholic universities should not attempt to offer graduate programs in theology, for which they are not equipped. It may well be, however, that they can offer courses which do not lead to a degree, but which bear on already existing degree programs. At Seton Hall, for example, Visiting Professor Barry Ulanov offers a course in the "Theological Dimensions of Contemporary Literature," to those in the graduate English program. Similar courses could be offered in the major secular universities which contain church-sponsored cluster colleges, which might be the only "theology" courses Catholics in such institutions would take.

97 John Donovan, *The Catholic Academic Man.*

98 Robert H. Knapp, "Changing Functions of the College Professor," in *The American College*, ed. Nevitt Sanford, John Wiley, 1962, pp. 290-311.

ing almost certainly held sway during the years when the "colleges" would more accurately have been called high schools; teaching probably moved to the fore around the turn of the century, when the Catholic Educational Association was formed;[99] and research has begun to loom large during the last decade. Faculty can be discussed in this context. Greeley describes the Catholic academic men he knows as the "new professors" and the "old professors." [100] This is of course an over-simplification, and Greeley is careful to point out that age is not the only variable here. But these ideal types can be used as heuristic devices for dramatizing some of the changes which are taking place.

Donovan found that the Catholic professors he studied had typically been good boys: "responsible, obedient, cooperative, and moderately ambitious." [101] Frequently aspiring to the priesthood during adolescence, a large proportion turned to teaching only after either ordination or a decision to leave the seminary. Many of Greeley's "old professors" seem to have had this sort of background, with a B.A. from either seminaries or the Catholic schools to which they returned to teach, after M.A.'s or Ph.D.'s from the same or another Catholic institution. Often given a position during the years when they were feeling some financial pinch—most likely because strict adherence to Catholic teaching meant growing families—these men felt a definite gratitude to the religious orders administering their institutions. (As Donovan shows, these professors tended to stay at the school where they first took positions.) The "new professor," on the other hand, is likely to have received his Ph.D. from a secular—often a leading—institution, and has been socialized to the values and rewards of his academic guild.[101a] What Greeley terms "his mobility, his professionalism, and his aloofness" set him

---

[99] Gleason, "Historical Perspective."

[100] Greeley, *Changing Catholic College.*

[101] John Donovan, *The Academic Man in the Catholic College,* Sheed & Ward, 1964, p. 85. For an indication that Catholic college professors—at least those in the Boston area—may still be more "responsible and obedient" than their secular school counterparts, see David J. Armor and his colleagues' unpublished paper, "Professors' Attitudes Toward the Vietnam War," Department of Social Relations, Harvard University.

[101a] Although these men, too, are more likely than their fellow doctoral candidates to have returned to the institution where they spent their undergraduate years. See Pattilo and Mackenzie, *Church-Sponsored Higher Education,* p. 110

apart from the "old professors," and are associated with a much greater interest in research.[102]

Even their backgrounds are different. As Gleason shows, utilizing the data of Donovan and Greeley to provide some telling comparisons, the student in a Catholic college in 1961 was three times more likely than his professor to be the son of a college-educated man (44% against 13%); only one-third of Donovan's professors of an older generation had professional or managerial fathers, compared to a majority of the 1961 Catholic college students.[103] In addition, the Donovan sample derived largely from the first of the Catholic immigrant groups, the Irish. These background factors have undoubtedly led to the difference orientations characterizing the "old" and "new" faculty. Donovan showed that interest in research was associated with having a college-educated father, particularly if he was a professional man.[104] Furthermore, the authority relationship with one's parents seemed to be crucial to the later academic values of an individual, with those coming from mother-dominated homes more interested in teaching, while those from homes where the fathers were family heads were oriented more toward research.[105] Although it is difficult to find supporting data, a number of social scientists have suggested that Irish families are especially prone to mother-domination. Whether or not the reader agrees with the last comment, there seem nonetheless to be several background differences between the "old" and "new" professors, and it is not too long a leap to suggest that they will approach their careers differently.[106]

The danger of painting in such broad strokes is obvious: much embellishment becomes impossible. Another risk is the possibility that a picture results which is not exactly the one intended. The

---

102 Chapter 7. For another indication of the importance of age, in dividing the "old" from the "new" professors—in this case, regardless of whether they were sisters or lay men and women—see chapter 4 of Hassenger, *Shape of Catholic Higher Education*. It sometimes seems that the "mobility, professionalism, and aloofness" to which Greeley refers here are the very qualities celebrated by Harvey Cox (*Secular City*), despite Greeley's differences with Cox (see Part III, "The *Commonweal* Debate," in D. Callahan [ed.], *The Secular City Debate*, Macmillan, 1966).

103 Gleason, "Historical Perspective," pp. 29-30. The Greeley data are from *Religion and Career*.

104 *Academic Man*, p. 141.

105 *Ibid.*, p. 145.

106 And it is of course to the point to note that considerable cultural changes have occurred: the "new professors" have grown up in a quite different climate than did the "old professors."

above should not be construed as suggesting that two distinct cultures are to be found on the Catholic campus; one of teaching-oriented, religious and fatherly locals, the other of research-minded, hip and professional cosmopolitans.[107] The Catholic professorial community is probably characterized by less antagonism and oneupmanship than most groves of academe. The high salaries which a young man with a quality Ph.D. can command have helped to raise the pay of those who outrank him, although they may have started at half his beginning salary (and would usually be able to command less in the current market); and the community which obtains in most Catholic colleges is most likely to blunt any incipient antagonism between the younger and older academicians.

Catholic college faculty can be dichotomized another way, however—into lay and religious—which is also a useful analytic device, but one fraught with even greater dangers with regard to oversimplification. We have some data at our disposal, here. The Donovan work seemed to show that laymen—particularly if trained in a non-Catholic graduate school—were more likely than the priest-professors in his sample to have primarily a research orientation.[108] The more strongly Catholic a family was, the less likely were the son-professors to be interested in research,[109] leading Donovan to suggest that strong religious influences inhibited the development of research values, and fostered a teaching orientation.[110]

But other factors operate to polarize these two groups—or at least have, historically. Almost four-fifths of the lay professors in Donovan's sample indicated that "lay-religious" problems were the

---

[107] To use Gouldner's terms. See Alvin Gouldner, "Cosmopolitans and Locals: Toward an Analysis of Latent Social Roles," *Administrative Science Quarterly,* **2,** 281-306 and 444-480 (1957-58). In fact, Catholic scholarship still leaves something to be desired. See the unimpressive record of faculty publication in major journals and receipt of government and foundation grants summarized in John H. Smith, "The Greater Glory: Scholarship and the Catholic University," in L.C. Vaccaro (ed.), *Toward New Dimensions of Catholic Higher Education,* Education Research Associates, 1967, pp. 37-55.

[108] *Academic Man,* Chapter 6.

[109] Which may help to explain the clerics' lack of research interest, since greater familial religiosity may also have led to entering the priesthood, and to Catholic school attendance for non-clerics. Greeley and Rossi (*Educ. of Cath. Americans*) found that family religiosity was a crucial predictor variable, when investigating the effectiveness of Catholic education.

[110] *Academic Man,* p. 145. Most likely it did not encourage an open-minded questioning, although the heavy teaching loads and low rewards of the system when these older men were starting out, and the broader social-economic forces of the 1930's, almost certainly had something to do with it.

chief source of frustration in their academic lives, compared to less than one-fifth of the religious faculty.[111] Almost 50 percent of the lay academicians felt that they were "second-class citizens," "necessary evils," and "without any significant voice." Greeley found some of the same criticisms, in his 1965 tour of Catholic colleges and universities.[112] Before turning to the very complex question of lay-clerical relations, at least a few things ought to be said about the priest-scholar.

It is perhaps inevitable that a layman writing on Catholic higher education concentrate on the problems of himself, his friends, and his senior lay colleagues (who are often, as suggested above, his own teachers from undergraduate days). But honesty will also compel him to point out that, whatever the atrocities of yesteryear—and the remnants of authoritarianism in such places as St. John's University on Long Island, and San Diego College for Women [113]—the current situation is a quite different one. Compensation in the best of the schools is at the B+ AAUP level, with promises of A— in the foreseeable future.[114] The teaching load is nine hours in the major institutions, with reductions if engaged in research. Already at least Fordham and Notre Dame are talking about standard six-hour loads in the years immediately ahead. If fringe benefits and

---

[111] *Ibid.,* pp. 183-84.

[112] *Changing Catholic College.* There were about thirty Catholic schools in the Greeley sample.

[113] St. Johns is discussed in the *AAUP Bulletin* and in John Leo, "The Faculty," in Hassenger, *Shape of Catholic Higher Education,* pp. 193-201; the San Diego case is referred to in *ibid.,* pp. 231 and 314-15.

[114] In 1966-67, the average AAUP Compensation Scales for the first four categories looked like this:

	AA	A	B	C
Professor	$24,510	$19,630	$15,630	$12,720
Associate	14,790	12,790	11,170	9,680
Assistant	11,210	9,890	8,810	7,840
Instructor	8,420	7,560	6,920	6,380

Source. AAUP Bulletin, 52, 151 (Summer, 1966).

Boston College led the list of Catholic schools in 1966-67, with an average of $12,108 total compensation for full-time faculty. Notre Dame was close behind, with $12,022. Catholic and other church-related colleges showed a greater percentage increase between 1965-66 and 1966-67 than did any other type of institution. In 1965-66, the total compensation figure at Boston College was $10,705, and at Notre Dame, $11,492. Thus, Boston College increased dramatically during that time period. Other total compensation figures for 1966-67: Santa Clara, $11,610; Catholic University, $11,560; Loyola of Los Angeles, $11,329; Detroit, $11,308; Marquette, $11,087; Georgetown, $10,825; Fordham, $10,824. *Source. AAUP Bulletin, 53,* (Summer, 1967).

academic citizenship have been slower in coming, every indication is that these, too, are close at hand.[115]

With this relative affluence of living and opportunity, it often happens that the special problems of the priest-professor are overlooked. But the suggestion can be made that, whatever the situation in the not-too-distant past, today's scholar—the "new professor" at least—is more free and has fewer problems than his clerical counterpart. For one thing, there is a rather general feeling on most Catholic campuses—among students and faculty (even religious) alike—that he is professionally inferior to his lay colleague. ("He" may of course be "she," but the faculty in coeducational universities is overwhelmingly male, and those in the Catholic women's colleges seems to be either "old professors" or Ph.D. candidates who depart the school upon donning the doctoral hood; the young sisters, especially, are often as well prepared as the best of these.) [116] For another, a religious faculty member is likely to be overworked, expected by his superiors, as Greeley put it, with only some caricature, to "teach twelve hours of class during the regular year as well as in summer session, hear confessions and say Mass on the weekend, moderate a Sodality, prefect a corridor of a residence hall, give nuns' retreats, teach a special course for a contemplative community, and serve as assistant sexton in the college chapel." [117] This, despite his Chicago or Princeton degree. Third, the cleric often has no contract and no tenure, and can be moved across the country if the "needs of the order"—which may mean a variety of things: it can be used to ship off the obstreperous—require it. (Or he may be appointed department head without seeking or even wanting it.) Fourth, the priest-professor is more likely than the typical lay scholar to be sought out by students for discussion of personal problems. And, if

---

[115] For example, only $1,025 and $1,010 at Boston College and Notre Dame, respectively, represented fringe benefits, such as faculty retirement. At Stanford and Northwestern, universities with which leading Catholic schools like to compare themselves, total compensation figures were $16,947 and $15,677, respectively, with $1,827 and $1,778 in fringe benefits. And a good liberal arts college, such as Earlham in Indiana, had a lower total compensation figure ($11,124) than either Boston College or Notre Dame, but paid $1,763 in fringe benefits, directly comparable to Northwestern, even though salaries at Northwestern are much higher. Newly established faculty senates may take care of some of the academic citizenship problems.

[116] And the women have been so long discriminated against that the sister or lay woman teaching in the university often seems to have to be better qualified than either priests or laymen.

[117] *Changing Catholic College*, pp. 7-40.

the new student mood [118] means that undergraduates are today more selective about whom they seek out, the most professional of the priest-scholars may be the very ones most sought after, by students who value competence.[119] Then there is the fascinating game of order politics, for those living in religious communities. More than one bright and ambitious cleric has found himself the victim of a conspiracy by an order clique who decide to "teach him humility," or, more honestly, to slow down or impede his rise to a position of greater visibility. It is interesting to speculate how many enlightened and progressive college presidents have been ambushed this way, *en route.* Finally here—there are probably many more difficulties, about which the layman is entirely innocent—the problem of censorship must be worried about. If more and more priest-scholars are ignoring an *imprimatur,* the threat of censorship or political repercussions must always be calculated. Not only work which might be construed as "dangerous to faith or morals," or even "imprudent," must be considered; the young cleric must also estimate the consequences of signing even a public letter or petition, which may be looked upon with disfavor by his typically more cautious superiors. All of these should be kept in mind, as discussion turns to the administration of Catholic colleges and universities.

ADMINISTRATION

It is virtually impossible to treat the administrative side of Catholic higher education without discussion of lay-clerical relations. This is seen in the most recent of the few studies of administration in Catholic colleges, by Andrew Greeley.[120] There is no need to rehearse the Greeley findings; they will be widely-discussed by the time the present volume appears. What will be said below will presume an at least general familiarity with the research of the NORC team.

If one word had to be chosen to describe the typical Catholic college administration, it would have to be "paternalism." [121] This is surely the most accurate description of the historical patterns of administrative control, and can still be found on more than a few

---

118 The reader is referred to the contribution of Hassenger and G. Rauch to *The Shape of Catholic Higher Education* (Chapter 7C).

119 See "Competence, the 'Pro,' and the Catholic College Student," by R. Hassenger, in *National Catholic Guidance Conference Journal,* **10**, 233-34 (Spring, 1966).

120 *Changing Catholic College.*

121 Meant to embrace its other form, "maternalism," as well.

Catholic campuses. Nor is this surprising. Not only were the administrators "fathers," but it was *their school:* one of their order founded it, past legions had devoted their lives to it, many were enshrined in buildings, scholarships, and trophies, and some were even buried on the grounds.

The Catholic colleges were founded to "save the faith" of young Catholic men and women, at a time when they were members of a distinct minority in the United States.[122] When higher learning was a virtual monopoly of the clergy among American Catholics—and at first, French or French-trained clergy—it was to be expected that the religious orders administering the colleges would define their roles in largely paternal terms. Thus, when Greeley describes paternalism as "the notion that the head of a given institution is responsible for all the decisions to be made in the institution and must himself provide for the welfare of those under him who are incapable of assuming any but the most minimal responsibilities," [123] those mindful of history will recognize this as not entirely inappropriate to the Catholic colleges of the late nineteenth century. (Nor is it specific to Catholic institutions, even in 1967.)

But paternalism is of course wholly anachronistic in the mid-twentieth century. When the administration of a Catholic women's college can cite a "master-servant" relationship in the California labor code as a partial basis for its justification in dismissing two lay instructors,[124] it seems fair to inquire what century they think they are in.[125]

The reference to communities of religious men and women is not gratuitous. It is, in fact, essential for understanding the present state of the question over "control" of Catholic higher education. Greeley found that "somewhere between three-fifths and two-thirds of the college presidents (they) interviewed would fall into the category of being good men from the religious order's viewpoint but not from the educational institution's viewpoint." [126] Qualities which would be appropriate to one who has taken vows of poverty,

---

122 See Leo R. Ward, *New Life in Catholic Schools,* Herder & Co., 1958.

123 In Chapter 8 of *Changing Catholic College.*

124 As did San Diego College for Women in the Spring of 1966 (see *National Catholic Reporter,* May 11, 1966).

125 One wag, speaking of the hopeless blundering which characterized a Catholic administration's dealings with its restive faculty, and the regulations governing life in at least one province of this order, suggested that: "They're fifty years ahead of their time: they live in 1850, and run——like it was 1900."

126 On page 88, *Changing Catholic College.*

chastity and obedience—especially the third—seem to have been looked for when the presidents Greeley describes were selected. In addition, selection is often in spite of a man's lack of interest in academic administration; as Greeley estimated, "perhaps 40 to 50 percent of the presidents, vice-presidents, and deans that we interviewed sincerely wanted to get out of their jobs." [127] Religious orders —particularly those in the monastic tradition—are structured by line authority. Docility to those who have the commission of religious office is observed.[128] Many of the difficulties facing Catholic higher education in the past quarter-century stem from an incomplete separation of the university community from the religious community. It is important to realize, in this connection, that little direct financial assistance has actually been provided to the college by the Church and its religious orders. Pattillo and Mackenzie found that less than half of the 339 Catholic colleges for which they had data received educational or general income from church sources, while about 12 percent received less than a tenth of their income from religious orders [129] What support is available is nearly always in the form of contributed services: three-fifths of the Catholic schools reported more than 10 percent of their educational and general income could be attributed to this indirect type of support (Table 5).

With the rapid growth of the large Catholic universities, and their increasing emphasis on graduate training and research, it is primarily the women's colleges that most depend on contributed services. Pattillo and Mackenzie reported that 91 out of the total teaching and administrative staff of Rosary College in 1964-65 were sisters of the Dominican order; this can be compared to the 119 of 608 full-time St. Louis University faculty who were Jesuits in 1965, and to the less than ten percent of the Notre Dame faculty who

---

[127] *Ibid.*, p. 8.10. Some of us who have done research on religious communities have been struck with a new style among the novices and scholastic (priests-to-be). The heroes of many of these seem to be King, Kennedy, and such social actionists as Michael Harrington and Saul Alinsky, and they appear to be joining religious orders like the Viatorians for the same reasons that their peers choose VISTA or the Peace Corps. In at least some of the orders re-tooling for "pastoral"—instead of intellectual—work on the campus, such a trend may increase.

[128] Indeed, for some, it seems that accession to the superior's chair is believed to confer a special kind of infallibility, and perhaps even special grace. Those in the Protestant tradition who become college presidents or bishops do not have such confidence (although there are parallels among some of the older generation of Negro college presidents).

[129] *Church-Sponsored Higher Education*, p. 45.

TABLE 5 PERCENTAGE OF EDUCATIONAL AND GENERAL INCOME OF ROMAN CATHOLIC INSTITUTIONS RECEIVED IN CONTRIBUTED SERVICES [a]

Percentage of Income	N	%
0	9	2.6
1-5	13	3.8
6-10	25	7.4
11-25	94	27.7
26-50	94	27.7
51-75	17	5.0
Over 75	5	1.5
Percentage not indicated	82	24.2
Total	339	100.0

[a] From M. M. Pattillo, Jr. and Donald M. Mackenzie, *Church-Sponsored Higher Education in the United States,* American Council on Education, 1966.

were Fathers of the Holy Cross.[130] Or again, there were 61 Jesuits, two other priests and 105 lay professors at Fordham in 1950; but in 1964, there were 99 Jesuits, 10 other priests, and 202 lay men and women. Laymen have held an increasing number of departmental chairmanships over the past decade, in major universities, and even begin to show up as chairmen in small Catholic women's colleges.[131]

---

[130] *Los Angeles Times,* February 21 and 23, 1966. With the respectable salaries now being paid by the major Catholic universities, however, the contributed services of even a relative few may add up to a considerable sum; it was estimated that the contributed services of the Congregation of the Holy Cross to Notre Dame amounted to about half a million dollars in 1965-66. David Riesman and Christopher Jencks note that some orders, "through whatever bookkeeping, think they make money from teaching in colleges, using this then to support the mother house or the seminary, with money turned back from contributed services and perhaps expecting retirement funds to take care of themselves when the time comes" (letter to the writer from Riesman, April 17, 1967).

[131] In both cases, it is more accurate to call these "heads," not "chairmen," since they are still appointed by administrations, not elected by colleagues. Many of those in the smaller schools seem to have no increments in salary, and often no secretarial help. Indeed, it would appear that the young laymen proudly taking over the headships of departments in such schools are getting too committed to such institutions, because their work loads increase enormously, and this takes the time they might be spending on the research and publication which would enable them to move on, to the more high-powered

In many ways, laymen in Catholic colleges are moving out of their roles as second class citizens; and in some sense, they are more free than young clerics, as has already been mentioned. When this chapter was being written, several leading Catholic universities were preparing to take steps which would solve the problems of the relationship between university and religious community.

In early 1967, a flurry of announcements heralded long-overdue changes in the boards of control at a number of Catholic colleges and universities. Although laymen had been represented on some boards of trustees for some time—Earl J. McGrath reports that at least six Catholic schools had lay representation on their boards even before the turn of the century [131a]—only a score or so had appointed laymen by 1940. But between a third and one-half of the Catholic institutions had laymen on their boards by 1967.[131b] Most likely to have lay trustees by 1967 were colleges and universities sponsored by a diocese or by an order of religious brothers.[131c] Ninety-four percent of the diocesan colleges in the McGrath sample had or would by 1968 have laymen on their boards, compared to eighty percent of those sponsored by brothers, and about two-fifths of those run by priests or sisters. A similar pattern is seen when the proportion of lay representation on present trustee boards is examined; McGrath found that about half of the boards of schools sponsored by dioceses were laymen, compared to 42% on boards of colleges run by brothers, and about a third at priest- and sister-sponsored institutions. Two-thirds of the responding schools which had no lay representation in 1967 indicated their plans to add laymen in the future. If they do, approximately eighty percent of the Catholic colleges would have some kind of lay participation in governance.

---

colleges and universities many of them long for. Some of the better older men, who concentrate on teaching rather than research, receive higher salaries and hold higher rank than they would command at a major university, where students might be more exciting.

[131a] Earl J. McGrath and Gerald E. Dupont, S.S.E., "The Future Governance of Catholic Higher Education in the United States." Unpublished paper, Institute of Higher Education, Columbia University, 1967.

[131b] Of the approximately 250 colleges and universities primarily for lay men and women, 168 four-year schools, and 20 junior colleges, responded to the request by McGrath and Dupont with usable data. This represents about three-quarters of the institutions queried.

[131c] It is perhaps not too cynical to point out here that these are most likely the types of institutions which most needed help, since relatively few secular priests or religious brothers have had experience in administering higher education institutions, and there is simply not the man- and woman-power available to, say, the Jesuits or Sisters of Mercy.

But reorganization schemes differ considerably. Three types of presently existing boards will be discussed here.

Although it is difficult to obtain accurate information as to just what steps are being taken in some universities, it seems that a number of Catholic schools are simply "expanding" their boards of control to "include" laymen for the first time (usually three or four on an average twelve to fifteen board members). Such institutions as John Carroll, Holy Cross and Fairfield—all Jesuit schools—are apparently only taking "exploratory steps" as this is written (Spring, 1967).

Much more dramatic are the changes announced for Webster College, in the St. Louis suburb of Webster Groves. If approved, the Webster reorganization would involve a yielding of the trusteeship of the College by the Sisters of Loretto, who founded Webster in 1915; the women's college would be turned over to an autonomous board of lay trustees. Webster's President, Jacqueline Grennan, stated that a mixed board of sisters and laymen would "still leave responsibility within the congregation," and she believes that "the very nature of *higher* education is opposed to juridical control by the Church."[132] If this change is finalized, other developments will undoubtedly follow, such as becoming closely tied to a major secular institution. Many wonder what it will mean for the College to become, in Miss Grennan's words, "a legally secular institution in which the power of Christian presence is an important force." [133]

But no less knotty a problem is posed by the third type of change to be mentioned here, best exemplified by Notre Dame and St. Louis Universities. Each has been described as having been "shifted to lay control." But it is important to determine just what this means; certainly not the same thing as Jacqueline Grennan means. Although the St. Louis and Notre Dame plans differ in small details, they are essentially the same, and I shall confine my discussion here to Notre Dame, for which I have the relevant documents.

Since 1947, the Board of Lay Trustees at Notre Dame had been

---

[132] *National Catholic Reporter,* January 18, 1967 (her italics). It was widely noted that Jacqueline Grennan—formerly Sister Jacqueline, S. L.—had been dispensed from her vows to return to secular life. For the time being, she stayed on as Webster's President, until her marriage in 1969.

[133] *Ibid.* She added: "Catholic colleges and universities are largely public corporations. We feel that the public to whom colleges respond must take a larger responsibility for the colleges. We chose to make the dramatic and therefore difficult decision to go all the way and push for a completely lay board of trustees, rather than a mixed board consisting partially of lay and partially of religious trustees."

the administrators of the endowment funds of the university. But these business and industrial leaders had no official voice in policy-making, which was the sole prerogative of a six-member Board of Trustees, all Holy Cross fathers, including the President of the University. As Notre Dame moved further up the excellence line, and began to spend upwards of thirty million dollars annually, the Lay Board was involved in more and more of the high-level decision-making. At the same time, of course, the faculty came to be dominated by laymen, as was indicated above.

The reorganization of the University involves the election of six from among the present Board of Lay Trustees to serve with the six Holy Cross priests as Fellows of the University. Members *ex officio* are the Holy Cross Provincial, the University President, Executive Vice-President, Vice President for Academic Affairs, and the Chairman and Secretary of the University Board of Trustees. (The latter were formerly called the Board of Lay Trustees.) Six of the Fellows must always, by statute, be Holy Cross priests. The President of the University is Chairman of all meetings of the Fellows. Power for governing the University is vested in the thirty to forty member Board of Trustees; the initial Board comprised thirty laymen, and seven Holy Cross priests. All Fellows are also members of the Board.

The Board is to meet at least twice a year, delegating its powers and functions to an Executive Committee between meetings. The Executive Committee can be seven to thirteen in number; *ex officio* Committee members are the Chairman and Secretary of the Board of Trustees, the President and Executive Vice-President of the University. The University President is its Chairman.

The Board of Trustees Chairman must be a layman, the President of the University "shall be elected by the Trustees from among the members of the Priests Society of the Congregation of Holy Cross, Indiana Province, after receiving recommendations made by the Nominating Committee of the Board." [133a] Further, the Nominating Committee must request a recommendation or recommendations from the Holy Cross Provincial, although it is also possible for recommendations to come from "other interested persons." So it is clear that the President of the University, who is also the Chairman of the Executive Committee, must be a member of the Order. Key day-to-day decisions are still being made by a Holy Cross priest. (At St. Louis, the new Board of Trustees comprises 18 laymen and 10 Jesuits, compared to the former Board of 13 Jesuits; there too,

---

[133a] By-Laws of the Notre Dame Board of Trustees, II, 2.

the President must be a priest of the Order, the Board Chairman, a layman. It might be noted that five of the ten Jesuits must come from Jesuit institutions other than St. Louis.) Notre Dame and St. Louis statutes can be altered only by two-thirds votes of the boards of control, slightly more than the number of laymen in the respective bodies.

One of the key Statutes at Notre Dame is aimed at a matter which must be considered here:

V(e). The essential character of the University as a Catholic institution of higher learning shall at all times be maintained, it being the stated intention and desire of the present Fellows of the University that the University shall retain in perpetuity its identity as such an institution.

Few people pretend to know the exact nature of the "Catholic university," in the late 1960's. The Notre Dame Statutes specify that the intellectual life of the University "should at all times be enlivened and sustained by a devotion to the twin disciplines of theology and philosophy," which are "viewed as being central to the University's existence and function." [133b] Similar language is used by the University President, in his Introduction to the new Notre Dame Faculty Manual, effective September, 1967. In the section on academic freedom in the Manual, the faculty member is reminded of his responsibility not to "maintain a position contrary to the basic

---
[133b] Notre Dame Statutes, V (f) 1.

aims of this Institution as outlined in the Introduction." [133c]   In a later secton defining criteria for dismissal from the University, one matter is "continual serious disrespect or disregard for the Catholic character of this institution." [133d]   And what is "Catholic character"? Sociologists are notorious for refusing to deal with such weighty concerns, and the present writer quite cheerfully passes up any invitations to provide a rationale for the separate existence of Catholic colleges and universities. In my own judgment, no one seems to have built one as this is written.   Jencks and Riesman suggest that, while they have not themselves heard a satisfactory answer to the classical question "What is a Catholic University?" the only answer may be that a Catholic college or university "should help its students explore the question 'What does it mean to be Catholic?' in an informed

---

[133c] Because of the importance of academic freedom questions in Catholic higher education, the entire section on academic freedom is reprinted here (from Art. III, Sect. 2):

"The University recognizes and supports the following principles of academic freedom: the freedom of the faculty member as teacher and scholar to seek the truth in research as he sees it, and as his particular professional training directs him to it; the freedom of the faculty member to publish the results of his research; the freedom of the faculty member to plan his courses and discuss his subjects according to the dictates of his training and knowledge; the freedom of the faculty member to speak or write on public issues as a citizen without institutional censorship or discipline.

"The faculty member, on the other hand, recognizing the responsibility of academic freedom, agrees to respect the following principles of that responsibility. In lecturing and teaching, he should not maintain a position contrary to the basic aims of this Institution as outlined in the Introduction. When speaking or writing as a citizen, he should remember that the public may judge his profession and his institution by his utterances; hence he should make every reasonable effort to be accurate, exercise appropriate restraint, show respect for the opinions of others, and indicate that he is not an institutional spokesman.

"Furthermore the faculty acknowledges its obligation to encourage the free pursuit of learning by the students of the University, to hold before them the best scholarly standards, and to respect the students as persons. Recognizing their role as intellectual guides and counselors, faculty members respect the confidential nature of the professor-student relationship and make every reasonable effort to foster honest academic conduct by the students and to evaluate students according to their true merit and accomplishment. Faculty members avoid any exploitation of students for private advantage and acknowledge in their scholarship significant student assistance."

[133d] The others: professional incompetence or continued neglect of academic duties or responsibilities, conviction of a felony, and causing notorious and public scandal (Art. II, Sect. 6, Subsect. a). It should also be noted that careful procedures to establish serious cause are also defined, meant to assure the protection of the individual faculty member.

and disciplined way." [134] A number of people have attempted to provide partial answers.[135] The query is outside the competence of the sociologist (although I have dealt with some aspects of the question, and can refer the reader to these contributions [136]). For the remainder of the chapter, I shall confine my remarks to a few comments on some of the things which have been touched on, above.

It might first be noted that a university or college seems unduly restricted if its president must come from the ranks of a particular religious order. There are undoubtedly many members of such Orders as the Jesuits and Holy Cross who would make admirable university presidents;[137] but such a requirement is bound to limit the choice, if only by the sheer law of averages. On the other hand, it should be pointed out that a certain "anti-authoritarian romanticism," as David Riesman put it,[138] seems to characterize the discussions of many young priests and laymen, who appear to believe that all of the problems of Catholic higher education will disappear once the universities are completely laicized. But of course they will

---

[134] In Chapter 7 of the draft, *The Academic Revolution.*

[135] See Frederick Crosson, "Personal Commitment as the Basis of Free Inquiry," in E. Manier and J. Houck (eds.), *Academic Freedom and the Catholic University,* Fides Press, 1967, 87-102; John E. Walsh, C.S.C., "The University and the Church," *ibid.,* 103-118; George N. Shuster, *Catholic Education in a Changing World,* Holt Rinehart, Winston, 1967; and William J. Richardson, "Pay Any Price? Break Any Mold?" *America,* 116, 624-642 (April 29, 1967).

In a widely-discussed article appearing about the same time, John Cogley entered his demurrer; he said, in part, "I do not believe that today *any* university can be uncritically committed as an institution to a particular philosophy, political system, to any one religion or to anti-religion. By the same token, the university can not exclude from thoughtful consideration any ideology, philosophy, political system or religion which living men of learning, by common agreement, deem worthy of consideration . . . . Futhermore, I do not believe it is within the competence of a university to 'give witness' to any proposition currently debated by responsible men. For one thing, the university is simply not in the business of 'giving witness' to anything but its own integrity as an institution where no controverted question is dogmatically foreclosed" (*Commonweal,* v 86, 310-316 (June 2, 1967). See the discussion of academic freedom by ten Catholic intellectuals in the same issue.

[136] In "The Future Shape of Catholic Higher Education," *Shape,* 295-334, especially p. 318 ff.; and in "Freedom and the Quality of Student Life," in Manier and Houck, *Academic Freedom,* 145-61.

[137] Although, as Greeley suggests in *Changing Catholic College* many first-rate men seem to be passed over just *because* they are innovative and free-wheeling.

[138] In his Foreword to *The Shape of Catholic Higher Education.*

not. For one thing, the lay trustees are more likely to be chosen from among businessmen and industrialists than from among educators and social critics, and the former may be even more likely than religious who attended graduate school to "see the Catholic colleges as turning out patriotic, sports-loving, smooth but unsophisticated young men and piously protected 'feminine' young women."[139] Then, too, the distinctive sense of purpose which some religious have seemed to have—a charisma stemming partly from a belief in the special grace discussed above, partly to the attribution of certain powers to them by subservient laity in the past—a single-mindedness which has forced change and contributed greatly to the vast improvements which have characterized several leading Catholic universities, may well be dissipated in a radical democratization that creates departmental or divisional baronies. As Jencks and Riesman point out, the great leap forward of several Catholic schools have been due in large measure to charismatic leaders, and institutions on the make cannot afford to spend their energies on internal pacification programs. With decentralization, mediocrity can protect and perpetuate itself.[140]

A brief comment about the changing roles of religious orders might also be made. One of the great dangers of the past, the tendency to identify an order's mission with the physical property of college or university, has largely disappeared as men in, for example, the Jesuits and Holy Cross, reason that it is better to hold a smaller place at a St. Louis or Notre Dame by competence than a much larger place by inheritance. But there also seems to be a close relationship between the increasing financial obligations of higher educational institutions, and disestablishment by some religious orders. It is as if they were saying, as Martin Marty once noted, "we can no longer compete so let's find a theology which justifies our transition and capitulation." While some orders seem to be characterized by a style and ethos—what Sister Roseanne Murphy terms an "organiza-

---

139 *Ibid.* Should this happen, the Catholic colleges will be faced with some of the same problems as universities in states where contractors and tycoons dominate the state boards of regents.

140 I am indebted to Jencks and Riesman for the ideas suggested here, both in their draft of *Academic Revolution* and in personal correspondence, Greeley makes some of the same points in *Changing Catholic College*. It is amusing that the very time when lay, but non-academic, men are coming to predominate on Catholic boards, a school of thought has developed which insists that American higher education would be better advised to put the academic profession in complete control of academic policy-making, to avoid the show-downs with non-academics which have characterized some major universities (e.g., California, Colorado, North Carolina).

tional stance"[141]—which is open to change, other religious groups are more wedded to the past, and appear to move toward greater lay participation more for expediency than because of sudden enlightenment.[142] If they cannot redefine their "apostolate," such orders may well find themselves lamenting their "loss of patrimony" in the years ahead.

Two recent brouhahas may be portents of things to come. The very week that the administration of St. John's University finally agreed to submit the cases of the 29 fired faculty members to the American Arbitration Association,[143] a crisis which had been brewing at another Catholic university began to boil over. After four faculty members were accused by another of "teaching heresy" in their theology and philosophy courses, the Archbishop of Cincinnati appointed a committee to investigate the charges at the University of Dayton. Although the final results of the investigation and the recommended actions are unclear as this is written—the largely priest-composed committee reported that the men at times had taught things "opposed to the teaching of the magisterium," but the President of the University and the Chairman of the Board of Trustees (both Marianist priests, the latter the Order's Provincial) seemed to criticize and partially reject the report, after which the Superior General of the Order in Rome insisted that traditional Church teaching must be adhered to—the important point to insist on is the implications of such an investigative process. If Catholic universities are to remain under "juridical control" of the Church for the foreseeable future, and if this means that what one teaches in class is subject to appraisal by an outside investigative body, then academic freedom has no meaning in that institution.

A dramatic confrontation on this issue occurred when it was announced in April 1967 that not only would a prominent young moral theologian at The Catholic University of America not be promoted to associate professor, as his department had recommended and the academic senate approved, but that he would be released from the University at the end of August. This followed an investigation and recommendation by a three-man committee of bishops

---

[141] See Roseanne Murphy's and William Liu's article later in the present volume.

[142] It has been suggested that the agreement to arbitrate the dismissal decisions in the now-famous St. John's case was due more to the danger of losing the accreditation of the Middle States Association than to principle.

[143] For a discussion of the St. John's case, see John Leo's contribution to *The Shape of Catholic Higher Education,* and the review of the AAUP investigation and subsequent censure in the *AAUP Bulletin,* Spring, 1966.

to the Catholic University Board of Trustees (composed of 33 American cardinals, archbishops and bishops, a third as many laymen). The firing of Fr. Charles Curran was apparently due to the theologian's mildly liberal position on several questions of "natural law," most notably birth control. But the University had been in a turmoil for some time, over such issues as the banning of four "liberal" theologians from the University in the early 1960's, and the attempt on the part of the rector and officials in Rome to merge departments over opposition from the departments themselves and from the academic senate. (In *The Changing Catholic College*, Andrew Greeley described the faculty of Catholic University—not identified by name in the book—as "completely demoralized." This was prior to the Curran affair, which rejuvenated the University.)

The disregard of faculty and senate recommendations in the case of Charles Curran—not only had approval been given for promotion, but the Dean of his School had not even been consulted on the firing—led to a unanimous agreement of the theology faculty to stop teaching until Fr. Curran was reinstated. Because no hearing had taken place, and because they believed their professional judgement had been repudiated, the entire Catholic U. faculty voted overwhelmingly (400-18) to cease functioning, in a demonstration of support.

The resultant nation-wide press and TV coverage made the case a *cause celebre* of Catholic higher education; in some ways, it was more dramatic than the St. John's and Dayton fiascos, because of the status of the school as the country's only Pontifical University. (Ironically, the blow-up occurred less than a month after the U.S. bishops, prompted by the Dayton situation, established a committee to explore the apparent conflict between the magisterium of the Church and the academic freedom of scholars.) The outcome of the Curran case is not the point here. The reversal of their action by the Board of Trustees (they claimed not to have "known the full circumstances" when they voted) and the promotion of Fr. Curran, plus the promises of structural reform for Catholic University, led some to consider the event the "Selma of Catholic higher education." [144] What is crucial is the whole matter of academic freedom in the areas of philosophy and, particularly, theology,[145] considered so central to the Catholic college. Catholic U. had long been dominated by clericalism and ecclesiastical paternalism; undoubtedly the

---

[144] Editorial, *National Catholic Reporter,* May 5, 1967.

[145] Primarily, because philosophy as a discipline has moved away from consideration of "ultimate" questions.

Board would not have dared to act so high-handedly (in spite of their lack of information) were they not predominantly bishops.[146] But the essential consideration is whether any Church authority can be allowed to interfere in the internal affairs of a Catholic university or college. Theology professors have long been viewed by Church functionaries as simply agents of the "magisterium"—which is why "investigations" have been possible. These authorities have felt responsibility for what is being taught in the schools. (Even the capitulation of the C.U. Board of Trustees was accompanied by a statement that the hierarchy should not be considered as having put their "seal of approval" [their term] on Fr. Curran's moral theology.)

Most Catholic educators believe that it is of the utmost importance to insist that no such seal of approval exists. Neil McCluskey, S. J., said this well:

The European and ecclesiastical tradition not withstanding, the discipline of sacred theology cannot be an exception. The Catholic university must arm its professors of theology with the same academic freedom that is accorded its historians, physicists, and sociologists. There is no more academic justification for the entry by a local bishop or provincial into the university discipline of theology than there is for the local mayor or governor to intrude into the field of political science. New concepts and different interpretations by scholars are put forth in the academic world to be examined, tested, proved, rejected or modified by a peer group which can challenge or approve because it has earned authority and competence through scholarship and learning.[147]

It is of the utmost importance to insist that anything short of violations of civil law must be handled within the university itself. Even if something is believed to be, in fact *known* to be, contrary to present Catholic teaching, any investigations must be by one's academic peers, with all the procedures of due process observed. If this is not assured, and if the local bishop, or papal nuncio, or any other Church official, can interfere with what occurs within a university, then it will make precious little difference whether deeds to

---

146 The eleven laymen were businessmen, most of them like those described by Riesman.

147 In a speech delivered at the University of Dayton, February 28, 1967. Some would go even farther, suggesting that not only theology, but all of the subjects taught in a Catholic university, should be pursued with no more restrictions than obtain in *any* American university. The AAUP, which has had a special sub-committee on problems of academic freedom at "committed" colleges and universities, is considering abolition of their separate set of guidelines for such institutions.

Catholic schools are in the hands of lay trustees, and it will be difficult to disagree with Jacqueline Grennan: higher education *will*, if not by its very nature, then in the practical order, be opposed to Church control.

Finally, something ought to be said about the matter of federal aid to Catholic higher education. Implicit in all the moves toward greater lay responsibility is the hope of obtaining federal and state funds. From its inception, Catholic education has had to contend with charges of disloyalty and divisiveness;[148] as this is written, more than a dozen cases are pending which deal specifically with the question of the constitutionality of public funds going to church-related schools. Although some from among the groups most opposed to aid for religiously-affiliated schools in the past now support it,[149] and Christopher Jencks has argued that public education would be forced to improve, if competing with private schools receiving support by federal aid to the students who preferred to attend them (especially the poor, who would then have their first real opportunity to choose schools for their children),[150] the Supreme Court seems to have been taking an increasingly dim view of the possibility of state and federal aid to private education. But some believe that funds for higher education raise different legal questions than public support for primary and secondary schooling.

These matters are outside our ken here. The important thing to note is the danger of counting too heavily on public support for Catholic institutions. In the Maryland case, state aid was ruled out because the three schools "projected a religious image," and this was held to be a violation of the Constitution. There are of course indications that many Catholic colleges and universities are moving

---

148 As late as 1951, the *Christian Century* ran an editorial which asserted that "a commonly shared education is the *sine qua non* of a homogeneous society," and that the proliferation of Catholic schools and organizations "means that a conscious and well-planned large-scale attempt (was) being made to separate Catholics from other Americans in almost every area of social life" (**68**, p. 703) [June 13. 1951].

149 Among these, Walter Lippman, *New Republic,* and Milton Himmelfarb, who argued that Jewish opposition to aid to Catholic schools "stands in the way of a more important good (and a more important safeguard of Jewish security), the best possible education for all" ("Church and State: How High a Wall?") *Commentary,* 42, 23-29 [July, 1966]. In addition, the chairman of the Anti-Defamation League recently proposed a review of its traditionally strong stand in opposition to federal aid to church-sponsored schools, suggesting that the educational needs of the country demand an inspection of this position.

150 Christopher Jencks, "Is the Public School Obsolete?" *The Public Interest,* 1, 18-17 (Winter, 1966).

away from such an image, to become increasingly like the formerly-Protestant schools. A fourth school in the Maryland Case, founded by a religious group, was judged to project in 1967 a "more secular image," and thus to be eligible for public funds. Should this happen to Catholic higher education—and there are many who think it will and, indeed, is—the question will arise as to the justification for its separate existence.

But distinctive or not, Catholic colleges and universities will continue to survive, for it is naive to expect that institutions so heavily invested in—financially and emotionally—will suddenly go out of business. The real questions they face, however, are the hard and pragmatic ones of how successful they will be in their quest for upward mobility. Both monetary and intellectual resources may continue to be in short supply, for the reasons which have been suggested throughout this chapter. The handful of universities that have charged ahead during the 1950's and 'sixties will probably continue to prosper, and one or two may become great (the smart money is on Fordham and Notre Dame, and possibly St. Louis). But their secular counterparts will not be standing still, and if it is encouraging to realize that the College Board Scores of 1967 Notre Dame Freshmen are not unlike those in many Ivy League colleges in 1957, it is frustrating to realize that the gap separating these institutions is still immense. Many second-rate Catholic colleges will die, not with a bang, but a whimper. As more and more American Catholics begin to question the wisdom of a separate system of higher education—and more to the point—begin to shop elsewhere for their children and for academic appointments—the majority may go under, or so drastically alter their character as to be unrecognizable.

I can think of no better way to end this contribution than to quote from a man who has had a profound influence on the present writer, and—more than he perhaps realizes—on Catholic higher education itself. At the conclusion of his Foreword to *The Shape of Catholic Higher Education*, David Riesman wrote: "But overall what (impresses me) is the simply tremendous energy liberated on the Catholic campuses in recent years and the kind of excitement that many Catholics are finding in examining their own institutions . . . People like myself who grew up in agnostic, permissive or unreligious homes almost envy the elan that comes to people moving out from encapsulation toward a wider world view, less ethnic, less ethnocentric and nationalistic, but Catholic in the original and broadest sense of the word. What will happen to these people in these institutions, of course, depends not only on them but on what happens to America itself, whether we cut ourselves off still more completely by war and affluence from the rest of the world, so that we force our critics back into an inner immigration, and whether the Catholic prophets can retain their sanity in the face of so many competing expectations, so many overpowering pressures, so many disappointments."

8

The Catholic Press in America

MICHAEL J. GREENE

Michael J. Greene Associates

SOURCE. Prepared especially for this volume.

Histories of the Catholic press in the United States can be found in virtually all of the standard reference works concerned with the Catholic church.[1] Professional, journalistic, and theological problems affecting member publications are discussed at every meeting of the Catholic Press Association and permanently recorded in the pages of the association's journal, *The Catholic Journalist*.[2] Read-

---

[1] Perhaps the best is the article in the *New Catholic Encyclopedia* published by McGraw Hill Book Company (New York: 1967).

[2] Published monthly by the Catholic Press Association, 432 Park Avenue South, New York, N.Y.

ership surveys (most of them designed to provide the advertising manager with sales ammunition) abound, particularly in the Catholic magazine field. But no systematic study of the goals and functions of the Catholic press as a social system has been done to date. The press has escaped the close study which John L. Thomas has given the Catholic family, Joseph Fichter the religious life, and Andrew Greeley the parochial school.[3]

At first glance the situation is more than a little puzzling. For at least in terms of its total circulation statistic, the Caholic press is a behemoth, and thus all the more vulnerable a target for behaviorally oriented Davids seeking likely Goliaths. *The Catholic Press Directory* for 1966-67 listed 497 publications with a combined circulation of 27,580,817.[4] Each week, 126 diocesan newspapers distributed a total of 4,813,820 copies. Four national newspapers (minus their diocesan editions) issued 846,492 copies weekly, and twelve foreign language newspapers contributed another 330,708 copies to the total. Magazines counted the lion's share of the total: Noted in the *Directory* were 335 magazines with a combined circulation of 21,589,797.

Despite the diversity of the publications blanketed by these statistics, the Catholic press has been the subject of many an easy generalization. Its critics have tended to overemphasize the extent to which the Catholic press can be regarded as a collectivity of publications rigidly unified within a single system. Its practitioners have tended to overstate the collective impact of the Catholic press on its publics within the church and without. On one hand the status and functions of the Catholic press have been identified with those of the mass media, and on the other, the Catholic press has been applauded for the excellence with which it performs certain group maintenance functions.[5] The union of the terms "Catholic" and "press" has created bewildering semantic problems.

When the Catholic press is considered only as a press, one finds points of similarity with the practice and traditions of the general press. What Robert E. Parks said of the general press can also be said of the Catholic press: It is not the "willful product of any little group of living men. On the contrary, it is the outcome of a historical process in which many individuals participated without

---

[3] The important work of Professor David Host of the College of Journalism, Marquette University, in directing the work of candidates for the master's degree should be mentioned here as a resource for all students of the Catholic Press.

[4] The *Directory* is published annually by the Catholic Press Association.

[5] See *The Catholic Journalist* for both points of view.

foreseeing what the ultimate product of their labors was to be." [6] But the Catholic press has unique historical reasons for its existence today. Albert Nevins, a former president of the Catholic Press Association, wrote of its origins:

"The Catholic Press in the United States was born in a spirit of apology. It was a defensive press, created to defend Catholic doctrine and to answer calumnies." [7] Yet today one may find publications of the Catholic press challenging the positions of ecclesiastical leaders (as on U.S. involvement in the Vietnam conflict) and endorsing the positions of those formerly cast in an anti-Catholic role (as in the areas of family planning and population control).

Edward Wakin recently described a historical progression within the Catholic press:

Historically the Catholic press developed in three phases, beginning with the immigrant period of the 19th century when publications mixed Catholicism and old-country nationalism with equal intensity. . . . Then from 1900 through World War II, the Catholic press became housebroken and docile, reflecting papal concern about the contentious, disturbing American Catholicism. From the vantage point of hindsight, it was also conservative, reactionary and painfully parochial, a hangover that still plagues both the image and the operation of the Catholic press. In the post-war period, the transfusion of competent and idealistic laymen upgraded the professional quality of many Catholic publications, and, also, created an uneasy partnership between lay journalist and ecclesiastical publisher.[8]

Wakin's analysis shows why the Catholic press cannot be viewed only in its relationship to the press as such, but must be viewed also in its relationship to the institutional church. Indeed, the dual character of the Catholic press as "Catholic" and as "press" is of first importance to the social scientist who will (one day, no doubt) undertake a systematic study—as it is of pressing importance to the practitioner within the Catholic press today. James O'Gara, editor of the well-known journal of opinion, *Commonweal*, suggested how nebulous—if not invisible—is the tie that binds "Catholic" to "press." In a reflective editorial, O'Gara asked:

[6] Robert E. Parks, "The Natural History of the Newspaper," *Mass Communications*, edited by Wilbur Schramm (Urbana: The University of Illinois Press, 1949), p. 7.

[7] A. J. Nevins, "The Catholic Press in the United States, *Twentieth Century Catholicism, A Periodic Supplement to the Twentieth Century Encyclopedia of Catholicism*, edited by Lancelot Sheppard (New York: Hawthorn Books, 1966) p. 31.

[8] "The Catholic Press: Parochialism to Professialism," *Journalism Quarterly* (Spring, 1966), p. 117.

Is *Commonweal* a Catholic magazine? . . . If to be Catholic means to be an organ of the Church or of some official organization in the Church, the answer is obviously "no." The hierarchy has certainly given us no special mandate to speak. Nor can we claim to be the voice of the Catholic laity as a group—who can? If these things are what is meant by being Catholic, we would have to abdicate all claim.

For all of its life, however, *Commonweal* has been accepted as in some sense a Catholic publication, and with reason. The magazine is and has always been published by a small group of journalists who are themselves Catholic. They are men who are concerned with Catholicism, and with the meaning of spiritual and temporal. It is this characteristic that has primarily distinguished *Commonweal* from other journals of opinion.

It is a fact, too, and not without significance, that most of our readers and many of our writers are also Catholics who have comparable interests. Such readers look to us for our views as Catholic laymen on the Church and the world, and such writers turn to us precisely because in our pages they can express these same concerns.

Then too we have many non-Catholic readers and writers, and this also we would cite as part of being Catholic. Our non-Catholic readers look to us for a certain kind of Catholic thinking. Our non-Catholic writers know they are welcome in our pages because of the Catholic spirit as one which welcomes good thinking and good writing, wherever found. In this sense too *Commonweal* has always been Catholic and thus always ecumenical, and I trust it always will be.[9]

O'Gara's comments are cited here not because they are typical, nor as an interesting sidelight on the contemporary scene, but to indicate the theoretical dimension of the practical question which must be asked by the editor as well as the research scientist: Is there a "Catholic press?" If so, how may it be identified and described beyond the listing of names and circulation figures from the *Catholic Press Directory?*

The first section of this paper deals with the question of identity and attempts to define a field of investigation which can legitimately be called a "Catholic press." A review of sociologically-grounded studies of the Catholic press follows, with an effort to correlate the available findings, and identify the goals and functions of the Catholic press. Finally, at the request of the editors, the writer reviews the implications of a Catholic press as a means of communication within the institutional church and between the institutional church and society at large, and looks to the future of the Catholic press.

---

9 O'Gara's comments appeared in *Commonweal*, May 19, 1967, p. 255.

I. THE PROBLEM OF IDENTITY

In the current American usage, "the press" refers to those publications engaged in the practice of journalism, that is, in gathering, handling, analyzing and commenting on the news. A long-time professor of journalism describes journalism as "the work performed with regular frequency, often daily, of publicly recording events and discussing them, especially in their bearing on men and communities. Reporting and editorializing are the accepted names of the two distinct but generally combined activities." [10]

The accepted meaning of "the press" has undergone an evolution, as has the meaning of news. Once seen as "anything which makes the reader say 'Gee Whiz,'" news is now more acceptably described by spokesmen for the press as "information which is essential to people who propose to govern themselves." [11] News need not be printed. Those who supply news may work for electronic as well as print media. But the press is the main component of the newspaper and the newsmagazine.

If the function of gathering, handling, analyzing and commenting on the news is essential to the concept of the press, then it is apparent that by far the largest segment of what is usually called the Catholic press does not fit precisely within the concept of the press. For (as the quick review above of Catholic press statistics suggests) the publications in the Catholic press concerned with news are fewer and account for a lower percentage of total circulation than those which are not, in the main, concerned with news.

The roster of the Catholic Press Directory includes *The Official Guide to Catholic Educational Institutions*, and *The Official Catholic Directory*, both published annually; *Orphan's Messenger and Advocate of the Blind* and *The Catholic Lawyer*, both published quarterly; the bi-monthly *Catholic Building and Maintenance;* as well as literary, scholarly, devotional and professional magazines and newspapers published monthly·and weekly. News does not dominate the content of Catholic publications—unless one considers news to be information which is useful for historical, religious, or other reasons. Further, many Catholic publications are eliminated from the category of the press by infrequency of issuance.

Real difficulties lie in the assumption that what is true of some or many Catholic publications is true of most or all. It is worth reviewing the most common assumptions to determine which apply to "the Catholic press" and in what sense.

---

[10] David Host, "Journalism, Catholic," *New Catholic Encyclopedia*, p. 1131.

[11] The latter phrase is attributed to Walter Lippman.

A. Assumptions—True and False

STRUCTURED WITHIN THE CHURCH. The comprehensive list of the Catholic press includes many influential publications which are not structured within the church, that is, not published by or for the constituents of a diocese, religious association or organization. Some examples are the magazines *Triumph, Critic, Commonweal,* and *Cross Currents,* and the newspapers, *The Wanderer* and the *National Catholic Reporter.*

FOCUS AND IDENTIFICATION. In content, publications of the Catholic press have to do with the church. When they deal with social, political or cultural issues isolated from the church, they do so in the context of an overriding concern with the church. Interestingly, there is no "Catholic" publication for the general reader which has as many nonCatholic readers as Catholic readers. Here it should be noted, too, that it is possible for a publication to opt in or out of the Catholic press by a change in focus—though not necessarily a change in values. The magazine *Ramparts,* for example, appeared in the *Catholic Press Directory* for 1965-66. Under the same editor and publisher, it soon adopted a policy of less frequent reference to the church, though with no discernable change in its position on social and political issues. *Ramparts* does not appear in the *Catholic Press Directory* for 1966-67. When it focused its attention outside the church *without frequent reference to the church,* it ceased to identify with the Catholic press. While *Commonweal,* in contrast, continues to focus much attention on the problems of society at large, it identifies itself with the church (though not as an official publication of the church). It seems that the Catholic publication need not be formally structured within the church to maintain an identification with the Catholic press, so long as it focuses on the church or sees itself performing a function for or within the church.

OWNERSHIP. While Catholic dioceses, religious orders and associations own many publications of the Catholic press, others are privately owned (including some diocesan newspapers) or owned by non-profit corporations which are not controlled by official representatives of the church.

EDITING. It is sometimes assumed that clergy control the content of the Catholic press. But laymen edit many diocesan weekly newspapers as well as magazines issued by religious societies and institutions. None of the publications mentioned as not structured in the church employ clergy on the editorial staffs.

SANCTION. A publication need not have the sanction of a bishop or bishops to publish under the name Catholic, and some of the most

influential do not operate under the sanction of ecclesiastical authority. *The Catholic Worker*, for example, has no sanction. Neither
must a Catholic publication be registered with the Catholic Press
Association. The association is voluntary. No publication in recent
years has retained its identification as Catholic directly against the
express mandate of a bishop, but some have gone against the teaching of a bishop. In early 1967 Bishop Helmsing of the Kansas City-
St. Joseph diocese repudiated the views of *The National Catholic
Reporter* on birth regulation (traditionally considered a matter of
marital morality) and clerical celibacy (a matter of church law and
discipline); yet the bishop did not attempt to suppress the newspaper, nor object to its use of the name Catholic.[12]

SERVING INSTITUTIONAL INTERESTS. Publications which propound
opposing interpretations of Catholic teaching, tradition and practice
abound. Notable opposites are *Triumph* and *Commonweal* magazines,
and *The Wanderer* and the *National Catholic Reporter* newspapers.
Among the "official" diocesan newspapers are those which have
taken pains to make it clear that none of the views expressed necessarily represent the views of the bishop or the church, unless labeled,
"official."

SHARING THE SAME SENSE OF PURPOSE. Whether the Catholic
press defines a field of interest, or a way of handling information,
remains a source of confusion. But it is clear that editors of similar
Catholic publications view their purposes in substantially different
terms. Thus in the report of a survey of Catholic newspaper editors
as to the editorial goal of a diocesan newspaper, 20 of 27 editors
quoted ascribed a teaching, spiritual guidance or church-advocacy
goal, such as: "To bring Christ to others; reflect moral values in
current society." "The promotion of diocesan interests." "To provide a Catholic viewpoint." [13]

Yet there were seven purely journalistic statements of purpose
among the responses; such as: "Objective reporting of news; take
editorial stands on social, moral issues." "To present significant news
of the life of the church and her members that is accurate, objective
and balanced; to present background and comment needed to make
the news understandable." "Publication of news which Catholics
need specifically as Catholics."

Obviously, some editors seek to influence, others merely to report.

---

[12] The bishop's views were published in *The National Catholic Reporter*,
January 18, 1967.

[13] The survey is reported in an NC News Service domestic release dated
February 2, 1967.

B. *Functional Criteria of the Catholic Press*

Since it seems that neither news content, nor frequency of distribution, nor ownership, nor editorship, nor sanction, nor the ability to serve institutional interests, nor a shared sense of purpose unifies "the Catholic press," what criteria may be used to define a valid field of investigation which might be called a Catholic press? Focus on the church and self-assertion of identification with the church would seem to be two criteria of a Catholic press. Still, some care should be exercised in the use of the term. Introducing his book, *Careers in Religious Journalism*, Roland E. Wolseley of the College of Journalism at Syracuse University, notes that the reader will probably take exception to the term, "religious journalism." Literally, "there is no such journalism," Wolseley writes. "What is meant is 'journalism that deals with religion.' " In the mainstream of the American tradition of the press, Wolseley adds, "Of course, journalism cannot be inherently religious." [14]

Following Wolseley one would say, "There is no such press as the Catholic press, but a press which deals with Catholicism." But using the term "press" in its ordinary current sense, we can, for the sake of inquiry, define the Catholic press to mean those publications which perform the commonly understood function of the press, namely, the gathering, handling, analyzing and commenting on the news. Of the 130 Catholic newspapers in the United States which may be defined in this manner, 115 call themselves "the official publication of the diocese of . . ." and another 11 describe themselves as the newspaper of a Catholic diocese. All are unmistakably associated with the institutional church. For the sake of clarity and convenience then, it seems best to apply the term "Catholic press" to mean the diocesan weekly newspapers in the United States—with apologies to the many important Catholic publications not in this group. To organize the empirical information available, we will use H. D. Lasswell's five-part question about the communications process: "Who, Is Saying What, To Whom, In What Channel, To What Effect?" [15] Of the 497 publications with a combined circulation of over 27 million, we refer below to 126 diocesan weekly newspapers with a total circulation of 4,813,820,[16] therefore defining the channel in advance.

---

14 New York: Association Press, 1955, p. viii.

15 Lasswell posed this formula in an essay titled, "The Structure and Function of Communication in Society," edited by L. Bryson, *The Communication of Ideas* (New York: Harper, 1949), pp. 180-222.

16 All Catholic press statistics from *The Catholic Press Directory*.

II. THE DIOCESAN WEEKLY NEWSPAPER

A. *The Organization of Control*

The key element in an answer to the question, "Who's talking in and through the Catholic press?" is sanction or control of the press, not, strictly speaking, legal ownership. The two do not necessarily co-exist. Thus the "official" newspaper of the Archdiocese of New York, *The Catholic News,* is privately owned, and its publisher and editor are laymen.

"Official" is the term ordinarily applied to newspapers to denote the existence of ecclesiastical sanction. When and where there is control by sanction the means of control may vary widely, from the power to hire and fire editors and writers, to the actual control of content by a priest-editor subject to ecclesiastical discipline.

Most Catholic diocesan newspapers are, in fact, owned by the diocese, or a corporation established and controlled by a bishop or a diocese. Forty-seven of the 126 diocesan newspapers are diocesan editions of two national newspapers, *The Register* and *Our Sunday Visitor,* and are therefore subject to a degree of editorial control in the dioceses of Denver (Colorado) and Fort Wayne (Indiana) respectively, as well as in the diocese of publication.

A 1954 study by Marian Anderson, published by the Institute of the Catholic Press at Marquette University,[17] and a 1966 thesis by Margaret Smith, submitted to the journalism faculty of the same institution,[18] offer points of comparison regarding the control of policy and content of the diocesan weekly newspaper:

1. Both find ownership concentrated in bishops and dioceses, although bishops ordinarily delegate priests to exercise operational control.

2. In the earlier study, one in three editorial employees were clergy; in the later study, one in two were clergy.

3. In the earlier study, half of the editorial workers entered the field of journalism by appointment of a superior rather than by choice. The later study makes this distinction: Most of the religious respondents would not have assumed their present responsibility except for the direction of a superior, while most of the laymen

---

[17] Research Report No. 2, "A Survey of the Editorial Staff of Catholic Newspapers" (Milwaukee: The Marquette University Institute of the Catholic Press, 1954).

[18] Unpublished master's thesis submitted to the College of Journalism, Marquette University, March 31, 1966.

would have sought employment in the Catholic press if the opportunity had not presented itself.

4. The earlier study found that 33 percent of religious staff members devoted only part time to the publication; but only four percent of the laymen devoted part time to the publication. In the later study, employees engaged in outside activities numbered two to one. Smith noted: "All priests had necessary duties to perform which are not in connection with the publication."

5. The earlier study said all clergy were concentrated in two positions, editor and associate editor, with laymen holding positions as news editor or reporter. The later study said priests exercised authority in all but two areas of decision-making; one exception was in the choice of which events were to be reported, and the other in decisions affecting mechanical production of the newspaper.

6. In neither study did the majority of editorial employees have either academic or professional background in journalism.

Smith, in the later study, found that priests remained in their jobs longer than laymen, the number of laymen declining as age and years on the job increased, with the number of priests increasing as age and years on the job increased.

The element of control affecting the diocesan newspaper is again apparent in the source of nonlocal news available to the diocesan newspaper editor. The primary news service for Catholic newspapers is NC, the news service of the Press Department, United States Catholic Conference (until 1966 called the National Catholic Welfare Conference). The conference is an agency of the Catholic bishops of the United States, regulated by an administrative board composed of bishops, archbishops and cardinals of the United States. Most of its correspondents within the United States are full-time editorial employees of Catholic diocesan newspapers.

From time to time, NC news service draws the fire of editors for failing to observe accepted journalistic standards. For example, in May, 1967, the board of directors of the Catholic Press Association issued a protest because NC had issued no news story concerning the revelation of the secret reports of the papal birth control commission by the French daily, *Le Monde*, and the American weekly, the *National Catholic Reporter*. A diocesan newspaper editor who regularly writes a column on the press in the Jesuit magazine *America*, Msgr. S. J. Adamo, wrote, "The source of the difficulty, I would reckon, is Bishop Paul Tanner, who acts as chief censor of the whole NC operation. Professional newsmen like Floyd Anderson (director of the news service) must get weary of trying to make events that happen fit into this conservative prelate's idea of what should be happening." [19] Issued not long before the incident was the Report of the Catholic Press Association-NC Liaison Committee's Continuing Study Group on Writing-Editing, which offered these observations:

Much too often, the news service's reports are "slanted"—that is, they are handled so as to suggest to readers certain points of view, or certain conclusions rather than being simply straightforward, objective factual news accounts.

It appears to the Writing-Editing Committee that the root of this fault is to be found in a tendency to view the news service not as such, but in some measure as a public relations or propaganda agency.

The committee set forth nine observations in all, concluding:

The news service falls into the fault of stretching to the point of absurdity to fit a story to an angle. For example, the Washington Letter of 12/7/66 came out with this completely unacceptable opening sentence: "Washington—Even as the feast of Christmas approached the question was asked here: How much crime is there in the world?" [20]

Strong voices speak for freedom of the press within the church. The United States Bishops' Committee for Social Communication issued a statement for World Communications Day (May 4, 1967) which said:

Man's right to be informed is a natural, inherent right. It is given by God Himself. It is not a privilege conferred by any authority. . . . If there have been abuses of this right by any authorities in the church, we members of the People of God can only regretfully acknowledge the fact and at the same time strive to amend our ways.[21]

The bishops' statement seems to represent the position which the Commission on Freedom of the Press adopted in 1947: "The

---

[19] Monsignor Adamo's comments appeared in *America* magazine of May 6, 1967. The protest issued by the C.P.A. board of directors is related on page one of *The National Catholic Reporter* for May 24, 1967.

[20] The undated report from which these quotations are taken was issued in Spring, 1967, over the names of Robert Olmstead, *The National Catholic Reporter;* John J. Ward, *The Voice;* and Joseph A. Breig, *The Catholic Universe Bulletin.*

[21] Quoted in *The New People,* newspaper of the Diocese of Kansas City-St. Joseph (Mo.), issue of May 5, 1967, p. 8.

press must be free from the menace of external compulsions from whatever source." [22]

Obviously, the Catholic press is responsive to elements of control within the institutional church. But the reader should keep in mind that the editors and reporters of the daily press in the United States are also responsive to elements of control. The investment-conscious publisher and the cause-conscious editor are familiar conflict-figures in the daily press. One significant step toward reducing editor-publisher conflicts in the Catholic press came with the formation of the Committee on Editor-Publisher Relations of the Catholic Press Association in 1956.[23] Nevertheless, stress between the control group in the church and the control group in the Catholic press has become a way of life.

B. The Communication Content

The pioneering work on content analysis of Catholic newspapers in the United States was published in 1965 by the Australian-born Jesuit, John Burton Bremner. Titled, "An Analysis of the Content of Catholic Diocesan Newspapers in the United States," Bremner's study focused on three consecutive issues of a carefully selected sample of forty diocesan newspapers throughout the United States.[24]

At the time of Bremner's survey there were 141 dioceses in the United States, 119 with newspapers in the English language. All but one were weeklies. Eleven dioceses were served by newspapers of neighboring dioceses. The largest newspaper in terms of circulation was the then new *Long Island Catholic* (circ. 195,875) and the smallest the *Catholic Sentinel* of Baker, Oregon (circ. 3,327).

Bremner constructed an "average" diocesan newspaper.[25] It had 12 standard eight-column pages, or 24 tabloid, five-column pages, and a mean circulation of 37,638. Its contents fell naturally into

---

22 George N. Shuster, founding editor of *Commonweal* magazine, was one of the 13 members of the commission whose historic report, *A Free and Responsible Press*, was published by the University of Chicago Press in 1947. The quote above appears on page 8. Theorists of the Catholic press began to arrive at many of the commission's conclusions following the issuance of the encyclical, *Peace on Earth* by Pope John XXIII. The encyclical termed freedom of information a natural right of mankind.

23 The first report of the committee was presented to the officers and board of the Catholic Press Association in August, 1966 by John A. O'Connor, chairman.

24 Bremner's dissertation was accepted for the Ph.D. in Journalism by the State University of Iowa in 1965.

25 Bremner, p. 19.

five categories: News (33.88 percent), Advertising (31.55 percent), Comment (20.58 percent), Art (10.57 percent) and Miscellaneous (3.42 percent).

Bremner cited as his major finding, "Enough empirical evidence to belie the charge that the Catholic press is monolithic." [26] His discovery of the existence of wide variances within the Catholic press should be kept in mind in the following review of his major findings:

1. *What is News for the Diocesan Press?* [27] Bremner found that about one-third of the content of the typical diocesan newspaper, and about one-half of its copy hole (total available space minus advertising) is news. News is about two-fifths local, between one-quarter and one-third American, about one-tenth foreign, but local news is less when there is some transcendent nonlocal story.

Analyzing the content of the news, Bremner found that more than three-fifths of local news consists of routine or handout copy, the remainder being "initiative news," that is, "news for which there is some internal evidence that a member of the staff or a correspondent covered the story, or that he showed some enterprise in getting facts other than a mere listing of who did, or will do, what, when, where."

Exactly half of the diocesan papers devoted more of their local news to diocesan organizations than to any other subcategory. Two papers devoted more of their local news to the local bishops than to any other subcategory; no paper ranked the bishop last in space consumed, but five papers ranked him second last.

The largest proportion of local news concerned organizations, school and parish, in that order, and the smallest proportion interfaith, expansion and entertainment news.

The percentages of solely religious news ranged from 87 percent *(Texas Catholic)* to 54 percent *(Catholic Star Herald)*, and the percentage of initiative news ranged from 67 percent *(The Catholic Reporter)* to 7 percent *(Southern Nebraska Register)*.

2. *Whence Does the Catholic Press Get Its News?* Sources other than the newspaper staff provide more of the news in the typical diocesan newspaper than the staff itself provides, Bremner found. NC news service and the newspaper staff provided approximately the same amount of news. Only about three percent of the local news officially came from the local bishop.

---

[26] Bremner, p. 165.

[27] Bremner's own questions and answers are summarized here. His full treatment can be found on pages 208-217 of his dissertation. In addition to editorial content, Bremner also studied advertising content and practices of the same newspapers.

3. What Is the Performance of the Diocesan Press in Reporting Religious-Political News? About one-quarter of the news content of the typical diocesan newspaper was religious news involving sociopolitical issues, and at least two-thirds of the news was solely religious, Bremner said. Less than two percent was solely political, and less than one percent neither religious nor political.

4. What Does the Diocesan Press Express Opinion on? Bremner found that about one-fifth of the content of the typical diocesan newspaper, and just less than one-third of its copy hole, was comment. The typical paper carried a column and a half of editorials, a column of letters to the editor, three columns of doctrinal instructions, a Question Box of one column, about three columns of family guidance, a column of entertainment advice, one literary column, and almost one column of sports. About one-sixth of the comment concerned local topics. Bremner found only one example of a newspaper expressing a difference of opinion with the local bishop *(Catholic Reporter*, Kansas City, Mo.).

5. Whence Does the Diocesan Press Get Its Opinion? Less than two-fifths of the comment content of the typical diocesan newspaper was original, Bremner found. More comment came from clerical sources than lay sources. Less than two percent of the comment officially came from the local bishop.

6. What is the Performance of the Diocesan Press in Expressing Opinion on Religiopolitical Issues? At least one third of the comment content of the typical diocesan newspaper was religious comment involving socioreligious issues, Bremner learned. About one-half of the comment was solely religious. About one-twelfth was solely political, about one-twentieth was neither religious or political.

Bremner rated three papers very good, eleven good, seventeeen mediocre, five bad, and four very bad. He listed the following general weaknesses.

"A lack of local news initiative, lack of human interest features, excessive reliance on the official Catholic news service, insufficient editing of news service copy, unprofessional headlining, style inconsistence, insufficient community involvement, unwillingness to entertain differences of opinion, excessive reliance on syndicated comment, insufficient comment on local issues, poor relationship between news and opinion, editorial touchiness, and, in general, a chip-on-the-shoulder attitude towards readers who might dare to draw a distinction between editorial opinion and incontrovertibility." He added a caution: "These, of course, are generalizations. Though all apply to some, not all apply to all. And though some apply to all, not all apply in the same degree. Indeed, the major conclusion to be drawn from this study of diocesan newspapers is their difference." [28]

Nevertheless, Bremner found the following significant relationships between dependent variables.

Percentage of initiative news and percentage of religiopolitical news; percentage of initiative news and percentage of original comment; percentage of non-NC news and percentage of original comment; percentage of original comment and percentage of local comment; percentage of original comment and percentage of nonclerical comment. [29]

Observably, where a vigorous journalistic thrust (manifested in initiative news) appears, the diocesan newspaper moved in the direction of reporting and commenting on events and issues in the sociopolitical area. The more intensely the newspaper involved itself in original comment and local comment, the less it depended on the official news service. The more comment originated from the staff, the more likely did this comment refer to local issues, and less likely it was written by a clergyman.

C. The Audience of the Catholic Press

To whom is the Catholic press speaking? Since it is "diocesan," the Catholic press is speaking primarily to "local" readers who, in most dioceses, will listen to the same radio stations, watch the same television channels, hear or read pastoral letters written by the same bishop, and usually live within half a day's automobile drive from one another. Many metropolitan daily newspapers share the same geographical dispersion of readers. Bremner's content study reveals that the diocesan newspaper does not have a perdominance of local news and comment, however. His analysis of local news by type shows that the largest segments are devoted to Catholic organizational news, parishes and schools, and that half of all news is solely religious. The diocesan newspaper cannot be said to address itself to non-Catholic readers; readers are predominantly Catholics who have strong ties to the institutional church. About one in ten persons in the Catholic population of the United States subscribes to a diocesan newspaper.

How is the audience selected? Many diocesan newspapers obtain "subscribers" not by direct solicitation of the potential readership

[28] Bremner, p. 19.
[29] Bremner, p. 165.

but by mandate of the bishop. The Catholic Press Association reports a survey of all diocesan newspapers, of which 103, or 73 percent responded.[30] Fifty-one newspapers said they used a "complete parish distribution plan (also called the 100 percent plan) or a variation thereof." Under the 100 percent plan, the cooperating parish or institution ordinarily assumes the responsibility of having the newspaper sent to the individual subscriber; the individual does not necessarily subscribe freely and assume the obligation of paying for the newspaper. Of the 52 respondents not using the 100 percent plan, four indicated they are considering adopting it.

An NC news service released to subscribers in February, 1967, said that 45 of the 63 papers reporting "derive most of their subscriptions through complete parish coverage, diocesan mandate, school crusades, or some other form of widespread campaign."[31] An explanation for this form of subscription sale suggests itself. The 40 newspapers surveyed by Bremner averaged 31.55 percent advertising. In the NC news service survey referred to above, 45 of 63 editors report that more than 50 percent of their total revenues are derived from circulation. Pressure for adequate operating monies may play a part in the means of selecting the readership of the diocesan newspaper, though surely there are apostolic or religious motivations operative in the decision to send the newspaper to a subscriber, regardless of his ability or willingness to pay for it.

D. Goals and Effect

When a communication or a medium of communication accomplishes the intended purpose, it can be said to be effective. Thayer put it plainly: "The only measure of communication effectiveness is the success a communication has in producing the desired effect."[32] It is useful to examine the purpose of a communication before risking any judgments as to its effectiveness—although indeed an effect may occur and evaluation of effect may be made without reference to the intended purpose of the communication. Here, the purpose seems especially relevant.

What does the Catholic press intend to do? Piecing together the discoveries of many researchers under the umbrella of Lasswell's "Who, Is Saying What, To Whom?" it comes clear that two message

---

30 A report of the survey appeared in the association's newsletter, *The Catholic Journalist,* **18** (12), 2.

31 The survey is reported in an NC News Service Domestic release dated February 2, 1967.

32 Lee O. Thayer, *Administrative Communication* (Homewood, Ill.: Richard D. Irwin, Inc., 1961), p. 83.

encoders are at work in the Catholic diocesan press: the institutional church, which sponsors, endorses, sanctions and to one or another degree staffs and controls the press, and the editorial staff, which selects, edits and writes certain kinds of information and comment appropriate to the newspaper as a form, and to the editor's idea of the newspaper's purpose, which may be journalistic or ecclesiastical. Here we might recall the purposes cited by editors who replied to the NC survey mentioned earlier.

Propaganda. ". . . Function as the organ of the bishop, aiming at propagandizing (in the right sense of the word) the people of God in the diocese."

Promotion of a Catholic Value System. "To provide a Catholic viewpoint . . ."

Teaching and Spiritual Guidance. "To bring Christ to others; reflect moral values in current society."

Other editors cited goals more closely related to the medium and less to the church:

Serve Reader's Needs. "Publication of news which Catholics need specifically as Catholics."

To Report the News. "Objective reporting of news . . ."

Put News in Perspective. "To present significant news of the life of the church and her members that is accurate, objective and balanced; to present background and comment needed to make the news understandable." [33]

The significant difference between these two sets of goals may be put simply by contrasting generally accepted dominant goals of the institutions of church and press.

Press	Church
To tell.	To convert.
To explain.	To persuade.
To serve.	To save.
To interest.	To educate.
To inform.	To form.
To make a profit.	To lay up eternal rewards.

When the two goals are encoded in a single medium, the criteria of one or the other tend to dominate the effect of a given message, although it is not necessarily true that one or the other set of goals will dominate all messages. The mix, however, may be confusing. Indeed, confusion seems to be the major finding of a 1965 attitude study by Michael E. Long, "Attitudes of 25 Subscribers toward

[33] NC, February 2, 1967.

Matters of Control and Authority in Their Diocesan Newspapers." [34]

Long's study was based on interviews with readers of Baltimore's *The Catholic Review*, a newspaper edited by laymen of high professional standing in the Catholic press, with a reputation for aggressive reporting and editorializing in the socio-political as well as socio-religious areas. Long attempted to assess the views of readers on matters of control affecting the editors, and to determine the readers' views of the authority of the newspaper.

Long found that readers are not confused as to whether control exists, but are confused as to how it is exercised with respect to the editorial policies and practices of *The Catholic Review*. No respondent thought that the archbishop wrote any of the editorials, but 17 of the 25 thought the archbishop saw the editorials before they were published. Asked if they thought the editorial writer tried to reflect the mind of the archbishop in the newspaper's editorials, 12 said yes, 12 said no, and one said he did not know. Asked what the "official" status of *The Review* meant to them, over half of the respondents used the words, "approved," "sanctioned," "backed," or "authorized by the archbishop or the archdiocese;" four said it meant "the only Catholic newspaper in the diocese."

Long found that readers exhibited considerable confusion both in attempting to distinguish religion and politics, and in attempting to identify those points at which religious beliefs can be said to affect political issues. Twelve replied in the affirmative and four in the negative when asked if they thought there was a Catholic stand on political matters; eight said they didn't know. Those who completely separated religion and politics, Long noted, exhibited a confusion that came to the surface in the comment that the paper was "getting into politics" when it commented on civil rights questions.

Finally, Long found confusion in attitudes about the obligation of readers to follow specific judgments and directives given in the *Review*.[35]

The rapid change of ideas and perspectives within the church, accelerated by the Second Vatican Council, would naturally cause, for some, situational ambiguity involving the Catholic press. Catholic newspaper letters columns reflect the concern of readers about the position of the church on birth regulation and war for example.

---

[34] Unpublished master's thesis submitted to the College of Journalism, Marquette University, May, 1965.

[35] All citations from Long can be found in Chapter 3 of the thesis.

Long's study suggests that readers may experience some confusion about who said what, and whether one is bound or not bound to believe or follow what is said.

To the extent that it succeeds in performing the work of the church, the Catholic press seems to foster the development of Catholic attitudes on general as well as specifically religious issues, and contribute to the compartmentalization of society along socio-religious lines which Lenski describes in *The Religious Factor*.[36] To the extent it succeeds as a press, it seems to foster a degree of independence from the institutional church, provide sufficiently unbiased information for the individual to maintain a perspective of some detachment, select among many options, and determine what guidelines he will accept or reject.

There are no compelling reasons to consider the effects of the Catholic press as parallel to the effects of the mass media; because of its identification with the church it stands apart. But the work of mass media researchers in the area of audience analysis may contain useful insights for the Catholic press in terms of goal definition. As Elihu Katz observed, "The model in the minds of early (mass communication) researchers seems to have consisted of: (1) the all-powerful media, able to impress ideas on defenseless minds; and (2) the atomized mass audience, connected to the mass media but not to each other.

"Empirical research rapidly dispelled this simple set of images and proved how difficult it is to 'convert' people by means of mass media alone. Dozens of studies, particularly in the field of public affairs, have failed to find any appreciable change in opinions, attitudes, or actions resulting from a mass media campaign. The audience, at least in a democratic society, exposes itself to what it wants to hear; even a captive audience engages in a kind of motivated missing-of-the-point when it finds its prejudgments under fire. So, the mass media were found to be far less potent than has been supposed (though popular writings still frequently equate the mass media with 'brainwashing')." [37]

E. Goals and Functions

Those who argue that the Catholic press has a predominantly institutional function may quote in support of their position one of

---

[36] Gerhard Lenski, *The Religious Factor* (New York: Doubleday/Anchor Books, 1962). See especially page 326.

[37] Elihu Katz, "The Diffusion of New Ideas and Practices," *The Science of Human Communication* edited by Wilbur Schramm (New York: Basic Books, 1963), p. 80.

the 16 documents issued by the Second Vatican Council, *The Decree on the Instruments of Social Communication.* The decree said:

Whether it (a Catholic press) is published or run by direct ecclesiastical authority or by Catholic laymen, let it be clearly edited with this goal: That it may form, strengthen, and spread public views which are in harmony with the natural law, and with Catholic teachings and precepts. . . .[38]

Those who argue for a press as an independent social institution —for a journalism which concerns religion, rather than a religious journalism—may quote Pope Paul VI:

A newspaper is as a mirror and must be an ample and faithful mirror. It obeys a fundamental requirement of its own: that of informing, that of reporting the news, that of telling things as they are, that of serving the truth, which we might describe as photographic, the truth of events, of facts, of daily happenings, the objective truth of the world which surrounds us and moves around us.[39]

Then, too, one finds those who apparently uphold both points of view, as Nevins, writing in *The Twentieth Century Encyclopedia of Catholicism.* At one point Nevins declares that the Catholic editor "realizes that he is part of the teaching magisterium of the church." [40] and later asserts, "The editor should have the right of individual decision, exercised responsibly." [41] But perhaps the final phrase, "exercised responsibly," is a qualification. For to whom or to what the editor is responsible seems generally to constitute a control factor which has consequences in content and effect and function.

The Catholic diocesan newspaper press functions at many levels —as a medium of information and social communication, as a public opinion forum, as advocate, guide and counselor, as bulletin board and official spokesman of the church—all with qualifications of degree from newspaper to newspaper. Confusion as to whether the Catholic press is a medium of organizational communication or a press for Catholics is apparent. Yet clearly the Catholic press conceives itself as serving both the church and the reader. Among its functions for the reader are the journalistic functions—information, commentary, analysis which makes it possible for the reader to know what he

---

[38] Walter M. Abbott, S J., ed., *The Documents of Vatican II* (New York: Guild Press, Association Press, America Press, 1966), p. 327, par. 14.

[39] The Pope's remarks, given May 2, 1964, to pilgrims from the Piedmont region of Italy, were occasioned by the announcement that the Catholic paper *Il Quotidiano* had suspended publication.

[40] Nevins, p. 38.

[41] Nevins, pp. 49-50.

needs to know in order to act according to his conscience for his own well-being and that of his community (in this instance, the church). Among its functions for the church are the propagation of teachings, traditions, ethical and moral standards, (or, in other language, ethicizing, status conferral, and the formation of patterns of personal and social life along religious lines). Some believe that both of these functions are preformed together and even simultaneously, by the Catholic press; that is,

The Catholic press informs.

The Catholic press persuades.

The Catholic press informs while persuading, and persuades while informing.

OR

The Catholic press explains.

The Catholic press teaches.

The Catholic press teaches while it explains, and explains while it teaches.

This notion is not so far-fetched as it may seem. Consider the secular daily newspaper whose goal is to serve the general welfare of the community. Its criteria for the selection of news and its norms for commentary will affect content, control and effect—and function. The publisher or editor of the daily secular newspaper who strives for no effect in his community beyond the transmission of information is not likely to be found. Though that effect may be consciously bland, it serves a social goal, (even if that goal is nothing more than the enhancement of the medium as an advertising channel).

The crucial matter affecting the function of the Catholic press, however, seems to be its inability to freely select either lofty community-interest or solely monetary gain goals. In serving the church the Catholic press comes under controls which are external to the press *because the church has adopted the press as a medium of communication.* The situation of the press in the church calls to mind Whitney Oates' observation that "one cannot whistle an algebraic formula." [42] The medium does not seem entirely appropriate to the message.

The unintended development of the press as an independent social institution within the church, however, constitutes an important functional problem involving the relationship of the church to the institutions of a democratic society. Indeed, it seems to this writer

---

[42] Whitney Oates, "Classic Theories of Communication," edited by Lyman Bryson, *The Communication of Ideas* (New York and London: Harper & Brothers, 1948).

that the Catholic press functions today as a model of how the institutional church works out its relationships with a secular institution—the press—and relates its message and performs its mission within the institutions of a society whose structure is basically different from its own.

III. SOME IMPLICATIONS OF THE PRESENT SITUATION OF THE CATHOLIC PRESS

In broad terms, the question of the Catholic press is the question of how a transcendentally oriented value system embodied in a strongly centralized social system functions within a humanistically oriented value system embodied in social custom and a political system. The Catholic press has not ignored the question.

In the last decade a serious discussion developed within the Catholic press centering on the question of the function of a press serving the church in the context of the secular order. The question was usually phrased something like this: Can the Catholic press move beyond those areas which can be clearly defined in their relevance to religious doctrine into the social, political, cultural context *without committing the church as an institution?* [43] In other words, can a press function apart from the structure but under the inspiration of the institutional church?

Editors who had seen in history enough of the unhappy consequences of the union of the church and state were careful to add the qualifying phrase at the end of the question. Often discussed were the means of accomplishing a social good through the instrumentality of a Catholic press. Seldom discussed was the nature of a church which cannot or should not be committed to the social, political and cultural institutions which constitute the framework of human life (one of those institutions being the press itself).

Charged with a specifically religious mission, the church looked beyond the good of social institutions in and of themselves.[44] Charged with a specifically social mission, the press looked directly to the social institutions of mankind. Thus journalists who sought to accomplish a social good for the church through the institution of the press aspired to perfect the Catholic press according to the inspiration of the church. Substituting inspiration for sanction and freedom

---

43 For an early discussion of the question by two journalists see Donald McDonald, *Catholics in Conversation* (Philadelphia and New York: J. B. Lippincott Co., 1960), pp. 230-232.

44 Abbot, *The Documents of Vatican II,* p. 241, par. 42.

for control seemed the way to find the identity of the Catholic press and fulfill its religious and social mission. Conceived in this way, the Catholic press could represent the church "unofficially" not officially, while functioning as an independent social force involved in the social institutions and movements of the secular order. But would this activity of the press be responsive to the church's notion of its role in society? No clear answer was forthcoming.

John G. Deedy, a former diocesan newspaper editor and one of the leading interpreters of the Catholic press,[45] once saw the problem as one of "adjusting the Catholic press so that it has the freedom to operate in the temporal order, without at the same time committing or seeming to commit the church as an institution." Today he finds the context of the problem changed. "The disconcerting thing," he writes, "is that suddenly this is not, as we once thought, the ultimate challenge which, when met, would solve all our functioning problems. For all of a sudden, the great challenge is the church itself, both as a religious and as an organized institution." [46]

From a position characterized by professional detachment and structural dependence, the press had become involved with the church during the Second Vatican Council.

In Vatican II, bishops of the church attempted to redefine and relate the church more closely to contemporary life and thought. That effort did not end with the close of the council. At least in part through the agency of the Catholic press, the effort of redefinition and relation continued, often focusing on the problems of the secular order with a new awareness that the church itself is a social institution. A conflict of ideas on the nature of the church, stimulated by contemporary social and cultural movements, followed the council. While reporting the church's internal struggle with the major question of its relationship to the social institutions of mankind, the Catholic press inevitably had to ask, "How is one to ascribe a role to the press whose *raison d'être* has been the church, when the *raison d'être* of the church is itself in question?" Thus the problem of the press is experienced as a problem of the church as well as the problem of editors who function at the intersection of ancient and modern traditions of communication.

As a press, the Catholic press faces dilemmas which derive from the conflict of two traditions of the press: the authoritarian and

---

[45] See Deedy's essay, "The Catholic Press," in *The Religious Press in America* (New York, Chicago, San Francisco: Holt, Rinehart and Winston, 1963), p. 65.

[46] Private communication to the author, February 23, 1967.

libertarian. In the authoritarian tradition it accepts another institution, the church, as the final arbiter of truth; it accepts some degree of sanction and control by the church, expressed by the designation, "official." It accepts a role in transmitting and in effecting the policies of peer groups within the Church selected by the editors.

At the same time the Catholic press shares many of the premises of the contemporary "social responsibility" idea of the press, the modern form of the libertarian tradition. It is jealous of its journalistic freedom but concerned that this freedom be exercised for the benefit of the society which it serves; it accepts the role of the press in attending to social, political and economic matters which affect the welfare of the people (and aspires to make religion relevant in these areas); it seeks to provide an informational service by which the individual can intelligently adapt himself to the circumstances of life and distinguish good from bad and right from wrong.[47]

At the core of the contemporary idea of the press is its informational responsibility and the idea that those who supply information must be above partisanship and self-interest. While the journalist is an employee, his responsibility is to serve the reader as his client, at no matter what cost to his publisher. A free press in the service of a free society is his goal.

At the core of the idea of the church is divinely revealed truth and a social mechanism through which truth is transmitted; implicitly, truth which is divinely inspired must be made available and relevant to the lives of men in all social institutions at all times. Deedy is one of many who fear a press which would teach truth at the expense of freedom.

For the press, freedom is a two-sided coin. On one side are impressed the rights of freedom; on the other, the responsibility thereof. The press' rights include access to pertinent public records and news sources; unimpeded ways and means in the gathering and presentation of news and opinion; liberty in expression; and freedom from manipulation, harassment, and the necessity to propagandize. Its responsibilities involve respect for the public trust, regard for the common good; honesty and accuracy in reporting; absence of bias and precommitment; and, ideally, the providing of a forum for the expression of contrary opinion. Freedom of the press exists in the nations and institutions of the world insofar as these virtues are honored.[48]

Books, magazines, pamphlets, television and radio—all more susceptible to the unilateral expression of a point of view—would

[47] See Siebert, Peterson, Schramm, *Four Theories of the Press* (Urbana: University of Illinois Press, 1956), pp. 1-2.
[48] Deedy, "Freedom of the Press," *New Catholic Encyclopedia,* Vol. 6, p. 127.

seem to offer more opportunities for the accomplishment of teaching, persuasion, conversion, propaganda and other church-related goals. Yet the Catholic press may be serving an indispensable service in exposing to public view the church's process of accommodation to a new era in its life. Painful as this may be, this exposure has the same salutary effects as the White House press corps has on the processes of government.

At the same time, it does not seem that the Catholic press, so long as it acts primarily with reference to the church, can move into a role larger than the one it now plays until a more functional answer is given to the question: "What is the church?" The alternative to prescribing a role for the press according to an idea of the church is, of course, prescribing a role based on a socially acceptable idea of the press. This would seem to entail focusing a Catholic press on the issues, events and problems of society at large, rather than within the confines of the institutional church, and involve substantial modification in the areas of control (official and unofficial status), content orientation (the secular and sacred orders), audience selection (forced or free circulation), media standards and goals (professional and church), intent (information and persuasion) and effect. Perhaps the most intriguing question to be asked regarding the possibility of change within the Catholic press is: At whose initiative is change to come? For as Siebert, Peterson and Schramm asserted, the press "reflects the system of control whereby the relations of individuals and institutions are adjusted." [49]

IV. LOOKING TO THE FUTURE

What new forms and new directions will emerge from the present situation of the church and the Catholic press? The following developments seem likely.

1. Newspapers and magazines with more ecumenical than denominational concerns. As the churches collaborate in the social order there will be more interest in identifying questions and issues which have religious implications and which concern all who share a religious outlook. Publications to serve this widely felt need of the religiously oriented are a logical outgrowth of the involvement of the churches in social issues.

2. A Catholic press more closely identified with local, national and international communities. Catholic diocesan newspapers have

---

[49] Siebert, Peterson, Schramm, p. 74.

tended to function as national papers published locally. With the growth of more vigorous national papers, specialization at the local level will fill a presently unmet need. The international, intercultural character of the church, as yet unexploited in any but specialized publications, is likely to generate a press concerned with the total involvement of the church in all cultures and nations.

3. New communications structures in the church. With increasing vigor, the Catholic press has tended to involve the entire community of readers in the decision-making process of the church. In fulfilling this role the press has demonstrated the inadequacy of existing structures for communications within the church. Senates of clergy and presynodal committees of laymen have already come into being; more structures are needed and will follow.

4. The development of a professional thrust within the Catholic press has established the need for an operative distinction between a press in the American newspaper tradition, and a press which is a medium of organizational communication. The potential value of good "house organs" for the church will be reexamined, and some diocesan newspapers will be sent in this direction, others set free from ecclesiastical control.

5. More experimentation in print and electronic media will take place. The growth of educational television will offer new opportunities for the church to reach a larger, more diversified audience. Print media will no longer carry the burden of communication between the institutional church and its publics—and this will reduce tensions concerning the activities of the print media.

6. Competition from the general press, at the local and national levels, will diminish the need for publications devoted exclusively to the church. Excellent reporting of religious events is now found in many secular daily newspapers and weekly magazines. A reduction of the number of Catholic publications is in progress. It seems likely that only the excellent (or defensive?) will survive.

7. As the press becomes one of many media in the spectrum of the church's communications, forced circulation plans will be abandoned. As the legitimacy of diverse views within the church is more widely acknowledged, bishops will be less inclined to establish or officially sanction publications. The absence of guaranteed revenue and insured acceptance will cause the disappearance of many of those diocesan newspapers which focus on the church, and the creation of a few which are "Catholic by inspiration" and focus on the needs of the commuity.

8. At least one Catholic university will establish a doctoral program in communications, and will generate attention to communications problems within the church.

9. More consideration will be given to the undergraduate education of students who desire to work in the communications media which affect all social customs and institutions as the responsibility of the church for social institutions and the welfare of all is clarified.

10. Serious studies of communications within the church will be funded by the church.

PART III

SOCIAL SYSTEM PATTERNS AMONG CATHOLIC AMERICANS

Catholic Americans are members of two relatively pervasive social systems: American society and Catholic culture. In an integrated social system, characteristic patterns of behavior among members of a society in interaction with each other, with their social institutions, and with members of outgroups are reasonably congruent with common cultural values and ideologies.

How effectively do the dual social systems represented in American Catholicism mesh? Do Catholic values and ideology or American values and ideology prevail in observable patterns of behavior? When values and ideologies conflict, are Catholic Americans more responsive to their society and its culture or to their religion and its tradition? Two reports focus on the American Catholic family as a social institution enmeshed in dual social systems. The fertility behavior of the American Catholic conjugal family—clearly an area in which traditional religious values, recently reinforced by papal pronouncement, conflict sharply with American social ideology—is examined by WESTOFF *and* RYDER. *They report a marked increase in conception control by other than the Church-approved "rhythm" method between 1955 and 1965, so that, by the end of that decade, more than fifty percent of American Catholic conjugal families no longer conformed to Church positions in their fertility behavior.*

Some effects of parental interaction in interreligious marriages are suggested by CROOG *and* TEELE. *The offspring tend to identify with the religion of the mother, whether Catholic or not, but few differences emerge in church attendance between offspring of religiously heterogeneous and those of religiously homogeneous marriages.*

HENRIOT *inquires into the relationship between religious and political liberalism among American Catholics. Although traditional Catholic doctrine in general and modern papal social teaching in particular seem more congruent with liberal than with conservative political ideology, liberal political attitudes seem to be associated with social class status, not with religion. In counterpoint,* LIU *reports that Catholic migrants to the south from northern cities display racial attitudes in such a way as to reflect both the religious reference system and the community reference system which, at a time of racial crisis in America, seemed incompatible. Perhaps Catholic values, thought not often effective, are not yet totally inoperative.*

9

Conception Control among
American Catholics

CHARLES F. WESTOFF

Princeton University

NORMAN R. RYDER

University of Wisconsin

SOURCE. Prepared especially for this volume. Based on "Methods of Fertility Control Used in the United States, 1955-60-65," William T. Liu (ed.), *Family and Fertility* (Notre Dame: University of Notre Dame Press, 1967).

The 1965 National Fertility Study provides the opportunity to examine changes over a decade in the methods of fertility control employed by married couples in the United States, because its design is comparable with those of the surveys conducted in 1955 and again in 1960.[1] Three circumstances make such an examination especially interesting at this time. First, the birth rate has been declining since 1957; this change cannot be explained without analysis of fertility regulation. In the second place, the oral contraceptive has recently emerged as a leading method of birth control.[2] Thirdly, the Catholic Church is currently reviewing its position on the subject of birth control.

COMPARABILITY OF THE SURVEYS

All three of the national sample surveys collected data for white married women, ages 18-39, husband present. The coverage of the 1960 study also included Negro women, and the upper age limit was extended to 44. The 1965 study provided a double sample of Negro women, and enlarged the age span further to include all married women, husband present, born since July 1, 1910. The data presented in this paper, however, cover only women, 18-39, from all three surveys.

In some respects the data included here are not completely comparable over time. In both 1955 and 1960, the methods of contraception ever used were determined by responses to a single general question on use; in 1965, the question was asked specifically for each separate inter-pregnancy interval and methods *ever* used were estimated by summing over all intervals. This change was introduced with the intention of increasing the accuracy of report; the consequence may have been to increase the incidence of methods used, at the expense of comparability. Another particular difference was a modification of the way in which information was obtained concerning the practice of douching for contraceptive purposes. A third difference was the ordering of options on the card to which the respondent was referred in replying to the question about methods used; it is suspected that a changed order is responsible for the substantial report of abstinence as a method in 1960 but not in 1955 or 1965. A fourth small difference is that age was defined in 1955 and 1960 as age at time of interview, but in 1965 as age at midyear,

---

[1] The principal reports of these studies are: Ronald Freedman, Pascal K. Whelpton and Arthur A. Campbell, *Family Planning, Sterility and Population Growth,* New York: McGraw-Hill, 1959; Pascal K. Whelpton, Arthur A. Campbell and John E. Patterson, *Fertility and Family Planning in the United States,* Princeton, N.J.: Princeton University Press, 1966.

[2] Norman B. Ryder and Charles F. Westoff, "Use of oral contraception in the United States, 1965," *Science,* 153 (3741), 1199-1205, September 9, 1966.

1965; in consequence, the women in 1965 are some four or five months older, on the average, than the women in the previous two surveys. Finally, the surveys of 1955 and 1960 were conducted by the Survey Research Center, University of Michigan while the survey for 1965 was conducted by National Analysts, Inc., Philadelphia. Differences between these organizations in procedures for obtaining a national sample do not appear to have affected comparability. With these exceptions then, the estimates for comparisons through time would appear to be reliable within the limits of sampling variability.

METHODS EVER USED

It is of some importance for interpretation of the results of this paper, which refer to using couples, that the proportion of couples

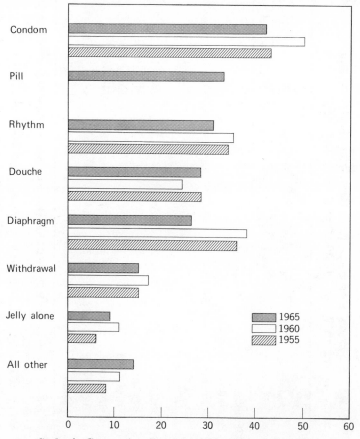

Styles in Conception Control for Three Time Periods

TABLE 1 PERCENTAGE OF USERS WHO HAVE EVER USED SPECIFIED METHOD OF CONTRACEPTION BY COLOR AND RELIGION OF WHITE WIVES (18-39), 1955, 1960, AND 1965

Method	White Total White 1955	1960	1965	Protestant 1955	1960	1965	Catholic 1955	1960	1965	Jewish 1955	1960	1965	Nonwhite[a] 1960	1965
Number of users	1,901	1,948	2,445	1,362	1,347	1,648	453	466	655	64	101	55	160	651
Percentage reporting:														
Condom	43	50	42	48	56	45	25	28	28	72	74	67	58	43
Rhythm	34	35	31	25	27	21	65	67	59	8	9	13	18	11
Pill	—	—	33	—	—	36	—	—	25	—	—	25	—	29
Douche	28	24	28	32	28	32	18	17	20	11	8	14	50	53
Diaphragm	36	38	26	41	46	31	17	12	11	56	51	45	30	17
Withdrawal	15	17	15	17	18	15	13	17	15	6	4	9	21	14
Jelly alone	6	11	9	8	14	11	2	4	4	2	8	2	19	19
All other	8	11	14	12	12	17	4	12	8	3	2	2	19	35
Total[b]	170	186	198	183	201	209	144	157	169	158	156	177	215	219

Source. Percentages for 1955 and 1960 adapted from Whelpton, Campbell and Patterson, op. cit., Table 156, p. 278 and Table 196, p. 360.

[a] The 1955 sample was confined to the white population.

[b] The total exceeds 100 because many couples reported two or more methods ever used.

reporting that they had ever used contraception [3] rose between 1960 and 1965 continuing a trend observed between 1955 and 1960 (see Figure 1). The increase is most evident among those who had the lowest rates of reported use—the nonwhites, the Catholics and the younger women. The general trend of fertility regulation will be the subject of another report; the focus here is on the different methods of fertility control reported by users. Between 1955 and 1960, the number of methods per using couple increased by ten percent (from 1.70 to 1.86); two methods showed statistically significant increases —condom, and jelly (alone). By 1965, the number of methods per using couple had increased to 1.98, perhaps in part because of the procedural change noted, but almost certainly also because of the availability of a new method, the oral contraceptive.

It is apparent from Table 1 that there has been a major change in the use of various methods between 1960 and 1965. For whites and nonwhites alike, the use of rhythm, diaphragm and condom decreased sharply in favor of the oral contraceptive.[3] First licensed for contraceptive prescription in June, 1960, use of the pill has increased at an amazing rate; by the time of our interviews in late 1965, 33 percent of white women and 29 percent of nonwhite women (see Figure 2) ever using any method reported having used the pill. It seems that the pill has been adopted primarily by couples who would otherwise have used, or were formerly using, the diaphragm, the condom, or the rhythm method. Although the douche shows an apparent increase in use, the change is probably artifactual.[4]

The residual category of "all other" methods is comprised principally of suppositories, foam, and the intra-uterine contraceptive device. The last of these, which did not become generally available until 1964, is reported as a method used by 1.3 percent of white users and by 2.8 percent of nonwhite users. These proportions may be expected to increase considerably in the years ahead. Supposi-

---

[3] Couples are classified as using contraception on a motive basis rather than on an action basis. This procedure excludes behavior which is contraceptive in effect but not in stated intent, such as use of the pill for medical reasons only. The extent of the latter activity is not insignificant, particularly for Catholics. (See Ryder and Westoff, *op. cit.*, p. 1200.) To the extent that there is dissimulation about reasons for using the pill, the estimates of use of oral contraception reported in the present paper are understated.

[4] Douching may be used for personal hygiene as well as for contraception. The reported figure refers only to women who asserted contraceptive intent. Furthermore, douching is frequently a supplementary technique to other methods of contraception. Much of the use reported in this paper involves techniques employed in combination.

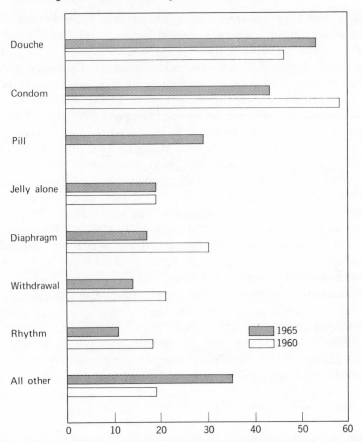

Styles in Conception Control for Two Recent Time Periods

tories were employed by 6 percent of white users and by 16 percent of nonwhite users in 1960; the proportions were approximately the same (5 percent and 17 percent respectively) in 1965. Use of the vaginal foam method was insignificant in 1960, but by 1965 the method had been employed by 7 percent of white users and by 15 percent of nonwhite users.

There are some important differences in the patterns of change in use of different methods among the major religious groupings of the white population. The methods most used by Protestant couples in 1955 and in 1960 had been the condom and the diaphragm; both declined substantially by 1965. Reliance on the condom and the diaphragm was even more pronounced among Jewish couples; by 1965, use of both had declined, but less so than for Protestants, and use of the pill is less frequent than for Protestants.

Among Catholic women the picture of change is dominated by the appearance of the pill between 1960 and 1965. The number of methods used per couple has increased from 1.57 to 1.69 and there has been a decrease in the proportion reporting that they have ever used the rhythm method. "Abstinence" as a method was reported by 9 percent of women using any method in 1960, and by less than 1 percent in 1965; the difference is probably attributable to the change of salience of the method in the questionnaire format.

CHANGES IN METHODS MOST RECENTLY USED

In Table 1, the methods described are those which the respondents have *ever* used. In consequence, the experience reported may extend for some of the women back over 25 years prior to the date of interview. In order to examine the most recent behavior of the samples, Table 2 has been prepared. It differs from Table 1 in that the methods are those used most recently; in temporal terms the appropriate comparison is between the techniques of fertility control employed by American couples during the first half of the 1950's and those of a decade later. A further difference between Tables 1 and 2 is that whereas methods *ever* used are described in Table 1— and thus many couples are included more than once—each couple is represented only once in the distributions of Table 2. The data for 1960 are omitted because the procedures followed in 1960 do not permit comparability.[5] While the bases for the 1955 and 1965 estimates are not exactly the same [6] they are more alike than either is with the 1960 study.

The impact of the pill on the distribution of methods used is revealed more clearly in the data on methods most recently used (see Figure 3) than in the comparison of methods ever used. Reliance on the condom, the diaphragm and rhythm—which amounted in terms of separate use to 74 percent in 1955—had declined to 41 percent by 1965. The pill which is responsible for this change has now become the most popular method of contraception used by American couples, a fact that would be even more pronounced if

---

[5] In 1960 the respondents were not queried about which method they used last if they were alternating use among two or more methods.

[6] In the 1965 study, unlike the 1955 investigation, the respondent who last used a method in an interval prior to the last pregnancy was not asked which method was used last if the couple used methods alternately. As a result, a higher proportion of couples interviewed in 1965 are classified in the category "Other Multiple Methods."

TABLE 2   METHODS OF CONTRACEPTION USED MOST RECENTLY, BY RE-
LIGION OF WHITE WIVES (18-39), 1955 AND 1965

Method	Total White [a]		Protestant		Catholic		Jewish	
	1955	1965	1955	1965	1955	1965	1955	1965
Number of users [b]	1901	2445	1362	1648	453	655	64	55
Percent total	100	100	100	100	100	100	100	100
Condom	27	18	30	19	15	15	56	44
Rhythm	22	13	12	4	54	36	2	—
Pill	—	24	—	27	—	18	—	22
Douche	8	6	9	7	4	4	—	—
Diaphragm	25	10	29	12	12	4	37	27
Withdrawal	7	5	7	5	8	7	3	—
Jelly alone	4	2	5	3	—	1	2	—
Other single methods	2	6	2	7	1	4	—	—
Condom and douche	1	3	1	3	1	2	—	—
Pill and any other	—	3	—	3	—	2	—	2
Rhythm and douche	2	2	2	1	3	2	—	2
Other multiple methods	2	8	3	9	2	5	—	4

Source. The 1955 data were tabulated in a slightly different form in Christopher
Tietze, "The Current Status of Contraceptive Practice in the United States,"
Proceedings of the Rudolf Virchow Medical Society, Vol. 19, 1960, p. 30.
[a] Totals include white women of other religions.
[b] Includes a small number of women who reported using contraception but for
whom specific method is unknown.

the comparisons were restricted to the younger women in the sample.
The method showing the greatest concomitant decline is the diaphragm followed by the rhythm method and the condom.

The patterns of change are not the same for couples of different
religions. Among couples with Protestant wives, use of the diaphragm and condom have declined appreciably and use of the rhythm
method has virtually disappeared. The pill now clearly dominates
the picture as the most popular method.

The patterns of change for Jewish couples seem reasonable,
although the numbers in the two studies are quite small. As with

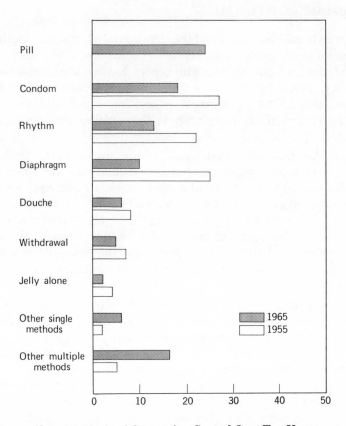

Change in Style of Conception Control Over Ten Years

Protestants, both the condom and diaphragm have declined in popularity with the adoption of the pill, but both methods continue to be used by Jewish couples much more extensively than by others. Thus 71 percent of Jewish couples still depend on these two mechanical methods compared with only 31 percent of Protestants and 19 percent of Catholics.

Among couples with Catholic wives, the major change has been a decline in reliance on the rhythm method—from 54 to 36 percent. The extent of use of the condom has not changed but the diaphragm has declined in use from 12 to 4 percent. The pill appears to have become the second most popular method of fertility control among Catholic couples.

CATHOLIC CONFORMITY

Although reliance on the formally accepted rhythm method is still the most common contraceptive practice by 1965, nearly two-thirds of the Catholic women who report having used some method of fertility control have at some time employed practices inconsistent with traditional Church doctrine, a position which although under review by ecclesiastical authorities at this writing was subsequently re-affirmed.

Since the data presented thus far are restricted to those who report use of some method of fertility regulation, and since Catholics who use no method are also conforming to doctrine, an assertion about conformity requires consideration of the behavior of all Catholic women. Table 3 therefore includes all Catholic women as well as those who reported ever having used a method. It should be emphasized that this analysis reverts to the concept "ever used"; although it includes recent behavior it is not confined to the immediate past.

The proportion of all Catholic women who have attempted to regulate their fertility by use of the rhythm method exclusively has changed only a little between 1955 and 1965 (from 27 percent to 31 percent to 25 percent); meanwhile the proportion using no method has declined from 43 percent to 30 percent to 22 percent. In consequence, the proportion not conforming (in this sense) has increased from 30 percent to 38 percent to 53 percent. In 1965 a majority of married Catholic women aged 18-39 reported having used methods inconsistent with the traditional Church doctrine on birth control.

Individuals differ widely of course in their adherence to religious values and church requirements and among Catholics at least such variation is associated with contraceptive behavior. To assess the significance of this dimension for the change over the years we include in Table 3 a simple breakdown of Catholic respondents by whether they attend church regularly or not.[7] As expected, the proportion conforming varies directly with the frequency of attendance. The more interesting observation however is that for both categories of attendance the trend over time is toward non-conformity. And this generalization holds regardless of whether the comparisons are based on all Catholic women or only on those who reported ever having used some method of family limitation.

---

[7] Additional more refined measures of religiousness are available in the 1965 study and will be included in subsequent reports.

TABLE 3 PERCENTAGE OF CATHOLIC WOMEN CONFORMING TO CATHOLIC DOCTRINE ON CONTRACEPTION BY FREQUENCY OF CHURCH ATTENDANCE, 1955, 1960, AND 1965

Year and Frequency[a] of Church Attendance	All Catholic Women						Catholic Women Ever Using Any Method	
	Number of Women	Percent Total	Total Con-formed	Non-Users	Used Rhythm Only	Used Other Methods	Number of Women	Percent Using Rhythm Only
Total								
1955	787	100	70	43	27	30	453	47
1960	668	100	62	30	31	38	466	45
1965	843	100	47	22	25	53	655	32
Regular								
1955	533	100	78	45	33	22	293	60
1960	525	100	69	32	37	31	357	54
1965	607	100	56	23	33	44	468	43
Less frequent								
1955	254	100	53	40	13	47	152	22
1960	143	100	35	25	10	65	107	13
1965	236	100	26	21	5	74	186	6

Source. Percentages for 1955 and 1960 adapted from Whelpton, Campbell and Patterson, *op. cit.*, Table 160, p. 285.
[a] "Regular" means "regularly" in the 1955 and "once a week" in the 1960 survey to questions on the frequency of attendance at religious services. In the 1965 survey the category means "once a week or more" to a question on attendance at Mass.

There is an understandable temptation to infer that the trend toward non-conformity among Catholic women is a response to the deliberations of Church officials about fertility regulation, reflecting confusion in the public mind about the possibility of change in the official position. Although this may be part of the explanation of the acceleration in the decline of conforming behavior between 1960 and 1965, it does not seem satisfactory as a complete explanation of the change because it represented a continuation of a trend already observed between 1955 and 1960. Furthermore, the acceptance of oral contraception, which is principally responsible for the increase in non-conforming behavior among Catholics between 1960 and 1965, is paralleled by an even greater adoption of the pill by non-Catholics. The most significant finding of our study to date has been the increase in the use by married couples of fertility regulation in general and oral contraception in particular, a proposition that holds for Catholics and non-Catholics alike.

10

Intermarriage: The Religious Behavior of Offspring

SYDNEY H. CROOG

Harvard University

JAMES E. TEELE

Harvard University

SOURCE. "Religious Identity and Church Attendance of Sons of Religious Inter-marriages," *American Sociological Review*, 1967, **32**, 93-103. Reprinted by permission.

Although there are powerful pressures toward homogamy in choice of marital partner, numerous marriages are formed in which partners come from disparate backgrounds, such as differing class, ethnic, religious, and racial origins. Recent empirical research and numerous theoretical observations have focused on the relative stability of

such intermarriages, on social and personal characteristics of intermarriers, and on the kinds of problems they meet.[1] However, many
questions in the area of long-term consequences remain for empirical
examination. For example, in instances of intermarriage, what factors determine the social identity of offspring? In what dimensions
of social behavior, if any, do offspring of intermarriages differ from
persons whose parents come from homogeneous social and cultural
backgrounds? Principles underlying the patterning of social identity
and the social behavior of children of intermarriage still remain to be
clarified through both national and cross-national research.

The issue of determinants of religious identity of offspring of
religious intermarriage is not a simple one. As has often been noted,
in American society affiliation with a particular religious group is
an important element of social identity.[2] Furthermore, persons engaging in exogamous marriages, as Cavan and others have shown,

---

[1] See, for example, James Bossard and Eleanor Boll, *One Marriage, Two
Faiths,* New York: Ronald Press, 1957; Lee G. Burchinal and Loren E. Chancellor, "Ages at Marriage, Occupations of Grooms and Interreligious Marriage Rates," *Social Forces,* 40 (May, 1962), pp. 348-354, "Factors Related to
Interreligious Marriages in Iowa, 1953-1957," Iowa Agricultural and Home
Economics Experiment Station, Iowa State University, Ames, Iowa, Research
Bulletin 510, November, 1962, "Survival Rates Among Religiously Homogam-
ous and Interreligious Marriages," *Social Forces,* 41 (May, 1963), pp. 353-
362; Loren E. Chancellor and Thomas P. Monahan, "Religious Preference
and Interreligious Mixtures in Marriages and Divorces in Iowa," *American
Journal of Sociology,* 61 (November, 1955), pp. 233-239; Joseph Golden,
"Patterns of Negro-White Intermarriage," *American Sociological Review,* 19
(February, 1954), pp. 144-147; Jerold S. Heiss, "Premarital Characteristics
of the Religiously Intermarried in an Urban Area," *American Sociological
Review,* 25 (February, 1960), pp. 47-55; August B. Hollingshead, "Cultural
Factors in the Selection of Marriage Mates," *American Sociological Review,*
15 (October, 1950), pp. 619-627; Ruby J. R. Kennedy, "Single or Triple Melt-
ing Pot? Intermarriage Trends in New Haven, 1870-1950," *American Journal
of Sociology,* 58 (January, 1952), pp. 56-59; Judson T. Landis, "Marriages of
Mixed and Non-Mixed Religious Faiths," *American Sociological Review,* 14
(June 1949), pp. 401-407; Murray H. Leiffer, "Mixed Marriages and Church
Loyalty," *The Christian Century,* 66 (January 19, 1949), pp. 78-80; Harvey
Locke *et al.,* "Interfaith Marriages," *Social Problems,* 4 (April, 1957), pp.
329-333; Simon Marcson, "A Theory of Intermarriage and Assimilation,"
Social Forces, 29 (January, 1950), pp. 75-78; J. L. Thomas, "The Factor of
Religion in the Selection of Marriage Mates," *American Sociological Review,*
16 (August, 1951), pp. 487-491.

[2] See, for example, the exposition of this point in Will Herberg, *Protestant
Cathiloc Jew,* Garden City, New York: Anchor Books, Doubleday and Co.,
Inc., 1960, Chapter 3, esp. pp. 36-41.

tend to be marginal in orientation to their own social groups [3] In the case of religious intermarriage, they must usually proceed in the face of powerful sanctions which encourage marriage within their own religious group. The children of these intermarriages, as they mature, may be influenced in various ways in choice of religion. First, they may identify with the religion of one parent on the basis of personal choice of theology, dogma, and set of practices. Second, their identity may be determined by a program of deliberate training by parents in one religion rather than in another. Third, in situations where offspring are permitted free choice, one parent may serve as a role model, exerting through the power of example and personality a determining influence upon the child.

In the case of religious intermarriage, there have been numerous speculations and observations concerning identity patterning and behavior of offspring. For example, Landis has suggested, on the basis of data from a study of midwestern Americans, that a child tends to follow the religion of his mother.[4] Similarly, Leiffer has maintained, on the basis of analysis of an urban sample of intermarriages, that "the mother is more important than the denomination" in determining the religious affiliation of the children.[5] On the other hand, recent research on differential patterns of power and influence in the family indicates that the roles of father and mother in decision-making vary in relation to specific issues and in terms of social status and situational variables.[6] Although evidence

---

[3] See the discussion in Ruth S. Cavan, "Subcultural Variations and Mobility," in Harold T. Christensen (ed.), *Handbook of Marriage and the Family,* Chicago: Rand McNally and Co., 1964, pp. 353-362.

[4] Landis, *op. cit.*

[5] Leiffer, *op. cit.*, p. 107.

[6] For example, see Robert O. Blood, "The Husband-Wife Relationship," in F. I. Nye and Lois W. Hoffman, *The Employed Mother in America,* Chicago: Rand McNally, 1963, pp. 282-305; Robert O. Blood and R. L. Hamblin, "The Effect of the Wife's Employment on the Family Power Structure," *Social Forces,* 36 (1958), pp. 347-352; Robert O. Blood and D. M. Wolfe, *Husbands and Wives: The Dynamics of Married Living,* Glencoe: The Free Press, 1960; David M. Heer, "Dominance and the Working Wife," *Social Forces,* 36 (1958), pp. 341-347, "The Measurement and Basis of Family Power," *Marriage and Family Living,* 25 (1963), pp. 133-139; Lois W. Hoffman, Parental Power Relations and the Division of Household Tasks," *Marriage and Family Living,* 22 (1960), pp. 27-35; R. Middleton and S. Putney, "Dominance in Decisions in the Family: Race and Class Differences," *American Journal of Sociology,* 65 (1960), pp. 605-609; Jesse R. Pitts, "The Structural-Functional Approach," in H. T. Christensen (ed.), *Handbook of Marriage and the Family,* Chicago: Rand McNally and Co., 1964, Chapter 3, pp. 51-124.

is contradictory in such studies, they offer ample reason to suspect that the matter of parental influence over choice of religion by a child is not simply patterned.

The fact that only a meager number of studies of offspring of intermarriages are reported in the literature thus far has been a handicap to clarification of speculation and contradictory observations regarding religious affiliation and church-attendance behavior of such persons. Furthermore, prior studies offer minimal information concerning the offspring of religious inter-marriage when they reach adult status.

The present paper is a report on the religious identity and church attendance of a population of young men who are products of religiously exogamous marriages. It constitutes an exploratory effort at delineating some basic patterns and identifying relationships in an area rarely investigated empirically. First, the report presents findings in regard to differential patterns of association between religious affiliation of offspring and social variables. Specifically, the variables included in the analysis are religious identification of the respondent, education of the respondent, religion of each of his parents, and parental social status.

The analysis is oriented to the following series of questions: Is the religious affiliation of the son a simple pattern of conformity to the religion of the parent of one sex rather than another? Does one religion tend to be dominant, in the sense that, regardless of parental affiliation, the son tends to adopt that religion? Does pattern of choice of religion vary by social status of the family of oreintation?

A second issue to be presented is the relationship between type of marriage and one dimension of religious behavior of the offspring: church attendance. The questions dealt with here are: Does the church attendance of male offspring of intermarriage differ from that of men who are the product of religiously homogeneous marriages? In the case of sons of religiously exogamous marriages, how are social status variables and type of intermarriage related to church attendance?

METHOD

The data for the present report were collected in connection with a large-scale study of Army inductees.[7] Two thousand three hundred inductees were chosen by a random selection technique as they were processed through the induction center at Fort Dix, New Jersey. As participants in the research, all completed a sociological questionnaire, in addition to carrying out other procedures required by the study design.

For the purpose of this report, two groups of men were identified: (1) sons of parents who engaged in religious intermarriage and (2) sons of parents who married within their own religion. Two criteria for differentiation were used: reported religion of each parent at birth and reported religion of the parent at the time of the study. Those men who identified their parents as being of different religions at present were classified as sons of interreligious marriages, provided that the present religion of each parent was the same as the reported religion at birth. Similarly, those men whose parents were reported as being of the same religion currently, were classified as sons of religiously endogamous marriages, provided the parent's current religion was the same as at birth. This technique for isolating two study populations was designed to eliminate from each group those men who were the sons of parents who converted to religions other than the ones into which they were born. In addition, converted respondents, i.e., sons of religiously endogamous parents who reported their own religion to be different from that of the parents, were also eliminated. Negro and foreign-born inductees were not

---

7 The study was undertaken in 1954 by the Neuropsychiatry Division of Walter Reed Army Institute of Research, Washington, D.C. It was designed to explore methods of prediction of the incidence of peptic ulcer. For examples of other publications reporting research on the inductee study population, see S. H. Croog, "Ethnic Origins, Educational Level, and Responses to a Health Questionnaire," *Human Organization,* 20 (Summer, 1961), pp. 65-69, "Relations of Plasma Pepsinogen Levels to Ethnic Origins: Implications in Duodenal Ulcer," *United States Armed Forces Medical Journal,* 8 (June, 1957), pp. 795-801; S. H. Croog and Peter Kong-Ming New, "Knowledge of Grandfather's Occupation: Clues to American Kinship Structure," *Journal of Marriage and the Family,* 27 (February, 1965), pp. 69-77; H. Weiner *et al.,* "Etiology of Duodenal Ulcer. I. Relation of Specific Psychological Characteristics to Rate of Gastric Secretion (Serum Pepsinogen)", *Psychosomatic Medicine,* 19 (January-February, 1957), pp. 1-10; P. G. Yesler, M. F. Reiser, and D. M. Rioch, "Etiology of Duodenal Ulcer. II. Serum Pepsinogen and Peptic Ulcer in Inductees," *Journal of the American Medical Association,* 169 (January, 1959), pp. 451-456.

included because of insufficient numbers of religious intermarriages and small representation in the original study population.

After procedures for isolating the study populations had been carried out, it was discovered that only Catholic-Protestant intermarriages were present in sufficient number to permit statistical analysis.[8] This report accordingly deals solely with this type of religious intermarriage. The final study group of offspring of such intermarriages consists of 281 men. A total of 1,066 Catholics and Protestant men who were the sons of religious endogamous parents were isolated on the basis of study criteria. This group consisted of 790 Catholic and 276 Protestant inductees.

The religious composition of the study population examined in this report owes its special characteristics in considerable part to the fact that the locus of the research was Fort Dix, New Jersey. The induction and training center is located in an industrialized, urban area with a large Catholic population. Because of the special characteristics of the inductees and the region from which they come, caution should be exercised in generalization of findings from the present study.

For purposes of brevity, the two types of religious intermarriage patterns are referred to in this report as follows:

FcMp = Father Catholic, Mother Protestant
FpMc = Father Protestant, Mother Catholic

Similar usage of letter symbols is made in regard to religious in-group marriages, with FcMc referring to Catholic and FpMp to Protestant marital combinations.

Traits of the Inductees. By virtue of their having been inducted into the Army, the respondents constitute a special group in several respects. Since all had met the physical and mental health requirements for military service, the possibility that physical or mental handicaps impeded opportunities for attendance at church services in civilian life was minimal. Further, the respondents were relatively homogeneous in age, with a mean age of 21.1 years. They were primarily urban in origin; approximately 40 percent designated their home as New York City. Less than 2 percent were from rural, farm backgrounds. About 80 percent came from two states, New York and New Jersey, while the remainder came primarily from the New England states.

---

[8] The frequency of mention of Jewish-Protestant and Jewish-Catholic parental intermarriages as well as intermarriages involving Greek Orthodox and Armenian Orthodox parents was minimal; these cases were accordingly omitted from the analysis.

On the basis of the age of the inductee respondents at the time of the study, it is estimated that the marriages of their parents were formed during the latter years of the 1920's and the early years of the 1930's. Since norms regarding religious intermarriage and principles of child rearing in religious traditions cannot be assumed to be constant over time, it must be emphasized that the patterns reported here cannot necessarily be generalized as predictive of outcome in marriages currently being formed.[9]

FINDINGS

Religious Identity. Among those men whose parents entered into an exogamous Protestant-Catholic marriage, what is the pattern of their current formal religious identification? In the study population the Catholic religion was clearly dominant in terms of reported identification by the inductees. Of the 281 men, 63 percent identified themselves as Catholic, 35 percent described themselves as Protestant, and the remaining 2 percent cited their religion as "None."

In view of the nature of Catholic norms regarding religious intermarriage, this finding at first impression would appear to support common stereotypes regarding general effects of Catholicism in intermarriages. Powerful influences are customarily exerted within the Catholic sub-cultural group toward assuring that the children of such marriages will be raised as Catholics. In fact, if a Catholic intends to form a religiously exogamous marriage which can be considered valid by his church, the Protestant partner must sign an Ante-Nuptial agreement. The agreement specifies that all children of the marriage will be baptized and educated as Catholics, even in the event of the death of the Catholic spouse. While we do not have information on the numbers of Protestant parents of the inductees who made the formal Ante-Nuptial agreement, the existence of this regulation is but one indication of the forces in such marriages turned toward assuring that offspring of the marriages will be adherents to Catholicism.

However, further consideration of the data reveals that there is no simple general effect of Catholicism in the intermarriages. Indeed, it is notable that over one-third of the men did not become

[9] For reports on historical variation in patterns of intermarriage, see Milton L. Barron, "The Incidence of Jewish Intermarriages in Europe and America," *American Journal of Sociology,* 11 (January, 1946), pp. 6-13; R. J. R. Kennedy, *op. cit.;* Claris E. Silcox and Galen M. Fisher, *Catholics, Jews, and Protestants,* New York: Harper and Brothers, 1934; and J. L. Thomas, *op. cit.*

Catholics. Obviously, factors are at work which reduce the influence of one religion over another, insofar as the upbringing of offspring of intermarriage is concerned. In this regard, two possible relationships which can be examined here are (1) the relative degree of influence of the maternal and paternal affiliations on the religion of the son and (2) variation in religious identification by social status level.

Variation in Terms of Parental Religious Affiliation. One factor commonly associated with choice of religion by offspring of religious intermarriage is the influence of the mother. This view has been supported in part by empirical evidence from studies noted earlier and in part by assumptions concerning the primary role of the mother in the socializing of the child.[10] Our data indicate that the relationship of maternal religious affiliation to that of the son is not a simple one. Of the 281 respondents identified as the offspring of religious intermarriages, 60 percent adopted the religion of the mother. However, an examination of the relationship between marriage pattern of the parents and the religion of the offspring indicates that the weight of maternal influence is greatly affected by whether the mother's religion is Catholicism or Protestantism.

As indicated in Table 1, in marriages in which the mother is Catholic and the father Protestant, 70 percent of the inductees identified themselves as Catholics. In those cases where the mother is Protestant and father Catholic, a slight majority of men follow the religion of the father, rather than that of the mother. On the basis of a chi-square test, the type of parental religious intermarriage is significantly related to the religious identification of the sons. In brief, although previous writers have contended that offspring of religious intermarriages follow the religion of the mother, regardless of her religious identity, we find that the particular religion of the mother makes a considerable difference. It is possible that the strength of the Ante-Nuptial agreement, i.e., the influence of the Catholic church, operates most markedly when the *female* partner in interreligious marriage is a Catholic.

---

10 For specific discussion of this point, see Landis, *op cit.* and Leiffer, *op. cit.* For more general commentary on material roles in child development, see, for example, John Bowlby, *Maternal Care and Mental Health,* New York: World Health Organization, 1951; E. Z. Dager, "Socialization and Personality Development in the Child," in H. T. Christensen (ed.), *Handbook of Marriage and the Family,* Chicago: Rand McNally Co., 1964, pp. 740-781; D. R. Peterson *et al.,* "Child Behavior and Parental Attitudes," *Child Development,* 32 (1961), pp. 151-162; Robert F. Winch, *Identification and Its Familial Determinants,* Indianapolis: Bobbs-Merrill, 1962.

TABLE 1   DISTRIBUTION (%) OF INTERMARRIAGE TYPE BY RELIGION OF RESPONDENT

| Religion of Respondent | Parental Intermarriage Type | | |
	Father Protestant Mother Catholic	Father Catholic Mother Protestant	Total
Catholic	70(115)	53 (62)	63(177)
Protestant	27 (44)	47 (55)	35 (99)
None	3 (5)	—	2 (5)
Total	100(164)	100(117)	100(281)

$\chi^2 = 10.89$; $p. < 0.05$. (Respondents reporting no religion are excluded from all tests.)

Obviously other variables may help to explain the patterning of religious affiliation of the offspring of the intermarriages. Although data on other possible factors are limited, we do have information on social status. One measure of status—educational level of the father—was employed as a control variable in the exploration of the relationship between religion of the respondent and the intermarriage pattern of his parents.[11] As may be seen in Table 2, in families where the father is either a high school graduate or where he has completed three years of high school or less, the pattern is similar to that reported in Table 1; some of the relationships are statistically significant. In both types where the mother is Catholic, the majority of inductees are Catholic. Where the mother is Protestant, the distribution of Catholics and Protestants among the sons of such families is about equal.

An exception is found in the families in which the father has had at least one year of college. Here the influence of the Catholic mother is apparently less. In fact, as may be seen in the first column, two-thirds of the sons of Catholic mothers identify their own religion as either "Protestant" or "None." No statistically significant difference was found in the religious identification of sons of marriages in which female Catholics were married to college-educated male Protestants and those in which college-educated Catholic males were married to

---

[11] Other measures such as occupational level of the father, social class of the father, and education of the mother were also employed in our analysis. Small numbers in cells preclude confident generalization about results. However, the direction of the relationships is similar to that which appears when education of the father is used as an index of status.

TABLE 2 DISTRIBUTION (%) OF PARENTAL INTERMARRIAGE TYPE BY
RELIGION OF RESPONDENT, WITH EDUCATION OF FATHER CONTROLLED
(*N* = 264)[a]

Religion of Respondent	Father Protestant Mother Catholic	Father Catholic Mother Protestant
Three years of high school and under [b]		
Catholic	74(71)	54(33)
Protestant	26(25)	46(28)
None	0 (0)	0 (0)
Total	100(96)	100(61)
High School Graduate [c]		
Catholic	74(34)	50(14)
Protestant	26(12)	50(14)
None	0 (0)	0 (0)
Total	100(96)	100(28)
One Year of College or More [d]		
Catholic	33 (5)	50 (9)
Protestant	33 (5)	50 (9)
None	33 (5)	0 (0)
Total	99(15)	100(18)

[a] 17 cases with insufficient data on father's education.
[b] $\chi^2 = 6.57$; $p < 0.02$.
[c] $\chi^2 = 4.45$; $p < 0.05$.
[d] $\chi^2 = 0$; n.s.

female Protestants. In sum, it would appear that, in at least one group, in which women married college-educated men, neither parental role nor religious group was statistically associated with the choice of religion made by the sons.

As previously noted, other studies dealing with areas of decision-making and power relations have reported differences between families of varying social levels. The findings here raise questions about differential patterns of influence and marital interaction. Although we have no data on attitudes or feelings of partners in the intermarriages, one might hypothesize that when Catholic women engage in intermarriage with college-educated Protestant men they feel only minimally compelled to carry out the normative requirements of their religion and to raise their children as Catholics. Indeed our

evidence indicates that those Catholic women who marry college-
educated men tend to be better educated themselves than Catholic
women who marry non-college men. Instead of molding their marriages along lines of Catholic cultural traditions, such women may
feel emancipated and inclined toward adopting the Protestant cultural system of their husbands. The fact that all of the respondents
who claimed they had no religion were the offspring of this category
of intermarriage may be an indication of the relative disinterest of
both mother and father in their own religious traditions.

Another possibility is that in these marriages a proportion of
the Catholic women are upwardly mobile. In adapting to the way
of life of their husbands, they may reduce their own religious ties
and affiliations, accepting in part at least the dominance of their
Protestant upper-status spouses. Certainly empirical findings of this
order suggest the need for more intensive research into religious
intermarriage patterns at differing social status levels and into the
psychological and social characteristics of persons who enter such
marriages.

Religious Intermarriage and Church Attendance. Although the

TABLE 3   DISTRIBUTION (%) OF PARENTAL INTERMARRIAGE TYPE BY FRE-
QUENCY OF CHURCH ATTENDANCE OF RESPONDENT, WITH RELIGION OF
RESPONDENT CONTROLLED ($N = 1312$)[a]

Religion of Respondent Parental Marriage Pattern	Frequency of Church Attendance		
	0-11 per Year	1-3 per Month	1+ per Week
Catholic [b]			
(A) FcMc	11 (90)	16 (124)	73 (576)	100 (790)
(B) FpMc	16 (16)	15 (15)	69 (70)	100 (101)
(C) FcMp	17 (10)	20 (12)	63 (37)	100 (59)
Protestant [c]			
(D) FpMp	36 (100)	38 (105)	26 (71)	100 (276)
(E) FpMc	23 (9)	56 (22)	21 (8)	100 (39)
(F) FcMp	53 (25)	43 (20)	4 (2)	100 (47)

[a] 35 cases with insufficient data.
[b] χ^2 with 2 d.f. for: $AB=1.71$ (n.s.); $AC=3.36$ (n.s.); $BC=0.80$ (n.s.).
[c] χ^2 with 2 d.f. for: $DE=4.98$ (n.s.); $DF=12.11$ ($p<0.01$); $EF=8.75$ ($p<0.02$).

religious practices of the children of religious intermarriages have only rarely been the object of empirical research, many speculations and assumptions in this area are current.[12] Systematic knowledge is limited concerning the degree to which mixed marriage influences beliefs and practices of offspring and the ways in which these patterns differ from those held by children of religious in-marriages. An assessment of the relationship between intermarriage and one dimension of the religious behavior of offspring—church attendance— is possible from the Fort Dix data. The research questions which interest us here concern: (a) the degree to which the church attendance of the sons of intermarried couples differs from the attendance of the sons of couples in religiously homogeneous marriages; and (b) the differences in attendance between the offspring of the various types of intermarriage. The extent of church attendance reported by Protestant and Catholic respondents is shown in Table 3.

Some notable differences in church-attendance patterns of Catholic and Protestant respondents can be seen. Parenthetically, Catholic respondents attend church much more frequently than Protestant respondents, a finding consistent with other studies. With respect to the Catholic soldiers, the church attendance of sons of intermarriers is similar to that of the sons of in-group marriers. No statistically significant differences were found: (1) when the sons of intermarriers were compared with the sons of non-intermarriers; and (2) when the sons of different types of intermarriers were compared with each other.

In the case of Protestant soldiers, the situation is different. In that group of men from FpMc families, the church-attendance pattern is similar to that of Protestant men whose parents were religious in-group marriers (FpMp). However, the attendance pattern of men from FcMp families is markedly different from those of the sons of homogamous marriages and the sons of FpMc intermarriages; the comparisons yield statistically significant differences. Only about 4 percent of the sons of these FcMp intermarriages attend church at least once weekly while over 50 percent are either non-attenders or irregular attenders. In brief, the results show that when the son in an intermarriage is Protestant, he is much more likely to attend church when the mother is the Catholic than when the mother is the Protestant. Or, to put it another way, a Protestant

---

12 For example, see Joseph H. Fichter, *Southern Parish: Dynamics of a City Church*, Vol. 1, Chicago: University of Chicago Press, 1951; Landis, *op cit.*; Leiffer, *op. cit.*; Joseph B. Schuyler, *Northern Parish: A Sociological and Pastoral Study*, Chicago: Loyola University Press, 1960, p. 294.

son is more likely to attend church when the father is Protestant in an intermarriage, than when the father is Catholic.

In the absence of detailed evidence on interpersonal relations and religious beliefs among intermarried parents and their offspring, it would be premature to accept easy interpretations of the data in Table 3. For example, explanations might be made in terms of common stereotypes about the role of the mother in religious training or about dominant effects of Catholicism. Thus, assuming that the mother plays a key role in the training of her offspring, one might suggest that Catholic mothers in the FpMc marriages may instill norms of regular attendance in their sons, even though the sons are being raised in another religion. Catholic emphasis on regularity of church attendance may be given expression through the mother, despite the fact of intermarriage and despite the fact that the child is a Protestant.

In contrast to this interpretation, however, one can also offer explanations through reference to the role of the father and to the influence of the Protestant religion as potent factors. For example, one can postulate that in the FpMc intermarriages involving Protestant respondents, it is the Protestant fathers who were primarily responsible for church attendance by the sons. The attendance pattern is, after all, similar to that of offspring of homogeneous Protestant marriages, unions in which the Protestant father also has the opportunity to exert influence on the religious training of his son. Such an interpretation is, of course, equally speculative in the absence of germane data.

Whatever the explanation, it appears that the two types of intermarriage patterns (FcMp and FpMc) are distinctive and that differing kinds of forces may be operating within each, with respect to adaptation to the fact of religio-cultural differences. Although easy explanation is possible through reference to popular stereotypes or logical assumptions, more research is clearly needed before more definite conclusions can be drawn.

Church Attendance Patterns with Educational Level Controlled. Positive relationships between church attendance patterns and social status level have often been reported in studies of Protestant and

Catholic respondents in American and European settings.[13] One of the common indices employed in such studies of status is educational level. In view of the utility of education as an index of status, we employed the variable as a control in the examination of data on church attendance. Indeed, the findings reported in Table 3 deserve further consideration in terms of underlying effects of education upon the results. The patterns reported in the table may, after all, be the consequence of differential distribution by educational level among the men whose parents form various types of religious-inter-marriage combinations. For example, it is possible that high church attendance may be the consequence of a concentration of college-educated men in a particular type of religious intermarriage.

As may be seen in Table 4, certain features of the general pattern of findings on church attendance reported earlier continue to hold when educational level is controlled. While interpretation of the table must be tempered with caution because of small numbers in particular intermarriage categories, some general trends can be noted. First, insofar as Catholic respondents are concerned, it appears that within each educational category the pattern of church attendance is similar, regardless of the type of parental marriage. Indeed, when statistical tests were carried out, no differences were found when the church-attendance patterns of men from homogeneous Catholic families were compared with those from religious-intermarriage families, nor were any found when men from the two types of intermar-

---

13 While the issue of the existence and direction of a relationship between social status and church attendance remains to be finally resolved, recent research has advanced the clarification of this matter. See, for example, the recent findings of Harry C. Dillingham based on a critical re-examination of data from four prominent American studies of church attendance. "Protestant Religion and Social Status," *American Journal of Sociology*, 70 (1965), pp. 416-422, esp. p. 421. Among those reporting clear-cut positive relationships between church attendance and education are Gerhard Lenski, *The Religious Factor*, Garden City, New York: Doubleday & Co., Inc., pp. 45-46 and Bernard Lazerwitz, "Some Factors Associated with Variations in Church Attendance," *Social Forces*, 39 (1961), pp. 301-309. See also the bibliography of studies reporting church attendance and social status in Rodney Stark "Class, Radicalism, and Religious Involvement in Great Britain," *American Sociological Review*, 29 (1964), pp. 698-706, esp. p. 699. For a report on pertinent European studies, see Louis Schneider, "Problems in the Sociology of Religion," in Robert E. L. Faris (ed.), *Handbook of Modern Sociology*, Chicago: Rand McNally Co., 1964, pp. 770-807, esp. pp. 795-798. In addition, positive relationships between church attendance and educational level were found by the authors in another study of the Fort Dix inductee data. The results were reported in Sydney H. Croog, David E. Lavin, and James E. Teele, "Social Status, Ethnic Origins, and Church Attendance," unpublished manuscript.

riage families were compared with each other. Hence, in the case of the Catholic respondent at least, it seems safe to assume from these data that the situation of having intermarried parents has no substantial effect upon church-attendance patterns.

For the Protestant respondents, on the other hand, there is a somewhat more complex picture. In the "Three Years of High School and Under" category, the proportion of non-attenders and minimal attenders (0-11 times per year) in intermarriage category FcMp exceeds that of respondents whose parental marriages are FpMp or FpMc. The same features are evident in the attendance patterns of men who have graduated from high school. Another notable feature of the distribution in these two educational categories is that the Protestant respondents with Catholic mothers report church attendance at levels somewhat higher than those of Protestant men from both FpMp and FcMp types of marriage. Indeed, it is striking that sons from this type of intermarriage should more frequently report regular church attendance than sons from homogeneous Protestant marriages.

Among the Protestant men who have completed at least one year of college or more, the relationship of church attendance to parental marriage pattern varies in a relatively distinctive way from that of men in the other two educational categories. Thus 30 percent of the college men whose parents are both Protestants report attending church at least once weekly. In contrast, college respondents from mixed marriages are much less likely to attend church weekly.

TABLE 4   DISTRIBUTION (%) OF PARENTAL INTERMARRIAGE TYPE BY FREQUENCY OF CHURCH ATTENDANCE OF RESPONDENT, WITH CONTROLLING RELIGION AND EDUCATION OF RESPONDENT CONTROLLED ($N = 1297$)[a]

	Frequency of Church Attendance			
	0-11 per Year	1-3 per Month	1+ per Week	100% =
Respondent Catholic				
I. Three Years High School and Under [b]				
(A) FcMc	21(37)	26(45)	53 (92)	100(174)
(B) FpMc	32 (7)	32 (7)	36 (8)	100 (22)
(C) FcMp	31 (4)	31 (4)	38 (5)	100 (13)
II. High School Graduate [c]				
(A) FcMc	11(35)	14(49)	75(259)	100(347)
(B) FpMc	12 (6)	10 (5)	78 (40)	100 (51)
(C) FcMp	21 (5)	25 (6)	54 (13)	100 (24)
III. One Year College or More [d]				
(A) FcMc	5(14)	12(30)	83(211)	100(255)
(B) FpMc	11 (3)	11 (3)	78 (21)	100 (27)
(C) FcMp	5 (1)	9 (2)	86 (19)	100 (22)
Respondent Protestant				
I. Three Years High School and Under [e]				
(A) FpMp	61(22)	28(10)	11 (4)	100 (36)
(B) FpMc	20 (1)	40 (2)	40 (2)	100 (5)
(C) FcMp	83(10)	8 (1)	8 (1)	100 (12)
II. High School Graduate [f]				
(A) FpMp	35(36)	39(40)	25 (26)	100(102)
(B) FpMc	6 (1)	59(10)	35 (6)	100 (17)
(C) FcMp	47 (9)	53(10)	0 (0)	100 (19)
III. One Year College or More [g]				
(A) FpMp	30(42)	40(55)	30 (4)	100(138)
(B) FpMc	41 (7)	59(10)	0 (0)	100 (17)
(C) FcMp	38 (6)	56 (9)	6 (1)	100 (16)

[a] Insufficient data in 50 cases.
[b] χ^2 with 2 d.f. for: $AB=2.01$ (n.s.); $AC=1.32$ (n.s.); $BC=0.015$ (n.s).
[c] χ^2 with 2 d.f. for: $AB=0.79$ (n.s.); $AC=4.84$ (n.s.); $BC=3.26$ (n.s.).
[d] χ^2 with 2 d.f. for: $AB=0.62$ (n.s.); $AC=0.42$ (n.s.); $BC=1.11$ (n.s.).
[e] χ^2 with 2 d.f. for: $AC=2.50$ (n.s.).
[f] χ^2 with 2 d.f. for: $AB=5.95$ (n.s.); $AC=6.21$ ($p<0.05$); $BC=13.60$ ($p<0.01$).
[g] χ^2 with 2 d.f. for: $AB=8.03$ ($p<0.02$); $AC=3.35$ (n.s.); $BC=1.21$ (n.s.).

Besides providing useful insights into church attendance patterns of men from differing types of parental marriages, the data in Table 4 raise questions in another area. As indicated earlier, a positive relationship between church attendance and educational level has often been found in studies of Protestant populations. Data in Table 4, however, appear to indicate that generalizations about the direction of the relationship deserve further study. As will be seen, the pattern of parental intermarriage appears to be a possible intervening variable in determining direction of the relationship between church attendance and education.

More specifically, an inverse relationship appears to exist between education and church attendance for the Protestant respondents from the FpMc type of marriage. On the other hand, an apparently direct relationship exists between attendance and education for all other types of parental marriages in the table. The hint of the inverse relationship is observable from a close inspection of the data for Protestant respondents in Table 4. By focusing on Protestant respondents and comparing successively the "A" rows with each other, and by doing likewise with the "B" rows and then the "C" rows, the reader can isolate the groups of data of interest here. Pearsonian coefficients were computed between respondent's education and church attendance, controlling marriage pattern and the religion of respondents (Table 5). As can be seen, the results confirm the appearance of an inverse relationship for the FpMc group and a positive relationship for all others.

Viewing Tables 3, 4 and 5, together, some major characteristics deserve underlining for the light they cast on common assumptions about the effects of intermarriage on the religious viewpoints of children of such marriages. First, a striking finding among the Catholic respondents is the lack of substantial effect of parental intermarriage on reported church attendance (Table 4). Catholic men who are the product of intermarriage are not significantly different in church attendance pattern from those men whose parents formed a homogeneous Catholic marriage. Second, as noted before, a somewhat mixed picture is presented by the Protestant respondents. Judging by the data, one cannot say with confidence that low church attendance among Protestants is related to parental religious intermarriage. Instead, church attendance by Protestant men varied by parental marriage type and by educational level. Thus, among Protestant respondents without college experience, some of the offspring of religious intermarriage (FpMc) attend church more frequently than sons of homogeneous religious marriages. These find-

TABLE 5   PEARSONIAN COEFFICIENTS BETWEEN RESPONDENTS' EDUCATION
AND CHURCH ATTENDANCE, CONTROLLING PARENTAL INTERMARRIAGE TYPE
AND RELIGION OF RESPONDENT $(N = 1297)$[b]

	Pearsonian Coefficient	N
Respondent Catholic		
FcMc	+0.27 [a]	776
FpMc	+0.29 [a]	100
FcMp	+0.43 [a]	59
Respondent Protestant		
FpMp	+0.21 [a]	276
FcMp	+0.38 [a]	47
FpMc	−0.45 [a]	39

[a] $p < 0.01$, two-tailed test.
[b] 50 cases with insufficient data.

ings suggest that religious intermarriage by itself is not automatically
a determinant of extent of religious observance by the offspring.
In other words, these data suggest caution in asserting that the
Protestant or Catholic sons of an intermarriage will be less diligent
practicers of the faith than those men whose parents share the same
religion.

A second major set of findings relate to patterning of church
attendance by educational level (Table 5). Among Catholic respondents, regardless of pattern of parental marriage, there was a
direct relationship between educational level and church attendance.
Among Protestant respondents in two of the three parental marriage
categories a direct relationship is also seen. However, among men
from the FpMc type of parental marriage, an interesting and puzzling exception appeared.

Since the relationship between education and church attendance
among sons of FpMc marriages varies so markedly from that of
sons of other types of marital combinations, the basis for this difference certainly merits further empirical investigation. It is possible,
of course, that the results reported here may be one product of
small numbers in cells, or they may arise from some idiosyncratic
factor. Nevertheless, in view of this deviant finding, it might be
wise to exercise particular caution before generalizing about church
attendance of sons of religious intermarriage. Certainly future in-

vestigators should be wary about making easy assumptions concerning the direction of any relations between church attendance and educational level. In particular, investigation of the interaction of family relationships and of the religious milieu of the home might prove fruitful in a further examination of these findings.

CONCLUSION

This paper has set forth empirical findings regarding relationships between religious intermarriage of Catholic and Protestant parents and the religious identities and church attendance of their sons. Briefly, it has been shown that differing patterns of religious identity of the sons are evident, depending upon whether the parental marriage involves Protestant father and Catholic mother or Catholic father and Protestant mother. In addition, it was seen that patterns of religious identity of the sons are mediated by social status of the family, as indicated in rough form by educational status of the father. In particular, having a Catholic mother tended to result in a predominantly Catholic identity among the sons in the lower status levels, while in the families of college-educated fathers, presence of a Catholic mother was associated more with non-Catholic identity in the sons. Furthermore, differential patterns of church attendance were found, depending upon whether the son was Protestant or Catholic and depending upon his educational level and the religious identities of his parents.

These data are, of course, only one manifestation of complex phenomena at work in the family settings from which the respondents come. To understand the basis for these findings, further empirical research might be followed through in a number of areas. At one level, for example, these data may constitute outcomes of (a), the situation of the triad, and (b) the rational and non-rational elements which enter into the decision-making process. They bear on problems of factors associated with power relationships and dominance-submission patterns within the family. At another level these data bear on matters which are only rarely the subject of sociological research, such as the mystical elements which may influence choice of religion or church-attendance pattern. Finally, the issues raised by religious intermarriage are linked also to larger questions of the social, psychological, and institutional consequences of exogamous and endogamous marriages in general, and the outcome in situations of interpersonal contact between individuals from differing cultures. The empirical findings of this study contribute to a foundation for future focused work in these problematic areas.

11

Political vs. Religious
Liberalism among Catholics

PETER J. HENRIOT, S. J.

Cambridge Center for Social Studies

SOURCE. "The Coincidence of Political and Religious Attitudes," *Review of Religious Research*, 1966, *8*, 50-58. Reprinted by permission.

How does a Catholic who knew in his heart that Goldwater was right react to the new emphasis in his church upon ecumenical activities? And what does a Catholic who looks at the world through Teilhardian-tinted glasses think of the AFL-CIO? These two questions point to the general subject which will be explored in this study: the coincidence in American Catholics of liberal and conservative views in political and religious matters.[1] The first task confronting us is to characterize (rather than to define) what we mean by liberal and conservative views in political and religious matters.

LIBERAL AND CONSERVATIVE CHARACTERISTICS

A political liberal has an internationalist outlook which leads him to favor greater participation of the United States in the United Nations and an expanded program of aid to needy foreign countries. On the domestic scene he supports federal activity in regulating the economy and in providing welfare programs, and is friendly toward labor unions. His interests include the movement to secure full enjoyment of rights by Negroes and the efforts to protect civil liberties such as free speech. On the other hand, a political conservative is antagonistic toward the United Nations and foreign aid programs, fears the expansion of federal government activities, and is slow to support the Negro cause or civil liberties.[2]

A religious liberal [3] is ecumenically-minded, and hence tolerant of Protestants and Jews. He views the world with an optimism, enthusiastic about the opportunities to make his religion relevant. His tolerance makes him cautious about imposing his ideas on others, for example, in the area of sex mores. His religious practice stresses more strongly personal responsibility, with less emphasis upon legalism and formalism. On the other hand, a religious conservative tends to be intolerant, showing hostility toward Protestants and Jews. His outlook on the world is fearful, marked by an emphasis upon the world's sinfulness and dangers, and by a longing for the

---

[1] The large area of the relation between religion and politics has been extensively examined from many different approaches by both political scientists and sociologists. The classic voting studies, personality studies, historical accounts of parties and elections, etc., all treat of the subject. For a general survey of the broad subject, see Murray S. Stedman, Jr., *Religion and Politics in America* (New York: Harcourt, Brace and World, 1964).

[2] Fichter uses attitudes on foreign aid and civil rights as the test for political liberalism and conservatism; see Joseph H. Fichter, *Priest and People* (New York: Sheed and Ward, 1965), p. 123.

[3] We are not speaking of religious liberalism in the older sense of nineteenth century "secularism" or twentieth-century "modernism." Nor are we characterizing religious conservatism as "fundamentalism." For clarification of these distinctions, see Robert Cross, *The Emergence of Liberal Catholicism in America* (Cambridge: Harvard University Press, 1958), pp. 206-224; and Daniel Callahan, *The Mind of the Catholic Layman* (New York: Charles Scribner's Sons, 1963), p. 159.

next life. He feels that the doctrines and morals of his religion, because they are the true ones, should be enforced upon everyone. A type of legalism influences his religious practices.

As we originally noted, these are *characterizations* rather than *definitions*. They are more "ideal types" than empirical categories. They merely attempt to delineate the general tendencies, orientations, outlooks, attitudes, etc, of those whom we will call liberals and conservatives in political and religious matters.[4]

This study is attempting to discover what coincidence, if any, exists between views in political matters and views in religious matters. The most basic question we begin by asking, then, is: Are the political liberals and the religious liberals identical? That is, do the same persons who have a generally liberal view in politics also have a generally liberal view in religious matters? The same basic question of identity is, of course, applicable to conservatives.

The initial response which we shall give to this question—a response admittedly based more on "common sense" observation than on strenuous empirical research—is *yes*. We are aware of the possibly misleading character of these "common sense" observations, and we agree with Lenski that there are "dangers inherent in the assumption that 'a liberal is a liberal is a liberal.' "[5] Nevertheless we will at least begin this study by assuming that the person whose attitudes are liberal in politics is likely to be liberal in religious matters, and that the one who is religiously conservative is probably politically conservative.

COINCIDENCE OF ATTITUDES

For an evident example of the coincidence of the attitudes about which we are speaking, let us compare two weekly Catholic newspapers of nation-wide circulation.[6]

The *National Catholic Reporter* (Kansas City) leaves us no doubt about its definite liberal orientation. In political affairs the newspaper leans strongly to the left, both in news coverage and in editorials. It supports negotiation in Viet Nam through the media-

---

4 For a detailed caution about constructing these characterizations, see Willard A. Kerr, "Untangling the Liberalism-Conservatism Continuum," *Journal of Social Psychology*, XXXV (February, 1952), 111-125.

5 Gerhard Lenski, *The Religious Factor* (Garden City, N.Y.: Doubleday and Company, Inc., 1963), p. 191; see also pp. 187-190.

6 For purposes of comparison, January and February, 1965, issues of these newspapers were read.

tion of the United Nations, endorses Medicare and the War on Poverty, and reports enthusiastically the demonstrations for equal voting rights for southern Negroes. This same newspaper also has strongly liberal religious views. Regular columns are written by prominent Protestant theologians; news of ecumenical interest is given extensive coverage. Actions of members of the hierarchy (even of the Pope) are openly analyzed and frequently criticized. Repeated calls are made for re-examination of the Catholic position on parochial schools, birth control, religious orders, etc. Reports in glowing detail are given of the spread of liturgical changes.

On the other hand (and definitely on the *right* hand), *The Wanderer* (St. Paul) is staunchly conservative in both politics and religion. Vigorously anti-Communist and anti-United Nations, the newspaper is also sharp in its attack upon the "socialistic" plans of the Great Society. It expresses repeated concern over the current agitation for civil rights and has been strong in its criticism of schools which have allowed "left-wing" speakers to appear on their campuses. In religious matters, front-page coverage is given to warnings by certain members of the hierarchy regarding the dangers of the ecumenical movement and the new theological trends. Columnists caution against excesses in the new liturgy and exhort readers to retain traditional devotions. Sharp criticism is made of those who call into question any of the long-accepted policies of the Catholic Church.

A look at these two Catholic papers (purposely chosen, of course, to give evident polar examples) provides support for the initial response which we gave to our basic question. But is there some effective way to empirically test the validity—and explicate the meaning—of the assertion of the identity of liberal and conservative positions in political and religious matters? Studies by Fichter,[7] Stouffer,[8] Lenski,[9] and Alford [10] contain some findings on the correlation between one's involvement in formal church activity and one's political and social attitudes. But involvement in church ac-

---

[7] Fichter, *op. cit.*, pp. 131-132.

[8] According to Samuel A. Stouffer, those who attend church regularly are less likely to be tolerant of non-conformists; see *Communism, Conformity, and Civil Liberties: A Cross-section of the Nation Speaks Its Mind* (Garden City, N.Y.: Doubleday and Company, Inc., 1955), pp. 140-149.

[9] Lenski says that regular involvement in the church is linked to a less liberal view on foreign aid and a narrow interpretation of free speech; *op. cit.*, pp. 171-173.

[10] Robert A. Alford, *Party and Society: The Anglo-American Democracies* (Chicago: Rand-McNally and Company, 1963), pp. 49-58.

tivity is *not* the precise religious phenomenon in which we are interested here. Rather, it is one's general religious outlook which we desire to correlate to one's general political outlook.

NORC SURVEY

Taking advantage of data recently gathered in a National Opinion Research Center survey on the effects of Catholic education,[11] we are able to examine the political and religious attitudes of some two thousand Catholics throughout the United States. We can make use of several special indices which were constructed from responses to various questions on political and religious subjects. The data supply us with the percentages of those scoring in such a way as to be designated as liberals or conservatives on each of these indices.

As a measure of political attitudes, we use three indices. The Social Teaching Index is constructed from responses to questions regarding the United Nations, foreign aid, labor unions, and government unemployed programs.[12] The Anti-Negro Index measures racial prejudices, and the Authoritarian Index measures attitudes toward free speech. A liberal political view is indicated by a high score on the Social Teaching Index and by a low score on the Anti-Negro Index and on the Authoritarian Index.

We use five indices as measures of religious attitudes. These are an Anti-Protestant Index and an Anti-Jewish Index, measures of Catholic tolerance toward non-Catholics. An Extremism Index is constructed from responses to questions which touch upon the influence of Catholicism in such practical matters as family limitation, Church-State relations, and religious legalism. Attitudes toward the world and the secular sphere are measured by a Manichean Index, and attitudes on sexual mores (principally related to birth control) are measured by a Jansenism Index. A liberal religious view is indicated by a low score on each of the five indices.

In order to supply some general information on the background of the respondents, use is made of the Duncan Index, indicating socio-economic status, and of an Educational Level Index, indicating the level of formal education completed. The Duncan Index relates

---

11 For a general description of this survey, see Andrew M. Greeley, Peter H. Rossi, and Leonard J. Pinto, *The Social Effects of Catholic Education* (NORC Preliminary Report No. 99-A; Chicago; National Opinion Research Center, The University of Chicago, 1964).

12 The "social teaching" referred to in this index is contained in recent papal encyclicals, such as John XXIII's *Mater et Magistra* and *Pacem in Terris*.

to occupational prestige, and by means of a ten-point scale it provides a rough indication of class.[13] Further information is supplied by a Secular Knowledge Index and a Religious Knowledge Index, constructed from responses to a set of general-knowledge questions.

HYPOTHESES TESTED

An initial set of hypotheses was drawn up in order to test whether or not liberal and conservative views coincide in political and religious matters. As a start, a gross distinction was made on the basis of political party affiliation.[14] We certainly recognize the significant differences between Northern and Southern Democrats, and between New York and California Republicans. Nevertheless, for the sake of a manageable starting point, we will consider Democrats as generally more liberal than Republicans.

1. More Catholic Democrats than Catholic Republicans will score as political liberals on the Social Teaching, Anti-Negro, and Authoritarian indices.

2. More Catholic Democrats than Catholic Republicans will score as religious liberals on the Anti-Protestant, Anti-Jewish, Extremism, Manichean, and Jansenism indices.

Next, using the Social Teaching Index to indicate the range of conservative-liberal political attitudes, the following hypotheses were tested for both Democrats and Republicans.

3. More of those indicated as political liberals on the Social Teaching Index will score as political liberals on the Anti-Negro and Authoritarian indices.

4. More of those indicated as political liberals on the Social Teaching Index will score as religious liberals on the Anti-Protestant, Anti-Jewish, Extremism, Manichean, and Jansenism indices.

In testing this initial set of hypotheses, the correlates definitely did not occur as predicted, and in many instances the differences were strikingly significant. As *Table 1* shows, there were more Catholic Republicans than Catholic Democrats who scored on the liberal side of the various political and religious indices. While it

---

13 A complete account of the construction and uses of this socio-economic index is found in Albert J. Reiss, Jr., *Occupation and Social Status* (New York: The Free Press of Glencoe, Inc., 1961), pp. 109-161.

14 Only respondents who identified themselves as either Democrats or Republicans were made use of in this study.

TABLE 1 N = BASE FOR %; PERCENTAGES SCORING HIGH ON POLITICAL AND RELIGIOUS INDICES

| | Political Indices | | | | | | Religious Indices | | | | | | | | |
| | Social Teaching | | Anti-Negro | | Authoritarian | | Anti-Protestant | | Anti-Jewish | | Extremism | | Manichean | | Jansenism | |
	%	N	%	N	%	N	%	N	%	N	%	N	%	N	%	N
Democrats	58.3	1177	50.1	1130	39.5	1142	44.2	1187	48.1	1182	53.4	1156	46.2	1179	51.4	1134
Republicans	44.2	256	43.1	252	38.3	243	42.2	263	40.9	264	43.4	249	44.5	261	46.4	248

is true that 14 percent more Democrats than Republicans scored higher on the Social Teaching Index, 7 percent more Democrats scored higher on the Anti-Negro Index. Percentages high on the Authoritarian Index were approximately even for members of both political parties. In the measure of religious views, there were consistently greater percentages of Democrats high on all of the indices, indicative of religious conservatism. Most striking was the fact that 10 percent more Democrats than Republicans scored high on the Extremism Index, and 7 percent more scored high on the Anti-Jewish Index.

The findings shown in *Table 2* were so contrary to the initial hypotheses as to cast some doubt upon the usefulness of the Social Teaching Index as a measure of conservative-liberal attitudes. It seems that among the Democrats the greater percentage of those scoring as political conservatives on the Anti-Negro and Authoritarian indices were among those who scored as political liberals on the Social Teaching Index. The pattern among Republicans is not as clear (some of the cells are very small), but it is still similar to the Democratic pattern. The picture of religious attitudes is as striking as that of political attitudes. With very little deviation, the higher percentage of Democrats who scored as religious conservatives were among those who scored as political liberals on the Social Teaching Index. While once again the Republicans do not present as consistent a pattern as the Democrats, it nevertheless is substantially the same. The findings would thus seem to indicate that the more one supports the United Nations, foreign aid, labor unions, and government unemployment programs, the more one is religiously intolerant, hostile toward the world, and puritanical.

From the data presented in *Table 3*, it is certainly evident that liberal scores on the Social Teaching Index did not correlate with liberal scores on the other two political indices, nor with liberal scores on the five religious indices. In order to test the validity of the Social Teaching Index, a complete breakdown of the Index was made. Each of the four questions, each with four possible answers, was compared with the scores on the seven indices. (In order to provide large cells, party affiliation was not considered in this test.) No particularly significant deviations were noted in this breakdown. The percentages of conservatives, as indicated by the Anti-Negro and Authoritarian indices and by the several religious indices, were in all but a few instances greater among those who endorsed the United Nations, foreign aid, labor unions, and government unemployment programs. A combined sampling from the findings of this

TABLE 2 PERCENTAGES SCORING HIGH ON INDICES, ARRANGED ACCORDING TO CONSERVATIVE-LIBERAL SCALE OF SOCIAL TEACHING INDEX

	Social Teaching Index	Political Indices						Religious Indices							
		Anti-Negro		Authoritarian		Anti-Protestant		Anti-Jewish		Extremism		Mani-chean		Jan-senism	
		%	N	%	N	%	N	%	N	%	N	%	N	%	N
Conservative	0	39.4	33	24.3	33	42.9	35	42.9	35	28.1	32	37.2	35	42.0	31
	1	41.2	136	39.0	136	40.6	138	43.5	138	44.8	136	38.4	138	48.9	135
Democrats	2	45.7	287	37.9	285	40.5	299	46.7	302	48.1	297	40.2	299	46.9	288
	3	52.1	403	41.0	398	44.9	414	51.5	412	47.5	404	50.0	410	51.6	401
Liberal	4	59.9	237	40.3	248	50.0	250	46.8	250	62.2	248	52.4	248	58.7	240
Conservative	0	42.8	14	7.7	13	42.9	14	46.2	13	15.4	14	35.7	13	15.4	13
	1	53.7	41	39.1	41	24.4	41	36.4	44	24.4	41	43.2	44	28.6	42
	2	56.3	80	44.6	74	33.3	84	40.5	84	51.3	78	45.8	83	51.3	74
Republicans	3	52.8	72	38.0	71	52.0	75	41.9	74	48.6	72	46.7	75	50.0	74
Liberal	4	44.0	34	32.4	34	58.3	36	37.8	37	47.8	35	42.4	33	58.8	34

breakdown is presented in *Table 3*. Those who answered "agree strongly" (a liberal response) to the questions on international affairs (United Nations, foreign aid) are compared in this table with those who answered "disagree strongly" (a conservative response) according to the percentages scoring as conservatives on a selection of the various indices. The same is also done for the questions on domestic affairs (unions and unemployment programs). The conclusion is that the larger percentages of conservatives are to be found among those giving the supposedly liberal responses to questions regarding international and domestic affairs.

We can thus see that the analysis of the data presented up to this point presents a quite unexpected picture. Democrats are found to be more Anti-Negro and more religiously conservative than Republicans. And those who endorse liberal international and domestic programs are found to be anti-Negro, anti-civil liberties, and staunch religious conservatives. What explanation can possibly be given for these surprising findings? A look once again at *Table 3* may offer us some clues. It has been noted that the larger percentages of respondents scoring as conservatives on the various indices are among those giving liberal responses to the international and domestic issues. Yet it should also be noted that these percentages are even larger in the domestic category. That is, in comparison to those who fully endorse the United Nations and foreign aid, more of those who fully endorse labor unions and government unemployment programs are indicated as conservatives on the other political indices and on the religious indices. Conversely, fewer domestic-issue conservatives than international-issue conservatives rank as conservatives on the various indices.

CLASS PHENOMENON

The higher percentages of conservatives among those endorsing unions and unemployment programs gives us a cue that this conservatism may possibly be a *class* phenomenon. Persons in the lower classes might reasonably be expected to be strong supporters of labor unions and of unemployment programs. Lipset has demonstrated the existence of what he calls a "working class authoritarianism." [15] He argues that those who have low incomes, low occupational status, and low educational level tend to have ethnic prejudices, to be

---

15 Seymour Lipset, *Political Man: The Social Basis of Politics* (Garden City, N.Y.: Anchor Books, Doubleday and Company, Inc., 1963), pp. 87-126.

TABLE 3 PERCENTAGES SCORING HIGH ON SELECTED INDICES, ARRANGED ACCORDING TO LIBERAL AND CONSERVATIVE VIEWS ON INTERNATIONAL AND DOMESTIC ISSUES

		Anti Negro		Authoritarian		Anti-Protestant		Extremism		Manichean	
		%	N	%	N	%	N	%	N	%	N
International Issues	Liberal	51.6	271	35.8	270	49.6	281	53.2	272	49.0	279
	Conservative	44.5	36	17.7	34	34.3	35	30.3	33	35.0	37
Domestic Issues	Liberal	58.1	299	37.0	249	57.2	304	55.8	297	54.4	297
	Conservative	32.4	37	20.6	34	40.5	37	25.8	37	32.3	34

politically intransigent and intolerant, to view most situations in narrow terms of black and white, good and bad, and to support fundamentalist religious groups. Studies have shown, Lipset notes, that "people poorly informed on public issues are more likely to be both *more liberal* on economic issues and *less liberal* on noneconomic ones."[16] Similarly, Stouffer has shown that the lower classes are more likely to be intolerant on issues of civil liberty.[17]

Is it possible, then, that in the data which is being analyzed here, the respondents from the lower classes are scoring as liberal on the Social Teaching Index, but as decidedly conservative on the seven other indices? This is the question which appears to be crucial, and is deserving of further examination.

Returning to the initial breakdown of all of the respondents according to political party affiliation, some interesting comparative facts can be presented regarding the socio-economic status and the education-knowledge level of Democrats and Republicans. As shown in *Table 4*, more Republicans than Democrats are to be found among those we might designate as "upper class" according to the ten-point scale of the Duncan Index. Fewer Democrats than Republicans finished high school and some college; and fewer scored high on the indices of secular and religious knowledge.

A similar set of findings is available in *Table 5*, which presents the socio-economic status and the education knowledge level of the Democrats and Republicans according as they place along the conservative-liberal scale of the Social Teaching Index. It can be seen from this table that the greater percentages of those scoring as conservatives on the Social Teaching Index are members of the upper classes and more highly educated.

The most revealing findings, however, are presented in *Table 6*. Here the Democrats and Republicans are divided into groups according to the Duncan Index as an indicator of class, and their percentages scoring high on the eight political and religious indices are compared. It is clearly seen that in every instance but one the higher percentages of both Democrats and Republicans scoring as conservatives on the indices are in the lowest socio-economic class. The one major exception, as would be expected from our previous discussion, is the Social Teaching Index. For on this Index, a higher percentage of the respondents who are members of the lower class score as liberals.

---

[16] *Ibid.,* p. 103.
[17] Stouffer, *op. cit., passim.*

TABLE 4 PERCENTAGES OF RESPONDENTS IN VARIOUS EDUCATIONAL AND CLASS LEVELS

	Educational Levels						Class Levels (Duncan Index)			
	At Least Some College		High Score: Secular Knowledge		High Score: Religious Knowledge		Lower (0-2)	Middle (3-5)	Upper (6-9)	
	%	N	%	N	%	N	%	%	%	N
Democrats	52.0	1251	49.5	1228	39.2	1252	47.3	34.8	18.1	794
Republicans	70.3	276	66.4	271	45.6	276	22.8	36.7	40.4	188

TABLE 5 Percentages of Respondents in Various Educational and Class Levels, Arranged According to Conservative-Liberal Scale of Social Teaching Index

Social Teaching Index		At Least Some College		High Score: Secular Knowledge		High Score: Religious Knowledge		Lower (0-2)	Middle (3-5)	Upper (6-9)	
		%	N	%	N	%	N	%	%	%	N
Conservative	0	77.1	35	57.7	34	45.7	35	27.2	50.0	22.7	22
	1	62.7	142	51.0	139	49.3	142	36.4	38.0	25.1	80
Democrats	2	58.4	312	54.4	306	40.4	312	39.7	41.4	18.8	186
	3	51.1	428	52.6	421	38.5	429	51.7	30.4	18.0	279
Liberal	4	41.8	258	44.5	254	36.4	258	53.2	31.5	15.2	184
Conservative	0	78.6	14	92.3	13	57.1	14	0.0	50.0	50.0	10
	1	86.3	44	77.4	44	47.7	44	9.4	40.6	50.6	32
Republicans	2	67.1	85	60.3	83	48.4	85	26.0	34.0	40.0	50
	3	73.6	76	73.8	76	39.5	76	25.0	35.8	39.3	56
Liberal	4	62.1	37	63.9	36	51.3	37	26.7	36.7	33.6	30

Note: "Educational Levels" spans the At Least Some College, High Score: Secular Knowledge, and High Score: Religious Knowledge columns; "Class Levels (Duncan Index)" spans the Lower, Middle, Upper, and N columns.

TABLE 6 PERCENTAGES SCORING HIGH ON INDICES, ARRANGED ACCORDING TO CLASS LEVELS

Class Levels (Duncan Index)	Political Indices								Religious Indices							
	Social Teaching		Anti-Negro		Authoritarian		Anti-Protestant		Anti-Jewish		Extremism		Manichean		Jansenism	
	%	N	%	N	%	N	%	N	%	N	%	N	%	N	%	N
Democrats Lower (0-2)	68.7	351	55.0	331	40.3	330	48.1	348	54.7	350	58.5	336	51.4	350	51.8	322
Middle (3-5)	54.5	262	47.8	257	35.6	258	43.3	268	48.6	265	52.6	254	48.7	261	48.7	252
Upper (6-9)	56.5	138	37.5	133	25.2	135	41.7	137	31.1	135	34.4	138	29.3	133	39.2	135
Republicans Lower (0-2)	57.8	38	68.6	35	54.3	35	52.6	38	64.1	39	67.6	34	60.5	38	52.8	36
Middle (3-5)	47.0	66	52.2	65	38.7	62	41.8	67	46.2	67	46.7	63	43.2	67	43.5	62
Upper (6-9)	44.6	74	37.9	72	22.1	68	43.5	76	29.3	75	23.9	71	38.4	73	37.5	72

CONCLUSIONS

What general conclusions, interpretations, and directions for further research is it possible to offer at this point? The findings in *Tables 4, 5, 6* seem to aid us to understand the findings presented in *Tables 1, 2,* and *3.* The variable which appears to be most influential in determining religious and political liberalism and conservatism is the socio-economic status of the respondent. This variable is, of course, a complex syndrome of many different factors. It should be carefully noted that "class" is not one single thing, and that these factors include at least such things as income, occupational status, and educational level.

It appears that on the political issues of the United Nations, foreign aid, labor unions, and government unemployment programs (especially the latter two), liberal respondents are more likely to be members of what we are designating as the lower class. But on the political issues of race relations and civil liberties, this same lower class is more likely to be conservative. Similarly, this class is more likely to be conservative according to the various measures of religious attitudes. The anti-Negro prejudice might *partially* be explained by the fact that lower class whites fear the threat to job security which they feel is posed by the Negroes. The religious conservatism might *partially* be explained by a less-educated understanding of the meaning and consequences of religion today.

Further study is certainly needed, however, to clarify the shades of differences of liberalism and conservatism, especially when class is held constant. For example, what are we to make of the fact that *Table 6* shows fewer upper-class Republicans than upper-class Democrats among those scoring as conservatives on the Authoritarian Anti-Jewish, Extremism, and Jansenism indices? Similarly, what is the meaning of the greater percentages of upper-class Republicans than upper-class Democrats scoring as conservatives on the Manichean Index? An important variable which deserves to be taken into account in further examinations of this topic is the area of the country in which the respondents live. Some observers of the Catholic Church in the United States have indicated various "styles" of Catholicism in different parts of the country.[18] This needs to be empirically researched. It may in part be found to be related to another variable worthy of notice, the ethnic background of the respondents.

In summary, we must recall that in entering into this attempt to analyze the coincidence of liberal and conservative attitudes in

---

[18] See, for example, the symposium on "Catholicism Midwest Style," *America,* CIV (February 12, 1966), pp. 221-230.

political and religious matters, an initial response of *yes* was given to the basic question: Are the political liberals and the religious liberals identical? But the data presented in this study gives fairly clear, although admittedly preliminary, indication that there is need for considerable qualification in this initial response. Political liberals according to the measure of the Social Teaching Index are definitely not identical with religious liberals, and are not even identical with political liberals according to the measure of the Anti-Negro and Authoritarian indices. A *lower class bias* appears to be the most significant factor accounting for the lack of identity. Thus the findings of this study direct our attention again to the caution of Lenski which we cited earlier: beware of the easy assumption that "a liberal is a liberal is a liberal."

12

Moral Values, Religion, and Racial Crisis

WILLIAM T. LIU

University of Notre Dame

SOURCE. "The Community Reference System, Religiosity, and Race Attitudes," *Social Forces,* 1961, 39, 324-328. Reprinted by permission.

This paper analyzes the attitudes of a group of Catholics who migrated from other regions, mainly the North, to Tallahassee, Florida, measured during the crises created by a series of racial tensions in 1957. As members of a religious minority group in a community in which the known sentiment is to preserve a segregated system, how do they perceive the situation and, consequently, how do they react toward such a situation?

307

Tallahassee is a small urban community located in the northern part of Florida. An estimated population of 38,000 was reported in 1955. The city is the state capital of Florida and is the seat of two segregated state universities, one white and one Negro. The economy rests upon white-collar work, and there is virtually no industrial base. The median family income in 1950 was $2,952 or about $600 higher than the state median income. The median number of years of school completed by persons 25 years or older in 1950 was higher than that for the state as a whole (11.9 as compared to 9.6 years). Negroes comprised 34 percent of the total population in 1950. The city follows the traditional southern etiquette of race relations, including the prohibition of social gatherings between students of the two state universities.

Like any southern community, the capital city is predominately Protestant. Before the turn of the present century, the Catholic congregation of Tallahassee consisted largely of early Irish and French settlers, few in number and generally poor. Even among these, many had drifted away, and by 1904 there were only four Catholics in the city.[1] Recent expansion of the city's population has been caused by the influx of incoming technical and professional personnel as a result of the expansion of the state government and the two state universities. Members of the only Catholic parish consist largely of newer migrants.[2] At the time of the racial crisis in Tallahassee, the local parish was the only integrated institution in which intermingling of two races was permitted and carried out in all regular church functions. Negroes comprised about 5 percent of the congregation.

During the spring of 1956 and in subsequent months, a series of precipitating events concerned with the Supreme Court's decision on the integration problem finally led to a bus boycott by the Negro population of Tallahassee, Florida. A complete report of this crisis was later presented by Killian and Smith.[3] Because of the importance of this event to the present research, it is necessary to describe briefly the incidents.

In the spring of 1956, two months before the beginning of the bus boycott, a study of the attitudes of Tallahassee white people toward desegregation was made by members of the two state univer-

---

[1] Dorothy Van Brunt, Father Hugon and the Early Catholic Church in Tallahassee (unpublished private manuscript), p. 8.

[2] Letter from the Department of Education, Diocese of St. Augustine, Florida (dated April 27, 1957).

[3] Lewis M. Killian and Charles U. Smith, *The Tallahassee Bus Boycott* (Anti-Defamation League of B'nai B'rith, 1958).

sities' sociology staffs. Interviews were conducted with 536 subjects, a 5 percent sample of the adult white population. In the study, which was primarily concerned with reactions to the Supreme Court ruling on school segregation, the general opinion was found to be overwhelmingly against the Court's decision. A series of precipitating events led to the ultimate episode of the well-publicized bus boycott which began on May 26, 1956.[4]

Between June, 1956, and the spring of 1957 several legal manifestations of the bi-racial conflict involving the city, the state, and the NAACP occurred.[5] By the time of the present study, the bus boycott movement had become relatively stationary. The desegregation attempt, however, did lead to: (1) clearly defined leadership among the Negro population, lacking before the crisis, and (2) the crystallization of the opinion of the community's white population with regard to the race problem.

THE PROBLEM

There are many avenues which might lead to fruitful investigation of the position of Catholic migrants with regard to the race crisis in Tallahassee. The investigator was repeatedly reminded that subjects being interviewed were members of a religious minority who were, at the same time, aware of the moral aspects of segregation issues. Secondly, the majority of subjects interviewed were members of middle or upper income groups.[6] As such, their behavior was subject to the pressure and sanction of the community's business and governmental groups. Finally, subjects interviewed were also migrants from other parts of the country, whose community satisfaction and the extent of their social participation were contingent upon their normative integration in the host community.[7] Having made a preliminary survey of opinions among several parochial leaders, the consensus seemed to be that unless these above-mentioned factors

---

[4] *Ibid.*, pp. 6-7.

[5] *Ibid.*, pp. 7-15, passim.

[6] The result of the first tabulation of data showed that the combined professional-technical-proprietors-managerial personnel comprised 64.2 percent of the total husbands' occupation. Of the remaining, 8.2 percent were students and members of the armed forces. About 75 percent of the couples owned their homes regardless of length of residence; yet about 26 percent of wives were gainfully employed; over 90 percent of the families had incomes higher than $4,000 annually.

[7] See William T. Liu, "Marginal Catholics in the South—A Revision of Concepts," *American Journal of Sociology*, 65 (January 1960), pp. 383-390.

were taken fully into account, it would be difficult to assess the true feelings of subjects interviewed in the study in regard to the desegregation issues.

The opinion of parochial leaders was later supported by the findings of a study made in Little Rock on attitudes among Protestant religious leaders toward the school crisis. In the Little Rock study, Campbell and Pettigrew focused sharply on the community reference system of subjects on the school problem.[8] The methodological framework of the Little Rock study thus further strengthens the theoretical implications of this study.

Based on the rationale mentioned in the previous paragraphs, a number of hypotheses were set forth: (1) attitude toward the race question will be related to the individual's degree of Catholic religiosity; (2) attitude toward the race crisis will be also related to the socio-economic status of the individual; and (3) the individual's lengths of residence and other factors concerning permanency and stability of residence will be related to his attitude toward the issue in question.

METHOD

To facilitate the analysis, only the white, married couples in which both are Catholics were used in the statistical analysis. Since there were only about 260 families in the congregation, a total enumeration of the parishioners' roll was made. The final sample consisted of 196 married individuals.

In the light of the above-mentioned hypotheses, the study did employ three independent variables—Catholic religiosity, socioeconomic status, and residential stability—and one dependent variable, a measure of race attitude.

To determine the degree of Catholic religiosity, two methods were used. Church attendance, frequency of participation in religious functions (Holy Communion, etc.), and the extent to which the individual was involved in parochial activities were used to assess the external behavior pattern in religious practices.[9] In addition to

---

8 Ernest Q. Campbell and Thomas F. Pettigrew, *Christians in Racial Crisis: A Study of the Little Rock Ministry* (Washington, D. C.: Public Affairs Press, 1959), and "Racial and Moral Crisis," *American Journal of Sociology*, 64 (March 1959), pp. 509-516.

9 This technique was first used by Joseph H. Fichter, S. J., in *Social Relations in the Urban Parish* (Chicago: University of Chicago Press, 1954). Fichter's classifications were modified here.

this method, two attitude scales were formulated according to the Cornell technique to measure attitudes toward doctrinal matters and toward birth control. These two scales were labeled as *Church Doctrine Scale* and *Birth Control Attitude Scale* respectively (CDS and BCAS). Significantly enough, the relationships between the external religious participation and the subjects' attitudes elicited by these two scales were highly consistent as shown in Table 1.

TABLE 1 LEVEL OF SIGNIFICANCE OF MUTUAL DEPENDENCY BETWEEN SCORES ON TWO ATTITUDINAL SCALES AND ON CATHOLIC RELIGIOSITY

Scale	Chi-square	$p <$ [a]
CDS	25.22	.001
BCAS	14.90	.01

[a] At 4 degrees of freedom.

The status categories employed were income, husband's occupation, and education of the respondents. All of those who had at least a college degree were considered "high" in education; the "middle" educational group consisted of those who had some education on the college level but did not have the degree; and those who had never been to college were indicated as "low." Families with an annual income of over $8,000 were grouped as "high," between $6,000 and $7,999 as "middle," and below $5,999 as "low." The high occupational group consisted of professionals and technical personnel; "middle" was for proprietors of small business and managers of chain stores and offices; and the rest were included in the "low." White collar occupations with high prestige—such as insurance broker —have been included in the "middle" group. All of the divisions were made according to the empirical distributions of data.

To measure the residential stability, two groups of criteria were used. On the objective level, length of residence, frequency of post-marital mobility, the respondents' age, and social participation of the individual in the community were used. Chapin's *Social Participation Scale* (SP) was used to measure the last mentioned item. On the subjective side, a six-item Guttman type of scale was used to determine the degree of the individual's regional identification [10] referred to in this study as the *Southern Identification Scale* (SIS). Distribution of the various groups is shown in Table 2.

[10] Coefficient of reproducibility at .918.

312   *Social System Patterns Among Catholic Americans*

TABLE 2   SOCIAL CHARACTERISTICS OF THE SAMPLE

Variables	High	Middle	Low	No. Inf.	Total
Catholic religiosity	70	74	52	—	196
Doctrine scale	73	60	61	2	196
Birth control scale	64	67	61	4	196
Status factors					
Education	70	48	74	4	196
Family income [a]	40	26	25	—	91
Husband's occupation	31	32	26	—	89 [b]
Residential stability					
Length of residence	66	56	70	4	196
Age	34	101	60	1	196
Mobility	59	78	55	4	196
Social participation	57	47	92	4	196
Southern identification	73	57	65	1	196

[a] Earnings for both the husband and the wife.
[b] Excluding students and unemployed.

The independent variable was defined by the scores on a five-term Guttman scale called the *Race Attitude Scale* (RAS) with a yielded reproductibility of .932. Four of the five items dealt with the race problem in general; the last item made specific reference to the local issue. Patterns of interdependency between each of the independent variables used and scores on the *Race Attitude Scale* were analyzed by Chi-square technique with rejection of null hypotheses set at the usual five percent level.

RESULTS

Religiosity and Race Attitude

The data failed to establish any relationship between the external pattern of religious participation and attitude toward the desegregation issues. The relationship between scale scores on doctrinal matters and race attitude was stronger than that between *Birth Control Attitude Scale* scores and *Race Attitude Scale* scores. Since the earlier analysis revealed that both of these scale scores were consistently related to the individual's external behavior in church attendance, some of the subjects were evidently inconsistent in their responses. These results are shown in Table 3.

Variable	Chi-square value	$p <$
Religiosity	1.95	—
CDS	9.53	.05
BCAS	5.41	—

Status Positions and Race Attitude

Turning then to the second general hypothesis on the relationship between socio-economic status and attitude toward the desegregation issues, the results are equally inconsistent. Of the three criteria used, only the education factor, with a chi-square of 21.18, was significantly related to the race attitude, i.e., more education was related to less prejudice. Table 4 shows the result.

Variable	Southern Identification		Social Participation		Race	
	Chi-square	$p <$	Chi-square	$p <$	Chi-square	$p <$
Income [a]	W— 3.31	—	W—17.32	.01	W— 6.29	—
	H—10.07	.05	H— 9.15	.1	H— 1.29	—
Education	6.60	—	19.41	.001	21.18	.001
Occupation	W— 1.47	—	W— 4.36	—	W— 5.67	—
	H— 3.76	—	H—14.62	.01	H— 7.93	—

[a] W indicates chi-square results for wives by using the family income.
H indicates results for husbands.

The Residency Factors and Race Attitude

One possible explanation of the unsuccessful attempt to establish confirmation of the hypothesis on socio-economic status and race attitude was that our subjects, being members of upper and middle income status groups, have failed to accept the community's feelings toward the race issues because they had not accepted the South or the community as a place in which to settle down. The identification of themselves as "sojourners" may be the contributory factor to such an indifferent attitude. Thus the test of the third hypothesis is related to the second hypothesis.

During the first step toward verification of the third hypothesis, all three variables used here—age, length of residence, and post-marital mobility—were found to be related to the *RAS* scores in the manner as anticipated. With the exception of age, stability factors were also related to the *Social Participation Scale* as well as the scores on *SIS*. Both of these results confirmed earlier assumptions. During the second step of the analysis, when the scores on *SIS* were used, it became more convincing that the individual's subjective identification with the South was responsible for the negative attitude toward desegregation issues. Table 5 shows the results.

TABLE 5   CHI-SQUARE RESULTS BETWEEN RESIDENTIAL STABILITY FACTORS, AND RACE ATTITUDE, SOUTHERN IDENTIFICATION, AND SOCIAL PARTICIPATION SCORES

Variable	Southern Identification		Social Participation		Race	
	Chi-square	$p <$	Chi-square	$p <$	Chi-square	$p <$
Length of Residence	38.48	.001	9.49	.05	27.16	.001
Mobility	15.68	.01	13.24	.02	12.57	.002
Age	22.83	.001	1.04	—	23.71	.001
SIS	—	—	—	—	14.46	.01

DISCUSSION

The hypothesis that attitudes toward desegregation issues among Catholics in Tallahassee, Florida during the bus-boycott crisis and its aftermath depended upon the individual's degree of Catholic religiosity receives partial support in this study. Those who adhered closely to Catholic doctrines showed more favorable attitude toward desegregation although the external behavior of church participation failed to be a predictive factor.

Data also showed that both the stability of residency factors and the social status factors are related to the individual's social participation in the community. The stability factors are significantly related to the individual's subjective identification with the South. Among the three status factors, only income seemed to be related to men's *SIS* scores who, in the majority of cases, are the breadwinners in the family. The hypothesis that class position is related to race attitude was not confirmed here. Education was found to be significant in the more favorable response to questions concerning desegregation.

Despite the unsurprising nature of the findings, this study nevertheless has confirmed observations made by Campbell and Pettigrew in the Little Rock study mentioned earlier. Significantly, subjects of the present study had been found to be operating between the religious reference system and the community reference system. Some of the subjects were aware of the expectation of the Catholic Church as well as its moral demand on the race issues, but only those who showed strong belief in doctrinal matters had also come to realize the moral aspect of segregation. The employment of the two attitude scales was able to give some evidence to justify the conclusion. One may also conjecture that the individual's identification with the community, as evidenced by the extent of social participation and the identification with the South, had provided a solid community reference system through which the desegregation issues were perceived. Unfortunately, because of the size of the Catholic community in Tallahassee in 1957, test variables such as mobility factors and aspirational patterns of the subjects could not be introduced to make statistical analyses of data meaningful. Both of these were expected to be factors of considerable importance and perhaps would have shed light on the socio-economic status element in relation to the attitude toward race issues. Further studies along this line seem to be desirable.

PART IV

SOCIAL PSYCHOLOGY OF BELIEF AND BEHAVIOR

Social psychology focuses its interest on the individual person, with his peculiar configuration of needs and behavioral dispositions, within the group, with its structure of norms and values. Behavior, from the social psychologist's frame of reference, is a function of the psychological self embedded within a particular social situation. It is further a truism of long standing that continued interaction between the person and the group leads the person to introject group norms and values, so that what was once external now becomes part of the internal press that the individual experiences.

Catholic Americans, caught as they are in the often-conflicting social situation that pits society against religion, represent fasci-

*nating subjects for social psychologists. When the pressure of con-
flicting group loyalties impinge upon the Catholic American, what
triggers his behavior? How much of what the Catholic American
carries about within his psychological core arises from internal disposition and how much from external group press? What consequences do conformity and nonconformity to group standards hold
for the individual? How does the individual resolve conflicts between his set of beliefs and cues for behavior emanating from an
"open" society?*

*In recent social psychological research, considerable attention has
been paid to structure of the person's belief system and to the way
in which beliefs are held. The principal issue is whether the person
accepts the beliefs of the group uncritically or whether he accepts
group beliefs provisionally to serve cognitive, integrative, or utilitarian purposes.*

In a now-classic study, ROKEACH, TOCH, *and* ROTTMAN *apply the
methods of modern behavioral science in a marvelously inventive
fashion to explore historical phenomena. They investigate the
amount of situational threat to Catholicism antecedent to each
ecumenical council convened prior to Vatican II, and they find positive relationships between threat and the pronouncement of absolute and punitive decrees.*

*Employing Rokeach's notion of the open and closed mind as a
principal construct,* FENDRICH *and* D'ANTONIO *report little relationship between dogmatism and involvement in religious and Church
affairs among college students. But they conclude that both open-
and closed-minded Catholics can find satisfaction within Church
social structures.*

*The effects of nonpunitive religious authority upon the social
perception of Catholics is explored in two experiments reported by*
PALLONE *and* YEANDEL. *In the first experiment, pressure to conform
applied by a priest causes subjects to deny their initial perceptions;
in the second, subjects conform uniformly to the perceptions of a
surrogate of religious authority, but not to those of a military
authority figure. The investigators conclude that conformity to
priestly authority constitutes an habitual response pattern among
Catholics.*

TAMNEY *applies social psychology's methods to the complex
phenomenon of religious conversion, distinguishing between persons
who change labels, those who change symbols, and those who change
beliefs. Religious conversion is thus interpreted as a psychological
phenomenon with strong social components rather than an event
issuing from mysterious spiritual forces.*

13

Threat and Dogma: a Behavioral Interpretation of Church History

MILTON ROKEACH

Michigan State University

HANS H. TOCH

Michigan State University

THEODORE ROTTMAN

Michigan State University

SOURCE. "The Effect of Threat on the Dogmatization of Catholicism," in Milton Rokeach, *The Open and Closed Mind* (New York: Basic Books, 1960), pp. 376-388. Reprinted by permission.

We feel quite justified in concluding from the evidence presented thus far that to a large extent the shape of a person's belief-disbelief system is relatively enduring, "carried around" within his personality

319

from one situation to another and accounting for many of the uniformities we can observe in his actions. But this does not mean that the situation itself cannot influence a person's behavior. Nor does it mean that a person's belief system is open or closed to the same degree at different times. We think of a person's belief system as possessing not only enduring properties, but also the property of expanding and contracting, of becoming more open, or more closed, in response to a specific situation in which the person finds himself. We assume that the more threatening a situation is to a person, the more closed his belief system will tend to become. Just as threat or anxiety built into the personality as a result of early experiences can lead to closed systems that endure, so should situational threats lead to similar effects that should last at least as long as the person experiences threat.

What holds true of people considered in isolation should also apply to people who hold beliefs in common and form groups, movements, or institutions. Here we would expect that if a threat to the collective belief system occurs, the people who hold it should develop a closed system. And we might predict that the degree to which this occurs should also vary with the extent of the threat.

In this chapter we will report on an investigation designed to test the broad hypothesis that situational threat will lead to more closed belief systems. There are no doubt many ways in which this hypothesis can be tested. The way we have chosen to do this is somewhat unusual because our analysis is at the institutional rather than at the individual level, and our method is historical rather than experimental. One motive for doing so is to try to extend the application of our formulations to institutional as well as individual behavior; a second motive is to extend the use of quantitative methods to the analysis of events long past.

The object of our attention is the Catholic Church as an institution. Throughout its history the Church appears to have weathered innumerable crises, some temporary and minor, other that shook the very foundations of the institution. Some of these crises originated in the Church itself, others in the secular world. Some were of short duration, while others lasted in one form or another for centuries. There were disputes among those high within the hierarchy concerning basic points of doctrine, disputes that affected adherents located throughout immense geographical areas. There were secular rulers intent on gaining control of the Church or limiting its authority. There were epidemics of personal misconduct and slackening of discipline involving sizable proportions of the Church's vast organization. Finally, there developed spontaneous movements among peoples under the jurisdiction of the Church, advocating new practices and beliefs and condemning current ones. A series of such movements culminated in the Protestant Reformation in the sixteenth century, ending the Church's spiritual monopoly over the Western world.

Whenever major crises occurred in the history of the Church, assemblies of ecclesiastical dignitaries and theological experts were convened to discuss the situation and to take appropriate action. Thus, only recently (January, 1959) Pope John XXIII announced his intent to convoke the twenty-first ecumenical council of the Catholic Church. The Vatican communiqué publicizing this news reported that the Pope "underlined the daily increasing perils threatening the spiritual lives of the faithful, notably errors which are infiltrating their ranks at various points and the immoderate attraction of material goods, which have increased more than ever with the advent of technical progress." The council, according to the communiqué, "aims . . . at the edification of Christian peoples" as well as representing "an invitation to the separated communities in quest of unity." According to the *Catholic Encyclopedia* (1908), ecumenical councils represent "a common effort of the church, or part of the church, for self-preservation and self-defense. They appear . . . whenever faith or morals or discipline are seriously threatened" (p. 424). It is at these Church councils, convened during times of crisis, that official Church doctrines, or dogmas, are formulated. A "dogma," in the Catholic sense of the word, is an authoritative religious truth enacted by an ecclesiastical assembly.

The official proceedings of Church councils may thus be taken as the institutionalized responses of the Catholic Church to the historical events preceding the councils. By analyzing these historical events we propose to gauge, at least in a rough way, the amount of threat to the Church. And by analysis of the content of council proceedings, we propose to ascertain the amount of dogmatization in the Church. In line with our hypothesis, we should expect to find that the degree to which the institutionalized belief system becomes closed should be a direct function of situational threat.

The most important councils are undoubtedly the Ecumenical Councils, which constitute the main landmarkes in the history of the Church since the days of Constantine. "Oecumen" means "empire," and Ecumenical Councils originally represented the Graeco-Roman Empire, the known inhabited world of that day.

The Ecumenical Councils were composed of ecclesiastics convoked from all over the world, meeting under the presidency of the Pope or his legates. They were assumed to speak for the Church. In the words of the *Catholic Encyclopedia,* they represented "the mind of the Church in action," and its "highest expression of authority."

The decrees of the Ecumenical Councils are official doctrine. Several of these decrees, in fact, constitute cornerstones of the belief system of the Church. One such basic tenet is the Nicene Creed, formulated by the First Council of Nicea, which was convened by Emperor Constantine in A.D. 325. The crisis prompting this council was a dispute over whether Christ was "coequal" with God. This dispute—the Arian controversy—had formed two enemy camps in the Eastern Church, and constituted a serious threat to its unity. Recognizing this threat, Constantine brought several hundred bishops and other ecclesiastics to Nicea at his expense. The Emperor himself took an active part in the Council, despite the fact that he was not a member of the Church hierarchy. He prompted the adoption of the Nicene Creed, which declared the equality of Christ with God, and the immortality of Christ. Arius and others of the losing faction (two bishops who refused to sign the Creed) were banished, and unity was temporarily restored.

This very brief account is introduced here to illustrate the function of councils and the origin of dogmas. A threatening historical situation leads to the convocation of a council; the council formulates doctrines or disciplinary measures which are designed to remove the threat.

Before proceeding to our study, it is relevant to mention briefly the nineteen other councils and to outline their main concerns. The Second Council (First Constantinople, 381) dealt with the question of the divinity of the Holy Ghost and amended the Nicene Creed to include relevant references. The next four councils (Ephesus, 431; Chalcedon, 451; Second Constantinople, 553; and Third Constantinople, 680-681) concerned themselves mainly with the identity of Christ. The controversies on this question were quite violent. For example, each of the opposing parties in the Council of Ephesus brought armed escorts to the proceedings. The Seventh Council (Second Nicea, 787) decreed that images should be "revered" but not "worshipped." The Eighth Council (Fourth Constantinople, 869) was mainly concerned with a jurisdictional dispute. The Ninth through the Fourteenth Councils (First, Second, Third, and Fourth Lateran, and First and Second Lyons) took place in the twelfth and thirteenth centuries. They dealt with various matters ranging from heresies (such as those of the Albigenses and Waldenses), Church discipline, Church-state relations, to the crusades and rules for the election of the Pope. The Fifteenth Council (Vienne, 1311-1313) considered complaints against the Knights Templar, but also took up such issues as Church reform, a new crusade, and the teaching of oriental languages at universities. Then followed two controversial "reforming councils" in the fifteenth century (Constance and Basle) which, among other things, condemned Jan Hus and attempted to pacify Bohemia. The Eighteenth Council (Fifth Lateran, 1518-1519) issued mainly disciplinary decrees. The next council was the famous Council of Trent, precipitated by Martin Luther and the German Reformation, which covered three two-year periods between 1545 and 1563. The Twentieth Council, the Vatican Council, convened in 1869 and 1870, affirmed the doctrine of papal infallibility by a vote of 533 to 2.

Our study includes only twelve of these twenty councils. Three of the twenty—the First and Second Constantinople and the Vatican Council—had to be excluded because they did not enact any disciplinary decrees. In the case of five others, there are historical indications which suggest that the proceedings are incomplete or that their records may have been altered. These are the Second Nicea, the Fourth Constantinople, the First Lateran, the Vienne, and the Fifth Lateran Councils.

All the canons to be considered in this study have been translated and compiled by Schroeder (1937, 1950). Since there is no reason to assume systematic distortions in translation, our material may be said to derive from primary sources.

In the case of institutional threat, the best source of material would be statements by Church officials of the period. These would be preferable to retrospective historical accounts because our primary concern is with the extent to which a given event is perceived to be threatening, rather than with the extent to which it is objectively threatening. The point has already been made by Znaniecki (1952) that "a transgression has to be viewed by the investigator as it is defined by participants in the system, for its disorganizing effect upon the system depends upon the importance which they ascribe to it" (p. 343). Since it did not prove possible to obtain contemporary Catholic statements, Catholic historical accounts seemed the best second choice. Fortunately, Schroeder's volume on the General Councils (1937) contains a running commentary of historical events leading up to each council. In the case of the Council of Trent, which is not included among those covered in Schroeder's book, we consulted Mourret and Thompson (1947), Wright (1926), and the Bull of Convocation to the Council of Trent, quoted in Schroeder (1950). All these works are written from a Catholic viewpoint, and carry the Imprimatur.

With these historical accounts before us, we proceeded to break them down into separate events. Some of these were judged to be events precipitating the convening of the council and others to be merely contributing to it. The total number of events we ended up with ranged from 4 for the Third Lateran Council to 40 for the Council of Trent. All these were then rated for degree of situational threat. This was accomplished with the aid of a seven-point rating scale, with $+3$ representing events posing dire threat to the continued existence of the Church, and -3 representing events ensuring the continued existence of the Church.

Schisms were rated $+3$. By way of example, we may cite the following event taken from Wright (1926): "In 1517, a German monk named Martin Luther . . . began by attacking the sale of indulgences, and ended by tearing down in North Germany the entire Catholic edifice of sacraments, priests, bishops, and papal supremacy" (p. 174). Another illustration of an event rated $+3$ concerns the Second Lateran Council: "The day that witnessed the election of Innocent II to the highest honor of Christendom, saw also a few hours later the election of Cardinal Pietro Pierleone as anti-pope" (p. 195).[1]

Ratings of $+2$ were assigned to events that seemed to imply less serious threat. One example, relating to the Council of Trent, is from Mourret and Thompson (1947): "While the preliminaries were dragging on, Maurice of Saxony . . . threatened the city of Trent at close range." Another example concerns the Council of Lyons: "In the Pope's mind, the chief purpose of the Council was the liberation of the Holy Land by means of a Crusade." Ratings of $+1.5$ or $+1$ were given to such items as: "The Council [First Nicea] dealt also with the controversy regarding the time of celebrating Easter" (p. 17), and "Philip . . . had been robbing the Church of France," the latter relating to the Council of Vienne.

In general, there were relatively few negative ratings assigned. Rated -1, for example, was: "The Pope was highly enthusiastic over the idea of a general council [Second Nicea] and promised his wholehearted cooperation" (p. 142). Rated -2 is the following event relating to the First Council of Constantinople: "With the death

---

[1] Page references for all historical statements, except those pertaining to the Council of Trent, are to Schroeder (1937).

of the Emperor in 378, a period of toleration set in. . . . Arianism in all its forms came practically to an end" (p. 61). The following item (from the Council of Basle) was rated —3: "The Greeks conceded to the Pope all the rights and privileges that he enjoyed before the schism" (p. 470).

Table 1 shows the mean ratings for situational threat for the precipitating and contributing events of each council. It may be helpful if we illustrate the distinction between these two kinds of events. Referring to the Council of Nicea, Schroeder (1937) states that the precipitating occasion for its assembly "was Arianism . . . by its warfare against the divinity of Christ." Arius preached "the heresy that would shake the church to its foundations" (p. 8). This precipitating event was judged to pose a maximum threat and, accordingly, is assigned a value of +3.

To assess the historical conditions more fully, we next take into account other events that contributed to the convening of the Council of Nicea. These include such occurrences as the Meletian Schism brought about by Bishop Meletius who attempted to form an alliance with the followers of Arius (+3), a general conflict between the Roman Church and the Eastern Church (+1.5), and Constantine's attempt to reconcile Arius and the bishop of Alexandria (+1).

Each of the contributing events were rated separately and averaged. This average was then combined with the average rating for the precipitating events. The final rating of situational threat is the mean of these two averages. For the Council of Nicea, then, the mean rating for the precipitating events is +3.00, and for contributing events, +2.00. The final rating is thus +2.50.

As seen in Table 1, the two councils that score highest with respect to the situational threat preceding them are Ephesus and Trent. The latter was convened to counter the threat of the Reformation. The Council of Ephesus was the culmination of controversy over the question of Christ's human attributes. This dispute, known as the Nestorian Controversy, became extremely bitter. Anathemas and counteranathemas were the order of the day, and the Pope (Celestine) as well as the Emperor (Theodosius II) and his family became embroiled. Scoring lowest on situational threat is Chalcedon.

To what extent are these ratings reliable? To answer this question, two judges independently rated the same events. The rank order correlation between the two judges was .95.

We will now describe how we went about assessing the degree of dogmatism reflected in the proceedings of the twelve councils.

Table 1 Ratings on Situational Threat for Twelve Catholic Councils

Council	Precipitating Events		Contributing Events		Combined Average
	No. of Events	Avg. per Event	No. of Events	Avg. per Event	
First Nicea (325)	1	3.00	6	2.00	2.50
First Constantinople (381)	4	1.75	5	0.50	1.13
Ephesus (431)	2	3.00	3	3.00	3.00
Chalcedon (451)	1	1.00	11	0.64	0.82
Second Lateran (1139)	3	1.83	3	1.66	1.75
Third Lateran (1179)	3	1.83	1	2.00	1.92
Fourth Lateran (1215)	2	2.00	6	1.08	1.54
First Lyons (1245)	3	2.33	6	1.58	1.96
Second Lyons (1274)	1	2.00	4	0.88	1.44
Constance (1414-1418)	1	2.50	6	0.67	1.59
Basle (1431-1449)	4	2.33	29	1.38	1.86
Trent (1545-1563)	6	3.00	34	2.85	2.93

In all, over 400 canons were enacted by these councils, ranging from 4 for the First Council of Constantinople to 137 for the Council of Trent. Each of these canons was rated twice: once to gauge the amount of punishment prescribed for violators of the canon, and once to assess the amount of absolute authority implied in it. Both variables were rated on a three-point scale, and the ratings for each council were averaged separately.

It may help to cite two short canons, to demonstrate how they were rated on these two variables. The first illustration is Canon 8 of the First Lateran Council. It is directed against the Normans who once had invaded the city of Benevento and held Pope Leo prisoner for a time:

Desiring with the grace of God to protect the recognized possessions of the Holy Roman Church, we forbid under penalty of anathema any military person to invade or forcibly hold Benevento, the city of St. Peter. If anyone act contrary to this, let him be anathematized.

This canon was given a high rating on both dimensions. It was rated high on punitiveness because it directed that infractors be anathematized. It was rated high on absolutism because it invoked the grace of God and the Holy Roman Church. By contrast, Canon 11 of the Council of Chalcedon was rated low on both punitiveness and absolutism. It reads:

All the poor and those in need of help when traveling shall after an examination be provided with ecclesiastical letters of peace only and not with commendatory letters, because commendatory letters ought to be granted to those persons only who are in high estimation.

However, a canon need not be necessarily high or low on both variables. The rank-order correlation between punitiveness and absolutism for the twelve councils is only .46.

Table 2 gives the mean punitiveness and absolutism ratings of one judge for each council and also shows the combined means. To check on the reliability of these ratings, thirty-six canons were selected to be independently rated by a second judge. This sample consisted of the first, middle, and last canon of each council. The rank-order correlation between the two sets of ratings on punitiveness was .81, and on absolutism, .65. These reliabilities are reasonably satisfactory.

We come now to the major question of this research. Is there any relation between degree of situational threat and the degree to which the Catholic belief system becomes closed, as reflected in the council proceedings? The results are shown in Table 3. Looking first at the rank order of ratings, which are obtained from Tables 1 and 2, certain facts become readily apparent. The Council of Ephesus ranks highest on situational threat and also highest on punitiveness and absolutism. The Council of Trent ranks second highest on threat, third highest on punitiveness, and second highest on absolutism. The First Council of Constantinople ranks next to the lowest on threat, lowest on punitiveness, and seventh on absolutism. The Council of Chalcedon, which ranks lowest on situational threat, ranks tenth on punitiveness and ninth on absolutism.

TABLE 2   MEAN PUNITIVENESS AND ABSOLUTISM RATINGS OF CANONS FOR TWELVE COUNCILS

Council	No. of Canons	Mean Puni- tiveness Score	Mean Abso- lutism Score	Com- bined Mean
First Nicea	20	1.85	2.08	1.97
First Constantinople	4	1.75	1.75	1.75
Ephesus	6	2.83	2.33	2.58
Chalcedon	28	1.89	1.70	1.80
Second Lateran	30	2.38	2.05	2.22
Third Lateran	27	2.17	1.72	1.95
Fourth Lateran	70	2.16	1.55	1.86
First Lyons	27	1.93	1.63	1.78
Second Lyons	32	2.11	1.55	1.83
Constance	7	2.14	1.92	2.03
Basle	15	2.27	1.83	2.05
Trent	137	2.32	2.18	2.25

TABLE 3   RANK-ORDER CORRELATIONS BETWEEN SITUATIONAL THREAT AND INSTITUTIONAL DOGMATISM

Council	A Situa- tional Threat	B Puni- tiveness	C Abso- lutism	D B and C Com- bined
First Nicea	3	11	3	6
First Constantinople	11	12	7	12
Ephesus	1	1	1	1
Chalcedon	12	10	9	10
Second Lateran	7	2	4	3
Third Lateran	5	5	8	7
Fourth Lateran	9	6	11.5	8
First Lyons	4	9	10	11
Second Lyons	10	8	11.5	9
Constance	8	7	5	5
Basle	6	4	6	4
Trent	2	3	2	2

A more global picture is obtained from the rank-order correlations among these variables. The correlation between situational threat and punitiveness is .52, and between situational threat and absolutism, .66. Both these correlations are statistically significant. When the punitiveness and absolutism ranks are combined, their average correlates .66 with situational threat. This is also statistically significant. We thus find good empirical support for the hypothesis that as situational threat increases there is a corresponding increase in institutional dogmatism.

Undoubtedly, the continued existence of an institution depends upon appropriate responses by its leaders to new situations. An important change in circumstances calls for corresponding changes in the institution. On the other hand, *groups also have to protect themselves against too much change, because beyond a certain point the group would change itself out of existence.* With too much modification, an Anabaptist is transformed into a Mennonite, and a Mennonite into an Amish. As Sorokin (1947) puts it, "If the component of meanings of the United States is replaced by that of the Buddhist Church, or that of Harvard University by that of the United Steel Corporation, the United States and Harvard University cease to exist, even if all their vehicles and personnel remain the same" (p. 381).

What are the "component meanings" that have to be preserved? Are the issues doctrinal, or is there something else at stake? There is an anonymous little poem that goes:

> The cheese-mites asked how the cheese got there,
> And warmly debated the matter;
> The orthodox said it came from the air,
> And the heretics said from the platter.

Actually, as far as the real point at issue is concerned, the positions in this memorable debate could just as easily have been reversed. For beyond the question of how the cheese got there, and beyond the question of who are the orthodox and who the heretics lies another issue—the issue of the legitimacy of the authority on which the belief system rests.

Speaking of the Inquisition, the Catholic historian Knox explains: "The head and chief offense, in their eyes, was the defiance of spiritual authority of which their other doctrines were merely the corollaries" (1962, p. *xiv*). In *American Inquisitors* (1928), Walter Lippman's fundamentalist tells Socrates: "You know and I know that the issue is not whether Adam was created at nine o'clock in the morning or whether he descended from an ape. The issue is whether there exists a book which, because it is divinely inspired, can be regarded by men as 'the infallible rule of faith and practice' or whether men must rely upon human reason alone and henceforth do without an infallible rule of faith and practice" (p. 63). In a letter published in Boston by Towgood (1748) a "dissenting gentleman" proclaims: "The Controversy betwixt us, Sir, I apprehend, may easily be brought to a *plain* and *short* Issue . . . It turns upon the single Point . . . *That the Church hath Power to degree Rites and Ceremonies and Authority in Matters of Faith*" (p. 6). The more concerted or widespread the attacks on authority or the authority's belief system (which amounts to the same thing), the more closed or dogmatic the reaction to be expected. Our results are consistent with this expectation.

A final word may be in order concerning the nature of our study. To our minds, the study suffers from certain methodological inadequacies. Our definition of what is an historical event was somewhat arbitrary; the canons might have been rated on other dimensions; the rating scale might have been more rigorously defined. What appears to us to make up for these possible methodological weaknesses is that this study represents a quantitative attempt to test a psychological hypothesis with historical material. As far as we know, it is one of the first attempts to apply quantitative methods to the analysis of a religious movement.

SUMMARY

We have investigated the effects of situational threat on the dogmatization of Catholicism. Positive correlations are found between independent measures of the amount of situational threat that preceded the convening of a dozen ecumenical councils of the Catholic Church and the degree of absolutism and punitiveness expressed in the canons enacted by these ecumenical councils.

REFERENCES

Knox, R. Introduction to Maycock, A. L. *The Inquisition.* London: Constable, 1926.

Lippman, W. *American Inquisitors.* New York: Macmillan, 1928.

Mouret, F., and N. Thompson. *History of the Catholic Church,* Vol. 5. St. Louis: Herder, 1947.

Schroeder, H. J. *Disciplinary Decrees of the General Councils.* St. Louis: Herder, 1937.

Schroeder, H. J. *Canons and Decrees of the Council of Trent.* St. Louis: Herder, 1950.

Sorokin, P. A. *Society, Culture, and Personality.* New York: Harper, 1947.

Towgood, M. *The Dissenting Gentleman's Answer to the Rev. Mr. White's Three Letters.* Boston: Rogers & Fowle, 1748.

Wright, C. *The Story of the Catholic Church.* New York: Boni, 1926.

Znaniecki, F. *Cultural Sciences: Their Origin and Development.* Urbana: University of Illinois Press, 1952.

14

Dogmatism and Religious Involvement

JAMES M. FENDRICH

Florida State University

WILLIAM V. D'ANTONIO

University of Notre Dame

SOURCE. Prepared especially for this volume.

Previous research has suggested that Catholics are more authoritarian and dogmatic than Protestants and Jews.[1] Although the

---

[1] T. W. Adorno, Else Frenkel-Brunswik, D. J. Levinson and R. N. Sanford, *The Authoritarian Personality*, (New York: Harper and Brothers, 1950); Milton Rokeach, *The Open and Closed Mind*, (New York: Basic Books, Inc., 1960); Daniel J. Levinson and Phyllis E. Huffman, "Traditional Family Ideology and Its Relationship to Personality," *Journal of Personality* (1955) 23, 251-273; S. Clark McPhail "Dogmatism, Self-Concept, Alienation and Religiosity" (unpublished paper); Frank Knopfelmacher and Douglas B. Armstrong, "Authoriterianism, Ethnocentrism, and Religious Denomination", *American Catholic Sociological Review* (1963) 24, 99-114; Leonard W. Moss, Freddie Subgihr, Don R. Steward, and Harold L. Sheppard, *An Exploratory Study of Psychiatric Aides at a Home and Training School for the Mentally Retarded*, (Detroit: Wayne State University, 1956).

findings may be important, they are difficult to interpret. Only nominal distinctions are made between religious groups, making it hard to pinpoint what characteristics of religious beliefs and action account for Catholics' high dogmatism scores and Jewish and Protestant low dogmatism scores. Another difficulty is the relatively high variance in dogmatism scores within each nominal grouping.[2] As an aggregate, Catholics score higher on dogmatism, yet within the research samples, there are many Catholic respondents who score lower than Protestants and Jews.

Since Catholics have often been associated with authoritarianism or closemindedness, this study was designed to examine in more detail aspects of Catholicism that might be associated with dogmatism. Various aspects of Catholics' religious involvement were explored to discover the degree of association with dogmatism. The concept of dogmatism has been defined by Rokeach as "(a) a relatively closed cognitive organization of beliefs and disbeliefs about reality, (b) organized around a central set of beliefs about absolute authority which, in turn, (c) provides a framework for patterns of intolerance and qualified tolerance toward others."[3] Religious involvement is used here to refer to participation in consistent patterns of activity that involve the promotion and acceptance of Catholic beliefs and social action.

Several dimensions were used to measure Catholics' religious involvement. In his study, Lenski developed four separate dimensions of religious involvement: (1) associational involvement (participation in formal religious activities); (2) communal involvement (the degree that primary relations are limited to one's own religious group); (3) doctrinal orthodoxy (a cognitive orientation that stresses intellectual assent to prescribed doctrines); and, (4) devotionalism (an orientation which emphasizes the importance of personal communion with God.[4]) Catholics scored higher on all four dimensions that Protestants or Jews.[5]

Lenski's findings suggest that each of the four dimensions of involvement may be related to closemindedness. For example, associational involvement is positively related to the amount of support given to the Catholic Church's authoritative pronouncements on the regulation of gambling, drinking, the distribution of birth

---

[2] Milton Rokeach, *op. cit.*, pp. 118-119.

[3] Milton Rokeach, "The Nature and Meaning of Dogmatism", *Psychological Review* (1954) **61**, 194-204.

[4] Gerhard Lenski, *The Religious Factor,* (Garden City, N. Y.: Doubleday and Company, 1961), pp. 22-25.

[5] *Ibid.*, p. 370.

control information and business operations on Sunday.[6] Lenski states that communal involvement "fosters and encourages a provincial and authoritarian view of the world." [7] Doctrinal orthodoxy is related to a compartmentalized outlook which separates and segregates religion from daily life.[8] This dimension of religious involvement appears closely related to Rokeach's closeminded personality who on the "belief-disbelief dimension" isolates conflicting beliefs.[9] Devotionalism is related to both the spirit of capitalism and a humanitarian outlook of problems of social justice.[10] Holding these often conflicting beliefs is considered to be a possible indicator that the highly devoted individual also isolates different beliefs within his belief system. Given these findings it was hypothesized that each of Lenski's four dimensions of religious involvement would be positively associated with dogmatism.

A fifth dimension of religious involvement was developed. It is similar to Glock's consequential dimension (the effects in the secular world of the prior four dimensions).[11] We prefer to label this dimension religious activism, i.e., involvement in promoting beliefs and actions in the secular world. From a religious orientation religious activism would refer to the person who commits himself to spread the light of Christianity rather than keeping his candle hidden under a bush. This dimension of religious involvement may be more telling because it involves participation in activities beyond normative prescriptions. The overt rewards are few and the attainment of goals frequently difficult. Within the larger society and to a certain extent within a Catholic subculture, the prestige associated with this dimension of involvement is generally not great and the idealistic goals of spiritual perfection and helping others are often beyond the hope of achievement. Religious activism should be strongly associated with the four other dimensions of involvement and should reveal a high degree of personal commitment. Therefore, it was hypothesized that religious activism would be positively associated with levels of dogmatism.

---

6 *Ibid.*, pp. 193-207.
7 *Ibid.*, p. 328.
8 *Ibid.*, p. 329.
9 Milton Rokeach, *op cit.*, pp. 36-37.
10 Gerhard Lenski, *op. cit.*, p. 329.
11 Charles Y. Glock, "On the Study of Religious Commitment," *Religious Education*, Research Supplement (July-August, 1962) 42, 98-110.

METHODOLOGY

Research Sample

In order to examine the association between the first four dimensions of religious involvement and dogmatism, a questionnaire was designed and randomly distributed to 400 male Catholic undergraduates attending a large Catholic university. The Ss represented approximately 9% of the on-campus student body. Two hundred and fifty-five, 63.8%, of the questionnaires were returned completed. This was considered to be a fairly high response rate. The percentage of students registered in the various colleges of the university was used to compare the sample to the population. The sample's proportions of students enrolled in the various colleges was not significantly different than the university population.

In order to measure religious activism the members of two voluntary groups were asked to complete the questionnaire at their regular meetings. The two groups were the Catholic International Lay Apostolate (CILA) and the Young Christian Students (YCS). The members completed thirty questionnaires. These were the only groups specifically working to promote Catholic actions and beliefs in the secular world. Other groups did exist; however, their main function was either to mirror a secular organization, e.g., Knights of Columbus, or to emphasize spiritual perfection through devotionalism, e.g., Sodality of Mary. The proportion of students actively involved in organizations promoting Catholic action and beliefs was quite small. The membership lists which included inactive members did not exceed 90.

Operational Definitions

Since the samples consisted of a relatively homogeneous group of young Catholic Ss, it was decided to modify some of Lenski's measures. The levels of religious involvement in a Catholic university environment were expected to be higher than the larger Catholic population. The first dimension, associational involvement, was measured by the frequency of church attendance and extent of elementary, secondary and college Catholic education. Catholics trained within their educational system interact within a milieu of Catholic symbolism. The socialization process within the symbolic milieu of the Catholic educational system is designed to train students to become "better" Catholics. Coleman and Neuwien report that parents send their children to Catholic schools to receive moral teachings, discipline and Catholic instruction.[12] Greeley and Rossi report the Catholic educational system is moderately successful.[13] Lenski reports his measure of associational involvement is positively associated with previous Catholic education.[14]

The second dimension, communal involvement, was measured by asking how many close relatives and close friends were Catholic. Since better than 96% of the student population was Catholic, close friends were limited to those not attending the university. Within the Catholic university it was assumed that most Ss would be very doctrinally orthodox, if the usual attitude items about belief in the divinity of God were used. Instead of using the above technique, it was decided the third dimension, doctrinal orthodoxy, could be measured by the extent to which Ss believed they had the right to question their church's teachings. In order to measure the fourth dimension, devotionalism, Ss were asked how frequently they received communion and went to confession. Within the Catholic subculture these acts are considered among the most perfect ways to be in personal contact with God.[15]

The fifth dimension, religious activism, was measured by the active membership in CILA and YCS. The mean scores on dogmatism for the random sample and the activists were compared to discover if the activists would score higher. The presidents of both groups were asked to describe the manifest purposes and activities of their organizations. The following statements of the presidents illustrate how the purpose and activities of the organizations reflect religious activism:

The president of CILA stated the purpose of the group was to make the individual Catholic layman aware of his responsibilities at the international, national and local levels and to create active Christians. The em-

---

12 James S. Coleman, *The Adolescent Society,* (New York: MacMillan Company, 1962), p. 63, and Reginald A. Neuwien, (ed.), *The Catholic Schools in Action: The Notre Dame Study of Catholic Elementary and Secondary Schools in the U. S.,* (Notre Dame, Ind.: University of Notre Dame Press, 1966).

13 Andrew M. Greeley and Peter I. Rossi, *The Education of Catholic Americans,* (Chicago: Aldine Publishing Company, 1966), pp. 53-76.

14 Gerhard Lenski, *op. cit.,* pp. 270-271.

15 For example see a classic work on devotionalism St. Francis De Sales, *Introduction to the Devout Life,* (New York: Harper and Brothers, 1950), For more modern works on devotionalism see M. Eugene Boylan, *This Tremendous Lover,* (Westminster, Md.: The Newman Press, 1957), Thomas Merton, *Seeds of Contemplation,* (New York: Dell Publishing Co., 1960), and Leo J. Trese, *The Faith Explained,* (Notre Dame, Ind.: Fides Publishers, Inc., 1959).

phasis on internationalism was due to the strongly held belief that the force of christianity can not be contained by political boundaries. At the time of the study CILA was trying to raise funds to send members to Mexico to work with the peasants in a rural area during the summer. The president felt the project would help to provide young, male, christian leadership to assist in work and educational projects. Subsequently, CILA members did go to Mexico.

The president of YCS defined his group as a "frame of Mind" rather than an organization. The purpose was to be alive in the Church; to practice Christian principles in everyday life. The president considered social action as a means of establishing a better society through Christian principles. He described his group as the force behind a student boycott against three local eating and drinking establishments that discriminated again Negro students. The members of YCS also had close contacts with the Catholic Worker Movement, which provided opportunities for part or full-time involvement after graduation from College.

The dependent variable was measured by Rokeach's 40-item dogmatism scale, which has been reported to be reliable and internally consistent.[16]

RESULTS

Chi-square was used to test the relationships between the first four dimensions of religious involvement and dogmatism. In order to facilitate analysis the dogmatism scores for the random sample were analyzed in quartiles. Table 1 Parts (a) through (d) report the associations between the indices of associational involvement and dogmatism. The first three tables report a rate of involvement greater than the Catholic adult population, suggesting a special sample of highly involved Catholics. Fifty-two percent of the sample attended church more than once a week, sixty-three percent received either seven or eight years of Catholic elementary education and seventy percent completed four years of Catholic high school. Although the Ss are highly involved on the associational dimension, the first three measures were not significantly related to dogmatism at the .05 level. Table 1d reports the association between year in college and dogmatism. There was a significant negative association. The greater the number of years of Catholic college education, the lower the dogmatism scores. Whatever the process of self and institutional selection, those students who continue through college to their senior year are less dogmatic than those who have attended three years or less of college.

---

[16] Milton Rokeach, *op. cit.,* pp. 89-91.

Table 1   Associational Involvement and Dogmatism

Part (a)

Church Attendance	Quartile 1 (84-137)	Quartile 2 (138-154)	Quartile 3 (155-168)	Quartile 4 (169-232)	Total
			Dogmatism		
Daily	15	15	21	11	62
More than weekly	12	19	15	24	70
Weekly	30	27	25	28	108
Less than weekly	6	2	4	3	15
Total	63	63	63	66	255

$X^2 = 11.07$ $df = 9$ $P. > .05$

Part (b)

Elementary School	Quartile 1 (84-137)	Quartile 2 (138-154)	Quartile 3 (155-168)	Quartile 4 169-232	Total
			Dogmatism		
7-8 years	42	44	39	35	160
1-6 years	9	8	13	18	48
None	12	11	11	13	47
Total	63	63	63	66	255

$X^2 = 6.35$ $df = 6$ $P. > .05$

Part (c)

High School	Quartile 1 (84-137)	Quartile 2 (138-154)	Quartile 3 (155-168)	Quartile 4 (169-232)	Total
			Dogmatism		
4 years	44	48	45	42	179
1-3 years	3	1	2	8	14
None	16	14	16	16	62
Total	63	63	63	66	255

$X^2 = 8.63$ $df = 6$ $P. > .05$

TABLE 1—Continued

	Part (d)				
	Dogmatism				
Year in College	Quartile 1 (84-137)	Quartile 2 (138-154)	Quartile 3 (155-168)	Quartile 4 (169-232)	Total
Freshman	22	24	16	30	92
Sophomore	13	21	26	17	77
Junior	8	14	13	11	46
Senior	20	4	8	8	40
Total	63	63	63	66	255

$X^2 = 25.46$ $df = 9$ $P. < .01$

Table 2, Parts (a) and (b) report the associations between the two measures of communal involvement and dogmatism. The extent of communal involvement was great: eighty percent of the Ss had all or most of their close relatives who were Catholic and sixty-five percent had all or most of their close friends not attending the university who were Catholic. Although the responses reveal a high level of communal involvement neither the number of close relatives nor close friends who were Catholic was related to dogmatism.

TABLE 2   COMMUNAL INVOLVEMENT AND DOGMATISM

	Part (a)				
	Dogmatism				
Close Relatives	Quartile 1 (84-137)	Quartile 2 (138-154)	Quartile 3 (155-168)	Quartile 4 (169-232)	Total
All	26	18	24	25	93
Most	25	33	28	24	110
Some	7	10	8	13	38
Few or none	5	2	3	4	14
Total	63	63	63	66	255

$X^2 = 6.98$ $df = 9$ $P. > .05$

T<small>ABLE</small> 2—Continued

Part (b)

Dogmatism

Close Friends	Quartile 1 (84-137)	Quartile 2 (138-154)	Quartile 3 (155-168)	Quartile 4 (169-232)	Total
All	7	14	11	14	46
Most	31	30	28	32	121
Some	17	8	10	12	47
Few or none	8	11	14	8	41
Total	63	63	63	66	255

$X^2 = 9.34$ $df = 9$ $P. > .05$

Table 3, Parts (a) and (b) report the association between the two measures of devotionalism and dogmatism. The extent of devotionalism was also great: Seventy percent went to Communion at least once a week and sixty-six percent went to Confession at least once a month. Neither variable was, however, significantly related to dogmatism.

T<small>ABLE</small> 3   D<small>EVOTIONALISM AND</small> D<small>OGMATISM</small>

Part (a)

Dogmatism

Communion	Quartile 1 (84-137)	Quartile 2 (138-154)	Quartile 3 (155-168)	Quartile 4 (169-232)	Total
Daily	16	14	20	12	62
More than weekly	6	20	13	17	56
Weekly	19	14	13	14	60
More than monthly	9	4	7	9	29
Less than monthly	13	11	10	14	48
Total	63	63	63	66	255

$X^2 = 14.69$ $df = 12$ $P. > .05$

TABLE 3—Continued

Part (b)

Dogmatism

Confession	Quartile 1 (84-137)	Quartile 2 (138-154)	Quartile 3 (155-168)	Quartile 4 (169-232)	Total
More than weekly	4	11	12	7	34
Weekly	10	12	9	8	39
More than monthly	26	24	20	26	96
Less than monthly	23	16	22	25	86
Total	63	63	63	66	255

$X^2 = 8.75$ $df = 9$ $P. > .05$

Table 4 reports the association between the measure of religious orthodoxy and dogmatism. The degree of religious orthodoxy was not as great as the other measures of involvement. Only twenty-one percent felt they did not have the right to question what the Catholic Church teaches. The extent to which Ss stated they had the right to question the teachings of the Catholic Church was not significantly related to dogmatism. Those Ss who stated that in all cases they had the right to question were slightly less dogmatic.

TABLE 4   RIGHT TO QUESTION CATHOLIC CHURCHES TEACHINGS AND DOGMATISM

	Dogmatism				
Right to Question	Quartile 1 (84-137)	Quartile 2 (138-154)	Quartile 3 (155-168)	Quartile 4 (169-232)	Total
In all cases	14	10	7	11	42
In some cases	39	41	39	40	159
In no cases	10	12	17	15	54
Total	63	63	63	66	255

$X^2 = 4.54$ $df = 6$ $P > .05$

In order to measure the effects of religious activism and dogmatism a difference of means test was used to discover if the random sample was significantly different from the activists. The respective M and S.D. from the random sample and the religious activists were: 153.8 and 24.9, and 149.4 and 23.7. Both M's were higher than

Rokeach's M (147.6) for Catholics attending public universities.[17] The rough comparison between Catholic college Ss attending a Catholic versus non-Catholic university suggests that those Ss attending a Catholic university are slightly more dogmatic. Within the Catholic university environment, however, the religious activists actually had lower scores on the dogmatism scale than the random sample. Therefore, religious activism is not positively associated with dogmatism.

The above finding is somewhat surprising given the activists' high level of involvement on the other measures. When compared to the random sample the level of involvement for the activist was similar on measures of education, communal involvement and doctrinal orthodoxy. Twenty activists received either seven or eight years of Catholic high school education. Twenty-three had all or most of their close relatives who were Catholic and twenty-one had all or most of their close friends not attending the university who were Catholic. Five out of thirty said they never had the right to question what the Catholic Church teaches.

When the religious activists are compared on the measures of church attendance, communion and confession they are more involved than the random sample. Twenty-six of the thirty activists attended church more than once a week. In fact, fifteen attended daily. Twenty-eight of thirty received communion at least once a week and fourteen went to communion daily. Twenty-four went to confession at least once a month. Nevertheless, the data reveal that religious activists score lower on the dogmatism scale than the random sample even though their level of religious involvement $\geqq$ than the random sample. Moreover, when the religious activists' other measures of religious involvement were associated with dogmatism scores, no positive phi-coefficients were significant at the .05 level. These data from both the random sample and the religious activists do not support the general hypothesis that individual measures of religious involvement are directly associated with dogmatism.

The above findings enticed the researchers to explore further the relationship between religious involvement and dogmatism. Outside of the special sample of religious activist, a high score on one measure of religious involvement does not necessarily imply a high score on other measures. It was possible the separate measures had additive characteristics. It was decided to explore the level of dogmatism for the range of religious involvement on all eight measures. Each of the eight measures was dichotomized into high and low

---

[17] *Ibid.*, pp. 90-91.

scores and given corresponding values of 1 and 0. A high level of involvement for each measure was considered to be:

1. Church attendance—more than weekly.
2. Catholic elementary school—7 or 8 years.
3. Catholic high school—4 years.
4. Close relatives Catholic—all.
5. Close friends Catholic—all or most.
6. Communion—more than weekly.
7. Confession—weekly or more.
8. Right to question—never.

Other responses to eight measures were scored as zero.

Table 5 reports the distribution of cumulative scores on measures of religious involvement and the mean score on the dogmatism scale for each level. A respondent could score high or low on each of the eight measures. The range of scores was from 8 to 0. The grouped data reveal no association between the level of religious involvement and the level of dogmatism. The product-moment coefficient for ungrouped scores was .02. Thus, the individual measures of religious involvement do not have additive effects on dogmatism.

TABLE 5   CUMULATIVE SCORES OF RELIGIOUS INVOLVEMENT AND DOGMA-
TISM

Levels of Involvement	Dogmatism		
	N	X	S.D.
High 8	2	148.5	19.5
7	11	153.0	19.8
6	38	155.5	20.3
5	45	152.8	22.1
4	51	154.3	28.2
3	55	154.4	20.8
2	26	148.0	21.2
1	15	156.9	32.8
Low, 0	12	151.8	15.8

r for ungrouped dogmatism scores = .02

DISCUSSION

In this study a random sample of 255 Catholic college undergraduates and a sample of members of two student religious organizations were used to explore whether five dimensions of religious involvement were directly related to dogmatism. The random sample was used to test the first four dimensions of associational, communal, devotional and doctrinal orthodoxy. Nine indices were used to measure the four dimensions: church attendance, extent of Catholic elementary, secondary and college education; number of close relatives and close friends who were Catholic, frequency of communion and confession, and the extent to which students felt they had the right to question their church's teachings. Only one of the nine indices was found to be significantly related to dogmatism. The relationship was, however, in the opposite direction than predicted. The greater the Catholic college education, the lower the dogmatism scores.

The remaining eight measures were reanalyzed to discover if the individual indices had additive effects when total scores were calculated. Each index was dichotomized into high and low religious involvement. The number of high scores for each respondent was summated. The total score of religious involvement was then associated with dogmatism and not found to be significant. Thus, both the individual and combined measures of the first four dimensions of religious involvement were not related to dogmatism.

The fifth dimension, religious activism, was measured by sampling from two student groups that actively attempted to carry Christian actions and beliefs into the secular world. It was hypothesized that the members of these two groups would be more dogmatic than members of the random sample. The mean score on dogmatism was actually lower than the random sample. Thus, the dimension of religious activism was not related to dogmatism. The weight of evidence would suggest that the five dimensions of religious involvement are not related to dogmatism.

There are two major limitations on the above findings. The first is the samples. The levels of religious involvement are relatively high for all students, except on the measure of doctrinal orthodoxy. Twenty-one percent felt they had no right to question the church's teachings and seventy-nine percent felt they had a right to question the teachings of the Catholic Church in some or all cases. Although the students have a high level of religious involvement on the other measures the sizeable majority appear to value intellectual autonomy. This select group of students reflect one end of the spectrum of religious involvement. It probably contains a larger proportion of what Walsh describes as the "New Breed" of American Catholics.[18] In the older, less educated Catholic population the level of religious involvement would probably be reversed, i.e., less Catholic education, less attendance at church, confession and communion and fewer close friends and relatives who are Catholic, but more doctrinal orthodoxy. A more heterogeneous sample of Catholics with a greater range of values on the measures of religious involvement might reveal a different pattern of relationships with dogmatism.

The second major limitation is that measures of the independent variable may be too crude. The nuances of different types of religious involvement may not be captured in the operational definitions. Finer distinctions may reveal stronger positive or negative relationships between types of religious involvement and dogmatism. This age of Vatican II in which both active "traditionalist" and "social gospel" Catholics are highly committed to associational, communal and devotional activities suggests the measures of religious involvement may be inadequate.

In conclusion, dogmatism varies among Catholics; however, its sources and supports may not be due to things Catholic in general, but due to specific Catholic forms of involvement, or to variables indirectly related to Catholic religiosity. As Knopfelmacker and Armstrong point out, the Catholic Church itself is a complex organization with a very high degree of internal specialization.[19] In its history the Catholic Church has been influenced by different interpretations of theological positions and by national, regional and ethnic accretions. These factors have caused a significant amount of internal variation. In short, both the open and closeminded Catholic can find what he is seeking within the complex organization.

---

18 Joseph L. Walsh, "The 'New Breed' of American Catholics," *Readings in Sociology,* edited by Edgar A. Schuler, et al. (New York: Thomas Y. Crowell, Company, 1957), pp. 744-750.
19 Knöpfelmacher and Armstrong, *op. cit.,* p. 114.

15

Religious Authority and
Social Perception

NATHANIEL J. PALLONE

New York University

FRANCIS A. YEANDEL

United States Air Force

SOURCE. Prepared especially for this volume. Data from Experiment I have also been reported in "Explorations in Religious Authority and Social Perception, I: The Collar and Conformity," *Acta Psychologica* (Netherlands), 1964, 22, 321-337; from Experiment II, in "Religious Influence and Social Perception, II: The Clear Triumph of Religious over Military Authority," *Journal of Social Psychology*, 1968, 75, 147-154. The views of the authors do not necessarily reflect those of the U.S. Air Force.

INTRODUCTION

From childhood onward, and perhaps especially from childhood onward, most of those convictions which men posit as partaking the character of "the true" have been *taught to* them, rather than *learned by* them of their own experience, and the "confidence interval" at which they are willing to risk positing "the true" is a function of their appraisal of the reliability of the "witnesses" who have told them what is true, who have offered them premises through which to define and organize the universe of the perceptible, the world of reality. According to one philosopher of religion, belief is a practical necessity in the conduct of life:

The area of immediate experience open to any individual is extremely slight—a mere slit in the world's expanse. Thus to say that we shall believe only what we can know directly is to reduce knowledge in a fantastic manner.... The conclusion to be reached, in view of our individual mental poverty, is that we cannot avoid reliance upon some sort of authority (Trueblood, 1942, pp. 66-67).

It is in this vein that Rokeach (1960 *b*, pp. 113-114) has defined *authority* as "any source to whom we look for information about the universe, or against whom we try to verify information we may possess about the universe," as a "cognitive liaison system mediating between the person and the world this person is trying to understand."

Few will disagree with such a position, or long argue that industrial man, encapsulated in the mass of human cognition which has produced his era, must yet place his hand in the side of the Risen Christ. Perhaps, then, the major question to be weighed can be phrased in some fashion similar to this: *About what* are *which* authorities to be believed? To what extent is authority to be relied upon, and in the face of what quality and quantity of contradictory evidence? Does absolute reliance upon the definitions of reality offered by authority in some provinces—those provinces of special competence which define authority as authority, in which authority is the "expert witness" in fact, and in which the individual person could rarely expect to reach "the true" save for reliance upon the expert—exempt from self-reliance one whose judgments in other provinces are contradicted by the same authority? What degrees of independence, of freedom to vary, obtain as one assesses *when* to rely upon authority and when upon himself?

It is in the decisions one habitually makes in such situations that Rokeach (1960 *b*, p. 115) finds meaning in the concept the *authoritarian personality*, specifically in the "notions about the nature of authority" and the "theories about the way to employ authority" one holds.

From these considerations evolved the investigations described in this report: To what limits can authority be extended beyond the province of special competence in which it is rooted? To investigate the fashion in which authority is capable of extension beyond the limits of its special competence to influence the way in which the individual perceives the world of physical reality, and to offer an elementary paradigm for the exercise of social authority in the "closed" society, the experiments described in this report were designed.

The first experiment investigated the operation of social influence in a "closed" religious society (the Roman Catholic Church), characterized by an authoritarian, hierarchial power structure, in terms of the social modification of members' perceptions of nonambiguous, clearly structured visual stimuli. Perceptual modification was induced through the application of conformity pressure by the appropriate surrogate of religious authority (specifically, a person introduced to and perceived by subjects as a member of the clergy, in which authority resides). For comparison, perceptual modification induced through conformity pressure applied by a "neutral" other (in contrast to the authority surrogate as a "significant" other for members of the closed society) was explored. Social influence was studied in the experimental situation in relation to relatively enduring personality factors predictive of conforming behavior and to the discrepancy between initial perceptions and experimentally offered perceptual "norms" as an additional "pull" toward conforming behavior. These predictor variables were arrayed by partitioning into subsets and conceptualized as levels of "conformity predisposition" within subjects. Stimulus objects exhibited high internal structure, the stimulus situation was relatively unambiguous, non-social frames of reference were available as perceptual anchorages, and neither positive nor negative sanctions were implied or imposed. The experimental task, judging the magnitude of visual stimuli, bore no relevance to the religious function of the authority surrogate.

The operation of social influence was studied in terms of immediate adherence to the norms of the experimental confederate while in his presence (*norm adherence*) and to the subsequent interiorization of those norms in the absence of conformity pressure (*norm interiorization*). Two degrees of severity of conformity pressure were employed by experimental confederates: *mild* conformity pressure was applied as the subject was required to report his perception of the magnitude of stimulus objects privately, in writing, in the presence of the confederate, and *severe* conformity pressure was applied as the subject was required to report his perception of stimulus objects publicly in the presence of the confederate. Two sequences of conformity pressure application, mild-severe and severe-mild, were employed by the religious authority surrogate in attempting to effect perceptual modification, while the "neutral" other applied pressure in the severe-mild sequence.

The second investigation explored the differential impact of social influence applied respectively by surrogates of religious and of military authority upon the perceptions of subjects who simultaneously held membership in a closed religious society (the Roman Catholic church) and a closed military society (an Air Force ROTC training unit). As in the first experiment, social influence was studied in terms of norm adherence and norm interiorization when subjects were required to estimate size in clearly structured, nonambiguous stimuli, in the presence of nonsocial frames of reference and in the absence of sanctions. However, in the second experiment, social influence was applied only in the *severe* degree of conformity pressure, by an appropriate authority surrogate in each closed society and by a "neutral other." Hence, the second experiment sought to determine whether the religious or the military membership group forms a more salient frame of reference in social perception.

These experiments, then, essayed to demonstrate the effect of social power held by the surrogates of authority in established social groups marked by authoritarian power structures, in which each member recognizes the symbols of authority. The experiments attempted to determine the extent to which social power legitimately exercised by authority surrogates in matters which properly fall within the purview of the closed religious or the closed military society is capable of influencing the behavior of members in arenas for removed from that purview. While the diversity of behaviors over which the closed military or religious society habitually or occasionally claims jurisdiction is protean, one does not often encounter the proposition that the perception of magnitude in physical objects indeed constitutes a behavior under societal jurisdiction. But the perception of a variety of other cognitive objects in the psychosocial environment often depends upon meanings attached by the closed societies, acting in tandem or in opposition to each other.

No direct correspondence is assumed between the results of these experiments and the operation of social influence in the diffuse "real life" situation. Rather, these experiments attempted to disclose, in Sherif's (1937, p. 98) phrase, "certain basic tendencies of the psychological organism" as it faces a highly structured stimulus situation, assesses the demands of the physical environment, or the structure of the stimulus field, on the one hand, and the demands of the social power structure, incorporated in the person of the surrogate of authority, on the other, and seeks to reconcile these forces in the performance of a casual perceptual task.

CONCEPTUAL FOUNDATIONS

Classical experimentation in social psychology tended to focus on variations and modifications of the behavior of the "one," the subject under consideration, which might be attributed to the presence or influence of the "other." The first experimental problem for inquiry into the dynamics of social behavior was framed, according to Allport (1954, p. 46), in a formulation similar to this: *"What change occurs in the individual's solitary performance when other people are present?"* It was to such a formulation that Triplett (1897) responded when he produced an early, if not the earliest, experiment intended specifically to study the effect of the group on individual performance.

The issue of the effect of group interaction and its significance for the individual is no longer *whether* the group is capable of influencing the behavior of the member or indeed of the nonmember. Rather, the principal objective in much contemporary research has become, as Borgotta (1963, p. 215) has suggested, the investigation of "how *with whom* ego participates affects ego's behavior." The exploration of the precise contingencies and parameters of the social stimulus situation, both physical and environmental, especially the role of "the other," constitutes a central concern in contemporary investigation of social interaction and of the stimuli which determine social behavior.

The present investigations were efforts to explore in the experimental setting the "contingencies" (conceptualized as mild and severe conformity pressure) and the parameters of "otherness" (operationalized as religious and military authority surrogation or neutrality) in relation to the modification of the complex behavior designated social perception.

Social Perception

Social perception, or the dynamics which govern perceiving when social pressures require that the individual perceiver define the stimulus situation and its significance in some fashion, has been recognized by experimenters and theorists as a pivotal issue in social psychology (Murphy, 1950). Reviewing the fairly well developed body of empirical studies devoted to perception and its social determinants, Bruner (1958, p. 85) suggested that the concern of the social psychologist in perception centers about "the manner in which social factors induce types of selectivity in what a person perceives and how he interprets it." After the process of socialization is essentially complete, the organized society is capable of exercising control not only over responsive and affective behavior, but over perceptual behavior as well (Bruner, 1958, p. 88): "Once a society has patterned a man's interests and trained him to expect what is likely in that society, it has gained a great measure of control on his thought processes, but even on the very material on which thought works—the experienced data of perception."

Psychologists and sociologists working in the area of social perception regard behavior as a function of the perceptual field. But the salient feature of perceptually anchored behavior for the social psychologist is the structuring both of experience and of the meaning or interpretation of experience in terms of perceptual anchorages implied in social interaction. Cartwright and Zander (1960, p. 167) have suggested that "Membership in a group determines for an individual many of the things he will see, think about, learn, and do. The nature of the stimuli in the environment of the individual is in large part affected by his group membership. Because of this relatively restricted range of events provided for its members by a group, they come to know, perceive and do things in a similar fashion." Affective and cognitive agreement about meanings engendered by the group upon objects of common perception seems essential to integrated group function (Bruner, 1958, p. 87), especially when the objective environment provides few stable or relevant cues about the significance of common perceptual experience (Cartwright and Zander, 1960, p. 170). Similarly, agreement about meanings attached to stimuli in the physical environment often serves as the "semantogenic" origin of group interaction (Cartwright and Zander, 1960, p. 168). The role of commonality of perception in establishing and maintaining group cohesion emerges as a key concept in group interaction. Present theories of the dynamics of social perception have developed as a result of a body of laboratory evidence bearing upon perceptual functioning and its social modification.

EARLY DEMONSTRATIONS. Early investigations into the effect of social influence upon perception concerned themselves primarily with the demonstration that such phenomena obtain in typical group interaction. As early as 1899, Slosson (1899, pp. 407-408) reported a classroom demonstration of "perception by suggestion." The suggestion of an instructor (who today would be regarded as a "high status confederate"), that the liquid contained in a vessel actually holding water exhibited highly unpleasant olfactory properties, served as sufficient stimulus to induce nausea in a majority of class members. In another descriptive study, Moore (1921) demonstrated the influence of "expert" and "majority" opinion upon moral and aesthetic judgments, indicating that subjects who are placed in an ambiguous stimulus situation with few frames of reference are generally receptive to the opinions of an expert or even of an unknown majority.

Efforts to explore the dynamics of social perception in controlled settings proceeded when psychologists focussed attention on the nature of social stimulus situations which affect individual perceptions and upon the types of pressure to which subjects respond when they modify perceptions or judgments. In a study involving contrived laudatory and derogatory editorials "planted" in a campus newspaper, Annis and Meier (1934) demonstrated that, when a stimulus situation is marked by relatively low structure, propaganda serves as the only frame of reference available to the subject as an anchorage for his judgments. Experiments by Lorge (1936) on change in rating verbal passages attributed such change to the influence of persons perceived as occupying positions of high prestige relative to the subject's own. Studies by Lewis (1947) confirmed Lorge's findings and suggested two conditions for the restructuring of the perceptual field as a result of the intervention of social influence: (1) the objective nature of the material to be judged, i.e., its evident truth or falsity, and (2) the frames of reference from which the subject views the total stimulus situation.

SOCIAL FRAMES OF REFERENCE. While these studies employed predominantly classroom groups, or perhaps aggregates, a series of experiments undertaken in the mid-thirties by Sherif (1935; 1936; 1937) sought to "create" groups in the laboratory setting, in order to investigate experimentally the genesis of group norms. In addition to providing important conclusions concerning social interaction in small groups, Sherif's investigations had the effect of subjecting observations from the disciplines of social psychology and sociology to rigorous laboratory control and to the methodology of experimental psychology. It was Sherif's model in experimental design which resulted in the conviction that one need assume no dichotomy between those laws of social behavior which are applicable to interaction in stable, organized groups and those which are applicable in less formal group settings.

Sherif proposed that social norms function psychologically much the same as objective, physical frames of reference, serving to give meaning to the stimulus field and to evoke in the subject a stable response set to the environment. The frame of reference which the subject brings to bear upon the stimulus field, Sherif suggested, influences how he perceives it and to some extent predetermines the meaning he will generate upon his perceptual experience; a social norm functions as a *social* frame of reference, serving to give meaning to one's experience and to provide the cues to a stable manner of relating to the environment. Sherif's design utilized the "autokinetic" situation. Subjects were introduced, in the typical experiment, into a darkened room, and a range of judgments concerning the direction and extent of movement in an immobile light were elicited. On the second trial, the subject encountered others engaged in the same experimental task, whose estimates of perceived motion differed from his own. On a final trial, his perceptual judgments tended to converge on the "norm" established by the group. Sherif concluded (1935, p. 135) that "When a member of a group is faced with the (experimental situation) subsequently alone, after once the range and norm of his group have been established, he perceives the situation in terms of the range and norm he brings from the group situation."

One of the chief characteristics of the autokinetic stimulus situation is its marked ambiguity. One of Sherif's most salient conclusions is that, in a highly ambiguous stimulus situation, in which the individual subject is unable to determine the "correctness" of his perception, he is dependent upon the group for his response. Similarly, the group limits the alternative behaviors available to the subject by establishing and defining an acceptable range. A paradigm is herein provided for the concept of *social reality* as the proving ground for one's perceptions and judgments. "Often there are no bases in logic, objective reality, or evidence of the senses which enable a person to arrive at a judgmental opinion; then the subjective reality and validity of the opinion comes to be established by the fact that other people hold similar opinions" (Cartwright and Zander, 1960, p. 170).

It is important to note that Sherif investigated not social norms in established groups, but formed new groups in the laboratory to study the development of entirely new norms. In focusing upon the emergence of norms which in fact effectively controlled behavior, his initial experimental design avoided the methodological criticism which Sherif and Sherif (1963, p. 84) have recently directed against much research into the dynamics of small groups: "Many of the experiments which have passed as small group research are studies of 'togetherness' situations, not of groups, i.e., studies of interaction among individuals without established reciprocities, but simply together in the experimental situation."

Publication of the early Sherif studies on social frames of reference provided a basic experimental design for a number of important investigations in group behavior, including the later studies of Sherif and Sherif on experimental group conflict (1956). The work of Luchins (1944) on the choice of stimuli and the series of experiments on the psychology of suggestion conducted by Coffin (1941), among others, tended to confirm Sherif's findings that social influences operate most effectively when the perceptual field is ambiguous and unstable. Walker and Heyns (1962, p. 23) have underscored the proposition that "conformity behavior can be expected to vary as a function of the degree of stimulus ambiguity in a social situation."

EXPERIENCE OF EXPERIMENTAL DISSONANCE. Cognitive conflict or "dissonance" is generated within a subject when he observes that his perceptions differ from those of others. Asch (1940; 1951; 1952), in a series of investigations which also exercised a marked influence on later research designs, sought to determine the conditions which cause the subject to deny the evidence of his senses and to alter his perceptions to conform to those of the group, despite the compelling objective properties and structural clarity of stimulus objects. In contrast to the ambiguous stimuli in Sherif's studies, Asch's stimuli allowed for little individual variation in perception.

In the usual Asch design, conflict is generated for the subject as he observes that his perceptions differ from the perceptions of others when he is placed in a group of experimental confederates coached to deliver objectively incorrect judgments. Asch determined that the tendency of the subject to deny sensory evidence in favor of group-anchored and group-supported perceptions is accelerated when (1) the quality of evidence presented by others is convincing because of unanimity of belief among them or because the subject evaluates their judgments as trustworthy; (2) the matter to be judged involves ambiguity of structure; (3) the discrepancy between his own perception and that of others is large; (4) the subject's confidence in the correctness of his own perception is low; and (5) he knows that others are aware of the disparity of his perceptions from theirs. Thus Asch concluded (1951) that conformity is related to (1) the character of the stimulus situation, especially its structural clarity, since the effectiveness of group pressure increases as structural clarity decreases, and (2) the character of group forces.

Asch (1940) identified the conditions under which conformity to group norms obtains as those which act to weaken the subject's confidence in the reliability of sensory evidence and to heighten the confidence he places in the perceptions of others. Cognitive dissonance arises from the awareness of disparity between sensate evidence and group norms (even though no direct attempt is made to influence the perception of the subject through the application of external pressure):

. . . The individual comes to experience a world which he shares with others. He perceives that the surroundings include him, as well as others, and that he is in the same relation to the surroundings as others. He notes that he, as well as others, is converging upon the same object and responding to its identical properties. Joint action and mutual understanding require the relation of intelligibility and structural simplicity. In those terms, the pull toward the group becomes understandable (Asch, 1952, p. 484).

Importantly, pressures toward conforming behavior originate in the individual subject under these circumstances, as he seeks to resolve his internal cognitive conflict, even in the absence of direct, externally applied pressure from the group. Lippitt and his associates (1952) have utilized the term "behavioral contagion" to describe an attempt to change behavior or attitudes in which the subject is not specifically aware that he is the target of an influence attempt.

Situational Variables and Social Conformity. Further experimental efforts have sought to refine methodology and to explore factors related to conforming behavior. Some experimenters have been concerned primarily with experimental conditions and characteristics of stimulus situations which accelerate the effect of social factors in producing modifications in the perceptual field; others have been concerned primarily with the determination of dimensions of personality functioning which accelerate the effect of external social influences.

To the clarity-ambiguity dimension of the stimulus field, Allport and Postman (1945) appended the dimension of "subjective stimulus salience." When an ambiguous stimulus field holds potential personal relevance for the subject, a subjective structuring process is called into play. "Its essential nature is an effort to reduce the stimulus to a simple and meaningful structure that has adaptive significance for the individual, in terms of his own interests and experiences" (Allport and Postman, 1945, p. 64).

Studying political behavior and attitude formation, Berelson, Lazarsfeld, and McPhee (1954) concluded that perceptual agreement is predicated upon stimulus clarity and personal relevance. Confirmed partisans tend to perceive the political positions and platforms of their party's candidates as clear and unambiguous on the one hand, and as similar to their own clear, unambiguous positions. Shifts in position engendered by the party leadership were not accompanied by corresponding shifts in the position of partisans, but the problems of social communication and the transmission of party "orders" tended to confute this finding.

Employing a complex stimulus field containing objects of varied degrees of stimulus clarity, Crutchfield (1955) found that "task-set" differentially affects conformity to social norms, or to norms which the subject is led to believe are shared by his peers. When subjects were asked to pronounce their personal preferences, rather than to render their perceptions or judgments, little pressure toward uniformity appeared to operate.

Tendencies toward uniformity in perception and behavior, Raven (1959) reported, arise more rapidly and operate more efficiently among subjects who are members of established groups with relatively long histories of member interaction, in contrast to subjects who are placed in newly organized groups in the laboratory, or in the "togetherness" situation.

In an experiment utilizing a variation of the Asch stimulus situation, Deutsch and Gerard (1955) confirmed the finding that group membership generates greater conformity than nonmembership or isolation. Persons with weak personal opinions appear more vulnerable to contrary group pressures than members with strong beliefs, and members who have not been urged to stand on their own beliefs accept the influence of others more readily than those who have been urged by the experimenter to stand on their own. As in Crutchfield's study of conformity and character, the subjects in the Deutsch and

Gerard study were more likely to conform if they were required to state their perceptions or judgments publicly rather than privately. But persons who were forced to behave publicly in a manner contrary to their beliefs, through the application of group pressure, were likely to retain those beliefs, whereas those who agreed to act overtly in a manner contrary to their beliefs tended to change those feelings, attitudes, or beliefs to bring them into congruence with overt behavior. In general, Deutsch and Gerard concluded, conformity to the perceptions of others is predictable when (1) subjects are required to state their perceptions publicly rather than privately, (2) they are members of established groups, and (3) heterogeneity of perception is not acceptable as a group norm.

In a series of studies which examined the mode of reporting, Dittes and Kelley (1956) presented results which suggest a paradigm for norm interiorization. Varying public and private modes of reporting, they found two patterns of conforming behavior related to feelings of acceptance by other group members: (1) the first consists of a high degree of genuine adherence to the norms offered by the group, evident in unquestioning conformity even under conditions of private reporting; and (2) a pattern of high conformity only under public reporting conditions. The first pattern was associated with subjects who enjoyed less than complete acceptance by the group but were made to feel the possibility of gaining such acceptance; the second pattern was associated with subjects who evinced the lowest degrees of group acceptance and who had been made to feel the likelihood of total rejection. For the latter group, public conformity was utilized as a method of forestalling total rejection. Though they had hypothesized in the opposite direction, Kelley and Volkart (1952) found that social influence directed against attitude change operated more effectively when postchange or postinfluence communications were made public to the group rather than revealed under private or confidential conditions. Raven (1959) found that subjects who privately record opinions which they do not entirely believe, and who are led to anticipate that others in the group who typically hold opinions divergent from their own will see their notes, are likely to change their internal beliefs. These subjects undergo the effects of internal pressure to change their internal beliefs, to align their public behavior with nonsocially disapprobated positions.

In an experiment designed to demonstrate the validity of Festinger's (1957) paradigm for the reduction of cognitive dissonance, Festinger and Carlsmith (1959) found that the subject who is induced to emit an overt or verbal behavior which is contrary to his internal or "private" opinion subsequently changes his opinion so as to bring it into accord with his behavior. This tendency, however, varies in inverse ratio to the strength of conformity pressure applied to elicit the initial conforming behavior beyond the "minimal elicitation threshold." Thibaut and Strickland (1956), investigating the effect of an orientation to group task vs. an orientation toward group membership upon social conformity, found that, as pressures become greater, and as subjects yield their own beliefs in favor of group-anchored beliefs, their confidence in their own initial view decreases and their resistance against group pressure is further reduced.

Research by Walker and Heyns (1962) into the process which has been conceptualized as "norm interiorization" introduces the dimension of familiarity with the cognitive or external object of the attitude, behavior, or perception which is to be the target of social influence attempts. According to Walker and Heyns (1962, p. 29), "The more familiar with the object of the attitude to be influenced by a norm the subject is, the less effective will be the pressure toward conformity." A second dimension investigated in the same series of studies is the level of confidence at which the subject has emitted an initial behavior which becomes the object of a social influence attempt (Walker and Heyns, 1962, p. 52): "A subject's use of a norm to derive a solution in an area with which he is not completely familiar will vary inversely with the degree of confidence he has in his own solution to the problem. The greater the disagreement between the norm and the subject's own experience, the less effective will be the norm in modifying the subject's behavior."

PERSONALITY VARIABLES AND SOCIAL CONFORMITY. While the major emphasis in the experimental investigation of social conformity has been the stimulus situation, an interest has been evinced in the exploration of the role of individual configurations of personality which facilitate the effects of social factors on behavior. Such studies, relatively small in number, have attempted to relate the fund of knowledge which deals with the dynamics of personality function to the social dynamics of interpersonal interaction. In this fashion, a gap in social psychological research is being filled:

Much experimental work in social psychology might be criticized on the ground that it ignores the role of personality and concentrates on the effects of behavior arising from the experimental manipulation of situational variables . . . Studies of the structure of a person can teach us as much about what constitute the consistencies we may expect of him in different situations, for it is what the person brings to the situation that gives meaning to it (Rokeach, 1960 *a*, p. 402).

Crutchfield's (1955) study of conformity in relation to character structure related a number of personality variables, derived from varied measures of intellectual competence, personality attributes, authoritarianism, and self-perception, to a continuum of behaviors extending from "independence" to "high conformity" at the poles. Results indicated that (Crutchfield, 1955, pp. 194-195) "as contrasted with the high conformist, the independent man shows more intellectual effectiveness, ego strength, leadership ability and maturity of social realization, together with a conspicuous absence of inferiority feelings, rigid and excessive self-control, and authoritarian attitudes." The high conformist, whose perceptions, preferences, and judgments depended virtually exclusively upon social reality for their validation, is described as submissive, inhibited, rigid, disorganized, unadaptive, and anxious. Variations in group pressure and stimulus clarity differentially affected groups at the polarities of the continuum.

Seeking to validate empirically the relationship between the inability to tolerate ambiguity and ethnocentrism advanced by Frenkel-Burnswik (1949) and incorporated into the schematization of the authoritarian personality by Adorno, Frenkel-Brunswik, Levinson, and Sanford (1950), a study by Block and Block (1950) supported the hypothesized relationship between ambiguity intolerance and ethnocentrism. But they were led to question the validity of ethnocentrism as a conceptual construct, preferring instead "ego control." Their findings suggest that rigid, inflexible subjects are unable to tolerate ambiguity and seek to define an ambiguous stimulus field in terms of subjective or social factors more readily than nonrigid, "normally" flexible subjects.

A congruent finding was reported by a Menninger Foundation research group (Klein, Schlesing, and Meister, 1951), which suggested that ego structure and perceptual organization serve as more pervasive determinants of the meaning of the stimulus field than situational cues. Investigating "agreeing" response set as a variable in psychological test results, Couch and Keniston (1960, pp. 173-174) determined that "yeasayers," or subjects who typically agree to stimuli and environmental cues, exhibit weak ego controls, accept impulses without reservation, and respond easily to pressures exerted upon them. Hochbaum (1954) weakened the confidence of subjects in one group and increased the confidence of others. Subjects who had been exposed to the confidence-weakening experience yielded more readily to subsequent group pressures. Hochbaum, however, investigated not the usual or typical level of self-confidence, which might be construed as a relatively enduring aspect of the subject's personality, but dealt only with situational determinants of confidence in the experimental situation.

The relationship between perceptual shifts and "typical" or non-situational anxiety was investigated by Mausner (1963). Projective measures of typical anxiety levels were related positively to shifts in perceptual judgments after the application of group pressure for Catholics and for eldest subjects. Mausner suggested that perceptual shifts among more confident and younger subjects represented more deliberate, less "unconscious" acts than for subjects for whom yielding to social pressure represents an avenue toward anxiety-reduction. Conformity can thus be conceived as a habitual mode of reducing typical or usual anxiety. Similarly, Crowne and Liverant's (1963) research confirmed their hypothesis that conforming behavior is related to low expectation of success in a socially evaluative situation, leading them to conjecture that conformity is either occasioned by or accompanied by a process of psychological self-defense. Utilizing an Asch design, Plant, Telford, and Thomas (1965) found that the subject who customarily tends to yield to others does so with greater frequency when confronted by public disagreement with his judgments. Zajonc and Wahi (1961), studying Indian students, concluded that the relationship between need for achievment, a relatively enduring personality trait, and conforming behavior is mediated by the instrumental value of conformity.

A number of investigators have studied the effects of the level of authoritarianism typical of subjects upon social conformity. Centers (1963) found that other-directed, more authoritarian subjects were more susceptible to social influence, from whatever source. Wilkins and DeCharms (1962) reported that, while subjects high in authoritarianism were not necessarily more sensitive to external behavioral cues issuing from social pressure, they were more influenced by such cues in making jugments. Similarly, Gerard (1965) reported that subjects tend to yield to the judgments of others quickly or not at all. But Vidulich and Kaiman (1961) concluded that closeminded, or highly authoritarian, subjects were receptive to social influence emanating only from confederates perceived as occupying high status; even when he tended to reinforce their initial perceptions, closeminded subjects resisted social influence applied by a low status confederate.

Social Influence

Social factors impinging upon the perceptual process appear to derive their force from two complementary sets of pressures: (a) the internal experience of "cognitive dissonance" arising within the person as he perceives incongruence between his own judgments and those of others, even in the absence of direct attempts at influence through the application of social power; and (b) forces initiated by other group members who seek directly to use social power to influence the behavior of the subject. These forces are considered complementary, rather than dichotomous, since internal cognitive conflict is generated and resolved by "group"-anchored norms for perceptual judgment interacting with internal predispositions toward independence or toward social approval. It is through investigation of the parameters and sources of social influence operating within the framework of the structure of established social groups that the elements of a response are likely to be outlined to Borgotta's (1963) formulation of the crucial research issue: "how *with whom* ego participates affects ego's behavior."

BASES OF SOCIAL POWER. Social power relationships existing within the structure of the group form the context for the operation of social norms. It is the ability of the "one" to influence the behavior of the "other" that forms for Cartwright (1959) the basis of social power. Abiltiy to influence others is especially evident when the group invests in a member, as the holder of a group-defined position or role, responsibility for execution of group-defined action. More generally, according to the formulation by Thibaut and Kelley (1959, p. 114), "Person A has power over Person B to the extent that by varying his behavior he can affect the quality of B's outcomes."

In offering a conceptualization of the development of social power, French (1956, p. 183) defined the basis of interpersonal power as the "more or less enduring" relationship between A and B in which the influence path from A to B is represented by direct communication, with no intermediary conveyor. The strength of the basis of social power is gauged in terms of the strength of force which A must exert on B to change B's behavior. According to French's paradigm (1956, p. 192), "The greater the bases of the power of A over B, the more influence A will have on B and subsequently on any other person P from whom there is a directed path from B to P." When A attempts to influence B's perception, judgment, or belief, French suggests, he marshals social pressure to exert on B in proportion to the strength of the basis of his social power.

Within French's schematic design, social influence is exerted directly as A acts on B but indirectly as B acts on P. Thibaut and Kelley (1959) have suggested that the presence of the influencer, or "norm-setter," in a unit of social interaction partially determines the effectiveness of social influence attempts. They distinguish three categories of social influence in order of dependence upon the presence of the social "agent" in the single unit of interaction:

In case one, B's conformity is contingent upon A's surveillance. This appears to imply compliance in the face of real or fancied sanctions which might be imposed. In case two, A applies positive sanctions for conformity; under these conditions, B can be expected to present evidence of his conformity to A in order to receive his reward, so A need not monitor B's behavior. This case generally implies some sort of identification of B with A. In case three, the task exercises behavior control over B and A's influence depends upon his ability to act as an expert or trainer in mediating between stages of the task and B's repertoire of behavior; this implies internalization (Thibaut and Kelley, 1959, pp. 253-254).

Previously cited empirical data and the rationales therefor offered by Sherif (1937), Asch (1952), and Festinger and Carismith (1959) suggest that, in what Thibaut and Kelley have specified as case one, A's surveillance of B's behavior may result in conformity as an avenue toward the reduction of cognitive dissonance, even in the absence or explicit denial of "real or fancied" sanctions.

In an empirical study designed to determine the dynamics of power relationships, Lippitt, Polansky, Redl, and Rosen (1952) found that adolescents who most significantly influenced behavior of others directly, when they actively sought to do so, were also more likely to have their behavior imitated by others in the absence of direct attempts to influence. In providing a conceptualization of these results, the researchers suggested that imitative social behavior frequently has the function of an attempt at locomotion on the part of the imitator toward the social power status of the norm-setter. The behavior of the high power group member was seen by some subjects as representing concretely the standards of the group, and his acts were interpreted as group-approved, since the exercise of social power provided him with a position of maximum interaction, conceived as an enviable social role. Tentatively, the researchers suggested that in some instances of imitative behavior there was involved an element of magical thinking, in which acting like the high power member has the effect of "becoming" that member and enjoying his status and prestige. Social power relationships, found to operate in a rather global context that overflows the parameters of group-defined interests and activities, are thus in part determined by group members' perceptions of the status of the norm-setter or exerciser of power.

To the extent that social power relationships are established and maintained by social influences exerted by high power members upon low power members, the operation of group standards hinges upon the power roles established and maintained by organized groups. French and Rave (1959) identified five bases of social power: (1) reward power, rooted in the member's perception that others have the ability to mediate rewards for him; (2) coercive power, rooted in the member's perception that others have the ability to mediate punishments; (3) legitimate power, rooted in the member's perception that others have a legitimate right to prescribe behavior; (4) referrent power, rooted in the member's sense of identification with the norm-setter; and (5) expert power, rooted in the member's perception that the norm-setter has some special knowledge in the task at hand. In related empirical research, French and Raven (1959) reported that attempts to apply social power beyond the scope of the basis for the exercise of power reduces influence. Resistance to influence varies in common with the perception of the legitimacy of the influence attempt. Somewhat congruently, Rudin (1961) found no relationship between the tendency to yield to rational authority and the tendency to yield to irrational authority. Social group members define specialized functions relevant to the execution of group objectives, establish positions or define roles which involve the performance of group-defined functions, and endow the occupants of group-defined positions and roles with social power necessary to ensure the effective execution of group-defined goals. It is within this context that Bellows (1963, p. 199) has defined authority as "institutionalized power," inhering in established, traditional patterns of group interaction. For Bierstedt, from a sociological viewpoint (1950, p. 731), authority is "a constraining influence which reduces the behavior alternatives" available to members of social groups; "it is that which influences or guides the behavior of a person (group member) under conditions in which the person does not participate in deciding about the behavior."

Investigating an illustrative case of institutionalized power, the power structure in a closed military society, Tannenbaum, Wechsler, and Massarik (1961) described the task of the military leader as that of transplanting orders, suggestions, and requests into group action. To accomplish his task, the military leader makes decisions which relate the demands of the social and physical environment to the capabilities of the men under his command. He judges the relevance of a number of stimuli, both internal and external to the group, arranges them in a psychosocial topography, then attempts to chart the course he will follow to communicate to members the action to be taken. Adherence to the decision of the leader rests not only on the application of strong sanctions, but on the members' expectations that his decision accounts their needs.

Merei (1949) studied the institutionalization of power in a children's play group, in an effort to relate leadership styles, malleability of group structure, and group cohesiveness. His findings indicate that the behavior of the group leader, as occupant of a group-defined role, is shaped by the *group* when lines of interaction have been traditionalized. Determinants of the group's ability to prescribe behaviors acceptable in the leadership role include the degree of crystallization of group tradition, the extent of collaboration between leader and members in executing group functions, and the degree of group cohesion. Eventually, however, even the leader who initially is forced to accept existing group norms exercises his role as leader relatively independently of initial traditions and reshapes role prescriptions, often by influencing the level of cohesion so as to permit him greater freedom.

ROLE PERCEPTION AND INFLUENCE. Besides investing the leader with authority to execute group-defined policy, the group specifies the channel of authority-exercise which it has defined as appropriate. The leader's effectiveness in influencing group behavior is partially determined by the congruence between his behavior and the group's perception of the appropriate channels of authority exercise, or, more simply, by the congruence between the way in which he exercises authority and the way in which the group expects him to exercise authority. Bellows (1963) empirically determined, in studying group response to leadership behavior, that leaders of children, pupils, or employees who attempt to substitute cooperative, democratic leadership in situations in which members had anticipated authoritarian leadership fail to influence members' behavior. The converse held for leaders who substitute authoritarian leadership when the group had anticipated democratic leadership. Apparently, in shifting the channel of authority exercise, such leaders were not fulfilling the group-defined channel of authority exercise. Accordingly, influence attempts were resisted.

A rationale for Bellows' results might be found in the research of Tagiuri, Bruner, and Blake (1953) on the congruence of self-other perception in the small group situation which suggested that group unity in behavior varies with congruence of perception of self-role by other and by self, and of other-role by self and other. Thibaut and Reicken (1955) found that subjects anticipated cooperation from high status confederates, whom they perceived as able and intelligent, and tended to attribute noncooperation to causes external to these confederates, while they perceived noncooperation as internal to low status confederates. Similar results are reported by Dannenmaier and Thumin (1964), who found that subjects regarded high status confederates as taller, and low status confederates as shorter, than actual.

Influence attempts initiated by members and directed toward leaders has been the subject of a series of investigations by Kelley (1951) concerning the interaction between social influence and communication. Results indicated that social structures which support several intermediate authority-exercising positions between those of member and leader, arranged in a hierarchial order, produce restraining forces against the communication of criticism or suggestion both from higher and from lower levels directed at other levels. But communication appears to serve some low-status members as a substitute for upward locomotion. Similarly, for some members, hostility results from perceiving persons at the higher level as the occupants of coveted but unattainable positions.

The dependence of the follower on the norm-setter or decision-maker has been discussed by Milburn (1963). The follower-leader relationship serves to perpetuate itself by perpetuating other-reliance and discouraging self-reliance. In Milburn's (1963, p. 226) formulation: "The perceived status of the relationship, now and anticipated, the amount of interdependence of the parties, the perception ... of the other, all serve to reduce the effectiveness of goal-oriented behavior and to decrease the likelihood that rationally adaptive, discriminating decisions will be made." Empirically, Milburn demonstrated that the manageability of one's social environment is related inversely to ambiguity and rate of change in the stimulus situation, factors which foster other-reliance.

REFERENCE GROUPS AND SOCIAL INFLUENCE. The role of reference and membership groups as sources of social norms has been the subject of investigations directed at the examination of the dynamics of norm-setting and the operation of social influence in existing social organizations. Reference groups, in which given subjects may or may not also hold membership, function as "social anchorages" in the subjective structuring of the perceptual field, as a social frame of reference for perceptual interpretation.

The reference group concept, however, is utilized in the behavioral sciences with three alternate referents (Shibutani, 1955): (1) as the group which serves as a point of comparison for perception and judgments; (2) as that group whose perspectives are adopted or assumed by the actor in the social arena; and (3) as that group to which subjects aspire. Most empirical studies dealing with group membership, social norms, or social perception have adopted no clear conceptual distinction in these usages, though the notion of social anchorages seems to imply both usages (1) and (2). The extent to which group pressure is capable of modifying individual behavior in the direction supported by the group serves as a gauge to the extent to which it has become a reference group in supplying social anchorages.

The effect of group-anchored norms upon the determination of members' perceptions and behavior appears to increase in proportion to the degree of cohesiveness. Back (1951) found that pressures toward uniformity in cohesive groups were highly effective in inducing behavioral and perceptual changes, while little change resulted in less cohesive groups. The strength of maximum pressure toward uniformity appeared to vary as a function of group cohesion. Thibaut and Strickland (1956) presented a realistically designed study which suggested that social pressures are highly effective in controlling behavior if the member or subject is concerned with maintaining membership in the group exerting influence. But if the subject is predominantly concerned with cognitive clarity, social pressures are ineffective. Thibaut and Strickland concluded too that contradictory pressures are decoded by the subject as disconfirmation of his own perceptions, but not as sufficient evidence on which to base acceptance of the judgments of others.

Experimental manipulation of the salience of group membership was an important variable in Kelley's (1955) study of group-anchored beliefs and behaviors of Catholics. His findings indicated that counterpressures exerted on group-anchored attitudes of Catholic subjects decreased in effectiveness as the salience of church membership was increased experimentally prior to influence attempts. Kelley's study additionally served to refine the concept of reference groups in terms of salience at any given moment for any given subject:

A member of a group often receives cues which make his membership prominent for him, heighten the salience of his group, are reminders that his group has standards which he is expected to adhere to. At one time, a person's beliefs and belonging to one group may be dominant, but at any given time, the dominant group largely determines his feelings and actions (Kelley, 1955, p. 276).

Charters and Newcomb (1958) conducted an investigation similar to Kelley's, in which the salience of religious identification was manipulated for Catholic, Protestant, and Jewish subjects. While results for Protestant and Jewish subjects were inconclusive, Catholic subjects for whom the salience of religious group membership was experimentally increased exhibited shifts in attitude in the direction of positions approximating "orthodox" views more closely than Catholics for whom awareness of group membership was not increased. No significant difference appeared between control and experimental subjects in attitudes whose cognitive objects were not relevant to religious identification, e.g., political, feminist, Jewish, and Protestant matters. Charters and Newcomb (1958, p. 281) thus concluded that "an individual's expression of attitudes is a function of the relative *momentary potency* of his group membership." Results in the investigations by Kelley (1955) and Charters and Newcomb (1958) thus suggest that social reality is defined by the membership group whose salience is most dominant for the individual subject, even when the subject's initial perceptions or judgments are in conflict with group-defined reality. "There are pressures to establish the correctness of an opinion," Schacter (1959, p. 128) has suggested, within the framework of group-defined reality, "when the precipitating situation is ambiguous or uninterpretable in terms of past experiences."

AUTHORITY IN THE CLOSED SOCIETY. A closed society is a social organization characterized by (a) an hierarchical power structure; (b) the maintenance, sanctioned by the society, of at least two "closed" estates; (c) the maintenance of a pathway for upward mobility from lower to higher estates; (d) formalized, intensive passage rites governing upward mobility, generally following prescribed regimens of training administered by the higher estates; and (e) the norm that power properly resides within and is exercised by members of the higher estate. Most societies organized as estate systems prohibit but do not exclude downward mobility; if downward mobility occurs, it is accompanied by strong negative sanctions and occasionally ostracism for the downwardly mobile. While a "caste" is a self-perpetuating class to which one belongs by reason of birth, an "estate" is a semirigid, but not self-perpetuating class. Upward movement is accompanied by initiation rites following a regimen of training, analogus to officer candidate training in the armed forces and to novitiate and seminary training in religious groups (Mayer, 1955, pp. 7-9).

Social power in a closed society typically rests upon a knowledge of secret rites and formulae, self-perpetuated by the members of the higher estate in which power and authority reside (Mayer, 1955). The symbols of authority include such badges of office as the officer's insignia in the military, types of costume representative of leadership positions in fraternal organizations, and clerical garb is closed religious societies.

In the closed religious society which forms the context for the present studies, authority and its exercise is based on the leadership role in religious ritual behavior, involving ancient rites and formulae whose possession and exercise are prerogatives of the higher estate. The closed religious society is organized primarily to provide an avenue for religious behavior. But attitudes, perceptions, judgments, or beliefs anchored in social reality as defined by the closed religious society can, according to Firth (1961, p. 239), "supply not merely a theory for social interaction, but also wider principles of order in the whole universe. They give an organizing medium for ideàs of social structure and a frame of reference for attitudes." In considering the organization of religious groups from the sociological viewpoint, Firth (1961, p. 247) thus defines religion as "a complex set of concepts and patterns of behavior for people in interaction, *dynamic in conditioning other kinds of behavior.*" Two important functions of religion are the investing of the religious leader with the power to define reality for the group and the prescribing of channels of authority exercise to implement such definitions through the direction of group action:

In the provision of authority and leadership functions, absolute criteria are given in the social relations of superordination and subordination, priest and parishoner. Analogically, priest and father are identified by the Catholic Church. The authority function of religion removes the dilemma of choice of action. If there is difficulty in the discovery of the right choice of action, then authority provides the answer for any difficulty. The church dogma of the infallibility of the Pope when he is speaking ex cathedra is a double locking of the authority principle by putting its immediate human interpreter beyond challenge. . . . Religion has one of its most important functions in the provision of meaning to human experience. In religions which are believed to have a universalistic quality meaning is highly canalized and submitted to some central authority in the last resort. The attribution of meaning to action, given with authority, offers a certitude which can be a powerful stabilizing mechanism for individuals in their personal and social relations. Religion serves to validate many of the choices made by individuals (Firth, 1961, pp. 233, 237-238).

Authority exercised by members of the higher estate in closed religious societies thus appears relatively unchallenged, even when authority exercise is not directed immediately upon an object of concern to the spiritual behavior central to the purpose of the society. In different dimensions, the social power of members of the higher estate issues from their roles as interpreters and leaders in spiritual matters and flows outward to other areas of human behavior. The bulletin of information of a well-known agent of socialization in the closed religious society declares in certain terms its views that (Pelton, 1963, p. 77), "At root, all problems of human living are theological." Once accepted, this proposition implies that every area of human behavior is subject to the jurisdiction of the authority-exercisers in the closed religious society and that the exercise of authority by the members of the higher estate, regardless of the task at hand, constitutes, from the internal frame of reference of the society, the use of what French and Raven (1959) have called legitimate social power.

Transferability of social power from one area of behavior to another, however, appears to represent a general characteristic of established prestige positions in closed social groups. Benoit-Smullyan (1944, p. 152), investigating interrelationships between status, prestige, and social power, suggested that prestige-derived deference exhibited by low-status members toward high-status members creates a halo effect behaviorally demonstrated by the "presumptive right to take the initiative." Similarly, Aron (1950, p. 141) maintained that the principal characteristic of the structural properties of existing social organizations is the "composition of the elite, that is, the relationship between the groups exercising power, the degree of unity or division between these groups, the system of recruiting the elite, and the ease or difficulty of entering it."

McCleery (1960, p. 73), studying the social organization of the prison, advanced the proposition that authoritarian power structures are supported by members to safeguard the cohesion and effectiveness of the group: "The authoritarian system seems to require censorship and control over communication for its own support and to ensure that those who make the decisions are, in fact, best informed to do so." In varying Kelley's (1951) earlier study of communication and locomotion, Cohen (1958) found that group members of low status communicate in such a way as to protect and enhance their relations with persons of high status who exercise power. This finding seems to suggest that self-protection is involved in submission to authority and in failure to criticize the exercise of authority outside group-defined limits.

Summarizing theory and research on the relation between religious identification and intergroup conflict, Williams (1956) suggested that religious group membership, especially when such membership imposes an obligation to defend the faith actively, imposes limits on the range of alternative meanings which can be engendered onto stimulus situations and on acceptable solutions to problematic situations. Religion-anchored value orientations rooted in sacred or nonempirical frames of reference may define the significance of the group to its members in such fashion as to hinder compromise on social issues or the interpretation of stimuli which appear to have a bearing either upon religious values or religious authority.

From the consideration of studies centering upon the social structure of the closed, religious society and upon the social dynamics of the exercise of power, authority invested in members of the higher estate emerges as self-perpetuating, since entry into that estate is controlled by present estate members; free from criticism by members of the lower estate, who may wish to safeguard themselves against retaliation by higher estate members; and relatively free from constraint of exercise in areas immediately within and beyond the jurisdiction of the closed society. Many of these characteristics of the closed society are analagous to communication patterns in other types of social organization, and absolute authority, exercised unquestioningly, has been seen as contributing to group cohesion.

DISCUSSION. Theoretical and empirical studies of the dynamics of social perception and the operation of social influence indicate several significant paradigms for the investigation of social influence in closed societies.

Stimulus ambiguity and the effectiveness of social influence emanating from several sources upon perception have been found to vary together. Group membership and the salience of the group to the individual appear to evoke conforming behavior to group standards, and conformity is predicated in part upon the mode of perceptual reporting required in the experimental task.

Though the bases of social power have been explored and the source of the norm has been found to contribute to the modification of judgment and perception, little empirical research has attempted to deal with the role of an institutionalized, traditionalized power-status relationship in the modification of social perception, and thus to capitalize on preexisting power structures meaningful to both group members and norm-setter. Though a paradigm has been offered for norm interiorization, little or no experimental study has been directed at the relative permanence of perceptual modification as a result of social influence operating within an established group. Little research has dealt with the operation of an enduring power structure upon social perception when the appropriate authority surrogate attempts to extend his authority to areas beyond the proper jurisdiction of his role-invested authority surrogation, at the same time underscoring the salience of the membership group.

The rationale for the selection of a highly structured stimulus situation in the present studies is rooted in the research of Sherif (1935; 1936; 1937), Walker and Heyns (1962), and especially Asch

(1940; 1951; 1952) on stimulus clarity and social perception, which indicates that sufficiently strong social influence operates to lead subjects to resolve cognitive conflicts in the direction of the perceptions of the significant other. Studies by Dittes and Kelley (1956) and Deutsch and Gerard (1955) on the effect of public versus private reporting upon social conformity suggested the experimental manipulation of what has been conceptualized as conformity pressure. The findings of Couch and Keniston (1960) on "yeasaying" as a response set and of Crutchfield (1955) on character structure and conformity influenced the selection of personality variables. The inclusion of the initial level of perceptual accuracy as a predictor was suggested by the research of Walker and Heyns, (1962), on familiarity with the cognitive object to be judged, and by the research of Asch (1951) concerning the effect of discrepancy between individual perception and social norms.

The findings of Raven (1959) and of French (1956) and the analyses of social power in existing groups offered by French and Raven (1959), Thibaut and Kelley (1959), Lippitt, Polansky, Redl, and Rosen (1952), Merei (1949), Firth (1961), and especially Kelley (1955) and Charters and Newcomb (1958) suggested the investigation of the limits of authority exercise in the closed religious society.

Evidence is available, however, which argues against the operation of social influence as hypothesized here. While Firth (1961) views the authority of the surrogate in the closed religious society as global, French and Raven (1959) have demonstrated that attempts to utilize social power outside the range of that power tend to increase resistance to social influence, and Charters and Newcomb (1958) have concluded that increased salience of religious group membership fails to influence significantly perceptions of matters not relevant to religious group identification. Similarly, the work of Bellows (1963) on role perception and influence suggests that attempts to exercise social authority outside the group-defined scope of authority tends to increase resistance.

Among the norms which govern "closed" societies and "authoritarian" power hierarchies often appear proscriptions against the scrutiny of the dynamics of power on which the exercise of authority in the society is based (Kelley, 1951; Cohen, 1958). Power vested in the higher estate is held to be closed to inspection by the lower estate to ensure maximum efficiency in group operation (McCleery, 1960). The secret rites and formulae which bind men into hierarchical organizations and govern initiation into positions of leadership, as Mayer (1955) and Firth (1961) have indicated, usually carry the injunction that the mode of exercise of social power shall hinge upon some basis other than the dynamics of interaction among independent personalities which constitutes the fabric of group belonging. Initiation ceremonies, the form of which has become the guarded tradition of the group, control communication and investigation of role function and dysfunction between occupants of leadership and followership roles, in primitive societies (Redfield, 1947), as in modern college fraternities and civic organizations, much as complex protocols and chains of command control behavior in military organizations.

Within the Roman church, a distinction has traditionally been made between the "sacred" sciences of philosophy and theology (and its branches, including canon law, which details the scope and mode of the exercise of "sacred" or religious authority), and the "profane" sciences which do not deal specifically with elements of the Divine Being as their focus of interest. Following this distinction, the contemporary Christian philosopher, Maritain (1953, p. 125), has urged that "Alike by the sublimity of its object, the certainty of its premises, and the excellence of its light, theology is above all merely human or profane sciences."

More particularly, De Lubac (1950, p. 179) has argued that the science of social behavior is inadequate to adumbrate interchange among members of the closed religious society which calls to itself the claim of divine origin, whether in fact that interchance is spiritual in nature or not: "Does not the psychology of a group of men freely associated in the service of some great cause show entirely different characteristics from those to be observed in crowd psychology, and does not the same term 'collective life' mean in the second case purely and simply fusion and in the first the exaltation of each personality?"

But Cartwright and Zander (1960, p. 138) have urged that "It should not be assumed that one set of laws applies to informal groups while another applies to formal ones," and that "Similarly, it should not be taken for granted that a specific field of special knowledge is required for groups having some particular objective."

EXPERIMENT I: THE COLLAR AND CONFORMITY

Experiment I sought to determine the effects of pressure to conform applied in two sequences (mild-severe and severe-mild) by a religious authority surrogate (RAS) upon members' perceptions of visual stimuli, in relation to the level of predisposition toward independent or conforming behavior characteristic of each subject. For comparison, effects of pressure to conform applied in a severe-mild sequence by a "neutral" other (NO) was also assessed.

This experiment was executed during 1963 in a relatively small (1,400) undergraduate liberal arts college for men conducted by an order of Roman Catholic teaching brothers. Located in a major urban area, the college draws its population, on a commuter basis, essentially from one diocese; a relatively nonrestrictive admissions policy prevails.

Ss were 120 randomly selected male undergraduates, of normal visual acuity, on the threshold of and in preparation for adulthood, concomitant with which is final separation into higher or lower estates in the society.

The personality factors *dominance* and *self-sufficiency* were measured through scales E and Q-2, respectively, of the *Cattell* (1962) *Sixteen Personality Factor Questionnaire, Form C.* The initial level of perceptual accuracy and perceptual modifications during and subsequent to applications of conformity pressure by experimental confederates were measured through "mean distortion error scores" (MDES) derived from exposure on various trials to the *Index of Visual Accuracy* (Pallone, 1964; 1966) an instrument developed for use in these experiments, which presents a series of 20 nonambiguous stimuli in the form of 35-mm. slides, which, when projected at a distance of 12 ft., range in area from one to 36 inches. The Index employs seven distinct sizes with gross intervals to decrease chance errors: one, four, nine, 16, 25, 30, and 36 square inches, respectively. Order of presentation was determined initially by random selection with replication, then held constant for each presentation for each S. Each slide was exposed for 12 seconds, with an interval of four seconds. Prior to each trial, nonsocial frames of reference were made available to S through three projections of slides of all seven sizes, in geometric order, which Ss were instructed to regard as standards for perceptual estimation. Ss were instructed to respond only in terms of the sizes presented in these standards in their subsequent perceptual estimates. MDES, an adaptation of the method of average error in psychophysical measurement, are calculated by summing algebraically each S's perceptual deviations from "objective" magnitude and dividing the sum by the number of estimates (20) rendered in each trial. Test-retest reliability is +.93, calculated from formulae for the coefficient of stability.

Experimental confederates offered Ss perceptual norms whose central tendency exceeded by three times the absolute magnitude of the S's initial perceptual estimates, as determined by the magnitude of S's initial MDES, and which veered in the direction (over- or under-estimation) opposite to that evident in the S's initial estimates, as demonstrated by the positive or negative algebraic sign attached to S's initial MDES. The criterion behavior was operationally defined as perceptual modification in the direction of norms offered by the RAS or NO under varying degrees of severity and sequences of conformity pressure. The discrepancy between S's initial perceptual estimates and the confederate's experimentally offered norms progressed geometrically; the larger the initial average error, the larger the discrepancy between the central tendency of S's initial perceptions and the central tendency of experimentally offered norms.

On successive days, Ss were exposed to the Index in five trials: (1) an initial trial for familiarization, (2) a trial for collection of initial MDES, (3) a trial under conditions of severe, or mild, conformity pressure, (4) a trial under the variant condition of conformity pressure, and (5) a final trial when the confederate was no longer present.

The experimental room was so arranged that S and the experimental confederate were situated at equal distances of twelve feet from the projection screen and approximately two feet from each other; the experimenter was seated some four feet behind them, at a control panel which triggered the slide projection mechanism. During initial, mild, and final trials, Ss recorded their perceptual estimates in writing on answer slips provided.

In the mild application of conformity pressure, S was requested to record privately, in writing, his estimate of the magnitude of each stimulus object, immediately after the confederate had delivered his norm-setting estimately orally. S reported his estimates, both in the mild and severe trial, in the presence of the confederate and E, who in each case appeared to be recording in writing the confederate's estimates. In the severe application, S was requested to report his estimate of each stimulus object aloud to E for purposes of recording by E, immediately after the confederate had delivered his estimate of each object orally and while in the presence of the confederate. It was anticipated that the S would experience the severe mode of pressure as placing him in the position of "public" disagreement with the norms offered by the confederate and thus increase S's awareness of experimentally induced cognitive dissonance. This position might be conceived as the "minority of one" role when S is faced with public disagreement with the surrogate of religious authority. During the final trial, when the confederate was no longer present in the experimental situation, S was requested to record his estimate privately in writing, as he had during the initial trial.

The RAS was introduced to S by E by name only, including clerical title. No effort was made to increase the salience of the membership group beyond the use of the clerical title of RAS and his clerical garb. The NO was presented to S by E by name only. Both were introduced as participants, along with S, in research relative to the correlates of visual acuity, and were so accepted. Either the RAS or NO participated in preliminary tests with each S to give credence to this masking device and were jointly instructed by E. Neither RAS nor NO was previously known to Ss. RAS and NO approximated each other in age and general appearance. Appropriate "masking" devices to conceal the purpose of the experiment from Ss were employed.

Predictor variables in this study were S's initial level of perceptual accuracy, self-sufficiency, and dominance. On the basis of Chi square treatments, self-sufficiency (Chi square = .2500) and dominance (Chi square = .3125) were found not to be significantly related to initial level of perceptual accuracy within the sample. As independent sources of conformity pull, these variables were partitioned, cross-partitioned, and double-cross-partitioned, to form subsets of the second-order construct, conformity-independence predisposition level within subjects. Partitioning produced eight-levels of conformity-independence predisposition, with level one, or high independence predisposition, characteristic of subjects who demonstrated high initial perceptual accuracy, high self-sufficiency, and high dominance, and with level eight, or high conformity predisposition, characteristic of subjects who demonstrated low initial perceptual accuracy, low self-sufficiency, and low dominance.

Ss were partitioned into three experimental groups, each identical with regard to eight levels of conformity predisposition. Forty Ss were exposed to influence attempts exercised by RAS in the severe-mild conformity pressure sequence, forty to mild-severe sequence applied by RAS, and forty to severe-mild applied by NO. Estimates of magnitude, measured through MDES derived from S's (1) non-influenced trial on the index, (2) trial under mild conformity pressure, (3) trial under severe conformity pressure, and (4) trial subsequent to two applications of conformity pressure, in the absence of the experimental confederate, were treated statistically through analysis of variance procedures for two-way classification. MDES were entered into analysis of variance tables in cells classified according to S's conformity predisposition level and according to conformity pressure conditions. Sources of variance thus were conformity predisposition, conformity pressure conditions, and interaction between predisposition and pressure conditions.

Norm Adherence

It had been hypothesized that norm adherence is a function of the severity of conformity pressure applied by the RAS, relatively independent of conformity predisposition within Ss. By implication, it was hypothesized that the NO does not significantly influence norm adherence. In analyzing sources of variance at play in norm adherence, MDES collected in trials 2 (initial), 3 (severe or mild degree of conformity pressure), and 4 (variant degree of conformity pressure) were investigated. The F ratio of interest in testing hypotheses relating to norm adherence is the "between columns" or conformity pressure condition ratio. Table 1 presents sources of variance and F ratios, in a two-way analysis of variance, for MDES in initial trials and in trials under varying degrees of severity of conformity pressure under classifications for each experimental group.

Inspection of Table 1 generates the following conclusions:

1. Norm adherence is a function of the sequence, not severity, of conformity pressure applied by the religious authority surrogate. Ss exposed to the severe-mild conformity pressure sequence applied by the RAS (Group B) tend to conform to his perceptual norms in his presence, regardless of internal predispositions. No appreciable interaction effect is noted. Ss exposed to the mild-severe sequence applied by RAS fail to conform (Group A). Variance arising from conformity pressure conditions for Ss in Group B reaches significance between .05 and .01; other sources are not significant.

2. The neutral other does not significantly influence norm adherence. Conforming behavior is evidenced in the comparison group (C) only for Ss highly predisposed toward conformity.

Norm Interiorization

It had been hypothesized that norm interiorization is a function of the interaction between conformity predisposition within Ss and sequence of conformity pressure applied by RAS; it had been expected that, while relatively independently disposed Ss might "acquiesce" to the RAS under conditions of severe conformity pressure, they would revert to their initial judgments in the final trial, when conformity pressure was no longer present. By implication, it was hypothesized that the NO does not significantly influence norm in-

TABLE 1   SOURCES OF VARIANCE AND F RATIOS FOR NORM ADHERENCE
TRIALS, EXPERIMENT I

Source	d.f.	Variance	F	P
Experimental Group A (Source = RAS; Sequence = MS)				
Conformity pressure conditions	2	3.13	.57	$\neq$ .05
Conformity-independence levels	7	4.34	.79	$\neq$ .05
Interaction	14	6.04	1.09	$\neq$ .05
Residual	96	5.52		
Experimental Group B (Source = RAS; Sequence = SM)				
Conformity pressure conditions	2	24.84	3.23	$.05 \neq p \neq .01$
Conformity-independence levels	7	4.36	.57	$\neq$ .05
Interaction	14	9.25	1.21	$\neq$ .05
Residual	96	7.69		
Experimental Group C (Source = NO; Sequence = SM)				
Conformity pressure conditions	2	3.87	1.35	$\neq$ .05
Conformity-independence levels	7	8.17	2.86	$.05 \neq p \neq .01$
Interaction	14	4.01	1.41	$\neq$ .05
Residual	96	2.85		

teriorization. In analyzing sources of variance at play in norm
interiorization, MDES collected in trials 2 (initial) and 4 (final,
no conformity pressure) were investigated. The F ratio of interest
in testing hypotheses related to norm interiorization is the interaction
ratio and the between columns, or conformity sequence effect, ratio
respectively. Table 2 presents ratios in initial and final trials for
each group.

Inspection of Table 2 generates the following conclusions:

1. Norm interiorization is a function of the *interaction* between
conformity predisposition levels within Ss and application of conformity pressure by RAS, regardless of the sequence in which conformity pressure is applied. Interaction F ratios for Groups A and
B both reach significance. Ss predisposed toward conforming behavior, including those exposed to conformity pressure in the mild-

TABLE 2   SOURCES OF VARIANCE AND F RATIOS FOR NORM INTERIORIZATION
TRIALS, EXPERIMENT I

Source	d.f.	Variance	F	P
Experimental Group A (Source = RAS; Sequence = MS)				
Conformity sequence effect	1	.002	.0001	$\neq .05$
Conformity-independence levels	7	.81	.39	$\neq .05$
Interaction	7	4.65	2.21	$.05 \neq p \neq .01$
Residual	64	2.10		
Experimental Group B (Source = RAS; Sequence = SM)				
Conformity sequence effect	1	27.44	7.43	$.01 \neq p$
Conformity-independence levels	7	21.23	5.75	$.01 \neq p$
Interaction	7	14.79	4.01	$.01 \neq p$
Residual	64	3.69		
Experimental Group C (Source = NO; Sequence = SM)				
Conformity sequence effect	1	1.97	.51	$\neq .05$
Conformity-independence levels	7	9.95	2.60	$.05 \neq p \neq .01$
Interaction	7	.59	.15	$\neq .05$
Residual	64	3.83		

severe sequence (Group A) who failed to adhere to his norms, tend
to interiorize the norms of the RAS following two applications of
conformity pressure.

2. Variance arising from interaction fails to reach significance
for Ss in either conformity pressure sequence applied by the RAS
during norm adherence trials (Table 1), but in the norm interiorization trials interaction for these Ss (Table 2) reaches significance
between .05 and .01 in the mild-severe sequence and beyond .01 in
the severe-mild sequence. For this reason, interaction between conformity predisposition and conformity pressure applications by RAS
appears to operate *cumulatively.*

3. Conformity pressure applied in the severe-mild sequence by
RAS produces highly significant norm interiorization, without regard to levels of conformity predisposition within Ss. Although only

conformity pressure conditions produce significant variance, between .05 and .01, in norm adherence trials, each of three sources of variance reaches a high degree of significance, beyond .01, in norm interiorization trials for these Ss.

4. The NO does not significantly influence norm interiorization. As in norm adherence trials, conforming behavior is evident in the comparison group only for Ss highly predisposed toward conformity.

DISCUSSION AND INTEGRATION. Conforming behavior observed in this experiment appears attributable to the significance of the religious authority role of the surrogate. Empirical results are interpretable in terms of role perception, role behavior reinforcement (specifically, of follower behavior in the presence of RAS), and the increased salience of the religious membership group as the RAS "enforces" his social authority through application of severe conformity pressure. In this experiment, self-behavior appears to issue from perception of self-role in relation to and dependent upon self's perception of other-role, in turn dependent upon environmental and situational cues which increase or decrease the salience of the social organization binding self and other, cues which demonstrate the malleability of the social structure and its tolerance for behavior deviant from norms established by social authority.

It may be conjectured that the initial contact with the RAS in the experimental situation established a perception of "self" and "other" roles within Ss both for their own roles and that of RAS, and that later contacts tend to reinforce this role perception and the behavior issuing therefrom.

Ss exposed to the severe-mild sequence applied by RAS apparently perceived the role of RAS as not permitting heterogeneity of perception, but tended rather to perceive him in such fashion that the salience of the religious membership group increased until it became the reference group in the experimental task, and social authority rooted in religious function but resident in RAS was free to operate outside the bounds of its "legitimate" exercise. The response set of these Ss, as they encountered mild conformity pressure in the second contact with the norm-offering RAS, was framed toward perceiving him as an effective norm-setter; perceptual disagreement produced cognitive conflict resolved in the direction of RAS's norms. Public disagreement is not "safe" in a situation in which behavior is emitted under the surveillance of the surrogate of the reference group, even though he threatens no sanction. It is proposed that Ss who experienced severe conformity pressure in the initial experimental contact with RAS perceived him as a norm-setter, accepted his role, adhered to his norms, and tended to interiorize his norms. Ss who had conformed to the norms of RAS under these circumstances, regardless of (perhaps even despite) their internal predispositions, were faced with "public" behavior divergent from initial behavior. Norm interiorization may represent for these Ss the resolution of cognitive dissonance in such fashion that initial perceptions are modified in the direction of public behavior. As the individual S seeks internal consistency, he perceives stimuli in the absence of conformity pressure in a manner not inconsistent with the way these stimuli appeared to him when social pressures were brought to bear upon perceptual process.

Role perception and response set appear to be differentially affected by mild conformity pressure applied in initial contacts. Ss introduced to RAS under conditions of mild conformity pressure either do not perceive his role in the experimental task as that of norm-setter, or reject this role perception, a situation which suggests a lack of salience for the membership group. Perhaps these Ss perceived RAS as attempting to exercise authority outside the limits of the scope of its legitimacy, and the closed religious society failed to function as the salient reference group in the experimental situation. The symbol of religious authority worn by RAS (i.e., the Roman collar) identified him as the legitimate surrogate of *religious* power to members of the closed society, but no other effort was made to manipulate group salience. If the S exposed to the mild-severe sequence applied by RAS perceived him as norm-setter in theological, philosophical, or social provinces, his initial contact with RAS in an experimental task claiming no relevance to religious function may have been perceived, in the absence of sanctions or other cues designed to increase salience other than RAS's garb of authority, as a "safe" opportunity for resistance to the attempts of the surrogate of religious authority to exercise behavior control in an area outside the province of religious behavior, or, more succinctly, as a safe opportunity to "rebel" against the authority structure of the closed society. Presuming that this conjecture approaches the psychodynamic processes involved, the response set of S in the mild-severe sequence to the second (severe) contact was that of safety in rebellion. But Ss internally predisposed toward conforming behavior were unable to *sustain* the experience of "safe" rebellion, in the face of a second application of conformity pressure. The tendency of such Ss to modify their perceptions, interacting with effects of the application of the mild-severe sequence, produced what has been considered a cumulative interaction effect upon social perception, evident in norm interiorization, in what might be viewed as successive approximations in the process of shaping behavior.

One may conjecture that the "neutrality" of NO provided an ambiguous stimulus in which the number of ways of perceiving his role was diffused, dependent not upon cues relative to social organizational hierarchies but only upon internal needs of S to project meaning upon NO. In this context, those Ss predisposed toward conformity were enabled, from inner need, to generate the meaning "norm-setter" upon NO. Though Ss exposed to NO may have felt that their own perceptions had been disconfirmed by his norms, they apparently felt no pull toward modification of their perceptions in that direction.

In an effort to conceptualize the psychological processes at play in the behaviors observed in this experiment, it has been suggested that conformity pressure applied in the severe-mild sequence casts the RAS, in the initial contact with S, in the role of the norm-setter whose norms are to be adhered to and interiorized and whose social authority is rooted in the power structure of the closed religious society, the salience of which increases as it becomes the reference group. Mild-severe conformity pressure sequence applied by RAS appears to provide a safe opportunity for rebellion from the exercise of religious authority outside the scope of RAS's special competence; the membership group fails to function as the reference group. Role perception establishes and reinforces a response set which serves as a frame of reference and a behavior prescription for Ss. The response set of Ss exposed to mild-severe sequence whose internal predisposition constitute them as capable of withstanding sustained "safe" rebellion to the exercise of religious authority by RAS is that of resistance; the response set of Ss exposed to severe-mild sequence exercised by RAS, regardless of level of internal predisposition toward independence, is that of yielding to authority rooted in the structure of the closed society and of denial of the direct testimony of one's perceptual faculties. Self-behavior is predicated upon role prescriptions imbedded in perception of self-role in relation to other-role.

EXPERIMENT II: THE TRIUMPH OF RELIGIOUS OVER MILITARY AUTHORITY

Experiment II investigated the differential impact of social influence, applied in a severe degree of pressure to conform by a military authority surrogate (MAS), a religious authority surrogate

(RAS), or a "neutral" other (NO), upon the perceptions of subjects who held membership simultaneously in a closed religious (Roman Catholic Church) and a closed military (Air Force ROTC training unit) society, in relation to the level of dogmatism characteristic of each subject.

The second experiment was executed during 1966 in a major midwestern university for men conducted by an order of Roman Catholic priests, primarily residential, drawing its student body on a nationwide, highly selective basis. Tuition costs and other economic factors lead one to speculate that subjects included in Experiment II represented typically families at higher socioeconomic status levels than subjects included in Experiment I.

The predictor variable, S's level of dogmatism, was measured through Rokeach's Dogmatism (D) Scale, Form E, a 40-item instrument designed to assess authoritarianism, intolerance, and openness-closedness of belief systems. Rokeach (1960 *a*) has reported reliabilities for Form E ranging from .88 to .93. This instrument was administered to the total 225 members of the Air Force Reserve Officers training program whose school records indicated membership in the Roman Catholic church and whose medical records indicated vision at, or corrected to, 20-20.

D Scale scores were arrayed for all 225 prospective Ss in descending order. The 42 prospective Ss with highest and the 42 with lowest D Scale scores were selected to participate in this experiment. Once the cooperation of these Ss to participate in what was presented as a study of visual accuracy in relation to reading habits had been elicited, Ss were randomly assigned to one of three "treatment" or experimental groups. Group A was to be exposed to influence attempts applied by MAS; Group B, to influence attempts applied by RAS; and Group C, to influence attempts applied by NO. Each group initially contained 28 Ss, 14 "high" and 14 "low" in relation to level of dogmatism. However, experimental data could be collected only for 24 Ss in Group A, 26 in Group B, and 22 in Group C. Mean D Scale scores for high and low dogmatic subjects in each group are reported in Table 3, along with *p* levels associated with *t* values for mean differences.

Initial perceptions, and subsequent changes in perception under conditions of social influence, were measured through *mean distortion error scores* derived from S's response to the 20 nonambiguous, socially neutral stimuli contained on a slightly revised version of the *Index of Visual Accuracy* (IVA). While the earlier version, used in Experiment I, had contained a 30 sq. in. area, this size had

TABLE 3   MEAN D SCORES ARRAYED BY EXPERIMENTAL GROUPS, EXPERIMENT II

Group	Norm Source	High Ss		Low Ss		P
		N	Mean	N	Mean	
A	MAS	12	183.58	12	126.42	$.01 \neq p$
B	RAS	13	182.92	13	121.31	$.01 \neq p$
C	NO	11	181.91	11	121.64	$.01 \neq p$
All		36	182.81	36	123.12	$.01 \neq p$

been eliminated from the instrument for Experiment II. Hence, the version of IVA employed in Experiment II contained 20 stimulus objects, which, when projected at a distance of 12 feet from S, vary in area from one to 36 square inches, with gross intervals between sizes (1, 4, 9, 16, 25, and 36 sq. in., respectively) to decrease chance errors. The order of presentation, determined by random selection with replication from among the six sizes, is reported in Table 4.

TABLE 4   IVA ORDER OF PRESENTATION, EXPERIMENT II (SQUARE INCHES)

1.	1	11.	1
2.	16	12.	25
3.	36	13.	1
4.	9	14.	16
5.	25	15.	9
6.	4	16.	25
7.	9	17.	4
8.	36	18.	16
9.	9	19.	4
10.	36	20.	16

In experiment II, each slide was exposed for 8 seconds, with an interval of 4 seconds, controlled by an automatic timing device. Prior to each trial—the trial for initial perception, uninfluenced; the trial for norm adherence, under conditions of severe conformity pressure; and the trial for norm interiorization, uninfluenced—nonsocial frames of reference were made available to S through one projection of all six sizes, in geometric order, followed by three projections of 1, 16, and 36 square inch slides, along with simultaneous tape recorded instructions to S to regard these as standards for perceptual estimates and to report his estimates in terms of the six IVA sizes only. MDES, an adaptation of the method of "average error" in psychophysical measurement, were calculated by summing algebraically the differences between S's estimate and the objective size of each stimulus object, then dividing by the number of estimates (20) rendered in each trial, as in Experiment I. Hence, MDES measures central perceptual tendency, with the algebraic sign indicating under- or overestimation, and the absolute magnitude of the arithmetic mean indicating the extent of average under- or over-estimation. For example, an MDES value of −1.5 indicates a tendency to underestimate size in stimulus objects by a mean 1.5 inches. Initial perceptions and subsequent changes in perception, concomitant with or following application of conformity pressure by experimental confederates, were measured through MDES derived from S's estimates of magnitude in IVA objects.

Experiment II was physically conducted in a light- and sound-proof room in a university building familiar to Ss. Two tables were placed 12 feet distant from a projection screen, a barrier was erected between them, and a projector, equipped with an automatic timing device, was installed atop the barrier. A tape recorder, to play taped instructions for each trial on the IVA, was placed behind the tables at which Ss were seated.

A number of masking devices were employed to lead Ss to believe that the experiment concerned the relationship between perceptual accuracy and speed of reading. A reading test was administered to Ss along with the D Scale; signs were erected near the experimental room proclaiming the site of the "reading factors study"; and, to explain the presence of experimental confederates, Ss were told that both students and adults from the general community were to participate as subjects in the experiment.

Ss were exposed to IVA objects under varying sets of experimental conditions on three successive days. During the first, or initial-perception, trial, Ss were instructed to report their estimates of stimulus objects privately, in writing, while in the presence of E and another S. Color-coded response sheets were utilized to indicate S's position to the right or left of the barrier between tables, a position which S maintained during the three trials. MDES collected during the initial trial were employed to determine the "norms" offered to S by experimental confederates during the subsequent, or norm adherence, trial. Ss whose MDES during the initial trial ranged between +1.0 and −1.0 were offered norms which systematically exaggerated the size of stimuli by increasing the magnitude of each object to the next larger size, with the exception of 1 and 36 sq in. stimuli. Hence, confederates estimated squares whose objective magnitude was 4 sq. in. as containing 9 sq. in., those containing 9 sq. in. as containing 16 sq. in., and so forth. Ss whose MDES during the initial trial fell above $+1.0$ or below -1.0, indicating general perceptual inaccuracy in the experimental task, were offered norms which were "objectively" correct.

During the second, or norm adherence, trial, Ss were exposed to social influence attempts applied by RAS, MAS, or NO. Upon appearing at the experimental suite, S was introduced by E to E's experimental confederate, presented as an adult who was also participating in the study of reading factors. Ss assigned to Group A were introduced to a confederate dressed in the uniform of a U.S. Air Force officer, wearing the rank insigniae of a captain. In fact, the MAS-confederate was a career noncommissioned officer, previously unknown to Ss. Ss in Group B were introduced to a confederate dressed in the garb (cassock, Roman collar) of a Roman Catholic priest. In fact, the RAS-confederate was a priest. Ss assigned to Group C were introduced to an adult male by name only. No information relative to the membership or nonmembership of NO in either closed society was supplied, though it is presumed that no S mistook NO for either a priest or a military officer.

Conformity pressure was applied during the norm adherence trial as S was required to report his estimates of magnitude in each stimulus object orally, immediately after the oral delivery of the confederate's "norm-setting" estimate. Tape instructions for this trial informed S that E was to record his response and that E would indicate whether the subject to the right or left of the barrier was to report his estimate first. Of course, in each case, E instructed the experimental confederate to deliver the initial estimate. This procedure, it is conjectured, had the effect of thrusting S into a position of public disagreement with the authority surrogate, in a situation in which S's behavioral deviations from the "norms" set by RAS or MAS lie open to the surveillance of the authority surrogate representing the closed society.

During the third, or norm interiorization, trial, Ss were instructed to report their perceptual estimate privately, in writing, as they had done during the initial trial.

MDES obtained for each of the three (initial, norm adherence, norm interiorization) trials on IVA were analyzed to determine shifts from S's initial perceptual estimates in the direction of estimates offered by experimental confederates. MDES were classified according to S's level of dogmatism (high or low) and according to experimental "treatment" conditions (pre-influence, influence attempt, post-influence), in a 2 x 2 analysis of variance design. Sources of variance were (1) level of dogmatism, (2) treatment condition, or presence or absence of conformity pressure, and (3) dogmatism-pressure interaction.

Norm Adherence

Norm adherence has been defined earlier as modification by S of perceptual estimates of magnitude in IVA stimuli under conditions of severe conformity pressure applied by RAS, MAS, or NO. Ss whose perceptual estimates during the "experimental" or "influence attempt" IVA trial differ significantly from estimates during the initial, pre-influence, trial are considered to have "adhered" to the "norms" of the confederate.

In analyzing sources of variance at play in norm adherence, MDES collected during trials 1 (pre-influence) and 2 (influence attempt) were investigated. Table 5 presents sources of variance and associated F ratios for MDES collected during "initial" and "conformity pressure" IVA trials for each experimental group.

Only the *F* ratio for "treatment condition" for experimental Group B, exposed to influence attempts applied by RAS, reaches significance. Since neither "dogmatism level" nor "interaction" *F* ratios for this group reach significance, it may be concluded that social influence applied by the surrogate of religious authority operates uniformly, as a single or isolated source of variance, in modifying Ss' perceptions, without regard to Ss' predisposition toward conforming or independent behavior (high or low dogmatism level). Hence, both high and low dogmatic Ss appear to be uniformly influenced by religious authority.

No similar effects obtain, however, when severe conformity pressure is applied by either MAS or NO. Since no *F* ratio reaches significance for Groups A and C, it must be concluded that conformity pressure applied by either a military authority surrogate or a "neutral other" fails to significantly influence S's perceptions, either considered as a single source of variance or in interaction with Ss' level of dogmatism. Further, if Ss exposed to influence attempts by MAS or NO experience cognitive dissonance in the experimental

TABLE 5   SOURCES OF VARIANCE AND F RATIOS FOR NORM ADHERENCE, EXPERIMENT II

Source	d.f.	Variance	F	P
Experimental Group A (Norm Source = MAS)				
Treatment conditions				
(columns)	1	.234	.132	$\neq .05$
Dogmatism level (rows)	1	.394	.223	$\neq .05$
Interaction: treatment condition x dogmatism level	1	.057	.032	$\neq .05$
Residual	43	1.767		
Experimental Group B (Norm Source = RAS)				
Treatment conditions				
(columns)	1	16.577	8.579	$.01 \neq p$
Dogmatism level (rows)	1	.683	.353	$\neq .05$
Interaction: treatment condition x dogmatism level	1	1.685	.872	$\neq .05$
Residual	47	1.933		
Experimental Group C (Norm Source = NO)				
Treatment conditions				
(columns)	1	3.339	2.005	$\neq .05$
Dogmatism level (rows)	1	2.219	1.333	$\neq .05$
Interaction: treatment condition x dogmatism level	1	.260	.156	$\neq .05$
Residual	39	1.665		

situation, even Ss high in dogmatism apparently fail to respond to these experimental confederates as "norm setters."

Hence, inspection of Table 5 generates the following conclusions:

1. As a single or isolated source of variance, severe pressure to conform applied by a surrogate of religious authority very significantly influences S's perceptions of visual, objective stimuli. This effect obtains uniformly, i.e., perceptual modification is significantly influenced neither by S's level of dogmatism nor by interaction between dogmatism and conformity pressure.

2. Pressure to conform applied by a surrogate of military authority or by a "neutral other" fails to influence S's perceptions of objective stimuli, either as a single source of variance or in interaction with S's level of dogmatism. Even high dogmatic Ss, who might be expected to resolve whatever cognitive dissonance they

experience in the experimental situation in the direction of norms offered by *any* other, fail to respond to either MAS or NO as to a "norm-setter."

Norm Interiorization

Norm interiorization has been defined earlier as modification by S of perceptual estimates of magnitude in IVA stimuli on a more than temporary basis, some twenty to twenty-four hours subsequent to the application of conformity pressure by RAS, MAS, or NO. Norm interiorization is thus regarded as a measure of the effect of social influence upon perception when conformity pressure is no longer an immediate determinant of behavior. Ss whose perceptual estimates during the final or "post-influence attempt" IVA trial differ significantly from estimates during the initial or pre-influence trial are considered to have "interiorized" the "norms" of the confederate.

In analyzing sources of variance at play in norm interiorization,

TABLE 6   SOURCES OF VARIANCE AND F RATIOS FOR NORM INTERIORIZATION, EXPERIMENT II

Source	d.f.	Variance	F	P
Experimental Group A (Norm Source = MAS)				
Treatment conditions				
(columns)	1	8.333	1.501	$\neq$ .05
Dogmatism level (rows)	1	.255	.046	$\neq$ .05
Interaction: treatment condition x dogmatism level	1	1.880	.340	$\neq$ .05
Residual	43	5.551		
Experimental Group B (Norm Source = RAS)				
Treatment conditions				
(columns)	1	9.563	7.989	.01 $\neq p$
Dogmatism level (rows)	1	2.957	2.554	$\neq$ .05
Interaction: treatment condition x dogmatism level	1	.185	.155	$\neq$ .05
Residual	47	1.197		
Experimental Group C (Norm Source = NO)				
Treatment conditions				
(columns)	1	1.995	1.181	$\neq$ .05
Dogmatism level (rows)	1	.670	.397	$\neq$ .05
Interactions: treatment condition x dogmatism level	1	1.393	.825	$\neq$ .05
Residual	39	1.689		

MDES collected during trials 1 (pre-influence) and 3 (post-influence) were investigated. Table 6 presents sources of variance and associated F ratios for MDES collected during "initial" and "post-influence" IVA trials for each experimental group.

The significance levels for F ratios reported in Table 6 are identical with those for corresponding F ratios reported in Table 5. Again, no F ratio reaches significance for Experimental Groups A and C, and only the "treatment condition" (pre- *vs.* post-influence) F ratio is significant for Experimental Group B, exposed to influence attempts applied by RAS. Ss in this group, uniformly influenced during the "experimental" trial by norms offered by the RAS, are also uniformly led to modify their perceptions of objective, visual stimuli when conformity pressure no longer operates in the immediate behavioral situation. Though it had been conjectured that, while low dogmatic Ss might "acquiesce" to the RAS under conditions of severe conformity pressure, they would tend to return to their initial perceptions in the post-influence IVA trial, no such result obtains. Rather, social influence applied by RAS is again seen to operate independently of S's level of dogmatism.

Similarly, Ss exposed to influence attempts by MAS or by NO fail to modify their post-influence perceptions as they failed to modify the perceptions they rendered under conditions of conformity pressure. Stated differently, the phenomena earlier conceptualized as norm adherence and norm interiorization simply *do not obtain* when Ss are confronted with either the military authority surrogate or the neutral other as a norm source. Clearly, social influence applied by the religious authority surrogate exercises a *decisive* role in social perception, while social influence applied by the military authority surrogate or the neutral other plays no significant role.

Thus, inspection of Table 6 generates the following conclusions:

1. Regardless of internal predisposition toward conforming or independent behavior, Ss exposed to conformity pressure applied by RAS uniformly interiorize the norms offered by the experimental confederate.

2. Ss exposed to conformity pressure applied by either MAS or NO fail to interiorize the norms offered by the experimental confederate, as they had failed to adhere to those norms.

DISCUSSION AND INTEGRATION. Results of Experiment II have demonstrated the clear triumph of religious over military authority in a social perception laboratory situation. Social influence emanating from the religious authority surrogate has been shown to exercise a decisive influence in norm adherence and in norm interiorization, under conditions of severe pressure to conform.

Under identical conditions, however, similar Ss are not influenced either by a military authority surrogate or by a neutral other. Apparently, S accepts RAS as a norm-setter and behaviorally responds to him as to a norm-setter, i.e., S's behavior in the experimental situation, in which he assumes the "follower" role, is analagous to his behavior in the religious situation. *Religious* authority is thus apparently capable of extension to provinces far beyond the spiritual bases in which it resides. It may be conjectured that S's perception of RAS is "global"; that is, S typically perceives RAS as the "leader," and himself as the "follower," regardless of the parameters or exigencies of the behavioral unit. Hence, the behavior of Ss exposed in this experiment to social influence attempts applied by RAS may be regarded as embedded in a perception of self-as-follower consequent upon a global perception of RAS-as-leader. Ss typically had been members of the closed religious society since shortly after birth, and thus subject to life-long reinforcement of self- and priest-role perception.

Only upon entering higher education, however, had Ss become members, or prospective members, of a closed military society. Nonetheless, since Ss aspired and were in training to become members of the higher estate in the closed military society, it had been expected that they would regard the higher military estate as a reference group, thus perceiving less social distance between themselves and the MAS. In these circumstances, the MAS might be expected to function as a model for emulation. Experimental results, however, have proved otherwise. Apparently, in the immediate behavioral unit required in the experimental situation, S does not perceive MAS as the occupant of a leadership role and himself as the occupant of a followership role. In this case, it may be conjectured that situational cues within the experimental situation fail to suggest to S the assumption of followership behavior.

Attempts by NO to influence S's perception have proved ineffective. Situational cues do not lead S to regard NO as a norm-setter, nor is even the high dogmatic S led to resolve whatever cognitive conflict he experiences in the direction of norms offered experimentaly by NO.

Identical experimental conditions have thus produced divergent results. While severe conformity pressure applied by the surrogate of religious authority very significantly influences S's perceptions in the immediate behavioral unit and further influences S's perceptions when pressure to conform is no longer immediately present in the behavioral unit, no similar effects obtain when conformity pressure is applied to otherwise similar Ss by the surrogate of military authority. Apparently cues for behavior are elicited from the repertoire of S's habitual personal behaviors. Equally evident, Ss in this experiment *apparently habitually perceive themselves as occupants of the "follower" role within the closed religious society* within any behavioral unit in which the member interacts with the leader. Since the experimental task—estimation of size in objective visual stimuli—is equally remote from the spiritual or military bases around which the two closed societies are organized, the parameters of the experimental task itself do not thrust the RAS or MAS into the role of leader in the experimental situation. Only the applicatino of "severe" pressure to conform, experimentally manipulated, serves to place the religious authority surrogate or the military authority surrogate in the leadership role, *unless* S's habitual perception of the authority surrogate is that he invariably occupies the leadership position in any mutual interaction situation, regardless of how remote it lies from the bases of legitimate social power he exercises.

Yet the "penalty" for failure to conform in the experimental situation is no more "severe" than the authority surrogate's notice. Ss socialized within the closed religious society, it may be conjectured, are unable to withstand public disagreement with the priest; hence, not only do they "acquiesce" to his judgments while in his presence, but they also internalize his judgments.

Within the closed military society, on the other hand, Ss in this experiment apparently perceive themselves as occupants of the "follower" role only when the immediate behavioral unit and its intrinsic properties require followership behavior. Both the physical and the social properties of the experimental task in this study, it is evident, fail to suggest to S assumption of the followership role. And the mere assertion of authority, or of superiority of judgment, or simply of difference in perception, on the part of the surrogate of military authority is not enough to evoke followership behavior, even among Ss predisposed toward conformity. In contrast, the mere assertion of authority, or simply of difference in perception, by the surrogate of religious authority is strong enough to elicit uniform followership behavior, even among Ss predisposed away from conformity.

SOCIAL AUTHORITY AND UNIFORM PERCEPTION

These experiments have investigated the effect of social influence exercised by the authority surrogate of a closed religious society, operating in a controlled laboratory situation. The criterion behavior, involving the estimation of magnitude in nonambiguous stimulus objects, in which external, nonsocial frames of reference were available as perceptual anchorages, was not related to the spiritual bases for the existence of the closed religious society, the membership of subjects in the society, or the possession and exercise of social authority by members of the higher estate. Stimulus objects to be judged, unlike those in Kelley's (1955) study of the salience of the religious membership group, bore no direct relevance to membership in the closed religious society, nor was the salience of the society as a membership group emphasized. Rather, membership in the closed religious society was globally implied for the subject who encountered the religious authority surrogate in a norm-setting role in the experimental situation, analogous to the norm-setting role he plays in the operations of the religious society.

The experimental task, like all experimental tasks, was artificial, contrived, remote from "real life" situations. It is probable that few, if any, Ss found themeslves deeply enmeshed in value conflicts when they were confronted by the demands of an authority surrogate. And perhaps not a single S found it difficult to yield to the demands of religious authority, for he had little of self invested in the experimental behavior. What results might have obtained had the experimental task in this study approximated "real life" thus remains a matter of speculation. Similarly, what *might* have occurred had Rolf Hochhuth's *The Deputy* intervened in the "internal affairs" of wartime Germany remains a matter of primary interest to the philosopher, not to the behavioral scientist.

But, though the stimulus objects were nonambiguous and though the experimental behavior bore no relevance to group membership, experimental results have demonstrated the underlying premise in which the experiments were rooted: Social influence inhering in the structure of a closed religious society with an authoritarian power hierarchy and organized for a specific purpose is applicable, under certain conditions, to situations and behavior far removed from the central purpose for which the closed society exists. The principal condition, within the limitations of these experiments, for the operation of social influence in the closed society, has been identified as the application of severe conformity pressure in initial contacts with members. In sum, the principal finding can be stated thus: When members of a closed religious society are forced by environmental situations to take a public stand in which disagreement with the surrogate of religious authority will lie open to his surveillance, they tend to adhere to and to interiorize his norms, even in the absence of implied sanctions, and in the presence of external, nonsocial frames of reference.

Uniformity of perception between norm-setter and norm adherer and interiorizer has, in these experiments, been shown to hinge upon the degree and sequence of pressure to conform applied by the occupant of the recognized religious leadership role. The religious leadership role has been shown to operate effectively in a situation which claims no relevance to the spiritual bases for leadership. In the internal operations of the closed religious society, it appears, conformity is predictable when the leader defines the group norm unambiguously and forces the position of public disagreement upon follower on the first occasion on which he announces the norm which shall become, in an authoritarian power structure, the group norm. Subsequent applications of conformity pressure reinforce the leader-defined norm and ensure its effectiveness in controlling follower-behavior.

In short, the closed religious society is enabled to maintain itself in an authoritarian power structure and to traditionalize and institutionalize its operations by the rigorous enforcement of group norms, which are both based upon and give rise to perceptions shared in common by members and leaders. When institutionalized group norms include intolerance of divergent perceptions, attitudes, or beliefs, however, a society, though insuring cohesiveness, tends to preclude movement from static positions, except insofar as such movement is dictated by leaders. The sacrifice in human quality implied in group-enforced perceptual uniformity, on which group-defined attitudes, beliefs, and values rest, was suggested by Rudolf Allers, a distinguished Catholic psychiatrist, when he declared that (1956, pp. 101-102) "the more the individual perceives, appraises, and evaluates in accord with the group's principles, the less able he becomes to contribute anything novel. . . . There is, in this process, some element which might be described as a movement toward a new primitivism. The world of modern man may be much wider than that of the primitive, but it runs the risk of becoming equally undifferentiated."

BIBLIOGRAPHY

Adorno, T. W., Frenkel-Brunswik, Else, Levinson, D. J., and Sanford, N. H. *The authoritarian personality.* New York: Harper, 1950.

Allers, R. The social implications of perception. In W. Bier (Ed.), *Perception in present-day psychology: proceedings of a joint symposium of the Amer. Catholic psych. assn. and the American psych. assn.* New York: Fordham Univ. Press, 1956.

Allport, G. W. The historical backgrounds of modern social psychology. In G. Lindzey (Ed.), *Handbook of social psychology.* Cambridge: Addison-Wesley, 1954.

Allport, G. W., and Postman, L. J. The basic psychology of rumor. *Transact N.Y. Adad. Sci. II,* 1945, **8,** 61-81.

Annis, A. D., and Meier, N. The induction of opinion through suggestion by means of planted contents. *J. soc. Psychol.,* 1934, **5,** 65-81.

Aron, R. Social structure and the ruling class, part II. *Brit. J. Sociol.,* 1950, **1,** 126-143.

Asch, S. Studies in the principles of judgments and attitudes. *J. soc. Psychol.,* 1940, **12,** 433-465.

Asch, S. Effects of group pressure upon the modification and distortion of judgments. In H. Guetzkow (Ed.), *Groups, leadership, and men.* Pittsburgh: Carnegie Univ. Press, 1951.

Asch, S. *Social psychology.* New York: Prentice-Hall, 1952.

Back, K. W. Influence through social communication. *J. abnorm. soc. Psychol.,* 1951, **46,** 9-23.

Bellows, R. Toward a taxonomy of social situations. In S. B. Sells (Ed.), *Stimulus determinants of behavior.* New York: Ronald Press, 1963.

Benoit-Smullyan, E. Status, status types, and status interrelations. *Amer. Sociol. Review,* 1944, **10,** 151-161.

Berelson, B., Lazarsfeld, P., and McPhee, W. N. *Voting.* Chicago: Univ. Chicago Press, 1954.

Bierstedt, R. An analysis of social power. *Amer. Sociol. Rev.,* 1950, **15,** 730-736.

Block, J., and Block, Jeanne. An investigation of the relationship between intolerance and ambiguity and ethnocentrism. *J. Pers.,* 1951, **19,** 303-311.

Borgotta, E. F. The effects of others on ego's behavior. In S. B. Sells (Ed.), *Stimulus determinants of behavior.* New York: Ronald Press, 1963, 213-233.

Bruner, J. S. Social psychology and perception. In E. Maccoby, T. Newcomb, and E. Hartley (Eds.) *Readings in social psychology.* 3rd ed. New York: Henry Holt, 1958.

Cartwright, D. A field-theoretical conception of power. In D. Cartwright (Ed.), *Studies in social power.* Ann Arbor: Institute for Social Research, 1959.

Cartwright, D. and Zander, A. (Eds.) *Group dynamics: research and theory.* 2d ed. Evanston: Row-Peterson, 1960.

Cattell, R. B., and Stice, G. F. *Handbook for the sixteen personality factor questionnaire.* Champaign, Ill.: Institute for Personality and Ability Testing, 1962.

Centers, R. Social character and conformity: differential in susceptibility to social influence. *J. soc. Psychol.,* 1963, **60,** 343-349.

Charters, W. W., and Newcomb, T. M. Some attitudinal effects of experimentally increased salience of a membership group. In E. Maccoby, T. Newcomb, and E. Hartley (Eds.), *Readings in social psychology.* 3rd ed. New York: Henry Holt, 1958.

Coffin, T. E. Some conditions of suggestion and suggestibility. *Psychol. Mongr.,* 1941, 46, 193-259.

Cohen, A. R. Upward communication in experimentally created hierarchies. *Human Relat.,* 1958, 11, 42-52.

Couch, A., and Keniston, K. Yeasayers and maysayers: agreeing response set as a personality variable. *J. abnorm. soc. Psychol.,* 1960, 60, 151-174.

Crowne, D. P., and Liverant, S. Conformity under varying conditions of personal commitment. *J. abnorm. soc. Psychol.,* 1963, 66, 547-555.

Crutchfied, R. S. Conformity and character. *Amer. Psychologist,* 1955, 10, 191-198.

Dannenmaier, W. D., and Thumin, F. J. Authority status as a factor in perceptual distortion of size. *J. soc. Psychol.,* 1964, 63, 361-365.

DeLubac, H. *Catholicism.* New York: Longmans, Green, 1950.

Deutsch, M., and Gerard, H. B. A study of normative and informational social influence upon individual judgments. *J. abnorm. soc. Psychol.,* 1955, 629-636.

Dittes, J. E., and Kelley, H. H. Effects of different conditions of acceptance upon conformity to group norms. *J. abnorm. soc. Psychol.,* 1956, 53, 100-107.

Festinger, L. *A theory of cognitive dissonance.* Evanston: Row, Peterson, 1957.

Festinger, L., and Carlsmith, J. Cognitive dissonance and the consequences of forced compliance. *J. abnorm. soc. Psychol.,* 1959, 58, 203-209.

Festinger, L., Schacter, S., and Back, K. W. *Social pressure in informal groups.* New York: Harper, 1950.

Firth, R. B. *Elements of social organization.* 3rd ed. Boston: Beacon Press, 1961.

French, J. R. P., Jr. A formal theory of social power. *Psychol. Rev.,* 1956, 63, 181-194.

French, J. R. P., Jr., and Raven, B. The bases of social power. In D. Cartwright (Ed.) *Studies in social power.* Ann Arbor: Institute for Social Research, 1959.

Frenkel-Brunswik, Else. Intolerance of ambiguity as an emotional and perceptual personality variable. *J. Pers.,* 1949, 18, 108-143.

Gerard, H. B. Conformity and commitment to the group. *J. abnorm. soc. Psychol.,* 1964, 68, 209-211.

Hochbaum, G. The relation between group members' self-confidence and their reactions to group pressures to uniformity. *Amer. Sociol. Rev.,* 1954, 19, 678-687.

Kelley, H. H. Communication in experimentally created hierarchies. *Human Relat.,* 1951, 4, 39-56.

Kelley, H. H. Salience of membership and resistance to change of group-anchored attitudes. *Human Relat.,* 1955, 8, 275-289.

Kelley, H. H., and Volkart, E. H. The resistance to change of group anchored attitudes. *Amer. Sociol. Rev.,* 1952, 17, 454-465.

Klein, G. B., Schlesinger, H. J., and Meister, D. The effect of personal values on perception. *Psychol. Rev.,* 1951, 58, 96-112.

Lewis, H. B. An experiment on the operation of prestige suggestion. In T. Newcomb and E. Hartley (Eds.), *Readings in social psychology.* New York: Holt, 1947.

Lippitt, R., Polansky, H., Redi, F., and Rosen, S. The dynamics of power. *Human Relat.,* 1952, 5, 37-64.

Lorge, I. Prestige, attitudes, suggestion. *J. soc. Psychol.,* 1936, 7, 386-402.

Luchins, A. S. On agreement with another's judgments. *J. abnorm. soc. Psychol.,* 1944, **39**, 98-111.

McCleery, R. Communication patterns as bases of systems of authority and power. *Theoretical studies in the social organization of the prison: Social Science Research Council Pamphlet 15.* March 1960, 49-76.

McDavid, J. L. Personality and situational determinants of conformity. *J. abnorm. soc. Psychol.,* 1959, **58**, 241-256.

Maritain, J. *An introduction to philosophy.* Trans. E. I. Witkin. New York: Sheed, Ward, 1953.

Mausner, B. The specification of the stimulus in a social interaction. In S. B. Sells (Ed.), *Stimulus determinants of behavior.* New York: Ronald Press, 1963.

Mayer, K. B. *Class and society.* New York: Random House, 1955.

Merei, F. Group leadership and institutionalization. Trans. Mrs. D. Rappaport. *Human Relat.,* 1949, **2**, 23-39.

Milburn, T. W. Design for the direct study of deterrence. In S. B. Sells (Ed.), *Stimulus determinants of behavior.* New York: Ronald Press, 1963.

Moore, H. T. The comparative influence of majority and expert opinion. *American J. Psychol.,* 1921, **32**, 16-20.

Murphy, G. Foreword. In Ruth Berenda. *The influence of the group on the judgments of children.* New York: King's Crown Press, 1950.

Pallone, N. J. Explorations in religious authority and social perception, I: the collar and conformity. *Acta Psychol.* (Netherlands), 1964, **22**, 321-337.

Pallone, N. J. Religious authority and social perception: a laboratory exploration in social influence. *J. soc. Psychol.,* 1966, **68**, 229-241.

Pelton, R. S. Announcement of the department of theology. *Bulletin of information, the graduate school, the university of Notre Dame.* Notre Dame, Ind.: Univ. Notre Dame Press, 1963.

Plant, W. T., Telford, C. W., and Thomas, J. A. Some personality differences between dogmatic and nondogmatic groups. *J. soc. Psychol,* 1965, **67**, 67-75.

Raven, B. Social influences on opinions and the communication of related content. *J. abnorm. soc. Psychol.,* 1959, **58**, 119-128.

Rokeach, M. (1960 a) *The open and closed mind.* New York: Basic Books, 1960.

Rokeach, M. (1960 b) Open and closed orientations to authority. In R. J. McCall and W. C. Bier (Eds.), *Three joint Amer. psych. assn.-Amer. Catholic psych. assn. symposia: proceedings of the Amer. Catholic psych. assn.* New York: Fordham Univ. Press, 1960.

Rudin, S. A. The relationship between rational and irrational authoritarianism. *J. Psychol.,* 1961, **52**, 179-183.

Schachter, S. *The psychology of affiliation.* Palo Alto: Stanford Univ. Press, 1959.

Sherif, M. A study of some social factors in perception. *Arch. Psychol.,* New York, 1935, No. 197.

Sherif, M. *The psychology of social norms.* New York: Harper, 1936.

Sherif, M. An experimental approach to the study of attitudes. *Sociometry,* 1937, **1**, 93-107.

Sherif, M. The concept of reference groups in human relations. In M. Sherif and M. O. Wilson (Eds.), *Group relations at the crossroads.* New York: Harper, 1958.

Sherif, M., and Sherif, Carolyn W. *An outline of social psychology.* 2d ed. New York: Harper, 1956.

Sherif, M., and Sherif, Carolyn W. Varieties of social stimulus situations. In S. B. Sells (Ed.), *Stimulus determinants of behavior*. New York: Ronald Press, 1963.

Shibutani, T. Reference groups as perceptual perspectives. *American J. Sociol.,* 1955, **60**, 562-569.

Slosson, E. E. Perception by suggestion. *Psychol. Rev.,* 1899, **6**, 407-408.

Tagiuri, B., Bruner, J. S., and Blake, R. W. Some determinants of the perception of positive and negative feelings in others. *J. abnorm. soc. Psychol.,* 1953, **48**, 585-592.

Tannenbaum, R., Wechsler, D. A., and Massarik, F. *Leadership and organization: a behavioral science approach*. New York: McGraw-Hill, 1961.

Thibaut, J. W., and Reicken, H. W. Some determinants and consequences of the perception of social causality. *J. Pers.,* 1955, **24**, 113-133.

Thibaut, J. W., and Strickland, L. H. Psychological set and social conformity. *J. Pers.,* 1956, **25**, 115-128.

Triplett, N. L. The dynamogenic factors in pacemaking and competition. *Amer. J. Psychol.,* 1897, **9**, 507-533.

Trueblood, D. E. *The logic of belief*. New York: Harper, 1942.

Vidulich, R. M., and Kalman, I. P. The effects of information source status and dogmatism upon conformity behavior. *J. abnorm. soc. Psychol.,* 1961, **63**, 639-642.

Walker, E. L., and Heyns, R. W. *Anatomy for conformity*. Englewood Cliffs, N. J.: Prentice-Hall, 1962.

Williams, R. W. Religion, value-orientation, and intergroup conflict. *J. soc. Issues,* 1956, **12**, 12-20.

Wilkins, E. J., and DeCharms, R. Results supporting theoretical position. *J. Pers.,* 1962, **30**, 439-457.

Zajonc, R. G., and Wahi, N. K. Conformity and need achievement under cross-cultural norm conflict. *Human Relat.,* 1961, **14**, 241-250.

16

The Social Psychology of
Conversion

JOSEPH B. TAMNEY

University of Singapore

SOURCE. Prepared especially for this volume.

A behavioral scientist interested in religious conversion begins by studying people who change social labels. Often conversion is identified with a shift from one set of values to another, but (1) we always begin with a much more crudely delineated sample, and (2) such an approach probably over-intellectualizes human behavior, reducing it to the concretization of preconceived values. Moreover, the use of a particular label is important in its own right: (1) the label we accept designates which authorities we will recognize as

399

legitimate, (2) this designation channels our financial support, and (3) the use of a particular label usually indicates a willingness to restrict changes in whatever is publicly associated with this appellation; a convert need not believe in the items that compose the social definition of a label, but he will probably defend it against attacks in order to preserve order in that part of the world associated with his identity. This paper, then, asks the question: why do people switch religious [1] labels?

Our approach is suggestive only. The research project on which this paper is based consisted of open-ended interviews with about seventy converts—people who had joined Catholicism, the Nazarene Church, a Neo-Hasedic group, and Zen-Buddhism.[2] Each told the story of his conversion to the writer. This type of study can prove nothing but suggest much. But the reader must be warned; on the one hand you will be struck with a sense of overflowing reality, i.e., any explanation will appear at best partial; on the other hand you will be dismayed by the lack of sufficient data to drive home the points I make; by and large these are intrinsic to the case study approach. The purpose of this paper, therefore, is to merely present a framework and some hypotheses that might be helpful in the study of religious conversion, and especially conversion to Catholicism.

TYPES OF CONVERTS

When a man converts because his wife is a Catholic and he is not, his act has little or nothing to do directly with the nature of the Catholic belief or ritual system. Similar are those who convert in order to receive rewards such as guidance or affection from religious functionaries. These types of cases, which have nothing to do directly with a religious system (i.e., the beliefs or rituals of a religion), we call reference converts because they represent a variation of what sociologists have called "reference group" theory. In other cases, religious phenomena are important because they symbolize significant people in our environment; we call such cases symbolic conversions. On the other hand, religious systems are themselves

---

[1] It is not necessary, for this paper, to discuss a definition of religion, but the one favored is: a radical solution to finiteness, i.e., a practice or belief that eliminates finiteness.

[2] For further information on the sample see Joseph B. Tamney, *An Exploratory Study of Religious Conversion*, doctoral dissertation, Cornell University, 1962.

of immediate relevance for at least three reasons: (1) they establish the existence of a nonvisual world of potential social relationships (these intrinsically nonvisual social bonds will be referred to as spiritual relationships); (2) some systems further self-destruction; and (3) religious systems can be important because they are relevant to the problem of meaning. This paper will consider, first, the reference converts, then the symbolic converts, and finally the three ways in which religious systems are themselves relevant; the conclusion will consider the possible significance of our ideas for the development of Catholicism.

Reference Converts

Of the twenty-seven converts to Catholicism we interviewed, at least fifteen seem to be reference converts, and some form of pressure for conformity appeared significant in every case. Our Catholic converts came entirely from small towns in the middle of New York State, and so have limited representativeness. But we were still impressed with the overwhelming importance of reference behavior for Catholic converts.

Is there anything about the Catholic Church that seems to make it more likely to have nonreligiously oriented converts? First, the insistence of Catholicism that children born to a Catholic and a non-Catholic must be raised as a Catholic increases the pressure to convert on those who marry Catholics. Children play a very prominent part in conversion.

The coming of a child defines two individuals, husband and wife, as one unit: parents. In the socialization process, adults do not feel that there is a significant division of labor as much as they believe in the importance of both parents' upholding the same code —or appearing to do so. There is a recognition that a child sees parents as a unit and that if there is a lack of agreement the child will become uncertain, possibly indifferent. Some of the converts seem to realize that a child must deal with both parents, that for the child they lose some of their individuality, and one therefore sacrifices a part of his identity, his religious difference, in order to remove an impediment to the child's experiencing his parents as a unit.

But children also introduce the possibility of loneliness into a marriage. Laura, for instance, was a Greek Orthodox who married a Catholic. Sometimes she went to church with her husband, sometimes she did not. But after the Baptism of her first child, Laura converted. She realized that hereafter her husband and daughter would be going to the Catholic Church; she, but not her husband, would be alone. Before parenthood, each spouse can attend his or her church without losing any advantage; both are equally isolated, or what seems more likely, neither one think in terms of loneliness or of being left out. In Laura's case however, a third member had joined the group; there were now fewer bonds uniting her with each of the others than existed between the other two members. Laura would probably not have been upset if the difference was sanctioned on the grounds of sex or age differences. But each religion is legitimate for all individuals, and thus religious differences can be experienced as a potential bond lost.[3] The movement from dyad to triad creates the possibility of loneliness, thus heightening the effect of religious difference.

The second reason that Catholicism seems more likely to attract nonreligiously oriented converts is that it makes comparatively few demands on its members. It is relatively easy to play the Catholic role. The only thing a person has to do to be considered a Catholic by his associates is to attend Sunday Mass fairly frequently (unless he loudly proclaims certain beliefs which might have him branded a heretic). Many Catholics do not even know a priest. Since the Catholic status is defined in minimum terms, it is easy to be an anonymous Catholic. On the other hand the Nazarene Church tends to define a member as one who leads an ideal life—who does not drink or smoke, who testifies during services, who partakes in church activities other than regular services, etc. To people who are not too involved in the institutional side of religion, and this seems to describe a majority of our reference converts, being a Catholic is a low price to pay for such things as family harmony or marrying the girl you love.

We suggest, therefore, that Catholicism, in part because of its strong stand on children and its minimal standards for membership, attracts many converts little interested in the religious specifics of Catholicism. Assuming that Catholic conversion losses are more religiously oriented (in part because outside Catholicism, the afore-mentioned conditions do not exist as strongly), the Roman Catholic

---

[3] Because religion is not restricted by sex or age in our society, shared religious activity can become a symbol of the solidarity of a unit. One convert who had an unhappy childhood was especially sensitized to symbols of unity such as family church attendance. The symbolic significance of common church attendance seems to have played a prominent part in her conversion to Catholicism. We see how an act which became important as a symbol of preexisting unit becomes used as a means of creating unity.

Church would seem over time to be turning into an organization composed of strongly committed leaders and a large, docile following.

Symbolic Conversion

The case of Loretta illustrates what we mean by overflowing reality and inadequate data, yet her story suggests an important point, and so we present it here.

Loretta was baptized a Catholic. A year later her father died; her mother remarried a Methodist, and became an Episcopalian. Loretta was raised an Episcopalian. As a child Loretta wanted to be a missionary to China; she likes missionary work because she likes people. Loretta does not know why she chose China. She was interested in Catholicism from about seven years of age; she frequently visited a Catholic Church. The first thing Loretta always saw was the altar; she knew God was supposed to be there. Loretta has always liked Communion; in all the churches she had attended, she has not once passed up an opportunity to receive Communion; Loretta believes it brings you closer to God. As a teenager she sometimes went to Mass, which intrigued her and filled her with awe; it was like participating in the mysterious. At Mass Loretta feels that she and all the people are united with the priest. During her first year of high school, Loretta began investigating other churches. She believed that the Episcopalian church lacked depth and consistency; moreover, she could not accept the control of the priest by the people. As a child, while reading the history of the Episcopalian Church, Loretta had discovered that the Anglican Church had broken from the Catholic Church; subsequently, in all the churches she visited, Loretta asked why they had split from Rome; she never got a satisfactory answer. Loretta left the Episcopalian Church and joined the Baptist Church. She liked the Baptists because they had active youth groups and a mission in China. After a while Loretta concluded that her attachment to the Baptist Church was emotional, and left. She then considered joining Catholicism, but the probable negative reaction of her parents prevented her. During the next several years Loretta tried various other churches, but none satisfied her. At twenty-one she went to Maine to teach. It was at this time that she found out she had been baptized a Catholic. Someone told her that a baptized person living outside the Church would go to hell. Loretta lived next door to a Catholic Church; she frequently visited it. During Mass she liked the stillnes and beauty—the beauty in the stillness. Finally Loretta went to the priest; he was old and partially deaf; when he found out that Loretta had not received any sacraments since her baptism, he called her a sinner. Loretta was hurt, and never returned to him. After first trying the local Community Church, Loretta gave up hope and became an agnostic. She believed all churches were full of hypocrisy. Then she moved to Boston, where her sister introduced her to an Anglican priest. He revived her interest in religion; Loretta planned to enter an

Anglican order of nuns with the understanding of going to China. The Anglican spriest satisfied her on every point except why his church broke with Rome. Loretta told her doubts to a Catholic friend, who suggested she see a Catholic priest. The Anglican priest agreed it was best. Loretta became a Catholic; it was like coming home, like being united with something you had always cherished. Loretta converted against the advice of her friends and family. That which she likes best about Catholicism is that it can trace its origin to Jesus.[4]

When the significant event(s) leading to conversion occur in early childhood, as in this case, we can not hope to satisfactorily piece the puzzle together. Four facts seem important, however: (1) Loretta was a Catholic at first like her deceased father; (2) from an early age Loretta wanted to go to China; I know to myself and others, China always represented the other side of the earth, the farthest-away place; Loretta's early and persistent desire to go there intimates a desire to escape an unhappy childhood; (3) her again early persistent discontent with the Episcopalian break from Rome seems both unusual in that it began at so early an age and exaggerated in that this break has been accepted by many without problems; Loretta's very early attraction to Catholicism suggests to this writer that she knew about her father's Catholicism as well as her own baptism; her dissatisfaction with the Episcopalian break from Rome would therefore be expressing her unhappiness that her mother was, in a sense, disloyal to her father, and at a deeper level it would express her longing for her mother and father to be together again; and (4) her comments about Catholicism seem to support this interpretation; for instance, Loretta likened her conversion to "coming home"; the fact that she so treasures Catholicism's ability to trace its origin to Jesus suggests a preoccupation with origin and could refer to her own origin, her lost father, and her desire to reestablish a relation with him. In short, it seems that Loretta's conversion was a wish fulfillment; she acted out her desire to regain her biological father, and her unhappiness with her mother. Loretta's conversion was like a dream.

When are conversions like dreams? In Loretta's case religions stood for people, as in dreams when parts apparently represent wholes. The key question, then, is under what conditions is religion likely to represent a person. In our society characterized by religious heterogeneity, we still place a premium on religious homogeneity in personal relations; as a result the development of such relations is

---

[4] The small-type story contains paraphrased or in direct quotation only the comments of the convert.

often accompanied by religious adjustments. If we are concerned about these relational changes, these adjustments force religion to stand out and to be strongly associated with the change. Thus religion becomes a very probable symbol of a new or lost relationship in our society. The inability of individuals living in a religiously heterogeneous society to tolerate such differences in their personal relations increases the likelihood of symbolic conversions in which the changes seem to be dream-like events.

SPIRITUAL RELATIONSHIPS. Religious systems are important because they "establish" the existence of a world beyond our vision. Christianity is especially significant in this respect; compared to Buddhism, for instance, Christianity is deeply committed to helping individuals maintain social relationships with beings beyond the possibility of perception.

As a result some people turn to these beings for power just as a boy may align himself with his older brother in moments of potential trouble. Consider the case of Jim.

Prior to entering the service, Jim did not take religion seriously. After his tour of duty he was very interested in religion. Life had made it plain to Jim that he was a small fish in a big pond: (1) while visiting Asia, he saw people living under miserable conditions; Jim thought, "Look at those people with nothing to hang onto, it could happen to me"; (2) he saw "plenty of blood"; Jim had picked up several pilots from his carrier who had crashed; "It made you think"; (3) he witnessed white slavery—people being pushed around like cattle. When Jim was discharged he had neither a job, nor plans, nor any real friends. He summed up how he felt with the word, insecure. Jim, then, met a Catholic girl, converted, and married her. Conversion, however, was not just an act of accommodation. Although Jim did not need Catholicism, he did need religion. His experience had forced him to realize how little control he had over his destiny. That this was the case is supported by his choice of incidents, which, he said, influenced his decision to become a Catholic: (1) his fiancee's grandmother was a religious woman; when she died, she did not seem at all worried; it was as though she knew where she was going; (2) two friends had a sick child; they entrusted him to God and everything turned out alright. These incidents illustrate the use of religion to overcome problems beyond human control.

Jim's experience burst the bubble of security in which he had lived. Is it sufficient, however, just to perceive these kinds of events? Regarding white slavery, Jim remarked: "Something should be done about it, but one person can't do much—maybe start something, but can't do much." These incidents brought home to Jim the powerlessness of the isolated individual. They drove him to religion because he felt isolated. While Jim was in the Navy these events made him start talking about religion, but he did not, then, become religiously active. Jim did convert after he was released, when he had no plans, no job, and, at first, no friends, in short, when he might have felt isolated. When a person is engaged in playing various roles, he is forcing the development of obligations on the part of others toward him; he believes that others will protect or help him. When a person is disengaged, he can experience the terror of being alone in an uncertain world. Jim's case suggests that if disengagement accompanies experiences of man's weakness, it will primarily lead to a search for security.[5] In Jim's case it appears that religion was used as a functional alternative to the societal framework established for controlling man's activities.

Although Jim might have joined another religion, the Catholic Church was very appropriate for someone suffering basically from fear. He liked the extensiveness and uniformity of Catholicism; the latter suggested to him that Catholics were close to each other, that they were more intimately related than members of other religions. We can easily understand how an insecure person would be attracted by a worldwide closely knit organization.

Spiritual relations also satisfy our desire for love and affection. Holiness churches seem more able to accomplish this because of their stress on the immediate, personal relation with Jesus. One convert to the Nazarene Church exemplifies what we mean.

Margie's husband was cruel; he forced her to violate her conscience and undermined her relation with their children. Moreover, because the family constantly moved, Margie had no close friends. She was trapped in an unhappy home. With the support of the Nazarene minister, whose church Margie joined,[6] she salvaged herself by developing a relationship with Christ. Margie now lives for Jesus; she even talks with him. Her spiritual relationship is a very real one, being immediate and two-way. It lacked the visual dimension, but as if to compensate for this, Margie generally devalues this means of sensing the environment; she stresses listening; thus she prefers radio to television and when attending religious services, she closes her eyes and just listens to the singing. Margie believes you do not have to see except with your spiritual eyes. To her, salvation does not require that you attend any church; it is a personal thing between God and man. Margie needed a positive relation of support and found it with Christ.[7]

---

[5] It might be true to say that while disengaged, Adam escaped into the world of philosophy, of ideas. Jim, on the other hand, was faced with reality, the actual behavior of men.

[6] She had been in the Church of Christ.

[7] Seven years after her conversion, but two years before the interview, Margie suffered a nervous breakdown, which suggests that like dreaming, spiritual relationships can relieve just so much of our frustration.

Such behavior is appropriate within the context of a church which emphasizes our immediate relation to Christ. Does anything similar happen in Catholicism?

A monastic life would seem a suitable situation for developing a deep dependence on a spiritual relationship.

Anna's father was Episcopalian, her mother a Catholic. She was raised a Catholic. Anna always had a questioning mind. She remembers asking on the first day of kindergarten: "Where do babies come from?" At seventeen a note was sent home from the Catholic school she was attending because Anna had questioned why it was necessary to obey all the church rules. "I was rebellious." During high school years, she was sent to the principal for having a book explaining Darwin's theory; her mother had given it to her. Anna attended a Catholic college of education. One Sunday she felt the closeness of God. Anna began to attend Mass daily. A year later she entered a teaching order of nuns. "I was in love with Christ." Later Anna realized her decision was an emotional one. She was very happy as a nun. She left the order because of "stomach trouble" and because she did not have enough time for contemplation. Anna taught for a while, then she entered the strictest order she could find, a cloistered order. The life disturbed her, however, and she had to leave. There was a time when Anna could not discuss her experiences in the cloister, now she can. She disliked having to tell on others. After a while she found herself seeking punishment; after leaving, Anna found it difficult to lose the habit of punishing herself. She became scrupulous, felt guilty if unable to properly meditate on God. She disliked the confinement to a cell, little sleep allowed, and sleeping on boards. Anna believes she was losing her personality, her self. She was being told things were evil that were not evil. "It really cuts you off." "Everything is against what you would tend to do." "They used fear a lot." Anna obeyed all the rules out of love of Christ. After nine months in the cloister Anna left, got a degree in education, and began to teach. At first she felt guilty doing various worldly things. She devoted herself to her job, to the exclusion of a social life. What there was of socializing centered on her relation with the children she taught. She realized that this was not right. She found herself doing various acts, e.g., keeping her eyes down, that she had had to do as a nun. Anna moved to New York City. She tried to teach, but had a difficult time controlling the kids. Anna entered nursing school. At time of graduation she was majoring in obstetrics, and became concerned about the Catholic stand on birth control. After some study she decided she disagreed with the church's position. At the same time Anna concluded that all the church rules and religious orders were not really what Christ wanted. Anna decided that if Christ came to earth, He would be an Episcopalian. She was influenced by: (1) her analysis; Anna had thought of going on to another field after nursing; she had an unstable personality, but analysis helped her to stick with nursing; analysis also taught her to seek reasons for rules; Anna believes that you can understand why various rules exist if you study the psychological condition of rule-makers; (2) some of her associates, who were doctors; they were fine men, but had no religion, and believed in birth control. Anna believes church rules are man-made, that there is no real reason for them (other than the rule-maker's psychological condition), and that no one should feel guilty for violating them. Anna does not believe her conversion was directly linked with analysis. She could never leave Catholicism for emotional reasons, although she had had reason to do so; she has witnessed the hypocrisy of Catholic doctors; however, she realizes that in every church there are good and bad. Anna does not believe that guilt was involved in her conversion. Anna studied various religions before she chose Episcopalianism. She chose this religion because it was her father's religion and a Christian religion. She was also influenced by an Episcopalian minister, with whom she is still in contact. Her analyst feared dire consequences from her conversion, because he believed Anna was more Catholic than the Pope. A year later Anna concluded her analysis, which had lasted about three years. She had to quit, because it was a crutch. Anna decided she had found herself. About a year after analysis ended, Anna became very ill. She was operated on, but still was near death. She prayed that she would not die until after marriage. "Sex was keeping me alive." Anna guesses that she wanted to partake of some of the frivolities of life, since she had been so serious, studying and all. Prior to her second operation, Anna experienced a state she believes is death. It was a state of nothingness—no guilt, or suffering, peaceful. She felt like she was leaving her body. After this Anna no longer needed a formal religion; she doubted the existence of God. She no longer feared death. She told her analyst about her experience. After questioning her, he concluded that she truly did not fear death. He told Anna that she had never looked better. She does not fear hell, because she does not believe she is doing wrong. Anna does not believe that analysis can give such peace to anyone with a religious problem. She is free. Anna does not believe her state of nothingness was like being drunk or drugged, or being under an anesthesia, or like dreaming. After the first operation she told the nurse she felt like jumping out the window. The nurse had bars put on the window. Anna and her doctor did not believe she was serious. Since her experience she does not need a personal God. Anna believes in something beyond, but does not try to be more specific. She believes morality has a purely naturalistic basis. She did not go to church last Sunday, and she does not feel guilty about it. Analysis helped to free her, but was not capable of actually freeing her, which resulted from her experience of death. Since this event her friends have noticed changes in her. She is easier to have a good time with, more joyous. Once Anna had been interested in worldly things, then she had given them up; now she is once more interested in them, but in such things as art. She can not agree with people who think you can be both holy and interested in material things like cars and minks; it is possible, but such things make it difficult to be holy. Anna has advised some non-religious people to study Catholicism. She believes it is alright for some people. She can not go out with Catholics; it is an emotional thing.[8]

This saga illustrates again what we meant by overflowing reality and inadequate data. A definitive explanation of Anna's conversion from Catholicism does not seem possible. On the other hand, it does seem possible to say that Anna's religious career most likely had little to do with religion and everything to do with her interpersonal relationships.

Our belief is that an understanding of this case would require the unravelling of Anna's relation to her parents with the skill of an analyst. But there seem sufficient signs to suggest Anna's conversion fits the basic Freudian model that spiritual relations become the stage on which the familial drama is symbolically played. Anna loved Christ; she finally chose Episcopalianism because first of all it was her father's religion; she finally decided that if Christ came to earth he would be an Episcopalian; it does not seem too far fetched to suggest that Anna's problem might have centered on her love, or possibly ambivalence, toward her father. All the relations Anna chose until her conversion, involved inherently asexual (on the crest level) objects—Christ, children, sick people, priests—like her father is supposed to be; that this is deliberate is supported by the eventual centrality of sex at the time of "death," which suggests it must have been operative in some manner previous to this event. This will help us understand her choice of obstetrics. Her "death," described as leaving the body, seems to have epitomized her entire existence up until this event. Finally Anna's life seems to have been continually guided by father-like figures: her analyst, the doctors she associated with, a minister, and Christ (who combines the qualities of lover and father). Anna finally rejected a *personal* God; to this writer her renunciation was less a conversion than a divorce.

But we are interested in more than emphasizing the spiritual world as the locus of reenactment of the personal drama. We are equally concerned about the structural attributes that allow this to take place. Anna's case suggests that the monastic life is a framework within which Catholics can develop a personal relationship with a spiritual being similar to that fostered by holiness religions. But Anna's case also highlights the modern weakness of

---

[8] The small-type story contains paraphrased or in direct quotation only the comments of the convert.

that approach. Catholicism allows this personal relationship only within a collective life; a personal relationship is allowed only after the individual has been depersonalized. No doubt religious orders differ, as do peoples' reactions to the various monastic-type procedures within these orders. But it still seems valid to us to suggest that Catholicism requires deindividualization before direct contact with the deity is allowed. In an individually oriented society, as ours generally is, this means that religions other than Catholicism would be structurally more attractive to those who turn to the religious arena for the re-creation of or substitution for their personal world.

But everyone interested in spiritual relations need not be so deeply troubled as Anna; for such people Catholicism might still work.

Mary Lou's parents are divorced. She lives with her mother, step-father, two step-brothers and two step-sisters. "My family life has been rather insecure because of my parents' divorce. Even today (at eighteen) I feel very insecure and worry too much—especially about losing the friendship or love of someone dear to me." "Mommy has done her best, but I hope to raise my children in the type of home I've always wished I had."

Mary Lou seemed most anxious to please; she thought of becoming a Catholic as a way of pleasing her boyfriend; several times during the interview she expressed the wish that she could be more helpful. If she left her fiance now, she would still become a Catholic. "I like the more 'material' things about the Church that makes it easier to actually worship God instead of just believing in Him; things like the rosary, not eating meat on Friday, etc.," Mary Lou liked the Catholic sermons because they were applicable to everyday life; she also appreciated the definite rules to follow in Catholicism. Mary Lou likes the dialogue Mass.

Insecure, concerned about the loss of love, Mary Lou seems to have turned to God for a secure affection. She underlined "worship," stressing her interest in relating to God, not just believing in Him. Similarly her appreciation of the many rules of Catholicism, such as not eating meat on Friday, reflected her desire to relate to God. We believe this emphasis on the spiritual relationship arose because Mary Lou realized that she, alone, controls this relationship, and that this tie will endure as long as she obligates God through obedience. Unlike man, we believe that Mary Lou's God has little control over His relationships. As long as we obey the rules, her "God" must love us. Like the rosary, reciting the Mass aloud is a series of acts expressing our acceptance of and dependence upon God—thereby obligating "Him." The dialogue Mass gives further contact in the spiritual relationship, helping to bind "God," and would for this reason seem to appeal to a person suffering from emotional insecurity.

Another convert who joined Catholicism believed you went to church to get close to God, and appreciated the fact that Catholicism makes people go to church. Most human relationships are characterized by mutual expectations; the various rules of Catholicism, by making explicit the demands of God, help to realize the spiritual relationship.

But the Catholic Church not only fosters spiritual relationships with deities; it also supports relations with deceased humans. Larry's conversion seems to have been greatly influenced by the fact of his daughters' joining Catholicism. However, also of some significance was a priest's explanation of how through prayer Larry could help his deceased mother get to heaven. At the time of being interviewed, Larry was very proud of his very generous contribution to the church-sponsored hospital fund; he plans to have his mother's name put on the hospital plaque commemorating donors. It is difficult to say how much stress should be put on Larry's relation to his mother. Yet it was of some importance. For our purposes it is sufficient to emphasize that Catholicism, with its stress on a community embracing living and dead, might have more appeal to those desiring or, perhaps needing,[9] to continue their relation with deceased individuals than the more individually oriented religions such as the holiness churches.

Christianity, and especially Catholicism, is patterned after our personal world, particularly the family. Catholic mythology helps to realize a world of spiritual relationships. It offers to frustrated men and women a vertical personal realm to replace their indifferent or punishing horizontal personal world. In a time in which personal relations are firmly patterned and routinely maintained, Christian mythology would be nourished by its building on the firm foundation of the personal network. In our world of flux and uncertainty, this

---

[9] Larry seemed to need the continuance of this relationship; possibly this was due to the strong ambivalence he must have felt toward his mother. In another case not reported, a mother seemed to have experienced similar ambivalence toward a deceased son, and to have identified with him; the case resembled the process discussed by Sigmund Freud, "Mourning and Melancholia," in *Collected Papers*. It seems possible that Protestant churches, to one of which this lady belonged, fosters such identification because they do not offer a mechanism for "keeping the relationship alive" as a spiritual relationship.

same mythology rather than elevating man above his immediate problems turns religion into a pseudopersonal realm.

SELF-DESTRUCTION. Many religious rituals are overt forms of self-destruction; they are often called transitional rites. Similarly, St. Paul talks about dying to our old self and being reborn. Self-destruction, usually accompanied by some form of rebirth, is a basic religious theme.

Goffman has pointed out that even when the situation does not require it, individuals may act in such a manner as to destroy their "selves."

In addition to profanation of others, individuals . . .

in varieties of situations give the appearance of profaning themselves, acting in a way that seems purposely designed to destroy the image others have of them as persons worthy of deference. Ceremonial mortification of the flesh has been a theme in many social movements. What seems to be involved is not merely bad demeanor but rather the concerted efforts of an individual sensitive to high standards of demeanor to act against his own interests and exploit ceremonial arrangements by presenting himself in the worst possible light.[10]

Self-destruction seems to be a basic human theme.

Yet we encountered no converts to Catholicism who were motivated by this desire. Of course, this could simply be due to the small number of people we interviewed. We did encounter one case, however, in which the person left Catholicism because it did not offer a satisfactory means of executing self-destruction; this story suggests the possibility that Catholicism is so structured as to minimize the appeal to individuals desiring to destroy their "selves."

Bret's parents didn't belong to any one church, nor did they regularly attend any church. They did send their children to Sunday School. The family frequently moved, so Bret never developed allegiance to any one church. When he was about sixteen, he attended a Nazarene Church for about six months. Bret liked the friendliness of the people, but religion was not important to him. Bret then moved north, where he spent the rest of his high school years. He did not go to any church. Bret went along with the gang, smoking and drinking; he married a Catholic and joined the Catholic Church. Bret did not like the idea that he could not go to other church services, or that he had to confess his sins to another man; moreover, he could not see the difference between doing servile work and playing football on Sunday. For the next four years, however, Bret and his wife regularly attended church. Bret knew the general ideas of the Mass, but it was the same ritual over and over again; it was not con-

---

[10] Erving Goffman, "The Nature of Deference and Demeanor," *American Anthropologist,* 58 (June 1956), p. 496.

structive because it was repetitious. The sermons, compared with those in a Protestant service, were very poor. The sermons were like lectures; he did not learn much from them. Bret did not respect confession; it was not used for its actual purpose. In his crowd it was not used as a breaking point between sin and not sinning, but to forgive sins committed. It did not appear to have much power, since the people went out and committed the same sins all over again. Bret wanted more spirit among the church goers, and a better atmosphere for the worship of God. Prior to his conversion several events occurred which indicated Bret's increased interest in religion, and his growing sense of guilt for his sins: (1) a younger brother who had recently been saved visited Bret; trying to excuse his own lack of religiousness, Bret asked him if he would have stood up for religion in a small town, i.e., if he would have proclaimed Christ and gone against the gang; his brother smiled and said "yes"; this disturbed Bret; (2) one day at work, a friend mentioned that smoking can give you cancer; Bret dropped his cigarette and never smoked again (he believed smoking was wrong); and (3) Bret and a friend were making the rounds of the bars around Madison Square Garden, when they saw that Billy Graham was in town. Bret felt guilty; soon after he went to hear Graham; he would have answered the altar call, except the thought his wife would never join a Protestant Church. Soon after these events, Bret's wife remarked that she was dissatisfied with their religious life; that was all Bret needed. They decided to visit other churches. Several Protestant churches appealed to them. They especially liked the friendliness of the people at these churches. Then they visited Bret's family. Saturday night one of Bret's sisters said that she believed that religion was going to come to some member of the family present in the room. Bret did not think it was he; others in the family could have used religion a lot more. Next day the family attended a Pentecostal church. Bret and his wife were saved. He can not remember that sermon. He cried. Afterwards Bret felt relieved of his burdens. When Bret returned home, he tried several churches and decided to join the Nazarene Church. He liked the enthusiasm of the minister and the fact that the people seemed to enjoy the service. Bret believes that he has always had a religious frame of reference; he always knew when he was doing wrong. Above all else, Bret believes in the necessity of experiencing a personal relationship with God to be saved. He sincerely feels that formerly his relation was with a church, but now, his relationship is with the Spirit, independent of any church. It is good to be affiliated with a church, however, because it enables one to be more effective in Christian work.

Granted Bret was probably never more than a nominal Catholic, but perhaps his case can still shed light on the effects of Catholic rituals.

Bret sought a "breaking point"; neither the mass nor confession seemed able to produce this. The basic repititiousness of the mass expresses Catholicism's concern for unchangeable truths rather than an interest in changing individuals. Concerning sermons, a remark of another convert who joined the Catholic Church seems relevant; he was very impressed by how people in one Catholic Church accepted a stuttering priest—a phenomenon not likely in the more liberal Protestant churches. This acceptance symbolized for him the strong, authoritarian character of Catholicism; sermons do not really have to be interesting because truth is already established and defended by the entire church organization. In short, the repetitiousness of the mass and the uninteresting sermons express Catholicism's concern with preserving established truths rather than an interest in aiding individuals through particular crises.

But why was the evangelistic service able to succeed where confession failed? Bret noted that people did not seem different after confession, but certainly that is true of most people before and after attendance at evangelistic services. What was significant probably was that after public testimony a person is different and more so than an individual after private confession. Why is public testimony more effective? Two considerations seem important: (1) if a person is to radically change he must get those he lives with to redefine him, thus presenting different expectations which will allow or even help him to be a new man; and (2) it is difficult for a guilt-ridden person to forgive himself; if we judge ourselves bad, we need evidence of a change, and of a basic change, before we can say we are a new man, and thus no longer have self-hate; ceremonies of self-defamation allow us then to figuratively kill ourselves, thus symbolically proclaiming even to ourselves the birth of a new man, but even more, such ceremonies involve such a radical departure from our customary way of behaving as to give concrete evidence that a new man has appeared. Public testimony, then, changes people's expectations of us and allows us to believe we have changed; both of these in turn help to actually produce a new man.[11]

We conclude that Catholicism might fail to attract converts interested in self-destruction both because of the absence of some form of public confession and because its central ritual, the mass, expresses more its certainty about its own truth than a concern for helping individuals find a new self.

But is it not strange that an old, established religion seems unable to serve what seems a fundamental religious problem, namely

---

[11] Catholicism would in general be failing to meet what Mowrer believes is a modern problem: the relative absence of structures that allow "confession" and communication among peers. O. Hobart Mowrer, *The New Group Therapy*, Princeton, New Jersey: Insight Book by Van Nostrand, 1964.

self-destruction? In fact, Catholicism had been able to service this desire; first, there were transitional rituals, such as confirmation and marriage, in which individuals were to some extent reborn; such a system would work within a society in which individuals all experienced their basic problems at the same point in their life, which in turn is possible if everyone is leading the same basic life pattern; in modern society, however, people lead such varied lives that a ritual system assuming uniform crisis points seems unreal and is ineffective; second, Catholicism did stress ceremonial silence—"This ceremonial silence signifies unconsciously being dead, just as in dreams . . ." [12] —the silence of the mass is of course being eliminated; but even if it were not, such silence would no longer work; for it signified the death of the individual into the group, whereas today as with Bret, individuals might seek to die but to be reborn as new individuals and not as parts of a collectivity. Thus the means evolved by Catholicism to handle self-destruction seem no longer appropriate for our times.

MEANING. Douglas [13] would have us alter our conception of religion "in the light of man's common urge to make a unity of all their experience and to overcome distinctions and separations in acts of at-one-ment." Religion is man's attempt to overcome all separations. This is what we refer to as the problem of meaning: the attempt to find wholeness.

Although we did not interview any converts to Catholicism who seemed to be motivated primarily by this search, we did talk with two such individuals, one of whom belonged to a Zen-Buddhist Institute and another who was really still searching; their stories, which because of their length cannot be presented in detail, seem worthy of some consideration.

The problem of meaning probably only occurs to the alienated; if someone is completely immersed in the social, he or she has found wholeness by reducing their awareness of reality. Religion becomes relevant when meaning becomes a problem, and this can only happen when people are no longer satisfied with the capabilities of social structures to produce wholeness. [14] But there are two basic ways of becoming an outsider. Miriam, one of our converts, had a very unhappy childhood; she began life feeling like an outsider because she was rejected by her family. On the other hand, Malcolm grew into the condition of being an outsider; he was influenced

---

[12] Theodore Reik, *Ritual,* Translated by Douglas Bryan, New York: International Universities Press, 1958, p. 140.

[13] Mary Douglas, *Purity and Danger,* New York: Frederick Praeger, 1966.

[14] See Douglas.

by: (1) the religious hypocrisy of his parents, each of whom went to a different church, but neither of whom seemed to practice their religion; (2) a religious experience he had while a youth painting out in the fields; he had this religious experience without playing the religious role;[15] and (3) while a soldier in World War II, Malcolm could not believe people were actually trying to kill him; when he was first bombed he had to stick his head up to see it; he did not believe all Germans or Japanese were evil, yet they were trying to kill him. All these experiences sharpened the distinction between the person and the role, and led Malcolm to look beyond the social structure for "something deeper." Outsiders, then, are of two types: the rejected and those who continue to live in society but sense something beyond it because of experiences that highlight the difference between person and role.

The first type searches for peace, the second for a path. As Miriam said—"I am looking for wholeness, a family with others to escape my loneliness." Miriam believes she is at the mercy of others, that being talented with extrasensory perception she is well aware of the attitudes and feelings of others; moreover, she has no boundaries of her own, accepting whatever attitudes she reads in others toward her as her own self-evaluations. In fact, Miriam seems to read all relations in terms of love and hate; for her there is no such thing as a bureaucracy; all relations evaluate her as a person. This must be an extremely trying way of life; we are not surprised to discover, therefore, that Miriam is searching for a means of producing a mystical experience; she longs for union with the universe. The religious ceremony Miriam likes best is the Quaker meeting; she loves the social silence—it allows communication with the divine yet a sense of participating with others in a significant experience. The extent to which interaction must be punishing for Miriam is probably reflected in this preference for truly silent relationships—contentless unions. We might say that in Miriam's case rejection led to an interest in religion as an escape. But this seems vastly inadequate. Miriam is truly outside, even outside religious structures. She is alone searching for a new way to get back in. Miriam is an intelligent, talented, possibly creative person. More and more pushed outside society Miriam may find a new reality. She cannot be satisfied with a path, with a promise; Miriam must break through

---

[15] Religious experiences, sexual attraction, and intuitive understanding are experiences that often undermine the social structure because they occur outside the appropriate social occasions for them.

or be broken. Miriam, to succeed, must search outside all communal religious roads.

Malcolm, on the other hand, settled for a path; he officially joined the Zen-Buddhist Institute. He reasoned that the people he met seemed intelligent and mature; the kind he could respect; so, Malcolm decided to try their method. He is self-confident enough that he does not see all relations as personal evaluations; therefore, he can associate with others and learn from them. But he is also basically an outsider; as a result: (1) he is attracted by a religion which puts stress on a method, not a doctrine; Malcolm is looking for a solution, but he must find it himself; for him the value of a religion is not related to the presence of ready-made solutions, but the availability of means that might help him make progress in better understanding the problem and possibly in moving towards its solution; Malcolm does not require solutions, nor can he accept them; and (2) Malcolm is not committed solely to the Zen method; he also tries yoga, for instance; since Malcolm sees religion primarily as a path rather than a solution it makes sense not to devote himself completely to one religion, but to be flexible enough to try several different roads. To self-confident outsiders, then, religion is a path and it makes sense not to commit oneself to a single path.

Both Miriam and Malcolm sought wholeness. For instance, Malcolm was attracted to Zen in part because it seemed able to be applied to all areas of life; there is a Zen way of living. However, both types are difficult to contain within a religious structure; those who are rejected must finally pursue the peace of mysticism which may or may not turn out to be a gate opening back into the social world; the Malcolmites are difficult to contain because of their basic mistrust of all structures and thus their tendency to try several.

CONCLUSION. Catholic leaders might use the ideas suggested in this paper to more deliberately shape the future of Catholicism. Should a church be receptive to all types of converts? The Malcolmite type would seem to be a desirable category; yet this is probably the least loyal. Religionists would probably agree that reference and symbolic conversions are not particularly desirable. But what about those seeking self-destruction? This has certainly been a traditional religious function, yet it seems to require an unnecessarily harsh condemnation of one's past. Can not growth occur without the exaggeration of self-destruction? Finally what should be Christianity's stand toward those whose devotion reflects their dependence on involvement in vertical, spiritual relationships? Does this not remove them from the horizontal world where they belong?

Catholic leaders might profitably attempt to answer these questions about the type of Catholic they want.

Having decided on the desirable qualities of membership, leaders might then take action to maximize these qualities within their church. Four basic approaches seem possible: (1) leaders might try to evaluate at least new members, and reject those lacking the preferred traits; this seems unsound both because we lack the precise methods needed for such evaluations and because it seems uncharitable and therefore inappropriate for a religious body; (2) leaders might try to affect society so as to eliminate the conditions generating non-preferred types; (3) they might alter characteristics of their religion that seem conducive to producing these desirable types; and (4) leaders might accept and allow all types while trying to move people toward the desired characteristics; this would require a flexible structure combined with a clear stand in favor of certain paths within the structure; leaders would not force individuals into a mold, but allow their preferences to be clearly understood. A combination of the last three alternatives would seem feasible and possibly desirable.

What types of things might religionists do to control the development of their church? Suppose Catholic leaders decided to maximize the Malcolmites. They might take the following actions: (1) reduce authoritarianism so as to appeal to people who believe they must make up their own minds; (2) stress the role of religion as a path rather than a solution; (3) try to increase religious tolerance so that religious differences can be more easily accepted in personal relations; this would help to minimize both reference and symbolic converts; (4) reduce the prevalence of evaluation in our society; this can be done by stressing the need to accept each other as we are, and by increasing the bureaucratization of the social world, which would mean that when evaluations were made they would not refer to the total person; bureaucracy lessens the psychological impact of evaluation; such action would help to minimize the number of people forced to turn to the vertical dimension for a sense of acceptance or value; it might also reduce the number of those seeking self-destruction; (5) depersonalize Christian mythology so as to make it harder to escape the horizontal into the spiritual dimension; and (6) further technological development and personal safety so as to minimize fear. This is, of course, only a crude sketch of a possible program. The significant thing is to recognize that we are at a point when religious leaders can attempt to control the destiny of their churches.

PART V

MARGINALITY, TRANSITION, AND RENEWAL

Growth, development, and change are as characteristic of viable social organisms as they are of physical organisms. But the processes of growth and maturation inevitably disrupt an organism's equilibrium. New modes of adapting and behaving must be explored and tested as these processes unfold. As a natural consequence of the disruption of its equilibrium, the organism tends in certain ways to resist change.

This section considers phenomena indicative of change, growth, and transition in the American Catholic community. First, LIU studies the social and religious attitudes of marginal Catholics in a Southern city, reporting that persons with a high degree of involvement in Church affairs also display high involvement in community

419

affairs. In the rural southwest, however, as DAVIDSON *and* SCHLANGEN *report, Catholics represent a numerical and social minority still subject to discrimination in political and religious matters.*

The Christian Family Movement, a midwest-based religious action group with obvious parallels to political populism, was once regarded as a subversive element in the Catholic community and is still darkly conceived as a growing field for such peripheral movements as the "underground Church." The process by which CFM progressed from a loosely knit tangential network into a formal social organization, a process accompanied by strain and conflict among members, is investigated by MAIOLO, LIU, *and* D'ANTONIO.

Of the casual and formal social groups that have sought to involve laymen more directly in religious affairs, perhaps none has more strident adherents or more vocal critics than the cursillo movement. In some ways similar to a rigidly "closed," secretively conducted retreat, the cursillo is customarily reported by its adherents to have dramatically changed their lives, while its critics fault the defensiveness, the secretiveness, and the manipulativeness of cursillistas. DRAGOSTIN *assesses his own experiences in a cursillo from the perspective of a priest who is a behavioral scientist.*

Post-Vatican II change in the institutional Church is evident in the liturgy, in the increased role of lay persons, and in the changed habits and lifeways of members of religious communities. In the final paper, MURPHY *and* LIU *investigate the role of "readiness" for change in three communities of nuns as evident in organizational structure and development.*

17

Catholics in Dixie: Marginality and Anomie

WILLIAM T. LIU

University of Notre Dame

SOURCE. "The Marginal Catholics in the South: A Revision of Concepts," *American Journal of Sociology,* 1960, 65, 383-390. Reprinted by permission.

The present study[1] was designed to re-examine the institutional approach to the concept of the marginal man by studying a group of migrants. Although the size of our sample is comparatively small,

---

[1] The writer is indebted to Professors Lewis M. Killian and Russell Middleton of Florida State University and to Professors William A. Botzum, C.S.C., and David H. Fosselman, C.S.C., of the University of Portland for their critical reading and suggestions.

the results should be significant because the social setting is quite different from that of other studies.

As part of the general trend of positivistic sociology, the ecological approach to migration studies emerged, spearheaded by Robert E. Park.[2] The international migration studies, which placed emphasis on the relationship between the values of the original group and the atttiudes of the individuals in terms of group solidarity, were highlighted by the work of Thomas and Znaneicki.[3] In the subsequent years the social psychological approach has benefited from the refinement of methodological tools and concepts. The tremendous volume of research on migration has produced a number of conceptual schema. Significantly, considerable efforts have been made toward the formulation of analytical variables which make possible the construction of a more sophisticated theoretical framework.

Park concluded that a more complete study of the adjustment of immigrants must also consider the social relationships between the immigrant group and host community. Hence he developed the well-known concepts of conflict, accommodation, and assimilation.[4] In the long run, the ultimate goal of immigrant adjustment lay in the process of assimilation of the symbols and values of the host culture.

In a further elaboration of the migration studies, Park developed the concept of the "marginal man," and the concept has been much extended by Stonequist. The term was used to refer to a "cultural hybrid," "a man living and sharing intimately in the cultural life and traditions of two distinct peoples . . . which never completely interpenetrated and fused." [5] The genesis of this concept seems to have been in the analysis of the social relations between the immigrants and members of the host group, since the marginal man is

---

2 The earlier works include E. Franklin Frazier, *The Negro Family in Chicago* (Chicago: University of Chicago Press, 1932); C. J. Galpin and T. B. Manny, *Interstate Migration of the Native White Population as Indicated by Difference between the State of Birth and State of Residence* (Washington, D.C.: Bureau of Agricultural Economics, 1934); and John N. Webb and Nalcom J. Brown, *Migrant Families* ("WPA Studies" [Washington, D.C.: Government Printing Office, 1938]).

3 William I. Thomas and Florian Znaniecki, *The Polish Peasant in Europe and America* (Boston: Gotham Press, 1919).

4 Robert E. Park, *Race and Culture* (Glencoe, Ill.: Free Press, 1950), p. 359.

5 Robert E. Park, "Human Migration and the Marginal Man," *American Journal of Sociology,* XXXII (May, 1928), 892. Cf. Everett Stonequist, "The Problem of the Marginal Man," *American Journal of Sociology,* XLI (July, 1935), 1-12.

essentially the product of the retarded process of assimilation. If this interpretation of Park's original work is correct, then the basic focal point of analysis is social relations, and the discussion lies properly in the sociological domain. However, the inner world of the marginal man rather than his social relationships has remained the object of observation. The analysis of the marginal man, therefore, has been the analysis of ambivalent personality maladjustment.[6] In other words, the main concern is no longer with the interactional process of the migrants and members of the receiving group but rather with the psychological analysis of the individual.[7]

In the years following the coinage of this term, several important criticisms appeared. Goldberg, for instance, believed that the marginal man need not live in a state of internal psychological conflict and that the marginal society may well develop a new cultural synthesis which provides its members with norms, behavior patterns, and goals which offer an adequate measure of security to develop what Goldberg called "marginal culture."[8] Closely allied to this cultural approach is that offered by Wardwell and elaborated by Fichter.[9] Fichter believes an important aspect of marginality is the imperfectly institutionalized role "which implies a kind of ambiguity and inconsistency in both the behavior of the marginal man and the sanctions attending his behavior."[10] The imperfectly institutionalized role, as it is termed, refers to the cultural adaptation of the individual, insofar as he recognizes its obligations. The point of reference here, whether that of the individual or that of his culture, is not readily apparent in Fichter's work. However, degrees of con-

---

6 For an orthodox interpretation see Melvin Tumin, "Some Fragments from the Life History of a Marginal Man," *Character and Personality,* XIII (March-June, 1945), 261-96.

7 The writer is indebted to Frank E. Jones on this point (see his "A Sociological Perspective on Immigrant Adjustment," *Social Forces,* XXXV [October, 1956], 39-47).

8 Milton M. Goldberg, "A Qualification of the Marginal Man Theory," *American Sociological Review,* VI (1941), 52-58. Further revision of this concept was offered recently by Paul C. P. Siu, "The Sojourner," *American Journal of Sociology,* LVIII (July, 1952), 34-44, and by Arron Anatonvsky, "Toward a Refinement of the 'Marginal Man' Concept," *Social Forces,* XXXV (October, 1956), 57-62. These two papers stressed the individual's perception of his life-goal and his position in the larger society.

9 Walter I. Wardwell, "A Marginal Professional Role: The Chiropractor," *Social Forces,* XXX (March, 1952), 339-48; Joseph H. Fichter, "The Marginal Catholic: An Institutional Approach," *Social Forces,* XXXII (December, 1953), 167-73.

10 Joseph H. Fichter, *Social Relations in the Urban Parish* (Chicago: University of Chicago Press, 1954), p. 57.

formity in role behavior, as it is conceptualized by Fichter, could be measured only by the importance to the individual of the prescribed pattern. Hence Fichter's approach still borrows heavily from the cultural perspective.[11]

The present study deals with the patterns of migration and adjustment of the Roman Catholic populaton of one southern community as an empirical test of the validity of the concept of the marginal man. (In this paper the word "Catholic," rather than the term "Roman Catholic," will be used). The Catholic migrants in the South are chosen because here are found a few conceptual areas where Catholic values are either contrary to or radically different from the traditional values of the South and because the newly acquired status of the migrants can be compared with their acceptance of attitudes prescribed by these many roles. In other words, the adjustment of the Catholic migrant families to the host community depends largely upon their capacity to perform successfully the inherent local social roles. This Catholic population here is not a distinct ethnic group in a strict sense [12] but is a migrant population composed of members of a religious minority. The stereotypical American Catholic is a recent immigrant, a member of the lower strata, a city dweller, and one who is sympathetic toward labor.[13] The American Catholics are regionally concentrated and, partly because of their pattern of immigration, have been identified with the Northeast and the Middle States regions.[14] On the other hand, the American South has few representatives of later immigrants and, with the exception of the French in Louisiana, is predominantly Protestant in faith. For this reason, and also because of the nature of the southern economy, much of the South's traditional way of life is still retained.

In the literature the concepts "adjustment," "assimilation," and "integration" have been frequently used synonymously; furthermore, there is no uniform agreement concerning the concept of adjustment

---

11 *Ibid.*, p. 62.

12 E. K. Francis, "The Nature of the Ethnic Group," *American Journal of Sociology*, LII (March, 1947), 393-400.

13 Will Herberg, *Protestant—Catholic—Jew* (New York: Doubleday & Co., 1955). A recent study suggested that, in rate of mobility, the Catholic segment of our population has kept up with other segments of it (see John Kosa and John Nash, "The Social Ascending of Catholics," *Social Order*, VIII [March, 1958], 98-103).

14 As defined by Howard W. Odum (see his *Southern Regions of the United States* [Chapel Hill: University of North Carolina Press, 1936]).

itself.[15] In the present study "adjustment" emphasizes both the normative integration of the migrant Catholics and the external evidence of the individual's identification with the values and sentiments of the receiving group. The components of the broad concept of "adjustment" include, then (1) the acceptance-rejection pattern of the migrant Catholics to the known values of American Catholicism; (2) the acceptance-rejection pattern of the migrant Catholics to the traditional values of the South; (3) the extent of the individual migrant's social participation in the host community; and (4) the degree of the individual migrant's self-identification with the host community.

Field work for this study took place in an urban community of northern Florida with an estimated population of 38,100 in 1955. Earlier Spanish missions in the community had completely withdrawn as early as the end of the nineteenth century, and the second wave of Catholic settlers consisted largely of Irish and French settlers. But this group of Catholics had also drifted away. In 1904 there were only four Catholics in the city.[16] A new influx of Catholic population occurred during World War II, and in 1957, during the period of field work, there were 268 Catholic families and 87 unattached individuals. Only the married, white, migrant couples were interviewed separately and 98 couples, or 196 individuals, were involved in the final analysis.

The questionnaire used in the present study comprises a battery of some sixty questions divided into four major parts: (1) background information on the individual; (2) the religiosocial attitude scales to elicit the subjects' values regarding race, church doctrine, birth control, and labor; (3) the Southern Identification Scale; and (4) Chapin's Social Participation Scale.[17] Pretest of the instrument was administered to 110 Catholic women college students during the spring of 1957, several months prior to the field work.

---

15 See Verne Wright, "Summary of Literature on Social Adjustment," *American Sociological Review,* VII (June, 1942), 407-22; Werner S. Landecker, "Types of Integration and Their Measurement," *American Journal of Sociology, LVI* (January, 1951), 332-40.

16 William T. Liu, "A Study of the Social Integration of Catholic Migrants in a Southern Community" (unpublished Ph.D. dissertation, Florida State University, 1958), Chap. III.

17 All attitude scales met the Guttman criteria. For scale items and details of scale construction see Liu, *op. cit.,* Chap. IV.

The independent variables [18] are Catholicity, education, residential status, religious training, age, post-marital mobility, family income, and husband's occupation (Table 1). Each of the eight independent variables is examined with the following dependent variables chosen for this study. These are (1) the Church Doctrine Scale (CDS); (2) the Labor Attitude Scale (LAS); (3) the Birth-Control Attitude Scale (BCAS); (4) the Race Attitude Scale (RAS); (5) the Social Participation Scale (SPS);[19] and (6) the Southern Identification Scale (SIS). For consistency, high scores on the CDS and the BCAS mean closer adherences to the Catholic teachings;

TABLE 1   EIGHT INDEPENDENT VARIABLES AND THEIR DISTRIBUTION

Variable	High	Middle	Low	No Information	Total
Catholicity	70	72	50	4	196
Education	70	48	74	4	196
Length of residence	66	56	70	4	196
Age	34	101	60	1	196
Mobility	59	78	55	4	196
Family income [a]	40	26	25	..	91
Husband's occupation [a]	31	32	26	2	91
Religious training	28	103	63	2	196

[a] Excluding six couples whose husbands were students, one unemployed.

similarly, high scores on the LAS and the RAS mean favorable attitudes toward labor unionism and toward desegregation issues. Table 2 shows the pattern of distribution.

---

[18] For practical reasons, Fichter's classification must be modified in this study (*ibid.*).

Fifty-five persons reported that they had not moved outside of the state since their present marriage. During the same period 78 persons made one move across the state line, and 59 individuals reported that they had made at least two moves since their present marriage. All individuals, however, in this category made moves prior to their marriages.

Data on family income and occupation of the husband have indicated that this group consists largely of middle-class families. It is necessary therefore to make arbitrary income-status divisions by marking the breaking points of the distribution.

[19] Chapin's scale was used here with a modified point-assigning system.

TABLE 2 SIX DEPENDENT VARIABLES AND THEIR DISTRIBUTION

Variable	High	Middle	Low	No Infor-mation	Total
Church doctrine	73	60	61	2	196
Labor attitude	53	72	70	1	196
Birth control	64	67	61	4	196
Race attitude	70	66	58	2	196
Social participation	57	47	92	0	196
Southern identification	73	57	65	1	196

THE RELIGIOSOCIAL ATTITUDES OF THE MIGRANT CATHOLICS

In many previous studies on migration and adjustment it was found that the breakdown of group solidarity and ideological values of the minority group generally preceded the gradual assimilation of such group members into the larger society. In the present study the employment of attitudinal scales is based on the assumption that the attitudinal deviance from the original group as well as the adaptation to the values of the host group should reinforce each other and simultaneously serve as the yardstick of measuring the general adjustment of the migrants in the host community. A general hypothesis was that there was a direct relationship between the degree of Catholicity and the scores on each of the four pertinent areas of attitudes—Catholic doctrine, race, labor, and birth control. A secondary hypothesis was that the social characteristics of the migrants would influence the attitudes.

Upon comparing Catholicity of practice with each of the four areas of migrants' values, it was found, first, that Catholicity was directly related to attitudes toward the church doctrines and the church's position on birth-control issues, while attitudes toward labor and race issues seemed to be independent of it.

Second, post-marital mobility was related to the attitude toward church doctrine, race questions, and the Catholic ideal of birth control. Mobility was inversely related to church doctrine but directly related to both the birth-control ideals and the attitude toward the race questions.

No significant relationships exist between religious education and each of the four areas. This was contrary to common expectation. Perhaps the explanation lies in the fact that there were too many individuals in the group who had no Catholic education (nearly 50 percent of the total) and too few people who had only Catholic education (about 13 percent). Furthermore, information regarding religious education was not complete without reports on the individual's Sunday-school attendance.

Age did not seem to be important in determining attitudes, except race issues. The expected result—that younger people are less conservative—was confirmed.

The husband's occupation was related to the wife's attitude toward birth control. The husband's attitude toward the same issue was not statistically significantly related, although there was a trend in this direction. It was found that the higher the prestige of the husband's occupation, the more favorable the attitude toward the Catholic position regarding birth control.

Although income and education are both related to occupation, income was shown to have little influence on attitudes toward the four issues. However, one might note that the frequency table showed the same general pattern of distribution as found in regard to occupation.

Excluding the birth-control issues, with which education formed the same pattern as income and occupation, attitudes toward race issues were highly influenced by educational attainment (Table 3). It is possible that the more highly educated rationalized their an-

TABLE 3   CHI SQUARES AND LEVELS OF SIGNIFICANCE OF INDEPENDENCE BETWEEN EIGHT INDEPENDENT VARIABLES AND RELIGIOSOCIAL ATTITUDES [a]

Variable	Church Doctrine		Labor Attitude		Birth Control		Race Attitude	
	X^2	$P<$	X^2	$P<$	X^2	$P<$	X^2	$P<$
Catholicity	26.22	.001	3.30	—	14.90	.01	1.95	—
Mobility	20.79	.001	1.69	—	11.00	.05	12.57	.02
Religious education	8.15	.1	3.69	—	3.67	—	5.92	—
Age	7.68	—	1.34	—	2.59	—	23.71	.001
Occupation:								
Husband	5.07	—	4.88	—	9.17	.1	5.69	—
Wife	1.29	—	4.40	—	11.62	.05	7.93	—
Income:								
Husband	5.47	—	6.56	—	6.71	—	6.29	—
Wife	2.35	—	5.93	—	9.34	.1	1.29	—
Residence	3.04	—	2.61	—	6.03	—	27.16	.001
Education	3.24	—	9.04	.1	9.59	.05	21.18	.001

[a] 4 d.f. for all Chi-square tables.

swers on the scale. Finally, length of residence was found significant in shaping attitudes toward race issues but not in the case of the other three issues.

Although Catholicity had decisive influence on two of the four areas, it was difficult to reach the conclusion that adherence to the Catholic church was the all-embracing factor in determining identification with the values and symbols of the host community: age, length of residence, socioeconomic status, and mobility each had a share.

THE PATTERN OF SOCIAL PARTICIPATION

As shown in Table 4, the extent of participation in the formal groupings was dependent on the socioeconomic status of the migrants and on their degree of Catholicity. The former was somewhat anticipated, since many previous studies had already established the relationship.[20] The latter finding—that the degree of Catholicity was directly related to the extent of social participation—was not at all expected. Since the auxiliary organizations of the parish were not included in the present data, it was first hypothesized that the extent

TABLE 4   SUMMARY AND COMPARISON OF EACH OF EIGHT INDEPENDENT VARIABLES AS RELATED TO THE SOCIAL PARTICIPATION SCALE [a]

Variable	X^2	$P<$
Catholicity	16.13	.01
Education	19.41	.001
Income:		
Husband	17.32	.01
Wife	9.15	.1
Length of Residence	6.45	—
Religious education	2.36	—
Age	1.04	—
Mobility	13.24	.02
Occupation:		
Husband	14.62	.01
Wife	4.36	—

[a] 4 d.f. for all Chi-square tables.

[20] Cf. Leonard Reisman, "Class, Leisure, and Social Participation," *American Sociological Review*, XIX (February, 1954), 30.

of secular social participation would be inversely related to the degree of Catholicity. One possible explanation is that, like members of the Protestant denominations, some Catholics in the South participated in the functions of the parish for the sake of general social conformity.

IDENTIFICATION WITH THE SOUTH

The degree of southern identification was influenced by the income of the family, the age of the individual, and the length of residence in the host community. Positive directions were indicated in all three factors, a result very much as was expected (Table 5). In other words, those who had high scores on the SIS were largely found among a more stable segment of the migrant population (i.e., the middle-aged, those of middle and high income, and the longer residents). What was not expected was that Catholicity and southern identification were found to be independent of each other (a x^2 of .64 at 4 d.f.).

The individual's self-identification with the host community was found related to the attitudes toward each of the four religiosocial issues. First, southern identification was found to be related to conservative views on race and labor problems. A significant Chi-square was found between degree of southern identification and

TABLE 5 SUMMARY AND COMPARISON OF EACH OF EIGHT INDEPENDENT VARIABLES AS RELATED TO THE SOUTHERN IDENTIFICATION SCALE [a]

Variable	X^2	$P<$
Catholicity	.64	—
Education	6.60	—
Income:		
Husband	10.07	.05
Wife	3.31	—
Length of residence	38.48	.001
Religious education	1.25	—
Age	22.83	.001
Mobility	15.69	.01
Occupation:		
Husband	1.47	—
Wife	3.76	—

[a] 4 d.f. for all Chi-square tables.

church doctrine, due primarily to the very large number of individuals simultaneously high in SIS and low in the Church Doctrine Scale. If the individual's subscription to the doctrinal matters were the real measure of the degree of Catholicity, one might conclude that identification with the South and the identification with the Catholic church are mutually exclusive. However, the fact remained that, although Catholicity as measured by Fichter's method [21] was related to the attitude toward doctrinal matters, it was not related to the degree of southern identification, as would have been expected.

Since we do not have any reason to believe that the community in which the present study took place should be different from similar southern communities of similar size, the findings may be verified in further studies.

A. *The individual's social involvement and identification with the host community depend upon the individual's social stability in the community.*

Three of the eight independent variables used here can be taken to indicate the degree of stability of the individual in relation to the host community: age, mobility, and length of residence. In the category southern identification, age and the length of residence were positively related, whereas mobility seemed to have a negative effect on self-identification with the host community.

B. *Social participation is related to socioeconomic status.*

The relationship between socioeconomic status and social participation is supported by the data. The probabilities of family income, husband's occupation, and the individual's educational attainment being related to the social participation ratings seemed statistically significant.

C. *Manifestation of attitudinal inconsistency seemed to have been distinctive of the "high" rather than of the "low" Catholicity group.*

First, it was statistically significant that Catholicity and the individual's social involvement in the host community were positively related. There were some indications that both Catholicity and social participation were all related to social standing in the community. Next, it was difficult to interpret the fact that Catholicity was independent of attitudes toward race and labor issues;[22]

---

[21] Fichter's typology is nuclear, modal, marginal, and dormant. Criteria used have been identified as the individual's external behavior in terms of religious duties and parochial participation. Since no dormant Catholics were used in the present study, Fichter's nuclear, modal, and marginal types were indicated by "high," "middle," and "low," respectively.

[22] The Catholic parish is the only desegregated institution in the community.

particularly, the data which showed that an individual's attitude toward the Catholic position on the race issue was positively related to his educational attainment. The latter, however, was inversely related to the stand on labor problems of the Catholic church. Finally, strong southern identification was found among the group who also showed a position contrary to Catholic belief on church doctrine, race, and labor.

One may conjecture that, in responding to the birth-control and the church-doctrine scales, those who were labeled "high" in Catholicity were influenced to make use of the Catholic church as a reference group; hence they would be more likely to respond to the statements in a manner prescribed for Catholics. On the other hand, these subjects made use of the South as their reference group when the race-attitude and labor-attitude scales were presented to them (see Table 6).

TABLE 6 TEST OF INDEPENDENCE BETWEEN THE DEGREE OF SOUTHERN IDENTIFICATION AND FOUR AREAS OF RELIGIOSOCIAL ATTITUDES [a]

Variable	X^2	$P<$
Church doctrine	14.02	.001
Labor attitude	9.76	.05
Birth control	2.07	—
Race attitude	14.46	.01

[a] 4 d.f. for all tests.

D. *The more distant from the center of the prescribed behavior norms of the original group (i.e., low Catholicity), the more the individual is detached from either social group and, therefore, the more anomic is he.*

Those involved less in the host community, as manifested either by actual social participation ratings, or by their values as revealed on the SIS, were also the very individuals who showed low scores on the BCS and on Catholicity rating. If Fichter's original scheme were employed here,[23] those found on the fringe of the circle of the Catholic parish were not involved intensively in either group. The individual on the fringe of the circle is not marginal but anomic.[24] No generalization beyond the present data is intended here. However, Fichter's theoretic formulation of the marginal Catholic must be re-evaluated in the light of the present findings, gathered not in a largely Catholic setting in Louisiana but in a predominately Protestant community in Florida.

E. *Among the migrant Catholics in the Protestant South, the "true" marginal Catholic is "high" in Catholicity and located in the inner sphere of the circle.*

It now becomes quite clear that the individual who is high in Catholicity is both dynamic and pluralistic and plays "multiple roles and occupies a potentially shifting status." [25] Since he endeavors to participate more both in parochial activities and in the secular community, and finds conformity promotes his acceptance by the host group in which he is making a new residence, he is compelled to make out his own blueprint in meeting new demands.[26] In so doing, he finds that the strain toward consistency is greater. If this interpretation can be accepted, marginality must be explained in terms of social relationships rather than of a "split personality,"

---

23 Fichter conceives that an institution may be represented by a circle, and an individual may be said to occupy a position somewhere inside the circle. The nuclear Catholic (i.e., high in Catholicity) is found in the core of the circle, and the "marginal Catholic" is still under some influence and control of the group, yet he may be very near its circumference, being pulled toward the center of one or more other groups (*Social Relations in the Urban Parish*, p. 59). The present findings seem to have suggested that the "marginal Catholics" in Fichter's framework are truly "fringe Catholics," low in Catholicity. For a comparative discussion on this view see William T. Liu, "Community Roles and Attitude Formation," *Research Reports in Social Science* (Florida: Florida State University Publication), I (June, 1958), 10-14.

24 Leo Srole described *anomia-eunomia* as a continuum seen from the "microscopic" view of individuals "as they are integrated in the total action fields of their interpersonal relationships and reference groups" ("Social Integration and Certain Corollaries," *American Sociological Review*, XXI [December, 1956], 709-16). Also see Robert K. Merton's "Social Structure and Anomia: Revisions and Extensions," in his *Social Theory and Social Structure* (Glencoe, Ill.: Free Press, 1949).

25 Fichter, *Social Relations in the Urban Parish*, p. 59.

26 For an excellent discussion on this point refer to Milton M. Gordon, "Social Structure and Goals in Group Relations," in M. Berger, T. Abel, and C. H. Page (eds), *Freedom and Control in Modern Society* (New York: D. Van Nostrand Co., 1954). Gordon has suggested that the individual's behavior must be placed on a point of the combination of several continua.

and the former are far more important in creating incompatibility in the individual's several institutional roles.[27]

Theoretically, findings under D and E may have suggested that area of difference between a man who is "marginal" and a man who is "anomic." The difference lies in the degree of normative integration of an individual in two or more groups.

A man can be marginal only if he has attained a degree of integration, in two or more groups simultaneously—a degree which in all the groups must be high enough to produce inconsistencies of behavior. If it is high in one group but low in another, the result will be what Siu described as "sojourn."

A man is anomic when he fails to attain the necessary degree of normative integration in any group, regardless of the form of adjustment in the larger society.[28] The present study, for example, shows that people with low Catholicity do not readily participate in or identify themselves with either the parish or the southern community. This may well raise the whole question of the integrative function of membership in one group in relations with all others. The fact remains, however, that Fichter's marginal Catholics may be more anomic than marginal.

---

[27] Data of the present study revealed that the Catholic migrant endeavored to accomplish what Gordon called both the "historical" and "participational" identification.

[28] For a discussion of the adjustment pattern see Robert K. Merton, *Social Theory and Social Structure* (rev. ed.; Glencoe, Ill.: Free Press, 1957), chaps. iv and v.

18

Cultural and Structural Assimilation among Catholics in the Southwest

JAMES B. DAVIDSON
University of Notre Dame

JOSEPH B. SCHLANGEN
University of Notre Dame

SOURCE. Prepared especially for this volume.

Historical and sociological data document the fact that during the late nineteenth and early twentieth centuries Catholics were a minority group in this country. Large numbers of lower-class Catholic immigrants confronted hostilities and discrimination as they migrated toward the urban centers of the Northeast.[1] A combination of factors—including a relative lack of education, low occupational status, and religious and ethnic heritages that differed from the dominant cultural characteristics of the Northeast—tended to retard the assimilation of Catholics into "the American way of life."

In 1957, however, O'Dea hypothesized that a shift in the social status of American Catholics had begun to occur. "From a despised minority," he suggested, "they have become, perhaps, a disproportionately large section of the new middle class." [2] There is considerable evidence now to support the contention that Catholics have made advances from the lower class into the middle and upper classes. Table 1 contains a comparison of the economic status of Catholics in 1943 and 1964.[3] According to these data, the percentage of Catholics in the upper economic class has nearly doubled in the past twenty-one years, while the percentage of Catholics in

[1] See John Higham, *Strangers in the Land: Patterns of American Nationalism* (New Brunswick, New Jersey: Rutgers University Press, 1955); John J. Kane, "The Irish Immigrant in Philadelphia, 1840-1880: A Study in Conflict and Accommodation," unpublished doctoral dissertation, Department of Sociology, University of Pennsylvania, 1950; Thomas McAvoy, C.S.C., *Roman Catholicism and the American Way of Life* (Notre Dame, Indiana: University of Notre Dame Press, 1960); Carl Wittke, *The Irish in America* (Baton Rouge, Louisiana: Louisiana State University Press, 1956); Thomas N. Brown, *Irish American Nationalism, 1870-1890* (Philadelphia: Lippincott, 1966); and William Shannon, *The American Irish* (New York: The Macmillan Company, 1963).

[2] Thomas O'Dea, "The Church in the Changing Community: An Area of Sociological Research," Publications in the Social Sciences I, Department of Political Philosophy and the Social Sciences, (New York: Fordham University Press, 1957); reprinted from *Thought*, Volume XXXI, Number 121, Summer 1956, pp. 251-270.

[3] Norval Glenn and Ruth Hyland, "Religious Preference and Worldly Success: Some Evidence from National Surveys," *American Sociological Review*, Volume 32, Number 1, February 1967, pp. 73-85. For additional data on the occupational, educational, and economic characteristics of Protestants and Catholics, see Bernard Lazerwitz, "Religion and Social Structure in the United States," in Louis Schneider, editor, *Religion, Culture, and Society* (New York: John Wiley and Sons, Inc., 1964), pp. 426-439; Leo Rosten, editor, *Religions in America* (New York: Simon and Schuster, 1963), pp. 283-285; Liston Pope, "Religion and the Class Structure," in Seymour Martin Lipset and Reinhard Bendix, *Class, Status, and Power* (Glencoe: The Free Press, 1953), pp. 316-323; Andrew Greeley, *Religion and Career* (New York: Sheed and Ward, 1963); Andrew Greeley and Seymour Warkov, "Educational Achievement and Parochial School Origins," *American Sociological Review*, Volume 31, Number 3, June 1966, pp. 407-414.

the lower economic class has been halved.[4] In contrast to the historical dominance of the white Protestant population over the Catholic minority in this country, Glenn and Hyland have summarized the current situation in the following way:

At the end of World War II, Protestants in the United States ranked well above Catholics in income, occupation and education; since then Catholics have gained dramatically and have surpassed Protestants in most aspects of status.[5]

TABLE 1   A COMPARISON OF THE ECONOMIC STATUS OF AMERICAN CATHOLICS, 1943 AND 1964 (PERCENT)

Economic Level	1943 (N = 485)	1964 (N = 2884)
Upper	21.6	41.0
Middle	48.1	43.3
Lower	30.2	15.6

Source. Adapted from Norval Glenn and Ruth Hyland, "Religious Preference and Worldly Success: Some Evidence from National Surveys," *American Sociological Review,* Volume 32, Number 1, February 1967, pp. 73-85.

While these national data reflect general changes in the status of American Catholics, they do not indicate the probable variations in the status of Catholics living under a variety of regional and ecological circumstances. A consideration of the regional and ecological distributions of the Catholic and Protestant populations suggests that changes in the status of Catholics probably have not been uniform throughout the country.

The Catholic population tends to be urban-oriented and clustered in the Northern states, while the Protestant population is typically

---

[4] Glenn and Hyland, *op. cit.,* p. 75. The data for 1943 were collected in a national survey conducted by the National Opinion Research Center of the University of Chicago. The data for 1964 is a composite of data gathered through Gallup polls from December 1963 to March 1965. Because these data were gathered by different organizations for different purposes, Glenn and Hyland suggest that "The change in relative economic status may not have been quite as great as these data suggest." This contention is supported by a comparison of the data in Table 1 with the data in the works cited in footnote 3. In general, however, the data in Table 1 are sufficiently accurate to indicate the substantial shift that has taken place in the status of American Catholics over the past several decades.

[5] Glenn and Hyland, *op. cit.,* pp. 84-85.

more rural and Southern in its distribution. For example, in eight Northern states Catholics constitute a larger proportion of the population than all Protestants combined.[6] At the same time, over 50% of the nation's Catholics reside in metropolitan areas.[7] Glenn and Hyland have argued that the high concentration of Catholics in these urban and "non-Southern" areas gives the Catholic population an "obvious and important advantage" in their efforts to alter their historical minority status. In these areas, they suggest, "earnings, occupational distributions, and rates of upward mobility are more favorable than in the typical home communities of Protestants." [8] In eleven Southern states Catholics constitute less than 10% of the population, while Protestants constitute from 40 to 80% of the population of these same states.[9] Hero suggests that, even in the South, Catholics have tended to congregate in the urban areas, leaving "much of the Southern interior almost entirely Protestant." Especially "in the lower two thirds of the educational and social spectra and in the rural and small-town locales" of the South, fundamentalistic Protestant churches have been a "major force in shaping values and attitudes." [10] These different regional and ecological circumstances, then, should have substantially different influences on the status of Catholics in these areas. The hypothesis that Catholics are no longer a minority group in this country seems more applicable to the Northern urban areas than to the rural South.

The purpose of this paper is to examine the status of a sample of Catholics in two Oklahoma communities which tend to reflect

---

6 Leo Rosten, *op. cit.*, p. 240. These data include only white Protestants and white Catholics during the 1950's. If Negroes were added, the percentages for both Protestants and Catholics, of course, would be increased. The increase, however, would be most noticeable for Southern Protestants.

7 Glenn and Hyland, *op. cit.*, p. 77. See, also, David Moberg, *The Church as a Social Institution* (Englewood Cliffs, New Jersey: Prentice-Hall, Inc., 1964), p. 35. The percentage distributions for urban and rural areas presented by Moberg do not correspond exactly with Glenn and Hyland's, but they do indicate a definite rural orientation for Protestants and a pronounced urban orientation for Catholics.

8 Glenn and Hyland, *op. cit.*, p. 85.

9 Leo Rosten, *op. cit.*, p. 240.

10 Alfred O. Hero, Jr., *The Southerner and World Affairs* (Baton Rouge, Louisiana: Louisiana State University Press, 1965), pp. 435-437. In a study of "Status, Residence, and Fundamentalist Religious Beliefs in the Southern Appalacians," Thomas Ford also found that fundamentalistic beliefs were most prevalent among (1) members of the lower socioeconomic classes, and (2) residents of rural areas. See Ford, *Social Forces*, Volume 39, Number 1, pp. 41-49.

the rural Southern conditions specified above.[11] One of the communities, for example, was distinctly rural,[12] with most of its 4,700 residents engaged in either small businesses or farm work. In this town there were only 75 adult Catholics attending one Catholic church. The other town had a population of approximately 12,000 residents, most of whom commuted to a near-by city for work. While the residents of this town had achieved somewhat higher levels of education and income than the residents of the former town, it did not constitute a distinctly urban area. In this community there were 340 adult Catholics, all of whom attended a single Catholic church. In short, Catholics constituted only about 3% of the population in these relatively small, but largely Protestant, communities.[13]

The data to be presented in this analysis were gathered by the authors during the summer of 1965 from a study they conducted of Protestant-Catholic relations in these towns.[14] To guide the analysis of the data, the concepts of "minority group" and "assimilation" will be utilized. The twofold problem that is addressed is: (1) whether Catholics in these towns were a sociological as well as a

---

[11] For other studies of Catholics in the South, see in particular William T. Liu, "The Marginal Catholics in the South—A Revision of Concepts," *American Journal of Sociology*, January 1960, pp. 383-390; Liu, "A Study of the Social Integration of Catholic Migrants in a Southern Community," (unpublished Doctoral Dissertation, Florida State University, Department of Sociology, 1958); George Anthony Kelley, *Catholics and the Practice of the Diocese of St. Augustine* (Washington, D.C.: The Catholic University of America Press, 1946). Joseph Fichter also has conducted extensive studies of Catholic religious practices in the South, but his work has focused on Catholics in an urban Louisiana parish where Catholics represent a sizeable portion of the population. See Fichter's *Southern Parish* (Chicago, Illinois: University of Chicago Press, 1951).

[12] The usage of the term "rural" in this paper does not conform to the U.S. Census definition (i.e., 2500 or fewer residents). Rather, it is utilized to contrast the milieux of the respondents from these two Oklahoma communities (1) with the distinctly urban-metropolitan setting of some Catholics in the South, and (2) with the urban-metropolitan areas of the Northeast where Catholics are a numerical majority.

[13] Fifty-nine percent of the Protestants and 52% of the Catholics in this study had lived in these communities at least ten years. Seventy-four and 64% of the Protestants and Catholics, respectively, had been raised in the South. Most respondents had been raised in the state of Oklahoma.

[14] This project was sponsored by the Extension Society of the Catholic Church, Chicago, Illinois. The authors especially thank Reverend John Sullivan, Director of the Extension Volunteers Program, for his capable assistance during the initial stages of the research.

numerical minority group, and (2) to what extent Catholics and Protestants were culturally and structurally assimilated in these communities.

MINORITY GROUP STATUS

Sociologists have traditionally distinguished between numerical and sociological minority groups. A numerical minority is simply any group which represents a smaller percentage of a given population than some other group(s). Protestants, for example, are a numerical minority in many Northern states, while in most Southern states, Catholics are a numerical minority group. Catholics in Oklahoma constitute only 4% of the state population, while well over 50% of the population is Protestant.[15]

The definition of a sociological minority, however, is more difficult. Louis Wirth,[16] Robin Williams,[17] and Arnold Rose [18] have suggested three definitions of a sociological minority group. Each of these definitions contains three elements which are considered to be necessarily associated with sociological minority status. First, the members of a sociological minority share some subcultural or physical characteristics which are not found in the dominant group. Second, on the basis of these differences, the dominant group

---

15 Leo Rosten, *op. cit.,* p. 240.
16 Louis Wirth, "The Problem of Minority Groups," in Ralph Linton, editor, *The Science of Man in the World Crisis* (New York: Columbia University Press, 1945), p. 347. Wirth's definition has been quoted extensively in other works, but it deserves mention in this context also. A sociological minority, according to Wirth, is "a group of people, who because of their physical or cultural characteristics, are singled out from the others in the society in which they live for differential and.unequal treatment, and who therefore regard themselves as objects of collective discrimination."
17 Robin Williams, Jr., *Strangers Next Door* (Englewood Cliffs, New Jersey: Prentice-Hall, Inc., 1964), p. 304. Williams defines sociological minorities as "any culturally or physically distinct and self-conscious social aggregates, with hereditary membership, and a high degree of endogamy, which are subject to political or economic or social discrimination by a dominant segment of any environing political society."
18 Arnold and Caroline Rose, editors, *Minority Problems* (New York: Harper and Row, 1966), p. 5. The Roses suggest that a group is a sociological minority "if it is the object of prejudice and discrimination from the dominant groups and if the members think of themselves as a minority. It is not a minority merely because its members have a distinctive racial or nationality background, or because its members adopt a certain religion or language, although minority status in the United States is attached to at least one of these four characteristics."

actively discriminates against the minority in an attempt to maintain some degree of social distance between the groups. Third, the members of the minority group share some belief in a common subjugation to the dominant group's discriminatory behavior. While these three characteristics are *commonly* found in sociological minorities, only two seem *necessary* for sociological minority group status: discrimination by a dominant group and the self-consciousness of the minority group. It seems that, regarding cultural differences in particular, and racial differences to some extent, latent ambiguities persist in the definitions provided by Wirth, Williams, and Rose.

These writers seem to have made two assumptions in their definitions. The first assumption is that, if people share some common national, racial, or religious identification, they also share some common cultural characteristics not found in the dominant group. It may be true that an ethnic group, when it first arrives in this or some other "foreign" country, has a system of cultural features that diverges from that in the "host" culture. Racial and religious groups may also have distinctly different subcultures. However, this assumption is subject to qualification. It is possible that, while the members of some group may still identify with their homeland to some extent, if they have been in a foreign country for some time, they may have altered their formerly distinctive ways to conform to the host culture. Similarly, while two religious groups may attend different churches, it may be that they do not differ in their attitudes, values, and beliefs.

The second assumption is that the dominant group's perceptions of the cultural or physical characteristics of religious, ethnic, and racial groups are basically accurate. Again, while this assumption may be sound in many cases, in others it may require qualification. It is possible that, although the members of a dominant group may *think* the members of some other group share cultural or physical characteristics not found in the dominant group, they actually *may not*. This situation may occur if the cultural characteristics of an ethnic group (1) once differed from those of the host culture, but now conform to them, or (2) the cultural characteristics of the host culture and the minority never differed at all. Even in the case of racial groups, the dominant group may think that certain people are members of a particular group because they appear to have physical features that are commonly associated with that group. In fact, however, the dominant group's perceptions may be quite erroneous. In the case of religious groups, our own data suggest that, while some groups perceived each other as very dissimilar, in fact, they were more similar along many dimensions of their relationship than they realized.[19]

Even if a minority group does not have real cultural or physical characteristics that differ from another group, insofar as the members of the dominant group think it does, when these supposed differences are negatively defined, discrimination is likely to follow.[20] The members of the group which is the object of this discrimination, in turn, are likely to develop some degree of in-group identification and self-consciousness. Moreover, this situation may result in the formation of real cultural differences within the minority group through the mechanism of the self-fulfilling prophecy.[21] For the reasons that have been advanced, in this paper a sociological minority group will be defined as any group that is subject to discrimination on the basis of real or supposed differences and whose members develop consciousness of common subjugation to this discriminatory behavior. This definition—like most others which have been made of sociological minority group—makes no references to the size of the groups involved. A sociological minority, then, may be either a numerical minority or a numerical majority in any given area. The lingering question of whether or not these groups have similar subcultures will be considered in a discussion of assimilation.

---

[19] William V. D'Antonio, James D. Davidson, and Joseph A. Schlangen, "Protestants and Catholics in Two Oklahoma Communities," unpublished report, Department of Sociology, University of Notre Dame, Notre Dame, Indiana. For example, Catholics perceived Baptists as being quite dissimilar and Episcopalians as the most similar of all the groups in this study. However, in terms of beliefs about the supernatural, for example, Baptists were the third most similar to the Catholics, while the Episcopalians were the most dissimilar of all the groups along this dimension. The authors have extended a discussion of this issue in an unpublished paper entitled, "On the Sociology of Ecumenism," presented at the annual meeting of the American Catholic Sociological Society, San Francisco, August 1967.

[20] This suggestion follows very closely W. I. Thomas' theorem that "If men define situations as real, they are real in their consequences."

[21] See, for example, Robert K. Merton's discussion of the self-fulfilling prophecy in his *Social Theory and Social Structure* (Glencoe: The Free Press, 1961), revised edition, pp. 421-436.

ASSIMILATION

Definitions of assimilation are distributed throughout the sociological and anthropological literature.[22] However, there probably never has been complete satisfaction with any of the ways in which this concept has been used. Students and researchers alike have frequently confronted difficulties in their efforts to apply the available models and analyses of assimilation to their data. The result has been a continuous effort to refine the definition of this bothersome concept.[23]

Implicit in previous definitions of assimilation have been at least two dimensions which should be clearly specified. One of these dimensions can be called *cultural assimilation*. Cultural assimilation refers to the extent to which, or the process by which, any groups approximate a complete sharing of a common set of attitudes, values, beliefs, and behavioral characteristics.[24] A second dimension of assimilation that must be taken into account is termed *structural assimilation*. This concept refers to the extent to which, or the process by which, the members of any groups approximate a distribution equal to that of other groups in the social structure of a given area. Structural assimilation, then, focuses on such things as income, occupational status, and educational achievement.[25]

Structural and cultural assimilation can be analyzed from two points of view. First, they can be considered over time, when longitudinal research or comparative data from two time periods are available. In this case, one could determine the process by which cultural and structural assimilation had become more or less complete over a period of time. A second point of view concerns the extent to which two or more groups are culturally and structurally assimilated at some point in time. In this case, there are no com-

---

22 Several definitions are contained in the following: Gordon Allport, *The Nature of Prejudice,* (Cambridge, Mass: Addison-Wesley, 1954), p. 231; Brewton Berry, *Race and Ethnic Relations* (Boston: Houghton Mifflin Company, 1965), third edition, p. 247; Charles Marden, *Minorities in American Society* (New York: American Book Company, 1952), p. 48; Bruno Bettelheim and Morris Janowitz, *Social Change and Prejudice* (Glencoe: The Free Press, 1964), p. 44; and Williams, *op. cit.,* p. 308.

23 For one of the most inclusive efforts, see Milton Gordon, *Assimilation in American Life* (New York: Oxford University Press, 1964).

24 This definition of cultural assimilation is very similar to the one proposed by Gordon, *op. cit., pp.* 70-71.

25 This definition of structural assimilation departs somewhat from the one proposed by Gordon insofar as the present analysis is only concerned with occupation, education, and income, not membership in voluntary associations.

parative data against which one could analyze change in the degree of cultural and structural assimilation. Since the current study was not longitudinal in nature, and since there were no data against which possible changes could be measured, assimilation will be defined in this paper as the *extent* to which, rather than the process by which, two groups approximate a common culture and are equally distributed throughout the social structure.

METHODOLOGY

The following denominations were sampled in both of the two Oklahoma communities: (1) Southern Baptist, (2) Roman Catholic, (3) First Christian, (4) Episcopal, (5) Methodist, and (6) Presbyterian. The Assembly of God and Missouri Lutheran churches were also studied, but each was sampled in only one town. During their study in the two communities, the investigators interviewed each of the clergymen and became acquainted with the members of each church. Copies of the membership rolls of each church were obtained from the clergymen and random samples were drawn from these rolls. The study, therefore, was concerned only with those people who had indicated some preference for involvement in an institutionalized religious group. Questionnaires were distributed at Sunday services during the last three weeks of the study.[26] Those people who were not in attendance at these services were contacted by mail. In three churches the questionnaires had to be mailed to all respondents. In a report of the major findings of the study, the responses from each subsample did not reveal consistent or substantial differences.[27] For this reason, the decision was made to collapse the two subsamples into one for the purpose of this paper. In addition, the responses from all Protestant churches have been collapsed for comparison with Roman Catholics. This decision is justified by the fact that almost all of the groups tended to share a

---

26 Many of the items in the questionnaire for this study were adopted from Charles Y. Glock and Rodney Stark's "A Study of Religion in American Life." Their complete instrument is now published in their volume *Christian Beliefs and Anti-Semitism* (New York: Harper and Row, Inc., 1966). Several other items were adapted from Gerhard Lenski, *The Religious Factor* (Garden City, New York: Doubleday Anchor Books, 1963) and Milton Rokeach, *The Open and Closed Mind* (New York: Basic Books, Inc., 1960).

27 For extended discussions of the methodology employed in this study, see D'Antonio, Davidson, and Schlangen, *op. cit.,* and Schlangen, "Religious Involvement and Dogmatism," unpublished Master's thesis, Department of Sociology, University of Notre Dame.

common identification with a "Protestant heritage" and, taken together, they formed the dominant group in these two towns.[28]

While cultural assimilation can include many aspects of the
cultural characteristics of any groups, in this paper the concept will
be restricted to only the more religious dimensions of the Protestant-
Catholic relationship in these communities. Three dimensions of
this relationship seem most relevant to this analysis of cultural
assimilation. The first dimension is the set of definitions that both
groups had of the supernatural. These definitions include only the
more sacred-oriented or "vertical" beliefs maintained by the members
of both groups. A second dimension includes the more secular-
oriented or "horizontal" beliefs. These beliefs pertain primarily to
man's relationship to other men and to other social institutions.
While they may ultimately be related to the supernatural, in the
main, these beliefs emphasize man's social relationships. Third,
Protestant and Catholic beliefs about the nature of the church as a
social institution will be considered. The analysis of this dimension
will entail an examination of church structure, the scope of church
responsibility and ability to deal with social issues, and the importance of church membership for salvation. Structural assimilation
will be examined by an analysis of Protestant and Catholic economic
status, educational achievement, and occupational status.

FINDINGS

To determine whether or not Catholics were a sociological as
well as a numerical minority group in these two towns, the data in
Tables 2 and 3 will be examined. Protestants reported in Table 1
that (1) attacks had been made on Catholic beliefs without any
real knowledge of these beliefs; (2) Protestants had tried to exclude
Catholics from political office; and (3) to a lesser extent, Protestants
had spread false rumors about Catholic priests and nuns. However,
only 17% of the Protestants felt that discrimination had occurred
against Catholics in terms of occupational status. These responses
suggest that Catholics in these towns were subject to some forms
of discrimination.

Catholic responses to these four items tend to reinforce this
finding. But more than that, the percentage differentials between

---

28 Some of the denominational differences which were found have been discussed
in the report of the major findings of this study. In that report these differences were compared to other sociological investigations of differences between Christian denominations.

Protestant and Catholic responses in Table 2 tend to indicate some degree of defensiveness or self-consciousness among Catholics. A large majority of the Catholics agreed that (1) Protestants have attacked Catholic religious beliefs; (2) Protestants have tried to exclude Catholics from political office; and (3) Protestants have spread false rumors about Catholic priests and nuns. Even when only 17% of the Protestants indicated that Protestants have attempted occupational discrimination, nearly 40% of the Catholics reported that such discrimination had occurred. All of these responses suggest that, even if this differential in Protestant and Catholic responses were due to a lag in perceptions of changes in the Protestant-Catholic relationship, there was evidence of a feeling within the Catholic population at the time of the study that they had been singled out for differential and unequal treatment. Our data suggest, then, that Catholics were subject to discrimination by the Protestant majority and that Catholics considered themselves to be objects of this discrimination.

Certain qualifications are necessary in this analysis of Catholic status in these communities. First, the data in Table 2 do not demonstrate actual discrimination by the Protestant majority against the Catholic minority. Instead, we must infer from these

TABLE 2   PERCENTAGE OF PROTESTANTS AND CATHOLICS AGREEING WITH FOUR STATEMENTS PERTAINING TO PROTESTANT DISCRIMINATION AGAINST CATHOLICS

Statements	Protestants ($N = 274$)	Catholics ($N = 64$)	Difference
1. Protestants attack Catholic religious beliefs without knowing anything about them.	76	95	19
2. Protestant employers often discriminate against Catholics, for example, by not hiring or promoting them.	17	38	21
3. Protestants have tried to exclude Catholics from political office.	69	91	22
4. Protestants have often spread false rumors about Catholic priests and nuns.	53	84	31

data that discrimination had occurred. The relatively high percentage of Protestants and Catholics agreeing with the items in Table 2 suggest that this inference is a valid one. Second, if discrimination has occurred, there are also indications in the data that this differential treatment has been selectively channelled along certain dimensions of the Protestant-Catholic relationship and not along others. It does not appear to be a generalized phenomenon. In a series of items similar to those in Table 2, Protestant responses indicate no consistently negative images of Catholics. For example, 87% of the Protestants felt that local Catholics were "as fair" as Protestants in their business dealings.[29] This response pattern tends to supply a rationale for the fact that only 17% of the Protestants reported that occupational discrimination against Catholics had occurred. Protestant responses in Table 3, and to item 3 in Table 2, however, suggest that the power dimension of the Protestant-Catholic relationship may be one of the more salient foci of discrimination. Nearly 70% of the Protestants felt that Catholics "tend to vote as a bloc for Catholic political candidates" and, closely associated with this, that "Protestants have tried to exclude Catholics from political office." While just over one-third of the Protestants believed that "Catholics try to impose their religious practices on others," fully 93% felt that "The Catholic Church is unfair to demand that children of a Protestant-Catholic couple must be raised Catholic." These responses suggest that Protestants felt, if the Catholic Church or Catholic political candidates were to achieve dominance in the area, the freedom of the Protestant churches would be threatened by the Catholic Church's supposed intolerance of non-Catholic beliefs.[30]

Additional supportive evidence for this position is derived from the 1960 Presidential election. Certain Protestant churches in these two towns were known to have publicly campaigned against the election of John F. Kennedy. For the first time in history, one of the counties in which these towns were located, and which had always voted Democratic, was carried by the Republican Presidential candidate. In short, then, discrimination against the Catholic population of these areas tended to be selectively channelled along certain dimensions of the Protestant-Catholic relationship (i.e., political and religious power), but not along other dimensions (i.e., economic).

---

29 For other data relevant to this point, see Lenski, *op. cit.*, pp. 60-73.

30 In this context "orthodox" means that these beliefs were consistent with traditional Christian teachings.

TABLE 3   PERCENTAGE OF PROTESTANTS AND CATHOLICS AGREEING WITH THREE STATEMENTS PERTAINING TO THE POWER DIMENSION OF THE PROTESTANT-CATHOLIC RELATIONSHIP

Statements	Protestants ($N = 274$)	Catholics ($N = 64$)	Difference
1. Catholics try to impose their religious practices on others.	36	11	25
2. Catholics tend to vote as a bloc for Catholic political candidates.	68	26	42
3. The Catholic Church is unfair to demand that children of a Protestant-Catholic couple must be raised Catholic.	93	29	64

Turning to the issue of cultural assimilation, the data in Table 4 suggest that Protestants and Catholics, to a considerable extent, tended to share a similar set of beliefs about the supernatural. Historical Christian beliefs such as the existence of God, the divinity of Christ, the reality of a life after death, and the need for belief in the Bible were strongly affirmed by most respondents in both groups. Some differences were found regarding belief in the divinity of Christ and the need for Baptism, but in both cases the differences were more than likely minimized by the extensive consensus of each group on these items. The most substantial differences pertained to the necessity for belief in Christ for salvation and the existence of the Devil. In general, then, it appears that Protestant and Catholic beliefs about the supernatural were quite similar, and in most cases were quite orthodox.[31]

Regarding the secular-oriented or "horizontal" beliefs about man in the world (see Table 5), Protestant and Catholic responses to our items exhibited somewhat less similarity than on the vertical belief items. Both groups reported that what we do in this life will determine our fate in the hereafter, that "loving thy neighbor" and "doing good for others" would at least help one gain salvation. While only 21% of the Protestants (compared to 39% of the Catholics) said that discrimination would "definitely" prevent sal-

---

31 There seems, then, to be some support in these responses for the hypothesis that a fear-threat factor may have been operative in the minds of the Protestant respondents when they answered questions regarding political and religious power.

TABLE 4 PROTESTANT AND CATHOLIC RESPONSES TO ELEVEN BELIEF ITEMS PERTAINING TO THE SUPERNATURAL (PERCENT)

"Vertical" Belief Items	Protestants ($N=274$)	Catholics ($N=64$)	Difference
1. Jesus walked on water ("completely" or "probably" true).	87	86	1
2. There is a life beyond death ("completely" or "probably" true).	93	95	2
3. Jesus was born of a virgin ("completely" or "probably" true).	92	94	2
4. I know God exists and I have no doubts about it.	84	81	3
5. Prayer ("absolutely necessary" or "probably would help" salvation).	89	93	4
6. Holding the Bible to be God's truth ("absolutely necessary" or "probably would help" salvation).	87	91	4
7. The miracles actually happened just as the Bible says they did (agree).	71	78	7
8. Jesus is the Divine Son of God and I have no doubts about it.	85	97	12
9. Holy Baptism ("absolutely necessary" or "probably would help" salvation).	77	91	14
10. The Devil actually exists ("completely" or "probably" true).	68	86	18
11. Only those who believe in Christ can go to heaven ("completely" or "probably" true).	67	48	19

vation, both groups agreed that it would at least "possibly" prevent salvation. Differences appeared in the responses to such items as drinking liquor, birth control, and man's propensity to evil. Protestants—more than Catholics—indicated that drinking liquor would "possibly" prevent salvation and that "Man cannot help doing evil."

Catholics, on the other hand, tended to define birth control as a religious issue, while Protestants tended not to. In summary, then, Protestant and Catholic responses to these horizontal belief items revealed a considerable amount of similarity, but somewhat less similarity than their responses to eleven vertical belief items.

The sharpest differences between Protestant and Catholic responses were found on items regarding the church as a social institution. In particular, the items on church structure yielded substantial differences (see Table 6). By church structure we mean the network of means which these churches establish to maintain state, national, and international affiliations, and through which authority is differentially allocated, decisions are made, and responsibilities are discharged. Protestants indicated more frequently than Catholics (1) that their churches were democratic in structure; (2) that they determined their own beliefs; (3) that they could

TABLE 5   PROTESTANT AND CATHOLIC RESPONSES TO SEVEN SECULAR-ORIENTED BELIEF ITEMS (PERCENT)

"Horizontal" Belief Items	Protestants ($N = 274$)	Catholics ($N = 64$)	Difference
1. What we do in this life will determine our fate in the hereafter ("completely" or "probably" true).	89	94	5
2. Doing good for others ("absolutely necessary" or "probably would help" salvation).	81	89	8
3. Loving thy neighbor ("absolutely necessary" or "probably would help" salvation).	84	92	8
4. Discriminating against other races ("definitely" or "possibly" prevent salvation).	74	84	10
5. Man cannot help doing evil ("completely" or "probably" true).	62	41	21
6. Drinking liquor ("definitely" or "possibly" prevent salvation).	59	36	23
7. Practicing artificial birth control ("definitely" or "possibly" prevent salvation).	12	78	66

TABLE 6   PROTESTANT AND CATHOLIC RESPONSES TO EIGHT ITEMS PERTAINING TO CHURCH STRUCTURE (PERCENT)

Church Structure Items	Protestants ($N = 274$)	Catholics ($N = 64$)	Difference
1. The laity's work in this life is as or more important than the clergy's.	81	63	18
2. The daily activities of the local church are planned by the laity and the local clergyman.	79	50	29
3. The structure of your church is somewhat or very democratic.	78	45	33
4. The laity's beliefs are determined mostly or completely by the laity.	43	—	43
5. The laity has the right to question church teachings in all matters of faith and morals.	78	30	48
6. The laity has a great deal or all the say in decisions that directly affect the local congregation.	74	23	51
7. The clergyman has no special powers necessary for the salvation of the laity.	60	9	51
8. The pope is infallible in matters of faith and morals.	13	86	73

participate fully in church decisions and question church teachings; and (4) that the clergy in their churches had no special powers that the laity did not possess.

Catholics, on the other hand, reported that (1) the pope is infallible in matters of faith and morals; (2) that the religious authorities in the Catholic Church were more responsible for what the laity believed than the laity; (3) that the Catholic Church was hierarchical in structure; (4) that the laity had a minimal amount of say in church decisions; and (5) that Catholics were not allowed to question church teachings as much as Protestants were. On most of the items there was a noticeable indication in the Catholic responses to reflect the values of a hierarchical organization and the investment of considerable authority in the clergy, while Protestants seemed to value democratic principles and independent judgment. These differences were large enough to suggest that church structure may be one of the most salient dimensions of the Protestant-Catholic differences found in the study.

A second series of questions on the church referred to the scope of church responsibility and ability to deal with social issues (see Table 7). Protestant and Catholic beliefs revealed more similarity on these items than on those about church structure. Both groups disagreed quite strongly with the statement that religious groups should concern themselves with exclusively religious matters and not "social and political questions." Both groups also disagreed with an item stating that "Aside from preaching, there is little that churches can really do about social and economic problems." Finally, Protestants and Catholics both tended to agree that churches should take public stands on political issues.

The final issue dealing with the church as a social institution pertained to the importance of church membership for salvation. Protestants and Catholics strongly agreed that membership in some Christian church would probably enhance one's chances of achieving salvation. They differed, however, on their beliefs about membership in their respective churches. While less than 50% of the Protestants felt that membership in their own churches would

TABLE 7   PROTESTANT AND CATHOLIC RESPONSES TO THREE ADDITIONAL ITEMS PERTAINING TO THE CHURCH AS A SOCIAL INSTITUTION (PERCENT)

Scope of Church Responsibility and Ability Dealing with Social Issues	Protestants ($N = 274$)	Catholics ($N = 64$)	Difference
1. Churches should stick to religion and not concern themselves with social, economic, and political questions (percent disagree).	62	62	—
2. It is proper for churches to state their positions on practical political questions to the local, state, or national government (percent agree).	56	59	3
3. Aside from preaching, there is little that churches can really do about social and economic problems (percent disagree).	81	69	12

either "probably help" or was "absolutely necessary" for salvation, as many as 77% of the Catholics reported that membership in their church would at least help. This pattern was not surprising, since it seemed to reflect traditional Protestant and Catholic teachings. Nevertheless, these differences may be a very important source of friction between these groups.

In summary, then, it seems reasonable to conclude that, along the dimensions we have considered, the major differences between the Protestants and Catholics in these two towns pertained to the nature of the church. Some differences appeared in Protestant and Catholic responses to the secular-oriented belief items, but very few differences were found in their beliefs about the supernatural.

Data regarding the question of structural assimilation are found in Table 8. Compared to Protestants in this sample, Catholics were slightly less educated, less likely to be in certain white collar occupations, and less frequently in the middle and upper economic classes. While 51% of the Catholics had not gone beyond high school, two-thirds of the Protestants had. Fifty-five percent of the Protestants said their families had an income of over $7,000 per year, while 45% of the Catholics reported this. Occupationally, Protestants (60%) were more frequently found in white collar positions than Catholics (47%).

Although there appeared to be a pattern of less than equal distribution of Catholics in the social structure, some qualifications are necessary. This sample of Protestants generally did not include many of the more fundamentalistic Protestant sects which were located in these two towns. These sects have traditionally been over-represented in the lower classes. For this reason, it can be assumed that the Protestants in this sample were somewhat more middle class than the general Protestant population in these communities. Therefore, while the data presented in Table 8 reveal less than complete structural assimilation, the data may exaggerate the differences between Protestants and Catholics.

SUMMARY AND DISCUSSION

The authors suggested in the introduction to this paper that the hypothesis that Catholics may no longer be a minority group in this country should take into account the variations in the regional and ecological distribution of the Catholic population. Data presented in the introduction also suggested that, if a change has taken place in the social status of American Catholics, quite probably

TABLE 8   PROTESTANT AND CATHOLIC DISTRIBUTION IN THE SOCIAL STRUCTURE OF THESE TWO OKLAHOMA TOWNS (PERCENT)

Occupation, Education, Family Income	Protestants ($N = 274$)	Catholics ($N = 64$)	Difference
1. Occupation of head of household			
(a) White collar (professional, sales, clerical, proprietor)	60	47	13
(b) Blue collar (crafts, laborers, operatives, household, service)	26	34	8
2. Education of each respondent			
(a) Beyond high school (some or finished college, graduate or professional school)	66	48	18
(b) Not beyond high school (some or finished grade school, some or finished high school)	30	51	21
3. Family income			
(a) $7,000 or more per year	55	45	10
(b) Less than $7,000 per year	40	45	5

the change has been most substantial in the urban and "non-Southern" areas of the country. The purpose of this paper has been the examination of Protestant-Catholic relations in two Oklahoma towns which reflect the set of circumstances associated with a rural-Southern category of regional and ecological differences. It was found that in addition to being a numerical minority in these towns, Catholics were also a sociological minority. They were subject to discrimination by the Protestant majority and the Catholics considered themselves to be objects of this discrimination on the basis of their church affiliation. In the discussion of discrimination, however, the selective character of the differential treatment of the Catholic population was emphasized. Discrimination against the Catholics did not appear to be generalized to all dimensions of the Protestant-Catholic relationship. Instead, discrimination was less likely to occur along the economic dimension than along the power dimension of their relationship. While Catholics, therefore, qualified as a sociological minority group by the definition established at the outset of this paper, the data should not be interpreted to mean that the Catholic's minority status in this sample corresponds to that of Catholics earlier in this century. Indeed, relative to the discrimination that Catholics once confronted along most dimensions of their relationship to the dominant white-Anglo-Saxon Protestant majority, Catholics in this sample might be considered "well off." However, the fact remains that on items in which political and/or religious power became the dominant issues, the responses indicated that Catholics still were objects of discrimination by the dominant Protestant group.

In terms of cultural assimilation, the data in this paper revealed few substantial differences between Protestants and Catholics in their beliefs about the supernatural and the social order. The major differences between Protestants and Catholics pertained to the church as a social institution. Protestants seemed to value independent judgment and democratic church organization, while Catholic responses reflected an orientation toward a more hierarchical church in which the clergy had considerable authority over the local congregation. Finally, regarding structural assimilation, compared to this sample of Protestants, Catholics were less than equally distributed throughout the social structure.

Since a substantial number of Catholics in the South live in predominately Protestant and rural communities, we suspect that the findings of this research may apply to other areas of the rural South. Assuming the validity of this influence, we suggest that in a considerable portion of this country, Catholics can still be considered a sociological minority group. Until further research yields evidence to the contrary, we must caution against unqualified acceptance of the hypothesis that Catholics are no longer a minority group in the United States. Such a general hypothesis tends to ignore the differential effects that regional and ecological circumstances may have on the status of American Catholics.

19

Structured Strain in a Social Movement: CFM

JOHN R. MAIOLO

University of Notre Dame

WILLIAM T. LIU

University of Notre Dame

WILLIAM V. D'ANTONIO

University of Notre Dame

SOURCE. Prepared especially for this volume.

The purpose of this paper is two-fold. We are concerned first with relating our observations of a socio-religious movement, namely, the Christian Family Movement, with respect to its transition to a routinized organization with clearly defined channels for decision-making and for airing and resolving differences among members. As the movement has become routinized, some of its early vigor has waned while problems of leadership succession and policy formulation have become the focal tasks. These factors have brought strain and conflict to the movement.

At the same time, we are concerned with the theoretical significance of our study of CFM. Much of the history and growth of the movement is clearly explicable in terms of existing sociological theory as we shall discuss below. As the movement has continued to grow, however, it has developed the capacity to withstand fragmentation and conflict and still continue to achieve its formally stated goals. Indeed, many of the existing means of goal-achievement are the chief generators of strain and conflict. It is at this juncture where extant social theory, specifically that which deals with social movements, contributes least to our understanding. It is imperative, therefore, that we draw from other corners of our theoretical structure, particularly from complex organizations theory, as we proceed with our empirical observations. In this manner, we hope to develop a more complete framework for the understanding of the internal dynamics and changes within social movements over time.

THE HISTORY OF CFM IN THEORETICAL PERSPECTIVE

The changes in the total American Social Structure over the past half-century have been quite dramatic; the changes in the Catholic sector may have been even more dramatic. Even as recently as the mid-1940's, Protestants ranked well above Catholics in income, occupation, and education. But by the 1960's, the situation had been reversed and Catholics ranked above Protestants in most aspects of status.[1] The educational aspiration differentials between the Catholics and Protestants gradually disappeared in the early sixties,[2] with the resultant alteration of the values and perceptions

---

[1] Norval D. Glenn and Ruth Hyland, "Religious Preference and Worldly Success: Some Evidence From National Surveys," *American Sociological Review,* 32 (February 1967), 73-85.

[2] Andrew Greeley, "Influence of the 'Religious Factor' on Career Plans and Occupational Values of College Graduates," *American Journal of Sociology,* Vol. 68, No. 4, pp. 658-671.

of a large number of Catholics in America. Many of the earlier ideas held by immigrant Catholic labor union militants and liberal Democrats have also changed, evidenced by the shifting of political behavior in election patterns.[3] Controversies also arose concerning "ideology" as a social force in shaping action patterns of minority groups.[4]

Since the inception of the Christian Family Movement during the post World War II years, a quarter of a century has elapsed. The Movement itself had as its immediate social background a period of economic depression and the interruption of the basic pattern of family living in America by war separations and mass rural to urban migration, which, among other changes, was followed by: (a) a rapid increase of birth rates accompanied by the post-war economic boom; (b) an ever increasing enrollment in higher learning institutions in America; (c) unprecedented social mobility both geographically and residentially throughout the United States; and finally (d) the involvement in mass leisure and the experiences of affluence never before witnessed by any society in the history of mankind. All of these social forces have directly influenced the basic unit of American society, i.e., the family system.[5] Leaders of the early Christian Family Movement were conscious of these changes and anticipated the pains of such transitions. Even sociologists and social critics became alarmed at the disruptions and questioned the capabilities of the average man in dealing with and handling problems resulting from such rapid changes. Theologians were caught napping and without ready-made answers to many of the changing problems; individual Catholics were left alone to interpret their own blueprints in sound Christian family ethics.[6] It is against this background of transitional change that we came to witness the conflict between ideology and formula which brought action-minded Catholics to the foreground. The birth and early

---

[3] Philip E. Converse, "Religion and Political Behavior," in Angus Campbell, Philip E. Converse, Donald E. Stokes, and Warren Miller, *The American Voter,* New York: John Wiley & Sons, 1965.

[4] Daniel Bell, "The End of Ideology in the West," in *The End of Ideology,* Glencoe, Illinois, Free Press, 1960; Edward Shils, "The End of Ideology?," *Encounter,* 5 (November 1955), 52-58; S. M. Lipset, "The End of Ideology?," in *Political Man,* Garden City, New York; Doubleday, 1960.

[5] William F. Ogburn and Meyer F. Nimkoff, *Technology and the Changing Family,* Boston: Houghton Mifflin Co., 1955.

[6] John Kosa and John Nash, "Social Ascent of Catholics," *Social Order,* Vol. 8, 1958, pp. 98-103; David Fosselm and William T. Liu, "Social Mobility Among Catholics in the Pacific Northwest," *Social Compass,* Vol. 11, 1961, pp. 52.

vigor of the Christian Family Movement were perhaps predictable consequences of such changes.

From a theoretical standpoint, then, the emergence and growth of the Christian Family Movement, like many other socio-religious movements, reflects the complexity and strains of modern living. Such characteristic urban conditions as segmentary relations, high mobility and transistory ties, the discontinuity of established values and norms across generations, the cross-purposes of institutions,[7] all have contributed to the emergence of a collective action program designed to promote religious values and family ethics. In short, CFM has both reflected and identified the shared discontent of mobile American Catholics in a transitional society.[8] Its main function is to link specific religious ideals to the changing conditions of the larger society.[9]

Social movements do not survive and grow without experiencing a rather predictable set of internal problems. The internal dynamics of an expanding, proselytizing movement includes the proliferation of leadership roles and the emergence of conflict and fragmentation. For example, Smelser notes that conflict must be considered as a normal and integral component of a movement's structure.[10] We see a universal built-in dilemma—there develops the necessity to organize and structure roles "vis-à-vis operational exigencies",[11] while such a development geometrically increases the probability of conflict and fragmentation.[12] Roche and Sachs note that the conflicts

---

[7] This by no means implies that movements are confined to an urban, indus- trialized society. On the contrary, Christianity and the major socio-religious movements of the East antedate urbanism and industrialism as we know them today. But, in a society where traditions are challenged and social heterogeneity is at a maximum, movements are notably more frequent than in a society where tradition dictates much of daily life, commitment to the status quo is at a premium, and homogeneity at a maximum. See C. Wendell King, *Social Movements in the United States,* New York: Random House, 1956, p.v.

[8] See, King, *op. cit.,* and Neil Smelser, *Theory of Collective Behavior,* New York: The Free Press of Glencoe, 1963, Chapters 9 and 10, pp. 270-381, for full treatments of conditions for social movements.

[9] See Eric Hoffer concerning beliefs and social movements: *The True Believer,* New York: 1964.

[10] Smelser, *op. cit.,* pp. 297-98 and 355-56.

[11] J. P. Roche and S. Sachs, "The Bureaucrat And The Enthusiast: An Ex- planation of Leadership in Social Movements," *Western Political Quarterly,* Vol. 8, 1955.

[12] Smelser, *op. cit.,* and see D. Miller and W. Form, *Industrial Sociology,* for their treatment of sub-ideologies and, consequently, cleavages in an indus- trial organization. The same principle, it is suggested, applies to movements.

that develop around decision-making processes do not occur at one point in time in a movement's career, but are constant features; there is a running battle among the various factions competing for control.[13]

It is at this point that some important, but unanswered questions come sharply into focus (from the perspective of a theory of social movements). For we suggest that, to the degree that it is true that conflict and fragmentation are constant features, and the movement continues in its quest for global-attainment, some sort of accommodating processes must be presumed. Moreover, accommodation in this sense points toward institutionalization in the conflict process, i.e., the organization of competing factions whose members are willing to settle for something less than internecine warfare, and where factions subscribe, at least minimally, to some sort of mutually satisfactory "ground rules."

It is to these problems that research must be directed and to which this paper is addressed; and we use CFM as our research base. We hope to show that patterns of leadership conflict and resolution in the Christian Family Movement are suggestive, if not illustrative, of routinized processes which can develop over time to accommodate internal strains in social movements. Our approach may be seen as an attempt to catalog the kinds of mechanisms that function to shape the sources of strain, set limits to internal cleavages in terms of their frequency and intensity, and accommodate competing factions.

But the multitudes of ideas and tactics which all movements have as alternative ways to attain broad objectives must have some minimum common take-off point. Without a basic overlapping interest among individuals involved in a social movement, there would not have been a movement in the first place. In order to describe the various factors which cause strains and conflict within the movement, it is also important to describe factors which minimize such conflict, i.e., those which function to develop and maintain equilibrium, which "stabilize" the base of collective action and which prevent disruptions which may endanger the existence and growth of such a movement. It is our assumption that the counterveiling forces which stabilize collective action may, at the same time, also go through several phases of change. The dynamic forces of the movement itself, in so far as movements in general are the results of conditions created by the on-going social changes occurring in the larger society, may cause stresses and strains. Our

---

[13] Roche and Sachs, *op. cit.*

attempt to describe the stabilizing forces does not mean that we make the a priori assumption that such factors operate in such a way as to weaken the dynamic nature of the movement from the beginning. Rather, we attempt to see the development of a movement as a result of several opposing forces at work. The specific strength of one force vis-à-vis the opposing force may determine the relative stability as well as vigor of the movement.

This paper is designed to be a preliminary statement. Data currently being collected at the present will considerably elaborate many of the ideas set forth here in future publications.

FACTORS PREDATING STRAIN

Several factors can now be identified as safety-valves to minimize internal cleavages during the course of the expansion of the Christian Family Movement. They are:

A. *Selective Recruitment*

Among the most important factors inhibiting the development of strains and internal cleavages in CFM is the recruitment process itself. Recruitment has been selective, in a manner analogous to that in other forms of social organization. In a recent analysis, Etzioni points up the nature of the impact of such a process with particular reference to internal control and goal-attainment. He notes that "a small increase in selectivity . . . results in a disproportionately large decrease in investments required for control." [14] Potential members who might deviate from normative prescriptions are screened out of the organization, thus allowing the organization to be less concerned about mechanisms of social control.

Thus, a latent function of selective recruitment would seem to be to minimize conflicts that might otherwise accrue from values, belief or social class differences. For, as long as a social movement selectively recruits in such a way as to maximize the compatability of members' values and interests consistent with structural expectations—i.e., activities consistent with the goals of the movement, a consequence would be to select members with similar background, ideology and values.

We suggest that selective recruitment is built into the Christian Family Movement not necessarily because of a concerted, conscious effort on the part of CFM to be a "closed group." It may be

---

[14] A. Etzioni, *Modern Organizations,* Englewood Cliffs, N. J.: Prentice Hall, 1964, p. 68.

analogous to a political organization in that a certain amount of selective recruitment is necessary because of the organizational requisites for goal attainment. While many political organizations recruit professional workers on the basis of commitment and ideology, their objective of promoting political loyalties from the mass may require use of a variety of mechanisms, cutting across class and value lines. The Christian Family Movement is, in this sense, a movement not directed towards the mass. It is not a mass movement where memberships are accepted without discrimination. Members of the Christian Movement must accept certain objectives and task assignments specified by the organization on one level or another. It, then, demands action rather than merely following, and it offers a more consistent, clear-cut program of objectives to potential members.

Evidence of selective recruitment was obtained from two earlier surveys of CFM.[15] While more reliable data are still lacking, pending results from the current study, the two previous surveys suggest a remarkable homogeneity of the Movement's membership. Table I shows that four out of five membership couples are middle class

TABLE 1   OCCUPATIONAL AND EDUCATIONAL PROFILES OF THE CHRISTIAN FAMILY MOVEMENT MEMBERS, MALES ONLY, COMPARED WITH U. S. CATHOLIC POPULATION IN GENERAL (PERCENT)

	Occupational Profile				Educational Profile		
	U.S. Catholics	CFM Survey	Fahey Survey		U.S. Catholics	CFM Survey	Fahey Survey
Non-manual	55	80	80	High school or more	68	79	85
Manual	45	20	20	Less than High school	32	21	15

Source. CFM Survey was conducted by CFM in an unpublished report dated 1965 with a total $N = 126$. The Fahey Survey was conducted by Father James Fahey in an unpublished report dated 1964 with a total $N = 67$. The U. S. Catholic data were collected by the University of Notre Dame Survey on American Parochial Schools and published in *Catholic Schools in Action,* edited by Reginald A. Neuwein, University of Notre Dame Press, 1966. Total $N = 24,502$, except for occupations data (22,663).

---

[15] The first was conducted by CFM through its publication *Act;* the second by Father James Fahey in 1964 in the South Bend, Indiana, area.

Catholic couples with white collar jobs and high school plus education, a figure significantly higher than the general profile of Catholic
population in the United States (see Table 1).

While the representativeness of the two surveys may be challenged, it would be difficult to hypothesize that a significant difference will be reported by the current study of the national CFM
membership profile. The homogeneity of membership means, *ipso
facto*, relative similarities in interests and values. That is, we are
dealing with a movement where a large majority of the memberships are "middle-class," with more than the average skills in
organizational and action experience.[16]

B. *Transitory Membership*

A characteristic feature of CFM membership is the transitory
nature of the membership. Though selective in process, it is easy
to make an entry into the Christian Family Movement and it is
easier to withdraw from it. The modal number of years during
which a member couple has membership is estimated to be about
3 years. This transitory nature of CFM membership produces
both stabilizing and non-stabilizing effects on the Movement *qua
movement*. First, there is the process of selection on the part of
the members; then the question of the extent to which the couple
will embrace the goals and activities of the Christian Family Movement. To many members, the action group of the Movement serves
primarily as a mediating agent for the couple to integrate into
other segments of the community life. This is true especially for
newcomers in the community. The homogeneity of CFM membership would contribute to the "mediating function" between the
couple member and the community. In this sense, the Christian
Family Movement is merely another community voluntary association; its functions may be analogous to the bridge club, the garden
club, or the League of Women Voters. For those who become
members of CFM primarily for such reasons, exits from membership can have a stabilizing effect within the group, since their commitment to the goals is low. Indeed, their continued presence
could have a disintegrative effect.

Secondly, there are those who join the Movement because of
high ideals which could not always be met in a concrete manner

---

16 This is based on our current knowledge of the behavioral correlates of socio-
economic status, combined with the fact that we are dealing with a population
that, until recently, has been exclusively Catholic; hence, our CFM population shares circumstances on three important variables in the "behavior-
shaping" process.

through membership in CFM. Such disenchanted members, if they chose to remain in the Movement, might have their disenchantment "rub off" on other members. Therefore, discontinuation of their membership also could have a stabilizing effect on the movement.

Thirdly, for those who drop out of CFM because of residential mobility, the positive effect of their membership in the Movement, however short in duration, may be indicated by their association with others and therefore help to "spread the good word of the Movement."

Finally, the transitory nature of the membership in the Christian Family Movement has an important effect on the leadership structure of the Movement, for it could contribute to a stable oligarchy on the one hand; but, on the other hand, produce certain degrees of discontinuity of programs and actions.

C. *The Role of Organizational Socialization: Guided Action Programs*

The process of becoming an action-oriented Christian Family Movement member may be described as that of a guided program experience to which everyone must be exposed during the membership tenure. Such guided programs include the education of members with regard to the central goals of the Movement as well as means to implement policies set forth by various local and national groups. The most notable brochure the newcomer receives is *For Happier Families*,[17] an introductory statement relating the Movements' objectives and tactics. Other literature includes annual inquiry books (guidelines for bi-weekly meetings) and *Act*, the monthly publication of the Christian Family Movement. Newcomers are also given the opportunity to have a senior member participate in the early organizing phases of their "action" groups to help in the preparations and procedures at meetings, the definitions of problems, and the overall theme for the Movement during that year.

Since members of the Movement are by and large above average in education and in occupational attainment, social stratification within the membership along the traditional lines is minimum. In addition to the general profile of the membership, insofar as it is relevant to the development of leadership, the structure of the Movement from the national to the local level is not so much "hierarchical" as it is "associational" and "representative," with interlocking controls and flows of communications. Under these two conditions, all members are potentially leaders. The lack of well-

---

[17] *For Happier Families,* Chicago: Christian Family Movement, 1965 edition.

defined "avenues" for organizational mobility makes it somewhat ambiguious as to what may be "legitimate" and what may be "extraordinary" ways in attaining leadership roles. Since everything—from policy to loosely defined objectives—is subject to discussion and consensus, articulation of ideas and protracted polemics are the normal activities characterizing CFM membership relations. The very forces which stabilize the Movement itself may also be the forces which create strains and conflict. In addition, several structural characteristics of the Movement may directly relate to the stresses and strains among members.

D. *The Decentralized Decision-Making Processes*

The Christian Family Movement is basically a movement based on associational interlocking relationships rather than a straight-line monolithic structure. It is a movement wherein "actions" take place on the lowest level; it is only through successive stages of debates and discussions that consensus is reached on the higher level. The national organization does not formulate policies, nor does it dictate to its associational members. It serves as a final stage at which consensus can be reached. The process of "from the bottom to the top" differs fundamentally from the "from top to the bottom" in that differential experience and regional variations are the underlying factors through which debates among members are carried out.

First, the "action" group represents the point from which the structure takes shape. This is the rank-and-file level. Second, the linkages that are built into the structure in fact prevent any of the action groups from being isolated from all other groups with regard to communications and influences. Such linkages are both vertical and horizontal in nature.

Third, special interests, views, grievances, etc., at the diocesan level are represented at the national level in two ways: (a) each diocese has a representative on the Coordinating Committee; (b) several dioceses are organized on an "Area" basis and each Area is represented on the Executive Committee.

Consequently, policy decisions made by the national committees, notwithstanding the differential accumulation of power, *must* reflect the broad spectrum of views emanating from the action group and diocesan levels. [17a] Policy decisions take on the characteristic of

---

[17a] Since "rule by the majority" is highly cherished in the decision-making process. This is further discussed below.

being very general as are action guidelines through published literature. For example, each year the movement publishes an *Inquiry Manual* consisting of guidelines for observing certain aspects of the life situation (around a common theme) which require action, e.g., the racial problems, family and leisure time. Table 2 presents a list of topics for use during the meetings of the 1966-67 school year,

TABLE 2   SUGGESTED INQUIRIES FOR 1966-1967. THEME: FAMILY IN TIME OF CHANGE

Meeting	Topic
1	The Challenge of Change—Preface Scripture-Liturgy: What is God Doing in History? Social Inquiry: Change in Patterns of Family Life? How to Lead Role-Play Role-Play Situations
2	Why Write a Constitution? Let My Children Go
3	The Church in God's Plan The Young Become Mature
4	The Spirit Works in the Church State of the Union
5	Evening of Reflection Authentic Love and Responsible Parenthood
6	Images of the Church in Scripture Communications in Marriage
7	Poverty and the Image of the Church A Matter of Judgment
(A look ahead to Meeting 9)	Introduction to the Home-Bible Vigil
8	Families Prepare for Christmas and Epiphany
9	Sex Education of Young Children Home Bible Vigil: The Prophet's Vocation
10	The People of God Families Open to the World
11	The Priesthood of the Faithful Tensions of Commitment
12	The Ties that Bind Home Bible Vigil: God's Desolate
13	Witness of Christ Seeds of Discontent

TABLE 2 — Continued

Meeting	Topic
(Can be used anywhere during program year)	Time Out to Evaluate
14	Meeting Our Fellow Man in God
	Families on the Move (I)
	Families on the Move (II)
15	Collegiality: A Community of Work
	Generations in Change
16	Evening of Reflection
	You Did It for Me
17	The Bishop: Symbol of Charity and Unity
	What Are their Names
18	A Familiar Question: What is a Layman?
	In the Midst of Plenty
19	The Hungry Hostages
	Home Bible Vigil: The Suffering Servant (I)
20	The Layman: Profitable Teacher?
	The War on Poverty: What are We Fighting For?
21	A Familiar Dialogue
	The War on Poverty: Who's on the Firing Line?
22	Evening of Reflection
	How the Council Sees the Church
23	The Call to Holiness
	Your Conscience and the Law
24	Let the Buyer Beware
	Home Bible Vigil: The Suffering Servant (II)
25	We are Pilgrims in the Church
	Big Daddy, Big Brother or Mother Hubbard?
26	Mary and the Church
	A Cross to Bear—and Share
27	Evening of Reflection
	The Church is People
28	A Look Back—A Look Ahead

the theme being *Family in Time of Change*.[18] As general as the guidelines are, one more element is added to the flexibility quotient,

---

[18] Chicago: Christian Family Movement, August, 1966.

i.e., the opportunity to adapt the guidelines to local situations. Note the following statement with respect to this idea:

> The leaders of such rural C.F.M. groups are encouraged to rewrite any of these social inquiries and to change any of the questions in any of these . . . inquiries whenever doing so will bring about a better discussion or a more fruitful action.[19]

This permissiveness, combined with the fact that some action groups do not even use the inquiry books, without fear of reprisal, indicates that deviation is not only provided for, but almost institutionalized. In this respect, one may speak of patterned and acceptable evasion at the local level as a result of ill-defined guidelines and/or the absence of sanctions for deviation in cases where guidelines may be defined.

Consequently, we suggest that the formal authority structure, the generalized policy and patterned evasion function on a latent, if not on a manifest basis, to minimize the number and intensity of conflicts that would arise out of differences about tactical operations in the goal-achievement process.

FACTORS WHICH PRODUCE & REGULATE ORGANIZATIONAL STRAIN

Still, conflicts do arise. Let us now discuss their source, consequences and means of coping with them.

A. *Incomplete Socialization*

A concerted, well planned, national guidepost for members may not always produce a uniform level of membership performance. The actual behavior of members varies not only from one action group to another, but individual conformity to the expected performance may also vary greatly. The differential pattern of socialization may be the result of many social and personal factors. On the social level, the local scenes and community programs may determine the kinds of receptivity of members with regard to the guidelines set by the national headquarters of the Movement. On the individual level, motivations underlying the participation in the Movement may differ greatly from one couple to another, with varying emphasis on social versus religious accent. The variations not only would reflect the kinds of things one action group may actually do; they

---

[19] *Rural Vistas, A Supplemental Inquiry Manual,* Omaha: Christian Family Movement (no date).

may also, in the long run, produce stresses and strains in the inter-actions between the local couples and other action groups on a different level. In the pilot study preceding the current investiga-tion, we discovered, among other things, that the use of the Move-ment's reading material is significantly related to the level of sat-isfaction among members in the Movement. Secondly, those who are classified as *non-readers* (of the Movement's literature), were also by and large ignorant about the various changes of goals and tactics of the Movement. In the previously cited Fahey study, sixty-five percent of the active members as compared to thirty-nine non-active members have used the Movement's literature con-sistently. Finally, fifty-three percent of the "readers" felt that their actions were effective and successful, while only thirty-seven percent of the "non-readers" felt that their actions were equally meaningful and effective.

Perhaps several hypotheses can be drawn from such data. First, the use of CFM literature may not be so much the direct cause of sustained commitment and membership in the Movement as it may be a device to promote shared interests and goal attainment activ-ities. These publications in fact become the "properties" of the group as well as the vehicle through which group norms are established and shared. It goes without saying that common socialization ex-perience serves to strengthen the communal feelings as it is the basis of group identification. Variations in reading habits and in socialization processes may both reflect and produce inconsistencies and stresses among leaders of the Movement as well as satisfaction or disaffection among members.

B. *Institutionalized Conflict*

There are three categories of phenomena in the movement which point to a strain toward conflict that has become institutionalized, viz., regulated channels for airing individual or collective views, ground rules for conflict, and means by which the conflict is resolved or accommodation achieved. In labor parlance these mechanisms may be said to constitute grievance machinery.

1. CHANNELS FOR EXPRESSION OF GRIEVANCES. From a policy standpoint, the meetings at the various decision-making levels and the monthly publication *Act* represent the two chief means for expressing views and airing grievances. Data from a pilot study of Diocesan leaders show unanimity on this point.

Meetings at all of the various levels are structured so that all those present can express their views. With respect to the former, some published statements document that fact:

A group needs some member who will help the members of the group consolidate their efforts. This person in CFM has been called the group leader . . . he must do all he can to create an atmosphere of freedom and ease . . . to keep the meetings running in such a way that all members of the group have a chance to express their opinions, to clarify their ideas, to contribute their experience to the group's decision, and to learn how to accept the group's decisions.[20]

Since the discussion must flow freely the discussion coordinator must show interest and attentiveness without disrupting the thinking or conversation of the group.[21]

What members expect from a leader . . . a share in this planning and work, and some understanding of the goals of CFM.[22]

Meetings of the Coordinating Committee provide an exciting example of expected and fulfilled conflict. These provide the arena for opposing groups like the enthusiasts with their utopian visions and, on the other hand, those with bureaucratic tendencies to meet head-on in wide-open debate. These meetings are, in fact, the places where the major policy decisions are made. Differences that exist on a regional basis intersect here. Several adjectives used by members to describe the meetings indicate the conjunction of differences, viz., wild, frustrating, fruitful, etc. One of the most powerful leaders in the movement had this to say about the meetings:

The Coordinating Committee is a clearing house for ideas . . . Everyone who has something to say gets his or her chance to speak at the Committee meetings.

Another made the following observation:

The . . . Coordinating . . . Committee meetings are really something. Everyone gets his feelings off his chest . . . When it's all over, there usually are no hard feelings . . . The end results are well thought-out ideas for the future and attempts to learn from our mistakes.

As noted above, *Act* also serves as a clearing house for ideas. There is a section in each issue for letters to the editor, many of which are critical of the policy and tactics of the movement. Many of the members take advantage of this means of expression (ap-

---

[20] *Leadership In the Christian Family Movement,* Chicago: Christian Family Movement, 1963.

[21] *Ibid.,* p. 25.

[22] *A Guide to CFM,* Chicago: Christian Family Movement, 1958.

proximately six new couples write in each issue) and rate it very high on their list of communication channels. Additionally, many members contribute articles to the magazine. Considering the potential readership of *Act* (200,000) the impact of new ideas and criticisms that are published could be considerable.

One of the newest issues of widespread importance in the movement relates to the structure of the decision-making itself, with respect to mobility into the top leadership positions. In theory, each leadership incumbent is elected, with *rotation* at any given level being the ideal. In practice, many top leadership positions are filled by "selection," to the growing dismay of many articulate members. Consequently, there is widespread activity pointed toward an elective process at all levels. Interestingly, not one leader who has been interviewed on this topic has expressed an objection to this change. The feeling seems to be, "anytime the people in a diocese or at any other level decide to develop an election process, it's fine with me. In fact, the sooner the better." It should be noted that early in the movement, selection of, say, an area leader was a necessary procedure in order to spread the movement and insure organization in a given area. As CFM becomes established in given areas, this procedure is no longer considered to be necessary. For once the movement has taken roots, settles down in an area and manifests continuity, the members opt for a voice in choosing their representatives and leaders. It then becomes less palatable to have leaders chosen for them by the decreasingly visible policymakers in Chicago.

2. THE HANDLING OF GRIEVANCES: GROUND RULES FOR CONFLICT. There are several components involved in the ground rules which are more or less subscribed to by CFM'ers (via the socialization process noted above). A widely cherished value in the movement is the premium placed on creativity. As noted previously, everyone is encouraged to participate in the decision-making process at *all* levels, recognizing, of course, that participation at broader levels is not presupposed for newcomers. The crux is that people are *expected* to participate and the rotating chairmanships and representative positions is living proof to the CFM'er. Moreover, to the degree that this expectation is internalized, one would expect that tolerance for disagreement would increase. Early evidence does indicate a high tolerance for disagreement (published documents, interviews) and this factor must be considered as a crucial ground rule.

The implications of this are obvious from the point of view of participation. One would expect (and evidence supports this) a spiral upward in terms of participation in operational decision-making. This participation is increasingly being channeled and structured with the use of the Committee concept, e.g., Coordinating, Program, Executive committees. And the opportunity for a couple to find their way into the decision-making apparatus is recognized by the CFM'ers. Pilot data show where all but a few members of a sample were in the mobility channels, i.e., opting for leadership positions. Most of those who were not were new to CFM. When asked what kinds of opportunities were available for participation in major CFM discussions, there was almost unanimous mention of obtaining some leadership position and participation in the national meetings.

3. THE HANDLING OF GRIEVANCES: CONFLICT RESOLUTION AND/OR ACCOMMODATION. "Rule by the majority" is the most widespread means of decision making in the movement. This value pervades all of the levels of CFM, from the Executive Committee to the Action group. At the same time, it must be recognized that many decisions on this basis will be difficult to accept by a minority, especially one that is very vocal. There seem to be three ways by which CFM'ers in a minority can adjust, individually or collectively, to a decision with which they did not agree.

First, there is the repression of their opposition for the "good of the movement." This is particularly true for leaders at the Diocesan level or above. Some leaders who were interviewed expressed their willingness to "drop the matter" in spite of the fact that they disagreed with some decisions. Others felt they would comply but hope to reverse the decision at a later date.

For those unwilling to accept the outcome of a decision, evasive factors are used which, given the lack of total communication, are difficult to spot. Even those who deviate that are known are not faced with any severe sanctions. Rather, encouragement to act with the majority is the usual case. This is particularly true for "renegade" dioceses, federations and action groups. The point to be made is that evasion is *expected* in some cases, and perhaps more important, *respected*. It is recognized that local adaptations must often be made. Even when the deviations are not a direct result of local problems, they are still respected and in at least a few cases on record, subsumed under the "local problems" category. There does seem an unwillingness to accept deviation from policy as simply a rejection of the policy.

Finally, insulation (in some cases, bound up with patterned evasion) is a latent mechanism for deviation and thereby circumvention of cleavages. This is particularly true at the broadest decision-making levels. In cases where neither resolution nor evasion is possible, where a minority is unwilling to give up a cause vis-à-vis a strong majority, boundaries emerge around the competing factions in an accommodation process. In 1956, for example, there were attempts to introduce a highly structured communication and records system. Several popular leaders felt this system was not feasible and the issue was hotly contested at the national level. The minority resisted the decision to drop the issue. The results took the following form: (1) leaders opposing the issue did not initiate conversation about it; (2) when the issue was brought up by members of the minority, majority members immediately attempted to bring the conversation to a close while giving the minority a chance to be heard; (3) when forced to prolong a discussion, the majority members suggested a trial period of the system at the local levels of the minority. The matter has never been brought up since that time.

SUMMARY AND DISCUSSION

We have examined the characteristics of CFM which seem most responsible for maintaining equilibrium on the one hand and producing strain and conflict on the other. In some cases, the very characteristics that make for equilibrium also seem to produce strain and conflict. Moreover, both tendencies seem to be related to the transition of CFM from primarily a social movement to an increasingly complex organization along bureaucratic lines.

Previous research on social movements has already shown that the ability of the movement to achieve its goals over time is related to its ability to balance ideology and emotional enthusiasm with bureaucratic organizational skill. It seems to us that what has not been stressed in the literature, however, is the way in which strain and conflict emerge and become a part of a social movement. From the theoretical point of view, it becomes important to understand at what point and under what circumstances strain and conflict begin to emerge, and the kinds of mechanisms or processes which are available to a particular social movement to help it control conflict and maintain some degree of equilibrium in order to survive as a goal-achieving organization.

It would seem from our general knowledge of social theory that strain and conflict are inevitable in any social organization[23] which persists over time and is founded on the principles characteristic of CFM. That is, democratic theory has as its key proposition that "who says democracy says effective opposition." The existence of effective opposition to those in control is the *sine qua non* of democratic organization as we understand it in the United States. CFM emerged as a social movement in a time of social disorder and change in the United States, as seen in the two World Wars and the rise of urbanism. It was a collective action movement aimed at giving the Catholic lay couple the opportunity to develop initiative and some autonomy for social action at the parish and community level.

An organization committed to local initiative and autonomy of action must expect to become the source for conflict and strain if it persists for any period of time. For conflict and strain are the stuff of the democratic process. This is ordered conflict, conflict within a set of ground rules which are generally accepted. As the work of Lipset and others has shown, there is a direct relation between social class, education, income and participation in the democratic process in American society.[24] CFM's recruitment has been largely from the upper classes, the better educated and financially more well-off Catholic couples, people who by their social background are tuned to the democratic game. The point is, and although it is commonplace to say it, it must be said again, that social movements like any other forms of social organizations do not operate in a vacuum. They are influenced by the larger and smaller social systems of which they are an inevitable part.

In this paper we have merely begun to explore the way in which these general propositions seem to apply to CFM. In Table 3 we have attempted to bring our observation on CFM together. As we have indicated, its peculiar history, and the character of its emerging goals, in combination with an emergent middle class Catholic population, have set the boundaries for recruitment. This fact, in turn, and in combination with a deliberately contrived socialization process, defines the areas that represent the sources for stability in the organization. But since neither recruitment nor

---

[23] Robert E. Lane, "The Decline of Politics and Ideology in a Knowledgeable Society," *American Sociological Review,* Volume 31, Oct. 1966, pp. 649-662.

[24] S. M. Lipset, *Political Man,* Garden City: Doubleday and Sons, 1960, and S. M. Lipset, *The First New Nation,* New York: Basic Books Co., 1963; see also W. V. D'Antonio and H. J. Ehrlich (eds.) *Power and Democracy In America,* University of Notre Dame Press, 1961.

TABLE 3 STRUCTURAL COMPONENTS SHAPING THE NATURE AND DIRECTION OF CONFLICT, RESOLUTION AND ACCOMMODATION

Entering the Group: Factors Lending Stability	Major Source of Conflict	Channels for Articulation of Differences	Factors Shaping Outcome: Resolution or Accommodation
Selective recruitment	Incomplete socialization	Decentralization	Rule by the majority
Socialization		Institutionalized grievance machinery	Patterned evasion
		Shared conceptions of "ground rule"	Insulation

socialization are complete and perfect, as perhaps they are not in any social organization, the sources for strain and conflict are inevitably present also.

The direction and early control of conflicts are shaped by the decentralized decision-making apparatus which functions (1) to generate broadly-based policy frameworks and (2) to set the stage, via inter-level linkages, for a patterned grievance type of machinery. The latter also implies that there exist shared conceptions of ground rules for conflict, e.g., that competing factions respect opposing viewpoints. In this respect, more or less everyone gets a chance to be heard; again, policy decisions are general; and compromise a likely outcome.

With respect to conflict resolution, rule by the majority is the norm. Since such a rule is difficult, if not impossible to implement in every case, this norm is complemented by two other processes of an accommodative nature, viz., patterned evasion at the local level and/or insulation of the competing factions. Consequently, via these processes, the movement is able to withstand conflicts that cannot be resolved through compromise or the acceptance of one point of view to the exclusion of the other(s).

Furthermore, conflict is reduced by the fact that it is so easy to become an ex-CFM'er. In fact, there seems to be some prestige attached to the status. It is fairly easy to drop out of CFM without negative sanction; as long as this fact is normatively accepted, it would seem to be another important conflict-reducing process (mechanism).

CONCLUSION

It appears that the Christian Family Movement as a social movement is dying. Like the Red Cross and YMCA-YWCA before it, in the place of a movement is developing a well-structured and routinized organization with flexible goals and adaptive latent functions, which appear to be satisfying an ever-changing membership. From the point of view of social theory we expect our study of CFM to help us better to understand the way in which movements become complex organizations, and what happens to the internal dynamics in the process, including not only questions of structure, but also of ideology and setting of goals.

From the point of view of the CFM members, it would seem that the study should help them to understand what is happening to them and to perceive more clearly the possible future directions which CFM can take in this society. In fact, it may well raise the question whether the changing nature of the movement merits the time and effort needed to help it succeed as a complex organization.

20

The Cursillo as a Social Movement

SIGMUND DRAGOSTIN, O.F.M.

University of Chicago

SOURCE. Prepared especially for this volume. Based on "The Cursillo—How It Works," *The Critic,* 1965, 24, 58-62.

The *Cursillo de Cristiandad* or "The Little Course in Christianity" has been and remains a matter of controversy in the Roman Catholic Church. There are those priests and laymen who are zealous supporters of the exercises. They point to their own experience and the obvious good effects experienced by others who have made the *cursillo*. Others are less enthusiastic and at times downright critical.

In 1962, Bishop Juan Hervas, the originator of the *cursillo*, published a lengthy article in *Christ to the World*. The article contained a full ten pages of endorsement by members of the Spanish and Latin American hierarchies, by priests in various parts of the world, and by laymen. In the United States, reaction in the press followed the first *cursillos* given in English. Sulpician Father Francis B. Norris, writing in the *Monitor*, the San Francisco archdiocesan weekly, stated that his deepest experience of our common life in Christ took place during the *cursillo*. Father John McLaughlin, S. J., wrote an approving article for *America* in which he said, "The proven value of the *cursillo* (as other true affiliations sacred or secular) is that it furnishes the conditions necessary for the individual to achieve his identity. It is within the context of this affiliation that the total Christian experience is most purely and unforgettably realized." Enthusiastic response came from far-off Japan. *The Japan Missionary Bulletin* carried an article by Eugene A. Walsh in which descriptions of the *cursillo* experience stretched for superlatives. Not to be overlooked is the fact that Pope Paul VI, at the request of Cardinal Benjamin de Arriba y Castro, Archbishop of Tarragona, named St. Paul the patron of *cursillos*. The document implementing this *motu proprio* mentions the good effects already achieved by the *cursillo* exercises.

On the other hand, the nasty voice of criticism has not ceased to be heard in the land. One of the first shots was fired by Bill Jacobs, writing in *Ave Maria* in early 1964. Chicago sociologist Father Andrew Greeley, and the *National Catholic Reporter's* columnist Gary Wills are among others who have raised critical questions about the training course. Most recently, Bishop Stephen S. Wosnicki of Saginaw has been critical of the fanatical fringe which ornaments the movement in his own diocese.

Reaction to the movement can be found at opposite ends of a continuum. Presumably, therefore, it can be found at many points in between. It seems to me that those who endorse the exercises most frequently speak from their personal experience of them. They are impressed with the cursillo's effectiveness in creating an atmosphere of Christian community and in implementing Christian attitudes. In assessing the *cursillo*, they generally speak about it with a theological vocabulary. Many give great emphasis to the effectiveness of actual grace and the power of the Holy Spirit.

Critics, on the other hand, are less likely to have made the *cursillo* personally. They tend to be concerned with the problem of social manipulation and respect for human freedom. At times, they indicate a greater acquaintance with the vocabulary of the behavioral sciences than the proponents and they tend to be concerned with the means used to achieve the good effects.

As far as my credentials are concerned, let me say that I made a *cursillo* in Cincinnati, Ohio in July, 1962. As a priest-sociologist with some acquaintance with current social psychology, I am disturbed by what seem to me to be undue pressures exerted on those making the exercises. A study of Bishop Hervas' *Leaders' Manual*, an extensive description of the *cursillo* running to some 300 pages, has done little to change this reaction.

Read from the viewpoint of pastoral theology, Bishop Hervas' manual does take some pains to achieve balance and points the way to obviate the more apparent pitfalls, e.g., lack of perseverence, cliquishness, and misdirected fervor. One should not blame on the *cursillo* the various mistakes that have been made in its name. On the other hand, I did not get the impression that the Bishop—whether by design or by accident—gives a fair description of the social psychological techniques involved. To be sure, there are enough general references to methods of good pedagogy and the lessons of modern psychology. But the actual description of the techniques of influence are mostly smothered in a smoke screen of pious vocabulary.

Having made the *cursillo*, I attempted an intuitive analysis of the social-psychological mechanisms at work in the exercises and, where possible, made references to empirical studies carried out in similar situations. To be sure, human interaction is far too complicated to be caught in a single conceptual net. The whole area of attitude change is a *mare magnum* to most psychologists. There are probably undiscovered continents in the geography of human behavior. With these reservations in mind, however, the subsequent study of Hervas' *Leaders' Manual* did little to change my original analysis of the social-psychological mechanisms being employed.

As is well known, human beings are profoundly modified as they acquire motives and attitudes through the process of interacting with others. One contribution of social psychologists has been to point out that these changes continue throughout life and that they occur dramatically in some situations.

How does interaction change people? More specifically, how does interaction affect a person's attitudes? Social psychologists distinguish at least five bases of social power, five ways people modify the behavior of other people: reward, punishment, legitimate power, expert power and referent power. It would be difficult to eliminate any of the bases of social power as possibly operating in the *cursillo*. But the *cursillo* seems to me to utilize referent power, or the power of the group, in a high degree.

Attitudes tend to become fixed as individuals acquire habitual frames of reference for seeing things—as they acquire background against which they can structure their perceptions. Individual frames of reference are socially influenced because people are motivated to belong to groups. The Asch (1958) and Sherif (1958) experiments with group norms and the host of studies in their tradition provide interesting statistical information on this point. Berelson and Steiner (1964) having catalogued much of what we know empirically about human behavior have concluded macroscopically: "behavioral-science-man is social man—social product, social producer, and social seeker. The traditional images of man have stressed, as prime motivating agents, reason, or faith, or impulse, or self interest; the behavioral science image stresses the social definition of all these.

"The individual appears less on his own, less a creature of the natural environment, more as a creature making others and made by others."

The *cursillo* attempts to structure and reinforce a particular religious frame of reference and value system not only through verbal persuasion of a somewhat intellectual kind, as in the retreat lecture or in the free give-and-take of the educational experience, but also to establish and use group relationships toward which the person is highly motivated. Many techniques of the training course seem aimed in this direction. The group discussion, public prayer, public commitment, and lay leadership help provide the added impetus toward change over the merely persuasive technique of the retreat lecture in much the same way that group discussion, group decision, and public commitment have been proven effective in changing everything from food habits to production standards. Group norms (Coch and French, 1948; Lewin, 1943) are more readily established if a person must make his opinion public, if the majority holding the contrary opinion is large, if the group is especially friendly or close-knit, and if the object of consensus is ambiguous. These conditions (Hare, 1962) are either inherently present in the *cursillo* situation or they are structured into it by conscious design.

But evidence suggests that the important element in change is not so much having the chance to discuss the matter at hand as in providing an effective method for breaking down the old value system before adopting a new one. It is here, precisely, that referent power comes into play. Theodore Newcomb (1959), among others, sees the stability of attitudes as a balance between supporting and opposing forces, a kind of equilibrium. Attitudes may remain unchanged because no new influences are met to upset the balance of forces. They may also remain unchanged because new forces which might undermine existing attitudes are countered by forces supporting existing attitudes. Among these supporting forces, ego-defense is a particularly strong force against change. Numerous studies support the hypothesis that ego-defensive forces, being aimed at safety in the face of threat, are much more likely to serve as resistance to change than are ego-supporting forces. The defensive person refuses to entertain alternate hypotheses and by that fact exercises selective perception.

Attempts to change attitudes must therefore go about it in ways that do not arouse defensiveness. You must generally do more than provide new influences to counteract old ones. If opposing forces are increased while supporting forces remain strong, then greater defensiveness may be aroused and greater resistance to change. For example, it is conceivable that all the intellectual arguments in the world, together with many threats of punishment, will not get the Latin male to church on Sunday if his culture and his important reference groups define such activity as feminine and he must symbolically emasculate himself to do so.

One way to weaken influences supporting attitudes is to weaken ego-involvement. But ego-involvement always presupposes a relationship between the self and some reference group. In order to weaken supporting influence, it is necessary to change the perceived relationship between the self and the reference group.

Insofar as religious values and attitudes are concerned, a full acceptance of such values might be blocked by seeing "religious people" as a negative reference group (so the importance in the *cursillo* of the talk on piety), by seeing the clergy as "different sort of people," by seeing religion, especially in a Latin culture, as a feminine pursuit, or, in other cultures, as "lower class," as "anti-intellectual", etc. Insofar as opposition to change is related to negative perceptions of this kind, then opposition to change can be overcome by substituting a positive group relationship for a negative one. In the *cursillo*, substitution of lay leadership for clerical, setting up a masculine atmosphere, the drawing of respected men from the community from many backgrounds (and this would be relative to the community), and carrying out the whole exercise in an atmosphere of "out with the boys" conviviality and great personal acceptance—all seem functional in reducing ego-defensiveness.

The dissolution of defensiveness and the establishment of new group relationships takes place through personal interaction within the small group discussions as well as interaction within the larger group. Because the exercises are of a religious nature and the men attending come with that in mind, salience could be expected to be operative for the majority of those attending (Charters and Newcomb, 1958). Members of a discussion group would be inclined to express opinions which they feel are in keeping with the task at hand. This is simply a case of putting one's best foot forward. The mutual reinforcement would be cumulative. Moreover, insofar as a trainee's self-idea includes a certain religious element, this new religious experience in a socially acceptable setting is also ego-supporting.

This is not to say that the talks given at the *cursillo* are not masterpieces of their kind. They present beliefs in a framework of philosophical and psychological credibility. But the group discussion does contribute to a kind of social confirmation, to what sociologists call consensual validation.

Since the effective change of norms requires knowledge of the new consensus, this can best be achieved by full participation with free feedback. Emotion would be particularly vulnerable to social influence. But even when a person conforms to the new consensus, he is likely to retain some reservations about his decisions. Think, for example, of a Catholic giving up the practice of birth control. These reservations are manifestations of a state of cognitive dissonance. The greater the attractiveness of the belief given up, the greater the dissonance following the decision. Various studies have shown that efforts will be made to reduce a dissonant state (Festinger, 1962; Festinger, 1956). Therefore, persons who conform may seek to convince themselves that there is a high value in their changed belief. This then adds to the stability of the new opinion. This phenomenon may account in part for the zeal some trainees frequently exhibit immediately following a training course. Insofar as those who do not change resolve their conflict by denying or downgrading the opinions of others, one might expect considerable hostility toward the *cursillo* on the part of those making the exercise who are not altered by it.

It is well known that when a person's attitudes have changed because group influences have lowered his resistance to change, then group influences should persist if the attitude change is to be enduring. This principle has been illustrated by group-induced changes in the attitudes of confirmed alcoholics. The *cursillo* trainee gains continued support for his newfound attitudes in the weekly small-group meeting with other personally selected trainees.

It is easily observed that the *cursillo* group goes through its own phases. Bishop Hervas describes the phases as follows: first phase, removing erroneous ideas or prejudices; second phase, what Christ has done for us; third phase, what I should do for Christ. It is interesting that this division of the material corresponds roughly with the empirically tested phases of collecting information, evaluating information, and pressing for a decision. Empirical studies prove that this decision point is the critical bottleneck in the process. Once the decision point has been passed, the rates of negative reaction usually fall off and the rates of positive reaction rise sharply. Joking and laughter, indicating solidarity and tension released, rise sharply. Bales and Strotdbeck (1951) in their original work on group phases posited precise conditions under which phase movements do appear. The conditions are all fulfilled in the *cursillo* setting in a high degree. Bishop Hervas is very much aware of the mood of the group as it moves through its various phases, and the talks are arranged accordingly—now logical, now straightforward, now enthusiastic, etc.

It is at the beginning of the decision phase that one reaches the critical bottleneck. According to Bishop Hervas' description, most *cursillistas* come to some kind of a crisis after the fifth talk, on piety. The priest-director is to have available the "penance" sheets before this talk begins. He is to use them "at the moment he deems it most appropriate." Presumably, this means that he is to use them to get the candidates through the bottleneck. When I made the *cursillo*, it was at this point that we were informed that others were doing rather severe penance on our behalf. The turning point in the control problem for many members took place at this time. From my observations, negative reaction and tendencies to withdraw (very real for some members up to this point) declined; positive reactions climbed rapidly during the rest of the course, cresting in great enthusiasm during the closing ceremony.

In the *cursillo*, the control problem is heightened by the fact that a person's whole style of life may be at stake. (Again, think of a Catholic giving up the practice of birth control.) Each member is expected to make a deep personal commitment to Christian beliefs which are increasingly becoming the norms of the group. Trainees are told that they have been especially chosen. They are told, "You and Christ are a majority." Imprudent helpers may well imply that the *cursillo* is a once-in-a-lifetime experience and that those who are unmoved by it are truly reprobate. When I attended the *cursillo*, two men from a table of eight showed rather great anxiety on this account.

Intuitive observation, then, leads to the conclusion that the *cursillo* is in large measure an example of group-induced attitude change.

The following hypotheses could be tested.

1. A person's attitude change in a *cursillo* setting will vary directly with the amount of his participation in the group—as measured by the amount of interaction initiated and received. Passive withdrawal from group activity will be detrimental to a person's adopting group norms and values.

2. Persons not sharing the dominant frame of reference and sub-culture of the group (agnostics, Protestants), to the extent of their differences, will be entirely unaffected or less affected by the experience. (Bishop Hervas says the cursillo is not a fitting means for these people.)

3. Persons who do not regard the priest-director as a high-status person or the Church as a high-status organization (some Catholic intellectuals) will be less affected by the exercise than those who do.

4. Persons who do not want to change their religious attitudes or their way of life will tend to be less involved in the interaction of the *cursillo* and will be less changed by it—unless they move toward wanting to change (This may seem a self-evident fact but empirically willingness to change would be a very important variable.)

5. In keeping with the theory of cognitive dissonance, persons who change after a personal struggle and who harbor some unconscious reservations will be more enthusiastic about their new-found beliefs and more zealous in spreading them.

6. Persons who make the exercise without being changed by it will tend to deprecate the training course.

7. Those aware of the social psychological mechanisms being employed in the *cursillo* will be less affected by it than those who are not aware.

Personality factors will also affect the way a person reacts to the *cursillo* and the amount of change he undergoes. Each person is different and to some extent perceives himself to be different from all other people. Therefore, each person sees group norms applying to himself in a unique way. The personality factor therefore enters the group process and modifies it.

One phenomenon of the *cursillo* that calls for explanation is its capacity to arouse the strain toward fanaticism in a minority of those who make it. I have a hunch that a straight-forward look at this fact may take us to the heart of the matter.

We all know that religious attitudes vary enormously from person to person. We have yet to develop an operational typology which can discriminate one type of religious attitude from another. Gordon Allport (1963) has suggested the beginning of such a discriminating typology. He speaks of extrinsic and intrinsic religion as one important measure of variability.

Extrinsic religion, he says, "may be used as a defense against reality and, most importantly, to provide a super-sanction for one's own formula for living. Such a sentiment assures me that God sees things my way, that my righteousness is identical with His." This is why, for example, utilitarian or extrinsic religiosity correlates positively with racial and ethnic bigotry and is widespread among churchgoers. In motivational terms, extrinsic religion is not an integral motive. It serves other motives: the need for security, the need for status, the need for self-esteem. The possessor continues to hold an egocentric view of the universe.

On the other hand, Allport describes intrinsic religion in the following terms. "Intrinsic religion is not an instrumental formation; specific needs are not so much served by as subordinate to an over-arching motive. This commitment is partly intellectual, but fundamentally motivational. It is integral, covering everything in experience and everything beyond experience; it makes room for scientific fact and for emotional fact. It is a hunger for and a commitment to an ideal unification of one's life, but always under the unifying concept of the nature of existence." Allport goes on to say that intrinsic religion is not primarily a means of handling fear, or a mode of conformity, or an attempted sublimation of sex, or a wish fulfillment.

Now it seems to me quite possible that religious fanaticism and other undesirable outcomes of the *cursillo* are possible to the extent that elements of the non-rational are used to bring about attitude changes in the individual. To that same extent, the *cursillo* is also a violation of human liberty. Given the techniques that are used, a person's egoistic motivational structure might very easily be vested with a cloak of religiosity.

What do I mean by elements of the non-rational? The defense mechanism of conformity is a case in point. To be sure, not all conformity, even as a generalized trait, is ego-defensive. But it can be. And in so far as one's new religious orientation is built on a non-rational need like conformity, it will be the type of extrinsic religion that Allport is talking about. Change based on appeals to non-rational self-esteem would be another case in point. Trainees are frequently told that they have been especially chosen. The elitist idea is built up.

Moreover, attitudes have affective, cognitive, and behavioral components that tend to be consistent with each other. Thus, change in one component leads to changes in another. The affective component has the most potency in attitude change and the cognitive component the least (Katz and Stotland, 1962). But it is just here in the area of affect and behavior that the *cursillo* candidate is given the least choice. His companions for the group discussion are chosen for him. There is also an effort to withdraw the candidate from the social support he might receive from friends and relatives who are attending the *cursillo* with him. People are being affectionate toward him in order to change him. Those who are shy and withdrawing are given special attention. His behavior, too, is subject to pressure. He is expected to pray publicly and personally before the tabernacle not because he has freely chosen to but because he is reacting to what social psychologists would call strong social contagion. His spiritual commitment toward the end of the course and his testimony of its value may likewise be made under similar pressure. The greater the lack of complete voluntariness in these matters, the greater the possibility that non-rational factors are being called into play. These are techniques we associate with propaganda rather than with the educational process. They do not seem well-calculated to bring a person to a mature spiritual outlook.

All of this may seem far too subtle to the person who has made a *cursillo* and found it an elevating spiritual experience. I have no doubt that this is the case for many who are spiritually mature (read: have intrinsic religious motivation) and who entered the exercises with complete voluntariness. Certainly, the secular definition of roles in contemporary society has left us rather inflexible as far as the expression of religious sentiment is concerned. I would welcome an atmosphere that provides a free and open opportunity for an individual to broaden his religious experience. But the extraordinary dramatic effect of the *cursillo* as well as its excesses seem directly related to the element of social manipulation. Bishop Hervas says that the *cursillo* is "not for minors or men without personality." This does not seem to me to be a very discriminating criterion. And *who* is to say which men may be helped and which may be harmed by such an exercise?

The fact that the *cursillo* inspires great enthusiasm as well as violent reaction seems to me to be related to several underlying issues.

First there is the question of the relative weight given to the free and transcendental character of the human person. There has been an historical development in man's consciousness of his own dignity. While the Church has come to see that political force is an improper instrument for bringing about religious consent, there are those within the Church who give very little attention to the moral and psychological means used to insure religious conformity. Between hypotism at one end of the scale and true education at the other there is available a whole bag of social psychological techniques that can be used to change people. Used by one person on another without his knowledge and consent, most of them are an affront to human dignity, autonomy, and freedom.

Second, there is the degree to which one realizes that social-psychological mechanisms can be as imperious as physical force. If a college fraternity on a prestige campus were to use the *cursillo* structure to initiate Roman Catholic students into agnosticism, we would certainly consider it a violation of fair play. No organization considering itself an educational institution would resort to such tactics.

Finally, there is the extent to which one emphasizes that the effects of the *cursillo* are the result of divine grace or the natural outcome of well-known social psychological techniques. This is not a question that lends itself to empirical evidence. If you insist that the effects of the *cursillo* are entirely the effect of Divine grace, then to whom do you attribute the non-random instances of fanaticism and the rare instances of complete personality disorganization? I would also like to know why God's grace habitually stops short with whole classes of people for whom the *cursillo* is not "a fitting means." The maximalists will answer that only the good effects are to be attributed to the Holy Spirit. When things go wrong, the human element is to blame. As I said, the question does not lend itself to empirical evidence.

As I read Scripture, it says the truth shall make you free. The *cursillo* implies that if you give up just a little of your freedom, it will make you true. They used to call that, "The end justifies the means."

REFERENCES

Allport, Gordon W. Behavioral Science, Religion and Mental Health, *Journal of Religion and Health,* 1963, 2, 187-197. Also, *The Individual and His Religion.* MacMillan, 1950.

Asch, S. E. Effects of Group Pressure upon the Modification and Distortion of Judgments. In Macoby, Newcomb, & Hartley, *op. cit.,* pp. 174-183.

Bales, Robert F. and Strodtbeck, Fred L. Phases in Group Problem Solving, *Journal of Abnormal and Social Psychology,* 1951, 46, 485-495.

Berelson, Bernard and Steiner, Gary A. *Human Behavior.* New York: Harcourt, Brace & World, Inc., 1964, p. 666.

Charters, W. W., Jr. and Newcomb, Theodore. Some Attitudinal Effects of Experimentally Increased Salience of a Membership Group. In Macoby, Newcomb, & Hartley, *op. cit.,* pp. 276-281.

Coch, Lester and French, John R. P., Jr. Overcoming Resistance to Change, *Human Relations,* 1948, I, 512-532.

Festinger, L. Cognitive Dissonance, *Sci. Am.,* October 1962.

Festinger, L., Riecken, H. W. and Schachter, S. *When Prophecy Fails.* Minneapolis: University of Minnesota Press, 1956.

Hare, A. Paul, *Handbook of Small Group Research.* The Free Press of Glencoe, 1962, p. 30.

Katz, D. and Stotland, E. A Preliminary Statement to a Theory of Attitude Structure and Change, in *Psychology: A Study of a Science, Vol. III,* edited by S. Koch, pp. 423-475.

Lewin, Kurt. Forces Behind Food Habits and Methods of Change, *Bull. Nat. Res. Counc.,* 1943, CVIII, 35—65.

Maccoby, Eleanor E., Newcomb, Theodore M., and Hartley, Eugene L. *Readings in Social Psychology,* 3rd ed. New York: Holt, Rinehart & Winston, 1958.

Newcomb, Theodore M. *Social Psychology.* New York: Henry Holt and Company, 1959, pp. 194-262.

Sherif, Muzafer. Group Influences upon the Formation of Norms and Attitudes, in Macoby, Newcomb, and Hartley, *op. cit.,* pp. 219-232.

21

Dynamics of Change in the
Religious Community

ROSEANNE MURPHY, S.N.D.

College of Notre Dame

WILLIAM T. LIU

University of Notre Dame

SOURCE. "Organizational Stance and Change,: A Comparative Study of Three Religious Communities," *Review of Religious Research,* 1966, 8, 37-50. Reprinted by permission.

One of the problems in the comparative study of different social organizations is that while it is easy to suggest contrasts and comparisons it is difficult to pin them down methodologically. Comparative studies of organizations oftentimes appeared in the form of case study descriptions of several organizations or in the form of examinations focused on some specific facets of several organizations. Since no two organizations are completely alike, attempts to locate one common denominator may lead to serious mistakes, as the observer may be looking at only one point of the changing processes while conveniently ignoring the entire and continuous historical processes of change.

The present study [1] is an attempt to describe the change dynamics of three religious communities of women in the United States. As previous studies on religious organizations of Sisters are lacking, our attempt here is both exploratory and systematic. It is systematic in that attempts are made to isolate the *regional* and *time* variations of the founding of the three communities, a point often neglected by other investigators when several organizations are compared. Furthermore, the historical milieu which shaped the original structural model of the organization is especially important in the study of organizational change.

Numerous studies on business, political and military organizations have pointed to certain variables in formal organizations which influence the pace of change. Selznick points to the *institutionalization process* [2] as a key factor in making change a personal threat to the members who have formed an "organizational image" or "character." Complex organizations need to develop a character to give the members moral support and to achieve the greatest efficiency in attaining their goals. On the other hand, the organizational character can lead to a resistance to change which then hinders organizational efficiency. This "displacement of goals" [3] puts the organization into a bind situation, which in turn leads to a consideration of another very important problem in organization, that of precisely defining their original goals since the goals of the organization most influence the development of its character.

Guest suggests in his study of Plant Y that *leadership* is the crucial variable influencing change. However, he admits that an important pre-condition for the effectiveness of leadership was what he called the "leeway to act" [4] in the organization. This "leeway"

---

[1] Conducted in 1965-66 at the Social Science Training and Research Laboratory, University of Notre Dame.

[2] Philip Selznik. *Leadership in Administration* (Evanston, Illinois: Row Peterson and Company, 1957), p. 15.

[3] Cf. Robert K. Merton, "Bureaucratic Structure and Personality" in *Social Theory and Social Structure* (Glencoe, Illinois: The Free Press, 1957), p. 199.

[4] Robert H. Guest. *Organizational Change: The Effect of Successful Leadership.* (Homewood, Ill.: The Dorsey Press, Inc., and Richard R. Irwin, Inc., 1962) p. 128.

is the organizational characteristic which defines the range of obligations for each person in the hierarchy.

Janowitz sees change in organizations, such as the military, as the result of technological advance and the historical development in tactical operations. Today it is imperative for military operations to *depend* upon the improvisation on basic principles by the individual soldiers who face constantly changing conditions in combat. Authority by domination has given way to "manipulative authority" by which he means ". . . influencing an individual's behavior by indirect techniques of group persuasion and by an emphasis on group goals." [5] A direct analogy can be made for active religious communities since the normal development has been that of a small group of persons engaged in one kind of work and directly under one superior to a large organization of many members scattered over a vast territory and engaged in numerous specialized activities.

As we turned to the study of religious communities, it became obvious that Selznick's model was more promising. This is so because from the very nature of religious communities—with a kind of communal economic life, distinct religious habits, special community prayers—the institutionalization process readily takes place and an organizational character develops which distinguishes one community from another. Since there are many similar, non-sectarian organizations engaged in the same kind of work as religious communities, the situation forces the latter to develop a unique type of religious or professional (or both) identification not to be found among non-sectarian organizations. To justify their existence, the organizational self-image must be strong enough to withstand outside pressures that would threaten organizational identity.

RELIGIOUS COMMUNITIES: CONSTANTS AND VARIATIONS

Religious communities in the United States today involve over 170,000 women in every type of educational, medical, and welfare work. From the sixth to the seventeenth centuries any woman wishing to dedicate her life in a religious community had to join a cloistered group whose main occupation was prayer and work, com-

---

[5] Morris Janowitz. "Changing Patterns of Organizational Authority: The Military Establishment." *Administrative Science Quarterly,* III (1959) p. 482. In a separate paper, Janowitz uses the constabulary concept of military to describe the change which occurred. *The New Military* (N.Y.: Russell Sage Foundation, 1964), pp. 11-38.

pletely separated from the world around them. Not until a French priest, Vincent de Paul, circumvented the law of enclosure for all female religious by founding a group he entitled the "Ladies of Charity" to care for the destitute of Paris did an "active group" come into being. Since then, hundreds of groups have been founded to meet local and contemporary needs. Each founder has given the group some unique characteristic usually representing his own particular interpretation of the needs of the time. However, each has a similar basic structure prescribed by the official judicial body in Rome charged with specifying the essential aspects of religious life, which qualify a group for official recognition as a religious community.

In spite of the centralized judicial power over religious communities, the continuous interactions among members of the congregation within the framework of common property tends to mark the religious community the kind of "total institution" suggested by Goffman.[6] The "total institution" concept, however, does not accurately describe a religious community, as most religious communities (exceptions being totally cloistered groups) participate actively in the larger society. Common community property and spiritual bonds among members of the same community do, however, give impetus to the continuous growth of *esprit de corps* in-

---

[6] Cf. Erving Goffman. "Characteristics of Total Institutions" in *Symposium on Preventive and Social Psychiatry* (Washington, D. C.: Walter Reed Army Institute of Research, 1957) Goffman's analysis of a "total institution", for which he applies to "convents" along with mental hospitals, military institutions, prisons, etc. He does not specify what he means by "convents" but seems to assume that they are all similar to his examples of a Benedictine monastery. The present study is concerned with active religious communities: those engaged in professional works such as teaching, nursing, social work, etc. These communities *do not* fit the description, "total institution," since they do not have the "totalistic features" listed by Goffman as: (1) "all aspects of life are conducted in the same place and under the same single authority; (2) each phase of the member's daily activity will be carried out in the immediate company of a large batch of others, all of whom are treated alike and required to do the same thing together: (3) all phases of the day's activities are tightly scheduled, with one activity leading at a prearranged time into the next, the whole circle of activities being imposed from above through a system of explicit formal rulings and a body of officials; (4) the contents of the various enforced activities are brought together as parts of a single overall rational plan reportedly designed to fulfill the official aims of the institution." One only has to think of the difference of activities in the lives of a college president, a surgery supervisor, an eighth grade teacher, or a nurse in an orphanage to imagine why active communities do not fit the characteristics of Goffman's total institution.

dividually marked and, therefore, interreligious community variations in spirit and in group processes inevitably develop.

Our attention has been called especially to the development of the unique organizational spirit found in each community. In the subsequent paragraphs, development processes will be presented which in turn will lead to an attempt to formulate a theoretical model capable of explaining variations in the change pace of three religious communities.

The wide range of variations, however, is found within the limits of certain constants of religious lives. All members of religious communities, for example, choose to make the vows of poverty, chasity, and obedience, by which they relinquish the act of proprietorship of any material goods belonging to the community and dedicate themselves through a life of celibacy. Obedience is the core of religious life through which members bind themselves to the rule of the community and to the dictates of all legitimate superiors. Although the vow of obedience does *not* mean a relinquishing of freedom of choice, the subject is bound by a normative expectation to obey a decision, reached either singularly or collectively, accepting the decision as "the will of God." The community constitutes for its members a *way of life* in addition to being the structure in which the individual carries out the works of teaching, nursing, or social work.

THE THREE COMMUNITIES STUDIED

The three communities studied were all founded in the same region of the United States, during the first decade of the nineteenth century and initially engaged in the same activity, namely, teaching. The fact that the three communities were founded within a radius of thirty miles indicates the acute need for education in the rapidly developing pioneer territory. For purposes of anonymity, the three communities will be known in this study by fictitious names, as the Sisters of St. Rose, St. Christine, and St. Martin. It is necessary to give a brief sketch of the background of each.

The Sisters of St. Rose

The Sisters of St. Rose began as a result of the efforts of one woman to conduct school for her many nephews and nieces since there were no schools in the area. As word reached other settlers that some children were being educated, requests for admission of their children came from all the neighbors. When the number of children to be educated exceeded the capacity of her brother's house, the young teacher, along with another young lady, moved the school to a log cabin adjacent to the house. Eventually, both decided to dedicate their lives as members of a religious community. They turned to the priest in the area to ask his advice and direction in founding a religious congregation and as soon as they had six members in the fledgling institution, they elected their first superior.

The pioneer priest who founded the Sisters of St. Rose spent most of his time on horseback attempting to take care of the spiritual needs of Catholics spread across a vast frontier territory. He had no intention of beginning a new community but only of helping the original group of six women who wanted to become religious and intended to have a sister from some established community in Europe come to the area to train the new sisters in the fundamentals of religious life. However, when he suggested such a plan, the sisters refused to have anyone but the priest guide them and received permission from the local bishop to start their community. This was a unique beginning in that they were not modeled, as most communities, on any other established community; it might be said that their "model" was original. Not having any traditions to fall back on or customs to maintain, the founder recognized from the beginning that the community would have to adapt readily to the ever changing conditions of a pioneer territory. The founder wrote to the sisters:

If you inquire whether I know what will come of you, this I cannot tell. But from any present experience, from the nature of things and from the condition of man, without pretending to any revelation or gift of prophecy, there is not a spark of doubt in my mind but you will undergo great changes from your present state. . . .

Built into the system, then, was a ratification, indeed, an *anticipation* of change which made it seem part of the natural growth process of the community.

The Sisters of St. Christine

In response to the need of the children for instruction in their faith as well as education in general, a French priest assigned to the territory appealed to the only other existing community in the United States to send some of their sisters into the area. However, since that community was enmeshed in its own problems of getting established and had not yet been officially recognized, he was told to try to start a community of sisters. Because the only community he knew as engaged in active work was that of the Sisters of Charity of St. Vincent de Paul in France, the rule of the first group of St. Christine Sisters was directly copied from the rule of St. Vincent. He had no intention of founding a separate community but thought he would help to get a group started, and he intended to ask a Sister to come from Europe. Although the Sister never came, the rule of St. Vincent was sent to the new community from France and with a few adaptations, the rule was used by the Sisters of St. Christine. Determined effort both on the part of the priest-founder and on the part of the Sisters was made to adhere to the rules and spirit of St. Vincent. For instance, when the first Mother General's term of office had ended, all of the sisters and the ecclesiastical superior wanted her to remain in office. She replied, "We must obey the rule," and held elections for her replacement, since St. Vincent had specified that no sister could be the Mother General for more than one consecutive term.

Identification with the rule was symbolized by the identification of the members of St. Christine's community with St. Vincent. The priest founder of St. Christine referred to St. Vincent as the "real" founder of the community. Shortly after their foundation, the conferences of St. Vincent's were sent to the St. Christine Motherhouse where they were read and re-read to all the sisters. One of the members said, "In the '70's and '80's we became terribly like the original Sisters of Charity of St. Vincent de Paul. The sisters didn't know how much we tried to imitate them."

St. Vincent had specified that his community was to be devoted to the works of charity which included every kind of educational, medical, and welfare work. The St. Christine group began by opening a school since education for the children of the settlers was considered to be of primary importance. However, when cholera and yellow fever plagued the settlers, the St. Christine sisters soon became involved in caring for the sick. Their Vincentian spirit urged them to respond to all kinds of needs. Since they were to engage in vastly different kinds of work, the one unifying element for the sisters and the major source of identification with the community became the rule of St. Vincent. The actual direction of any one of the sub-organizations, such as a hospital, orphanage, school, or mental institution, *had* to be left to the discretion of the administrator in charge. The areas of concern on the part of the higher superiors were those regulations directing the religious lives of the members of the community and the prescriptions laid down by St. Vincent. In fact, when one group of sisters asked for permission to engage in some parish work *not* specified by the rule, the Mother General advised them that any sisters who wished could start their own congregation, but since that work was not mentioned by St. Vincent, they could not remain Sisters of St. Christine if they undertook it. Consequently, a group of sisters did break off from the St. Christine community and started their own congregation which eventually developed into a congregation as numerous as the Sisters of St. Christine.

The Sisters of St. Martin

The Sisters of St. Martin, founded ten years after the other two communities, had a very different origin. The priests of St. Martin who were established in the same region as the Sisters of St. Rose and St. Christine wanted to start a "secondary order" of St. Martin in the United States. A "secondary order" of St. Martin, as structured in Europe, meant a *cloistered* order of sisters organized on a monastic pattern. However, recognizing the dire need for teachers, the founder of the Sisters of St. Martin in the United States directed them to teach the poor children of the area although he intended that, as soon as other provisions for the children could be made, the order of sisters would become a cloistered one and the members would devote their lives to prayer and sacrifice. The model proposed, then, was of a cloistered group of sisters with exception being made temporarily to allow them to teach. Even in the vow formula taken by the first sisters, the members stated that they would make simple vows (characteristic of active communities) until such time as they could make solemn vows (characteristic of cloistered orders). Exceptions had to be made for those sisters involved in teaching as they could not be with the community to recite the community prayers during the school hours.

ORGANIZATIONAL STANCE

The history of the origin of each community led the investigators to hypothesize that the original structure of the community would markedly influence its subsequent developmental pace. For instance, if the St. Martin community was originally intended to have been a cloistered, monastic type community, any adaptation of the rule necessary for an active community would be looked upon as an exception and, therefore, as taking the community away from its original goal. Change, in such a case, would be looked upon as something deviant, or at least threatening to the identity of the community as monastic. In the case of the St. Christine group whose rule constituted an important source of organizational identity for its members scattered in various occupations, change of the rule would be regarded as particularly threatening since variations in the professional commitments already tended to separate its members. Finally, with a built-in tendency toward change in the original St. Rose structure with all the members working in the same profession, change would be more readily accepted and implemented. Three factors seemed to be most responsible for the variance of organizational development among the communities. First, the model upon which the organization was first patterned; that is, its organizational base. Second, the orientation which that model imposed upon the organization; that is, whether the goal was specific as being that of a previous organizational model as in the case of the St. Martin community, or diffuse as in the case of the St. Christine community (see Chart 1), or more specific as in the case of the St. Rose community's concentration on teaching (see Chart 2). Third, the perception of the underlying value of organizational change as it

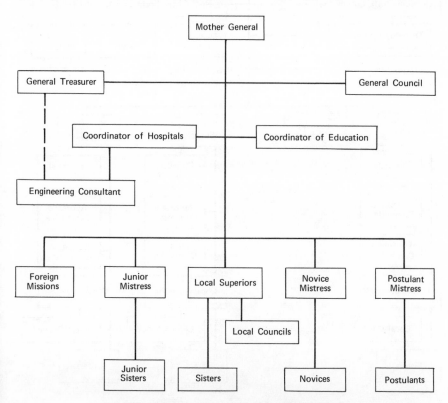

CHART 1. Organization of Sisters of St. Christine

was structured from the beginning. These factors constitute what is known in this study as the "organizational stance" of each community.

The sociological concept of the "organization image" or "organizational character" discussed by Selznick comes closest to the description of the phenomenon expressed by the concept, "organizational stance." It encompasses the idea of attitudes and behavioral consequences resulting from the structure of the organizational apparatus influencing the perception of change and causing tensions regarding it. It also includes Selznick's concept of "organizational weapon" by which he means that once the goals of the organization are specified, the organizational apparatus used to implement these

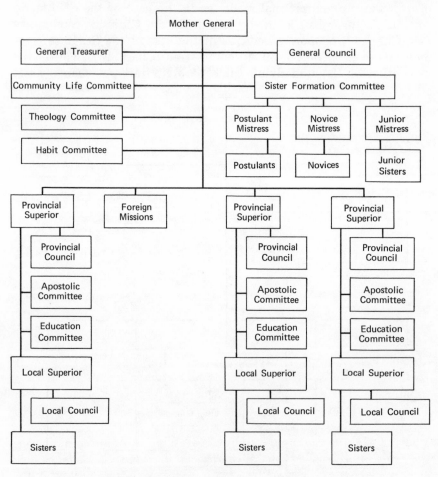

CHART 2. Organization of Sisters of St. Rose

goals is set up and becomes the means by which the goals are achieved. The question of the possibility that organizations may have the same goals but with different organizational models was neither raised nor discussed. In the case of the religious communities studied, all three eventually had one goal in common, namely, teaching, but they all had different models of structuring the organizational apparatus to implement this goal. The original model, or the lack of one, seems to have influenced the subsequent perception of change and therefore, the acceptance or rejection of it.

In summary, the three communities demonstrated the organizational stance shown in Table 1.

TABLE 1   ORGANIZATIONAL STANCE AT THE TIME OF FOUNDATION

Community	Model	Goals	Change Orientation
St. Rose	Original	Teaching	Originally ratified.
St. Christine	Active European	Teaching	Change of rule perceived as a threat to organizational identity.
St. Martin	Monastic	Cloister (later teaching)	Change of rule perceived as an exception—for accommodation to temporary needs. Later—as a threat to the monastic tradition.

ORGANIZATIONAL STANCE AND ORGANIZATIONAL DEVELOPMENT

The differences in the organizational stance of each community resulted in differences in their present organizational structure and their developmental pace.

St. Rose Community

Quantitatively, there have been *more* changes in the St. Rose community than in the other two. Qualitatively, some of the changes that have occurred in all three communities occurred *earlier* in the St. Rose group when social pressures were *against* such change, whereas when some changes have been made in other communities, they were made during a time when social pressures had been created in the opposite direction, i.e., when so many communities in the United States had made the changes that there were pressures *to* change. A good example of this is the introduction of the juniorate program through which the new members of the community are kept in college work until completing their bachelor's degrees before going into the classroom. When all teachers were content to get a normal school training, most sisters were put into the classroom after two years of college work. However, when teaching standards were raised, the Sister Formation Conference, an inter-community organization, urged all communities to have their young sisters complete their college work before entering the profession. The St. Rose community wanted to start their juniorate program in 1946 but could not get the pastors in charge of the parochial schools to allow fewer sisters to be put into their schools. However, in 1952, the General Chapter [7] of the St Rose community passed the resolution to keep all their sisters in college until they completed their undergraduate work *in spite of* protests from some of the clergy. The formal organization of the Sister Formation Conference was not officially recognized until 1954, two years later, after which time it proved to be the greatest pressure group for the institutionalization of juniorate programs in all U.S. communities. When the juniorate program was started in the St. Christine community in 1959 and in the St. Martin community in 1961, there was considerable pressure from outside the community to do so.

The St. Rose community has demonstrated the pioneer mentality characteristic of the people with whom they originally worked. When asked if she felt that a pioneer mentality was rather characteristic of her community, a sister of St. Rose replied:

Yes it is. In fact sometimes maybe we're too independent. We all have our own ideas all right, and we feel free to discuss them—but I guess that's good, too, because if people disagree with you, they let you know and then we come to some sort of solution. I guess it's our pioneer mentality that's helped us to move ahead.

A former Mother General commented:

One thing I think we did which is characteristic of the Church in general— we spread ourselves so thin—we never had enough sisters. The fact that we did spread out so much and were so scattered made us more aware of the needs of the Church. For instance, Mother—in the Southwest they had permission to make changes if they were needed. It has created a pioneer mentality. I don't think it hurt us.

---

[7] A General Chapter is the highest policy-making body in any religious community. Ordinarily, the elected members of a general chapter along with the Major Superiors meet every six years to review the status of the congregation, decide on changes, and elect a new Mother General.

A rather striking example of this willingness to innovate was shown in 1899 when the Mother General of St. Rose sent three sisters to a graduate school which was originally a Methodist Divinity School. Consideration of the fact that very few women were going to college then, much less doing graduate work, emphasizes the willingness on the part of the Mother General to move ahead.

The General Chapter of 1964 initiated some major changes in the St. Rose community. Changes in increased contact with the laity, such as visiting private homes, visits to their families, not always having a companion sister when going out, dropping the rule of silence during the day, and changing the religious habit to a more contemporary garb, were ratified. One of the resolutions passed which was most indicative of the changed climate of the community was that which stated that any recommendation made by Vatican Council II about religious communities would be implemented immediately without the necessity of convoking another General Chapter.

St. Christine Community

"Prudence" seems to be the key word in the responses to questions concerning community changes for the Sisters of St. Christine. As one said, "Reverend Mother warned us to be prudent—not to change for the sake of change." Another summarized:

We've been by and large—all the way through—an extremely prudent community. We have moved slowly—we got catapulted into this modern period without being perhaps quite ready for it because of this extreme Vincentian spirit—that we shouldn't be too modern. There's a danger of moving too fast—we might lose our moorings. We have to consider our demographic background and see first where we are going.

As far as future changes are concerned, one of the sisters commented:

. . . I'll tell you what will happen. We'll wait and see what the other communities are going to do. Then if it works, we'll probably eventually adopt it.

One of the factors responsible for the reluctance to introduce changes is the deference toward the clergy which was extolled by St. Vincent for his followers. Originally the Vincentian rule specified that there be an ecclesiastical superior for the community. This had resulted from the fact that St. Vincent was determined to keep the community he founded from being taken over by any one bishop in any one diocese—the usual case with communities in his day. However, in 1910 the St. Christine community became a pontifical organization.[8] Even after becoming pontifical, as one sister said:

One thing has been characteristic of our community all through its history. We have been trained to have extreme deference to the clergy. We always do whatever they want.

Even with pontifical status, then, the bishop of the diocese in which the motherhouse is located has had, traditionally, about as much authority over the St. Christine community as he would have if they were a diocesan congregation. An example of this last point is that the sisters had asked twelve years ago for the bishop's permission to divide into provinces. It was not until 1965 that provinces were established.[9] Getting the bishop's permission was a matter of deference—it was not required.

The same spirit was, in part, responsible for the juniorate program not having been started until 1959. An administrator in education commented upon the beginning of the program:

Our biggest obstacle was the pastors. We had been supplying them with teachers as fast as we could and they just couldn't understand why we wanted to keep the sisters back to finish their degrees. We had been catering to their wishes just too long. Finally Mother— simply kept the sisters here (i.e., at the college) to finish—no matter what the pastors said. We're finally beginning to realize that we've simply got to establish policies about things like this and stick with them. If they (i.e., the pastors) don't like it that way, there are plenty of other places who want our sisters. They're beginning to realize that they can't be as demanding as they used to be. They expected us to do everything.

The General Chapter of 1960 introduced some remarkable changes considering the traditional attitude about lay intervention in the governing of religious communities. Recognizing the need for expert advice in the governing, building, and renovation of the multi-million dollar investment of the community in hospitals, schools, orphanages, and other institutions, the St. Christine community hired a full-time

---

8 A Pontifical Institute is one in which the Mother General is responsible to the Sacred Congregation of Religious in Rome, has a Cardinal Protector, and is not confined to the work of one diocese. A Diocesan Institute, on the contrary, is under the direction of the bishop of the diocese in which the sisters work and in most cases is one in which the sisters work in one diocese only.

9 A "province" represents a decentralization in the authority structure. A congregation may be divided geographically and/or numerically into provinces, each having a provincial superior who takes care of granting many of the permissions ordinarily given by the Mother General. She also cares for many other administrative tasks such as opening or closing schools, assigning sisters to positions, buying or selling community property, structuring the educational program of the sisters, etc.

engineering consultant who, together with the General Treasurer, works directly with the Mother General and her Council in administrative decisions regarding property holdings. At that same Chapter, two new offices were created: Educational Coordinator and Hospital Coordinator. Both Coordinators are General Councilors of the community who have been released from all other duties in order to work on such matters as long-range planning, studying the use of personnel, and advising the Mother General on preparing sisters in various fields where they will be needed. There is, too, some *centralization* of decision-making going on since the vast spread of personnel into all the "works of mercy" has tended to threaten efficiency of administration. One superior commented:

We just grew like Topsy. Everyone was so involved in the work she was doing we didn't take time to get together. Eventually we realized that we should pool our resources and use the experiences of those in the work. That's why lately we've been trying to do a lot more collaboration—so we can all benefit from each other's experience. Many times a sister can be saved a lot of worry and avoid mistakes if someoue who has been in the work can tell her how it's done.

This centralization took the form of committee formation and the functioning of the two offices mentioned above.

Apart from some minor changes, the St. Christine community does not seem to be considering a contemporary habit. When asked if the sisters ever talked about a radical change of dress, a respondent answered:

I haven't heard much discussion about it. Most of us want to be recognized as sisters of—(St. Christine) and really, our present habit is very simple.

Others changes have taken place in minor details but most of the respondents in the St. Christine community could not think of changes within community life since its foundation. Chart 1 shows the formal structure of the community.

The St. Martin Community

Any changes taking place in the St. Martin community are measured against what is called the "St. Martin" spirit. Every two years, all the presently autonomous groups of sisters of St. Martin (there are over thirty of them) send their major superiors to a meeting to discuss how each group is carrying on the "Martin" spirit. The function of the meeting is to reinforce adherence to the original model. The tradition of St. Martin was described in the 1957 report of the Martin Conference as consisting of "recitation of the office, the study of sacred doctrine, monastic observance, silence, austerity, promotion of devotion. . . . and meditation together." Excerpts of the report are as follows:

Besides the three solemn vows . . . regular life with monastic observance, the solemn recitation of the divine office, and assiduous study of sacred truth. . . . these can never be changed. Our convents [are] to be houses of *regular* observance with traditional monastic ascetical practices, as indicated in the Rule and respective constitutions.

The Mother General is in the situation of being subjected to strong pressures for maintaining the status-quo while having to have the sisters prepared professionally to carry out the works of the community to which they are committed. The monastic-professional dichotomy creates opposite pressures on those in authority which inevitably results in conflict situations. A simple example of this is the conflict between the need to attend professional meetings in the evenings and the traditional attitude regarding cloister and having the sisters return to the "monastery" before evening. Going too far away from the "monastic observance" exhorted as the Martin "spirit" makes a Mother General subject to criticism of not being "true to the Martin spirit." Not making changes requisite for the professional competence of the sisters makes her subject to crticisms of being ultra-conservative and not aware of professional demands.

The more changes the Mother General initiates, the more she makes the community "un-Martin-like" and the more threatened the organizational image of the sisters becomes. Caught in such a dilemma, it is difficult for the Mother General to have much "leeway to act." One of the sisters commented:

Poor Mother—. No matter what she does she's going to be criticized. I never thought about it until you mentioned it but it really must be hard for Mother to make changes and still maintain the (Martin) spirit.

Apparently, the role of the Mother General is one of preservation. That is, she is expected to preserve the model upon which the community was originally based. Theoretically, there is a definite role-model; namely, the head of the monastery of the secondary order founded by St. Martin himself. Although there is ready acceptance of the fact that the present Mother General must make adaptations necessary for a teaching community, there is, nonetheless, a normative expectation that she will be truly "Martin" the more she emulates the superiors of the past. Small wonder that one of the sisters commented: "Mother—is upset by all this talk of change. She just doesn't want to talk about it."

However, some changes *are* being made, such as changes in the juniorate program, allowing more freedom to attend professional meetings, and more flexibility in the schedule. One sister commented:

Changes have been made. For instance, last summer we had two days when we could sleep as late as we wanted. I know we'd never do things like that at the Motherhouse ten years ago. I can see some changes. . . . I know we're not changing as much as the other communities . . . but we *are* changing.

As to the question of a contemporary habit, the following comments are typical of the usual responses:

We'll probably never change. You know what it would mean if we did— we would think we weren't St. Martin sisters anymore.
Well, if we *do* change, we'll probably be the last ones to go into a suit. We'd probably wait until we're the only group left who hasn't changed.
No, I don't think we'll ever give up the (St. Martin) habit. I'd like to see us go into a suit but I know we won't. Right now there are other more important things which need changing anyway. The habit really isn't that important right now.

Chart 3 shows the formal structure of the community.

COMMUNICATION FLOW AND ORGANIZATIONAL STRUCTURE

Given the differences in the organizational stance of each community and the change in climate resulting from it, differences in organizational structure and communication flow were anticipated. A comparison was made of the use of opinion-gathering techniques [10] as indices of communication flow within each community. As was anticipated also, the monastically-based community demonstrated greater rank-ordering which tended to hinder communication flow.

In a monastic setting, rank-ordering of all members for community functions is a common practice. Monasteries, having been the strongholds of learning during the Dark and Middle Ages, became places where members after joining the community grew in secular knowledge as well as spiritual. The custom developed of ranking members according to age in community and it has prevailed to some extent in all religious communities ever since. The behavioral consequences of organizations where ranking is considered important results in

---

[10] "Opinion-gathering techniques" here refer to the use of written questionnaires and/or discussion groups.

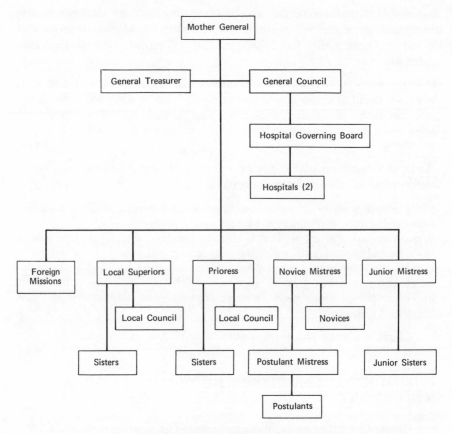

CHART 3. Organization of Sisters of St. Martin

expectations of (1) the longer the time in the monastery, the greater the competency of its members; and (2) a long time in the monastery is necessary to acquire the competency required for responsible and prudent decisions. As a result, rank-ordering tends to be inhibitive of communication among members.

An example of this is the attempt to have discussion groups among the sisters to encourage them to express their opinions. The problem of getting discussion groups started in the St. Martin community seems to be overcoming the built-in tradition that any issues are settled from the top down. One sister of St. Martin indicated that some change was beginning to take place when she said, "Well, at least now occasionally a younger person can say something. It used to be that, if you were the young one in the group, you must keep quiet." Formalized discussion groups have yet to be started in the St. Martin community. One reaction to them was "It's just impossible at our house." Table 2 shows a comparison of the three communities in rank-ordering and opinion-gathering techniques.

The structural results of the organizational stance of each community in the variation in centralization of decision-making as well as the formation of committees is shown in Table 3. The differences in organizational complexity bear out the hypothesis that differences in organizational stance influence the organization's structural development and communication.

SUMMARY AND CONCLUSION

Any exploratory study of necessity results in tentative hypotheses only. The historical analysis and comparative design used in the present study of three religious communities has led the investigators to conclude that the paramount factor influencing organizational change and structural development is the concept of "organizational stance." Organizational stance has been defined as encompassing (1) the model upon which the organization was first patterned; that is, its organizational base; (2) the orientation which the model

TABLE 2   COMPARISON OF THE THREE COMMUNITIES IN RANK-ORDERING AND OPINION-GATHERING TECHNIQUES

Community	Rank-Ordering	Questionnaires
St. Martin	All community exercises except recreation	None [a]
St. Christine	Dropped for the most part	1. Job satisfaction
		2. Habit modification
St. Rose	Dropped	1. Change of prayers
		2. Summer work
		3. Change of habit
		4. Personnel study (i.e., job satisfaction)
		5. Recommendation for administrators

[a] The exception already mentioned was in the form of a ballot sent to the sisters in 1950s asking them their preference regarding the change of the veil. Since the ballot simply required a "yea" or "no" answer, it is not considered here to be a questionnaire.

imposes upon the organization; and (3) the perception of the underlying value of organizational change as it was structured from the beginning.

TABLE 3

Community	Discussion Groups	Committees
Rule-oriented	None—Formalized	None
Task-oriented	Formalized about two years ago. Topics suggested by Mother General. Informal communication to members of heirarchy	1. Educational Coordinator (a) Sister formation (b) Secondary and Elementary school committees 2. Hospital Coordinator Hospital Administrators
Profession-oriented	Formalized four years ago. Official reports to Motherhouse. General Councillor outlines topics, suggests related reading	1. Apostolic Committee 2. Education Committee 3. Theology Committee [a] 4. Community Life Committee 5. Habit Committee [a]

[a] Temporary Committees

Observing the results of differences in organizational stance some interesting questions arise. If organizational goals so influence the later development of each community, what can be said of the future of those communities that seem to have more of a built-in resistance to change than others? The change pressures on religious communities are going to increase proportionately as communities begin to introduce changes which will precipitate more change, etc. The differences between those communities which change and those which do not will heighten the pressures on the latter considerably. What is the future of the non-change communities? How will change-pressures influence the restructuring of non-change communities?

Although only suggestive, the present study opened the door to the sociological investigation of religious communities and the picture inside the room is full of interesting possibilites. Future research using longitudinal studies on communities to see at what point communities re-define their goals to legitimize necessary changes would tell us much about the change-dynamics of formal organizations. The study of the impact of the organization on leadership development and of the impact of strong leaders on the communities could lead to greater insights into the influence of organizational structure on personality and the converse. Could it be that different types of individuals are found to enter different religious communities even though all are engaged in the same kind of profession?

Some of the changes taking place in religious communities today offer a rich field for research to social scientists. The fact that this study was *able* to be done is testimony to the fact that religious communities *are* changing. Using the techniques of the social scientist in studying communities as formal organizations can help us to ferret out the "sacred and profane" aspects of religious life. The present study is just a beginning to what promises to be a rewarding field for students of complex organizations and change.[11]

----

[11] It should be noted that this study has not mentioned all of the changes that have taken place in the three religious communities since the research terminated in the winter of 1965. As is the case in all such studies, a certain space limit had to be taken into account.

Reprise: Prospects for Social Change

It is perhaps not accidental that the members of the Washington Laymen's Association staged their protest of an American Cardinal within months and days of social protest movements in a number of segments of American society. The social climate seemed, if not to favor, at least to tolerate strident dissent from respected pediatricians no less than from student "radicals." From the mid-1960's on, the spirit of protest seemed contagious, if not epidemic. But protest remains an American, not a Catholic, phenomenon.

There is now wide subscription to the late Crane Brinton's view, first expressed in *Anatomy of a Revolution*, that revolution is triggered by hope, not by hopelessness, by progress, not by intolerable oppression. When there is no hope for change, men dissipate their energies in activities that distract them from their hopeless condition; when hope is present, men are energized for traumatic change. Furthermore, progress produces ever more demanding supplications for yet more radical change. It is, on the basis of Brinton's notions, not fortuitous that Black Americans began to burn the urban ghettos only after a decade of progress in racial justice, not after three centuries of despair.

In recent months, many apparently radical statements have been made in prediction of a schism between the American Catholic community and the Vatican. The same months have witnessed the publication of an unpopular, if not downright reactionary, papal encyclical condemning contraception practices in which, according to Westoff and Ryder, more than half the American Catholic com-

513

munity engages. And a low-comedy wrangle between an American Cardinal and a group of West Coast nuns over the length of the hemline has eventuated in a partition between progressivists and traditionalists in a religious community—a partition sanctioned by Rome. In some dioceses, senates of the clergy have petitioned for the right to elect their ordinaries, perhaps a portent of a return to the custom of the early Roman church, when bishops were elected by the laity.

What predictions for future social change can be made on the basis of the perspectives one gains about American Catholics and about Catholicism from behavioral science research? It seems clear that social change will indeed continue, at a pace never before known, both in American society and in the American Catholic community.

The ties Catholic Americans once felt with the old country and its folkways now seem all but dead. The Catholic American's identity as an American is, if anything, strengthened by the introduction of English into the liturgy, by liturgical experimentation, and by such democratic—not religious—phenomena as the establishment of a nationwide congress of bishops and of local senates of priests. Catholic Americans are now predominately situated in or near the middle class, with a consequent decline in the role of the kinship family. The life experience of today's Catholic American differs radically from that of his forebears.

Change has been as characteristic of the American Catholic community as of American society generally, although in an earlier day the pace of change may have been slow and imperceptible. Now there are organized efforts for drastic and traumatic change, stimulated not only by the aftermath of Vatican II, but also by the American sociocultural experience. The end of ideology in American life has already been translated into sometimes wholesale changes in the belief and behavior of Catholic Americans. In a knowledgeable society, there is little place for authority, religious or otherwise.

One can prognosticate with some assurance that change will continue, but it is more difficult to prognosticate the direction and the specific dimensions of social change in American Catholic life. Still, on the basis of the perspectives of the behavioral sciences on social change in the American Catholic community, certain telling questions emerge: After the papal position on birth control is either retracted by Rome or disavowed by the American hierarchy, after church properties have been added to the civic tax rolls, and after priestly celibacy is dead—what next?

Author Index

Subject Index